1

Dictionary of Polish Literature

Dictionary of Polish Literature

Edited by E. J. Czerwinski

GREENWOOD PRESS
Westport, Connecticut • London

Library of Congress Cataloging-in-Publication Data

Dictionary of Polish literature / edited by E. J. Czerwinski.
p. cm.
Includes bibliographical references and index.
ISBN 0–313–26222–5 (alk. paper)
1. Polish literature—Dictionaries. I. Czerwinski, E. J. (Edward Joseph).
PG7007.D5 1994
891.8'509'0003—dc20 93–49540

British Library Cataloguing in Publication Data is available.

Library of Congress Catalog Card Number: 93–49540
ISBN: 0–313–26222–5

First published in 1994

Greenwood Press, 88 Post Road West, Westport, CT 06881
An imprint of Greenwood Publishing Group, Inc.

Printed in the United States of America

The paper used in this book complies with the Permanent Paper Standard issued by the National Information Standards Organization (Z39.48–1984).

10 9 8 7 6 5 4 3 2 1

Contents

Introduction

Work on the present volume began in 1986, at a time when the entire population of Poland seemed to be on strike. Most scholars refused to collaborate on any project, even one as nonpolitical as a *Dictionary of Polish Literature,* meant primarily for an English-speaking audience. They were, in a word, demoralized.

Four years later a new Poland was born: In 1990 the dictatorship of the Communist Party was broken and the Polish people began to regain their moral and political rights, not only for themselves but for all of East Europe and the Soviet Union as well. "For your freedom and ours!" rang out again as it did many times before during Poland's fight for freedom and self-government. As Poland changed, so did the format and contents of this project.

The first draft of the *Dictionary* was completed in December 1989. Factual material was supplied by those scholars who contributed to the two-volume *Literatura Polska: Przewodnik Encyklopedyczny,* edited by Czesław Hernas and Julian Krzyżanowski. Published in 1984–85, the encyclopedia, unfortunately, was dated long before it was published. Censorship prohibited an honest evaluation of many writers' work and the inclusion of controversial figures. It was not until the triumph of Solidarity that Polish scholars awakened from their lethargy. As a result the first draft of the *Dictionary* became obsolete and our efforts had to be redirected to an honest, open reevaluation of Polish writers and Polish literature and culture in general.

What remains of the first draft are the general format, the biographical and factual material, and the entries. Even in the original plans, of course, controversial authors were included. After 1990, however, critical evaluation was unhindered by censorship and materials on banned authors became available.

The editor was fortunate in obtaining the services of two outstanding specialists: Halina Gerber and Jan Wojnowski, who, together with the editor, wrote the entries, supervised final revisions, and established contacts with numerous Polish scholars who contributed to the final draft of the book. The assistant editor, Joanna Radwanska Williams, and the editorial assistant, Dorothy Pasich, guided the dictionary to its conclusion. Bożena Wojnowska also significantly contributed to the volume. Thanks are also due to Barbara Dancygier for various translations from the Polish.

No caveats were imposed on the work of these scholars, except a reminder that the book was intended for an English-speaking audience with a very limited knowledge of Polish literature. The editors also hoped that scholars would find the book useful. In order to effect this delicate balance the format of each entry includes information that will prove useful to both layman and scholar: in the case of authors, name, date of birth and death, a brief biographical review of the author's works, an in-depth discussion of the author's most important and most representative work, and a brief statement regarding the author's development, his or her use of themes, his or her place within the Polish tradition, and his or her importance in world literature. The bibliography for each section includes the following information: the definitive edition of the author's works in Polish, a list of works in English translation, and, whenever possible, the most important critical work in English. A General Reference Bibliography is also included at the end of the book. A great deal of the information on each subject can be found in the primary bibliographical source provided after each entry. The entry itself, however, was compiled and critically analyzed by the cited scholar (where appropriate) or by the editor. The editor takes full responsibility for changes made in submitted entries and for all critical analyses of literary works.

The work also includes entries for literary periods, universities, individual works, major publications, and movements. When an author with a separate entry appears in the discussion of literary periods, movements, or trends, an asterisk appears after his or her name. Cross-references are noted at the end of the text of an entry and in the List of Entries. Wherever possible available translations into English of an author's works have been included in the bibliographical entries. Primary sources in Polish have also been provided.

The editor wishes to thank several graduate students in the Department of Germanic and Slavic at SUNY Stony Brook: Donna Jesaitis, Maria Pavelock, John Kubiniec, Dorothy Pasich, Timothy Hamilton, and Darin Menlove. The final corrections on the manuscript were made with loving care by Barbara Gajer, to whom I am deeply grateful.

Special thanks to the secretary in the Department of Germanic and Slavic at SUNY Stony Brook, Debbie DeBellis, who processed the entire manuscript, making corrections and inserting new materials. Without her, the dictionary would have been delayed for at least a year. Our appreciation for editorial assistance also goes to Patricia O'Brien, who selflessly worked extra hours in order to bring the book to fruition.

Research for this book was supported in part by two grants from the International Research and Exchanges Board (IREX), with funds provided by the National Endowment for the Humanities and the United States Information Agency, and the U.S. Department of State, which administers the Soviet and East European Training Act of 1983 (Title VIII).

Without the earnest work of Polish scholars, past and present, this dictionary would have been impossible to complete within one's lifetime. The word processor can alleviate many anxieties and make the tedious work of recopying a thing of the past, but human intellectual effort has yet to be replaced by either animate or inanimate means. The work of Polish scholars in Polish literature is indeed of high quality, but it has only been in recent years (post–World War II) that American scholars have contributed significantly to Polish scholarship. Perhaps the most important figure in this regard is the Polish scholar Manfred Kridl, whose *A Survey of Polish Literature and Culture,* translated from the Polish by Olga Scherer-Virski (The Hague: Mouton and Company, Printers, 1956), and anthology of Polish literature provided young American students of Polish descent the opportunity to discover the riches of a country that was almost erased from the map of Europe.

Kridl was followed by other internationally renowned Polish scholars: Wiktor Weintraub, Professor of Polish Literature at Harvard University, known especially for his work on Adam Mickiewicz (*The Poetry of Adam Mickiewicz* [The Hague, 1954]); Czesław Miłosz, the Nobel Prize recipient, Professor Emeritus of Polish Literature at the University of California at Berkeley (*The History of Polish Literature* [London and New York: 1969]); as well as scores of excellent American scholars who are cited in this volume. Recently Polish publishers have added two volumes to the library of Polish criticism available in English: Julian Krzyżanowski, *A History of Polish Literature,* translated by Doris Ronowicz (Warsaw: PWN—Polish Scientific Publishers, 1978), and Bogdan Suchodolski, *A History of Polish Culture,* translated by E. J. Czerwinski (Warsaw: Interpress Publishers, 1986). It is the hope of the editors that this volume will in some small way contribute to the further study of Polish literature.

The editor would like to express his sincere gratitude to Grzegorz Boguta, director of Polish Scientific Publishers (*PWN*), for permitting use of material from the two volumes, *Literatura Polska: Przewodnik Encyklopedyczny,* edited by Czesław Hernas and a core of Poland's finest scholars.

Without the encouragement, scholarly guidance, concern, and interest of Professor Czesław Hernas, this book could not have been completed. I humbly dedicate it to my friend and mentor.

Dictionary of Polish Literature

A

ABRAMOW-NEWERLY, JAROSŁAW (born 1933), playwright, son of the writer Igor Newerly, was one of the cofounders of the Students' Satirical Theater (*STS*). His first satirical pieces and monologues written for *STS* were published in the volume *Myślenie ma kolosalną przyszłość* (Thinking Has a Colossal Future, 1957). They contain satirical views of myths, national stereotypes, and contemporary social and moral changes. A number of his short plays were adapted for the radio, such as *Licytacja* (The Auction, in *Dialog,* 1961), *Śmierć po latach* (Death Years After), and *Wielki kochanek* (The Great Lover)—all three produced on the stage under the title *Remanent* (Inventory) in 1962. His comedy *Duże jasne* (Big Bright, coauthored with A. Jarecki), produced in 1962 and published in 1965, enjoyed considerable success, as did his play *Anioł na dworcu* (The Angel at the Station, staged in 1965 and published in 1967, with an introduction by Helmut Kajzar), which received the S. Piętak Award. According to Szczepan Gassowski, in 1965 his style and content changed from mere anecdote to a generalization on the relativity of facts and truths. He created a new type of "theater within a theater," which combined the features of the avant-garde theater and folk culture. He contrasted the old, vanishing cultural traditions with the new reality in his plays *Derby w pałacu* (Derby in the Palace, in *Dialog,* 1966, staged in 1966) and *Klik-klak* (Click-Clack, in *Dialog,* 1972, staged in 1972). One of his favorite themes involves the freedom of man, who is being lost among the existing social norms and laws (e.g., *Ucieczka z wielkich bulwarów* [Escape from Great Avenues], in *Dialog,* 1969, staged in 1969, *Darz bór* [Hail, Well Met], in *Dialog,* 1974, staged in 1974, and *Maestro* [1984]). In these he mixed realistic plots with a pure nonsense type of humor. He is the author of numerous plays for television, and the composer of songs, notably to lyrics written by Agnieszka Osiecka. His main publications include *Dramaty* (Dramas, 1975);

a selection of satirical pieces, *Co pan zgłasza?* (What Do You Submit?, 1977); and plays for radio, *Pięć minut sławy* (Five Minutes of Fame, 1978). His novel *Pan Zdzich w Kanadzie* (Mr. Zdzich in Canada, 1991), based on the experiences of Polish emigrants in Canada, enjoyed great success. His works have been translated into several languages.

ANDRZEJEWSKI, JERZY (1909–83), novelist, short-story writer, and journalist, made his debut in 1932. Beginning with his early short stories inspired by a Catholic morality (the collection *Drogi nieuniknione* [Inevitable Roads], 1936), his works reflect the search for permanent spiritual values, depicted through the drama of human weakness. His characters undergo a continued pattern of defeat. His style varies from lyrical, heroic pathos and irony to satire and grotesque. For Andrzejewski, man's spiritual life is moral to the very depths of his being; it is a service, a duty, a realization of an idea. His characters often undergo sudden reversals and make an ideological decision which does not require rational justification (*Ład Serca* [The Order of the Heart], 1938). Andrzejewski's experiences during the Nazi occupation were recounted in his short stories, published in the collection *Noc* (Night, 1945), in which he analyzed, in the ethical spirit of Joseph Conrad, human beings facing the final disaster, as well as the tragedy of Polish Jews, destined for mass extermination by German occupiers. Among other works one can cite *Wielki Tydzień* (Holy Week), stories about the uprising in the Jewish Ghetto. His most important postwar work is the novel *Popiół i diament* (Ashes and Diamonds, 1948), which poses dramatic moral and political questions. After several works published in the fifties, expressing his approval of Marxist ideology—the period Miłosz* scathingly attacks in his portrait of Andrzejewski (as Alfa) presented in *The Captive Mind*—Andrzejewski entered a period of ideological disillusionment. In this post-Stalinist period, ideology is presented as a fatal power, which manifests itself through lies and depravation of innocent minds as in his metaphoric novel from the history of the Spanish Inquisition, *Ciemności kryją ziemię* (Darkness Covers the Earth, published as The Inquisitors, 1956), and in the novel about the Children's Crusade to the Holy Land, *Bramy raju* (The Gates of Paradise, 1960). His most important novel of his later period is *Miazga* (Smithereens), a portrait of modern Polish intelligentsia. It was first published underground and fifteen years later, in 1981, officially appeared in print. The period marked a time when Andrzejewski abandoned the Communist Party and parted with Marxism and, finally, became a "nonperson" because of his membership in the Committee for the Workers Defense (*KOR*). During this period his works were not published; he was also strongly attacked in the press. *Miazga* is a multilayered book; the intertwined plot combines fictive stories with autobiographical fragments and pieces of journalism. The object of analysis is the artistic milieu of the capital; the isolated elite with its intrigues, its idleness, and cynicism; the elite in conflict with state authorities. The compromise that both sides hope to achieve is never effected, and the value that emerges, after the dust settles, is the creative talent, understood as a manifestation of the rebellious Dionysian spirit from which art derives its vital strength. This last motive Andrzejewski developed in his novel *Idzie, skacząc po górach* (He Cometh Leaping over the Mountains, 1963), a perfidious portrait of a brilliant contemporary artist (his portrait reminds one of Pablo Picasso). Andrzejewski's literary diaries from the years 1972–79 were published under the title *Z dnia na dzień* (From Day to Day, Volumes 1 and 2, 1988).

Andrzejewski's books have been translated into over thirty languages. Perhaps because of Wajda's superb movie or perhaps because Andrzejewski managed to freeze a moment of cataclysmic change in a Socialist world, *Popiół i diament* (Ashes and Diamonds) remains Andrzejewski's most popular work, published in more than thirty languages. Printed in 1947 in the weekly *Odrodzenie* (March 22, 1947), under the title *Zaraz po wojnie* (Right After the War), it was published in 1948. The novel covers three days, May 6–9, 1945; the place is the district city of Ostrowiec. The country is still in a state of turmoil connected with the rise of a new government, with the migration of people returning from the war, and, above all, with the activities of the underground organizations opposing the new Communist system. A group of young people, led by Maciek Chełmicki, the main character of the book, and Andrzej Kossecki, his superior in the organization, prepare to assassinate the Communist activists. The assassination of Stefan Szczuka, the secretary of the district committee of the party, forms the central theme of the dramatic story. Maciek wants to withdraw from the organization and start a new life with Krysia Rozbicka, whom he has just met, but shooting Szczuka is the price he is forced to pay to be free from any further obligations. He does his job, but is accidentally shot soon after by a police patrol. The novel presents the image of a society which is dispersed and exhausted, paralyzed by the nightmare of the occupation, dramatically antagonized by the revolutionary changes it is subject to and the ideological and moral choices it is forced to make. The young generation, the rare survivors of the war, still live with the ideas that have emerged during the difficult years of the occupation and their underground struggle. They are faithful to their soldierly ideals of loyalty, honor, and discipline, but are also aware of their own demoralized status under the new circumstances. They are convinced that further resistance is pointless, offering no chance of success (Andrzej Kossecki); among the youngest the underground ethos is deformed into moral nihilism (the group consisting of Alek Kossecki and Jurek Szretter). The posts in the new government attract mainly opportunists and pushers. The concluding scene during the night banquet at the Monopol Hotel evokes Wyspiański's ghostly dance in his play *Wesele* (The Wedding, 1901). How can a new society be created? How can one save or create the values necessary in order for new social bonds to take shape? This is the main question posed by the author, the question that appears also in the title and the motto of the novel, taken from Norwid's drama *Za kulisami* (Behind the Scenes). The tragic death of Maciek Chełmicki is meant to symbolize the ideological confusion of the young generation tied with the Home Army (*AK*), the generation which has been somehow cheated by history. The novel was suggestively reincarnated in another medium, Wajda's film version, with Zbigniew Cybulski playing Maciek (1959). On the other hand, the reputation of the novel itself has suffered greatly: contemporary criticism questions the truthfulness contained in the depiction of the underground that struggled for independence and the self-imposed Communist regime and shows the various propagandistic stereotypes which the author submitted himself to during the period in which he was fascinated with Marxist ideology.

(See Contemporary Polish Literature.)

BIBLIOGRAPHY

English

The Appeal, A Novel (Apelacja), translated by Celina Wieniewska, preface by Jan Kott, Indianapolis: Bobbs-Merrill; London: Weidenfeld and Nicolson, 1971.

Ashes and Diamonds (Popiół i diament), translated by David F. Welsh, London: Weidenfeld and Nicolson, 1962; New York: Penguin Books, 1980.

The Gates of Paradise (Bramy raju), translated by James Kirkup, London: Weidenfeld and Nicolson, 1963, 1962; London: Panther, 1967.

He Cometh Leaping upon the Mountains (Idzie, skacząc po górach), translated by Celina Wieniewska, London: Weidenfeld and Nicolson, 1965; London: Panther, 1968.

The Inquisitors (Ciemności kryją ziemię), translated by Konrad Syrop, New York: A. A. Knopf, 1960; Westport, Connecticut: Greenwood Press, 1976.

A Sitter for a Satyr (Idzie, skacząc po górach), translated by Celina Wieniewska, New York: Dutton, 1965.

Critique in *Modern Slavic Literatures,* Volume II, edited by Zbigniew Folejewski and Bogdan Czaykowski, New York: Frederick Ungar, 1976.

ANHELLI (See Słowacki).

ASNYK, ADAM (pseudonym Jan Stożek) (1838–97), a poet, was born in Kalisz of a petty-gentry family. His father participated in the November Uprising. For a while he studied medicine and agronomy. He took part in the conspiratorial movement and was imprisoned in the Citadel in 1860. After his release, he left for Paris and Heidelberg, where he studied the social sciences. He returned to Poland in 1863. After the failure of the uprising, he escaped abroad. He completed his studies in Heidelberg and received a doctorate in philosophy in 1866. In 1864–65, he published his first literary works in the *Dziennik Literacki* (Literary Daily) in Lvov. In 1869 he published his first volume of poetry, *Poezje* (Poems). After 1870 he made his home in Cracow, keeping ties with a few close friends, among them Mieczysław Pawlikowski and I. Maciejowski. He traveled to Italy, Tunis, and Algeria (1888), as well as to Ceylon and India (1894). He also made several excursions into the Tatra Mountains and was one of the first members of the Friends of the Tatras. He was also a member of the city council of Cracow (1884) and a deputy to the country's *Sejm* (Parliament), representing the so-called Democrats (1889). In 1882 he joined the editorial board of the daily *Reforma* (Reform), which from 1883 became *Nowa Reforma* (The New Reform); from 1889 he was its editor-in-chief. At the same time, he wrote for *Kłosy* (Ears of Grain), *Bluszcz* (Ivy), and other periodicals, where he published poetry and drama, as well as social-political and literary studies. In the nineties, struck with tuberculosis, he began to withdraw from social life. In 1896 he went to Italy to recuperate. He returned to Poland, infected with typhoid fever, and, after a few months, died. He is buried on the Skalec.

Asnyk's poetry was a significant expression of the consciousness of his generation, which experienced the failure of the January Uprising. During his first period (1864–72, *Poezje* [Poetry], Volumes 1–2, 1872), a note of extreme pessimism dominated his poetry; the main theme was the fate of those banished from their "native shores," who as a result of the curse on the nation lost their reason for living. The poet contrasted the past with the present; he spoke about the ties with the world of the "graves" and about the isolation in the living world; he blamed his contemporaries for discarding the ideals of the people in the name of "the right of the state." His method of depiction, the motives and plot, his style and versification are witness to his dependence on the poetry of Romanticism, especially on the works of Słowacki.* The main work of this period was the poem *Sen grobów* (Dream of Graves, 1865), written in Dante's terza rima, a settlement of accounts with the political figures during the time of the January Uprising, a work filled with Romantic symbolism. During this period he also composed numerous love lyrics, which feature an extensive scale of moods, a simplicity and directness of response, a precision in the building of the poetic line and verse, for example, *Między nami nic nie było* (There Was Nothing Ever Between Us), *Gdybym był młodszy* (If I Were Younger), *Jednego serca . . .* (Of One Heart . . .), *Ty Czekaj mnie* (You Wait for Me). In the most typical irony of these verses Heine's influence can be detected. Later (*Poezje* [Poems], Volume 3, 1888; Volume 4, 1894) Asnyk's works became saturated with a philosophic statement. In his eclectic but compact system he included, among others, a conception of the history of the Polish nation based on evolution. The ideas concerning independence of the past were treated by the poet as a living legacy, which, enriched by the spiritual labor of contemporary generations, would contribute to the regeneration of future generations. The most complete statement of these views can be found in the cycle of thirty sonnets *Nad głębiami* (Over the Depths, in Volume 4, *Poezje* [Poetry], 1894). Poems of a more direct character are tied in with these poems, which formulate a more concrete ideology (*Przeminął czas* [Time Has Gone], *Daremne żale* [Complaints in Vain], *Do młodych* [To the Young]). A significant role was also played by the poetry based on Tatra themes (the cycle *W Tatrach* [In the Tatras]), poetry dedicated to contemporary social problems (e.g., *Szkic do współczesnego obrazu* [A Sketch for a Contemporary Painting]), as well as satire directed against the conservative politics of the Stańczyks (*Historyczna nowa szkoła* [A Historical New School], *Dzień wczorajszy* [Yesterday], and others). Asnyk's poetic language, with the exception of his youthful period, is marked by clarity and simplicity. It shows a profusion of prosaisms, a paucity of metaphors, operating with the construction of developed sentences that are close to the language of contemporary journalistic works.

His poetic artistry appears here mainly in the versification, in the sophisticated rhymes, in the varied building of lines. For these reasons this poetry was quite popular in the nineteenth and at the beginning of the twentieth century. On the other hand, Asnyk's dramas and drawing-room comedies (e.g., *Gałązka heliotropu* [A Branch of Heliotrope], 1869, in the style of Musset) have not retained their popularity. Nor have his social dramas any significance today: *Bracia Lerche* (The Lerch Brothers, 1888), *Żyd* (The Jew, 1875). His historical dramas, formulated along Shakespearean lines, have suffered the same fate: *Cola Rienzi* (1873) and *Kiejstut* (1878). Asnyk's short stories comprise his marginal work, based mostly on autobiographical elements. Asnyk was also the author of critical and literary works, among others studies on Sophocles' *Antigone* (*Bluszcz* [Ivy], 1874) and Słowacki's *Król-Duch* (King-Spirit) (*Przewodnik Nauki i Literatury* [A Guide to Science and Literature, 1879]).

(See Positivism.)

BIBLIOGRAPHY

Pisma, oprac. i wstęp S. Krzemiński, T. 1–5, Warsaw, 1898.
Pisma, oprac. F. Hoesick i W. Prokesch, T. 1–3, Warsaw, 1916.
Wybór poezji, oprac. E. Kucharski, wydanie 3, Cracow, 1935 BN I 67.
Pisma, oprac. H. Schipper, wstęp I. Chrzanowski, T. 1–2, Warsaw, 1938–39.
Listy, opracował F. Bielak, J. Mikulska, S. Papierz, Wrocław, 1972.
Wiersze wybrane, wybór i wstęp, J. Z. Jakubowski, Warsaw, 1973.
Poezje, wstęp S. Lichański, Warsaw, 1975.

B

BACZYŃSKI, KRZYSZTOF KAMIL, (pseudonym Jan Bugaj) (1921–44), earned his reputation as a poet after his death. During his student days he had ties with a leftist organization of the young. He was graduated in 1939, when the war broke out. In 1943 he became a member of the militant fighting underground (the famous scout battalion *Zośka* of the Home Army). He was killed during the Warsaw Uprising in 1944. His wife, Barbara, died several weeks after his death.

Baczyński is mainly a poet of the occupation. Apart from two small collections of poems printed in 1940 (only seven copies), he published only two collections of poems, both in the underground: *Wiersze wybrane* (Selected Poems, 1942) and *Arkusz poetycki* (Poetic Folio, 1944). The first volume had very favorable reviews (one by Kazimierz Wyka). Baczyński was well known and highly esteemed in the literary underground. All of his handwritten works have survived the war: approximately five hundred poems, including several longer ones; approximately twenty short stories and prose pieces; and a poetic drama. His works, unusually mature, often referring to the Romantic tradition, underscore his personal, symbolic vision of the experiences of his generation: the understanding of the historical moment, man's patriotic duty to fight, the tradition of such a struggle in the past, the catastrophic feelings and fears raised by the Nazi threat to the spirit of history. These are counterbalanced by a lyrical longing for the beauty of nature. Finally, there is the awareness of the necessity to choose between the position of an artist and patriotic duty. Baczyński also composed subtle love lyrics dedicated to his wife. His remaining poems were published for the first time after the war in the collection *Śpiew z pożogi* (Song from the Blaze, 1947).

According to Kazimierz Wyka, Baczyński is considered the most outstanding poet of the war generation. He has become an object of unusual esteem and has inspired a cult following among each new generation.

BIBLIOGRAPHY

Utwory zebrane (Collected Works), edited by A. Kmita-Piołunowa, introduction by Kazimierz Wyka, Cracow, 1961; second edition, Volumes 1–2, 1970.

Poezje (Poems), selected by K. Wyka, introduction by J. Strzelecki, Warsaw, 1977.

BAL MANEKINÓW (The Ball of Mannequins) (see Jasieński).

BAŁUCKI, MICHAŁ (pseudonym Elpidon, Załęga) (1837–1901), author of comedies, prose writer, poet, journalist, made his debut as a poet in 1859. He was coeditor of a number of journals, mainly published in Cracow.

In the early period of his work Bałucki expressed democratic and revolutionary views; he also advocated the independence of Poland. He took part in the conspiratorial activities of 1863–64 and was imprisoned by the Austrian authorities. He insisted that literature should openly make a statement regarding important, controversial moral and political issues. Such views are reflected in his works from the 1860s: the short story *Przechrzta* (1861) and his novels *Przebudzeni* (The Awakened, 1864) and *Młodzi i starzy* (The Young and the Old, 1886), which elaborate on the uprising from the point of view of the "Reds." In his youth he also wrote poetry; he was the author of the text of the popular song *Góralu, czy ci nie żal* (Highlander, Are You Not Sad?, 1874).

In the 1870s Bałucki espoused positivist ideas. His protagonist is no longer simply a freedom fighter, but rather the hero of an organic work, that is, a man actively involved in the development of the economic and humanitarian aspects of the country. This is reflected in the novels, such as *Błyszczące nędze* (Shining Destitution, 1870) and *Żydówka* (The Jewish Woman, 1870). Bałucki's arguments with some of the positions held by the positivists can be seen in his portrayal of social utopias (*Z obozu do obozu* [From Camp to Camp], 1874) and religious reformism (*Siostrzenica księdza proboszcza* [The Niece of the Parish Priest], 1872; *Biały Murzyn* [The White Negro], 1875), and in his reserved attitude toward some postulates of the progressive middle class, for example, emancipation of women (*Sabina,* 1873).

Bałucki's satirical comedies of the period express similar social views (*Polowanie na męża* [Hunting for a Husband], 1869; *Radcy pana radcy* [The Councillor's Counsellors], 1871; etc.). More fundamental changes in his work became apparent in the eighties. On the one hand, Bałucki became more critical of social realia; his optimism was undermined; his theses became less obvious; the positivist hero almost disappeared (e.g., *Pańskie dziady* [Royal Beggers], 1881), as in his best novel, *Pan burmistrz z Pipidówki* (The Mayor from Pipidówka, 1887), whose title town became the symbol of misery and backwardness, and as in his comedies such as *Sąsiedzi*

(The Neighbors, 1882) and *Ciężkie czasy* (Difficult Times, 1889). Subtle and not so subtle tones of anti-Semitism appeared (the novel *W żydowskich rękach* [In Jewish Hands], 1885). On the other hand, a series of good-humored or sentimental works appeared, presenting the petit bourgeois or si simple folk—who lived in the old traditional way, not asking for too much—depicted rather satirically, but as good and honest. It was Bałucki's attempt to escape from upsetting reality. The works representing this trend were mainly comedies; the two best known ones are *Dom otwarty* (Open House, 1883) and *Grube ryby* (Fat Fish, published 1900, staged in 1881). The latter, which became immensely popular, created a one-sided, generally accepted image of Bałucki's point of view and gave rise to the term *bałucczyzna,* which literally meant an approving image of the bourgeoisie—lazy and thoughtless, modestly well-off, enclosed in a world of food, taking a walk and a nap and playing a game of whist. An evaluation of Bałucki's entire literary output indicates that he was not uncritically approving of such a way of life, although in the 1880s he did indeed escape into it from time to time.

During the period of *Młoda Polska* and later, *bałucczyzna* became an object of criticism, synonymous with the worst vice of the petit bourgeois. Bałucki's works in the 1890s were a continuation of the previous period, but on a lower artistic level. Only one play written during this period became popular—*Klub kawalerów* (The Bachelor's Club, staged in 1890, published in 1911). Bałucki became involved in polemics with the modernists. He wrote pamphlets on them (*Pamiętnik Munia* [Muń's Memoirs], 1900) and was in turn severely attacked by members of the group. The difficulties he faced as a writer—loneliness and the constant attacks of critics—resulted in severe depression, which he fell deeper and deeper into and ended with his committing suicide. In 1911 the people of Cracow celebrated his memory by erecting a monument, which now stands in the *Planty,* the park that surrounds the Old City.

Grube ryby (Fat Fish), a comedy, presented in various theaters in Warsaw and Cracow in 1881, was published in Warsaw in 1900. In this play, Bałucki gave up writing "meaningful" plays and abandoned the bitter satire of his earlier works. He presented the world of the bourgeoisie as somewhat comical (a keen observer in this respect), with minor imperfections, not really serious, and evoked an understanding and sympathetic smile rather than anger—consider the old couple, the Ciaputkiewiczes; their servant and their daughter-in-law; and even their guests and card playing partners Wisłowski and Pagatowicz, who are ridiculed a bit more ruthlessly. This view of the petit bourgeois of Galicja was referred to as *bałucczyzna.*

Dom otwarty (Open House), a comedy, was first performed in Cracow in 1883, and published in Lvov during the same year. It presents an episode in the life of an honest, though slightly comical, middle-class family who, driven by snobbery, begin to imitate a way of life basically foreign to them.

The ball that the Żelskis organize results in an avalanche of problems for the family and their friends. The play praises modesty and restricting oneself to family life (although the author himself had criticized that view in his earlier works, e.g., *Młodzi i starzy* [The Young and the Old]. *Open House* consists of many comical situations and caricature portraits (e.g., Wicherlowski, his wife, Pulcheria, and Fikalski), the chief reasons for the play's continued popularity.

BIBLIOGRAPHY

Pisma wybrane (Selected Writings), Volumes 1–12, edited by T. Drewnowski, J. Skornicki, and A. Żyga, introduction by T. Drewnowski, Warsaw, 1956.

English

Lad from the Highlands (Góralu, czy ci nie żal), in *The Golden Book of Polish Songs*, edited and translated by Adam Harasowski, London: Alma Book, 1955.

BARAŃCZAK, STANISŁAW (born 1946), poet, literary critic, theoretician of literature, translator, is now Professor of Polish Literature at Harvard University. Having graduated from Poznań University, he worked there as a lecturer (Polish Philology). He made his debut as a poet and critic in 1965; he soon became one of the leaders of the poetic current called "The New Wave" (along with R. Krynicki and A. Zagajewski), which dominated the face of young Polish poetry at the end of the 1960s and early 1970s. However, it did not succeed in developing fully because of restrictions imposed by political censorship. Barańczak was not allowed to publish during the period 1976–80. In 1977 he was forbidden to carry out his duties at the university. The reasons for his difficulties were his activity in the Committee for the Defense of Workers (*KOR*), in which he was a member from 1976, and his participation in the publications of *Drugi obieg* (Independent Publishers): Barańczak was one of the founders and editors of the first underground literary journal, *Zapis* (Record), published in Warsaw. He returned to his position at the university in 1980 as a result of the intervention of the newly organized Solidarity. Nonetheless, in 1981 he left for the United States, where he was offered the chair of Polish Literature at Harvard University. He has retained his position to this day and at the same time has assumed the position of editor-in-chief of *The Polish Review* (from which he resigned in 1991), published in New York, and co-editor of the émigré journal *Zeszyty Literackie* (Literary Notebooks), published from 1983 in Paris. His collections of poems include *Korekta twarzy* (A Correction of Face, 1968), *Jednym tchem* (In a Single Breath, 1970), *Dziennik poranny* (Morning Diary, 1972), *Sztuczne oddychanie* (Artificial Respiration, 1974), *Ja wiem, że to niesłuszne* (I Know That It Is Not Right, Paris, 1977), *Tryptyk z betonu, zmęczenia i śniegu*

(Triptych of Concrete, Weariness and Snow, 1980). In his poetry he expresses the moral anxieties of his times, combining a moralistic and contentious stance with a keen observation of patterns of everyday behavior in contemporary Polish society. His style is marked by a "distrustful," analytic approach to the clichés of speech, both colloquial and official, spoiled by the stereotypes of the Communist "Newspeak"; it is reflected in his intricate rhetoric, something akin to "linguistic poetry." In his later poetry, included in his collections *Atlantyda i inne wiersze z lat 1981–1985* (*Atlantyda* and Other Poems from the Years 1981–1985, published in London in 1986) and *Widokówka z tego świata i inne rymy z lat 1986–1988* (Picture Postcard from This World and Other Rhymes from the Years 1986–1988, published in Paris in 1988), new elements of a reflective and metaphysical nature appeared. As a literary critic Barańczak has collected his articles, sketches, and reviews in the following volumes: *Nieufni i zadufani: Romantyzm i klasycyzm w młodej poezji lat sześćdziesiątych* (The Distrustful and the Arrogant: Romanticism and Classicism in the Young Poetry During the Sixties, 1971), *Ironia i harmonia* (Irony and Harmony, 1973), and *Etyka i poetyka* (Ethics and Poetics, published in Paris in 1979 and in Cracow in 1981). He also wrote separate studies on the works of Miron Białoszewski, *Język poetycki Mirona Białoszewskiego* (The Poetic Language of Miron Białoszewski, 1974), and Zbigniew Herbert, *Uciekinier z Utopii, O poezji Zbigniewa Herberta* (A Fugitive from Utopia: The Poetry of Zbigniew Herbert), published in London in 1984 and in the underground press in Poland in 1985. He was also fascinated by the function of stereotypes of mass culture under conditions existing in a Communist government: *Czytelnik ubezwłasnowolniony, Perswazja w masowej kulturze literackiej PRL* (The Incapacitated Reader, Persuasion in Mass Literary Culture PRL), published in Paris in 1983; *Książki najgorsze 1975–1981* (The Worst Books 1975–1981), published in 1981, expanded in 1990. In his collection of essays *Tablica z Macondo: Osiemnaście prób wytłumaczenia po co i dlaczego się pisze* (Blackboard from Macondo: Eighteen Experiments of Explanation Why and for What Reason One Writes), published in London in 1990, spins a thread regarding the confrontation between American and European civilization. The anthology *Poeta pamięta: Antologia poezji świadectwa i sprzeciwu 1944–1984* (The Poet Remembers: An Anthology of Poetry of Testimony and Resistance 1944–1984), published in London in 1984, edited by Barańczak, is an important document for an understanding of the fate of Polish poetry during the past half-century. His rich contribution in the area of translation, chiefly of English authors, includes *Antologia angielskiej poezji metafizycznej XVII stulecia* (An Anthology of English Metaphysical Poetry of the Seventeenth Century), published in 1982; and separate collections of poetry by Donne, Hopkins, Cummings, and Dylan Thomas and the Russians Osip Mandelshtam and Jozif Brodsky. His translations of Shakespeare's plays have gained him an enviable position among Polish translators of Shakespeare.

BIBLIOGRAPHY

Poezje wybrane (Selected Poetry), Warsaw, 1990.
159 wierszy, 1968–1988 (159 Poems, 1968–1988), Cracow, 1990.

English

Under My Own Roof, translated by Frank Kujawinski. Portland, Oregon: Cogito Press, 1980.
Where Did I Wake Up? (poem), translated by Frank Kujawinski. Portland, Oregon: Cogito Press, 1978.
Breathing Under Water and Other East European Essays. Cambridge, Massachusetts: Harvard University Press, 1990.
A Fugitive from Utopia: The Poetry of Zbigniew Herbert, Cambridge, Massachusetts: Harvard University Press, 1987.
Spoiling Cannibals' Fun: Polish Poetry of the Last Two Decades of Communist Rule, edited by Stanisław Barańczak and Clare Cavanagh, foreword by Helen Vendler, Evanston, Illinois: Northwestern University Press, 1991.

BARBARA RADZIWIŁŁÓWNA (see Feliński).

BAROQUE (*Barok*) was a literary epoch which appeared between the Renaissance and the Enlightenment; the period encompasses the seventeenth century, although there are signs of the Baroque at the end of the sixteenth and to the middle of the eighteenth centuries. The term "Baroque" is also employed in the history of art and in the history of culture. In Poland the tradition of the Baroque dates from the time of F. Bentkowski (1814), who isolated "the teleological-panegyric Period," 1622–1760. The literature of the Baroque was negatively evaluated by critics with Classical criteria and tastes. Much of the literature of the period was first published in the nineteenth century from manuscripts (see J. A. Morsztyn,* W. Potocki,* etc.). Regarding it as an epoch whose "tastes were lowered," critics of literary history narrowed the margins of the period (M. Wiszniewski [1840] situated the Baroque from 1650 to 1750). According to Czesław Hernas, the present boundaries of the Baroque are usually assigned to the late Renaissance–early Baroque (1580–1620) and the late Baroque–early Enlightenment (1740–64).

The term "Baroque" is a borrowing from the history of art. The first Polish critic to employ the term was E. Porębowicz (1893), in evaluating the poetry of J. A. Morsztyn.* I. Chrzanowski* used the term Baroque in his handbook (1908), followed by S. Dobrzycki (1927) and J. Krzyżanowski* (1939). A. Brueckner, on the other hand, introduced the term "Sarmatian Baroque," and opened up the study of the period. H. Wolfflin's study *Renaissance und Barock* (1888) introduced a comparative approach to the period; his research was continued by R. Pollak in his study *Od renesansu do baroku* (From the Renaissance to the Baroque, 1923).

Polish literature of the Baroque was largely shaped by examples from Italian literature, as in the lyrics of Marino, as well as from examples from popular poetry and prose, for example, Tasso and Boccaccio. Italian and Spanish theater and drama also greatly influenced the Polish Baroque. From the middle of the seventeenth century French culture played an important part in the development of Polish literature, especially in the areas of Court Theater and the romance. The main influence, however, was Classical literature, especially in the area of poetry and the translations and adaptations, not only of Horace, but of other Classical writers, such as Seneca, Lucan, and Persius.

Poland's influence during the Baroque is rather due to social and political writings than to literary works. A secure place among European writers was granted M. K. Sarbiewski,* a poet and theoretical writer, one of the leading codifiers of Baroque conceptions.

The early Baroque was formed at the end of the sixteenth and beginning of the seventeenth centuries (around 1580–1620), after the death of Jan Kochanowski* and while Renaissance literature was still taking shape, especially at the famed Zamoyski Palace. Alongside the most important poets of the late Renaissance (Klonowic, Szymonowic,* Paprocki) appeared writers who critically evaluated the theory of Renaissance humanism, which tried to come to terms with worldly and eternal values, with finding worldly happiness and harmony. The new poets Sęp-Szarzyński* and Grabowski understood life as being a transformation, that is, an episode opening up a way to eternal life. They referred to the dualism of man's nature, pointing out that only that which is spiritual is lasting and the only thing of value. These attributes were part of the trend in Polish metaphysical poetry—intellectual, difficult, with roots in the Christian tradition. This poetry sought to answer the eschatological questions of existence: "What is man? Who am I?" Sęp-Szarzyński and Grabowski gave voice to these questions. Both writers searched for new means of expressing their ideas in versification, new poetic forms, composition, stylistics, and complicated structure in order to give a dramatic form to poetic thought. Employing similar means, both poets created various models, each evaluating differently man's ability to comprehend his place in the universe. Sęp-Szarzyński believed that man was capable, through his intellectual capabilities, of distinguishing between permanent values and appearances. He advocated an attitude of heroic action. Grabowski, on the other hand, skeptically evaluating the possibilities of mortal man and emphasizing man's helplessness and solitude, suggested that man flee this earthly world and maintain a naive belief in God, thereby creating a condition of religious quietism. Alternatives to these two views were expressed in the poetry of other writers of the Baroque, who sought examples in the poetry of the Middle Ages. Terror and the macabre were often emphasized; that emphasis, during the late Baroque, led to the trend in poetry of dwelling on the "Last Judgment" and the finality of life.

The new theories of humanism and the novel approach to man's condition expressed in the metaphysical poetry projected a distinct profile during the early Baroque and led to a controversy regarding values. An extreme view in this controversy was expressed by the poetry of "worldly bliss," represented then by H. Morsztyn, the young K. Twardowski, and Sz. Zimorowic. This attitude was propagated in the anonymously published anthologies which today are referred to as "songs, dances, and Paduans." Morsztyn emphasized the singular makeup of man, his noble spirit, creating a poetic variant of the ideal earthly condition. On the other hand, Zimorowic emphasized love, which he characterized as "greater than death." Zimorowic based his poetry on Italian and French models, Classical examples, and Polish folklore. The authors of "songs, dances, and Paduans" also based their poetry on these models, presenting two different models of love—courtly and mundane. J. A. Morsztyn* became the most important representative of this trend during the full-fledged Baroque.

A somewhat neutral stance within the controversy was maintained by *ziemiańska* (gentry) poetry, which proposed a model of moderate stoicism and a moderation in earthly providence (one rich village should suffice). Restraint in divining eternal matters was also urged. The country manor became a place of refuge from worldly contradictions and from obligations. The tendency to praise and glorify the beauty of village life continued to the end of the epoch. The obligations of the gentry were strongly debated and became a part of the discussions concerning the cult of "golden freedom," best represented later in the works of W. Potocki.

A distinct current also appeared in the poetry referred to as *mieszczańsko-plebejska* (bourgeois-plebeian), the main theme of which was the confrontation between this world and eternity. The universal rights of man became part of the philosophic foundation of these discussions in which all of society seemed to take part—merchants, craftsmen, peasants, the village presbyteries, the school, and so on. Most often the hero of these works was the parish schoolteacher. A great number of writers of such literature came from this milieu. The genre is often referred to as "Rogue" (*sowizdrzalska*) or "Minstrel" (*rybałtowska*) literature. Their ideological stance was similar: discovering the beauty and conflicts of the town (A. Władysławiusz and Jan from Kijan), the heroism of the physical work of miners and ironmasters (W. Rozdzieński), and so forth. *Rybałt* (Minstrel) Comedy also sprang up within this milieu. Within the tradition of the Mystery, a trend in folk theater can also be observed during the Baroque. At the end of the sixteenth century, *szkolny* (School) theater developed within Catholic and Reformation circles.

Religious and polemical writing dominated prose. Piotr Skarga was perhaps the greatest prose writer of the period. His sermons combined an intelligent discussion of the changes within society and a poetic imagination, which placed his writings between literature and social prose. The period also witnessed a birth of new forms—the anecdote, war diaries, home or agenda diaries, itineraries of journeys, and so on.

The Counter-Reformation also witnessed a flowering of printing houses, especially those set up by the Jesuits. A reorganization of censorship also followed in 1603, 1604, and 1617; "preventive" censorship was established around 1618. The censorship was not only directed at the various religious sects but also at the acceptance or rejection of various ideas from Classical and Renaissance literature.

Literature during the fully fledged Baroque (around 1620–80) developed under quite restricted conditions, and a great deal of the literature of the period remained in manuscript form. Because of repression, various trends ceased to exist, especially the Minstrel and Bourgeois-Plebeian groups. The Polish Brethren, whose center was located in Raków, regarded as a philosophical and religious opposition of the Counter-Reformation, also came under attack. The Arian poets, in line with their beliefs, fought for tolerance and freedom of conscience. The war against "coercion" opened up a new road regarding a change in the theories of humanism, free of dogma. The most forcible exponents of the rights of man were Z. Morsztyn* and W. Potocki* (also after accepting Catholicism). The same ideas can be found in the works of J. A. Morsztyn,* and even in those of the foe of advocacy the Catholic W. Kochowski, who fought in defense of restricting the freedom of literature and severely hounded writers whose religious bent differed from his own.

A synthesis of these ideas was attempted by M. K. Sarbiewski,* a theorist and writer of Latin verse, who sought a new relation to Christian poetry and Classical and Renaissance poetry. K. Twardowski (1628) and L. Opaliński (around 1661) attempted to define these changes on the local level.

Rhetoric became the center of controversy regarding style: simple (Classical) versus ornamental (Baroque). Sz. Starowolski championed a Classical style, while F. Birkowski and J. Mijakowski, among others, urged the Baroque, which finally became universally accepted. The Opaliński brothers also urged a return to the Classical, although Baroque elements can be found in their poetry.

The master of Baroque poetry was undoubtedly J. A. Morsztyn, who in his masterfully crafted lyrics sought the means to express the collision of love and civilization. He structured a libertine confrontation between love and religion and presented a courtly and primitive exposition of this confrontation. In his works he strove to test the limits of poetic language as a means of expression.

During this period an attempt was made to develop the knightly epos.

The model for this genre, translated by P. Kochanowski, was Tasso's *Gofred*. S. Twardowski tried his hand at various kinds of epics, although his best work was in romances. The finest expression of war experiences can be found in the lyrics of Z. Morsztyn,* based on his own experiences, dating from the middle of the century.

In the area of theater, the most important event was the establishment of a permanent court theater in 1637 by Władysław IV. Baroque opera was the staple of the theater; French Classical tragedy was later introduced (Corneille's *Cyd*). S. H. Lubomirski wrote a number of court comedies, written under the influence of Italian and Spanish writers.

Memoirs were also written (the Maskiewiczow brothers, A. S. Radziwiłł, J. Jerlicz, etc.). M. Borzymowski combined personal experiences and Classical models involving sea journeys and planted the seeds of maritime literature in Poland.

The late Baroque (ca. 1680–1740) saw a diminution of creative activity. During the first twenty years, three outstanding writers continued their work: W. Potocki,* W. Kochowski, and S. H. Lubomirski. Unfortunately, the character of their output changed drastically. Potocki began his paraphrases of the Bible and published his collections of epigrams and reflections (*fraszki i rozważania*)—*Ogród* (The Garden) and *Moralia*. Kochowski, after problems with censors, published *Psalmodia polska* (Polish Psalmody). Lubomirski stopped writing comedies and turned to religious and political writing (*De vanitate consiliorum*).

These three writers did not have any followers in the first half of the eighteenth century. Writers began to turn to French models, translating the fables of La Fontaine, Corneille, Racine, and so on. Censorship became more severe, leading to the pronouncement of the death sentence on K. Leszczyński (1689).

The theater was less affected by the censorship crisis. The Court Theater, after weakening in the second half of the century, had a rebirth during the reign of the Saxons. Memoir writing flourished and was not susceptible to censorship. It was during this period that the finest example of memoir writing appeared, the work of J. Ch. Pasek. Spiritual romances were also a popular genre (Lubomirski, W. Chrościński, S. Piskorski, and M. Kuligowski).

The tradition of Baroque literature continued not only during its transitional period but even later into the Enlightenment.

BIBLIOGRAPHY

Dramaty staropolskie (Old Polish Drama), t. 1–6, opracował J. Lewański, Warsaw, 1959–1963.

Julian Krzyżanowski, *Od średniowiecza do baroku* (From the Middle Ages to the Baroque), Warsaw, 1938.

Czesław Hernas, *Barok* (Baroque), wydanie 3, Warsaw, 1978; wydanie 1, 1973.

Słownik literatury staropolskiej (A Dictionary of Old Polish Literature), Redaktor T. Michałowska. Wrocław, 1990.

BENIOWSKI (see Słowacki).

BERENT, WACŁAW (1873–1940), a novelist, essay writer, and translator, came from a Warsaw middle-class family. He studied the sciences in Munich and received his doctorate from the University of Zurich in 1895. He lived in Warsaw but traveled a great deal—in Poland—to Cracow, Zakopane, and abroad to Italy, Austria, and Germany. In 1920–21 he became one of the editors of *Nowy Przegląd Literatury i Sztuki* (A New View of Literature and Art); in 1929, of *Pamiętnik Warszawski* (The Warsaw Diary); he received a literary award from the city of Warsaw and in 1933 a state award. He was a member of the Polish Academy of Literature (PAL). He published his first stories under the pseudonym Władysław Rawicz; Nauczyciel (The Teacher), in *Ateneum*, 1894; *Przy niedzieli* (On Sunday), in *Gazeta Polska* (The Polish Gazette), 1894; *W puszczy* (In the Forest), in *Bibliografia Warszawska* (Warsaw Bibliography), 1896. Berent presents characters in conflict with their environment, which displays the author's pessimistic approach. His first novel in the series of works concerning contemporary times was *Fachowiec* (The Expert, 1895), preserved in the realistic convention of the penetrating critical foundations of positivism (that is, a hero, a young writer, an avid champion of the idea of organic work, who becomes of his own choice a laborer in a factory and, because of this decision, experiences defeat in both the social and human arenas). Several years later (1903) he wrote *Próchno* (Dry Rot)—a study of the cosmopolitan modernist *boheme.* His treatise on *Źródła i ujścia nietzscheanizmu* (The Sources and Estuaries of Nietzscheanism, 1906), in which Berent appears as both a follower and an opponent of Nietzsche's philosophy, is a commentary to *Próchno.* In his study *Idea w ruchu rewolucyjnym* (Ideology in the Revolutionary Movement, 1906, signed S.A.M.) Berent presented himself as an opponent of the revolutionary struggle and gave a perspicacious warning against the destruction of the intellectual achievement of the past. According to Janina Gorbaczowska, as an admirer of the national tradition and a follower of Nietzsche, Berent felt that Poland should take its place in the revolutionary movement: he viewed it as an opportunity for creating an alliance of the most outstanding personages of the nation. The shock brought about by the revolution was presented in *Ozimina* (Winter Corn, 1911), Berent's last novel set in contemporary times. After *Ozimina,* Berent presented his point of view in historical novels and "tales," although he remained a steadfast supporter of moral nationalistic ideals. He chose those periods of the past which were marked with historical and cultural breakthroughs, in which new ideas confronted old ones: the height of the Middle Ages and the Renaissance in *Żywe kamienie* (Living Stones, 1918);

the fall of the Polish state and the awakening of hearts and minds of the Polish people to patriotic action, both in the defensive battles in the Polish Legions at Napoleon Bonoparte's side and in the battle to preserve the intellectual culture of the nation in *Nurt* (The Current, 1934), *Diogenes w kontuszu* (Diogenes in a Nobleman's Field-Coat, 1937), and *Zmierzch wodzów* (The Twilight of Military Leaders, 1939)—a story about the times of Prince Konstanty in Warsaw, about the last days of General Jan Henryk Dąbrowski, and about the famous November night of 1830. Similar themes appeared in his inaugural speech delivered to members of PAL, entitled *Onegdaj* (Once upon a Time, 1933), which was devoted to the *Towarzystwo Przyjaciół Nauk* (Popular Scientific Society) in Warsaw, to Stanisław Staszic and the poet Cyprian Godębski. These works make up a clear, ideologically and formally consistent whole. The main motive is the tragic fate of creative individuals, freedom fighters, and advocates of intellectual progress. The past has a double role in these works: a picture of the bygone days and an analogy to the present. In the experiences of the past Berent wanted to find the source of his disappointment and hope; he unmasked people's spiritual passiveness and praised active participation, viewing the pursuit of one's goal as the highest value. His writings are strongly connected to the life of the nation, whose history showed him the "lamps of life" of past generations that gave light and guidance to generations that would appear later. He dug into the past, criticized it, but also treated it as a model for the present, always sensitive to the current situation. Just before World War II broke out, he wrote *Zmierzch wodzów,* the story which unmasked the "false glitter" of public life before 1830 and the political immaturity of the November Uprising, thus giving expression to a foreboding of defeat. The structure of Berent's works is solid and concise; the style differs from novel to novel, always well calculated, but difficult to read because of the complex syntactic structures and numerous inversions—the main formal characteristics of these outstanding works. Berent was also a translator of Nietzsche, Hamsun, Hearn, Ibsen, Maupassant, Rolland, and others.

Próchno (Dry Rot), first printed in *Chimera** in 1901 and then in Warsaw in 1903, concerns an international group of modernist *boheme.* The place is one of the great cities in Germany, reminiscent of Munich and sometimes of Berlin. The main characters are the actor Borowski, the journalist Jelsky, the musician Hertenstein, the poet Mueller, the playwright Turkul, and the painter Pawluk. They are followers of Nietzsche's idea of a superman. Like Nietzsche they also feel contempt for women, hate the state as an oppressive institution, and feel like the tragic victims of the urban civilization that surrounds them. These misfits of the "mob" despise spending their time in cabarets and cafés on idle conversation about art, wasting their talents, as well as their personal lives. Borowski leaves his wife to accept a good part in the theater; Jelsky commits suicide in a café.

Mueller, who is in love with Borowski's wife, and Hertenstein, who has an incestuous affection for his sister, choose to die of drug abuse, hoping to find peace in nirvana. The two men who are saved are Turkul, thanks to his ruthlessness, and Kunicki, a doctor, who finds his satisfaction in working for society. They are both observers, who defend moral standards and condemn the other characters of the novel for their decadent lives. However, this severe criticism of unhealthy decadent moods is, on the one hand, an accusation and, on the other, a defense of the artist's existential drama. In his *List autora Próchno,* Berent avers that he believes the products of decay become the fertilizer for future art. *Próchno* presents the inner selves of the characters, mainly through lyrical dialogues full of dramatic suspense. Descriptions (e.g., of the town, the cemetery, or the cafés) are impressionistic in style, although they combine features of the expressionist style, which Berent developed and employed in his later novels.

Ozimina (Winter Corn), a novel published in Cracow in 1911, describes the course of one winter night in Warsaw in 1904, prior to the Revolution of 1905. The soirée in the salon of Baron Nieman—similar to the wedding hut in Wyspiański's *Wesele* (The Wedding)—becomes the background for the confrontation of various attitudes and views of Polish society, from the conciliation of the aristocrats and plutocracy to the patriotic and revolutionary involvement of young conspirators. (A Russian colonel is a Chekhovian character, who respects the Polish tradition of the national insurrections.) The news of the outbreak of the Russian-Japanese War carries the action of the novel to the streets, where a revolutionary cortege is assembling in which among the workers and peasants can also be found the young conspiratorial intelligentsia. The marchers are dispersed by the Cossacks. The blood of those killed is actually the seed of the winter corn of future freedom. With this Eleusinian symbol of the renewal of life through death the author comes close to Wyspiański's *Noc listopadowa* (November Night).

Żywe kamienie (Living Stones) (first published as *Opowieść rybałta* [The Minstrel's Tale] in 1917–18 in *Zdrój,* and then in a definitive edition in Poznań 1918) is a novel about a group of medieval traveling artists at the turn of the thirteenth and fourteenth centuries who enter a city sunk in idleness, material well-being, a state of passive stupor, suffering from the "illness of the soul" called in Latin *acedia.* The visit of the group, led by a singer-poet, is a shock for all the inhabitants of the city. The newcomers try to oppose *acedia* with the help of three old men: a maker of bronze armor to the glory of knights; a Franciscan friar and illuminator of manuscripts named Łukasz; and a scholar, the prior of the Franciscan monastery. What brings them together is their creativity, their spiritual anxiety, the idea of eternal longing, as symbolized by the Holy Grail. Several people are not affected by *acedia*—an acrobat, a woman who embodies the Dionysian joy of living, and a doctor, a follower of the maxim *Probate omnia.*

These "live stones" are personages from sculptures, legends, and medieval songs. The novel shows the dying of the theocratic ideology of the Middle Ages and presents the tragic lonely fighters who are aware of the change. When the poet dies, pure, brave, unselfish poetry dies with him. The armor maker ends his life, feeling that the middle class needs a different type of art from the one he practices. The prior and Łukasz represent Franciscan ideals, which look forward to the future. The doctor and the acrobat choose to become part of the new life, since they approve of life in general. The young artists who make their living after the poet's death by performing for the crowd are treated with understanding, but the achievements of those who had to die appear more valuable. The poet's ideals are bound to rise again in the souls of his followers. The expectation is an allusion to the writer's contemporary times, which he emphasized in his epilogue. The idealism and the sensual down-to-earthness of the Middle Ages are presented in archaic language, sometimes highly elevated, sometimes ribald. The narration is interspersed with poetry and dramatic elements. Medieval allegories go hand in hand with modern symbolism.

(See *Młoda Polska.*)

BIBLIOGRAPHY

Dzieła wybrane (Selected Works), Volumes 1–6, Introduction by J. Wilhelmi, Warsaw, 1956–58.

Próchno (Dry Rot), edited by J. Paszek, Wrocław, 1979.

Ozimina (Winter Corn), edited by M. Growiński, Wrocław.

English

"Critique of Wacław Berent," *Modern Slavic Literatures,* Volume II, edited by Zbigniew Folejewski and Bogdan Czaykowski, New York: Frederick Ungar, 1976.

BIAŁE MAŁŻEŃSTWO (White Marriage) (see Różewicz).

BIAŁOSZEWSKI, MIRON (1922–83), poet and playwright, attended school in Warsaw. He studied Polish philology at the underground university during the war. At the time of the 1944 uprising he was in Warsaw; after the defeat he was sent into forced labor in Germany. Upon his return, he worked at the Main Post Office, and in 1946–51 he was a reporter for a daily newspaper; he continued with his studies during this period. His first works included the poems *Chrystus powstania* (The Christ of the Uprising, Warsaw, 1947) and *Fioletowy gotyk* (Violet Gothic, in *Odrodzenie,* 1949). He also wrote song lyrics and books for children in order to make a living. In 1955 he became a cofounder (together with L. Hering and L. Murawska) of an experimental theater called Theatre on Tarczyńska Street (they worked and performed in the apartment of L. E. Stefański). Later the name was changed; the theater continued until 1963 as the Separate Theatre. Białoszewski produced five works there, most based on his own texts. In 1956 the first collection of his poems was published under the title *Obroty rzeczy* (The Evolution of Things). It consisted of a selection of his works, edited and selected by A. Sandauer. This delayed debut evoked a very lively response from the critics and brought the writer considerable popularity. At first his poetry was viewed as part of "the 1956 generation," although the only characteristic Białoszewski shared with this group was the date of his appearance on the literary scene, for his works are deeply rooted in the experiences of the war generation. Approval along with confusion were also the reactions to his next collections of poetry: *Rachunek zachciankowy* (An Account of Whims, 1959), *Mylne wzruszenia* (Deceptive Emotions, 1961), *Było i było* (It Was and It Was, 1965). Only *Pamiętnik z powstania warszawskiego* (Memoir of the Warsaw Uprising, 1970) was more unambiguously successful; the book received the award of the Minister of Culture and Art in 1971. *Memoir* strikes an original note in Polish literature, especially in its treatment of personal remembrances regarding the Warsaw Uprising, which according to rule have a combative and heroic character. Białoszewski's work is related by a civilian who does not take part in the battles; he is the sole witness of the terrible fate of the civilian population and the annihilation of the city, whose history is re-created with extraordinary chronological and topographical compactness, in a manner completely free of pathos, stylistically equivalent to recollective oral narration. In 1973 a collection of his dramas written during the period 1955–63 was published under the title *Teatr Osobny* (Separate Theater, with an introduction by Arthur Sandauer). This was followed by several volumes of prose: *Donosy rzeczywistości* (Reports of Reality, 1973), *Szumy, zlepy, ciągi* (Noises, Conglomerates, Sequels, 1976), and *Zawał* (Heart Attack, 1977). His next collection of poems, *Odczepić się* (To Lay Off), appeared in 1978. In 1980 he received the literary award from the city of Warsaw. The following collections appeared after his death: *Stara proza, nowe wiersze* (Old Prose, New Poems, 1984), in which he related a story, connected with his trip to New York, undertaken by Białoszewski a year before his death to accept an émigré literary award presented by the Jurzykowski Foundation.

According to Janusz Sławiński, Białoszewski's early poetry was distinguished by its reference to the peripheries of contemporary culture—which ran contrary to the traditional view of art. His imagination was attracted by objects which occupied the lowest position in the hierarchy of objects of everyday use—old and devastated things, junk and rubbish, and so on. The material of his imagery contains things and situations alien to the high-tech civilization: the cheap glitter of a village fair, flashy souvenirs, the landscape of a little town or suburb, holy images in roadside shrines, the reality evoked by songs sung by street musicians. He tried to express all this through language which also belonged to the periphery of daily use. He was intrigued by speech that was crippled, laughable, clumsy, incoherent; that went beyond the limits of meaning, grammar, or style. Considered one of the main representatives of the so-called linguistic poets, he based his poetry on the language that violated norms of communicative efficiency and aesthetic standards, especially colloquial speech in its most disorderly and substandard form. He wanted to exploit in poetry delinquent speech, with all its mistakes and clumsiness, the realm of empty blather, slips of the tongue, and thoughtless logorrhea. What the poet does with such language is often a parody, but it can also be a reflection of his sincere solidarity with the "low" language, in which—against the existing tradition—he is able to find expression for lyricism, for moral ideas, and for narration. The majority of Białoszewski's plays are based on linguistic concepts: the story is developed from a pun, from an unclear and ambiguous word, or from a phraseological cliché. In the late sixties the focus of his poetry shifted to the normal course of life, to chaotic and unpredictable links among events, to conversations, overheard stories, memories, and dreams. His texts resembled diary entries or family chronicles. Gradually, they became more and more proselike, beginning with "small narratives," like hasty notes, or anecdotes, then short stories, and culminating in prose narratives in *Pamiętnik* (Diary) and *Zawał* (Heart Attack). As in his poetry, he tried in his prose to stay as close as possible to the naturalness of colloquial spoken language.

In all of his writings Białoszewski consistently presented himself as "a private person," as someone trying to preserve his independence by remaining on the outskirts of the world, as someone who ignored—completely, though without ostentation—all the motivations and patterns of behavior which were obligatory in the world struggling for prestige, domination, position, wealth, higher social status, and participation in institutionalized public activity. By rejecting all temptations to climb to a high position in the world, he was able to keep his unique place and retain the authenticity of his ego.

(See Contemporary Polish Literature.)

BIBLIOGRAPHY

Wiersze (Poems), selected by the author, introduction by J. Sławiński, Warsaw, 1976.

Poezje wybrane (Selected Poems), selected and with an introduction by the author, Warsaw, 1976.

English

A Memoir of the Warsaw Uprising, edited and translated by Madeline Levine, Ann Arbor, Michigan: Ardis, 1977; Evanston, Illinois: Northwestern University Press, 1991.

The Revolution of Things: Selected Poems, translated and with an introduction by Andrzej Busza and Bogdan Czaykowski, Washington D.C.: Charioteer Press, 1974.

Critique, *Modern Slavic Literatures*, Volume II, edited by Zbigniew Folejewski and Bogdan Czaykowski, New York: Frederick Ungar, 1976.

Shifting Borders: East European Poetries of the Eighties, edited by Walter Cummins, Rutherford, New Jersey: Fairleigh Dickinson University Press, 1993, 274–75.

BOBKOWSKI, ANDRZEJ (1913–61), an essayist and prose writer, was educated as an economist (he studied at the Main School of Trade in Warsaw). He left Poland in 1939, several months before the outbreak of the world war, to take a position in a Polish export company in Paris. In 1940, after the German invasion, he was evacuated to the south of France; he later returned to Paris, where he spent the period of occupation maintaining contacts with the resistance movement and Polish émigré circles. After the war he remained in Paris, where he worked with such émigré periodicals as the Paris *Kultura* (Culture) and the London *Wiadomości* (News). Until 1949 he also sporadically published in Poland, in periodicals such as *Tygodnik Powszechny* (The Universal Weekly). In 1948 he left Europe and settled permanently in Guatemala, where he lived until his death in 1961.

The single book published during his lifetime, the diary *Szkice Piórkiem* (Sketches Made with an Ink-Pen, Paris, 1957), has brought him popular acclaim. The diary covered the period 1940–44, from the beginning of the German occupation of Paris until its liberation by the American army. The notes of an attentive observer of the realities of daily life in occupied France, who is also receptive to the sensuous beauty of the world (description of a bicycle journey through southern France), are intertwined with extensive parts of a meditative-essayistic nature, in which he ponders the situation of Europe at the time of its endangerment by fascist and Stalinist totalitarianism. He analyzed the causes and effects of the military breakdown and the mass murders, which he considered to be the expression of the spiritual catastrophe of Europe. Bobkowski ponders Europe's inability to counter the nationalist-fascist and Communist ideologies effectively and at the same time manifests his personal convictions as an avid defender of man's right to individual dignity and freedom. From this standpoint Bobkowski also sharply criticizes the patriotic-martyrological stereotypes cultivated by the Polish intelligentsia, taking a stand similar to that of Witold Gombrowicz. His short stories, collected in the volume *Coco de Oro* (Paris, 1970), concentrate on the Conradian ethical questions of moral choice, fidelity, and righteousness and are set among the exotic realities of life of Polish émigré groups in Central America. The writer also represented his independent point of view in his journalism published in the Paris *Kultura* (Culture) and in the correspondence he maintained with his colleagues.

BIBLIOGRAPHY

M. Pieczara, "*Latarnik:* O Twórczości Andrzeja Bobkowskiego" (*Lamplighter:* About the Creativity of Andrzej Bobkowski), *Więź* (Bond), Number 7, 1983.

S. Gębala, "W tym jest trucizna" (In This Is Poison), *Zdanie* (Opinion), Number 3, 1986.

BOGURODZICA, the oldest Polish poem in print, is a Polish medieval religious song, preserved in various manuscript copies from the fifteenth and early sixteenth centuries. The oldest text, the so-called Cracow Text I, comes from 1407 (in manuscripts dating after 1408 we find the form *Bogarodzica*). The poem was published in the Statut Laskiego in 1506.

The Cracow Text I has two stanzas, the first of which is addressed to the Holy Mother, the second one to Jesus Christ: both end with the refrain *Kyrie elejson.* The Cracow Text II has fourteen stanzas; the Warsaw Text (second half of the fifteenth century) has nineteen. The original text was here enlarged to include the Easter Song and a Passion Song. Later, litanies to various saints were added.

According to Długosz, *Bogurodzica* was sung as *carmen patrium* in the battle of Grunwald against the Teutonic Knights in 1410. It was the coronation anthem of the first Jagiellonians, the song of the dynasty or the state. It lost its meaning in the second half of the sixteenth century ("You don't hear it these days; it was given to women," says the author of *Albertus z wojny* [Albert from the War, 1596]). In the seventeenth century M. K. Sarbiewski translated it into Latin, but the venerated song was finally rescued from oblivion in the patriotic poetry of the nineteenth century. Niemcewicz included it at the beginning of his *Śpiewy historyczne* (Historical Songs, 1816); Słowacki welcomed the 1830 uprising with a paraphrase from the song, while Norwid devoted a treatise to it. The tradition of *Bogurodzica* as the "Grunwald Song" was strengthened in Sienkiewicz's novel *Krzyżacy* (Knights of the Cross) and incorporated in his novel *Potop* (The Flood). More recently, poems written during the time of the Nazi occupation have referred to the song: *Modlitwa do Bogarodzicy* (Prayer to Bogarodzica) by K. K. Baczyński and *Modlitwa żołnierska* (Soldier's Prayer) by T. Gajcy.

The origins of *Bogurodzica* (Mother of God) present a complex problem, which outstanding scholars in literature and language, such as Julian Krzyżanowski, have attemped to solve. The tradition, inherited from a note added to the first printing by Jan Laski (1506), attributed its authorship to Saint Wojciech (Adalbert). The explanation has long been considered improbable, for the Czech bishop's visits to Poland were of too short duration and too infrequent for him to have become conversant with the language well enough to write *Bogurodzica.* The idea was again revived by Józef Birkenmajer (1937), who claimed that Saint Wojciech was acquainted with Byzantine culture in Italy, and that certain linguistic elements of *Bogurod-*

zica came from Greek liturgy. Another advocate of the idea of the early origin of *Bogurodzica* was T. Lehr-Splawiński (1936), who attributed the language of Bogurodzica not so much to Saint Wojciech as to Czech influences; he suggested that it was created sometime between the tenth and twelfth centuries. The hypothesis concerning Saint Alexander's authorship was challenged by Brueckner (after 1901) and by scholars who looked for the sources of the song in Latin paraliturgy and its melody, or who saw it as a *lais* (J. Fijalek, later Jerzy Woronczak—who dated the song from the second half of the thirteenth century; and Ewa Ostrowska, who dated it much earlier, to the eleventh or twelfth century). Krzyżanowski noted the similarity of some parts of *Bogurodzica* to Latin hymns and took into consideration the suggestions made by scholars from other Slavic countries (Jagić, Franko, Shevelyov) attributing the content of the first two stanzas to traditional Byzantine iconography. He saw the language of *Bogurodzica* as being influenced by Old Church Slavonic and contemporary Ruthenian. According to Krzyżanowski, the song was created in the late fourteenth century, in the early period of the rule of King Władysław Jagiełło, who felt attached to Ruthenian culture through his family bonds, who had many Ruthenians at his court, and who often sponsored Ruthenian artists. The hypothesis was further supported by the fact that the text mentions the king's wife, Sophia, and the king's sons, probably Kazimierz and Władysław Warneńczyk, and also by the fact that the song remained the anthem of the Jagiellonians throughout the fifteenth century.

The remarkable poem was memorialized in 1962, in a richly illustrated volume, which contains two hundred reprints of the text. The definitive edition did not solve the problem of the song's origin, but it laid the ground for further study.

The preceding studies were further supplemented in 1978 by S. Urbańczyk, who suggested that the origin of *Bogurodzica* lay against the background of Latin religious songs that existed earlier in medieval Poland. He emphasized the complexity of its verse and musical score, which, in his opinion, proved that the text dated from a later period, probably from the fifteenth century. A comparative linguistic analysis of *Bogurodzica* and similar national songs in Czech confirms the vernacular origin of the song, and also admits Czech cultural inspiration, especially that of the Czech song *Hospodine pomiluj ny,* which enjoyed a revival as a battle song and a coronation hymn in the thirteenth and fourteenth centuries. The hypotheses concerning the dating of *Bogurodzica* differ and the problem remains.

BIBLIOGRAPHY

Bogurodzica, opracował J. Woronczak, E. Ostrowska, H. Feicht, Wrocław, 1962.

BOGUSŁAWSKI, WOJCIECH (1757–1829), an actor, director, and playwright, came from a poor gentry family. After completing high school, he took a job in the army, but later resigned and joined the National Theater, against the wishes of his father. In 1778 he made his debut as an actor, a playwright (he adapted a French comedy), and an opera singer. In 1781–82 he performed in the theater in Lvov, then returned to the National Theater where he became the administrative director during the years 1783–85, 1790–94, and 1799–1814. In 1783 he opened his own theater in Poznań; then in 1785–90 in Wilno; and in 1795–99 in Lvov. When he became head of the National Theater for the third time, his group toured Łowicz, Kalisz, Poznań, Białystok, Kraków, and Gdańsk and became known throughout Poland. Connected with the educated nobility, Bogusławski was associated with the Reform Party and was a member of the *Sejm* (1788–92). He was very much respected in society. He was a member of the conspiracy which prepared the Kościuszko uprising in 1794 and a member of the government after Warsaw was liberated. After the fall of the Polish state he was forced to make many concessions to the occupying force (offering a pledge of allegiance, running a German group in the theater alongside the Polish one). This was the price he had to pay for the uninterrupted development of his theater, where he always managed to smuggle in political texts, ignoring the conflicts with the authorities that ensued. In 1814 he returned to his role as an actor in the National Theater, which toured Kalisz, Poznań, Wilno, and Minsk. In 1823 he was in charge of the theater's tour of Płock, Poznań, and Kalisz; in 1826 he became a member of the board which ran the theater; he made his last appearance on the stage on November 20, 1827.

In 1811 Bogusławski set up a Drama School at the National Theater; he prepared four volumes of his lectures, which were published in 1812 under the title *Dramaturgia, czyli nauka sztuki scenicznej* (Dramaturgy, or the Science of Theatrical Art; Volume 3, however, was never published). In Volumes 1 and 4 of *Dzieła dramatyczne* (Dramatic Works, Volumes 1–12, 1820–23) he published his memoirs, entitled *Dzieje Teatru Narodowego* (History of the National Theater), which contained portraits of actors and actresses of his time. These volumes are a priceless source of information regarding the early history of public theater in Poland.

Bogusławski wrote over eighty plays, sixty-two of which were published; fifteen are known in fragments or only by their titles; the authorship of five plays is disputable or doubtful. The majority of works are translations or "adjustments," which are in accordance with the theory and practice of literary translation during the period of the Enlightenment. The character of these works resulted, to a large extent, from the conditions in which Bogusławski worked—running a theater as a private enterprise. His own plays formed the core of the repertoire, which was always decided upon with the audience's tastes in mind. Brought up respecting French Classicism, Bogusławski gradually departed from the ideals (honor and duty), which were still being preached in circles close to King Stanisław August, and later had something of a renaissance during the first quarter of the nineteenth century. Besides French Classical tragedies that he staged (in translations other than his own) under the pressure of the literary milieu, he introduced Shakespeare to the Polish stage (translating *Hamlet* himself, on the basis of a German version and also Lessing's *Emili Galotti*) and eagerly produced drama, a genre then taking root. In his best comedies he followed the English models (*The School for Scandal* based on the play by Richard B. Sheridan, 1793), as well as Italian works (*Spazmy modne* [Fashionable Spasms], based on the play by Albergati Capacelli, 1797). He devoted most of his energy to creating an opera house: he was the initiator and the author of the greatest achievements of national opera (see his *Cud mniemany czyli Krakowiacy i górale* [Supposed Miracle, or Cracovians and Highlanders], 1794). Apart from the financial profit that the operas brought, Bogusławski's interests were also influenced by his own artistic and vocal gifts, which predestined him for the roles of basso buffo caricato. The experience he gained in such roles was later put to use during the period of his maturity as an actor and as a writer, when he created—obviously under the influence of sentimentalism—the character of a skeptical, yet serene, plebeian old sage, who expresses himself most adequately in a song: consider Old Dominik in *Taczka occiarza,* based on L. S. Mercier (1790), a work extremely popular on the Polish stage; Ferdynand Kokl from *Henryk VI na łowach* (Henry VI at the Hunt), Bardos in *Cud Mniemany* (Supposed Miracle), and so on. Bogusławski's talents were further stretched in works where he was at his best as a director: exotic dramas (*Iskahar* and *Król Guaxary,* 1797, exploiting a popular theme, the struggle of the Incas against the Spanish invaders), and especially in "great operas," such as Saberi's *Axur* and *Król Ormus* (1793), Mozart's *The Magic Flute* (1802), and Cherubini's *Les deux journées* (Two Days of Fear, 1804).

According to Zbigniew Raszewski, after 1812 Bogusławski became more and more obsessed with the classics; he was undoubtedly laying the ground for Romanticism. He led the Polish theater in the direction of the Romantics; he demanded, as did Mickiewicz, that the theater awaken idle minds. Bogusławski developed these patriotic goals not only in his plays, but also in the songs which gained popularity independently of the plays or operas they came from, such as songs from *Cud mniemany* or Song to the Sun from *Iskahar.* Not surprisingly, only the Romantics adequately evaluated Bogusławski's role, especially after the fall of the Polish state. He was called the "father of Polish theater" by his contemporaries, in appreciation of the fatherly care he bestowed on it. But to subsequent generations the name in fact implied that he was the actual founder of the national theater. Many theaters in Poland today bear his name. In 1936 a monument to his memory was erected in Warsaw (it was destroyed during the war and reconstructed later in front of the Great Theater). He became a colorful character in many literary works.

Cud mniemany, czyli Krakowiacy i górale (Supposed Miracle, or Cracovians and Highlanders), a comic opera by Bogusławski (probably based on some earlier unidentified text), with music by J. Stefani, was composed in 1793–94. The last work in the genre of "country opera" (during the times of King Stanisław August), it enriched its tradition by its links with folk poetry. For the first time in Polish theater, two regional groups come in conflict with one another: Cracovians from the village of Mogiła and Highlanders, who attack the former to take revenge and steal their cattle. The conflict involves a girl from Mogiła, Basia, who refuses to marry Bryndas, one of the Highlanders. Bryndas had earlier been promised Basia's hand by her stepmother, Dorota, who is in love with Basia's fiancé, Stach. The conflict is resolved in favor of the Cracovians by "a poor student," Bardos, who impresses the simple folk by employing an electrical machine.

The opera (first performed March 1, 1794) was received enthusiastically and "set the minds on fire" with the thought of Kościuszko's uprising against the Russians. F. Karpiński notes "its arias which were so well suited to the situation in Poland, and very expressive." After the third performance Russian censorship forbade that the opera be performed; it reached the stage again only during the uprising. It was produced again in Lvov in 1796, and later was performed everywhere in Poland up to the middle of the nineteenth century. It was modernized to suit current tastes at times; a popular version by Jan Nepomucen Kamiński, *Zabobon, czyli Krakowiacy i górale* (Superstition, or Cracovians and Highlanders), appeared. The folk opera returned to the stage of many theaters in Poland after the famous production by Leon Schiller (in Łódź, 1946). Among the preserved manuscripts, there is no text of the first performance.

(See Enlightenment.)

BIBLIOGRAPHY

Dzieje Teatru Narodowego . . . oraz Wiadomość o życiu sławnych artystów (History of the National Theater . . . as well as Information on the Life of Famous Artists), photo-offset edition, 1965.

Cud mniemany czyli Krakowiacy i górale (Supposed Miracle or Cracovians and Highlanders), third edition, edited by S. Pietraszko, Wrocław, 1960.

Z. R. Raszewski, *Bogusławski,* two volumes, Warsaw, 1972.

BOROWSKI, TADEUSZ (1922–51), prose writer, poet, and journalist, spent his childhood in Ukraine, in an area which after the Bolshevik Revolution found itself under Soviet control; for a number of years during his childhood he was placed under the care of distant relatives because both his parents were sent to forced labor in far-off regions of the Soviet Union. In 1932, as a result of the Act of Repatriation, he moved with his parents to Warsaw. He finished his secondary education in an underground school during the Nazi occupation (1940) and later also studied Polish philology in the underground university, associating with leftist circles (after 1943 they were gathered around the journal *Droga* [The Way]). On February 24, 1943, he was arrested, and after a short time spent in Pawiak, he was sent to Auschwitz (he was an orderly in the camp hospital). After August 1944 he was sent to the camp at Natzweiler-Dautmergen, then to Daschau-Allach. Liberated by the American army (May 1, 1945), he spent a short time in the DP camp in Freimann, and later worked for the Poles who were still in Germany and other Western countries (among other things, he was one of the founders of the Red Cross organization, which helped people find lost relatives). In June 1946 he returned to Poland. He finished his studies and then worked in Korbutianum, and for papers such as *Świat Młodych* (The World of the Young), *Pokolenie* (Generation), and *Nurt* (Current). In 1948 he joined the Communist Party. He had an important post in the organization of the pro-Communist World Congress of Intellectuals (in Wrocław 1948) and edited the Congress paper. During 1949–51 he worked in Berlin for the Polish Information Agency, at the same time carrying out intelligence work at the request of the Ministry of Public Safety. He also worked for the paper *Rzeczpospolita* (The Republic, 1949), and after 1950 was coeditor and chief journalist of *Nowa Kultura* (New Culture). A year later he committed suicide.

Borowski made his debut as a poet with the cycle *Gdziekolwiek ziemia* (Where Ever the Earth, underground edition 1942), a manifesto regarded as a bitter confession of the war generation. In his camp poems (the anthology *Imiona nurtu* [The Names of the Current], Munich, 1945) he created a horrific image of the fall and degradation of man. The poems develop the theme of the tragedy of one's personal guilt and responsibility to the millions who died. These obsessive motifs of his poetry were expressed vividly in two series of short stories: *Pożegnanie z Marią* (Farewell to Mary, 1948) and *Kamienny świat* (Stone World, 1948), which reveal the mechanism of moral destruction and degradation of man under circumstances created by the concentration camps and show the crisis of humanistic ethical ideals during the Holocaust. In contrast to the message found in other "camp literature" of the time, Borowski felt that the concentration camps were a logical consequence of a certain trend in European culture, the model for a new social order and new experiments with mankind. According to Tadeusz Drewnowski, these claims were regarded as blasphemy at the time and produced a wave of violent discussions and protests, and accusations (especially among Catholic circles) that Borowski was being cynical and nihilistic. Borowski's stories oppose the "martyrological" view by presenting a cruel vivisection of the "daily life" of the camp, which set in motion psychological mechanisms of adjustment and acceptance which inevitably blurred the distinction between victim and tormentor. In his later works Borowski became one of the main propagators of Socialist Realism and a spokesman for the radical cultural policies connected with it. (His political stand was analyzed by Czesław Miłosz, who made Borowski one of the heroes of his monumental work *The Captive Mind.*) In the short stories written shortly before his death and regarded as a continuation of his expressive political journalism, Borowski attempted to present current problems: *Opowiadania z książek i gazet* (Stories from Books and Newspapers, 1949), *Mała kronika wielkich spraw* (A Small Chronicle of Great Matters, 1951), *Na przedpolu* (In the Foreground, 1952), *Czerwony maj* (Red May, 1953). This creative period turned out to be artistically and ideologically catastrophic: it remains solely as a document of Stalinistic orthodoxy and a survey of its typical trend, known as Socialist Realism (an aggressive attack on contemporary European culture as a product of degenerative bureaucratic civilization, an obsessive hunt of the infiltration of "American imperialism," oratorical propaganda, panegyrics in honor of the Soviet Union and Communism, etc.). He also wrote some erotic poetry (*Arkusz poetycki* [Poetic Sheet] in *Droga* [The Way], Number 2, 1944, an underground edition), a poetic brochure *Poszukiwania* (Searches, 1945, with K. Olszewski), and a documentary volume, *Byliśmy w Oświęcimiu* (We Were in Auschwitz, 1946, the first edition in Poland 1958, with K. Olszewski and J. Nel-Siedlecki). Borowski's letters and his diary from Freimann entitled *Z pamiętnika* (From a Diary) were published in *Polityka* (Politics, 1961, 1970); a fragment of his treatise *O poezji i poecie* (On Poetry and the Poet) appeared in *Twórczość* (Creativity, 1971). Borowski's works have been widely translated into German, French, Dutch, Czech, English, and Russian; some were dramatized for the stage and screen (for example, the film by Andrzej Wajda *Krajobraz po bitwie* [Landscape After the Battle], 1970).

Pożegnanie z Marią, a collection of short stories, was published in Warsaw in 1948. Two stories come from the volume *Byliśmy w Oświęcimiu* (We Were in Auschwitz, Munich, 1946): *Dzień na Harmenzach* (A Day at Harmens) and *Proszę państwa do gazu* (This Way for the Gas, Ladies and Gentlemen); the other three were written after his return to Poland (*Pożegnanie z Marią* [Farewell to Mary], *Śmierć powstańca* [Death of an Insurgent], *Bitwa pod Grunwaldem* [The Battle of Grunwald]). After the writer's death the title was used to refer (acceding to the author's wish) to a larger series of stories (including also *Chłopiec z Biblią* [The Boy with the Bible], *U nas, w Auschwitzu. . .* [At Our Place, in Auschwitz], *Ludzie, którzy szli* [The People Who Walked], *Ojczyzna* [Fatherland], *Ofensywa styczniowa* [January Offensive]). The collection is considered Borowski's main literary work and one of the best in this genre in world literature.

This collection of stories presents its own vision of the times of the Holocaust, and especially of the concentration camp. The vision is markedly different from what we find in the war literature of the time. What links all stories together is the character of the narrator, Tadek, a student and poet from Warsaw, later a prisoner in Auschwitz and other Nazi camps, where he tries to survive by accepting various auxiliary tasks in the hospital, in the storeroom, in the reception center where Jews were prepared for the gas chambers. Vorarbeiter Tadek, who is himself starved, tortured, and cheated, accepts the rules of camp struggle for survival as a natural reality in which one can save one's life only through selfishness and learning to adjust, by obeying the orders of the tormentors, and by being ruthless to fellow prisoners. In the world of a concentration camp, which Tadek sees through his "adjusted" mind, all elementary emotions and all moral values of the outside world—sympathy, honesty, solidarity, dignity—are thought to mean nothing at all. The concentration camp, as the author sees it, is a model of the Nazi order, an extreme, but logical consequence of the system of exploitation, invasion, and terror. The violation of human values is particularly tragic here, for criminal goals are also imposed on the victims who, in turn, are forced not only to obey, but also to accept the crime and their own participation in it. Borowski sees similar symptoms in the reality of the occupation, which is governed by fear, violence, lies, and an unscrupulous struggle for survival, in the chaos of the postwar period, and, generally, in the climate of that era of the degradation of humanistic values of European culture. The provocative character of these stories is emphasized in its rigidly used naturalistic style, which resembles the styles of American behaviorists with its avoidance of any authorial comment, and in the character of the narrator, whom the author gives his own name, as if accepting responsibility for all of Tadek's faults (hence the ungrounded claims that the author was actually Tadek). Borowski's stories were widely known from the start, but they were received quite critically, regarded as symptoms of the author's moral nihilism; even today the ruthless moralistic tone in his works is the subject of critical disputes and arguments. The main problem that intrigues the scholar investigating the life and works of Borowski is the riddle, as formulated by Jan Kott, of the transformation of a writer who was "the greatest hope of Polish literature" into "a disciple, apostle, and inquisitor of the Communist Party."

(See Contemporary Polish Literature.)

BIBLIOGRAPHY

Utwory zebrane (Collected Works), Volumes 1–5, edited by J. Andrzejewski, T. Drewnowski, J. Piórkowski, and W. Woroszylski, Warsaw, 1964.

English

This Way for the Gas, Ladies and Gentlemen and Other Stories, edited and translated by Barbara Vedder, introduction by Jan Kott, New York: The Viking Press, 1967; New York: Penguin Books, 1967; 1976.

BOROWY, WACŁAW (1890–1950), historian and critic of literature, began his studies in Lvov, then continued at the Jagiellonian University (Polish Philology, also English). In 1920 he participated in the Polish-Soviet war as a volunteer. He worked as a high school teacher and a librarian in the University of Warsaw library (1920–28). In 1921 he became one of the founders of *Przegląd Warszawski* (Warsaw Review), where he was coeditor for two years; he was also one of the founders and active members of the Warsaw Scientific and Literary Club. In 1930–35 he was professor of Polish Philology in the School of Slavonic Studies of London University. In 1936–38 he was the head of the University Library in Warsaw. In 1938 he became professor and chairman of the Department of Polish Literature at Warsaw University. During the occupation he lectured in the underground university; he also contributed to the underground press. He was one of the coauthors and editor of a collective work on the losses of Polish culture during the occupation; the book was secretly sent to London and published there (*The Nazi Kultur in Poland,* with a foreword by John Masefield, 1945). After the Warsaw Uprising, he helped save various Polish libraries. In 1945 he started teaching again at the university and became the supervisor of the English Studies Program.

According to Zofia Stefanowska, Borowy belonged to the generation of researchers who modernized Polish literary studies. He was the first to use the Dibelius method in Poland. He emphasized the importance of writing techniques and literary convention and stressed the merits of modern comparative methodology (*O wpływach i zależnosciach w literaturze* [On Influence and Dependence in Literature], 1921); he also worked on the history of Polish verse and the role of rhythm in prose (*Rytmika prozy Żeromskiego* [The Rhythm of Żeromski's Prose], 1937). He opposed traditional biographical and psychological approaches, as well as new trends in literary criticism: phenomenological and formalistic ones (*Szkoła krytyków* [School of Critics], 1937; *Prawda w poezji* [Truth in Poetry], 1939). He treated literary history as a form of criticism whose aim was to discover the poet's individual features in order to reveal universal, emotional, and imaginative factors of the work which make the reader react to it. The description of the work, the study of its poetics, and the interpretation were elements which permitted an evaluation which reflected the critic's overall taste. Thanks to his comprehensive knowledge and methodological rigor these assumptions (inspired partly by Anglo-Saxon criticism, and by Benedetto Croce's aestheticism) did not give way to impressionistic evaluations, though they did at times bring about changes in the generally accepted hierarchy of Polish men of letters; for instance, in the anthology of Polish poetry *Od Kochanowskiego do Staffa* ([From Kochanowski to Staff], 1930, revised edition 1958); in essays on *Lilla Weneda* (1949) and *Gody zycia* (The Feast of Life, 1946) by Dygasiński; in his critical study *O poezji polskiej w wieku XVIII* (On Polish Poetry in the Eighteenth Century, 1948, second edition 1978), a collection of twenty excellent studies and literary portraits which emphasized purely poetic values of the literature of the epoch, rather than the public service performed by the authors. His critical acumen led him to revise his own views: an enthusiastic admirer of Żeromski (see, among others, *O "Przepióreczce" Żeromskiego* [On Żeromski's "The Quail"], 1925), he later gave a much more reserved evaluation of the novelist's works in his articles published in 1936 (then in the collection *O Żeromskim* [On Żeromski], 1960 and 1964).

Borowy's interests were concentrated mainly on the literature of the eighteenth century, Romanticism, and the period of Young Poland; he emphasized the special position of Mickiewicz in Polish literature; he devoted several essays and a series of university lectures to Mickiewicz (published from a manuscript *O poezji Mickiewicza* [On the Poetry of Mickiewicz], Volumes 1–2, 1958). An expert on Norwid, he wrote about the poet in *Pamiętnik Literacki* (Literary Diary, three series, each under the title *Norwidiana*) and in independent reviews. His overall interpretation of Norwid appeared in two sketches: *Norwid poeta* (Norwid the Poet) and *Główne motywy poezji Norwida* (Main Motifs in Norwid's Poetry, second edition, in the collection *O Norwidzie* [On Norwid], 1960). He also compiled a bibliography on Norwid and was editor of the reprint of Norwid's *Vademecum.* He displayed his comprehensive knowledge of European literature, especially English and French, in comparative works and in analyses of translations (*Boy jako tłumacz* [Boy as a Translator], 1922; *Przekłady Shakespeare'a i teatr* [Translations of Shakespeare and the Theater], 1947–48; *Dawni teoretycy tłumaczeń* [Old Theoreticians of Translation], 1950). He introduced Polish readers to the work of G. K. Chesterton (a monograph published 1929) and T. S. Eliot (sketches 1935, 1936). He amassed a great deal of source material on Polish-English cultural relations, but published only a small part in journals; the rest was destroyed during the war. He was also editor of numerous works (Żeromski, Mickiewicz, Kniaźnin). Only a small number of his works were included in two book collections that he published: *Kamienne rękawiczki* (Stone Gloves, 1932) and *Dziś i wczoraj* (Today and Yesterday, 1934). A master of prose style, he was able to combine acute reasoning with elegance of style, keen observation with high originality, in formulating general problems anew; for this reason, his short sketches remain important contributions to Polish and world literatures.

BIBLIOGRAPHY

Studia i rozprawy (Studies and Debates), Volumes 1–2, edited by T. Mikulski, S. Sandler, and I. Ziomek, Wrocław, 1952.

Studia i szkice literackie (Studies and Literary Sketches), Volumes 1–2, edited by Z. Stefanowska and A. Paluchowski, Warsaw, 1982–83.

BRAMY RAJU (The Gates of Paradise) (see Andrzejewski).

BRANDSTAETTER, ROMAN (1906–87), playwright and poet, first studied Polish philology (1924–29) at the Jagiellonian University, then spent two years in Paris doing research on the political activity of Mickiewicz. He spent the war years in the Near East. During 1947–48 he assumed the duties of cultural attaché in Rome: in 1948–49 he became the literary director of *Teatr Polski* in Poznań. He received the State Award for an opera libretto in 1951 and the Pen Club Award for translations from the Hebrew in 1972.

Brandstaetter's works combine general humanistic motifs, above all philosophical, moral, and aesthetic ones, with traditional ideas of Christian thought. His lyrics, classical in style, are frequently based on motifs taken from the Bible (*Jarzma* [The Yokes], 1928), *Królestwo Trzeciej Świątyni* [The Kingdom of the Third Temple], 1934), *Faust zwyciężony* [Faust Defeated], 1958), *Pieśń o moim Chrystusie* [Song of My Christ], 1960), *Hymny Maryjne* [Hymns to Mary], published in the collection *Pieśni* [Songs], 1963) or from antiquity (*Dwie muzy* [Two Muses], 1965). Among his poetic output are translations and paraphrases of biblical poetry (the anthology *Słowo nad słowami* [Word Above All Words], 1964; a revised abridged edition, *Cztery poematy biblijne* [Four Biblical Epics], 1972, and *Psałterz* [Book of Psalms], 1968) and various translations of Shakespeare's works. Brandstaetter's dramas are mainly based on historical themes. According to Leslaw Eustachiewicz, his heroes are usually embodiments of tragic moral conflicts: *Powrót syna marnotrawnego* (Return of the Prodigal Son, staged in 1947, published in 1948), based on the life of Rembrandt; *Przemysław II* (produced in 1948); selections from the volume *Noce narodowe* (National Nights, 1954), among others, about Mickiewicz and Towiański (produced in 1949); and *Król i aktor* (The King and the Actor), based on the life of W. Bogusławski (produced in 1952). Events occurring during World War II appear in *Upadek kamiennego domu* (The Fall of the Stone House, 1958), *Dzień gniewu* (Day of Wrath, 1962, revised edition, 1971), and the highly macabre *Zmierzch demonów* (The Twilight of the Demons, 1964); contemporary political problems were explored in *Milczenie* (Silence, 1957), a work which was ultimately censored. He returned to historical Polish traditions (in his comedy *Marcholt,* 1954) and to Greco-Roman traditions (in his collection of poetry and drama *Śmierć na wybrzeżu Artemidy* [Death on the Shore of Artemis], 1961). In his tetralogy *Jezus z Nazarethu* (Jesus of Nazareth, 1967–73), a transposition of the Gospel, he presented an image of the epoch, deeply rooted in the everyday reality of the lives of the Judeans, but colored with poetic vision.

Brandstaetter also published a collection of pamphlets, *Zmowa eunuchów* (The Eunuchs' Conspiracy, 1936); pieces of literary journalism, *Kroniki Asyżu* (Chronicles of Assisi, 1947); impressionistic miniatures in the same mode, *Inne kwiatki Świętego Franciszka z Asyżu* (Other Flowers of St. Francis of Assisi, 1976); and essays, *Krąg biblijny* (The Biblical Circle, 1975).

BIBLIOGRAPHY

English

Silence (Milczenie), translator anonymous, *Dialog,* Number 6, 1956.
Day of Wrath (Dzień gniewu), translated by H. C. Stevens, 8 Foster Close, Brundell, Norfolk, England, 1957.

BRANDYS, KAZIMIERZ (born 1916), a prose writer, was also coeditor of the Marxist weeklies *Kuźnica* (Forge, 1945–50) and *Nowa Kultura* (New Culture, 1950–52, 1956–60). A member of the Communist Party, recipient of state literary awards (1948, 1950, 1955), after 1956 he cut off ties with Marxism and with time drew nearer to circles of democratic opposition. In 1970–71 he lectured at the Sorbonne. From 1981 he has lived abroad, at first in New York, and later in Paris.

In his works he attempted to capture the social and historical conditioning of the fate and awareness of an individual and to reveal the motives of one's choices, opinions, and decisions. He especially tried to express experiences of the Polish leftist intelligentsia, its conflicts of conscience, hopes, and disappointments. In his novel *Drewniany koń* (The Wooden Horse, 1946) he presented an ironic portrait of a young intellectual, whose alienation from the community under the Nazi occupation leads to his moral and political defeat. A similar motive is undertaken in the tetralogy *Między wojnami* (Between the Wars), an epic story of the years of the advent of fascism, of the Nazi occupation, and of the period of postwar revolutionary metamorphoses (*Samson,* 1948; *Antygona,* 1948; *Troja, miasto otwarte* [Troy, the Open City], 1949; *Człowiek nie umiera* [Man Does Not Die], 1951, joint edition, revised, 1962). Drawing equally from Marxist views and the then modern tendencies derived from French existentialism, the writer endeavored to realize the thesis that, although the fate of people is determined by their social background and the course of history, they still can save their personal dignity through a "correct" ideological choice and involvement in the struggle for the right cause—even if chances for victory are minute. Two of his novels are devoted to Warsaw: its heroic war activities (*Miasto niepokonane* [The Unvanquished City], 1946, with numerous reprints) and postwar reconstruction (*Obywatele* [Citizens], 1954, regarded during its time as an exemplary realization of "Socialist Realism"). Short stories from the collection *Czerwona czapeczka* (The Little Red Hat, 1956) document the vital and moral catastrophe of many devoted members of the Communist Party resulting from moral compromise, political opportunism, and disappointed enthusiasm. Similar themes appear in *Matka Królów* (The Mother of Kings, 1957), where the arguments of the Communist revolution "horrifying for one's children" are contrasted with the instinctive knowledge of truth and moral righteousness, whose exponent is a simple mother-worker, mother of several party activists. The novel was made into a movie by J. Zaorski; it was held up for several years by censorship, and released only in 1987.

Brandys's early penchant for arbitrary judgments was later replaced by a lack of faith in the possibility of reaching a unique evaluation of the acts and intentions of a man caught in a net of involvement, experiencing the inconceivable turns of history or the cruelty of the war. In *Listy do pani Z.* (Letters to Mrs. Z., Parts 1–3, 1958–62) Brandys combined the presentation of his views on the objectives of literature with an essay-style review of the various problems of contemporary life (e.g., the present status of Polish traditions of the intelligentsia and the model of civic values emerging from it). The story *Jak być kochaną* (How to Be Loved) and others from the collection *Romantyczność* (Romanticism, 1960), as well as the novel *Sposób bycia* (A Way of Being, 1963), reflect the drama of a man losing his sense of psychological identity or dangerously deformed by circumstances which favor the loosening of ethical norms and turning of history into a fetish. His conviction that one can and has to shape one's own fate and his awareness of the moral meaning of what one does are best seen in his later works: *Dżoker* (The Joker, 1966), *Rynek* (Market Place, 1968), *Pomysł* (Idea, 1974), *Nierzeczywistość* (A Question of Reality, 1977), all published underground, as well as *Rondo* (1982) and *Sztuka konwersacji* (An Art of Conversation, London 1990). An interesting novel in letter form, *Wariacje pocztowe* (Mail Variations, 1972), a pastiche of Polish literary trends from the Baroque to contemporary times, is in its contents a recapitulation of the vicissitudes of several generations of Poles. These works also consider the relationship between literary fiction and reality. Brandys's latest works also reflect his attitude as a sympathizer of the democratic opposition and an émigré writer, especially in his reflective diaries *Miesiące* (Months), covering the period 1978–87 and published in Paris, 1981–87 (Volumes 1–4).

BIBLIOGRAPHY

English

A Question of Reality (Nierzeczywistość), translated from French by Isabel Burzun, New York: C. Scribner's Sons, 1980; London: Blond & Briggs, 1980; 1981.

Sons and Comrades, translated by David T. Welsh, New York: Grove Press, 1961; London: Allen Unwin, 1961.

A Warsaw Diary (Pamiętnik Warszawski), translated by Richard Lourie, New York: Random House, 1983; New York: Vintage Books, 1983; 1985.

Letters to Mrs. Z. (Listy do pani Z.), translated by Morris Edelson, Highland Park, Illinois: December Press, 1987.

Paris, New York, translated by Barbara Krzywicki-Herburt, New York: Random House, 1988.

BRANDYS, MARIAN (born 1912), a historical writer, journalist, brother of Kazimierz Brandys, studied law and economics at the University of Warsaw from 1930 to 1935. In 1939 he participated in the Polish-German war. Taken prisoner, he spent the remainder of the war in a German prisoner-of-war camp in Waldenberg. After liberation, as a war correspondent, he witnessed the capture of Berlin by the Red Army. From 1945 he was a member of the Communist Party, and in the early stages of his career as a writer (i.e., the documentary *Początek opowieści* [The Beginning of a Tale], 1951), he was included in the official criticism in the group of Socialist writers. Later he became associated with the group of Marxist revisionists under the leadership of Leszek Kołakowski. In 1966 he gave up his membership in the Communist Party and, in the seventies, he attached himself to the democratic opposition (his wife, Halina Mikołajska, a well-known actress, was a member of *Komitet Obrony Robotników* [Committee for the Defense of Workers]).

Brandys has worked out his own form of "a report of the past," in which he utilizes the experiences and methods of contemporary reporters for an analysis and description of remote historic events. His most prominent works are the series *Kozietulski i inni* (Kozietulski and Others, Volumes 1–2, 1967), and *Koniec świata szwoleżerów* (The End of the Cavalrymen's World, Volumes 1–5, 1972–79), which tells the story of the Polish participants in the Napoleonic Wars. They were the officers of the famous regiment of Napoleon's guards who fought on various battlefields for the freedom of Poland. After Napoleon's defeat they tried to find a place for themselves in the new reality of the Congress Kingdom (a quasi-autonomous Polish state created by Napoleon), which had fallen under Russian domination. A few attempted to reconcile working for their country as industrialists, military and civilian officials, financiers, and sponsors of art and culture, with loyalty to the self-imposed foreign government. Others entered conspiracies aimed at Poland's independence. For both the former and the latter the November Uprising of 1830 became the key event in their lives, which forced them to give up all in the face of the necessity to make an explicit moral and political choice. This typically Polish dilemma, faced time and time again by the Polish people in the nineteenth and twentieth centuries, also exists in Brandys's biographical works: *Nieznany książę Poniatowski* (The Unknown Prince Poniatowski, 1960), *Oficer największych nadziei* (The Officer of the Greatest Hopes, 1964), *Kłopoty z panią Walewską* (Problems with Mrs. Walewska, 1969), and *Generał Arbuz* (General Arbuz, 1988). The motif of inevitability of moral and political choices also returns in those works dealing with Polish contemporary reality: the collection *Z dwóch stron drzwi* (From Both Sides of the Door, published by the underground house NOWA) and the volumes *Moje przygody z historią* (My Adventures with History, 1981) and *Strażnik królewskiego grobu* (The Guard of the Royal Grave, 1984). The characteristic trait of Brandys's writing is his merging of documented accounts of historic events with observations made by contemporary researchers and writers who re-create not only facts but also the customs and morals of the epoch, the personalities of the heroes, and the moral and intellectual justifications for their actions. The writer shares with the reader the problems of his own research workshop, uncovering the traces of his own investigations, suppositions, and hypotheses, which give his books a note of authenticity.

BREZA, TADEUSZ (1905–70), an essayist and prose writer, entered the Benedictine Order in 1926, but after a few months resigned and began his studies at the University of Warsaw. He continued his studies in London, where he was a press secretary in the Polish Embassy in 1929–32. On his return to Warsaw he became director of the Cultural Department from 1933 to 1937 and director of the theatrical agency, *Młody Teatr* (Young Theater), founded by T. Boy-Żeleński. His first literary success came with the novel *Adam Grywald* (published in 1936). During the Nazi occupation Breza took active part in underground literary activities. After the war he became literary director of the *Stary* (Old) Theater in Cracow (1945–46). He also carried on a theatrical debate in the weekly *Odrodzenie* (Revival) (1946–48). In 1955–59, he became the cultural attaché in the Polish Embassy in Rome and in 1961–65 assumed the same duties in Paris.

Breza's postwar works have not withstood the test of time. His ambitiously intended cycle of political novels, *Mury Jerycha* (The Walls of Jericho, 1946), as well as *Niebo i ziemia* (Heaven and Earth, Volumes 1–2, 1949–50), a rather obvious lampoon of the prewar Polish elite politicians, have been doomed to the simplistic propaganda of that time. Greater recognition was accorded the writer for his two books based on his experiences in Rome: the essayistic diary *Spiżowa brama* (The Bronze Gate, 1960) and the novel *Urząd* (The Office, 1960), describing the church-government (the Vatican) as an institution of centuries of tradition, as well as of a complex bureaucratic structure searching for its place in the contemporary world. Both works, distinguished by a knowledge of the realia of the life of the Roman Curia in the final period of Pope Pius XII's pontificate, turned out to be, however, far from the mark in their diagnosis and prognosis of the course which the evolution of the church already had embarked upon after the Vatican Council. During the sixties numerous translations in various languages appeared; some critics succeeded in finding in them a perfidious allusive analysis of all functions—including the Communistic—of the mechanisms of power. Certain analogies were also raised by critics linking *Urząd* (The Office) with Kafka's *The Trial.*

BIBLIOGRAPHY

T. Drewnowski, *Krytyka i giełda* (Criticism and the Marketplace), Warsaw, 1969.
W. Maciąg, "Droga pisarska" (The Writer's Road), in *Nasz chleb powszedni* (Our Daily Bread), Cracow, 1966.

BRODZIŃSKI, KAZIMIERZ (1791–1835), a poet, historian and theoretician of literature, journalist, and translator, came from an impoverished gentry family and early in life became acquainted with the lives of simple folk. His knowledge of literature was gained through a formal education and the influence of his brother, Andrzej (in whose volume of poems he made his debut in 1807), who introduced him to sentimental poetry. From 1809 to 1813 he served in the army of the Grand Duchy of Warsaw, established by Napoleon; he took part in the battle of Lipsko and later became a clerk. In 1818 Brodziński started teaching literature, first in high schools, then at the University of Warsaw. From 1815 he worked exclusively with the periodical *Pamiętnik Warszawski* (The Warsaw Diary); he was coeditor from 1822 to 1823. He became a member of *Towarzystwo Przyjaciół Nauk* (Society of Friends of Science [TPN]) in 1821.

According to Alina Witkowska, his literary talent and view of the world matured during his experiences as a soldier, which made him sensitive not only to the sentimental and melancholy aspect of man's life, but also to the constant presence of pain and inevitable coming of death. These humanistic thoughts went well with the Freemasons' ideals which Brodziński advocated in his poems (he became a Freemason in 1814). This combination of constant awareness of the approaching end and stoical acceptance of this fact allowed Brodziński to go beyond prevailing artistic conventions and the philosophy of consolation which were typical of sentimental elegies: he created those still moving lyrics about the bitter sense of human existence (*Duma nad grobem* [Reflections over the Grave], *Na piasku piszem rachuby* [We Write Reckonings on Sand], etc.). Brodziński himself wanted, above all, to be a writer of idylls (*sielanki*). He wrote several in various literary conventions, beginning with imitations of the idylls of Theocritus and Virgil, and evolving into very mature idylls, country idylls like *Wiesław* (1820) and city idylls like *Staś i Halina* (1821), later known as *Czerniaków*. Brodziński endeavored to overcome eighteenth century conventions regarding the idyll—their highly emotional, Rococo-like style. He wanted to adapt them to contemporary ideals of simplicity and to moral standards of the "honest life" praised during his time, as well as to the realistic scenery of the country landscape. In this respect he borrowed ideas from old Polish sentimental poetry and contemporary German idylls (e.g., Goethe's *Herman und Dorothea*), as well as from German literary criticism (Herder, Jean Paul, and Schiller). In his critical writings (*O klasyczności i romantyczności tudzież o duchu poezji polskiej* [On Classicism and Romanticism as Well as the Spirit of Polish Poetry], 1818; *O idylli pod względem moralnym* [On the Idyll from a Moral Viewpoint], 1823; both in *Pamiętnik Warszawski*) the idyll appears not as a literary genre, but as a moral and aesthetic category, as a philosophical stance which could be realized in life as well as in art: the main principle was to seek happiness by limiting one's demands, remaining calm and modest. His interests were guided not only by a poetic spirit, but by the tenets held by historians and ideologists—trying to understand the nation's past and future. He wanted to get at the national character of Poles and draw conclusions for literature. With his treatise *O Klasyczności i romantyczności* he became one of the outstanding representatives of Slavophilism—with its glorification of national history and its belief in the outstanding moral character of Poles. These virtues were to stem from the ideals of a farmer's life—his patriarchal gentleness, his love of the land, and his patriotism and courage.

Brodziński's views on literature were given their best expression in two treatises: *O krytyce* (On Criticism) and *O egzaltacji i entuzjaźmie* (On Exaltation and Enthusiasm) in *Pisma rozmaite* (Various Writings, Volume 1, 1830). In these two works Brodziński fiercely opposed Romanticism, whose passionate, uncompromising spirit and gloomy imagery threatened the ideals of sentimental literature. In return, his opponents (M. Mochnacki, J. B. Ostrowski) accused him of spreading imitation sentimentalism, of terrorizing opponents, and, above all, of ignoring the changes in the contemporary world.

His views changed radically after the November Uprising (1830–31). After that time he began to interpret the history of his nation with a messianic spirit. In *Mowa o narodowości Polaków* (Speech on the Nationality of Poles, May 3, 1831) he suggested that the Polish nation was appointed by God to spread Christianity, freedom, and brotherhood, paying for the privilege with great suffering. In *Posłanie do braci wygnańców* (A Missive to Brothers in Exile, written in 1835, published in 1838) he emphasized the similarity between the history of Poland and Christ's pain and resurrection. Brodziński's notion of Poland's messianic role is passive in nature—people ought to wait patiently until they are rewarded for their suffering. It disagreed with the dynamic messianism represented by, among others, Mickiewicz and Towiański.

Brodziński was also a translator of the works of Schiller, Goethe, Herder, Grillparzer, Scott, and others.

(See Romanticism.)

BIBLIOGRAPHY

Poezje (Poetry), Volumes 1–2, edited by Cz. Zgorzelski, Wrocław, 1959.

Pisma estetyczno-krytyczne (Esthetic-Critical Writings), Volumes 1–2, edited by Z. J. Nowak, Wrocław, 1964.

BRONIEWSKI, WŁADYSŁAW (1897–1962), a poet and translator, came from a family with lively patriotic traditions. Already in secondary school he was a member of an underground organization struggling for Poland's independence. In 1914 he edited a paper of young independence fighters, which he practically monopolized with his own poems. In 1915 he joined the Polish Legions and fought at the front until 1917, when he was placed in an internment camp. In 1918 he started his studies at the University of Warsaw but shortly thereafter returned to the army and took part in the Polish-Soviet War (1919–20), in which he served as a captain and was awarded the Cross of Valor a number of times. In 1921 he went back to his studies. He soon became attracted to the ideology of leftist circles. In 1924 he was on the editorial board of *Nowa Kultura* (New Culture), where he published his first poem, signed with his real name—a translation of a poem by Mayakovsky. A year later he published his first collection *Wiatraki* (Windmills), followed by the "poetic bulletin" *Trzy salwy* (Three Salvos, together with W. Wandurski and S.R. Stande—the first manifesto of the so-called proletarian poets in Poland). From 1925 to 1936 he worked for *Wiadomości Literackie* (Literary News) and published many reviews and articles. He was not a member of the Communist Party, but participated in many of its activities: he founded and ran a worker's theater, edited a political paper in 1928, and was on the editorial board of *Dźwignia* (The Lever, 1927–28) and *Miesięcznik Literacki* (Literary Monthly, 1929–31). He was arrested together with other editors and spent two months in prison, from which he was released through the influence of friends who served with him in Piłsudski's Legion. After his release he continued working for leftist papers; in 1934 he spent a few weeks in the Soviet Union.

In September 1939 he enrolled in the army as a volunteer and went to Lvov to find his unit; the city was soon occupied by the Russians. In early 1940 he was arrested by the Soviet Secret Police (NKVD); after serving time in a number of prisons, he was released in September 1941 as a result of the amnesty accord reached by the Polish government in exile and the Soviet Union. First he went to Kuibyshev (Samara), where he worked for the paper *Polska* published by the Polish Embassy; then he joined the Polish army which was then being formed in the Soviet Union under General Anders's command. Evacuated along with others, he found himself in the Near East. In 1943 he was granted a leave of absence and went to Jerusalem, where he was coeditor of the paper *W drodze* (On the Way). In 1945 he returned to Poland, first to Łódź and then to Warsaw, where he lived until his death.

According to Feliksa Lichodziejewska, Broniewski's works progressed not only in close relationship with his biography, but also with the history of Poland and its proletarian movements. His poems are revolutionary and patriotic in content and have great emotional impact. After the first eclectic collection, *Wiatraki* (Windmills), he was able to develop his own poetics and his own style, which combined the tradition of Romanticism with a moderate avant-garde, exaltation and pathos with everyday language and the phraseology of political propaganda, traditional verse with modern assonance. His collections published between the wars (*Dymy nad miastem* [Smoke over the City], 1927; *Troska i pieśń* [Worry and Song], 1932;

Krzyk ostateczny [Final Cry], 1938; and *Komuna Paryska* [The Paris Commune], 1929, first confiscated by the censor) are mainly political in character: they explore revolutionary ideals, but at the same time relate back to the romantic myth of Promethean sacrifice, presenting heroes imbued with courage and loneliness, savoring both bitter defeat and glorious hope for future victory. His war collections are similarly complex (*Bagnet na broń* [Present Arms!], 1943; *Drzewo rozpaczające* [The Lamenting Tree], 1945). Patriotic themes are interwoven with nostalgic memories, the urge to fight intermingled with despair, the awareness of unity with the whole nation along with feelings of being lost and alienated. His postwar poems of the early period (the collection *Nadzieja* [Hope], 1951, and the lengthy poem *Słowo o Stalinie* [A Word About Stalin], 1949) are above all political, dealing with the "revolutionary struggle," with the "creative effort exerted in the reconstruction of the country." They are typical representatives of Socialist Realism. Broniewski is one of the characters described in Miłosz's *The Captive Mind.* Miłosz was not the only critic surprised by the unbelievable combination of Romanticism and Socialist Realism, Polish ardent patriotism, and an apologetic attitude toward Stalin and Soviet Russia in Broniewski's poems. (A provocative interpretation of this phenomenon was given by Marek Hłasko in *Piękni dwudziestoletni* [Beautiful Twenty-Year-Old]). Later Broniewski turned to lyrical motives in his poetry: the beauty of the Polish landscape and a reflection on his life and works (*Mazowsze* [Mazovia] and *Wisła* [Vistula], 1951 and 1953). After the death of his daughter (1954), he wrote one of his most impressive cycles of poems, *Anka* (Annie, 1956). He also translated a number of Russian classics.

Broniewski was a very popular and respected poet. Even those who criticized his political views considered him highly talented. His works often circulated in handwritten copies, were recited at political meetings, and, indeed, had the power to mobilize people. During the war his patriotic poems were often published in the underground papers, in Poland and abroad. He received many important awards and medals.

(See Contemporary Polish Literature.)

BIBLIOGRAPHY

Wiersze zebrane (Collected Poems), 1948; Fifth edition, Warsaw, 1956.

Wiersze i poematy (Poems and Narrative Poems), 1962, thirteenth edition, 1978. Works omitted from the Polish edition of his collection were published in *Wiersze* (Poems), Paris: Instytut Literacki, 1962.

BROSZKIEWICZ, JERZY (born 1922), prose writer and playwright, was connected with many cultural journals and magazines (*Odrodzenie* [Rebirth], *Teatr* [Theater], *Listy z teatru* [Letters from the Theater], *Nowiny literackie* [Literary News], *Przegląd Kulturalny* [Cultural Review, 1953–

63], and *Muzyka* [Music]). He had his own cultural program on Polish radio. For many years he was the literary director of *Teatr Ludowy* (The People's Theater) in Nowa Huta (Cracow). His interests as a writer are very broad, ranging from psychology to politics, history, and adventure. His best known novels include the following: *Oczekiwanie* (Awaiting, 1948), the story of one year in the life of the ghetto, where his characters are torn between patience and despair, hope and determination; *Kształt miłości* (The Shape of Love, 1951), about the development of the artistic talents of Chopin; the cycle *Dziesięć rozdziałów* (Ten Chapters, Volumes 1–2, 1970–71), a picture of the intricate fate of Poles in our century; and *Doktor Twardowski* (Doctor Twardowski, Volumes 1–2, 1977–79) about the problems of contemporary science presented against the background of the old Polish legend of Master Twardowski. He was also a well known playwright: *Imiona władzy* (The Names of Power, in *Dialog*, 1957, produced in 1957) is a triptych presenting three models of the struggle for power; *Skandal w Heidelbergu* (Scandal in Heidelberg, produced in 1961) shows the helplessness and terror caused by the renascence of fascism in Germany; *Koniec księgi VI* (The End of Book VI, in *Dialog*, 1963, produced in 1964), a play about Copernicus, deals with the responsibility of a researcher for what he discovers. His plays are characterized by a lack of uniformity in terms of the literary genre they represent. Two dramas are more clearly grotesque in character: *Jonasz i błazeń* (Jonah and the Jester, produced in 1958) and *Dziejowa rola Pigwy* (The Historical Role of Quince, produced in 1960). His novels for younger readers combine an interesting plot with a moral lesson; their setting is contemporary reality (*Wielka, większa, największa* [Great, Greater, Greatest], 1960, adapted for the screen 1963); sometimes they reach out into outer space (*Mój księżycowy pech* [My Moon Ill Luck], 1970). Broszkiewicz also wrote plays for TV and radio, sometimes adapted novels for the stage, and authored several screenplays. He has received many awards, among others the award of the Minister of Culture.

BIBLIOGRAPHY

Utwory sceniczne (Theatrical Works), Cracow, 1973.

English

E. J. Czerwiński, *Contemporary Polish Theater and Drama, 1956–1984*, Westport, Connecticut: Greenwood Press, 1988.

BRYLL, ERNEST (born 1935), a poet, prose writer, and playwright, graduated from Warsaw University in the school of Polish philology. He was connected with several cultural magazines. He was also on the board of *Współczesność* (The Contemporary, 1959–60); the literary director of the film studios *Kamera* (since 1968) and *Silesia* (since 1978); the literary director of *Teatr Polski* (The Polish Theater) in Warsaw (1971–74); the director of the Polish Cultural Institute in London (1975–78); and an ambassador to Ireland (since 1991).

The main trend in Bryll's writings is his critical reconsideration of the national literary tradition; in his early works he expressed an antiaestheticism and the feeling of being disappointed and discouraged (*Wigilie wariata* [Christmas Eves of a Madman], 1958; *Autoportret z bykiem* [Self-Portrait with a Bull], 1960). Later he turned to moral reflection on politics and historicism. He evaluated modern times by unmasking the habits developed in people's minds—falsifying reality with dreams and illusions, making it better than it really was. He opposed the pompous seventeenth and eighteenth century gentry ("sarmatian") patterns deeply rooted in Polish literature and argued for the ideals of plebeian vitality and sober political realism; instead of glorifying national defeats and dilemmas, he claimed, literature should propagate those values that could prove useful in modern times. In poetry (*Twarz nie odsłonięta* [A Face Not Uncovered], 1963; *Sztuka stosowana* [Applied Art], 1966; *Mazowsze* [Mazovia], 1967; *Muszla* [The Shell], 1968; *Piołunie piołunowy* [Bitter Wormwood], 1973) these thoughts are expressed through the constantly varying moods of the lyrical character, through self-contradiction, irony, and self-irony. In Bryll's poems during the 1980s a catastrophic tone appeared simultaneously with Solidarity and the nation's subjection to repression during Martial Law. In the poetry of this period a major role was played by religious motives (in his collection *Advent,* London in 1986, with drawings and an afterword by Andrzej Wajda).

Bryll's ideas are further developed in his poetic dramas, which juxtapose contradictory views and refer to the tradition of Romantic drama: *Rzecz listopadowa* (A November Matter, in *Dialog,* 1968, produced in 1968), *Kto ty jesteś?, czyli Małe oratorium na dzień dzisiejszy* (Who Are You? or a Small Oratorium for Today, in *Dialog,* 1970, produced in 1970), and a stylized morality play *Życie jawa* (A Life Awake, in *Dialog,* 1972, produced as *Co się komu śni* [What One Dreams], 1972). Bryll often juxtaposes a sarcastic tone with general humanistic reflection, with metaphysical and eschatological elements (*Oratorium pastoralne "Wołaniem wołam cię"* [Pastoral Oratorium, "By Voice I Call You"], 1974; *Zwierzątko* [The Little Animal], 1975). The conflicts he presents in his poetry and dramas are expressed through a variety of contrasting means: crude words and plain imagery, sophisticated metaphors, and references to the style of old Polish and Romantic literature (especially Norwid and Słowacki). He employed the folk tradition in his pastoral drama *Po górach, po chmurach* (On Mountains, On Clouds, 1969, produced in 1968) and in his folk musical play (*śpiewogra*) *Na szkle malowane* (Painted on Glass, in *Dialog,* 1969, produced as *Janosik, czyli . . .* [Janosik, or . . .], 1970), the verse drama *Wieczernik* (Cenacle), a transposition of evangelical trends suggestively setting up a mood of desperation and of hope which prevailed in society during the eighties. Suppressed by the censor, it was produced to great success in various churches (directed by Andrzej Wajda) and was only published in 1990. His prose belongs to the tradition of realism and presents a sociological portrait of Polish peasants, both in historical perspective (World War II and the postwar period) and in contemporary times. He also wrote mininovels—*Studium* (A Study, 1963), *Ciotka* (Aunt, 1964), *Ojciec* (Father, 1964), *Jałowiec* (Juniper, 1965)—and short stories: *Gorzko, gorzko* (Bitter, Bitter, 1964) and *Drugi niedzielny autobus* (The Second Sunday Bus, 1969). He has also translated Old Irish poetry.

BIBLIOGRAPHY

J. Kwiatkowski, "Zgrabna niezgrabność" (Shapely Unshapeliness), in *Remont pegazów* (Overhauling Pegasuses), Warsaw, 1969.

English

Shifting Borders: East European Poetries of the Eighties, Rutherford, New Jersey: Fairleigh Dickinson University Press, 1993, 276–77.

Spoiling Cannibals' Fun: Polish Poetry of the Last Two Decades of Communist Rule. Evanston, Illinois: Northwestern University Press, 1991, 132–35.

BRZOZOWSKI, (LEOPOLD) STANISŁAW (pseudonym Adam Czepiel) (1878–1911), a literary critic, philosopher, journalist, and novelist, came from an impoverished gentry family. He started his studies at the University of Warsaw, but was soon dismissed for participating in an anti-Russian demonstration. In 1898 he was arrested and spent a month in prison, where he contracted tuberculosis.

Brzozowski's first works (critical pieces, the novels *Pod ciężarem Boga* [Under the Weight of God], 1901, and *Wiry* [Whirlpools], 1904–5, and a drama, *Mocarz* [The Potentate], staged in 1903) were written in the spirit of modernism, emphasizing the decay of all values. Thus his works are rooted in modernism, but even his modernist manifesto (*My młodzi* [We the Young], 1902, in *Głos* [Voice]) signals the coming change, arguing in this piece the differences between early modernism, as represented by the Cracow magazine *Życie* (Life), and its later social ideals regarding working in society for society, as embodied in the works of Stefan Żeromski. His position was made still clearer in his campaign against Henryk Sienkiewicz, which he initiated and published in *Głos* (Voice), and summed up in his treatise *Henryk Sienkiewicz i jego stanowisko w literaturze współczesnej* (Henryk Sienkiewicz and His Position in Contemporary Literature, 1903). The young critic gave priority to the social and ideological role of literature, and condemned Sienkiewicz not as an artist but as an ideologist of the conservative nobility. A year later he ran a similar campaign against the influential critic, advocate of the ideals of "art for arts' sake," Zenon "Miriam" Przesmycki, and more specifically, against treating art as a mystic ideal not to be understood by the profane. He was thus supporting his earlier position, that is, a view of modernist thought different from the one advocated by Miriam.

According to Andrzej Werner, Brzozowski's philosophical views developed alongside his understanding of art. They were often referred to as "the philosophy of acting," after the title of his specific understanding of the works of Nietzsche, Fichte, and Kant. Acting, man's free creative effort, distinguishes him from other beings: it gives an individual his freedom in the world and constitutes his subjectivity. The creative act does not lead to a goal which can be attained permanently; it constantly recreates itself, for achieving a goal would simply mean becoming a slave of the things already done. Philosophy, art, criticism, any intellectual activity can be evaluated only in terms of "the quality and quantity of acting it gives rise to." There is no barrier between those intellectual activities and life itself; they are a form of living in one's consciousness. Brzozowski opposed all theories which make man dependent on already established entities, whether material or spiritual, and considered them erroneous and harmful. His criticism was mainly directed against various forms of "positivist naturalism" or "scientism," that is, seeing man as a link in the evolutionary chain, and the consequences of such a stand, from epistemology to social practice. He held similar views on Marxism, which he understood as "a theory of automatic progress in history." His writings of the period were later published in the volume *Kultura i życie* (Culture and Life, 1907).

Later Brzozowski's view of Marxism changed drastically, to a large extent as a result of the 1905 Revolution. The writer's links with the progressive circles became strictly political, though he was never a member of any organization. He gave many talks (in Zakopane, Cracow, Lvov); he gave two series of lectures in the Lvov Technical University. At that time his views radically changed, from a "philosophy of acting" to a "philosophy of work." His new ideas developed his earlier way of thinking and now he saw the works of Marx in a totally different light. Work is a collective act of mankind which creates the foundations for an independent existence in our struggle with nonhuman elements, with nature. The collectiveness of the effort is the only guarantee of the act being effective and changing history into man's conscious creation. Hence the Promethean role of the proletariat, for mankind can be freed only through the emancipation of work, through making it a conscious act of self-creation. There is no freedom outside work; avoiding work means self-destruction in history. Every human activity is sanctioned only through its connection with work. Intellectual activity, too, which is not based on such a foundation can produce only harmful illusions. Brzozowski's work as a critic at the time (after 1906) presents a unique phenomenology of such illusions. Individual pieces combine into an imposing overall critical analysis of cultural phenomena in Poland and Europe from the early nineteenth century to contemporary times. It found its best expression in *Legenda Młodej Polski* (The Legend of Young Poland, 1910), the fundamental critical study of the consciousness of the Polish intelligentsia, reflected in the literature of the period. Earlier, in 1906 and in 1907, Brzozowski wrote two shorter works, *Współczesna powieść polska* (The Contemporary Polish Novel) and *Współczesna krytyka literacka w Polsce* (Contemporary Literary Criticism in Poland). His ruthlessly thorough evaluation done from the point of view of the philosophy of work was directed at intellectual trends and artistic programs in general, not at particular works or authors. According to Brzozowski the task of a critic was to juxtapose his own point of view on the one expressed in the work—whether consciously or not. In order to achieve this, the critic first had to reconstruct the ethical foundation of the work, which was revealed mainly in its form. As a result, Brzozowski's critical works, apart from being uncompromisingly evaluative, contain very deep-reaching and often sympathetic portraits of authors and analyses of their works. He was particularly subtle in his sociological analyses. The comprehensiveness of his outlook is seen at its best in his own novels (*Płomienie* [Flames], 1907, based on authentic facts about the activities of groups of Russian and Polish revolutionaries who attempted to assassinate Tsar Alexander II; and *Sam wśród ludzi* [Alone Among People], the history of an ideologically mature hero, a representative of the Polish Romantic intelligentsia, whose fate comes into conflict with the intellectual currents of Europe at the beginning of the nineteenth century).

In 1907 Brzozowski went to Italy with his family and never returned to Poland. Soon after that he was unjustly accused of being an agent of the tsarist police. He defended himself in the press; many outstanding writers also spoke up in his defense—the authors of the accusations, the Socialists, could not risk their prestige and called off the charges. The case was never brought to any conclusion.

During the later years of his life, Brzozowski's philosophical views evolved even further. Under the influence of Sorel and Bergson his philosophy of work adopted the irrational claims of the philosophy of life. The concept of the nation was now given a more prominent role as "the deepest reality," the source of the collective will. At that time Brzozowski became fascinated with English literature. He was moving further and further away from the Marxist ideas in his philosophy of work. His critical approach to Marx did not mean a lack of coherence in his thought, for it resulted from assumptions taken earlier, and the main questions of his philosophy remained unchanged. The "religious breakthrough" in his work was not a sudden deviation. Brzozowski was under the influence of Catholic modernism (mainly J. H. Newman), but the Catholic beliefs were not a matter of faith for him, but rather an intellectual argument.

The last years of his life were filled with physical and moral pain: he was sick, lived in poverty, but worked as hard as ever. He never finished all he wanted to do, yet he remains one of the most outstanding critics in the history of Polish literature.

He was a very talented novelist, although he did not achieve much (the two early works mentioned and an unfinished novel, *Książka o starej kobiecie* [Book About an Old Woman], 1908–10). They show human life from the point of view of the bare facts of human existence, emphasizing the obstacles history and nature place on man's road to fulfillment. The life of an individual is evaluated not with regard to the values that Brzozowski fought for, but rather to the effort put into finding one's own truth.

Brzozowski's output exerted a great influence on the political and literary thought of the twentieth century. It gave inspiration to many, though sometimes conflicting, intellectual trends. Its role was not only that of direct stimulation of certain views, but rather that of a negative or positive point of reference. There is still no complete edition of his works; many pieces remain scattered in numerous periodicals.

(See Positivism.)

BIBLIOGRAPHY

Dzieła wszystkie (Complete Works), Volumes 4, 6, 8, 11, edited by A. Górski and S. Kołaczkowski, Warsaw, 1936–38 (edition not completed).

Kultura i życie (Culture and Life), wstęp A. Walicki, Warsaw, 1973 (augmented and edited).

Listy (Letters), t. 1–2, edited by M. Sroka, Cracow, 1960.

BURSA, ANDRZEJ (1932–57), a poet, prose writer, journalist, studied Polish philology at the Jagiellonian University. He was a reporter for *Dziennik Polski* (The Polish Daily). He first started publishing poetry in 1954, in magazines, mainly in the student newspaper *Zebra.* According to Jadwiga Zacharska, his poetry addresses conditions of his times; it is rebellious, reacting violently against injustice and lies; uncompromising and provocative, in its conscious brutality and cynicism. At the same time his poetry probes permanent humanistic values, combining naturalistic acuity of poetic vision with surrealist imagery and hidden lyricism. Apart from poetry, Bursa also wrote several short stories, reminiscent of the parables of Franz Kafka (the situation of an individual threatened by the anonymous machine of law and power), and a novel, *Zabicie ciotki* (The Killing of the Aunt), inspired by Dostoevsky's *Crime and Punishment,* whose main theme is the effects of senseless killings on a young man who commits the murders. He also tried his hand at drama, in which he emphasized the macabre and grotesque. His literary output was published after his death: *Wiersze* (Poems, 1958), *Utwory wierszem i prozą* (Works in Verse and Prose, edited by S. Stanuch, 1969, 1973), and *Poezje wybrane* (Selected Poetry, 1977). After his untimely death, Bursa became a mythic figure of his generation.

BIBLIOGRAPHY

M. Chrzanowski, *Twórczość Andrzeja Bursy* (The Creativity of Andrzej Bursa), Cracow, 1978.

C

CATHOLIC UNIVERSITY OF LUBLIN (*Katolicki Uniwersytet Lubelski*), better known as *KUL*, was founded in 1918 as a private school of higher learning. Until 1928 *KUL* was known as *Uniwersytet Lubelski* (Lublin University). The rector of the Petersburg *Akademia Duchowna* (Academy of Religious Studies), I. Radziszewski, was instrumental in establishing the secular school. In 1938 *KUL* was officially authorized to grant degrees of higher learning under the same mandate as the state universities.

At the present time *KUL* has four divisions. Besides scientific and teaching activities, the university is also involved in social and popular undertakings, offering basic courses to the public at large. The following were on the university staff during the twenty-year period between the wars: Radziszewski, M. Straszewski, B. Rutkiewicz (Philosophy), L. Bialkowski, S. Ptaszycki, S. Zachorowski (History), J. Manteuffel, and W. Strzelecki (Classical Philology). During the Nazi occupation professors of the university carried on underground studies in Lublin (1939, 1941–42), in Warsaw (1943–44), and in Kielce (1943–45). After the war the following scholars joined the faculty: in the area of Philosophy—S. Świezawski, S. Kamiński, M. A. Krąpiec, and Karol Wojtyła; in the area of History—A. Wojtkowski, M. Żywczyński, and J. Kłoczowski. Under the auspices of *KUL*, *Biblioteka Uniwersytecka Lubelska* (The Library of Lublin University) publishes five series of scientific studies. The articles of university professors appear in the publication *Odrodzenie* (Rebirth), sponsored by the Union of Polish Catholic Intelligentsia and Christian Learning (*Wiedzy chrzesciańskie*). In 1930 the university began to publish a series devoted to dissertations and seminar papers.

In 1934 the academic Senate appointed *Towarzystwo Naukowe KUL* (Scientific Society of *KUL*) as the coordinating center for organizational and scientific activities of all publications, separate from the university.

Among the activities of the publishing center are the following: research sources and monographs, as well as various treatises, dissertations, and commissions. The Humanities Yearbooks include the following categories: Polish Literature, History, Classical Philology, Neo-Philology, History of Art, and Linguistics.

Polish Philology was created within the Division of the Humanities. Linguistics developed in the direction of comparative and general studies (W. Porzeźiński, J. Baudouin de Courtenay, and T. Milewski), as well as research in the history of the Polish language and stylistics (H. Gaertner; S. Szober; W. Doroszewski; W. Kuraszkiewicz, the initiator of the study of Lublin dialects; M. Dłuska; and T. Brajerski).

In the area of Polish literature, Romanticism was stressed. An emphasis was also placed on Old Polish Studies. The oldest traditions of research involved the history of literature, especially the history of drama. Later studies included the theory of literature and methodology of literary research. Among the early staff members were the following: S. Ptaszycki (1918–26; in 1927 he was elevated to the position of distinguished professor); P. Bańkowski, who lectured on the history of literature after the partitions (1918–24); C. Pecherski (1918–25), a specialist in sixteenth-century literature, who also lectured on poetics and the analysis of literary works. The directors of the two departments of the History of Polish Literature were W. Hahn (1921–39), whose research included an emphasis on the works of Słowacki and dramatic literature of the sixteenth century, and H. Życzyński (1927–39), whose areas of interest included aesthetics of Romantic thought and the theory of drama, who also lectured on poetics and stylistics and the problems of *Młoda Polska* (Young Poland*). J. Krzyżanowski (1925–26) lectured on seventeenth century literature, Polish Romantic elements in the sixteenth century, and Polish syntax. L. Kamykowski (1934–36) specialized in Baroque literature. With the outbreak of the war, the university was unable to carry on normal educational activities. A number of professors were killed, among them J. Birkenmayer (who joined *KUL* in 1939) and Życzyński. A number of professors were arrested by the Nazis and interned.

After 1944 a new stage in the development of KUL began with professors of other universities, especially of Jagiellonian University, taking on various duties. The first staff of the Department of the History of Literature included J. Kleiner (1944–49), F. Araszkiewicz (1948–66), S. Sawicki, M. Jasińska-Wojtkowska, S. Kawyn (from 1945), and Cz. Zgorzelski (from 1950).

The Department of Comparative Literature was headed by J. Parandowski (1944–50). Romanticism continued to be the chief area of research, with the following staff: Kleiner (on Mickiewicz and Krasiński) and Kawyn (history of the cult of Mickiewicz). After 1950, the following joined the staff, concentrating especially on Mickiewicz, Słowacki, and research on the problems of the art of poetry, and the epic: Zgorzelski and his former students M. Maciejewski, D. Zamęcińska-Paluchowska, I. Opacki, and A. Paluchowski. Norwid was also emphasized by the following researchers: I. Sławińska, W. Achremowiczowa, and Sawicki. Old Polish Literature was the main research interest of J. Nowak-Dłużewski (1953–56). In 1971 J. Sokołowski became the head of the Department of Old Polish Literature. Araszkiewicz introduced positivism and the literature of *Młoda Polska* as a permanent research area in the department, including the history of the Polish novel in the second half of the nineteenth and the twentieth centuries. S. Fita and H. Filipkowska also worked in this area. In 1975 the Department of Contemporary Literature was set up under the directorship of Jasińska-Wojtkowska.

Kleiner and M. Dłuska were instrumental in developing the area of the theory of literature. From 1949 Sławińska (director from 1950 to 1975) emphasized research on the problems of drama and theater and the theory of the novel and the lyric. Sawicki contributed to the development of the area of methodology, while the following carried on research in the theory of literature, methodology, and semantics and semiotics: Jasińska-Wojtkowska (theory of the novel and literary biography), Opacki and Zgorzelski (theory of the lyric and ballad), and W. Górny (stylistics and linguistics).

In 1976 the Department of Drama and Theater (directed by Sławińska) was set up.

The research in Polish studies appears in *Roczniki Humanistyczne* (Humanities Yearbooks) published by *Towarzystwo Naukowe* (Research Society) of *KUL* in the notebooks of *Polish Literature* (edited by Kleiner, and subsequently by Sławinska, Aroszkiewicz, T. Brajerski, and Jasińska-Wojtkowska), as well as in the quarterly *Zeszyty Naukowe KUL* (The Research Notebooks of *KUL*), edited by W. Granat, and subsequently by F. Grygielewicz, M. A. Krąpiec, A. B. Stepień, and W. Hryniewicz.

BIBLIOGRAPHY

S. Fita, *Polonistyka KUL, 1944–1974* (Polish Studies at KUL, 1944–1974), *Biuletyn Polonist,* 1975.

Rocznik Humanistyczne 17 (1969), *Zeszyt* 1. (Dedicated to KUL).

CHIMERA, a literary-artistic magazine, was published in Warsaw 1901–7 (with breaks in 1903 and 1906). The editor-in-chief was Zenon Przesmycki (pseudonym Miriam); the secretary of the board was S. Korab Brzozowski; then, for some time, Jan Lemański. Originally, *Chimera* was planned to be a monthly, but it was not published regularly. There were thirty issues in ten volumes altogether. The artistic program of the magazine, which was characteristic of the main trends in modernism, could be summed up in

Miriam's thought "Great art is always symbolic in its form and metaphysical in its content." According to Jerzy Kądziela, the modernists assumed that art had to be indifferent to moral systems and practical purposes (art for art's sake) and worshiped great artists, who were said to form the elite, the "spiritual aristocracy." Conflicts between the artist and society or the petit bourgeois were considered "the eternal laws of art"; intuition was treated as the main component of creativity. Such views were criticized by many intellectuals (S. Brzozowski, J. Marchlewski, W. Nałkowski). The works of the modernists were certainly given preference in *Chimera.* The following were published: Berent's *Próchno* (Dry Rot) and *Źródła i ujścia nietzscheanizmu* (The Sources and Estuaries of Nietzcheanism); J. Kasprowicz's *Hymny* (Hymns) and *Narodziny marcholta* (The Birth of Marcholt); T. Miciński's *W mroku gwiazd* (In the Darkness of Stars); translations by Przesmycki and his study on Rimbaud; S. Przybyszewski's *Synowie ziemi* (The Sons of the Earth); Stefan Żeromski's *Leśmian, Dygasiński, Reymont, Wyspiański, Staff, Zawistowska, Komornicka,* and *Nałkowska.* The editor deserves credit for publishing Norwid's works and for rescuing him from oblivion (Volume 8, 1904, was devoted to Norwid). Miriam also raised the quality of translations and widened the circle of foreign authors to include translations of the main representatives of European symbolism and Parnassism, as well as publishing the Romantics, to whom contemporary literary trends related so often (Ch. Baudelaire, P. Verlaine, S. Mallarmé, E. Verhaeren, J. Keats, R. W. Emerson, W. B. Yeats, H. von Hofmannstahl). Miriam also published texts by Nietzsche and Kirkegaard, and English, Scottish, Scandinavian, Spanish, and Provençal ballads, translated by E. Porębowicz. *Chimera* was also distinguished (among other magazines in Europe) by its very high level of graphic design—artists who worked permanently for *Chimera* included Józef Mehoffer, Edward Okuń, and Jan Stanisławski. Jan Lemański and Maria Komornicka, together with Miriam, were responsible for the section *Kronika miesięczna* (Monthly Chronicle), which published reviews and critical articles on new books in Polish prose and new translations, as well as notes on painting and music. Miriam's high standards were the reason why the magazine did not appear very regularly. The last volume contained an anthology of young poets from the so-called *Chimera* School.

BIBLIOGRAPHY

Programy i dyskusje literackie okresu Młodej Polski (Literary Programs and Discussions during the Period of Young Poland), edited by Maria Podraza-Kwiatkowska, Wrocław, 1973.

CHŁOPI (The Peasants) (see Reymont).

CHMIELOWSKI, PIOTR (1848–1904), a critic and historian of literature, was one of the creators of Polish literary positivism and represented its moderate trend. He was connected with *Przegląd Tygodniowy* (Weekly Review, 1867–72), *Opiekun Domowy* (The Home Guardian, 1872–76), and *Niwa* (Soil). He published several ideological papers (*Geniusz i masy* [Genius and the Masses] and *Utylitaryzm w literaturze* [Utilitarianism in Literature], 1872; *Pozytywizm i pozytywiści* [Positivism and Positivists], 1873; *Niemoralność w literaturze* [Immorality in Literature], 1872) and theoretical treatises (*Geneza fantazji* [The Origin of Fantasy], 1872; *Artyści i artyzm* [Artists and Artism], 1873). He studied in Leipzig 1873–74, where he received his Doctor of Philosophy degree. From 1903 he taught at the University of Lvov. He was also a member of the Academy of Sciences (1893) in Cracow.

According to Henryk Markiewicz, as a literary critic Chmielowski followed the positivist beliefs of social utilitarianism in literature; later he placed more emphasis on the realistic presentation of the contemporary world. In his ideological evaluations he applied the criteria of liberal progressiveness; from the artistic point of view he paid attention to the accuracy of observation, the form of narration, the structure of the work, and the psychological probability of the characters. Approving realistic prose, he treated modernist poetry with reserve, but he admired Wyspiański's work. He was exceptionally productive (over two thousand works) and was able to cover all the important phenomena in literature from 1864 to the beginning of the twentieth century. His reviews and articles were published in the following volumes: *Współcześni poeci polscy* (Contemporary Polish Poets, 1895), *Najnowsze prądy w poezji naszej* (Newest Currents in Our Poetry, 1901), *Dramat polski doby najnowszej* (Polish Drama of the Most Recent Times, 1902), *Henryk Sienkiewicz* (1901), and *Jan Kasprowicz* (1904). His synthetic view of the period was presented in *Zarys literatury polskiej z ostatnich lat szesnastu* (Outline of Polish Literature of the Last Sixteen Years), 1881; fourth edition enlarged, *Zarys najnowszej literatury polskiej* (Outline of the Newest Polish Literature, 1898).

As a historian of literature Chmielowski was, at least theoretically, a follower of Hippolyte Taine. In fact he was mainly interested in the relation between the writer's work and his cultural background; he tried to characterize the ideological content of the work and remained historically oriented in his evaluation. He was mainly interested in nineteenth century literature. Apart from his monographic studies—*Adam Mickiewicz* (1886), *Józef Ignacy Kraszewski* (1888), *Studia i Szkice z dziejów literatury polskiej* (Studies and Sketches from the History of Polish Literature, Volumes 1–2, 1886), and literary portraits, *Autorki polskie wieku XIX* (Polish Female Authors of the Nineteenth Century, 1885), and *Nasi powieściopisarze* (Our Novelists, S. 1887–95)—he wrote studies of literary genres in all areas of Polish literature: *Nasza literatura dramatyczna* (Our Dramatic Literature, Volumes 1–2, 1898) and *Dzieje krytyki literackiej w Polsce* (History of Literary Criticism in Poland, 1902). One work which became very popular and had many editions was *Kobiety Mickiewicza, Słowackiego i Krasińskiego* (The Women of Mickiewicz, Słowacki and Krasiński, 1873). His book *Liberalizm i obskurantyzm na Litwie i Rusi* (Liberalism and Obscurantism in Lithuania and Russia, 1898) was an excellent study of eighteenth century culture. His vast research was summed up in his *Historia literatury polskiej* (History of Polish Literature, Volumes 1–6, 1899–1900), which was meant for nonscholars. He used the same method as in his other works: briefly presenting the literary facts, emphasizing the influence of the writer's cultural background, and then characterizing the problems touched upon in the works. Chmielowski was also the editor of many Polish classics. He was also a pedagogue, an editor, a publisher, and a translator.

(See Positivism.)

BIBLIOGRAPHY

Pisma krytyczno-literackie (Writings in Literary Criticism), Volumes 1–2, edited and with an introduction by H. Markiewicz, Warsaw, 1961.

Prace z metodyki literatury i stylistyki (Works on the Methodology of Literature and Stylistics), selected, edited, and with an introduction by K. Lausz, Warsaw, 1961.

CHRZANOWSKI, IGNACY (1866–1940), a historian of literature, studied in Wrocław, in Berlin, and later at the Sorbonne and College de France. A Professor at the Jagiellonian University from 1910, a member of the Academy of Sciences, the recipient of two doctorates *honoris causa,* he worked for many magazines and publishing houses and the serial publications *Wiek XIX: Sto lat myśli polskiej* (The Nineteenth Century: A Hundred Years of Polish Thought). In 1911–39 he published, at his own expense, a series (approximately fifty volumes) of works written by his disciples. In November 1939, he was arrested along with other professors of the Jagiellonian University and imprisoned in Wrocław and later in concentration camps, located in Sachsenhausen and in Oranienburg, where he died.

Chrzanowski made his debut with the treatise *Tragedia Szymona Szymonowicza "Castus Joseph" w stosunku do literatury obcej* (Szymon Szymonowicz's Tragedy "Castus Joseph" in Relation to Foreign Literature) in 1892. His early works were typically philological in character, but he soon abandoned strictly academic studies and devoted his attention to interpretation, both aesthetic (related mainly to the works of Dibelius) and ideological. His criteria were both moral and patriotic. He saw literature as "a means and a symptom of the struggle for the existence of the nation" (*O literaturze polskiej* [On Polish Literature], 1910) and expected literary works to be imbued with educational values. Brought up on the ideals of Romanticism and educated to be a positivist, he combined both approaches. According to Ewa Kondyjowska, he never followed any one definite philosophical trend or a given variant of poetics. His writings are characterized by a direct and emotional attitude toward the work under analysis, with a broad humanistic outlook and delivered in a beautiful style. First he concentrated on the literature of the sixteenth and eighteenth centuries (*Z dziejów satyry polskiej XVIII wieku* [From the History of Polish Eighteenth Century Satire], 1909); later his main subject was Romanticism (*O komediach Aleksandra Fredry* [On the Comedies of Aleksander Fredro], 1917; sketches and treatises in collections such as *Z epoki romantyzmu* [From the Epoch of Romanticism], 1918; *Wśród zagadnień książek i ludzi* [Among Questions on Books and People], 1922; *Literatura a naród* [Literature and the Nation], 1936; *Studia i szkice, rozbiory i krytyki* [Studies and Sketches, Analyses and Criticism], Volumes 1–2, 1939). His most popular work remains *Historia literatury niepodleglej Polski* (History of Literature in Independent Poland, 1906; fourteenth edition, 1975); its continuation—*Historia literatury Polski porozbiorowej* (History of Literature in Poland Under the Partitions)—remained in manuscript. The book had a specific didactic goal: it displayed the glory of Polish culture in the past and claimed that the nation had the right to live at the level reached by its culture; he praised the patriotic values of some works and condemned the lack of such ideas in others. The book was supplemented by readers' texts. It was first meant to be used in secondary schools; in 1930, enlarged and completed, it became a university textbook. It is not flawless in its presentation of facts and the interpretations are controversial, but the work still has undeniable informative and educational value.

(See Baroque.)

BIBLIOGRAPHY

O literaturze polskiej (On Polish Literature), selected by A. Biernacki, Warsaw, 1971.

Optymizm i pesymizm polski: Studia z historii kultury (Polish Optimism and Pessimism: Studies in the History of Culture), selected by A. Biernacki, Warsaw, 1971.

CHWISTEK, LEON (1884–1944) a philosopher, mathematician, theoretician of art, painter, journalist, and writer, studied in Cracow, Göttingen, and Paris and later became Professor of Logic in Lvov. In philosophy he represented critical rationalism and pragmatism, arguing against metaphysical speculative philosophy and dogmatism; later his views approached materialism and Marxist thought. A follower of epistemological relativism, he developed his original theory of "multiple reality" (1921), which assumed the existence of four mutually exclusive types of reality, which corresponded to independent forms of experience: common (the reality of things), scientific (the physical reality), psychological (the reality of impressions), and artistic or religious (the reality of images). On the basis of this division he developed his own aesthetic typology (see, among others, *Wie-*

lość rzeczywistości w sztuce [The Multiplicity of Realities in Art] in *Maski* [Masks], 1918), which distinguished four types of art: primitive, realistic, impressionistic, and visionary—which he considered to be the domain of modern trends in art.

His ideas gave a theoretical foundation to the early Polish avant-garde, in which Chwistek was actively involved. He was a theoretician of formism, a member of the group called *Formiści Polscy* (Polish Formists, formed in 1917), and coeditor of their periodical, *Formiści* [Formists]; he participated in some "happenings" of the futurists, was coeditor of *Nowa Sztuka* (New Art, 1921/22) and *Zwrotnica* (The Switch, 1922); he wrote on avant-garde art, poetry, theater, and architecture; and he was a painter, practicing his own doctrine of "strefism." What he appreciated most in the new art was the freedom of imagery, experimental daring, with its variety and optimistic liveliness and playfulness. He was engaged in polemics with the representatives of academic aesthetics (e.g., Roman Ingarden); he was often criticized, mainly by Karol Irzykowski and S. I. Witkiewicz—his former friend and intellectual colleague, who later became his main antagonist (*Krytyka teorii sztuki Leona Chwistka* [A Criticism of Leon Chwistek's Theory of Art] and *Leon Chwistek—demon intelektu* [Leon Chwistek: Demon of the Intellect]). He was also a publicist (e.g., *Zagadnienia kultury duchowej w Polsce* [Questions of Spiritual Culture in Poland], 1933), criticizing anachronous forms of social and cultural life in a spirit akin to that of Boy-Żeleński. Competing with Witkacy, he wrote some experimental novels: *Kardynał Poniflet* (Cardinal Poniflet, written in 1906, destroyed in 1917) and *Pałace Boga* (The Palaces of God), a grotesque fantasy filled with philosophical, religious, ethical, social, political, artistic, and erotic motives (written 1932–33, fragments published in *Czas* [Time] in 1934, an "attempted reconstruction" by L. B. Grzeniewski, 1968).

BIBLIOGRAPHY

Wielość rzeczywistości w sztuce i inne szkice literackie (The Multiplicity of Realities in Art and Other Literary Sketches), selected and with an introduction by Karol Estreicher, Warsaw, 1960.

Pisma filozoficzne i logiczne (Philosophical and Logical Writings), introduction by K. Pasenkiewicz, Volumes 1–2, Warsaw, 1961–63.

CLASSICISM (see Enlightenment).

CONTEMPORARY POLISH LITERATURE (*Współczesna Literatura Polska*), according to most Polish critics, begins in 1918, when Poland regained its independence and literature and the arts and culture began to take on new forms and once more flourished. Various literary institutions sprang up, including the Union of Writers and the international PEN Club (1924). In 1926 a law guaranteeing authors' copyright was passed.

Ideological and political upheaval dominated the period between the wars, 1918–39. New social conflicts arose as a result of Poland's gaining independence. The problems of Europe became manifest in Poland. The Socialist revolution in Russia, the rise of Communism, the great economic crisis (1929–33), nationalism, fascism, and the menace of a second world war left their marks on Poland. Polish literature proved fertile ground for the evolving creative, artistic, and scientific movements of the period. In literature all types of experimentation took place: extreme subjectivism and an attempt at objectifying the picture of the world, expressionism and "the new realism," psychoanalytical penetration of the subconscious, and the documentation of "literature of fact." A search for a moral, spiritual, and meaningful social system, built upon the tenets of Communism and Catholicism, was attempted. Urbanization, industrialization, movies, radio, and social factors dictated the road that Poland was to follow.

The older generation of Polish writers played a major role at the beginning of the period between the wars, especially those writers associated with modernism: Żeromski* and Berent* in prose; Kasprowicz* and Lange* in poetry. Staff* championed the return to everyday reality while Leśmian* urged a closer relationship between fantasy and concrete observation and experimentation with language. The group of poets gathered around the journal *Skamander** (founded in 1920), rejected the program of *Młoda Polska**, and experimented with Romantic themes and lyrical language (Tuwim*), reflective rhetoric (Słonimski*), Romantic pathos (Lechoń*), biological optimism (Wierzyński), and stylized irony (Iwaszkiewicz*). Women poets appeared under the aegis of *Skamander*, especially Iłłakowiczówna* and Pawlikowska-Jasnorzewska,* who in their poetry displayed a deep sensitivity and intellectual irony.

A group of writers from Poznań developed a program of Expressionism (J. Kaden-Bandrowski),* which also appeared in the early works of the Skamandrites (J. and W. Hulewiczów, J. Stur, E. Zegadłowicz, and J. Wittlin* (*Hymns*, 1920). At the same time, a group of writers from Cracow and Warsaw espoused the doctrines of futurism (J. Jankowski, T. Czyżewski*, B. Jasieński*, S. Młodożeniec, A. Stern, and A. Wat*), publishing manifestos calling for a radical departure from traditional works and a search for new sources of poetic inspiration. The Cracow avant-garde gathered around the journal *Zwrotnica* (Switch, 1922–27), under the theoretical leadership of Tadeusz Peiper.* He was joined by J. Przyboś*, J. Brzękowski, and J. Kurek. Cubism was also espoused, especially by the poet A. Ważyk.* Social and revolutionary poetry also had its adherents (W. Broniewski*, S. R. Stande, W. Wandurski, and Jasieński*).

In prose the problems brought on by war and the winning of independence were explored, especially the theme of "lost illusions" (Nałkowska's *Romans Teresy Hennert* [The Romance of Teresa Hennert], 1924), Strug's *Pokolenie Marka Świdy* [The Generation of Marek Swida], 1925), and specifically Żeromski's* *Przedwiośnie* (Early Spring, 1924). The seizure of power was graphically depicted by Kaden-Bandrowski* (General Barcz, 1923). A deeply humanistic approach to the fate of village people was presented by Maria Dąbrowska* in her collection of short stories *Ludzie stamtąd* (People from Yonder, 1925).

In the area of drama Żeromski's* dramas (*Uciekła przepióreczka* [A Little Quail Got Away from Me], 1925), together with the works of members of *Młoda Polska**, were quite popular. Expressionism was represented by the works of K. H. Rostworowski.* Comedy was a major genre, especially the works of W. Perzyński, S. Krzywoszewski, A. Grzymała-Siedlecki, S. Kiedrzyński, W. Grubiński, K. Wroczyński, and B. Winawer. Avant-garde drama was brilliantly represented by Stanisław Ignacy Witkiewicz, whose works influenced source of Polish and world drama and theater of the absurd.

With the death of Reymont,* Żeromski,* and Kasprowicz,* a new generation of young writers appeared: under the patronage of *Skamander*—J. Liebert, S. Napierski, S. Karpiński, and J. Paczkowski; gathered around the weekly *Wiadomosci Literackie* (Literary News, 1924–39)—more liberal democratic writers like Słonimski.*

In the area of cultural criticism, T. Żelenski* defended rationalist traditions and translated some of the finest works of French literature. He was joined by K. Irzykowski,* a penetrating critic of literature between the wars (*Walka o treść* [A Battle over Content], 1929).

Revolutionary literature, a mixture of Polish Romanticism and social themes, became quite popular during this period (see Broniewski*). Members of the young generation of writers, which gathered around *Kwadryga* (Quadriga), included the following: S. R. Dobrowolski, S. Flukowski, K. I. Gałczyński,* W. Sebyla, W. Słobodnik, A. Maliszewski, S. Ciesielczuk, and M. Piechal. In drama the symbolic mood pieces of Jerzy Szaniawski* appeared, together with the psychological dramas of Nałkowska (*Dom Kobiet* [House of Women, 1930]) and the satirical comedies of Słonimski.*

The thirties were marked by an interest in social and economic problems, exacerbated by the Great Depression of 1929. The Polish Academy of Literature (*Polska Akademia Literatury*) was established in 1933 under the leadership of W. Sierowski, who was instrumental in setting up the journal *Pion* (Plumb-Line, 1933–39).

The novel became the most outstanding genre in the thirties: *Noce i dnie* (Nights and Days, 1932–34) by Dąbrowska; *Granica* (The Border, 1935) by Nałkowska; and the novels of Iwaszkiewicz,* Kuncewiczowa,* and Gojawiczyńska. It was marked by a return to the realistic tradition and psychological exploration. Proletarian literature was also popular (Kruczkowski and Wasilewska), emphasizing a new, more revolutionary view of the past. Writers who would play an important role in postwar literature also made their debut: Andrzejewski,* Breza,* and Rudnicki.

Three writers occupy a foremost place in the literature between the wars: S. I. Witkiewicz (*Pożegnanie jesieni* [Farewell to Autumn], 1927, and *Nienasycenie* [Insatiability], 1930), W. Gombrowicz* (*Ferdydurke,* 1937), and B. Schulz* (*Sklepy cynamonowe* [Cinnamon Shops], 1933, and *Sanatorium Pod Klepsydrą* [The Sanatorium Under the Sign of the Hourglass]).

During World War II and the German occupation, Polish literature and culture suffered severely. Most institutions, universities, and schools were closed and literary publications were silenced. Writers were either forced to go into hiding or interned in camps or ghettos. Polish writers, accustomed to battling censorship and the cruelty of the occupying forces, with few exceptions refused to collaborate with the authorities. Conspirational activities flourished, private apartments became literary and political meeting places, and underground cultural activity became a staple for a nation at war. Over fifteen hundred pamphlets and books were published underground, with more than two hundred of these of a literary character. Hundreds of collections of poetry were also published and private presses collected manuscripts for eventual publication. Most larger cities had a conspiratorial press. In Warsaw a number of publications appeared: *Sztuka i Naród* (Art and the People), edited by O. B. Kopczyński, W. Bojarski, A. Trzebiński, and T. Gajcy; *Sprawy Naroda* (Affairs of the People), edited by J. Dobraczyński; *Kultura Jutra* (Tomorrow's Culture), edited by J. Braun; *Prawda* (Truth), edited by Z. Kossak-Szatkowska, among others; and *Droga* (The Way), edited by E. Pohoska and S. Marczak-Oborski. In Cracow the most important publication was *Miesięcznik Literacki* (Literary Monthly), edited by T. Kwiatkowski.

Poetry was the most popular genre among the older generation of poets and those making their debuts during the war years and occupation. Staff,* Jastrun,* and Miłosz* continued publishing, the latter poet issuing his books of poetry himself after 1940. Individual collections appeared conspiratorially: Zagórski, Bąk, Zuławski, and Gamska-Lempicka. The following anthologies were among those best known: *Pieśń niepodległa* (Independent Song), *Słowo prawdziwe* (The True Word), *Wierne płomienie* (Faithful Fire), and *Śpiew wojny* (Song of War). Young poets born after World War I made their debut during this period, including Baczyński,* Borowski,* Gajcy, Trzebiński, Stroiński, and Bojarski.

Jerzy Andrzejewski's early novels appeared in typewritten manuscripts. The main themes in these works concerned the moral problems of the world of prisoners in the ghettos and war camps. A. Kaminski's documentary novels were also popular, as were those dealing with the war and ghettos (*Obóz śmierci* [Camp of Death] by N. Zarembina, *Golgota* [Golgotha] by Z. Kossak-Szatkowska, and *Na Oczach Swiata* [Before the Eyes of the World] by M. Kann). The works of eyewitnesses to the tragedy of the ghettos and camps offered a rich storehouse of materials for future literary critics and historians. The following writers have left great personal documents to the treasury of war literature: Nałkowska,* Irzykowski,* Bobkowski,* W. Szlengel, H. Lazowertówna, Janusz Korczak, M. Borwicz, Gałczyński,* Nowicki, Sułkowski, Górska-Romanowiczowa, and G. Chrostowska.

On the territory not occupied by the Germans in 1939, in the area of today's Ukraine and Belarus, a number of Polish writers gathered around the Communist literary monthly, *Nowe Widnokręgi* (New Horizons), published in Lvov (Lviv) under the editorship of W. Wasilewska in Polish. The contributors included the following writers: Borejsza, T. Żeleński,* J. Pański, J. Przyboś,* J. Putrament,* A. Ważyk,* J. Broniewska, H. Górska, M. Jastrun, and K. Kuryluk.

A special role was played by writers who emigrated to France, England, and the United States during the years 1940–41. The earliest literary effort was organized in Paris in 1939–40. The journal *Polska Walcząca* (Poland Fighting), under the editorship of T. Terlecki, was first published at this time, followed by *Wiadomości Polskie Polityczne i Literackie* (Polish Political and Literary News) under the editorship of M. Grydzewski and Z. Nowakowski. The following writers were active in England: A. Słonimski,* S. Baliński, M. Pawlikowska-Jasnorzewska,* Z. Nowakowski, K. Pruszyński, and the president of the Polish PEN Club in Exile, M. Kuncewiczowa.*

In the United States writers continued publishing. Julian Tuwim wrote his most celebrated volume of poetry, *Kwiaty Polskie* (Polish Flowers), during the war. Other poets who continued writing in Polish were J. Lechoń,* K. Wierzyński,* and J. Wittlin,* who together edited *Tygodnik Polski* (The Polish Weekly) in New York (to 1947). Polish writers who found themselves beyond Poland's borders continued to publish Polish literature abroad: Gombrowicz* in Argentina; K. Iłłakowiczówna* in Romania; S. Vincenz in Hungary; Broniewski,* Wańkowicz,* and Parnicki* in the Soviet Union; J. Łobodowski in Spain; and J. Stempowski in Switzerland.

Polish literature during the war years and occupation was created in the free world, in occupied Poland, and in prisons and war camps. This literature dealt with the eschatological questions of life, offering hope in the future in a free world. Philosophical and moral themes were intertwined with social, ideological, and political problems. The mistakes of the recent past were analyzed by such disparate writers as Andrzejewski,* Nałkowska,* Breza,* K. Brandys,* S. Dygat,* and by the literary critic Kazimierz Wyka* in his sketches.

The literature of the Polish People's Republic came into existence shortly after the war. Various literary organizations, journals, and publishing houses were founded. The Union of Professional Polish Literary Writers (*Związek Zawodowy Literatów Polskich*) was again set up and in 1949 became the Union of Polish Literary Writers (*Związek Literatów Polskich*).

Warsaw was rebuilt after being almost completely destroyed and soon became the center of literary and cultural activities. Writers of all generations took part in creating a new literature, many returning from years in exile. Not all agreed with the new political reality and either remained abroad or emigrated, especially after 1949, when the doctrine of Socialist Realism was adapted by the Union of Polish Writers. The simpleminded and objectionable tenets adumbrated by the government's puppets proved anathema to the majority of Polish writers, who demanded freedom of expression. In 1955–56 a partial victory was achieved by the liberal wing of the Union of Writers. After this time, Polish literature found itself on a roller-coaster ride, sometimes reaching the heights of artistry, at other times experiencing the nadir of literary defeat.

As a result of the partial victory, which witnessed the overthrow of Socialist Realism, a number of literary organs sprang up, offering writers the opportunity to disagree and present various points of view. The following journals provided high-quality writers a place to publish their works: *Współczesność* (Contemporaneity, 1956); *Odra,* 1957; *Nurt* (Current, 1965, set up in Poznań); *Dialog;* 1956, published in Warsaw; *Kultura* (Culture, 1963); *Poezja* (Poetry, 1965); and *Miesięcznik Literacki* (Literary Monthly, 1966).

In 1968 a "new wave" (*Nowa fala*) of young writers appeared. The short-lived weekly *Literatura* (Literature, 1972) allowed writers with radical views that differed from the Party line to publish their concerns. The feeling of exhilaration was fleeting, and writers began to search for other unofficial sources to publish their works; this led to the events in the eighties with the declaration of Martial Law on December 13, 1981, and a decade of underground literature (see *Drugi obieg*).

After 1944 prose became the dominant genre. Kazimierz Wyka* expressed his views on realism in his book *Pogranicze powieści* (Border Novels, 1948). The following critics sided with the ideological-political views of the authorities and established *Kuźnica* (Forge): J. Kott,* S. Żółkiewski, and A. Ważyk.*

The psychological climate of the occupation was described by the following writers: J. Iwaszkiewicz,* in his collections of short stories *Stara cegelnia* (The Old Coal-Mine) and *Młyn nad Lutynią* (The Mill over Lutynia, 1946) and in his novel *Matka Joanna od Aniołów* (Mother Joan of the Angels, 1946); Z. Nałkowska* in her relation of accounts of witnesses to Hitler's crimes in *Medaliony* (Medallions, 1946); and J. Andrzejewski,* who expressed the moral conflicts of the war generation, in his short stories *Noc* (Night, 1945) and in his *Popiół i diament* (Ashes and Diamonds, 1948), in which he created a sharply satirical and tragic picture of the young generation weighted with the problems precipitated by the war. The martyrology of the Polish Jews was tragically delineated by A. Rudnicki* in his collections of short stories entitled *Epoka pieców* (The Epoch of Ovens), *Szekspir* (Shakespeare, 1948), and *Żywe i martwe morze* (The Living and Dead Sea, 1952). T. Breza's* novels (*Mury Jerycha* [The Walls of Jericho], 1946 and *Niebo i Ziemia* [Heaven and Earth], 1949–50) examined the psychological-political aspects of the contemporary elite. J. Putrament* also dealt with the reaction to the war on people who lived through it, especially in his short stories (*Święta Kulo* [O Holy Sphere], 1946). His novel *Rzeczywistość* (Reality, 1947) explored the fate of the young leftists during the time of the purge. The war novel was popular with many Polish writers, especially W. Żukrowski (*Z kraju milczenia* [From the Country of Silence], 1946, and *Dni klęski* [Days of Defeat], 1952). J. J. Szczepański also dealt with the moral and psychological problems that resulted from the September defeat (*Polska jesień* [Polish Autumn], 1955). S. Dygat's* novels explored the fate of a troubled intellectual in *Jezioro Bodenskie* (Lake Boden, 1946) and *Pożegnanie* (Farewell, 1948). P. Hertz tackled the problem of the naive individual who comes in contact with fascism (*Sedan,* 1948). K. Brandys's* epic *Między wojnami* (Between the Wars, 1948–51) dealt with those individuals who were out of step with the rhythm of history in a pathetic and sentimental way. Personal reflections and publicistic commentaries were written by some of the leading writers of the day: Jan Kott,* M. Dąbrowska,* Pruszyński, E. Osmańczyk (*Sprawy Polaków* [The Affairs of the Polish People], 1946), and K. Wyka* (*Życie na niby* [Life As If], 1957).

The finest writer among the war generation (known as *Kolumbów* [Columbuses]) of young talents was Tadeusz Borowski. His two collections *Pożegnanie z Marią* (Farewell to Maria) and *Kamienny świat* (Stone World, 1948) examined the psyche of the prisoner-of-war and was at the same time a diagnosis of fascist ideology. His contemporary, B. Czeszko,* related the experiences of leftist youth fighting conspiratorially in occupied Warsaw (*Pokolenie* [Generation], 1951). R. Bratny described the fate and experiences of young soldiers in the *A K* (Home Army) in his novel *Kolumbowie, rocznik 20* (Insurgent Columbuses, Age-Group 20), published in 1957.

Maria Dąbrowska* achieved great success with her realistic observations of actual social changes, especially with *Na wsi Wesele* (A Village Wedding) from her collection, *Gwiazda zaranna* (Morning Star, 1955). J. Parandowski* turned to classical themes and to antiquity in his sketches and short stories (*Godzina śródziemnomorska* [Mediterranean Hour], 1949, and *Alchemia slowa* [Alchemy of the Word], 1951).

In poetry K. I. Gałczyński* achieved the greatest fame, uniting in his poetry criticism of anachronistic myths with sentimental feelings and utilizing conventional poetic means and a fairy-tale-like, grotesque imagination, best illustrated in his collection *Zaczarowana dorożka* (The Enchanted Coach, 1948); his long poem, *Niobe* (1951); and his miniature theater pieces, *Zielona Gęś* (The Green Goose). W. Broniewski* voiced the anguish of the nation trying to cope with the new reality, especially in his elegiac poem, *Mazowsze* (1952) and in his cycle of threnodylike verses,

Anka (1956). Among the avant-garde in poetry, Juliusz Przyboś* combined the reality of history with a subjective tone in his collections *Miejsce na ziemi* (A Place on Earth, 1945) and *Najmniej słów* (As Few Words, 1955). Jastrun's lyrics enjoined reflective philosophy and a revaluation of ideology (*Rzecz ludzka* [A Human Thing], 1946, and *Poezja i prawda* [Poetry and Truth], 1955). The older generation of poets also continued to publish remarkable poetry: L. Staff* (*Martwa pogoda* [Lifeless Weather], 1946, and *Wiklina* [Wicker], 1954); J. Tuwim* (*Kwiaty polskie* [Polish Flowers], 1949); Iwaszkiewicz* (*Warkocz jesieni* [Braid of Autumn], 1954); and new collections by Slonimski,* Iłłakowiczówna,* and Miłosz* (*Ocalenie* [Salvation], 1945).

Satirical verse was also a popular genre (S. J. Lec,* L. Pasternak, J. Mińkiewicz, and A. Marianowicz), as was parody (A. M. Swinarski*). Among those making their debut, the most outstanding was Tadeusz Różewicz* (*Niepokój* [Anxiety], 1947). His poetry encompassed the existential experiences of the war generation and the ethical crisis confronting humanity. Other poets also made significant contributions: Z. Bieńkowski, who combined symbolism and the avant-garde in his visionary verses; B. Ostromęcki, and J. Ficowski, who described the minute changes in people's lives in their chamber poetry. A. Międzyrzecki* and A. Kamieńska combined Classical and colloquial idioms in their poetry, while W. Woroszylski employed popular dance hall elements in his revolutionary verses.

In drama L. Kruczkowski* dominated the stage, first with *Odwety* (Retaliations, 1948) and then with *Niemcy* (The Germans, 1949), which portrayed the moral problems related to fascism confronting the German nation. J. Szaniawski employed realistic and symbolistic elements in his finest play, *Dwa teatry* (Two Theaters, 1946). In his cycle of monologues (*Professor Tutka,* 1954), Szaniawski created a type of mood piece, utilizing a combination of *skaz* (village lore) and dramatic techniques. J. Zawieyski* dealt with moral and spiritual problems in his parabolic dramas (*Rozdroże miłości* [Crossroads of Love], 1946), while Hołuj returned to the traumas associated with the death camps in his drama *Dom pod Oswięcimiem* [The House Outside Oswiecim], 1948). Various writers turned to historical events: R. Brandstaetter,* S. Flukowski, A. Maliszewski, L. H. Morstin,* H. Auderska, and K. Korczelli; Adam Tarn and J. Lutowski dealt with controversial contemporary themes.

Around 1956 Poland's literary life entered a new phase. A wider degree of latitude in the arts and in daily life was permitted. A more balanced view of the various ideologies was also allowed. The first example in literature of this new-found openness can be found in Iwaszkiewicz's *Sława i chwała* (Fame and Glory, 1956–62), whose epic canvas spans the years from the First World War to the Warsaw uprising. The same type of epic format is seen in Dąbrowska's *Przygody człowieka myślącego* (The Adventures of a Thinking Man, 1970). It was only after 1956 that the novels of Maria Kuncewiczowa* could be published: *Zmowa nieobecnych* (Conspiracy of Those Absent), which describes the confrontational situation of Polish émigrés in England with the reality in Poland; *Leśnik* (The Forester), a study of the complexity of Poland in the second half of the nineteenth century; and the novel *Tristan 1946* (1967), in which Kuncewiczowa attempted to combine mythic elements and psychological probing.

In 1957 Witold Gombrowicz's works were allowed to be published: *Trans-Atlantyk,* a parodistic rendering of the country's Polish complex; the allegorical, existential drama *Ślub* (The Wedding Ceremony); and the farce *Operetka* (Operetta). Breza exposed the ramifications of the governing process in the Vatican in his novels *Spiżowa brama* (The Bronze Gate, 1960) and *Urząd* (The Office, 1960). A. Kuśniewicz analyzed the cultural roots of fascism in his novel *Eroica* (1963). Experimentation with time and structure in the novel was carried out by Buczkowski and Gomolicki. J. Stryjkowski* described the daily life and culture of the Polish Jews in *Głosy w ciemności* (Voices in the Dark, 1956), *Austeria* (1966), and *Przybysz z Narbony* (The Stranger from Narbona, 1978).

Stanisław Lem* became Poland's most famous writer abroad with his science fiction novels, which combined philosophical problems and an interesting form of narration (anachronism, stylization of language, etc.)—*Dzienniki gwiazdowe* (Star Diaries, 1957), *Solaris* (1961), *Cyberiada* (1965)—and in his essays devoted to this genre, *Fantastyka i futurologii* (The Fantastic and Futurology, 1970).

Interest in existentialism and man's place in the universe, combined with the limits of man's autonomy, grew in the 1960s with the triumph of the theater of the absurd and the publication of works by Gombrowicz* and Witkacy (S. I. Witkiewicz).* It was Leszek Kołakowski* who adumbrated the philosophical program of the absurd in his essay *Kapłan i błazen* (The Priest and the Jester, 1959). Kołakowski advocated "a negative vigilance in the face of all absolutes." Andrzejewski* examined the phenomenon of power in his novels *Ciemności kryją ziemię* (Darkness Covers the Earth, 1957), *Bramy raju* (The Gates of Paradise, 1960), and *Idzie skacząc po górach* (He Goes Leaping over the Mountains, 1963), in which he examined the myth of the artist and freedom to create. Alienation and man's loss of direction were explored in the novels of K. Brandys,* in his cycle *Listy do Pani Z* (Letters to Mrs. Z., 1958 and after), and in his collection of short stories *Romantyczność* (Romanticism, 1960). The world of illusion was explored by S. Dygat* in his novel *Podróż* (The Trip, 1958). A lyrical mood was sounded in A. Rudnicki's* novels (*Niebieskie kartki* [Blue Cards], 1956, and *Krowa* [The Cow], 1959). Putrament,* in his multivolume personal account *Pół wieku* (A Half Century, 1961 and subsequent volumes), described his experiences as a political activist and writer. His autobiography, *Wybrańcy* (The Privileged Ones, 1978 and subsequent volumes), painted a rather flattering portrait of a not always ethical writer. The short stories of H. Worcell gave an account of the situation in the Silesian villages (*Natrudniejszy język swiata* (The Most Difficult Language of the World, 1965), where Polish settlers go head to head with the German population. Other regional writers also created a storehouse of Silesian literature: Szewczyk, Paukszta, Pierzchała, Baumgardten, and Jesienowski. The new developments in Poland found fertile ground for both old and new writers: Hołuj's *Osoba* (Person, 1974), Auderska's cycle of novels *Ptasi gościeniec* (Birds' Gathering, 1973) and *Babie lato* (Indian Summer, 1974), and Machejka's *Czekam na słowo ostatnie* (I'm Waiting for the Last Word, 1975). The following writers also published significant works: Broszkiewicz, J. S. Stawiński, J. Hen, B. Kogut, L. Prorok, and L. M. Bartelski. J. Kawalec explored the problems of people whose roots were with the soil and peasant culture: *Ziemi przypisany* (Attributed Lands, 1962) and *Tańczący jastrząb* (The Dancing Hawk, 1964). Sea novels also appeared by such writers as S. M. Saliński, J. B. Rychliński, F. Fenikowski, and A. Necel, who described the life of Kashubian fisherman.

The war generation continued to write novels in which the traumas of the not too distant past crisscross with present reality, resulting in intense psychological probings of man's psyche. Tadeusz Konwicki* best exemplified the writer trying to make sense of apocalyptic events in light of present chaos: *Sennik współczesny* (The Contemporary Dream-Book, 1963), *Nic albo nic* (Nothing or Nothing, 1971), and the novels published unofficially, *Kompleks polski* (The Polish Complex, 1977) and *Mała Apokalipsa* (The Minor Apocalypse, 1979). The conflicts resulting from a clash of war experiences and present reality were explored by Czeszko in *Tren* (Threnody, 1961) and *Powódź* (The Flood, 1975). Bratny also developed these themes in his novels (*Losy* [Destinies], 1973), as did Zalewski (*Pruski mur* [Prussian Wall], 1964) and J. S. Stawiński.

The younger generation of writers also returned to the traumas resulting from childhood experiences during the war and the cruelty of present-day existence: S. Grochowiak,* A. Kijowski, W. Odojewski,* J. Krasiński, B. Drozdowski, J. Krzysztoń,* M. Białoszewski* (*Pamiętnik z powstania warszawskiego* [A Memoir of the Warsaw Uprising], 1970), and B. Wojdowski (*Chleb rzucony umarłym* [Bread Thrown to the Dead], 1971). The younger generation also dealt with the changes affecting culture in the countryside and the reaction of the people to the ever-present specter of war, agricultural reforms, and the advances made in society. The following writers created an outstanding body of such literature: T. A. Nowak,* in his novels *A jak królem, a jak katem będziesz* (And If You Will Be a King or an Executioner, 1968) and *Diabły* (Devils, 1971); Ernest Bryll,* who described changes and social conflicts; W. Myśliwski, in his lyrical, balladlike novel

Pałac (The Palace, 1970); and E. Redliński, who accurately captured the spirit of village life in his parodic, humorous, highly popular novel *Konopielka* (The Female Scarecrow, 1973).

A new sensibility can be detected in the mixture of lyricism and brutality in M. Hłasko's* novel *Pierwszy krok w chmurach* (The First Step into the Clouds, 1956). A. Bursa's* poetry also contained this quality of lyrical cruelty. On the other hand, M. Nowakowski searched for a means to express the concerns of those living on the margins of society. I. Iredyński* also explored similar themes and experimented with the language of those on the fringes of society (*Dzień oszusta* [The Day of the Swindler], 1962). Several writers were assigned to the movement of "little realism" because of their concentration on the particular social problems inherent in the system: A. Augustyn, A. Twerdochlib, and J. Głowacki.*

After 1956 poetry developed at a rapid pace. Iwaszkiewicz continued to explore the "new realia" (*Mapa pogody* [Weather Map], 1977). The older generation (Iłłakowiczówna, Brzostowska, Swirszczyńska, etc.) as well as Polish writers living abroad (Wittlin,* Lechoń,* Wierzyński,* etc.) were published and had a ready audience. Czesław Miłosz,* after years of suffering censorship, became one of the most popular writers in Poland. A number of his works were published for the first time: *Traktat poetycki* (Poetic Tract, 1957), the autobiographical *Rodzinna Europa* (Native Realm, 1959), *Wiersze wybrane* (Selected Poetry, 1980), and *Poezja* (Poetry, 1981).

Przyboś continued to lead the avant-garde with his collections of poetry *Narzędzie ze swiatła* (Instruments Made of Light, 1958) and *Kwiat nieznanego* (A Flower of an Unknown Person, 1968), and in his sketches *Linia i gwar* (The Line and Din, 1959), *Sens poetycki* (Poetic Sense, 1963), and *Zapiski bez daty* (Notes Without Dates, 1970). J. Brzękowski added to Przyboś's remarks in his volume *Wyobraźnia wyzwolona* (Liberated Imagination, 1966).

The older generation continued to publish outstanding poetry: A. Stern's* *Poezja zbuntowanna* (Rebellious Poetry, 1964), partially dedicated to his experiences with futurism; Ważyk's *Wagon* (Carriage, 1963) and *Dziwna historia awangardy* (The Strange History of the Avant-Garde, 1976), experiments with surrealism and the avant-garde; and the works of A. Wat, S. Młodozieniec, and M. Czuchnowski.

A historical skepticism appeared in the verses of Jastrun* and in his reflective collections of essays *Mit Śródziemnomorski* (Mediterranean Myth, 1962) and *Wolność wyboru* (Freedom of Choice, 1969). The paradoxes of historical time were formulated by Lec in his aphorisms *Myśli nieuczesane* (Unkempt Thoughts, 1957 and subsequent volumes).

Tadeusz Różewicz* became the father of the young generation of poets and simultaneously, the father of the Polish theater of the absurd. His volumes of poetry contained his customary pessimism and concern for the artist in an apocalyptic world: *Formy* (Forms, 1958) and *Twarz* (Face, 1964). A similar note of resignation and pessimism was detected in his most successful play, *Kartoteka* (The Card File, 1960). His contribution to Polish drama continued throughout the 1960s and 1970s, culminating in *Białe Małżeństwo* (White Marriage, 1973) and *Pułapka* (The Trap, 1981). After Martial Law was declared on December 13, 1981, Różewicz returned to poetry. *Płaskorzeżba* (Bas-Relief) was published in 1991, the year Różewicz received the doctorate *honoris causa* from the University of Wrocław.

Similar expressions of doubt and despair can be detected in the works of other poets published during this time, in the colloquial lyrics of Woroszylski, in the Classically inspired poetry of Międzyrzecki and Kamieńska, and in the humorous and ironic verse of Szymborska (*Wielka liczba* [A Great Number], 1976).

Zbigniew Herbert was recognized as one of the leading poets of his generation. Ironic distance and original function of Classical motives mark his poetry, which is usually accompanied by a gentle skepticism: *Struna swiatła* (A String of Light, 1956), *Studium przedmiotu* (A Study of an Object, 1961), *Napis* (Inscription, 1969), and *Pan Cogito* (1974).

Białoszewski* slowly gained recognition with his volume *Obroty rzeczy* (The Revolution of Things, 1956). Nowak's *Psalmy* (Psalms, 1971) contained motives from mythology and cultural realia. S. Grochowiak, considered the representative poet of the "contemporary" generation, combined a subtle lyricism and a Baroque vision in his critical view of the status quo: *Ballada rycerska* (A Knightly Ballad, 1956), *Rozbieranie do snu* (Undressing for Sleep, 1959), and *Nie było lata* (There Was No Summer, 1969). The works of a number of poets contained a reflective character and a lyrical component: T. Śliwiak, H. Poświatowska, U. Kozioł, T. Kijonski, R. Śliwonik, and M. Grzesczak. The new generation of poets, most critical of the political system, found disfavor among the government authorities. They included the following: E. Lipska,* S. Barańczak,* R. Krynicki, R. Wojaczek, K. Gąsiorowski, and poets who made their debut after 1970 (Kornhauser, A. Zagajewski).

Polish theater and drama entered a golden age in the early sixties. Kruczkowski's* plays marked the end of realism and less emphasis on the war and its aftermath (*Pierwszy dzień wolności* [First Day of Freedom], 1960, and *Śmierć gubernatora* [Death of the Governor], 1961). Sławomir Mrożek's* satirical plays together with Tadeusz Różewicz's* pessimistic but humorous works shaped Polish theater and drama. *Tango* (1964) and *Emigranci* (Émigrés, 1975) became as popular as any present-day series. Różewicz, Mrożek, Gombrowicz, and Witkacy (S. I. Witkiewicz) became the staple of practically all sixty-five Polish theaters devoted to drama. They were joined by other dramatists who contributed to Poland's rich reservoir of drama: Grochowiak, Iredyński, Karpowicz, Drozdowski, Abramow, Bryll, and Krasiński.

During the decade of Martial Law Polish literature literally went underground, along with theater and the visual arts. Few writers published in the official press. Alternative sources of publishing were employed (see *Drugi obieg*). Many actors went into exile, finding work in films in Germany and France. Writers, including Mrożek, emigrated and published abroad. Some, like Janusz Głowacki, found themselves stranded in a foreign country after the declaration of Martial Law and happily shaped a career abroad.

Głowacki managed to solidify his position as an American writer on the basis of his two plays, written while in exile: *Hunting Cockroaches* (1986) and *Antigone in New York* (1992). He is probably the best known "Polish" writer in the United States today.

BIBLIOGRAPHY

Azja i Afryka: Antologia poezji polskiej na Środkowym Wschodzie. (Asia and Africa: An Anthology of Polish Poetry in the Near East), edited by J. Bielatowicz, Palestine, 1944.

Z lat wojny: Poezja polska, 1939–1945. (From the War Years: Polish Poetry, 1939–1945), edited by K. Wyka, Cracow, 1945.

Antologia "Nowej Polski" (An Anthology of "New Poland"), edited by A. Słonimski, Łódź, 1946.

Konspiracyjna publicystyka literacka, 1940–1944 (Conspirational Literary Journalism, 1940–1944), edited by Z. Jastrzębski, Cracow, 1973.

Antologia współczesnej poezji polskiej, 1918–1938. (Anthology of Contemporary Polish Poetry, 1918–1938), edited by L. Fryde and A. Andrzejewski, Warsaw, 1939.

Antologia polskiego futuryzmu i Nowej Sztuki (Anthology of Polish Futurism and the New Art), edited by H Zaworska, introduction and commentary by Z. Jarosiński, Wrocław, 1978.

K. Czachowski, *Obraz wspólczesnej literatury polskiej, 1884–1933* (An Outline of Contemporary Polish Literature, 1884–1933), Volume 2. *Neoromantyzm i psychologizm* (Neo-Romanticism and Psychologism), Lvov, 1934.

Kolumbowie i współcześni: Antologia poezji polskiej po roku 1939 (Insurgent Columbuses and Their Contemporaries), second edition, edited by A. Lam, Warsaw, 1976.

Antologia opowiadán polskich pirsarzy współczesnych (Anthology of Short Stories of Contemporary Polish Writers), edited by W. Maciąg, Warsaw, 1973.

Antologia dramatu (Anthology of Drama), edited by J. Koenig, Cracow, 1976.

K. Wyka, *Pogranicze powieści: Proza polska 1945–1948* (Border Novels: Polish Prose, 1945–1948), second edition, Warsaw, 1974.

R. Matuszewski, *Literatura po wojnie* (Literature After the War), Warsaw, 1948.

A. Sandauer, *Moje odchylenia* (My Deviations), Cracow, 1956.

K. Wyka, *Rzecz wyobraźni* (A Thing of the Imagination), second edition, Warsaw, 1977.

Słownik wspólczesnych pisarzy polskich (A Dictionary of Contemporary Polish Writers), S. I, 1–4, Warsaw, 1963–66; S. II, 1–3, Warsaw, 1977–80.

A. Lam, *Wyobraźnia ujarzmiona* (A Subjugated Imagination), Cracow, 1967.
W. Maciąg, *Literatura Polski Ludowej 1944–1964* (The Literature of People's Poland, 1944–1964), Warsaw, 1973.
A. Sandauer, *Poeci czterech pokoleń* (The Poets of Four Generations), Cracow, 1977.
Polscy pisarze współcześni: Informator (Contemporary Polish Writers: A Directory), edited by L. M. Bartelski. Warsaw, 1977.

COSMOS (see Gombrowicz).

CUD MNIEMANY CZYLI KRAKOWIACY I GÓRALE (Supposed Miracle or Cracovians and Highlanders) (see Bogusławski).

CUDZOZIEMKA (The Foreign Woman) (see Kuncewiczowa).

CYBERIADA (The Cyberiad) (see Lem).

CZAPSKI, JÓZEF (1896–1993) (Jozef Hutten-Czapski), a writer, painter, and art critic, came from a landed nobility family related to the German aristocracy. He spent his childhood at his family estate in Belorus, and his youth in Petersburg, where he was educated in the elite Corps of Pages. In 1917 he enlisted in a Polish cavalry regiment, formed in Russia amid the revolution. After Poland regained its independence, he settled in Warsaw but soon was assigned the mission of finding Polish officers missing in Russia. He returned to his regiment to participate in the Polish-Soviet war in 1920. In 1921 he began to study painting at the Cracow Academy of Fine Arts and continued his creative activity from 1924 to 1932, in Paris, where he led a group of Polish post-Impressionist painters organized into the so-called *Komitet Paryski* (Paris Committee), otherwise known as *kapiści.* In 1939 he was drafted into the army and later captured by the Soviet Army and was held in the prisoner-of-war camp in Starobielsk in the Ukraine. He was liberated in 1941 after a treaty was signed between the Polish government in exile and the Soviet authorities. He then enlisted in the Polish army which was being formed on the territory of the Soviet Union under the command of General Anders. On behalf of the Polish army he conducted a futile search for Polish prisoners-of-war, captured by the Red Army in 1939 (it was later discovered that almost all of the sixteen thousand prisoners were murdered by the NKVD in Katyn, Kharkov, and Tver). In 1942 he was evacuated with the Polish army to the Middle East; he later took part in the campaign in Italy and, after the end of the war, chose emigration and settled in Paris. He is one of the founders of the monthly *Kultura* (Culture) and the Literary Institute, which was the main publishing center of Polish emigration.

Among the most prominent works of Czapski are his memoirs *Na nie-*

ludzkiej ziemi (On Inhuman Ground, published in Paris in 1949 and in Poland in 1990): the main motif in this work is his account of the search for Polish prisoners-of-war conducted in the Soviet Union during the years 1941–42. The stories about the misfortunes of Poles imprisoned in the gulag camps or exiled to Siberia are joined by descriptions of Soviet life and the functioning of the apparatus of the Communist government, along with general remarks about laws governing the Stalinist system of coercion and terror. The book also sounds a clear moral message: it is a homage paid to the millions of victims of the Soviet empire, not only to the Poles but also to the Russians and other inhabitants of the Soviet Union whose suffering and fate find a compassionate and sympathetic expression in Czapski's work *Wspomnienia Starobielskie* (Memoirs from Starobielsko, Rome, 1945 later reedited in the volume *Dwugłos wspomnień* [Duet of Memories]), with his sister, Maria Czapska. Essays on painting, in which he meditates on formal and artistic questions together with ethical dilemmas, were collected in the anthologies *Oko* (Eye, Paris, 1960) and *Patrząc* (Looking, Poland, 1983). Literary essays (among others about Russian and French writers dealing with moral-religious questions) were published in *Tumult i widma* (Turmoil and Phantoms, Paris, 1981) and *Czytając* (While Reading, Poland, 1990). He also published *Dzienniki-wspomnienia-relacje* (Diaries-Memories-Accounts, 1988).

CZECHOWICZ, JÓZEF (1903–39) (pseudonyms Henryk Zasławski, Józef Surmacz, Zygmunt Klimuntowicz), an outstanding poet, came from a very poor family, spent his childhood in the country, and started working as a teacher in 1921. In 1920 he took part in the Polish-Soviet war as a volunteer. Actively involved in the Lublin poetic group gathered around the magazine *Reflektor* (Reflector), in which he made his debut with *Opowieść o papierowej koronie* (The Story of the Paper Crown) in 1923, he published his first collection, in a series also sponsored by *Reflektor,* in 1927. During his studies in Warsaw (1928–29) he became associated with the literary group *Kwadryga* (Quadriga). In Lublin he wrote for the local daily and later cooperated with various literary magazines, such as *Droga* (The Way), *Zet* (Z), *Pion* (Plump-Line), and *Kamena.* In 1933 he moved to Warsaw, where he worked for *Głos Nauczycielski* (Teachers' Voice), for the children's magazines *Płomyk* (Little Flame) and *Płomyczek* (Tiny Flame), and after 1934 for *Miesięcznik Literatury i Sztuki* (Monthly of Literature and Art). In 1937 he became the editor of *Pion;* he also worked for Polish Radio. After 1934 he tried to organize various young poetic groups into one movement. In 1938–39 he edited a collection of works by twelve poets whose careers spanned several generations. When the war broke out he went to Lublin, where he died in one of the bombing attacks on the city.

Czechowicz's lyrics form the basic core of his writings (the collections *Kamién* [Stone], 1927; *Dzień jak codzień* [A Day Like Everyday], 1930;

Ballada z tamtej strony [A Ballad from the Other Side], 1932; *Stare kamienie* [Old Stones], together with F. Arnsztajnowa, 1934; *W błyskawicy* [In the Lightning], 1934; *Nic więcej* [Nothing More], 1936; and *Nuta człowiecza* [A Human Tune], 1939). He wrote several articles, reviews, and short stories; he also worked on a novel (*Berło* [Scepter]), which was not preserved. He wrote a few short plays for theater and radio, and poetry for children. He rendered a number of translations from French and Slavic languages; he was one of the first translators of T. S. Eliot and James Joyce.

According to Tadeusz Kłak, Czechowicz's lyrics are characterized by an overlapping of two opposing trends: idyllic and catastrophic. The first trend, markedly though discreetly lyrical, is evident in numerous poems which are inspired by the landscape of the countryside and the small towns of Poland, mainly in the region of Lublin (e.g., *Stare kamienie,* the cycle *Prowincja noc* [The Province Night] from the collection *W błyskawicy* [In the Lightning]), and in poems devoted to his mother. The second trend reflects Czechowicz's obsessive attraction to death (e.g., *Ballada z tamtej strony* [A Ballad from the Other Side]), his war memories, and his existential fears and anxieties, which led to a catastrophic vision of the world. The apocalyptic image of destruction of the world is present in many literary trends of the time prior to World War II (e.g., *Tren* [Lament] from the collection *Nuta człowiecza* [Human Tune]). In spite of a few similarities with the artistic program of the Cracow avant-garde—the elliptical style of Czechowicz's lyrics—his writings developed in conscious opposition to its intellectual rigor. The poet claimed his position to be Romantic and visionary (after Słowacki); he defended the role of the symbol as a means of allusive and ambiguous expression in poetry (here he referred to Blok, to the poets of French symbolism, and to Polish modernism). He made creative use of folklore, not so much in terms of form, but on a deeper level—he introduced elements of myth, the folktale, and a magical view of the world, which can be discerned, for example, in his frequent use of magical formulae, especially incantations, which express the prophetic catastrophism of his lyrics. The combination of motives from folk songs and symbolist inspiration resulted in a highly refined musical quality in his poetry, with its rich repertoire of means of acoustic expression—from distant sound allusions to expressive dissonance.

Among the poets of the period between the wars, Czechowicz quickly won a recognized, though independent position. He was clearly in opposition to the orientation of the *Skamander* group, and at the same time quite distant from the extreme views of the early avant-garde. Conservative critics either ignored or attacked him, while those of the younger generation valued his work highly. He was later generally approved of as the leader of the young generation of poets (the so-called second avant-garde). After 1955 his poetry underwent something of a renaissance, with many new editions, studies, and memoirs.

BIBLIOGRAPHY

Wiersze wybrane (Selected Poems), edited and with an introduction by S. Pollak and J. Śpiewak, Warsaw, 1955.

Wiersze (Poems), collectively edited, Lublin, 1963.

Wiersze wybrane (Selected Poems), selected and with an introduction by Tadeusz Różewicz, Warsaw, 1967; third edition, 1987.

Wybór poezji (Selected Poems), selected and with an introduction by Tadeusz Kłak, 1970; second enlarged edition, Warsaw, 1985.

English

Bogdana Carpenter, *The Poetic Avant-Garde in Poland, 1918–1939;* Seattle: University of Washington Press, 1983.

CZYŻEWSKI, TYTUS (1880–1945), a painter, poet, theoretician, and art critic, studied art in Cracow and Paris. He was cofounder of the Polish literary and artistic avant-garde. In 1917, together with the Pronaszkos, he founded a group of Polish expressionists, which later accepted new members and changed its name to *Formiści Polscy* (Polish Formists). Czyżewski was also among the founders and editors of the group's magazine *Formiści* (The Formists). Together with B. Jasieński and J. Młodożeniec he participated in the first happenings of the futurists and published in the collective manifestos of the movement (e.g., *Hymn do maszyny mego ciała* [Hymn to the Machine of My Body] in *Jednodniówka futurystów* [One Day Publication of the Futurists], 1921). He worked in the diplomatic corps, and later (after 1930) in Warsaw as a literary critic. His works written during the period of the war were lost in the Warsaw Uprising.

He began his literary career with an ironic stage poem, *Śmierć fauna* (The Death of a Faun, 1907, produced in 1934). His early poetry from the collections *Zielone oko: Poezje formistyczne, elektryczne wizje* (Green Eye: Formist Poems, Electric Visions, 1920) and *Noc-Dzień: Mechaniczny instynkt elektryczny* (Night-Day: The Mechanical Electric Instinct, 1922) gave a unique interpretation to the assumptions of futurism, dadaism, and other avant-garde trends: it presented the ideal of man freed from the bonds of tradition; it expressed the cult of nature and instinct and at the same time of modern urban civilization and products of modern technology; the artifacts were seen as biological creatures which inspire, at the same time, admiration, awe, and catastrophic expectations. According to Jan Wojnowski, his works combine the tradition of modernistic impressionism with the attempt at liberating poetic expression from the "chains of logical sentences and syntactic structures." Czyżewski exploits the mechanical juxtaposition of semantically distant concepts and words, but also employs the techniques used in film editing to combine different observations and impressions. He also applied experimental graphic techniques. He evinced interest in primitive folk art: his collection *Pastorałki* (Pastoral Carols, 1925 in Paris) is one of the best examples of folk stylization based on Christmas rituals. Czyżewski preserved the naive charm and humor of the original songs, at the same time creating an original synthesis of folk dialect, shepherds' calls, and lullaby songs, placing greater emphasis on the acoustic side of the work, a trait characteristic of dadaism. His poem *Lajkonik* (from the collection *Lajkonik w chmurach* [Lajkonik in the Clouds], 1936), full of grotesque fantasy, an absurd sense of humor, and mockery, is based on the urban folklore of Cracow. There is also a lyrical trend in Czyżewski's writings, where one can trace the influences of Rimbaud, Apollinaire, and the Spanish Baroque. Czyżewski also wrote two visionary poems based on philosophical and historiosophical ideas: *Robespierre* and *Rapsod,* published in 1927 together with his sketch *Od romantyzmu do cynizmu* (From Romanticism to Cynicism), and several short avant-garde plays written in the convention of parody and the grotesque: *Wąz, Orfeusz i Euridika* (Snake, Orpheus and Eurydice), 1922; *Osioł i słońce w metamorfozie* (The Donkey and the Sun in Metamorphosis); and *Włamywacz z lepszego towarzystwa* (The Burglar from High Society), published jointly in 1922.

BIBLIOGRAPHY

Pastorałki (Pastoral Carols), *drzeworyty* (woodcuts) T. Makowski, II wydanie, Cracow, 1985.

D

DĄBROWSKA, MARIA (née Szumska) (1889–1965) was a novelist and publicist. She was brought up in the country, in an impoverished gentry family with strong patriotic traditions. She studied in Losanne and Brussels. In 1911 she married M. Dąbrowski, an emigrant activist for the Socialist Party. In 1913 she published her first short story *We Francji . . . ziemi cudzej* (In France . . . An Alien Land) in *Echo Literacko-Artystyczne* (Literary-Artistic Echo). During World War I, she was an activist of the peasant independence movement and coeditor of *Chłopska Sprawa* (Peasant Affair, 1915) and *Polska Ludowa,* 1915–16. After 1918 Dąbrowska was involved in many types of activities: she was a devotée of the Cooperative Movement, organized courses for farmers and workers, worked for the PEN Club and the Union of Polish Writers, took part in the actions of protest against violations of human rights (to demonstrate her own disagreement with the treatment of political prisoners, she refused to accept membership into and an award from the Polish Academy of Literature). She spent the period of the Nazi occupation in Warsaw, taking part in underground cultural and educational activity. She received many important awards, and an honorary doctorate from the University of Warsaw.

Dąbrowska started her literary career writing short stories on social themes (cooperatives) and for the young (the collections *Dzieci Ojczyzny* [Children of the Fatherland], 1918, and *Gałąź czereśni* [The Cherry Branch], 1922). She was highly appreciated by critics and readers for the cycle of short stories *Uśmiech dzieciństwa* (The Smile of Childhood, 1923), based on her own childhood memories of the life in the country. Her innovative form of narration, similar to that of Marcel Proust, created a lyrical image of the world moving irrevocably into the past. Her great success came with another cycle of stories, *Ludzie stamtąd* (People from Yonder, 1926), which combines the rough realistic description of the life of the so-called country proletariat with a subtle presentation of the richness of their spiritual life. Her main work, the tetralogy *Noce i dnie* (Nights and Days, 1932–34), gives an expressive picture of the changes that Polish society was undergoing at the turn of the nineteenth and twentieth centuries. Dąbrowska's humanistic beliefs can be seen in her short stories from the collections *Znaki zycia* (Signs of Life, 1938) and *Gwiazda zaranna* (Morning Star, 1955), which express the author's belief that the tragic suffering of the war and occupation was not in vain. The pieces in the collection *Na wsi wesele* (Wedding in a Village), both fiction and nonfiction, attempt a psychological and sociological analysis of the changes that people's attitudes were undergoing after the war. Her unfinished novel *Przygody człowieka myślącego* (Adventures of a Thinking Man, 1970) analyzed the roots of the contemporary intelligentsia. Her historical dramas supplement the themes undertaken in her novels (*Geniusz sierocy* [Orphan Genius], 1939, produced in 1959, and *Stanisław i Bogumił* [Stanislaus and Bogumił], in *Twórczość* [Creativity], 1945–46; definitive edition 1948, produced in 1966). Her aim was to create a type of drama which would reflect contemporary problems by reaching into history. She called her plays "dramas of attitude" and tried to dramatize in them the various conflicting threads of national awareness. She wrote many works for children (*Wybór pism dla dzieci* [Selected Writings for Children], 1948) and patriotic and educational stories for young readers (*Marcin Kozera,* 1927; *Przyjaźń* [Friendship], 1927; *Czyste serca* [Clean Hearts], 1936); she also translated works from Russian, Danish, and English (*Diaries of John Pepys*). As a literary critic Dąbrowska wrote several articles on Polish writers (Mickiewicz,* Słowacki,* Prus,* Orzeszkowa,* Kasprowicz,* Wyspiański,* Żeromski,* and others) and a number on foreign writers (Gogol, Tolstoy); some of them were included in the collection *Myśli o sprawach i ludziach* (Thoughts About Problems and People, 1956). Another important contribution is her collection of essays *Szkice o Conradzie* (Sketches on Conrad, 1959). Her critical writings analyze contemporary realistic prose from the point of view of philosophical and artistic value. She often commented on her own prose as well. She also wrote a great deal as a publicist, mainly on the problems of cooperatives and agriculture. Highly regarded are Dąbrowska's *Diaries,* kept from her youthful years (published in a collection, edited by T. Drewnoski, Volumes 1–5, 1988), including a personal commentary and penetrating creative observations alongside historic events. The whole stands as an important document, depicting the vicissitudes and attitudes of the Polish intelligentsia of the twentieth century.

Dąbrowska's writings span the period between the positivist model of literature and contemporary realism. She was influenced by the traditions of national literature; she highly valued the ideological aspect of art, the psychological appeal of characters, and a well-constructed plot. At the same time, she was influenced by twentieth century philosophy and sociology and often commented on the artistic experiences of such outstanding writers as Conrad, Chekhov, Proust, and Thomas Mann. Her deep faith in the sense and value of history made her independent of those philosophical trends which stem from distrust in civilization and from those who felt human existence to be seriously threatened.

Noce i dnie was published in Warsaw 1931–34: Volume I, *Bogumił i Barbara* (Bogumił and Barbara, 1931); Volume II, *Wieczne zmartwienie* (Eternal Worry, 1932); Volume III, Parts 1–2 *Miłość* (Love, 1933); and Volume IV, *Wiatr w oczy* (Wind in the Eyes, 1934). It is an epic story of several generations of a gentry family during the second half of the nineteenth and early twentieth centuries, against the background of important historical events. The story begins in the 1880s and extends to the beginning of World War I, but the period actually presented goes back to 1863. The characters, and especially Barbara Niechcicowa (née Ostrzeńska), often remember the January Uprising of 1863, the defeat which changed the living conditions of the nobility and forced the coming generations of gentry to make difficult changes from the advantages of the privileged class relegated to the position of employees, having to work to make a living. Bogumił Niechcic was still a boy when he took part in the uprising; he had to leave his country and spent a number of years abroad. After his return, he married Barbara, who also came from a once wealthy family, and began working as an administrator of other people's estates. Presenting the story of her heroes, Dąbrowska showed not only the typical social changes ("the falling apart of a certain way of life in Poland based on the tradition of family estate"), but also the changes in the minds of her characters, who establish themselves in their environment and accept their new way of living, thinking, and behaving. Barbara's brother and his wife—Daniel and Michalina Ostrzeńscy—settle down in the town of Kaliniec and become part of the local petit bourgeois intelligentsia. The charitable activities of the ladies from Kaliniec go hand in hand with their growing skill in handling problems; Anzelm Ostrzeński, Barbara's nephew, becomes a clever businessman, developing commercial relations with the Russian empire. Barbara and Bogumił's daughter, Agnieszka, who is the main character in Volumes II and III, enters yet another environment. Having finished school, she goes abroad to study and there becomes engaged to a political emigrant and a revolutionary activist, Marcin Śniadowski. Under his influence she becomes involved with various democratic unions of the young, which are paving the way for the independence of the country. Together with a rich social and historical background, Dąbrowska also created characters of great psychological depth. Barbara is a common and yet unique personality, whose life gradually soothes the wounds of her youth: the disappointment of her first love affair, her unfulfilled aspirations and spiritual needs, her feeling of alienation in the world of peaceful existence and hard work, the world which is different from the romantic ideals on which she was brought up. Bogumił is very active and his attitude is affirmative; exaltation is alien to him, but he is capable of being deeply moved; he represents a type of straightforward and righteous man similar to some of the characters in works of Conrad, for whom duty, honor, and respect for work are dominant motives in life. In relating the story of their marriage, which was not free of misunderstandings and mutual feelings of unfulfillment, yet loyal and lasting, Dąbrowska gave a subtle analysis of the complex nature of love and marriage. The contrasting characters and beliefs of Barbara and Bogumił are harmoniously combined in the personality of their daughter, who finds an outlet for her feelings and aspirations in collective work.

According to Zbigniew Folejewski, *Noce i dnie* (Nights and Days) is a novel which stems from the tradition of the great realistic novel of the nineteenth century (Prus,* Orzeszkowa*), modernized and developed into a so-called family saga; it also draws upon the experiences of naturalism and modernism in prose and refers to contemporary achievements in sociology and psychology (Bergson, Durkheim, Freud, and the Polish Socialist E. Abramowski). The author was able to present the lives of her characters in a double perspective: historical and existential. The novel depicts typical social and historical processes through the consciousness of the characters, which is conditioned by their class and their environment. The historical period covers the background of the experiences of individuals and social groups: they shape their consciousness, determine the sense and goals of their existence and their role in the human community in the actual course of history and under its influence. The perspective of human existence (which Bergson calls "lasting") thrusts the heroes of *Nights and Days* into the flow of time, of passing away as parts of nature, beings not conscious of their destiny, but experiencing the mystery and tragedy of existence, trying to understand the higher meaning of life and sometimes reaching it in contact with nature, in work, in being with other people. In the novel the continuity and rhythm of time are determined by the cycle of nature, by births and deaths, by customs, daily rituals, and work. The concept of historical time is optimistic here; it derives from the belief that the course of history will eventually bring a fair solution to all the problems of this world. This belief, its trust in the goodwill and moral value of man, is best expressed in the ending of the novel, because it is only when war breaks out that the homeless Barbara is eventually filled with calm and places trust in the future. The perspective of timelessness introduces a philosophical dimension: for this reason *Nights and Days* can be compared with a classical epic, which considers the problems of everyday life in terms of a pattern of a higher level imposed by God or by fate. Critics recognize the value of the novel and consider it to be an outstanding achievement of twentieth century prose, especially in regard to its narrative technique, based on apparent reported speech, and its style—simple and natural, but also sophisticated, naturally combining colloquial speech, in its individual and social variations, with the reflection of the narrator. Some objections were raised against later volumes of the cycle, especially *Miłość,* in which the story of Agnieszka is related with too much detail and through introspection, which undermines the epic harmony of the whole. Dąbrowska took part in discussions of *Nights and Days* and published some of her comments (*Jak powstały "N.i d."* [How "Nights and Days" Came to Be] in *Kultura,* 1932, Number 7; *Kilka myśli o "N. i d."* [Several Thoughts on "Nights and Days"] in *Ateneum,* 1938, Number 4/5). The detailed realism of the novel gives an impression of authenticity, which is a result of the fact that the book was written on the basis of Dąbrowska's own life, and Marcin is modeled after the writer's husband. The novel went through many editions (a total of twenty-three up to 1979) and was made into a film, and into a TV series by J. Antczak.

(See Contemporary Polish Literature.)

BIBLIOGRAPHY

Noce i dnie (Nights and Days), edited and with an afterword by E. Korzeniewski, Warsaw, 1972.

Pisma wybrane (Selected Writings), Volumes 1–3, introduction by J. Przyboś, Warsaw, 1956.

Dramaty (Dramas), Warsaw, 1957.

Opowiadania (Short Stories), selected and with an introduction by W. Maciąg, Wrocław, 1972.

Pisma wybrane (Selected Works), Warsaw: Czytelnik, 1956.

English

A Village Wedding, and Other Stories (Na wsi wesele), Warsaw: Polonia, 1957.

Zbigniew Folejewski, *Maria Dąbrowska,* New York: Twayne, 1967.

DAMY I HUZARY (Ladies and Hussars) (see Fredro).

DISNEYLAND (see Dygat).

DŁUGOSZ, JAN (1415–80) is regarded as Poland's first historian. Descended from a poor gentry family, he studied at the academy in Cracow. In 1436 he was a canon of Cracow; just before his death he was raised to the rank of archbishop of Lvov. In 1431–55 he was a secretary to Zbigniew Oleśnicki, a bishop of Cracow and a politician who opposed the king's power in regard to that of a bishop. He traveled to Italy as a diplomat and participated in a pilgrimage to the Holy Land. Having opposed King Kazimierz Jagiellończyk, he left Cracow. Regaining the king's trust during the war with the Teutonic Knights (1454–66), he was instrumental in negotiating various diplomatic decisions with the defeated Order. After the war he became a tutor to the king's sons: he later helped the oldest one, Władysław, to ascend to the Czech and Hungarian throne.

Długosz worked intensively as a historian during his entire life, writing a variety of works in Latin, including a description of Teutonic standards won at the battle of Grunwald in 1410 (*Banderia Prutenorum,* written in 1448, published in 1850, and translated from Latin into Polish in 1958); the armorial *Insignia seu clenodia . . . Regni Poloniae* (written in 1454–80, published in 1851); lives of Polish saints: *Vita S. Stanislai* (written in 1460–65, published in 1511), *Vita S. Cunegundis* (written in 1471–74, published in Polish in 1617); catalogues of Polish bishops in six dioceses; a description of the Cracow diocese; and his monumental work, *Annales seu Cronicae Regni Poloniae* (written in 1455–80, a partial edition entitled *Historia Polonica,* published in Dobromil 1614–15, and the full edition entitled *Historiae Polonicae libri XII,* published in Leipzig in 1711), which covers the history of Poland from legendary times to 1480. According to Julian Krzyżanowski, his work, which is written as a chronicle, is based on the research of Polish and foreign predecessors and contains a thorough analysis of documents in which he assumed a modern, critical approach. He followed Livius in his so-called pragmatic method, linking the facts he described into a casual chain. A writer and a patriot, and understanding the greatness of his own epoch, he revealed a great literary talent in his colorful description of people and problems. Długosz's work was the first and, for an entire century, the only attempt to give a scholarly synthesis of Polish medieval history, which accounts for its unique status in the history of Polish research.

(See Renaissance.)

BIBLIOGRAPHY

Opera omnia, edited by A. Przeździecki, Volumes 2–14, Cracow, 1878–87 (including a translation by K. Mecherzyński, *Dziejów polskich ksiąg dwanaście* [Twelve Books on the History of Poland]).

Annales seu Cronicae incliti Regni Poloniae, Liber I–XI, edited by Jan Dąbrowski, Krystyna Pieradzka, Józef Garbacik, and others, Warsaw, 1964–85; Polish edition, *Roczniki, czyli kroniki sławnego królestwa Polskiego, księga I–XI* (The Annals, or A Chronicle of the Famous Polish Kingdom, Books I–XI), edited by Jan Dąbrowski, Krystyna Pieradzka, Józef Garbacik, and others, Warsaw, 1965–85.

English

Book Two of the Chronicles of Jan Długosz, translated by William Faix, 1976.

DOM OTWARTY (Open House) (see Bałucki).

DRUGI OBIEG The Polish phrase has no adequate equivalent in English. "Second circulation," "second estate," "underground press," "independent culture," and even "book-legging" have all been used by various writers in an attempt to render an English equivalent to the Polish phrase. Each of these English phrases capture various aspects of the phenomenon known in Polish as the *Drugi obieg,* but, equally important, each of these phrases fails to capture some important aspect of it. They are either too narrow, too broad, or simply inaccurate.

One can make a threefold distinction in Polish cultural life prior to spring 1989: the officially sanctioned cultural activities; the independent, but not anonymous, cultural activities; and finally the independent and anonymous cultural activities. The most important distinction is between the first (also known as "official circulation" or in Polish, *Pierwszy obieg*) category and the other two categories.

The latter two categories are usually lumped together under the heading *Drugi obieg.* For this reason it is inappropriate to translate *Drugi obieg* as the underground press, because only a part of it can be properly described as "underground." It should be noted as well that the word "underground" revives memories of the underground press in Poland during World War II, as well as the conspiratorial activities which aimed at the overthrow of the Communist regime.

In the West the phenomenon most often associated with the *Drugi obieg* is the publishing and distribution of uncensored materials. It is also helpful to view independent publishing in the overall context of independent culture in Poland, which includes independently published written materials, audiocassettes, videocassettes, and art exhibitions.

Jacek Federowicz in an article in *Uncaptive Minds* (September–October 1988) quotes a statistic from an unnamed official source that there are approximately one million video recorders in Poland, or alternatively, there is approximately one video recorder for every thirty-six Poles, a ratio which puts Poland in the top ten in per capita ownership. Anyone who wanted to could view banned films or uncensored versions of films released for general circulation. The most well-known example of this is *Przesłuchanie* (Interrogation), which was seen by virtually everyone who wanted to see the film before it was released officially to be shown in movie theaters. As of fall 1988 there were four independent producers of video films. Today there are scores of independent producers who deal with both movie and video films.

Federowicz also maintains that there are two forms of independent culture not so well known in the West: home theater and private lectures, the latter being the most common manifestation of popular culture. These are not well known outside Poland for the simple reason that it is easier to send books and posters through the mail and thereby printed materials lose none of their immediacy.

In addition to home theaters and private lectures, the Flying University of the nineteenth century and of World War II was revived in the middle of the 1970s under the name *Towarzystwo Kursów Naukowych* (Society for Academic Courses). Courses in those areas most distorted by official ideology included history, economics, sociology, philosophy, and other disciplines in the humanities. The lectures for the Flying University were often reprinted and distributed through *KOR* (Worker's Defense Committee) and its affiliated organizations. The Flying University was active before 1981 and the declaration of Martial Law.

Against this background the *Drugi obieg* can be seen as part of a larger phenomenon: at once as a revolt against a too strict censorship and control of information and as an assertion of national identity. One should, however, avoid dichotomizing Polish cultural life from the mid-1970s until the end of the late 1980s into the simplistic categories of official and independent, as if authentic cultural expression could only be found in the independent press. Not only would this be a falsification of the actual history of independent culture in Poland, it would also belie the heterogeneity of independent culture. There were polemics, controversies, and critical reviews of books appearing in the independent press. It would be a presumption of agreement and unanimity where in fact there is none.

While there was no great odium attached to appearing in the official press, a great deal depended upon which publication was involved. Obviously there would be a great difference between an interview for *Czerwony Sztandar* (The Red Standard), the official Party newspaper, and an interview with a Catholic weekly, even though the latter was also subject to strict censorship. The single most important effect of the rise of independent culture was that it gave both the creative intelligentsia and the public at large a choice in its patronage. Once the larger independent publishers were able to compete with the state-sponsored publishing houses for a writer's work it was clear that independent culture was going to remain on the cultural scene for some time.

This choice provided by independent culture gave an artist the opportunity to avoid a quid pro quo with the authorities. Thus, if the state, for example, wanted to stage an exhibition called "Socialism and Art," an artist could safely refuse, without fear of retribution. In the worst case, he might have to exhibit in churches, but this would have only enhanced his reputation. An artist could submit work without compromising himself. Of course, collaboration on any sort of propaganda effort was decidedly out of the question.

After Martial Law the situation for writers and artists did not change appreciably: there were official journals to which it was taboo to contribute, and there were official journals to which it was acceptable to contribute. There was, however, a very successful actors' boycott which lasted for five years—from the declaration of Martial Law in 1981 until the release of political prisoners in 1986. Those who took part did not appear on television but did appear on stage. Whenever an attempt was made to film a performance, the camera crews were expelled bodily from the theater. Until the release of political prisoners in 1986 it was most definitely damaging to one's credibility to appear on television, actor or not. After 1986 it was somewhat suspicious but not as it had been, according to Jacek Fedorowicz.

From a developmental perspective the history of the *Drugi obieg* can be divided into two periods: before and after August 1980, Solidarity's first rise to power. From 1976 with the founding of *KOR* the number of uncensored publications gradually increased until about 1980, when with the legalization of Solidarity the number of publications and publishers increased dramatically. With the founding of Solidarity a locus of activity was provided. Solidarity functioned as an umbrella to the various political and cultural groups belonging to the opposition. This provided a certain degree of cohesion, uniformity, and organizational and funding conformity. With the declaration of Martial Law many of the regional representatives and national leaders were interned and the opposition fragmented. This resulted in the formation of a large number of opposition groups each with its own, often irregularly appearing journal which described its political program and planned activities.

Unfortunately bibliographical information of a comprehensive nature is lacking. The only period adequately covered is between December 13, 1981, and June 1986, recorded by Józefa Kamińska, who compiled bibliographical information on 1,424 periodicals and almost 2,000 books and pamphlets. According to Kamińska, thirty-five publishing houses were founded by August 1980. With the emergence of Solidarity after the Gdańsk strikes over 160 illegal publishing houses and printing shops came into existence.

The amount of material which appears is considerable. Kamińska estimates the total number of issues of periodicals from this period of time to be twenty-five thousand. Most of these periodicals were short-lived and only of regional and specialized interest. During the time of Martial Law people were most interested in information on detainees and reliable news about the effects of Martial Law. It should be noted as well that in the Chernobyl incident it was the independent press which responded most quickly with reliable news and recommended measures to be taken against the radiation. Given the amount of material and the scope of interests and concerns involved it is impossible to provide more than a cursory overview of the published materials.

PRIOR TO AUGUST 1980

The independent and unofficial press in Poland had its start in 1976 with the founding of *Komitet Obrony Robotników* (*KOR*), the Worker's Defense Committee. *KOR* (June 25, 1976–September 28, 1981) was founded to aid in the defense of workers and their families who lost their jobs as a result of participating in the strikes and protests in Warsaw and Radom at the URSUS tractor factory.

The modus operandi of *KOR* was "open opposition," not a conspiracy conducted in secret. Its membership was known to all. The members of *KOR* took their stand on the letter of the constitution and demanded only that the authorities honor their commitments in an open and legal manner.

KOR's program of action was simple: to document systematically the abuses of power committed by representatives of the government. It also published various journals in the independent press exposing the arbitrariness of the government. The rationale for its founding was to help victims of persecution to obtain financial, legal, and medical help. In order to facilitate the activities *KOR* established a communications network between factories.

KOR refused to draw up a political program or to become a party of any kind: the protection of human rights provided a sufficient purpose for its activities. As a result, it functioned as an umbrella organization for various and sundry activities in trade unionism, culture, and politics. Following *KOR*'s founding a large number of uncensored journals and newspapers appeared. Some of these were published by *KOR*, others by other opposition groups, and some were joint efforts. The lectures of the Flying University were published by NOWA, one of the publishing houses associated with *KOR*.

The first publication under *KOR* auspices was *Apel do Społeczeństwa i Władz PRL* (Appeal to the Society and Authorities of the PRL), in which the formation of *KOR* as the first openly active but illegal organization in the opposition was enunciated. The general outline of its activities was included as well. *KOR*'s publications included *Komunikat, Biuletyn Informacyjny, Robotnik, Głos, Krytyka,* and *Placówka.* Publications put out jointly included *Zapis, Puls, Robotnik Wybrzeża, Biuletyn Dolnośląski, Tematy, Sygnał, Kurier Akademicki,* and *Tarnowskie Wiadomości. KOR* was also involved in the formation of two publishing houses: *Biblioteka Głosu* and *Krąg.*

Biuletyn Informacyjny KOR (KOR Information Bulletin) was the first publication of *KOR*. Originally it was a bulletin of information on the activities of *KOR;* later it became a monthly and still later a bimonthly, providing information and publicizing *KOR*'s activities. The Bulletin consisted of approximately fifty pages, of which twenty to twenty-five pages in roman numerals were used by the communicants of *KSS "KOR"*—as *KOR* was later called. It published descriptions of incidents of repression and information about independent groups and their activities and programs. Permanent features included "Themes of the Day," "Culture and the Censor," "*Bez Debitu*" ([Without Debit]; debit is the officially given right to circulate and publish books, audiotapes, magazines, etc.), and

"Church and Belief." On the title page of each issue there appeared information representing the goals and aims of the magazine. The title of the magazine referred to the *Służba Zwycięstwu Polski* (Service of the Victory of Poland) and to the later Home Army. The first issue appeared in September 1976 and the last appeared with the date October–November 1980.

Komunikat (Communication)—also called *Komunikat KOR* or *Komunikat KSS "KOR"*—first appeared on September 29, 1976. The first two issues contained information about *KOR*'s activities along with news about the opposition's activities. Originally it was edited by Antoni Macierewicz, and then by Anna Kowalska, then by people acceptable to *KOR*. After several months it was published jointly with *Biuletyn Informacyjny KOR* and later again separated from *Biuletyn Informacyjny KOR*. The first few issues were typewritten and copied. It appeared once a month.

Robotnik (The Worker) was active from October 1977 to December 1981. *Robotnik* started as a biweekly of four pages, primitively printed in four hundred copies. One year later it had a circulation of twenty thousand, thanks to the technical improvements instituted by Witold Łuczywo; in the summer of 1980 it reached a circulation of sixty thousand. The name of the paper referred to the prewar *Robotnik* (Worker), and as the title suggests was aimed at a working audience. It was edited by Jan Lityński, with the assistance of Henryk Wujec, Ludwika Wujec, Helena Łuczywo, Witold Łuczywo, and Bogdan Boruszewicz.

Głos (Voice), a monthly, first appeared in October 1977. It was devoted to the theory and discussion of the movement for democratization. *Deklaracja Ruchu Demokratycznego* (A Declaration of the Democratic Movement), an analysis of the crisis facing the country, appeared in the first issue. It asserted that the root cause was the gulf separating the general populace and the governing authorities. The monthly had a circulation of three thousand to five thousand with length varying from twenty-eight to forty-eight pages. Thirty-five issues appeared before December 1981. After the introduction of Martial Law the magazine came out irregularly. The first issue appeared with the date February–March 1982 (pp. 1–36) and a special edition in May–June 1983 (pp. 2–43) with the group's program, under the editorship of Antoni Macierewicz. The themes ranged from articles about the character of political programs of various opposition groups to current events and problems relating to the Church. From 1989 it has been officially published through *Zjednoczenie Chrześcijańsko-Narodowe* (The Union of National Christians).

Krytyka (Criticism) is one of the few publications of the opposition dating back to 1978. It is a political quarterly originally edited by Jacek Kuroń. In the first part of its history, it had a circulation of two thousand to three thousand with an average length of two hundred pages. Throughout its history *Krytyka* was reprinted by *ANEKS* in London. The editorship also published a series under the name *Biblioteka Kwartelnika Politycznego Krytyka* (The Library of the Political Quarterly Krytyka). *Krytyka* was published by the *NOWA* and *Krąg* (Circle) publishing houses.

The title *Krytyka* (Criticism) was taken from a Cracow periodical from the nineteenth and twentieth centuries. The first issue was jointly edited by Stanisław Barańczak, Konrad Bieliński, Miklos Haraszti (Hungary), Stefan Starczewski (editor-in-chief), Václav Havel (Czechoslovakia), Jacek Kuroń, Jan Lityński, Adam Michnik, Jan Walc, and Roman Wojciechowski. Nine issues appeared before December 13, 1981. From 1982 to 1987 it was edited anonymously (number 10 to number 16). Beginning with number 26 it was again openly published. The present editor is Jan Kofman, who assumed duties during the early days of its inception, in 1982, under the pseudonym Włodzimierz Mart. *Placówka* (Outpost) was also published through the auspices of *KOR*.

KOR's joint publications included the following: *Zapis* (The Record), a literary quarterly, was typewritten by a group calling itself Uncensored Publishers—*Niecenzurowana Oficyna Wydawnictwa* (*NOWA*)—from January 1977 to 1981. It was mostly edited by members and coworkers of *KSS "KOR"* who were authors of the articles appearing in *Zapis* (Record). The subtitle announced that the quarterly would be made up of prose, poetry, and essays. The major motivation for the formation of *Zapis* was the continued confiscation of uncensored texts. The editorial board of *Zapis* was made up of a number of known writers: Jerzy Andrzejewski, Jacek Bocheński, Stanisław Barańczak, Kazimierz Brandys, Tomasz Burek, and Wiktor Woroszylski.

Appearing as separate issues of *Zapis* were the following: Tadeusz Konwicki's *Kompleks Polski* (The Polish Complex) in issue number 3, *Mała Apokalipsa* (The Little Apocalypse) in issue number 10, and his *Wschody i Zachody Księżyca* (The Risings and Settings of the Moon) in issue number 21; Julian Stryjkowski's *Wielki Strach* (The Great Fear) appeared in issue number 14. Except for the first issue all other issues were published either by *NOWA* or *Krąg* publishing house. The entire set was published in the West by Index on Censorship.

Puls (Pulse) is an irregularly appearing literary quarterly whose first issue dates from the fall of 1977. Numbers 1 to 12 appeared in Poland uncensored; issue numbers 2, 3, 9, and 10 were reissued in London in a reedited format. The thirteenth issue was prepared before Martial Law but was not published. From issue number 14 onward *Puls* has been published in London. At the beginning Jacek Bierezin was editor-in-chief; J. Chodakowski took over from 1983. The magazine has a number of standard features: *Pojedynki* (Duels), *Archiwum Emigracyjne* (The Archives of the Emigration), *Półtytuły Pólprasy* (Polish Titles and Press), *Muzeum Ruchu Wolnego* (The Museum of the Movement for Freedom), to name only a few. Issue number 18 was devoted to contemporary Russian literature, and number

25 to Czech literature. From 1991 it has been published officially in Warsaw and in London (under the editorship of, among others, Antoni Libera and Zbigniew Hentzel).

Robotnik Wybrzeża (Worker of the Coast) was the journal for the *Komitet Założycielski Wolnych Związków Zawodowych Wybrzeża* (The Committee for the Founding of Free Trade Unions on the Coast). *Robotnik Wybrzeża* was to some extent a variation of *Robotnik*. It was edited by Bogdan Borusewicz, Joanna Duda-Gwiazda, and other members of *WZZ* (Free Trade Union). Information and news of regional interest were printed.

Biuletyn Dolnośląski (Lower Silesian Bulletin) was founded in June 1979. Until 1981 it did not have a clear program. It finally settled on a program that included self-defense, self-organization, and independence. Much space was devoted to the problems of the USSR. The monthly was at first closely affiliated with *KSS "KOR,"* but from July 1980 until December 1981 it was independent. After December 1981 it became closely affiliated with *Solidarność Walcząca* (Fighting Solidarity).

The remaining periodicals mentioned here were used by *KOR* to establish communications and to provide a forum for interaction between factories, regions, and segments of the population.

Krąg (Circle) was founded on February 15, 1981, in affiliation with *KOR*, mainly through earlier activity with *Głos* (Voice). This publishing house separated itself from *Głos*, earlier known as *Biblioteka Głosu* (The Voice Library), because of a desire to publish works mainly of a political nature. *Krąg* was not affiliated with any political group.

Its founding purpose was to publish works concerned with the history of Poland and the history of its neighbors. This included politics, economics, and literature which characterized the epoch.

The first items were printed with a silk-screen press and through primitive printing methods. The later items were printed on a small offset press. Since 1981 over 160,000 titles have been published. Before December 13, 1981, it was edited by Witold Ferens, Marek Tabin, and Andrzej Rosner; after the introduction of Martial Law it went underground. On December 16, 1981, the staff decided to print magazines: *Głos* (Voice), *Tygodnik Mazowsze* (Mazovian Weekly), *Tu Teraz* (Here Now), *Syrenka* (Mermaid), *Druk* (Press), *Solidarność Narodu* (Solidarity of the Nation), *Replika, Wola* (Will), and *Słowo* (Word)—but only a few issues. Part of the staff organized the monthly *Fakty* (Facts), which was also published by *Krąg*.

From mid-February 1982 *Krąg* began to print books and brochures. On the average books were printed in quantities of fifteen hundred to eight thousand; an exception was *Solidarność* by Jerzy Holzer in ten thousand copies.

Krąg reprinted translations, works by émigré authors, as well as original works. The subjects included history, memoirs, philosophical and literary works, literary criticism, political publications, and religious works. Some issues of *Krytyka, Nowy Zapis,* and reprints of *Aneks* were printed as well as *Res Publica* before it went official, along with reprints of émigré periodicals, such as *Puls* (Pulse), *Aneks* (Annex), *Zeszyty Historyczne* (Historical Notebooks), and the best-known titles of *Krąg* (Circle), for example, *Najnowsza historia Polski Andrzeja Alberta* (The Newest History of Poland of Andrew Albert) by Wojciech Raszkowski.

In 1988 *Krąg* was a signatory of the *Fundusz Wydawnictw i Konsorcjium Wydawniczego* (The Publisher's Fund and Consortium) but withdrew at the end of the year. It is functioning again with the lifting of censorship.

Głos was originally founded as *Biblioteka Głosu* in conjunction with *KOR* during the fall of 1977. The writers and editors of the publishing firm included Krzysztof Łaczyński, Piotr Naimski, Wojciech Fałkowski, and Antoni Mackiewicz. Its main activity was publishing its own magazine, of which thirty-five issues appeared before December 1981. Forty books and brochures appeared as well. With *Krąg, Głos* also copublished *Wiadomości* (News), of which 163 issues were printed between December 17, 1981, and October 6, 1985.

Głos was one of the first independent publishing houses to resume activity after December 13, 1981. The one-hundredth book published was *Krótki kurs historii wyborów do rad Narodowych* (A Short Course of History of Elections to the Nation Council), by Ludwik Dorn; *Czas morderców* (The Time of Murderers), *Kulisy Zamachu na Papieża* (Scenes of the Attempt on the Life of the Pope), by Claire Sterling, was the one-hundred-twenty-ninth book published. After 1985 *Głos's* level of activity began to decline. Among the best-known titles was *Myśli staroświeckiego Polaka* (Thoughts of an Old World Pole), by Piotr Wierzbicki. The publishing house continues to function since the lifting of censorship.

Probably the best known independent publisher in Poland is *NOWA** (*NOWA* is an acronym for *Niezależna Oficyna Wydawnicza* [Independent Publishing Office]. It was founded in the winter of 1976–77 by Janusz Krupski, Antoni Macierewicz, and Mirosław Chojecki. Earlier Krupski and Piotr Jegliński suggested traveling to the West in order to procure printing equipment which would then be taken back to Poland. Jegliński bought the printing equipment with his own money. A hectographic printer was taken to Lublin.

In June 1977 the first issue of *Zapis* appeared printed by *Nieocenzurowana Oficyna Wydawnicza* (The Uncensored Publishing Office). A change of name was suggested by M. Chojecki, who was also coauthor of *NOWA*'s program. Among the editors of the publishing house were Grzegorz Boguta and Konrad Bieliński. Adam Michnik also influenced the programs of the organization.

NOWA was founded with the specific aim of breaking the government's monopoly on information and publishing. In accordance with this *NOWA* did not identify itself with any specific political orientation. It wanted to serve a variety of creative efforts.

NOWA printed books and brochures about history, memoirs, documents, poetry, prose, lectures of the Flying University, essays, journalistic articles, satires, and press articles. During and after the rise of Solidarity the following series appeared: *Biblioteka Robotnicza* (The Workers' Library), *Biblioteka Krytyka* (The Critical Library), and *Seria Współczesna* (Contemporary Series). *NOWA* also worked with the émigré publications, *Kultura, Aneks,* and *Polonia Publishing*. In Poland it worked with *Oświata Niezależna* (Independent Education) and *Komitet Kultury Niezależnej* (The Committee of Independent Culture). Items published by *NOWA* were also reprinted by other independent publishers in Poland. After the rise of Solidarity, *NOWA* actively participated in the formation of a printer's union. By this time it was acting for all intents and purposes publicly and openly.

After the introduction of Martial Law the staff of *NOWA* was interned. As a result, activity was minimal. At this time a separate group under the direction of Adam Kersten formed *NOWA 2*.

In the first half of the 1980's *NOWA* began to produce audio and video cassettes. Its periodicals included *Krytyka* (Criticism), *Puls* (Pulse), and *Zapis* (The Record). It has continued to function since the lifting of censorship.

There was another opposition group besides *KOR* worthy of description: *Ruch Obrony Praw Człowieka i Obywatela* (The Movement for the Defense of Human and Citizens' Rights), sometimes abbreviated as *ROPCZIO* or simply *RO* (1977–81). Among the editors and staff were Leszek Moczulski, Wojciech Ziembiński, and Andrzej Czanma. The formation of *RO* was made known to the *Sejm* and to the episcopate through the publication of *Apel do Społeczeństwa* (Appeal to Society). The founding of *RO* occurred three weeks after Poland's ratification of the International Pact of Citizens' and Political Rights, but it was announced earlier through *U Progu* (On the Threshold).

RO published the independent monthly *Opinia* (Opinion, first issue April 30, 1977). It was first published in 1980. In some large cities meeting places were organized in which there were lectures and independent publications, for example, *Gospodarz* (Farmer, or Landholder, December 1977 to some time in 1979).

The student oriented magazine *Bratniak* (Student Organization), whose name was taken from a former students' organization, was loosely affiliated with *RO*. It was put out from October 1977 until 1979, when it merged with *Ruch Młodej Polski* (The Young Poland Movement) and *Ruch Związkowy* (The United Movement), a magazine published through the *Komitet Założycielski Wolnych Zwiazków Zawodowych* in Katowice (The Committee for Founding Free Trade Unions).

In 1979 the activities of *RO* were reported in the independent *Aspekt.*

In 1978 *RO* split into two factions during the national meeting, during which various speakers traded accusations during their speeches. This led to the formation of two distinct groups: *Rada Sygnatariuszy* and *Rada Funduszu Praw Człowieka* (The Council of Signatories and the Council for the Foundation of Human Rights). *Rada Sygnatariuszy* was affiliated with *Opinia,* and the *Fundusz Praw Człowieka* became the new publications *Droga* (Road or Way, July 1978) and *Gazeta Polska* (Polish Gazette, February 1979).

Some members affiliated with *Fundusz Praw Człowieka* announced the formation of the *Konfederacja Polski Niepodległej* (Confederation for an Independent Poland) on the first of September 1979.

The founding charter of the *KPN* was signed by thirty-four people representing various opposition groups. The principle of self-determination was declared to be dependent upon free expression of the will of society in matters of international relations, in social and political organization, and in the guidance and direction of the state. The founder and guiding spirit behind *KPN* was Leszek Moczulski. After 1989 *KPN* became a legally sanctioned political organization.

The *KPN* was repeatedly attacked in the official press. An example of this is the book by Marian Reniak *KPN, kulisy, fakty, dokumenty* (KPN, Scenes, Facts, Documents). In the Western press it was often presented as a nationalist movement.

Cecuda in his *Leksykon* (Lexicon) links thirty-eight publications and two publishing houses associated with the *KPN.* He gives only the most rudimentary information for nine and none for the remaining twenty-nine. He briefly describes the *Wydawnictwo Polskie* but gives no information about the *Wydawnictwo Reduta.* His *Leksykon* seems to be reliable for what is included; however, the fact of a given publication's exclusion does not necessarily reflect a lack of value of the publication. To give an idea of the problems involved, Kamińska lists approximately fourteen hundred magazines—monthlies, weeklies, irregulars, and so on—and Cecuda lists only 435 titles. Moreover Kamińska's bibliography covers only the period between December 13, 1981, and June 1986, whereas Cecuda's work covers the period from 1976 to 1989.

AFTER AUGUST 1980

Before 1980 the *Drugi obieg* is relatively simple to describe and delineate: it consisted of a few major opposition groups with their own publications and publishing houses. With the rise of Solidarity the situation changed. Money was given to finance regional efforts and during the euphoria of Solidarity's legal existence any semblance of secrecy or underground activity was largely given up. Many regional chapters of Solidarity had earlier begun to collect archival material from the *Drugi obieg*. As a result, when Martial Law was declared the Interior Ministry became the possessor of one of the world's largest collections of pre-1981 *Drugi obieg* materials.

With the suppression of Solidarity, the world's attention focused on Poland. This resulted in contributions of money and equipment. According to Karpiński, on November 28, 1986, a truck arriving on a ferry at the Polish port of Świnoujście disembarked, as was officially announced, with over eight tons of computer, radio, printing, and telecommunications equipment, as well as several thousand books in Polish printed in the West.

While there was no doubt some sort of distribution network and organization in the opposition, no information has been made public. It should not be forgotten that there were quite a number of small organizations unaffiliated with any group, each publishing its own journal with its own "publishing house." As might be expected, the smaller the publishing house, the poorer the type quality; and the larger, the better the print quality. In these smaller publishing houses improvisation was the rule.

After the internment of most of the regional and all of the national leaders of Solidarity, the opposition fragmented. This made the task of providing an overview of the *Drugi obieg* enormously difficult. All the world has heard of Solidarity, and as a result of this, more space will be devoted to less well-known publishers. It should be noted that it would be quite easy to write a great deal about Solidarity's publishing efforts alone, without considering the smaller groups. Because of this only two of Solidarity's publications, *Tygodnik Solidarność* (Solidarity Weekly) and *Tygodnik Mazowsze* (Mazovian Weekly), will be described. It should also be noted that all of the regional committees sponsored several publications; *Tymczasowy Komitet Koordynacyjny* (The Temporary Coordinating Committee) was also heavily involved in independent publishing.

Tygodnik Mazowsze was published during Martial Law and afterward. Number 2 appeared with the date February 11, 1982. The first number did not appear. The thirteenth issue appeared with the date of June 27, 1985. *Tygodnik Mazowsze* printed short news stories and discussed the strategy that Solidarity should adopt. With the founding of the *TKK* and of the Regional Executive Committee for Mazowsze, *Tygodnik Mazowsze* published its own statements and declarations. It appeared until 1989.

Tygodnik Mazowsze was published by *NOWA* and *Krąg*. Until the thirty-second issue there was no charge. Standard features included interviews with Solidarity's activists, *Tydzień w Tydzień* (Every Week), *Więźniowie polityczni* (Political Prisoners), and *Opór* (Resistance).

Tygodnik Solidarność was the central newspaper of *NSZZ. Solidarność* was published from March 31 until December 11, 1981. Each issue had a circulation of over half a million, with the exception of one issue in September at the time of the National Congress, which was printed in one million copies. Solidarity's policy declarations were published in *Tygodnik*

Solidarność, as well as information relating to Solidarity's activities and the discussions with the government. Articles of a social, historical, and political nature also appeared.

Tygodnik Solidarność was published by the *Krajowa Komisja Porozumiewawcza NSZZ Solidarność* (National Commission NSZZ Solidarity). The future prime minister of Poland, Tadeusz Mazowiecki, was its editor-in-chief. *Tygodnik Solidarność* was reprinted by *Słowo* (Word) in Toronto. It was officially renewed in May 1989; its initial editor was Tomasz Mazowiecki, followed by Jarosław Kaczyński and Andrzej Gelberg.

Solidarność Walcząca (Fighting Solidarity) was organized as a result of a split in the regional strike committee of Solidarity in Lower Silesia. The development of the organization took place against the background of further tactical activities, and in June 1982 *Solidarność Walcząca* was formed. Its overriding goal was the fight for Poland's independence. The founding artist and leader of Fighting Solidarity was Kornel Morawiecki. The original charter was called *Manifest programowy* (Manifest Program), in which the goal of a democratic and parliamentarian form of government was put forth. The economy would be based on the laws of the market with the exclusion of privately owned real estate. Human and political rights would be protected by institutions that would be held accountable and by an independent judiciary. There was also a strong emphasis on independent trade unions united on the basis of voluntary membership open to all professions. *Solidarność Walcząca* also supported independent movements in other Communist countries.

The propaganda, information, and publishing activities had the formation of social awareness as their goal, and the development and improvement of the structure of *Solidarność Walcząca*. Special groups were formed for street demonstrations. *Solidarność Walcząca* was an organization that consisted of careful conspirators: anyone could become a member after a thorough background check, and by swearing an oath.

Solidarność Walcząca worked with *MRK Solidarność* (MRK Solidarity) and *Liberalno-Demokratyczna Partia Niepodległość* (Liberal-Democratic Independence Party) as well as with the social and political movement *Pomost* (Platform), which was active in the United States. In 1990 Fighting Solidarity legally became *Partia Wolności* (Freedom Party).

It had a lively publishing arm in the form of stamps, books, audiocassettes, placards, pictures, and regularly appearing publications. Its press organ was *Solidarność Walcząca* (founded during the second half of 1982, with a circulation of over twenty thousand). In addition to these were the following publications:

Czas (Time) was a politically oriented bimonthly which appeared in Poznań in 1984–85.

Europa was a journal of the Institute of Eastern Europe. The first issue appeared in 1987 with 127 pages. The aim of *Europa* was to liven up the intellectual climate in Poland. The intention of the editors was to publish material about the functioning of Socialist states. It was also eventually to include poetry, prose, and reviews from Polish and Western sources.

Galicja (Galicia) was published in Rzeszów from December 1984 until some time in 1985.

Gencjana (Gentian) first appeared in 1985 in Jelenia Góra. It was published irregularly.

Myśl (Thought) was a monthly which appeared in Jelenia Góra in 300 issues.

PIK—Podziemny Informator Katowicki (Underground Directory of Katowicki) is a monthly which has appeared in Katowice since 1983.

Wiadomości Historyczne (Historical News) was a monthly printed in 300 issues. It was free to students.

Wolna Polska (Free Poland) first appeared in 1985 in Wrocław.

In addition to these publications *Solidarność Walcząca* had regional publications in Wrocław, Lublin, Łódź, Cracow, Pruszków, Warsaw, Kalisz, Poznań, and Gdańsk. It also had representatives in various cities in the West. In addition to periodicals devoted to culture and the fine arts, essays, criticism, and translations it published periodicals with a more political and action-oriented program:

Arka (Ark), a quarterly published from 1983 in Cracow. The editorial board included Ryszard Legutko and Tadeusz Nyczak. It has appeared in the official press since 1990.

Kultura Niezależna (Independent Culture), a monthly sponsored by the Committee of Independent Culture, was published from 1984 in Warsaw: the editor-in-chief was Andrzej Osęka. The editorial board included A. Kawczyński (pseudonym Leon Bohev), Janusz Sławiński, and Jan Walc. From 1990 to 1991 it appeared officially.

Wezwanie (Summons) was a periodical published in Warsaw from 1982 to 1988. The editor-in-chief was Tomasz Jastrun.

Obecność (Presence) was a periodical published in Wrocław. The editor-in-chief was Lothar Herbst.

The following are descriptions of the larger publishers not mentioned in the first section of this entry.

CDN was founded in the winter of 1982 by Czesław Bielecki, writing under the pseudonym of Maciej Poleski. The group published over 130 items; it stopped publishing in 1990. At first it did not have a high public or political profile; neither did it have a developed political program. Its ambition was to stimulate contemporary social and political activity. This was done in several ways: independently of its printing activities, audiocassettes, films, and albums were delivered and distributed. The production of films was the special activity of the *CDN* Film Unit. The distributor was the Solidarity Information Office in London, which simultaneously transferred funds to Poland for the purpose of developing *CDN*'s activities. The various books published included the most current historical accounts, politics, political commentaries, literature, and literary essays.

The foreign representative was the *Publishing House Puls Publications. Puls Publications* also created the *CDN* Fund and appealed for financial support for *CDN*'s activities in Poland. Support was provided by *Instytut Literacki* (Literary Institute) in Paris and included the following publishers: Libella, Kontakt, Spotkanie, Aneks, Archipelag, the Foundation for Polish Culture, Polonia, The Independent Polish Agency, and Bicentennial Publishing in New York.

CDN is a signatory of the Foundation for Independent Publishing, and its representative sits on the Council for Independent Publishing. Because of the decrease in items published by *CDN*, it now conditionally remains in the consortium which directs the financial policies of the Foundation for Independent Publishing. *CDN* stopped functioning in 1990.

Oficyna Literacka (Literary Publishing House) was initiated in Cracow in 1982. It began as an independent publishing house, *Krakowska Oficyna Studentów* (Student Publishing House of Cracow [*KOS*]), which was active from 1978 to 1982. *Oficyna Literacka* probably published more literary texts than any of the other publishing houses associated with *Drugi obieg*, among others *Seria Biblioteka Poetów* (Literary of Poets Series). Its first publications appeared during Martial Law. These were signed *Nieobecni* (The Absent); later other names were used. The primary concern was to publish literary works, essays, history, and politics. However, the primary concern was always literary, hence the name. The reason for this is that a number of other independent publishers were publishing contemporary history, politics, economics, sociological studies, and so forth. Literary publishing efforts were marginal. Because the primary orientation was literary rather than political, the editorial staff valued artistic quality over political orientation. *Oficyna Literacka* is a signatory of the *FNW*, *Społeczna Rada Wydawnictw Niezależnych* (The Social Council of Independent Publishers [*SRWN*]) and *Konsorcjum Wydawnicze* (The Publishing Consortium [*KW*]). It has cooperated extensively with independent publishers based in Cracow. The Committee for Independent Culture awarded *Oficyna Literacka* a prize for its editorial efforts in 1986. *Oficyna Literacka* published *Zeszyty Literackie; Aneks*, a quarterly consisting of articles selected from *Kultura* from 1984 to 1987; and several numbers of *Brulion* (Rough Copy), *Bez Dekretu* (Without Decree), *Almanach Humanistyczny* (Humanistic Almanac), and *Polityka Polska* (Polish Politics). Approximately a hundred and fifty publications and one hundred books have appeared under *Oficyna Literacka* auspices. Among the artists and editors of the publishing house are Henryk Karkoszasz and Andrzej Mietkowski. It has continued to function since the lifting of censorship.

Przedświt (Daybreak) was founded in November 1982. It was formed with the intention of spreading independent Socialist traditions of the Polish Socialist Party—Revolutionary Faction. Among the artists were Wacław Holewiński and Jarosław Markiewicz. This journal failed to materialize. During 1983 *Przedświt* developed an interest in other literary forms. The Warsaw Independent Publishers of Poets and Painters worked under *Przedświt* auspices. *Przedświt* also cooperated with *NOWA* in the initiative of creating a special literary fund. From 1982 to 1990 over 130 books and brochures appeared under *Przedświt* auspices. It also carried the series *Biblioteka Myśli Krytycznej* (The Library of Critical Thinking) and *Biblioteka Wezwania* (The Call Library), the latter named after a paper of the same name. Other periodicals included *Karta* (Card), *Wezwanie* (Summons), and *Kultura Niezależna* (Independent Culture).

In June 1989 *Przedświt* split into two firms having the same name, one of which was legalized. Both have full rights to the works and traditions of the earlier firm. It continues to function since the lifting of censorship. Two separate publishing houses were formed in 1990. Some of the more famous publications of *Przedświt* were *Oni* (They), by Teresa Torańska, and *Konspira* (Conspire), edited by three writers.

Rytm (Rhythm) was created in Warsaw in 1983, with three major aims: first, to publish books and brochures forbidden by the censor; second, to keep its own printing shops ready to support Solidarity; and third, to provide financial support to Solidarity's resistance groups.

The first item printed was a brochure, *The Fourth Partition of Poland in Documents.* Since 1986 the firm has published a sociopolitical quarterly, *21,* edited by Lech Wałęsa's advisers. From 1983 to 1990 *Rytm* published over sixty items, each with a circulation of two thousand to five thousand copies. The firm also prints Solidarity "postage stamps," calendars, posters, and factory newspapers and bulletins. *Rytm* has also cooperated in publishing *Tygodnik Mazowsze.* Among the artists and editors of the publishing house are Marian Kalarski and Teodor Klincewicz. Some of the most important periodicals of *Rytm* are *Solidarność* (Solidarity) by J. Holzer and *Droga nadziei* (Road to Hope) by Lech Wałęsa.

Myśl (Thought) was also known as the General E. Nila-Fieldorf Publishing House, and the Gdańsk August Publishing House. Originally it was known as the 3rd of May Constitution Publishing House and was affiliated with *Ruch Obrony Praw Człowieka i Obywatela.* The present name was approved in 1983. It published *Pogląd* (View), the political quarterly; *Akces* (Access), which consisted of reprints from the Western press; *Szkice, Nowa Koalicja* (Sketches, the New Coalition), dedicated to the problems of East European nationalities; as well as several other periodicals.

In 1987 *Myśl* began to reprint *Kultura. Myśl* has published several dozen books, including *Przyszłość demokracji* (The Future of Democracy) by Samuel Huntington, *Oni* (They) by Teresa Torańska, *W obliczu wojny* (In the Face of War) by Cornelius Casoradis. It also published *Biblioteka Lit-*

eracka, in which such titles as the following appeared: *Brak tchu* (A Loss of Breath) by Janusz Anderman, *Podróż w czasie pułapki na ludzi* (A Journey During the Time of Trapping People) by Piotr Wierzbicki, and *Twardy człowiek* (A Tough Man) by Marian Brandys. Under the imprint General Nil-Fieldorf, such titles as the following appeared: *Rok 1920* (The Year 1920) by Józef Piłsudski, *Wspomnienia Starobielskie* (Starobielsko Reminiscences) by Józef Czapski, and *W i N na szlaku AK* (W and N on the Trail of *AK*) by Stanisław Kluz. Under the banner Gdańsk August *Grudzień 1970: Wybór Dokumentów* (December 1970: A Selection of Documents) and *Gdańsk-Gdynia-Elbląg* were published. Generally speaking, *Myśl* was concerned with social journalism, politics, economics, historical monographs, poetry, and prose.

In 1988 it helped found the *Wydawnictwo Prasowe Myśli* (A Publication of Publishing Thoughts), which provided general access to general printing services: printing, typing, and proofreading. According to a statement issued by *Wydawnictwo Prasowe Myśli* the prices of these services were to be below actual cost. As a result over 130 titles in twenty centers were printed from 1977 to 1990. In some regions publishing houses were started, for example, *Górnośląska Oficyna Wydawnicza. Myśl* also worked with other publishers in printing books. An example of this is Piechur, which published *(Nie) realny socjalizm* ([Un] Real Socialism) by Jerzy Drygalski and Jacek Kwaśniewski. Marek Latyński's *Nie paść na kolana* (Don't Fall on Your Knees) was also published in this way. It continues to flourish since the lifting of censorship. Other important publishing houses include the following: *Oficyna Literatów* (Artists Publishing House), founded in 1978 and directed by Janusz Korwin-Mikke. It published over seventy titles since the lifting of censorship in 1990 and continues to function. *Pokolenie* (Generation), founded in 1983, published over 120 titles before 1990, from émigré literature to political commentary. *Pomost* (Platform), founded in 1986 as *Most* (Bridge), published over 130 titles on various subjects, ranging from memoirs to politics and culture.

As mentioned earlier, several publishing houses cooperated in founding *Fundusz Niezależnych Wydawnictw* (The Independent Publishers' Fund) at the beginning of 1985. The main aims of the *Fundusz Niezależnych Wydawnictw* were to support publishing initiatives, to subsidize editorial staffs, and to pay for translations. Newly formed publishing houses, as well as established publishers, were given financial support. To improve the distribution of funds a distinction, based on the level of activity and length of activity of the publishing effort, was drawn. A printing house was something different from a publisher. A publishing firm was not a publisher if it had existed as an organization for less than one year; had published fewer than twelve books or titles of publications (e.g., *Arka, Krytyka*); had been absent from the market for longer than nine months; and did not respect laws concerning the rights of authors and publishers.

In specific cases, a firm might be limited to publishing only books without any editorial work being done by the organization. The executive council of *Fundusz Niezależnych Wydawnictw* decided on who or what fulfilled such conditions. The board members included *CDN, NOWA WSKoS-Warszawa, Krąg, Oficyna Literacka, Przedświt,* and *Komitet Kultury Niezależnej.*

Wiktor Kulerski presided over the people associated with the publishers' movement who judged the quality of submitted proposals. *Fundusz Niezależnych Wydawnictw* took care of laws concerning authors' rights, as well as those of independent publishers involved with the Western market.

Originally it was determined that the price of a book could not exceed 4.5 zlotys (4.50zl) for an offset print copy. The publishers' syndicate provided *Fundusz Niezależnych Wydawnictw* with financial support. The founding charter was signed by *CDN, NOWA, Krąg, Przedświt, WSKoS-Warszawa,* and *Oficyna Literacka—Kraków.* The regulations for dividing up the profits were as follows: 45 percent for the founders of the firm, 45 percent for dynamic and artistically high-quality printing houses, and 10 percent in reserve. After some changes were introduced, 75 percent was designated for the most active publishers of the previous two years, in both output and quality of the books published. The remaining 25 percent went to support editorial staffs and initiatives showing promise. From 1986 until the end of 1987 loans and other support were given to forty-eight printing houses. There were plans to issue a brochure detailing and helping in coordinating printing plans, in order to prevent unnecessary repetitions. As of 1988 the members of *Fundusz Niezależnych Wydawnictw* included the following: *CDN, IWA, Krąg, NOWA, Przedświt, Oficyna Literacka, Wydawnictwo Grup Politycznych Wola,* and *WSKoS.* After 1991, when censorship was partially lifted, most of these groups disbanded and published sporadically.

DRUGI OBIEG AND THE FUTURE

Drugi obieg came into existence as a reaction against an overly strict and arbitrary censorship. In the simplest definition *Drugi obieg* consists of those publishing efforts which did not first obtain official permission to publish. Thus, high school announcements, advertisements, brief newsletters, and so on, technically qualify for inclusion. Contrary to common belief both in Poland and in the West censorship laws and a censor's office still exist. The Catholic weekly *Tygodnik Powszechny,* for example, failed to submit a copy for review. A copy was finally presented, but only after it had been printed. The censor did not grant permission to distribute that issue. One of Solidarity's Regional Committees wanted to print a calendar with a map of Poland, pointing out the Russian military bases and the motto across the top, "Poland Has Always Been" in Polish, and in Russian "Always Free." Needless to say, the calendar was not cleared for publication.

The constitution has been changed, but the censorship laws remain.

There is, however, a great deal of discussion about changing or repealing these laws. When there is no more censorship in Poland, will there still be a *Drugi obieg*? No doubt what will remain is the so-called *Trzeci obieg* (Third circulation), which is anonymous and "highly critical of the government, Mazowiecki, Jarużelski, and everything and everyone else." Even today, Jarużelski remains a topic of discussion with critics wishing to prosecute him. It is quite unlikely that independent publishing will continue in its old ways, if for no other reason than that it has always depended upon foreign contributions. With the reform process well under way, it certainly appears that that war has already been won.

DULLES GRIET (see Grochowiak).

DWA TEATRY (Two Theaters) (see Szaniawski).

DYGASIŃSKI, (TOMASZ) ADOLF (1839–1902), a writer, novelist, publicist, and pedagogue, took part in the January Uprising (1863) and was, as a consequence, imprisoned for several months. He studied history and philology in Warsaw but had to interrupt his studies for financial reasons. He earned his living as a private teacher; among others, he taught the famous painter Jacek Malczewski. In 1871 he opened an educational institution in Cracow and also opened a bookstore, where he published several popular publications. He was also an editor of a fashion magazine and the literary journal *Szkice Społeczne i Literackie* (Social and Literary Sketches). He was strongly opposed by conservative circles for popularizing positivist ideals and Darwin's theory. After his bookstore went into bankruptcy, he moved to Warsaw, where he started teaching again and worked with several major cultural and literary magazines. He was among the main spokesmen (along with Antoni Sygietyński and Stanisław Witkiewicz) of the group gathered around the magazine *Wędrowiec* (The Wanderer). The group used the columns of this magazine to promulgate naturalism in art and literature. He initiated a pedagogical journal and coedited an ethnographic magazine, *Wisła* (The Vistula). As a correspondent he traveled to Brazil, France, and Italy. In 1901 he returned to Warsaw, where he died a year later.

He began his work translating philosophical writings, pedagogical studies, and journalistic pieces. He was also a literary critic (e.g., two studies on Prus, his polemics with Maria Konopnicka concerning dialect). He made his literary debut quite late, with a short story, "*Za krowę: Opowiadanie z życia ludu*" (For the Cow: Stories from the Life of the People) in *Przegląd Tygodniowy* (Weekly Review), 1883. In 1884, with the advent of naturalism, he published *Nowele* (Novellas), *Seria I* (Series I), which began his career as a writer of short stories (a total of 131). His early stories are mainly concerned with two themes: life in the country and the world of animals. In his naturalistic images he portrayed the rough truth about the fate of poor farmers much more faithfully and poignantly than any of his contemporaries. The world of animals was portrayed sympathetically and with great knowledge. These two themes remained forever present in his writings. In 1885 he published two more series of *Nowele:* in 1886 a collection of short stories, *Z ogniw życia* (From the Chainlinks of Life, Volumes 1–2); and in 1887 *Z siół, pól i lasów* (From Villages, Fields and Forests, Volumes 1–2). The early period of his work was climaxed with *Beldonek* (1888), the most mature of his works, both in subject matter and in artistic form. Retaining the style of folk narration (*gawęda*) and written in a dialect, the novel relates the adventures of two village peasants who travel through the poor villages and towns of the writer's childhood (around Kielce); the work gives a wide panorama of the life of the Polish people during the second half of the nineteenth century. According to Jan Zygmunt Jakubowski, Dygasiński was much less convincing in his working of themes of urban life and the proletariat (*Nowe tajemnice Warszawy* [The New Mysteries of Warsaw], Volumes 1–2, 1887). The rural themes, in which he best displayed his skill, returned in the novels *Właściciele* (The Owners, 1887) and *Pan Jędrzej Piszczalski* (Volumes 1–2, 1890). In 1890–91 Dygasiński traveled to Brazil, where he became acquainted with the fate of Polish emigrants. He portrayed their extreme poverty in his *Listy z Brazylii* (Letters from Brazil, 1891) and the novel *Na złamanie karku* (At Breakneck Speed, 1893), passionately accusing Polish upper classes of having led the farmers to such desperate straits, from which they could only escape abroad.

In the second period of his activity as a writer Dygasiński published several more works on rural life, the novel *Gorzałka* (Vodka, Volumes 1–2, 1894); a collection of short stories, *Wywczasy młynowskie* (Millers' Vacations, 1895); the novels *Dramaty lubadzkie* (The Lubadz Dramas, 1897) and *W Swojczy, czyli Żywot poczciwego włościanina* (In Swojcza, or the Life of an Honorable Landowner, 1899); and a didactic novel, *Przygody młodzieńca, czyli Robinson polski dla młodzieży* (The Adventures of a Young Man, or a Polish Robinson for Young People, 1891). In 1896 the novel *As* (Ace) appeared. The main hero of this work is, as could be expected, a dog. *Cudowne bajki* (Wondrous Tales), a collection of stories, was published in the same year. *Pióro* (The Pen), a satirical view of Poland's journalist circles, appeared in 1897. His school memories, *W Kielcach* (In Kielce), were published in 1899. The themes of the second period are synthesized in the novel *Zając* (The Hare, 1900), one of Dygasiński's most popular works, a lively tale of life in the wilderness of both people and animals. The final period brought one of Dygasiński's most beautiful short stories, *Łabędzia woda* (Swan Water, 1901), and the novel *Margiela i Margielka* (1901). In 1902 he published his last work, *Mysikrólik, czyli Gody życia* (Kingmouse, or Feast of Life, 1902), a kind of poetic-naturalistic treatise, in which he created a mythology both Christian and pagan. The philosophical inferences of the work—treating art as a salvation preferable to the suffering of life—brings this work closer to modern literature (Young Poland). Though overshadowed by the great realists of the late nineteenth century, Dygasiński has a special position in Polish literature: he introduced folk themes into national literature; he was a lover of nature and animal life and enriched the Polish literary language with a rich dialect.

(See Positivism.)

BIBLIOGRAPHY

Pisma wybrane (Selected Writings), Volumes 1–24, edited by B. Horodyski, Warsaw, 1949–53.

J. Z. Jakubowski, *Zapomniane ogniwo: Studium o Adolfie Dygasińskim* (Forgotten Link: A Study of Adolph Dygasiński), Warsaw, 1961, 1978.

DYGAT, STANISŁAW (1914–78), a prose writer and playwright, studied philosophy and architecture during his early youth. He was relegated to an internment camp in Romania in 1939 and returned to Warsaw in 1940. He later lived in Cracow, Łódź, and Wrocław, and finally returned to Warsaw. In 1952 he joined the staff of *Przegląd Kulturalny* (Cultural Review) and was associated with that journal until his death.

According to Włodzimierz Maciąg, almost all of Dygat's works attempt to capture the conflicts between man and his social and cultural environment and to reveal the humor inherent in such clashes. Dygat was particularly sensitive to the forms of social convention. His characters are people who are struggling to free themselves from the chains of the social norm through provocation, scandal, or complete escape. The theme of escape (which resembles that of Gombrowicz), the ever-occurring dream of living in a different environment in which there would be no boredom and grayness in the activity of quotidian life, recurs in Dygat's main novels and gives them a nostalgic and poetic mood. Escaping invariably appears to be a vain activity, but there is no tragic sense to it: a melancholic mockery is shaped, in which situations underscore the contrast between human naïveté and the wisdom of experience. Dygat's early novels include *Jezioro Bodeńskie* (Lake Boden, 1946) and *Pożegnania* (Farewells, 1948, film version by Wojciech Has, 1958). In these works he linked the escape motif with the experiences of the occupation, when the old social structure fell completely apart. In his later novels, *Podróż* (The Journey, 1958), *Disneyland* (1965), and *Dworzec w Monachium* (A Station in Munich, 1973), his characters pursue other goals—an idealized world of freedom and a luxurious life, romantic love, and a return to the ideals of one's youth. The special value of Dygat's prose is his ability to combine a nostalgic and poetic mood with jocular unmasking of the make-believe world produced by our imagination. The inner life of his characters is presented as if it were unstable and ambiguous, tending to render the narration less literal, poetic, and melancholy; on the other hand, however, his characters clearly see the practical side of things. Dygat's favorite hero is someone inconspicuous—a clerk (*Podróż*), a young man "with no future" (*Pożegnania*), sometimes a sportsman (short stories and the novel *Disneyland*)—who wants to test his own value by seeking success and fame but is at the same time entangled in the network of relations with other people and institutions. Dreaming of a different life becomes merely a product of the hero's imagination, an attempt at overcoming the facts of life with mental mythology. These people are not aware, however, that the images created by their imagination are just as stereotypical and conventional as the life they lead in reality: in escaping they merely manage to fall into a different convention.

Similar themes are developed in Dygat's short stories and pieces, published while he was a journalist. They appear in the collections *Pola Elizejskie* (Elysian Fields, 1949), *Słotne wieczory* (Rainy Evenings, 1957), *Różowy kajecik* (The Pink Exercise Book, 1958), *Rozmyślania przy goleniu* (Meditations While Shaving, 1959), *W cieniu Brooklynu* (In the Shadow of Brooklyn, 1973), and *Na pięć minut przed zaśnięciem* (Five Minutes Before Falling Asleep, 1960). His writings are filled with skepticism and common sense; Dygat questions the fossilized rules of social and intellectual conventions, ridiculing mystification and pose. On the other hand, Dygat himself willingly wears a clown's face, regarding this pose as one of the important pleasures in life. Dygat also wrote two plays: *Zamach* (The Coup, 1946, with T. Breza) and *Nowy Świętoszek* (The New Tartuffe, 1950, with Jan Kott). He composed several pieces for children and was also a translator.

His novel *Jezioro Bodeńskie* (Lake Boden), written in 1942–43 and published in 1946, marked Dygat's debut. It is narrated in the first person as memory from an internment camp for foreigners organized by the Germans during World War II in Constanca on Boden Lake. The young hero is involved in a constant drama of self-creation; his imagination imposes on his mind reminiscences from literature which are subtle deformations of his actual situation. While flirting with a French girl, the hero identifies himself with a romantic artist, suffering for his tormented fatherland. He dreams of escaping, realizing his great patriotic duty, awakening the conscience of his compatriots—only to find out with relief that in reality escaping is impossible. Through his own experience he unmasks the traditional conventions of national literary mythology. The critic Kazimierz Wyka assigned this novel to the so-called novels of squaring up, which revealed the clash between the anachronous stereotypes of national consciousness and the historical reality of 1939–45. A quite popular work, the novel has been republished frequently (seventh edition, 1976).

(See Contemporary Polish Literature.)

BIBLIOGRAPHY

English

Cloak of Illusion, translated by David Welsh, Cambridge, Massachusetts: M.I.T. Press, 1969.

Disneyland, translated by David Welsh, Cambridge, Massachusetts: M.I.T. Press, 1969.

DZIADY (Forefathers' Eve) (see Mickiewicz).

E

EMANCYPANTKI (The Emancipated Ladies) (see Prus).

EMIGRANCI (The Emigrés) (see Mrożek).

ENLIGHTENMENT (*Oświecenie*) is a period in Polish culture and literature which occupies the second half of the eighteenth and beginning of the nineteenth centuries. The term Enlightenment was based on the German use of the term, propagated by, among others, Immanuel Kant. Until recently, the period was considered the final link with Old Polish culture and literature. Today it is regarded as the first epoch of modern culture in Poland. The problem of dating the period, however, exists to this day. For some critics the Enlightenment strictly encompasses the rule of King Stanisław August, that is, 1764–95. In general, critics agree that the boundaries lie between Saxon times (1740) and the period of Classicism, the final phase after Stanisław August's reign.

When speaking of the Enlightenment, one is referring to currents within the social and cultural fabric of a nation. It is characterized by a critical stance toward reality and saturated with a desire to free man from feudal ties, to participate in the reforms of the world in the spirit of the principles of humanity and righteousness. In Western Europe (Holland, England, and France) these tendencies had already appeared by the end of the seventeenth century; in Eastern Europe (Poland and Russia) these currents appeared only during the second half of the eighteenth century. In Poland the period is tied in with the country's efforts to extricate itself from a backward civilization and to raise itself to a higher level. During this period the bourgeoisie and the peasants began to take an active part. It marked the beginning of modern institutions and forms of cultural life, for example, in journals advocating reforms, shaping social and aesthetic views, as well as tastes.

The beginnings of the movement can be observed during the reign of August III, when the Załuski brothers founded their library and publishing house in Warsaw (*Biblioteka Załuskich*). S. Kotlarski reformed the school system (in 1740 *Collegium Nobilium* was opened). W. Mitzler de Kolof began his publishing activities (among others, the first scholarly writings in Poland). During Stanisław August's reign, the *Narodowy* (National) Theater was inaugurated. The Knightly School (*Szkoła Rycerska*) was also set up to educate the young nobility in the spirit of patriotism and according to the new pedagogy. In 1773, the first Ministry of Education in Europe was established and contacts with the outside world were made through publications and libraries.

King Stanisław August played a critical role in the literary and artistic life of the nation. His royal program to modernize Poland was best realized in the area of culture. He initiated a number of projects and was responsible for setting up a number of cultural institutions and inspired A. Naruszewicz to create his project on the History of the Polish Nation (*Historia narodu polskiego*). He also encouraged the writing of didactic satire (F. Bohomolec, A. Naruszewicz,* I. Krasicki,* and S. Trembecki). He was a patron of the arts and bountifully assisted artists and writers.

The main characteristics of the period were the development and changes in methodology of education and learning. Research was based upon empiricism; the law of nature became the basic principle governing human relations, the innate right in spite of any differences—"one and invariable." The Society of Writers (*Towarzystwo literatów*) was established. In Poland a very important place in the development of the Enlightenment was the flowering of social and political thought. An attempt to improve social conditions was already effected in the first half of the eighteenth century in the writings of S. Leszczyński and Konarski, who advocated a restriction or even an abolition of the right of *liberum veto*. They championed changes in the treasury, army, and political administration. The desire for reform appeared in all forms of writings—tracts, memoirs, publicistic materials, and, in literature, in novels, satires, and plays. A great many of the writings were published anonymously, and, only after years, as in the case of J. Pawlikowski, could their authorship be traced. Radical elements appeared during the Warsaw *Sejm* (Diet) within the group known as *Kuźnica Kołłątajowska* (Kołłątaj's Ironworks). Revolutionary accents were discerned in the writings of the Polish Jacobins, during the time of the Kościuszko Uprising. The writers of the period were bound by the idea of social change for the peasants and the bourgeoisie.

Literature played a distinct role during the Enlightenment. Passionate satire can be found in poetry as well as in novels and plays. Writers found their themes largely within the gentry milieu, but they also derived inspiration from folk motif, often painting vivid pictures of village life. A rich gallery of gentry types can be found in the satires of Naruszewicz and Krasicki, and in the comedies of F. Zabłocki* and J. U. Niemcewicz.* They appear also in the poetry of T. K. Węgierski and in the depiction of life in Warsaw (J. Ancuta and J. Czyż). Contemporary life (especially plebeian customs and mores) began to take shape in the novels of the period, especially in those of Krasicki* (*Mikołaja Doświadczyńskiego przypadki* [The Fortunes of Nicholas Doświadczyński] and *Pan Podstoli* [Mister Podstoli]), M. Krajewski's *Wojciech Zdarzyński,* and J. K. Kossakowski's *Ksiądz Vicar* (Father Pleban). These same elements can be found in Trembecki's descriptive narratives (*Powązki* [Cemetery] and *Polanka* [Open Field]) and even in Krasicki's* comic-heroic epic *Monachomachia* and Węgierski's *Organy* (Organ). During the Enlightenment, didacticism and rationalism were the means of expression. Fables were written by almost every major writer, including Naruszewicz,* Krasicki,* Trembecki, F. D. Kniaźnin,* Węgierski, and Niemcewicz.* Fables were a popular genre because in them the writer could comment on universal ideas, touch upon man's innate nature, and reflect upon social and political matters. They contained contemporary themes and often defined the current political situation.

Didacticism can also be found in the novels and poetry of the period. In the novels of Krasicki* and Krajewski, the hero learns religious tolerance and the way to a better social and political life. Krasicki's Nicholas Doświadczyński becomes a new man. Influenced by life's experiences, he changes from a callow youth to a good provider and a model citizen.

In philosophy, skepticism, utilitarianism, rationalism, and empiricism were the major currents. Man's natural right to build a better society was championed. In matters of religion, a decided free-thinking attitude was advocated (Trembecki, Węgierski, and J. Jasiński). A hands-off policy regarding religion in personal and social matters was championed by these writers.

During the final years of the Republic, during the Warsaw *Sejm* and the Kościuszko Uprising, satire changed dramatically from a social to a political means of expression. Anonymity among the writers became common. The pamphlet became the most popular genre (Niemcewicz*). Satire, riddles, and epigrams were employed to express the anger and frustration of the public. Poems advocating a call to arms for freedom, the use of the guillotine, and the abdication of the king appeared.

Lyric poetry also developed during this period. Based upon Classical models, the poetry followed those regarded as sentimental or Rococo. The favored form for those poets employing sentimentalism was the *sielanka* (pastoral). A new way of expressing intimacy was being explored: sadness, grief, longing, and tears found expression in the works of Karpiński,* for example, in his *Pieśni nabożne* (Religious Songs), in his elegy *Powrót z Warszawy na wieś* (A Return from Warsaw to the Village), and in his pastorals *Do Justyny* (To Justine) and *Tęskność na wiosnę* (A Yearning During Spring). Similar themes can be found in the lyrics of Kniaźnin,* with the difference that in his anacreontic and erotic verse elements of Rococo style are discerned. Similar elements distinguish the verse of J. Szymanowski. The three poets were connected with the Czartoryski manor in Puławy, where sentimentalism developed quite strongly.

Classicism, sentimentalism, and Rococo were not the only currents in the poetry of the Enlightenment. Scholars point out the pre-Romantic elements in some of the poetry of the period, as well as folk motifs, expressed most strongly in Wojciech Bogusławski's* *Cud mniemany czyli Krakowiacy i górale* (Supposed Miracle or Cracovians and Highlanders). Baroque elements can also be found in the poetry of K. Benisławski, Naruszewicz,* and Zabłocki,* and in the prose of J. Kitowicz.

The theater played a decided role in propagating the social and political ideas of the Enlightenment. During Stanisław August's times, and even during the Saxon period, the theater became a means of propagating cultural and political ideas, as well as educating the public in social matters. Various currents and tendencies can be discerned in its development, from anti-Sarmatian comedies (championed by King Stanisław August), for example, Bohomolec's *Małżeństwo z kalendarza* (Marriage from the Calendar), to realistic comedies, containing irony but maintaining poetic distance, like Zabłocki's *Fircyk w zalotach* (The Dandy Goes Awooing). Other trends were also present: parodistic and fantastic comedies (Zabłocki's *Król w Kraju Rozkoszy* [The King in the Kingdom of Bliss]), sentimental comedies, and libertine pieces.

Two trends were present in the development of the national opera: the French comic opera and the Italian opera buffo. Foreign operas were adapted to Polish tastes and the action was often moved to Poland. A. K. Czartoryski set down the theory of these adaptations in his foreword to *Panny na wydaniu* (Marriageable Ladies). During the last years of the Republic a number of plays with a political bent, urging reforms, appeared: Niemcewicz's* *Powrót posła* (The Return of the Envoy), Zabłocki's* *Henryk VI na łowach* (King Henry VI at the Hunt), and Bogusławski's* *Cud mniemany czyli Krakowiacy i górale* (Supposed Miracle or Cracovians and Highlanders). Tragedy was not a staple of the time: not until 1817, with A. Feliński's* *Barbara Radziwiłłówna,* did a work of quality appear.

The decline of culture and literature of the Enlightenment came at the beginning of the nineteenth century. After the dismemberment of Poland, political activity gave way to an attempt to preserve what was left of the country and to strengthen social and cultural institutions. The most evident sign of this attempt was the work of *Towarzystwo Przyjaciół Nauk* (Society of the Friends of Learning). The most active members were J. Ch. Albertrandi, S. Staszic, and Niemcewicz.*

According to Zdzisław Libera, the literature of the Enlightenment left much that is lasting and worthwhile. Its development under difficult conditions included battling Sarmatism (Old Polish prejudices and thought) and gentry conservatism. Basically, the period is marked by a sensible and level-headed approach to political and social problems, although it is true that in the late eighteenth century radicalism and revolutionary thought became apparent.

BIBLIOGRAPHY

Nauka polska w okresie Oświecenia (Polish Education During the Enlightenment), oprac. i wstęp Bogdan Suchodolski, Warsaw, 1953.

Poezja polskiego Oświecenia (Poetry of the Polish Enlightenment), oprac. i wstęp Jan Kott, wyd. 2, Warsaw, 1956.

Poezja polska XVIII wieku (Polish Poetry of the Eighteenth Century), oprac. i wstęp Zdzisław Libera, Warsaw, 1976.

M. Klimowicz, *Oświecenie* (The Enlightenment), wyd. 3, Warsaw, 1977; first edition, 1972.

F

FANTAZY (see Słowacki).

FARAON (The Pharaoh) (see Prus).

FELDMAN, WILHELM (1868–1919), literary critic and historian, journalist, playwright, and prose writer, was born and brought up in a poor Jewish family. During his entire life he worked for the assimilation of Jews. He became a member of a democratic youth organization and cofounded (with A. Górski, F. Nowicki, and K. Tetmajer*) the magazine *Ognisko* (Bonfire), a journal published by university students with a Socialist orientation (he later portrayed the group in his novel *Nowi ludzie* [New People], 1894). He was also active in educational movements. In 1896–97 he was editor of the radical paper *Dziennik Krakowski* (The Cracow Daily); from 1901 to 1914 he edited the literary monthly *Krytyka* (Criticism), which under his leadership played a major role in the intellectual life of Young Poland. In 1905 he was associated with the followers of Józef Piłsudski; in 1914 he joined the *Legiony* and was soon sent to Berlin as a press representative of the National Independence Committee.

As a literary critic and journalist Feldman was an enthusiastic propagator of Young Poland. He regarded it as a great movement, a renaissance of artistic culture, poetic language, and idealist thought but, above all, of social, patriotic, and national independence—the goals and ideals of Romanticism. Hence his cult and worship of Wyspiański and Żeromski and his dislike of the aesthetic programs of the journal *Chimera* and its editor "Miriam" (Zenon Przesmycki). For him the main duty of a critic was to find an intuitive insight into the writer's inner life and creative activity, first recognizing his specific physical and psychological predispositions. According to Jan Wojnowski, Feldman regarded this as a precondition of a fully adequate, "cocreative" interpretation of literary phenomena, grounds for determining the role of a creative individual in the development of social, aesthetic, and philosophical thought, which eventually would stimulate the entire society. According to Feldman, the role of a critic was that of an artist and moralist, who absorbed the work of art, experienced it intensely, and reproduced his impressions in an individual, personal form: thus he awakened the reader's understanding, his enthusiasm, and the cult of the ideal. On these grounds Feldman opposed academic literary studies, especially the representatives of the philological-historical school, accusing them of degrading the individuality of a genius by tracing secondary influences and considering unimportant anecdotes and gossip as adumbrated in his brochure *Pomniejszyciele olbrzymów* (The Demoters of Giants, 1905). His main achievement as a critic is a synthetic work, *Współczesna literatura polska* (Contemporary Polish Literature). The first edition, entitled *Piśmiennictwo polskie ostatnich lat dwudziestu* (Polish Literary Art of the Last Twenty Years, Volumes 1–2, 1902), was updated and developed in subsequent editions, supplemented with reading pieces (e.g., *Wybór poezji Młodej Polski* [A selection of Poetry of Young Poland], 1903), and further developed after his death. The book is written in a very emotional style, impressively prolix and full of pathos, clearly manifesting the ideological and artistic preferences of the author. It became the basis for numerous polemics and exerted a strong and lasting influence on the opinions of the literary intelligentsia; later critics found Feldman's work to be highly informative and accurate in its selection and ranking of literary works. His historical studies (*Stronnictwa i programy polityczne w Galicji 1846–1906* [Factions and Political Programs in Galicia, 1846–1906], Volumes 1–2, 1907, and *Dzieje polskiej myśli politycznej w okresie porozbiorowym* [The History of Polish Political Thought Under the Partitions], Volumes 1–3, 1914–20) were similarly journalistic and polemic in style.

Feldman's literary output was quite large, but not valued highly by critics from an artistic point of view; his works display strong influences of the positivist roman à these and of contemporary modernist trends. His works describing the life of orthodox Jews still have a documentary value (especially his novels *Piękna Żydówka* [A Beautiful Jewish Woman], 1888, and *Żydziak* [The Jew], 1889, and his dramas *Sądy Boże* [God's Judgments], 1899, and *Cudotwórca* [The Miracle Worker], 1900). Feldman also undertook classical modernist themes (e.g., the psychology of a woman) in his novels *W okowach* (In Fetters, 1890) and *Ananke* (1898) and in his plays. He also published several historical dramas, a comedy, and several collections of prose writings.

BIBLIOGRAPHY

A. Jażowski, *Poglądy Wilhelma Feldmana jako ktrytyka literackiego* (The Views of Wilhelm Feldman as a Literary Critic), Warsaw, 1970.

FELIŃSKI, ALOJZY (1771–1820), a playwright and poet, was born in Wołynia (Volhynia). He made Warsaw his residence during the years of the Great *Sejm* and the Insurrection. In 1794 he became one of the secretaries to Kościuszko. After the failure of the insurrection, he returned to his family's roots and took up duties in the village. He maintained contacts, however, with Warsaw's literary and scholarly groups. He was a member of *TPN* (1818) and undertook the duties of director and professor of the Polish secondary school in Krzemieniec, one of the finest in Poland at that time.

Feliński is one of the most talented representatives of Polish Classicism in its later phase, after the death of King Stanisław, known at one time as Warsaw Classicism. He is the author of the tragedy *Barbara Radziwiłłówna* (produced in 1817), which is still held to be the best drama of the Classical period in Poland. He also wrote some poems and religious songs, of which the most important was *Hymn na rocznicę ogłoszenia Królestwa Polskiego* (Hymn on the Anniversary of the Proclamation of the Polish Kingdom); it was written in 1816 in honor of Tsar Alexander I. During the November Uprising of 1830, after minor narrative changes, it attained patriotic significance; it is sung to this day as a celebratory national-religious song: "*Boze, coś Polskę przez tak liczne wieki . . .*" (God, Who Saved Poland Through Such Countless Ages . . .). He was also a well-known translator (J. Delille's *Gentry, or French Landed Aristocracy,* 1816) and the author of a treatise on Polish orthography.

Barbara Radziwiłłówna, a tragedy in five acts, was written during the period 1809–11, produced in Warsaw in 1817, edited in 1820. The plot centers around the conflict between the last king, Zygmunt August from the Jagiellonian dynasty, and the *Sejm* (Parliament) over legalizing the king's marriage to Barbara, a commoner and not of royal blood like the Radziwiłłs, which eventually ends in Barbara's tragic death. The historical truth (the story of the relationship, the alleged poisoning of Barbara by the queen mother, Bona) and the sequence of actual events are treated with a great deal of artistic freedom for the sake of coherence and brevity, as well as for the preservation of the unity of place and time. These features are characteristic of Classical drama, as are the strong idealization of characters (especially that of Barbara), the elevated and sophisticated style, and the story's being related rather than acted out.

The play was very popular and highly praised by critics (it was also translated into German and French) because of its superb language and differentiated versification, but above all, because of its patriotic and political message: showing the bygone power of Poland, the moral issues (the emphasis on the king's respect for the law), and patriotism as the supreme value of the state, and, finally, positing the obvious analogy between the tragic death of the innocent queen and the partition of Poland. According to Zdzisław Libera, the tragedy was harshly criticized and neglected by the

Romantics, who influenced the opinion of future generations. The play's literary and theatrical values were confirmed in productions by Kazimierz Dejmek (1958, 1962).

(See Enlightenment.)

BIBLIOGRAPHY

Dzieła (Works), Volumes 1–2, Wrocław, 1840.

FERDYDURKE (see Gombrowicz).

FIRCYK W ZALOTACH (The Dandy Goes Awooing) (see Zabłocki).

FRASZKI (Trifles) (see Kochanowski).

FREDRO, ALEKSANDER (1793 [or 1791]–1876), a superb writer of comedy and a fine poet, came from a family of modest means, but through his own work and the dowry brought by his wife his financial status and social prestige were augmented (Fredro received the title of a count in 1822). In 1809 he joined the Polish army, which fought alongside Napoleon, took part in the war of 1812, was taken prisoner by the Russians, but escaped. In 1815 he returned to his family estate, Benkowa Wisznia, near Lvov and remained connected with Galicja for the rest of his life.

He was married in 1828 to Zofia née countess Jabłonowska countess Skarbkowa, after waiting ten years for her divorce from her former husband; the experiences during this period of uncertainty influenced his misanthropic moods. During the years 1850–55 the Fredros (with their daughter) remained mostly in Paris, where their only son lived until 1957; upon their return they settled permanently in Lvov. Fredro became a member of *TPN* in 1830 and a member of the first Polish Academy of Science in 1873.

Fredro did not write regularly: periods of artistic activity are interspersed with periods of silence (1823–24, 1828–30, 1842–54); after 1854 he started writing again, but never published or produced his works. The reasons for his refusal to publish, about which he never changed his mind in spite of being insistently asked to do so, are not clear. It is certain, however, that his decision was at least partly influenced by the attacks of the critics who accused him of being indifferent to vital questions of national existence (S. Goszczyński, A. Dunin-Borkowski). According to Kazimierz Wyka, Fredro felt alienated from the Romanticism, which was triumphant in émigré circles. His artistic testament can best be found in his memoirs of the Napoleonic era, *Trzy po trzy* (Three by Three, written 1844–46, first edition 1880; complete edition 1968). His dramatic output falls into two groups, only one of which was known in his lifetime. The group includes (1) full-length comedies: *Pan Geldhab* (Mr. Geldhab); *Mąż i żona* (Husband and Wife); *Cudzoziemczyzna* (Foreignness); *Przyjaciele* (The Friends), written in 1826; *Ciotunia* (Auntie), written in 1883); *Śluby panieńskie* (Maiden Vows); *Pan Jowialski* (Mr. Jovial); *Zemsta* (Vengeance); and *Dożywocie* (Life Annuity); (2) vaudeville skits, farces, and grotesque plays: *Nowy Don Kiszot, czyli Sto szaleństw* (The New Don Quixote, or a Hundred Crazy Deeds), written in 1822; *Damy i huzary* (Ladies and Hussars); *Nocleg w Apeninach* (Overnight Stay in the Apennines), written in 1825; *Gwałtu, co się dzieje!* (Good God, What's Happening!), written in 1826; and *Dyliżans* (The Carriage), written in 1827; and (3) several one-act masterpieces: *Intryga na prędce, czyli Nie ma złego bez dobrego* (Intrigue on the Run, or There Is No Evil Without Good), written in 1815, produced in 1817, later rewritten as *Nowy Don Kiszot* (The New Don Quixote); *Zrzędność i przekora* (Nagging and Contrariness), written probably in 1819–20; *Pierwsza lepsza, czyli Nauka zbawienna* (The Best That Comes Along, or Salvation Arts), written in 1823; *Odludki i poeta* (Misanthropes and the Poet), written in 1825; *List* (The Letter), written in 1825; *Nikt mnie nie zna* (Nobody Knows Me), written in 1825; and *Obrona Olsztyna* (The Defense of Olsztyn), written probably before 1830. Simultaneously, Fredro wrote a number of poems, deeply personal, mostly lyrical in character, and several fables.

Fredro's dramatic works were created in close relationship with the theater itself; he was able to learn a great deal from his direct contact. He had an excellent understanding of the actor's role and also had close relationships with people working in the theater, in spite of the social gap that existed. His one-act pieces rely on common, everyday experiences of the theater of his time and on some invariable principles of reaching the viewer, especially the uneducated one. In his full-length comedies of the first period, on the other hand, one can trace the formal and thematic influence of the Polish comedy of the Enlightenment: these plays center around a character whose vice and humorous traits motivate the plot to some extent, providing links with the actual problems of the epoch. The same tradition accounts for the meaningful names of characters: Geldhab (having money), Raptusiewicz (easily led to anger) and Milczek (silent man) in *Zemsta* (Vengeance), Birbancki (a fop), and Twardosz (a tough man) in *Dożywocie.* Among Fredro's early comedies, *Pan Geldhab* and *Cudzoziemczyzna* bear the strongest relationship to Enlightenment comedy; *Mąż i żona* (Husband and Wife) is the most original, most daring, and best written of all Fredro's comedies before 1830. As for Fredro's experiences in Napoleon's army, the funniest image can be found in *Damy i huzary.* His favorite device, the folk motif, can be found in *Gwałtu, co się dzieje!:* the plot is based on two ancient folk themes—about a locksmith who is guilty and a blacksmith who is unjustly hanged in his stead, and about a world ruled by women. The best of his comedies were written after 1830. Staged in Lvov, the following were produced in sequence: *Pan Jowialski, Śluby panieńskie,*

Zemsta, and *Dożywocie.* Fredro became fully mature as an artist when he liberated himself from the heritage of the traditional comedy; at the same time, he was influenced by Romanticism, that is, to the extent to which Romantic ideals could be reconciled with his realism. *Zemsta* and *Dożywocie* can be called "Galician" comedies, for they were clearly situated in the Austrian partition of Poland. *Pan Jowialski* is the most complex of Fredro's comedies; *Dożywocie* is the harshest in its evaluation of the power of money, but at the same time it is the funniest of his works.

Fredro unexpectedly began writing comedies again after a break of more than ten years, upon his return from Paris; the comedies of this period (which lasted until 1870) probably appeared in the following sequence: *Wielki człowiek do małych interesów* (A Great Person for Small Business), *Wychowanka* (The Ward), *Co tu kłopotu!* (What Trouble Here!, 1858), *Ożenić się nie mogę* (I Cannot Marry, around 1859), *Rewolwer* (Revolver), *Godzien litości* (Deserving of Pity, 1862), *Z Przemyśla do Przeszowy* (From Przemyśl to Przeszowa, after 1864), *Ostatnia wola* (Last Will, 1867); and one-act plays, in verse and prose, *Dwie blizny* (Two Scars), *Pan Benet* (Mr. Benet), *Lita et Compagnie, Koncert* (Concert), *Jestem zabójcą* (I Am a Murderer), *Świeczka zgasła* (The Candle Has Gone Out), and *Teraz* (Now). Certain themes developed during the first period are absent in these pieces and not one can be found. Contemporary interest was no longer focused on the times of Napoleon, sentimental feelings toward nobility, or the traditions of the eighteenth century. On the other hand, Fredro's techniques changed drastically, probably influenced by what he saw in the theaters in Paris. He now chose his representative characters quite differently; he constructed conflicts in a new way and found motivations for the characters' actions within bourgeois society, stressing its cult of money. Thus, almost all of Fredro's characters in his late comedies either have a firm grip on their estate and money, or—and these are the majority—pursue money ruthlessly, pestered by debts, unable to work or to run a real business, counting on some inheritance or some sort of shady deal. These themes can clearly be seen in the recurring motif of marriage between members of different classes, treated purely in terms of a financial deal (*Lita et Compagnie, Godzien litości,* etc.). The secondary characters are drawn sharply and show that Fredro remained a keen observer of the human condition. The plots are rooted in Galicia with its specific human fauna: a clerk, a rebellious peasant, impoverished noblemen, common visitors to the horse market, conspirators, and Polish officers serving in the army of the occupiers. A specific role is assigned to women: they are quite independent (confirming the advent of the emancipation movement), for example, Matylda in *Wielki człowiek . . . ,* Laura Łęcka in *Godzien litości,* the teacher Paulina in *Ostatnia wola.* These women are clearly predecessors of Orzeszkowa's heroines; however, these female foils are merely Romantic "lionesses," whom Fredro treats with a great deal of irony. Three comedies of this period deserve special mention, each for a different reason: in *Wielki człowiek do małych interesów,* Fredro employed the old structure of the play for the last time, comparing it satirically with the political stagnation in Galicja; *Wychowanka* is a ruthless analysis of the morality of the contemporary magnate's home; *Rewolwer* is a grotesque piece, quite modern in form and presenting very definite political views. Produced after Fredro's death, these comedies disappointed many critics and were later considered inferior to his earlier plays. The latter is a superficial evaluation: Fredro returned to writing when he was about sixty, and went on until he was almost eighty—an unprecedented example in Polish or in any literature. His works of the period are simply different, as if written by someone else. In some ways they resemble the antibourgeois comedies of the period of Young Poland; thus his ideas seem almost modern.

Apart from his works for the theater, Fredro also wrote poems, fables, and lyrics. He also tried his hand at short stories and composed aphorisms. Among the lengthy poems, *Szewc i diabeł* (The Cobbler and the Devil), written around 1854, seems to stand out, with its bourgeois-folk theme and political allusions. Fredro's fables, on the other hand, are written in the best tradition of narrative fables. They became so popular that they entered the domain of national folk literature, where the name of the author is almost superfluous: such works as *Paweł i Gaweł* (Paul and Gaul) and *Małpa w kąpieli* (The Monkey Takes a Bath). Fredro's lyrics are varied in themes. They are an important source of knowledge regarding the author's character, both in the pieces where he gives vent to his feelings and in those in which he presents his bitter reflections on his long life and rich experiences. The reflexive lyrics are more numerous during the late period of his life, when he wrote with self-irony of his own strange artistic fate, or reflected on the past, or addressed his contemporaries. During the same period he wrote a collection of aphorisms, *Zapiski starucha* (Notes of an Old Man, published in 1880), which deal with the bitterness of ideology and politics, and, above all, with human vice and the Polish national character.

An overall evaluation of Fredro's work must take into account the course of his career—so long lasting, paradoxical, and unique that the author of *Zemsta* (Vengeance) cannot be compared with any other of the great Polish writers. His artistic activity lasted over fifty years, with periods of idleness, but his personal and historical experience covers the period from the times of Napoleon to the rise of Prussia after 1870. To the "younger Fredro," the one belonging to the Napoleonic Wars and post-Enlightenment heritage, we owe the most valuable plays, those that animate Polish national theater even today: the "older Fredro" left us a heritage of a different genre, yet rich enough to elevate his artistry to classic heights.

Although his works were often produced on the Polish stage, Fredro was less lucky with publishers. They were never fully published until S. Pigoń began a complete critical edition in 1955.

Zemsta (Vengeance), a comedy in four acts, written in verse, is probably his masterpiece. In the Russian partition, it was performed and published under the title *Zemsta za mur graniczny* (The Revenge for the Boundary Wall), in order to satisfy the demands of the censor. Written probably in 1833, produced in Lvov in February 1834, it was published in 1838. The locale of the play is the actual castle of Odrzykoń near Krosno, which was part of the dowry of Fredro's wife, Zofia. The text does not mention time nor place: the action probably takes place soon after the partition, when in the depths of the country the old ideals of the nobility were still very lively. The plot centers around the conflict between two local dignitaries: the Cup-Bearer Raptusiewicz and the Notary Milczek, who live as neighbors in an old castle divided into two parts. The story begins when the Notary attempts to repair the wall separating the two parts and the Cup-Bearer makes his task impossible. The Cup-Bearer wants to take revenge on his neighbor and uses a trick to get the Notary's son, Wacław, into his home, where he forces him to marry his daughter, Klara, not realizing that the couple has loved each other in secret and that Wacław was simply acting according to their wishes. When it is discovered that Klara is the heir to a fortune which was originally to go to Podstolina, an elderly widow whom Raptusiewicz wanted to marry and whom Milczek wanted to have as a daughter-in-law, everyone accepts the situation and the argument is ended. An important role is given to Papkin, a cowardly liar, a great comic character, who enlivens the conflict between the Cup-Bearer and the Notary.

The value of *Zemsta* lies in its fast developing plot, full of unexpected turns; a masterful characterization of the main heroes; the quality of the dialogue; and the superb form of the verse. Fredro praises the ideals of the nobility as an embodiment of the national character. The parts of the main characters were always played by the best actors in the history of Polish theater.

BIBLIOGRAPHY

Pisma wszystkie (Complete Writings), Volumes 1–15, edited by S. Pigoń, 13–15, edited by K. Czajkowska; introductions in Volumes 1 and 7 by K. Wyka, Warsaw, 1955–80.

Pisma wszystkie (Complete Works), edited by S. Pigoń and K. Wyka, Warsaw: Państiwowy Instytut Wydawniczy, 1955–57.

English

The Major Comedies of Alexander Fredro, translated by H. B. Segel, Princeton, New Jersey: Princeton University Press, 1969.

Ladies and Hussars (Damy i huzary) (comedy in three acts), translated by Florence Noyes and George Rapall Noyes, New York: Samuel French, 1925.

Husband and Wife (Mąż i żona) (comedy in three acts), translated by Anna Gelperowich, Monash University, Clayton Victoria Australia, 1980.

Maiden's Vows, or The Magnetism of the Heart (Śluby panieńskie) (comedy in five acts), translated by A. P. Coleman and M. M. Coleman, Schenectady, New York: Electric City Press, 1940.

Vengeance (Zemsta), translated by Harriet Eleanor Kennedy, introduction by M. M. Coleman, *Alliance Journal,* Number VII, 1957.

FRYCZ MODRZEWSKI, ANDRZEJ (1503–72), the finest political writer of the Polish Renaissance, was also a social reformer, moralist, and theologian. He came from a noble, but not particularly rich family, and studied at the Cracow Academy. He worked in the office of the primate Jan Łaski; he was long associated with this family, and especially with the primate's nephew, the well-known humanist and reformer J. Łaski, with whom he spent a long time in Germany studying at the University in Wittenberg, where he met Martin Luther and Philip Melanchton. After the death of Erasmus of Rotterdam, he spent time shipping his library, purchased by Łaski, to Poland. In 1547 he was nominated secretary to King Zygmunt Stary (the Old); in this capacity he took on a number of diplomatic missions. After 1553 he lived in his family estate of Wolbórz but had to escape in 1556, because he was persecuted by Church authorities for his reformist views. Without changing his beliefs, he nonetheless maintained close contacts with Calvinists and Polish Arians (as well as with centers of the Polish Reformation), attempting to understand the views of others through the means of dialogue. Later he was given protection by means of a letter issued by the king and continued writing.

Frycz began his activity as a writer in 1543, with an attack on the rules of punishment for murder, which made the punishment dependent on the social status of the criminal and his victim (*Lascius, sive de Poena homicidii*): the treatise was written in the form of a senate speech delivered by Hieronim Łaski; the subsequent three texts on the same subject retained the same form. All his works were written in Latin. Another important work was *Oratio Philatethis peripatetici* (1545), an attack on the law which forbade townsmen from possessing land, which was reserved strictly for the gentry. His first conflict with the Church was generated by the speech *Ad Regem, Pontifices . . . et Populos Poloniae . . . oratio* (1546), arguing in favor of sending secular representatives along with clergymen to the Council of Trident. He believed that representatives of non-Catholic beliefs should take part. After 1546 he wrote his main work, *Commentatorium de Republica emendanda libri quinque.* The history of editing of this work was far from easy: the Church censor did not allow the work to be published in its entirety. After a truncated publication in Cracow (1551), the complete edition only appeared in 1554 in Basel. The Polish translation dates from 1577. The treatise, which relies on the traditions of antiquity and of Christianity, was strongly influenced by contemporary social, political, religious, and educational ideas (Erasmus, Melanchton). It was a great humanistic proposition of reparation—above all, a moral one—of man and government, which ought to be a monarchy, having as its goal a common good, strong enough to keep the social balance and protect the weaker classes against the stronger ones. Frycz argued for limiting the growing feudal dependence of the peasants; he also demanded that townsmen be given access to important offices and have the right to possess land. The main idea of his program was the legal equality of all citizens, and the primacy of law in the state. He also wanted the state to take control over education and the Church; he demanded that education be raised to a higher level and prepare people to assume public responsibilities. He also suggested that funds be taken from rich monasteries and Church institutions. According to Janusz Tazbir, he envisaged the Church as a national institution with a democratic internal structure, which would be completely independent of the papacy and be controlled by society as a whole. Opposing all forms of violence, and a follower of Erasmus' idea of peace among all religions, he argued for tolerance and freedom of religion. His work reveals his trust in human nature and reason and is the best embodiment of the social and political thought of the Polish Renaissance.

(See Renaissance.)

BIBLIOGRAPHY

Opera omnia, Volumes 1–5, edited by K. Kumaniecki, Warsaw, 1953–59.

Dzieła wszystkie (Complete Works), Volumes 1–5, Volume 1, edited by S. Bodniak; Volume 2, edited by K. Koranyi; Volumes 3–5, edited by K. Górski, Warsaw, 1953–59.

G

GAJCY, TADEUSZ (pseudonyms Karol Topornicki and Roman Oścień) (1922–44), a poet, prose writer, playwright, and literary critic, studied Polish philology underground at the University in Warsaw after 1941. He was a cofounder and editor of the underground paper *Sztuka i Naród* (Art and the Nation), around which gathered the most talented poets of the young generation, who made their debut under the conditions of the Nazi occupation. A soldier in the Home Army, he died in the Warsaw Uprising.

A follower of the artistic program advocated by *Sztuka i Naród* (Art and the Nation), Gajcy strongly criticized his predecessors, accusing the poets of the Skamander group of opportunism and lack of ideological involvement and those from the Cracow avant-garde of being "intellectual acrobats." According to Ewa Zuberbier, he considered the poets of his own generation to be continuators of catastrophism, but he opposed the passive attitude of such catastrophists as Czechowicz and Miłosz. He advocated active participation and, as a result of his Catholic beliefs, a heroic acceptance of man's tragic fate. His poems reflect his wish to free himself from the obsession of death and present the poet's role as that of a national educator, one who could reveal the mystery of existence. Gajcy presents reality through visionary and symbolic imagery, rich in metaphors. He often employs the convention of a dream and combines realistic elements with fairy tale effects. He also wrote ballads, tales, carols, and songs. In his poems *Z dna* (From the Bottom), in which he refers to the defense of Poland in 1939, and *Widma* (Specters, published in 1943 in his first underground collection), and an answer to Borowski's cycle *Gdziekolwiek ziemia . . .* (Wherever the Earth . . .), he presents an apocalyptic image of destruction. In the musical play *Misterium niedzielne* (Sunday Mystery, written in 1943) he tries to overcome the catastrophic themes by presenting the world under siege in grotesque dimensions, mixed with references to the folklore of Warsaw in a form which is a parody of national drama. His poetic play *Homer i Orchidea* (Homer and the Orchid, produced in 1946) is a metaphor of his own life, the life of his generation, and the fate of a poet, who pays with suffering for being one of the chosen with visionary capacities. The mystic sense of sacrificing oneself in the name of love of other people and of one's country is the leading motive in Gajcy's collection of poems *Grom powszedni* (Everyday Thunder, published in the underground press, 1944), especially in his poetic testament, *Do potomnego* (To Posterity), filled with monumental images inspired by sculpture and architecture, influenced greatly by the poetic technique of Norwid. Gajcy also wrote several short stories, an unfinished autobiographical novel, and a number of reviews of debut collections of poems written by his colleagues.

BIBLIOGRAPHY

Utwory zebrane (Collected Works), Warsaw, 1952.
Pisma (Writings), introduction by L. M. Bartelski, Cracow, 1980.

GAŁCZYŃSKI, KONSTANTY ILDEFONS (1905–53), a poet, came from a lower-middle-class family. Evacuated with his parents, he spent the period of World War I in Moscow. He started writing in 1915 and published his first poem in 1923. He studied English and classical philology for a time and began writing regularly after his military service (1926–28). He joined the poetic group *Kwadryga,* whose bohemian style had already attracted him as a student. He also worked for the satirical weekly *Cyrulik Warszawski* (The Warsaw Barber), which was connected to the Skamander group. In 1930 he married Natalia Awałow, the lyrical heroine of most of his erotic poems. During 1931–33 he lived in Berlin, working in the cultural section of the Polish consulate. In 1934 he settled in Wilno. Having received an invitation to work for *Prosto z mostu* (Straight Talk), he moved to Warsaw in 1936 and lived in the nearby village of Anin. Mobilized in 1939, he was taken prisoner on September 17 and spent all of the war in German camps. After liberation he lived some time abroad (Paris, Brussels, Rome), then returned to Poland in 1946 and settled in Cracow. There he worked for various journals—*Przekrój* (Cut Through), *Tygodnik Powszechny* (Universal Weekly), *Odrodzenie* (Rebirth)—and with the satirical cabaret, *Siedem Kotów* (Seven Cats). In 1948 he moved to Warsaw, with long summer breaks in Pranie, on Mazurian Lake, where he wrote his best poems during his late period.

In his early works Gałczyński was influenced by the Skamander group, although even here the specific lyrical style he was so fond of can be discerned: mocking and grotesque or decadent and bohemian. His first book was a poetic novel, *Porfirion Osiełek czyli Klub Świętokradców* (Porfirion

Osiełek or the Club of Perpetrators of Sacrilege, 1929), a grotesque fantasy. During the period when he was associated with *Kwadryga,* two trends are evident: the first, reminiscent of Villon and Rimbaud, creates the image of a poet as a kind of bohemian or clown, eager to escape from reality into the world of poetry (e.g., *Szekspir i chryzantemy* [Shakespeare and Chrysanthemums], *Serwus Madonna* [Hello Madonna]); the second trend can be called catastrophic grotesque (*Koniec świata. Wizje świętego Ildefonsa czyli satyra na wszechświat* [The End of the World: The Visions of St. Ildefons or a Satire on the Universe], 1929), in which the mask of jocularity and mockery hides the ominous note concerning Poland's social and political situation. Searching for permanent values amid the absurdity of reality surrounding him, Gałczyński showers praise for a job well done (the only person saved in *Koniec świata* is a carpenter, a good tradesman). The same motive appears in *Pieśń cherubińska* (The Cherub's Song), in which he lauds honest, hardworking people. His stay in Berlin produced *Bal u Salomona* (The Ball at Solomon's, 1931), which the poet himself called "a stream of inspiration." The technique of this poem resembles the surrealist technique to some extent; it is a free, alogical chain of associations. During his association with *Prosto z mostu,* Gałczyński introduces a new theme into his poetry—a lyrical hero who springs from the petit bourgeois and lumpenproletariat. The lives of these heroes are contrasted with the opportunism of the intelligentsia, a group he severely and repeatedly attacked and continued to castigate even after the war. During the same period he wrote poems ridiculing the excesses of *sanacja,* Pilsudski's followers after 1926 (*Zima z wypisów szkolnych* [Winter from a School Reader] and *Skumbrie w tomacie* [Mackerels in Tomatoes]). Being linked to the *Prosto z mostu* group gave him the feeling of literary stability (the paper paid for the publication of his *Utwory poetyckie* [Poetic Works], 1937, for which he received an award in 1938) and also presented him as an advocate of rightist-nationalistic ideology. The dependence on his sponsor soon became a burden for him (see especially, *Impresario i poeta* [The Impresario and the Poet], *Nieporozumienia* [Misunderstandings]). His last work before the war was the lyrical cycle *Noctes Aninenses.*

During the war years and his imprisonment he wrote a number of well-known patriotic and nostalgic poems (*Pieśń o żołnierzach z Westerplatte* [Song of the Soldiers of Westerplatte], *Pieśń o fladze* [Song About the Flag], *List jeńca* [The Prisoner's Letter], *Matka Boska Stalagów* [Mother of God of the Stalag]), often relying on religious motives or prayers. His stay abroad produced a lengthy poem, *Notatki z nieudanych rekolekcji paryskich* (Notes from Unsuccessful Paris Recollections), which reflects his hesitation about returning and having to take a stand on the political changes Poland was undergoing after the war. The poet's popularity (which is evidenced by the three volumes of poems published in one year, 1946—one appeared in Poland, the other two in Rome and Hanover) became still more firm during his Cracow period (especially the collection *Zaczarowana dorożka* [The Enchanted Carriage], 1948). In 1945 he began composing pieces for the *Teatrzyk Zielona Gęś* (Theater of the Green Goose), microdramatic grotesque pieces, ruthlessly ridiculing the intelligentsia, the petit bourgeois, and Poland's "national character." The absurd sense of humor was irresistible to many but outraged others. He delved still further into the absurd with the pieces he wrote for *Przekrój* (Cut Through), 1946–50, "mock letters to the editor," called *Listy z fiołkiem* (Letters with a Violet), a selection published in 1964. Gałczyński was later severely attacked by Marxist critics as a deviationist and did his best to meet their demands to compose optimistic political poetry in the obligatory spirit of Socialist Realism. He wrote some popular songs, such as *Ukochany kraj* (Beloved Country) and the collections *Ślubne obręczki* (Wedding Rings, 1949) and *Wiersze liryczne* (Lyrical Poems, 1952). In this regard Gałczyński was later "analyzed" as one of the characters in Miłosz's *The Captive Mind.* It should be pointed out, however, that few remember his political poetry, even his verse lament after Stalin's death (1953), while he was and still is adored and idolized for his lyrics and his sense of humor. During the late period of his life Gałczyński was concerned, above all, with the function and role of art (see especially, *Śmierć Andersena* [Death of Andersen], *Na śmierć Halasa* [On The Death of Halas], *Wielkanoc Jana Sebastiana Bacha* [The Easter of J. S. Bach]). This theme is most conspicuous in *Niobe* (1951), where Gałczyński emphasizes the permanence of art and gives expression to his poetic program. It is also evident in *Wit Stwosz* (1952), where the old motive of the tradesman-artist is developed around the fate of the great medieval sculptor. According to Marta Wyka, his poetic testament can best be seen in the cycle *Pieśni* (Songs, first edition, 1953; definitive edition, 1965), in which he sums up his output and addresses the readers' memory. Gałczyński also wrote several cabaret monologues, songs, radio plays, pieces for children, and a number of translations.

Gałczyński created an individual lyrical pattern and created the model of a bohemian poet characteristic of such poetry. He freely changed poetic conventions, switching from grotesque and lyrical images of everyday life, family, or nature, to realism and fantasy. He combined the capacity of sensing the social climate or the expectation of his reader (or sponsor) with a skeptical and ironic attitude toward all ideological mythologies. He respected tradition, availed himself of city folklore, and gave a fresh interpretation to old lyrical clichés.

Zaczarowana dorożka (The Enchanted Carriage), 1948, is probably his finest work. A collection of poems published since 1946 in journals and magazines, it has a tone that is mainly satirical or grotesque in character. The poems are rooted in postwar reality, with references to the poet's personal situation, to authentic people, and to actual events. The characteristic feature of this collection is the passage from deep depression, in those poems written abroad, such as *Ulica Skarg* (Street of Grievances) and *Notatki z nieudanych rekolekcji paryskich* (Notes from Failed Paris Recollections), full of personal questions concerning his attitude toward the political changes in postwar Poland, to joyful optimism on returning to familiar people and places (*Powrót do Eurydyki* [Return to Euridice], *Liryka, liryka, tkliwa dynamika* [Lyrics, Lyrics, Tender Dynamics]). Gałczyński was also enchanted with the atmosphere of Cracow (*Czterdziesty-szósty Kraków* [The Forty-Sixth Cracow], *Zaczarowana dorożka* [The Enchanted Carriage]). A number of important poems are included in this volume, such as *Wjazd na wielorybie* (Entrance on a Whale) and *Ars poetica,* which present his poetic program, that of a poet seen as a trademan who has to see his output in commerical terms, able to find a "buyer" (reader or sponsor). On the other hand, a poet is a bohemian, a magician, a cynical scoffer; he ostentatiously avoids unanimous declarations or taking on obligations, and never tries to be a moral authority or an ideologue. This attitude is developed in his attack on the Polish intelligentsia, its anachronous attitudes, its snobbish tastes and self-serving posing for martyrdom. The wide variety of poems also describe the charms of everyday life; some comic and absurd pieces are also included. The collection is a representative review of Gałczyński's characteristic motives; it gave him great popularity, but also generated bitter polemics and contradictory critical opinions.

(See Contemporary Polish Literature.)

BIBLIOGRAPHY

Dzieła (Works), Volumes 1–5, Warsaw, 1957–60; second edition, 1979.
Wybór poezji (Selected Poems), introduction by M. Wylere, Wrocław, 1982.

English

Niobe, translated by Adam and Ann Czerniawski, Celle: Moech Verlag, 1967.
Green Goose (Zielona Gęś), translated by Daniel C. and Eleanor S. Gerould, in *Twentieth Century Polish Avant-Garde Drama: Plays, Scenarios, Critical Documents,* Ithaca, New York: Cornell University Press, 1977.
Heart of the Night (Serce Nocy) (a song), translated by Ann and Adam Czerniawski, Cracow, PWM Edition, 1974, 1963.

GALL ANONIM (anonymous, called Gall) who lived during the turn of the eleventh and twelfth centuries, was the author of the first Polish chronicle, written in Latin. His real name is not known; the name *Gall* (which means French) was ascribed to him by M. Kromer. While living in the court of King Bolesław Krzywousty, Gall Anonim wrote the history of Poland (probably in 1113–16) with the help of the chancellor Michał Awdaniec and Bishop Paweł. He modeled his work on contemporary Western sources, and, by employing the form resembling the epics of the court, he composed the *gesta* (histories), that is, stories about the martial achievements of knights. The main hero of the chronicle is Young Bolesław Krzywousty (Wrymouth), who lived during the period 1085–1138, ruling as a Polish prince from the year 1102.

The chronicle has three parts, each of which begins with a dedication written in the form of a letter and a versified introduction. Part 1 contains the legends of Great Poland (the old west province of the Polish state) and the story of the Piast dynasty until the birth of Krzywousty; Part 2 covers the period between 1086 and 1108; Part 3 (unfinished) continues to 1113. In his chronicle Gall Anonim gives expression to Polish political ideas of the time, supporting Krzywousty's attempt at reviving the Kingdom of Poland. He depicts three clear portraits of the three great Bolesławs from the Piast dynasty: the Brave, the Bold, and the Wrymouth. He was also the king's spokesman in his presentation of the conflict between Bolesław Śmiały and Bishop Stanisław. The language of the work is prose, often rythmic prose; some parts also have rhyme. The text of the chronicle was preserved in three manuscripts, the oldest of which is from the fourteenth century (it can be found in the National Library).

BIBLIOGRAPHY

G. A. Chronicon, edited by Julian Krzyżanowski, Warsaw, 1948.

Kronika polska (Polish Chronicle), fourth edition, translated by R. Grodecki, introduction by M. Plezia, Wrocław, 1975.

GENERAŁ BARCZ (see Kaden-Bandrowski).

GŁOWACKI, JANUSZ (born 1938), a prose writer, playwright, and journalist, studied Polish philology in Warsaw. In 1964 he worked as a columnist for *Kultura* (Culture). The pieces were published in two collections—*W nocy gorzej widać* (At Night One Sees Worse, 1972) and *Powrót hrabiego Monte Christo* (The Return of Count Monte Christo, 1975). Głowacki in these pieces appears as a master of irony and grotesque. He published several collections of stories: *Wirówka nonsensu* (Centrifuge of Nonsense, 1968); *Nowy taniec la-ba-da* (New Dance la-ba-da, 1970)—the story *Polowanie na muchy* (Hunting for Flies) was made into a film by Andrzej Wajda in 1969; *Paradis* (Paradise, 1973); *My sweet Raskolnikov* (1977, together with a grotesque play, *Obciach* [The Shame], produced in 1976); *Skrzek* (Croak); and *Coraz trudniej kochać* (Ever Harder to Love, 1980). In these stories he presents an ironical and bitterly funny image of the times of "the little stabilization" (a term first used by Tadeusz Różewicz)—the uselessly rebellious young, the conformism of the adults, the loss of authentic intellectual and ethical values, the cult of financial success and its obvious symptoms. Głowacki seems to regard the majority of people around him as stupid, uneducated, vulgar, and greedy—the real children of the system. His early interest in concrete patterns of behavior was later replaced by a tendency toward a parabolic transformation of reality. His play *Kopciuch* (Cinders) was produced in 1979, published in Warsaw in 1981, and later staged by Joe Papp at the Public Theater in New York. His published works include selections of stories (*Polowanie na muchy i inne opowiadania* [Hunting for Flies and Other Stories], 1974), *Opowiadania wybrane* [Selected Stories], 1978) and a film scenario, *Trzeba zabić tę miłość* (One Has to Kill This Love).

After the strikes of 1980 and the rise of Solidarity Głowacki wrote a mininovel, *Moc truchleje* (Power Shudders), published underground, which presents the events from the point of view of an ignorant, unqualified worker, practically a lump of clay, who merely watches the developing situation but eventually becomes politically mature and involved. The book is written from Głowacki's usual perspective—slightly grotesque, free of any pathos, rational, and down to earth. Probably the keenest and most objective observer in contemporary Polish literature, Głowacki stayed in the West after Martial Law was declared (December 1981), first in England (where he had gone for the premiere of his play *Cinders* at the Royal Court Theater), then in the United States. His play, *Polowanie na Karaluchy* (Hunting Cockroaches), was produced by Joe Papp at the Public Theater in the East Village and was proclaimed one of the ten best plays of the year by New York critics in 1987. In 1990 Głowacki's three "American" plays were published by Northwestern University Press: *Hunting Cockroaches, Cinders,* and *Fortinbras Gets Drunk.*

Głowacki is the only Polish dramatist who has been able to break into the highly competitive American market. Neither Mrozek nor Rózewicz (to mention only the most popular of Głowacki's contemporary peers) has gained comparable acceptance. In fact, only the Czech Vaclav Havel has generated similar excitement about his work. But in the case of Havel, politics plays an important role. Głowacki has managed to attain prominence on talent alone.

Głowacki's American period (there will be no further Polish period, according to Głowacki in an article that appeared in *The New York Times*—"A Playwright Is Free [So Now What?]" (March 4, 1990)—began with the production of *Cinders* at Joseph Papp's Public Theater (opening night: February 20, 1984). Reminiscent of Ireneusz Iredyński's *A Christmas Play—Moderne,* where inmates in a concentration camp are rehearsing a nativity play, *Cinders* takes place in a prison where the female prisoners are rehearsing a film production of the Cinderella story. Głowacki outdoes Iredyński (and Jerzy Kosiński as well) in sexual innuendo and exploitation. The juxtaposition of a prison locale and a fairy tale wonderland destroys the Cinderella myth and highlights the injustice of prison life. Głowacki's play was perfectly timed: a production in England was taking place on the eve of Solidarity's temporary defeat on December 13, 1981. *Cinders* has great appeal for audiences and directors all over the world. Głowacki's puzzle is difficult to piece together. Whom does Cinderella represent? In destroying one myth, another insinuates itself and takes its place. But there is no question about Głowacki's attitude toward authority—local or from the outside. Bars do not a prison make: the warped minds of those in charge and those under their charge create the prison. *Cinders* is a disturbing play that does not depend on the Polish scene.

Hunting Cockroaches, produced at the Manhattan Theater Club at City Center Theater (opening night: March 22, 1987), is a truly American play in which the contemporary dream/nightmare is placed in historical perspective. It is a very "wise" play, without one false note. It provokes laughter through pain, recognition through the icon of émigré poverty, and a sense of urgency about the plight of the dispossessed artist, no longer at home in his native country, nor comfortable in his adopted land. The émigré couple's vicissitudes with the professional world inhabited by American artists and entrepreneurs are almost too real to be taken as fictive depictions. Głowacki knows too well what it is to be a lonely artist in America. Like Wajda, he shows a more than superficial acquaintance with Dostoevsky's mass of insulted and injured. The copious rain of laughter in his play falls gently on an artist's despair.

These two plays have had over one hundred productions throughout the world. His play, *Fortinbras Gets Drunk* (1988–89), begins and ends with moments from Shakespeare's *Hamlet,* but what remains in between is pure Głowacki. Far more innovative and less dependent on verbal fireworks than Tom Stoppard in his play *Rosencrantz and Guildenstern Are Dead,* Głowacki's *Fortinbras* contains an exciting plot, colorful characters, and a humor reminiscent of Elizabethan ribaldry. *Fortinbras Gets Drunk* is a dark comedy with tragic overtones. The story line is dependent on a superficial knowledge of *Hamlet* and is, therefore, easily accessible to all audiences.

There is a sexual undertone in all of Głowacki's plays. In *Cinders* and *Hunting Cockroaches* Głowacki experiments with role reversal (the Prince in *Cinders* is a woman playing a man both onstage and in prison). In *Hunting Cockroaches* the émigré couple seem to have forgotten how to have sex and have practiced sexual abstinence for over a year. This underlying sexual theme gives his "American" plays an added layer of dramatic tension. In *Fortinbras* Głowacki succeeds in duplicating the Elizabethan penchant for low comedy. Sexual nuance, it would appear, is a staple of his dramaturgy.

His latest play, *Antygona w Nowym Yorku* (Antigone in New York, 1993), had its world premiere at the Ateneum Theater in Warsaw, under the direction of Izabella Cywińska.

BIBLIOGRAPHY

English

Cinders (Kopciuch) (a play in two acts), translated by Christina Paul, New York: Samuel French, 1985.

Give Us This Day (Moc truchleje), translated by Konrad Brodziński, New York: St. Martin's, 1983; London, Andre Deutsch, 1983.

Hunting Cockroaches (Polowanie na karaluchy) (a play), translated by Jadwiga Kosicka, New York: Theater Communications Group, 1986; New York: Samuel French, 1987.

Hunting Cockroaches and Other Plays (Polowanie na karaluchy i inne sztuki), translated by Jadwiga Kosicka and others, Evanston, Illinois: Northwestern University Press, 1990.

GOMBROWICZ, WITOLD (1904–69), novelist, playwright, essay writer, and memoirist, came from an old gentry family. He studied law in Warsaw, then philosophy and economy in Paris. After a brief period of working as a lawyer, he devoted himself totally to literature. In 1934, Gombrowicz began writing literary reviews for papers and magazines (mainly *Kurier Poranny* [Morning Courier]). In August 1939 he left for Argentina; he was there when World War II broke out. He never returned to Poland; he lived in Argentina until 1963, spent a year in West Berlin, and then settled down in France. In 1967 he received the Prix Formentor. After the war the only publisher Gombrowicz had was the émigré press *Instytut Literacki* (Literary Institute in Paris; in Poland—except for brief periods—his works were banned by the censor until the late 1980s).

He began his literary work with partly fantastic stories devoted mainly to strange psychological cases (a collection of these pieces appeared in *Pamiętnik z okresu dojrzewania* [A Diary from a Time of Maturation], 1933; enlarged edition, *Bakakaj,* 1957). He drew critical attention with his grotesque novel *Ferdydurke* (1937), in which he unmasked various cultural and behavioral models and outlined the main themes of his later work. Before the war broke out he published his first play, *Iwona, księżniczka Burgunda* (Yvonne, Princess of Burgund, published in *Skamander,* 1938, definitive edition 1958, produced in 1959), and an unfinished novel, *Opętani* (The Possessed), published in daily papers in 1939. After a prolonged break, while in Argentina, he wrote the play *Ślub* (The Marriage) and the novel *Trans-Atlantyk* (Trans-Atlantic, published jointly in Paris, 1953, and in Poland, 1957, with the author's commentary). *Ślub*, produced in Poland in 1974, is, at the same time, a transcription of a dream and a parody of a Shakespearean tragedy. In his novel *Trans-Atlantic,* he formulated, among other things, his attitude toward Polish cultural traditions. He later wrote two more novels: *Pornografia* (Paris, 1960) and *Kosmos* (Cosmos, Paris, 1965). The plot of *Pornografia* is situated in the transformed setting of Poland during the occupation; he concentrated on what some critics regard as the sexual fascination aroused by youth. In *Kosmos* he delved deeply into erotic psychology, analyzing the relations between chance and the meaning of events. His third and last play is a parodistic, philosophically grotesque libretto, appropriately called *Operetka* (produced in Poland in 1975). He published *Operetka* (Operetta), along with Volume 3 of his *Dziennik* (Diary, Volumes 1–3, Paris, 1957–66), which he had been writing since 1953 and in which he mixed personal, incidental notes with provocative polemics and philosophical considerations, thus painting perhaps the most peculiar self-portrait in Polish literature.

According to Jan Błoński, Gombrowicz's works center around two major themes, adherence to form by adults and immaturity, both of which are gradually enriched with complex meanings. A man, in his view, is never just himself: watched by others he conforms (like the hero of *Ferdydurke*) to the cultural, intellectual, and social forms (conventions) that exist among people. As he demonstrates in *Kosmos,* there is some internal logic in the development of forms, which a man can only guess at, never sure that he is not being deceived by his own mind. The freedom of an individual is revealed first in his ability to destroy the forms, especially through laughter: it leads a man into discovering that the maker of forms is not any transcendental power (e.g., God, nature, historical necessity), but a concrete man, even if his own power frightens him (*Ślub*). Life runs concomitantly with fossilizing forms and shapeless chaos, and progress is stimulated, paradoxically, by immaturity, "inferiority" loaded with energy. The obtrusiveness of immaturity, in which Gombrowicz sees the source of beauty, makes him center his writer's curiosity on ugliness (*Iwona, księżniczka Burgunda*), on schoolboys' pranks (*Ferdydurke*), and on the primitivism of traditional Polish traits (*Trans-Atlantyk*). In time it achieves a more erotic sense, which is most fully expressed in *Pornografia* and *Operetka.* For Gombrowicz art is born out of fascination with the shapeless, but it always leads to complete forms. In order to overcome this contradiction, the writer advises that one has to keep "a distance from form," remaining youthful and skeptical at the same time. Trying to combine insignificance and greatness, comicality and seriousness, a whim and a pattern, he proposes, in *Dziennik,* a model of personality which is dynamic and internally ambivalent: a measure of a man's (an author's) authenticity is the number of metamorphoses he is able to go through, not the stability of his psychological features or his intellectual views, which would be a sign of fossilization. The intellectually daring works of Gombrowicz combine the criticism of contemporary culture with a spiritual attitude that he wants to impose. His views are sometimes close to existentialism, but they differ from it with regard to the tones of skepticism and anarchism and to the form he gives to his message, which is dominated by parody and a masterful, grotesque sense of humor. Since 1960, Gombrowicz's works have enjoyed great success around the world and have been translated into almost every language.

In *Ferdydurke,* the main character, Józio, is a thirty-year-old writer just beginning his career; he is transferred into adolescence by the embodiment of "teacherhood," Professor Pimko. Thus he finds himself in school, where he has to suffer the tortures of adolescence along with the torment of old-fashioned education: he is forced to "adore" the national poets and classical grammar and is witness to absurd, pseudoideological arguments among his colleagues, which are crowned and terminated with a "face-making duel" between Miętus and Syfon and a chaotic fight that follows. Living in a rented room, he gets to know the family of the engineer Młodziak and has to stage a scandal to get away from the charms of "a modern, emancipated schoolgirl," Ziuta. Together with a friend, who is overcome with the desire to "fraternize" with simple folk, he goes to the country, where Miętus's ideas cause the collapse of the ancient hierarchy of the noble house of the Hurleckis and give rise to a kind of fantastic revolution as a result of which Józio has to escape, entangled in a nonsensical love affair and completely paralyzed by the childish daughter of his hosts.

The unusual plot enables Gombrowicz to come up with a brilliant, grotesquely comical criticism of the culture of the period between the wars in two of its embodiments: the educational, traditional and modeled after the ethos of the gentry, and the liberal-progressive. It also reflects the psycho-sociological conviction of the author that people's behavior depends on the opinions held by others (*gęba*) and on forms (conventions) which constantly arise and collapse in human interaction. A man always feels that he is "below" the social norm and that is why he is threatened with falling into immaturity (*upupienie*), from which he derives his anarchical and rebellious energy. Gombrowicz states his point of view in allegorical tales, each preceded by a short preface, which interrupt the flow of the story. The novel was received with great interest, at the same time causing confusion among the critics. Positive and enthusiastic reactions (B. Schulz, A. Sandauer) were accompanied by aggressive attacks of spokesmen of different orientations, from the right (S. Piasecki), to the left (I. Fik). In time, *Ferdydurke* achieved the status of a classic, one of the best novels of the interwar period.

Ferdydurke remains an amazing phenomenon: for, though published only once in Poland (1934), it was known by absolutely every educated person. Gombrowicz's neologisms (*zrobić gębę* [make a face], *pupa* [rump], *upupić* [make an ass of]) entered Polish colloquial language and are still used today.

(See Contemporary Polish Literature.)

BIBLIOGRAPHY

Dzieła zebrane (Collected Works), Volumes 1–10, Paris, 1969–73.

Dzieła (Works), Volumes 1–9, Cracow: Wydawnictwo Literackie, 1986. (The text of *Diary* was severely cut by the censor.)

English

Cosmos (Kosmos), translated from French and German by Eric Mosbacher, London: MacGibbon & Kee, 1967; New York: Grove Press, 1967.

Ferdydurke, translated by Eric Mosbacher, London: MacGibbon & Kee, 1961; New York: Harcourt, Brace & World, 1961; second edition, New York: Grove Press, 1967.

A Kind of Testament, edited by Dominique de Roux, translated by Alastair Hamilton, Philadelphia, Pennsylvania: Temple University Press, 1973; London: Calder & Boyars, 1973; London: M. Boyars Merrimack Book Service, 1981.

The Marriage (Ślub), translated by Louis Iribarne, New York: Grove Press, 1969; London: Calder & Boyars, 1970; Evanston, Illinois: Northwestern University Press, 1986.

Operetta (Operetka), translated by Louis Iribarne, London: Calder & Boyars, 1971.

Pornografia, translated from French by Alastair Hamilton, London: Calder & Boyars, 1966; New York: Grove Press, 1966; 1967; 1968.

Possessed or the Secret of Myslotch (Opętani), translated from French by J.A. Underwood, London: Boyars, 1980, 1982; London: Merrimack Book Service, 1981; London, New York: M. Boyars, 1988.

Princess Ivona (Iwona, księżniczka Burgunda), translated by Krystyna Griffith-Jones and Catherine Robins, London: Calder & Boyars, 1969.

Ivona Princess of Burgundia (Iwona, księżniczka Burgunda), translated by Krystyna Griffith-Jones and Catherine Robins, New York: Grove Press, 1969.

Three Novels: Ferdydurke, Pornografia, and Cosmos, New York: Grove Press, 1978.

Trans-Atlantic, translated by Walter Tiel, Pfullingen: Neske, 1964.

Alex Kurczaba, *Gombrowicz and Frisch: Aspects of the Literary Diary,* Bonn: Bouvier Verlag, 1980.

Cosmos, Pornografia, New York: Grove Press, 1985.

Diary, translated by Lillian Vallee, Evanston, Illinois: Northwestern University Press, 1988.

GOSZCZYŃSKI, SEWERYN (1801–1876), a poet, publicist, and political activist, was the son of an impoverished nobleman. He never received a thorough education. In 1820 he arrived in Warsaw, where he became acquainted with several men of letters and subsequently joined an underground independence organization. He tried to reach Greece and take part in its struggle for independence, but did not get beyond the Ukraine, where he lived from 1821 to 1830, working for underground organizations, studying, and writing a great deal, treating literature as a form of political expression. In 1824–25 he wrote his revolutionary lyrics; in 1826–27, a Romantic novel, *Zamek Kaniowski* (Kaniowski Castle), appeared (which made him a representative of the so-called Ukrainian School, which included A. Malczewski and J. B. Zaleski). In 1828–29 he spent some time in Vienna and Cracow; in 1830 he traveled to Warsaw, where he participated in the preparations for the coming November Uprising. He later took part in the attack on Belvedere. After 1831 he became associated with *Nowa Polska* (New Poland), writing patriotic poems.

After the defeat of the uprising he moved to Galicia, where he continued his underground political activity. Wanted by the Austrian police, he hid in the houses of noblemen in Podkarpacie and Podhale (hence his *Dziennik podróży do Tatrów* [Diary of Travel to the Tatras], published in 1853). He planned another poetic novel, *Kościelisko* (Bone Cemetery), in which the highlanders were to play a role similar to that of Cossacks in *Zamek Kaniowski*—a patriotic impetus to events. However, because of the lack of historical evidence which would make of the Cossacks a symbol of a free people, he never finished the work. He expressed his views on the ethnic problems in literature in *Nowa epoka poezji polskiej* (A New Epoch of Polish Poetry, 1835). During this time he also composed a collection of poems, *Trzy struny* (Three Cords, 1839), which included a cycle of Ukrainian lyrics. Constantly in danger of arrest, Goszczyński emigrated in 1838 to France, where he worked mostly as a publicist, writing political and social articles and pamphlets against rightist émigré circles. Among his literary works of the period is the novel *Król zamczyska* (Castle King, 1842).

In August 1842 Goszczyński joined Towiański's group and became its secretary. Former friendships were broken as a result, and since Słowacki and later Mickiewicz were moving further and further away from Towiański's influence, Goszczyński felt more and more lonely and abandoned, his emotions intensified by his extreme poverty. He stopped literary work for years, and his articles of this period are marked with mysticism, revealing deep changes in the realistic outlook of the former democrat and freedom fighter. He did not always agree with Towiański but remained faithful to his ideals. In 1872 he returned to Poland and settled in Lvov.

Zamek Kaniowski, his poetic novel, was written in 1826–27 and published in *Dziennik Warszawski* 1827–28 (definitive edition, Warsaw, 1828). The theme is taken from Ukrainian folk stories about the Uprising of 1768. Goszczyński made use of various folk materials, the relationship between the real and the supernatural, and between people and nature. The creation of the main character was influenced by European Romantic literature (Byron); the theme of revolution reflects Goszczyński's own experiences as a conspirator and political activist. The plot of the novel centers around the character of Nebaba, a Cossack who joins the rebellious unit of the ataman Szwaczka, seeking revenge on the lord of the castle of Kaniów, who has deceitfully taken away his beloved Orlika. After his famous speech, in which he accuses the lords and urges his soldiers to fight, he is able to convince part of the unit to ally with him. The castle is set on fire and Orlika dies, having first killed her husband. Later, after his defeat in the battle with the Polish army, Nebaba dies impaled on the ruins of Kaniów. Nebaba has the features of a Cossack ataman, but also typical traits of a Byronic hero—a rebellious individual, whose conscience is tormented with a crime he has committed (seduction and attempted murder of the insane Ksenia). According to Maria Grabowska, in the novel events are motivated in two ways: the social background of the revolution intertwines with the fatalistic view of human fate, according to which man is condemned to evil, which is an active force that always threatens the world. Here it is revealed both in the actions of individuals and in the collective act of rebellion and punishment. The infernal vision of the world is emphasized by "the aesthetics of horror": blood, fire, violence, murder, raging people, elements, and infernal forces.

The novel, as Mickiewicz said, "as if it had set fire to the ancient building" of Slavic poetry, was received with indignation and disgust among traditionalists and advocates of the idyllic model of national literature; on the other hand, it was highly evaluated by the Romantic critics (especially M. Mochnacki). Along with Malczewski's *Maria* and Mickiewicz's *Konrad Wallenrod,* it is one of the outstanding Polish poetic novels; it is also an important achievement in Goszczyński's career and one of the first Polish works on revolution.

(See Romanticism.)

BIBLIOGRAPHY

Dzieła zbiorowe (Collected Works), Volumes 1–4, edited by Z. Wasilewski, Lvov, 1904.

GRANICA (Border) (see Nałkowska).

GROCHOWIAK, STANISŁAW (1934–76), poet, prose writer, playwright, and publicist, was born in a provincial town in the area of Great Poland. He, together with his parents, was displaced by the Germans; the period of the Nazi occupation and the Warsaw Uprising of 1944 he spent in Warsaw. In 1951 he began studying Polish philology in Poznań (he never completed his degree). In the same year he made his poetic debut in the local newspaper. After 1955 he lived in Warsaw, working in the PAX publishing house (1955–56), then on numerous magazines: *Za i przeciw* (For and Against, 1957–58), *Współczesność* (Contemporary, 1958–60; editor-in-chief, 1959–60), *Nowa Kultura* (New Culture, 1961–63), *Kultura* (Culture, 1963–70), *Poezja* (Poetry, 1972–75), and *Miesięcznik Literacki* (Literary Monthly, 1975–76). He was the recipient of numerous literary awards.

He published his first books, the novel *Plebania z magnoliami* (The Rectory with Magnolias) and the collection of poems *Ballada rycerska* (The Knight's Ballad), in 1956. The latter immediately attracted the attention of the critics. Under the influence of Tuwim, Liebert, and Gałczyński, Grochowiak at the same time demonstrated his individuality with his ostentatious antiaestheticism, his penchant for the brutal grotesque, his parodistic and ironic violations of poetic convention, and, finally, his references to old literature, especially Baroque. This style became more mature in the collections *Menuet z pogrzebaczem* (Minuet with a Poker, 1958),

Rozbieranie do snu (Undressing for Sleep, 1959), and *Agresty* (Gooseberries, 1963), in which he expressed his fascination with the phenomena generally considered "unpoetic," with what is crippled, poor, and ugly—both with objects that surround man in everyday life and with the landscape or states like senility, death, biological decay, and emotional disappointment. Hence the term "turpism" (from Latin *turpis*—ugly) used by Julian Przyboś in his *Oda do turpistów* (Ode to Turpists) in *Przegląd Kulturalny* (Culture Review, 1962) to describe this aesthetic stand often manifested in the young poetry of the time, especially in Grochowiak's works. According to Janusz Maciejewski, Grochowiak himself preferred to call his approach *miserabilism* (from Latin *miser*—poor, unhappy, tormented), putting emphasis on its ethical source, since he regarded his point of disagreement with the existing reality, with the existing hierarchy of values, with the unfairness of the very evaluation in terms of "beautiful" and "ugly," where beauty is not deserved and ugliness is not a fault. Grochowiak's later poetry was marked with various stylistic allusions to Leśmian, Norwid, Baudelaire, Villon; to the poetics of the Baroque; and to painting (the old Dutch school and surrealism). In the collections *Kanon* (1965), *Nie było lata* (There Was Not a Summer, 1969), *Polowanie na cietrzewie* (Hunting for Grouse, 1972), *Bilard* (Billiard, 1975), and *Haiku-images* (1978) his rebellious stand was toned down; he demonstrated a stronger tendency to stylization, while "turpism" and his penchant for rough aesthetic means became milder, because of Classical inspirations (e.g., *Rok polski* [Polish Year]). At the same time the social themes in his works received more emphasis, especially those associated with the recent experiences of the nation—the last war, the events of 1968 and 1970 (*Totentanz in Polen,* 1969, and the poems *Mamy tych braci* [We Have These Brothers], *Nie było lata* [There Was Not A Summer]).

Grochowiak's dramatic works, presented in the theater, on radio, and on television, are formally close to the form of gloomy grotesque or poetic parable: *Szachy* (Chess, produced in 1961), *Partita na instrument drewniany* (Partita for a Wooden Instrument, produced in 1962, and made into a film in 1976), *Król IV* (King IV, produced in 1964), and *Chłopcy* (Boys, a successful television production, 1966). His other plays, including *Okapi* (1974), *Dulle griet* (1976), *Po tamtej stronie świec* (On the Other Side of Candles), and *Lęki poranne* (Morning Fears), were collected in the volumes *Rzeczy na głosy* (Things for Voices, 1966), *Rzeczy na wersety i głosy* (Things for Verses and Voices, 1973), and *Dialogi* (Dialogues, 1976). In these works, as in his prose writings (the short stories *Lamentnice* [Lamentations], 1958; the novels *Trismus,* 1963, and *Karabiny* [Rifles], 1965), the exactitude of realistic detail, portraying the brutal and disgusting aspects of life, is linked with problems concerning dignity and moral decay, death and passing, moral and ideological choice in extreme situations. As a journalist Grochowiak spoke about the social and cultural problems of his generation, which was called, after the name of the journal he was the editor of, "the generation of *Współczesność*" (Contemporaneity).

(See Contemporary Polish Literature.)

BIBLIOGRAPHY

Wybór wierszy (Selected Poems), Warsaw, 1965.
Poezje wybrane (Selected Poetry), Warsaw, 1968.
Wiersze wybrane (Selected Poems), Warsaw, 1978.

English

"Dulles Griet," in *Pieces of Poland: Four Polish Dramatists,* translated by E. J. Czerwiński and Janusz Wilk, *Slavic and East European Arts,* Volume 1, Number 2, 57–110, 1983.

GRUBE RYBY (Fat Fish) (See Bałucki).

GRYNBERG, HENRYK (born 1936), a novelist, short story writer, and poet, comes from a Jewish family, who before World War II lived in the village region of Northern Mazowsze. During the German occupation he and his family hid from the Germans until their deportation to the death camp in Treblinka. After the war he studied journalism at the University of Warsaw, but upon completing his studies in 1959, he began work as an actor in the Jewish Theater. At the same time, he started his literary career, making his debut in 1959 with the short story *Ekipa Antygony* (Antigone's Crew), published in the journal dedicated to young talent *Współczesność* (The Contemporary). During the tour of the Jewish Theater in the United States in 1967, he asked for political asylum and became an émigré. In 1971 he completed his degree in Slavic Literature at the University of California in Los Angeles. He next worked on the editorial board of the magazine *Ameryka* (America), designed for the Polish audience; from 1973 he became associated with the Polish Section of the Voice of America. He continued his literary work, contributing to various Polish émigré journals published in Paris (*Kultura* [Culture]) and in London (*Wiadomości* [News] and *Puls* [Pulse]), as well as to other publications. Beginning in the eighties, his books, after having been banned for a long time, began to be published in Poland.

Grynberg belongs to the last generation of writers who gave witness to the martyrdom of the Jewish people during World War II, on the basis of his personal experiences. He is also a penetrating observer of the continuing tragic fates of the freed heroes, already uprooted from the traditions of their forefathers, attempting at the same time to assimilate within a different environment, as well as to renew their Jewishness in the postwar world. In his collection of short stories, *Ekipa Antygona* (Antigone's Crew, 1963), as well as in his novel *Żydowska wojna* (The Jewish War, 1965), the theme of the Holocaust pervades, witnessed through the eyes of the child-hero. His later novels, constituting a cycle of a decidedly autobiographical character (*Zwycięstwo* [Victory], 1969, *Życie ideologiczne* [An Ideological Life], 1979, *Życie osobiste* [A Personal Life], *Życie codzienne i artystyczne* [An Everyday and Artistic Life], 1980, and *Kadisz* [Prayer], 1987), deal with the history of the Polish Jews who survived the horrors of the war and who, after the war, became entangled in the Polish-Jewish conflicts. They came in contact with expressions of anti-Semitism and the allurements of Communism or tried to begin life anew as émigrés in the United States or Israel. The Jewish motives are also intertwined with Grynberg's personal and lyrical reflections in his published collections: *Swięto kamieni* (Holiday of Stones, 1964), *Antynostalgia* (Anti-Nostalgia, 1971), *Wiersze z Ameryki* (Poems from America, 1980), *Po zmartwychwstaniu* (After Resurrection, 1982), *Wśród nieobecnych* (Among the Absent, 1983), *Pomnik na Potomakiem* (A Memorial on the Potomac, 1989), as well as in the country's elections, *Wróciłem* (I Returned, 1991). In the essays collected in the volume *Prawda nieartystyczna* (Inartistic Truth, 1984, published in Poland in 1990), Grynberg took up, among other themes, the problem of the causes and the psychological-moral consequences of the Holocaust, as well as the similarities and differences between Christianity and Judaism.

H

HARASYMOWICZ, JERZY (or Harasymowicz-Broniuszyc) (born 1933), a poet, spent his youth in the foothills of Southern Poland (Beskid Sadecki). He later moved to Cracow. A poet of a rich, artistic imagination and an expressive talent, Harasymowicz gained instant attention with his first collection of poems, *Cuda* (Miracles, 1956), and in the volumes that followed, *Wieża melancholii* (Tower of Melancholy, 1958) and *Przejęcie kopii* (Emotion of Duplicates, 1958). In his poetry Harasymowicz transformed the motives of the foothill beauty of the Beskid Mountains as well as the folklore and traditions of the people who lived on this land during the war. (The Lemkows differ from the inhabitants of other Polish territories; among other differences their religion is closer to Christian Orthodoxy than to Catholicism.) Harasymowicz often sought inspiration in the rich landmarks of culture and art in Cracow, as well as in primitive folk art (his collections *Pastoralki polskie* [Polish Pastorals], 1966, and *Madonny polskie* [Polish Madonnas], 1969). The traditions of the Baroque especially interested him, as well as the richness of Old Poland (the volumes *Barokowe czasy* [Baroque Times], 1975, *Banderia Prutenorum, 1976, Polowanie z sokolem* [Hunting with an Eagle], 1977, *Klękajcie narody* [Kneel Down, Nations], 1984, *Kozackie bunczanki* [Cossack Standard-Bearers], 1991, and *Lichtarz ruski* [Russian Candlestick], 1987). Harasymowicz's poetry has been widely translated in the United States.

BIBLIOGRAPHY

English

Shifting Borders: East European Poetries of the Eighties, edited by Walter Cummins, Rutherford, New Jersey: Fairleigh Dickinson University Press, 1993.

*Spoiling Cannibals' Fun: Polish Poetry of the Last Two Decades of Communist

Rule, edited by Stanisław Barańczak and Clare Cavanagh, foreword by Helen Vandler, Evanston, Illinois: Northwestern University Press, 1991.

HERBERT, ZBIGNIEW (born 1924), poet, playwright, and essay writer, in 1943 began studying Polish philology in the underground university. He was a soldier of the Home Army. He spent his early years in Lvov, first in independent Poland, and later, in turn, under Soviet, Nazi, and once again Soviet occupation. In 1944 he left Lvov and settled in central Poland. After the war he completed his studies in law and economics and attended lectures on art and philosophy. He lived a very simple life, maintaining himself with second-rate office work. *Struna światła* (A String of Light) was a selection of his poems from a period of fifteen years. As a poet he made his debut in the press in 1950; however, his decided opposition to the official doctrine of Socialist Realism and his aversion to the Communist Party's controlling the literary life of the country caused his first volume of poetry to be published only in 1956. Herbert vented his attitude toward Communism and his motives for refusing participation in the Sovietization of cultural life during the Stalinist epoch—polemicizing to a certain extent with Czesław Miłosz's analysis in *The Captive Mind*—in his extensive conversation with Jacek Trznadel in his well-known book *Hańba domowa* (Home Shame), published in 1986 in the underground press. He later published several other collections: *Hermes, pies i gwiazda* (Hermes, a Dog and a Star, 1957), *Studium przedmiotu* (A Study of an Object, 1961), *Napis* (Inscription, 1969), and *Pan Cogito* (Mr. Cogito, 1974). In 1965–68 he was a member of the editorial board of *Poezja* (Poetry). In 1983 the underground publication *Oficyna Literacka* (Literary Publishing House) published his volume *18 wierszy* (18 Poems) in Cracow; an expanded version was published at the same time in Paris, under the title *Raport z oblężonego miasta* (Report from the Besieged City, 1983). The famous title poem, an apology for uncompromising heroism, became known as the most accurate statement of Polish determination in the battle with the regime that called for Martial Law and the Communist threat. His latest volume of poetry, *Elegia na odejście* (Elegy on Leaving, 1990), was also published in Paris. He has traveled to a number of countries, giving lectures on Polish and European literature; from 1987 he has lived in Paris. He is the recipient of two prestigious awards from Austria: the N. Lenau award (1965) and the G. Herder award (1973).

According to Jerzy Kwiatkowski, Herbert's works are strongly associated with the renaissance of Polish poetry that occurred in the midfifties. Sensitive to the moral questions of the time which were raised in regard to the political and cultural changes of the contemporary world, he was able to endow his poetry with a universal perspective, employing the poetics of great metaphor or parables grounded in myths, works of art, elements of nature, and the symbolic status of some personages in history and literature. His works combine respect for the European cultural tradition with a modern means of expression, philosophical contemplation with the simplicity of poetic language, the significance of ethical and existential questions with a sense of irony and humor. The most outstanding achievement is the collection *Pan Cogito,* whose hero, who experiences the basic problems posed by Herbert, is depicted in a discreetly humorous manner, with a slightly diminished perspective which eliminates pathos and, paradoxically, emphasizes the heroic moral sense of the poems. The intellectual character of Herbert's poetry, its cultural roots and links with tradition, and its specific tragic tone and sense of proportion have led some critics to assign these works to the new, twentieth century Classicism (Neoclassicism). As the author of stage and radio plays Herbert preferred short pieces quite varied in their themes: from philosophical allegory (*Jaskinia filozofów* [The Philosopher's Den], *Rekonstruckcja poety* [The Poet's Reconstruction]) to realistic, almost mundane sketches (*Lalek, Drugi pokój* [Second Room]); his plays were collected in the volume *Dramaty* (Dramas, 1970). As an essay writer (see his collection *Barbarzyńca w ogrodzie* [The Barbarian in the Garden], 1962) Herbert specializes in problems of history, art and culture, usually treated in the form of a travel diary (France, Italy, Greece). These essays, like his other works, are permeated with the spirit of humanism and philosophically grounded muted humanitarianism. Herbert is one of Poland's contemporary poets best known abroad. His works have been widely translated. A periodical published at the Pacific University in Oregon is entitled *Mr. Cogito,* after his collection of poems.

(See Contemporary Polish Literature.)

BIBLIOGRAPHY

Wiersze zebrane (Collected Poems), Warsaw, 1971.
Wybór poezji (Selected Poetry), Warsaw, 1973.
Wybór wierszy (Selected Poems), Warsaw, 1983.

English

Selected Poems, translated by Czesław Miłosz and Peter Dale Scott, London: Penguin Books, Penguin Modern European Poets, 1968; translated by John and Bogdana Carpenter; Oxford, New York: Oxford University Press, 1977; translated by Miłosz and Scott, Manchester, England: Carcanet, 1985; New York: Ecco Press, 1986.

Barbarian in the Garden (Barbarzyńca w ogrodzie), translated by Michael March and Jarosław Anders, Manchester, England: Carcanet, 1985; San Diego: Harcourt Brace Javanovich, 1985; 1986.

Report From a Besieged City and Other Poems (Raport z oblężonego miasta i inne wiersze), translated by John Carpenter and Bogdana Carpenter, New York: Ecco Press, 1985; Oxford, New York: Oxford University Press, 1987.

"The Philosopher's Den" (Jaskinia filozofów), translated by Paul Mayewski, *Twór-*

czość, Number 9, 1956; also in *The Broken Mirror, a Collection of Writings from Contemporary Poland,* New York: Random House, 1958.
The Mature Laurel: Essays on Modern Polish Poetry, edited by Adam Czerniawski, Chester Springs, Pennsylvania: Dufour Editions, 1991.

HERLING-GRUDZIŃSKI, GUSTAW (born 1919), distinguished prose writer and literary critic, during his studies at the University of Warsaw (1937–39) was involved with several literary journals (among others, literary editor of *Orka na Ugorze* [Ploughing the Fallow Field]). Participant in the war in 1939, during the Nazi occupation he first lived in Warsaw (cofounder of the underground organization *PLAN,* and of the newspaper *Biuletyn Polski* [Polish Bulletin], 1939–40). Later he found himself in Lvov, soon occupied by the Red Army, where he was imprisoned and forced into various labor camps in the northern Soviet Union, near Archangelsk; freed after the signing of the treaty between the Polish government and the Soviet powers, in 1942 he managed to join the Polish army. He took part in the Middle East campaigns and later fought in the battle of Monte Cassino. After the war he took part in the émigré literary life in Italy, France, and England. In 1945–47 he was literary editor of the weekly *Orzeł Biały* (White Eagle); in 1947 he was a constant contributor to the Paris monthly *Kultura* (Culture); during his stay in London, 1948–52, he worked for the émigré weekly *Wiadomości.* In 1955 he settled in Naples and continued working for *Kultura.* Written from 1971 and published systematically in *Kultura* (Culture), the *Diary* was successively published in book form (Volumes 1–4, Paris, 1973–89; Volumes 1–3, Warsaw, 1990). Herling-Grudziński's stories, consciously continuing the traditions of this type of prose, ingeniously constructed, are dedicated to a philosophic-moral problem—the mysterious suffering and tragic nature of the existence of man, who himself in his conscience stands in relation to the problem of guilt and punishment. His first major publication was the collection of essays *Żywi i umarli* (The Living and the Dead, Rome, 1945), devoted, among others, to Joseph Conrad, Cyprian Kamil Norwid, Wacław Berent, and Karol Irzykowski, in whose works he found models of moral heroism and nonconformism. These issues also dominate his later stories and sketches, which were published in the collections *Skrzydła ołtarza* (The Wings of the Altar, Paris, 1960), containing the stories *Wieża* (The Tower) and *Pieta dell' Isola* and *Drugie przyjście* (The Second Coming, Paris, 1963). In Poland his works have been banned by the censor for decades; only after the establishment of *Drugi obieg** (The Alternate Press) in the 1970s were they available to the public at large. Since 1989 all of his most important works have been published in the official press, and in 1991, after almost a half-century, the writer was able to visit his homeland for the first time. At that time he received a doctorate *honoris causa* from Poznań University. His reflective *Dziennik pisany nocą* (A Journal Written by Night, Volume 1, Paris, 1973) is a documentation of his philosophic considerations, polemics, and comments on books he had read, on political events, on the situation of an emigrant, and on his obligations to European and national culture. A special position in Herling-Grudziński's output is occupied by *Inny świat* (A World Apart, English edition, London, 1951, with an introduction by Bertrand Russell; Polish edition, London, 1953, Paris 1965), a documentary report of his experiences and observations from the prisons and forced labor camps of Stalinist Russia, which at the same time offers a penetrating study of psychological and sociological mechanisms leading to the degradation of man and of the breaking of relations among people. *A World Apart,* published in numerous editions and translated into over twenty languages, stands together with the works of Solzhenitsyn as the chief literary documents that present the truth about the Soviet camps—*The Gulag Archipelago.* He was also editor of an anthology, *W oczach pisarzy: Wybór opowieści wojennych 1939–1945* (In the Eyes of Writers: A Selection of War Stories, 1939–1945, Rome, 1947). He devoted much attention to foreign literature, especially Russian: Fyodor Dostoyevsky, Boris Pasternak, Anna Akhmatova, Osip Mandelshtam, Aleksander Solzhenitsyn and others, in whose works he recognized "another Russia" which neither the Bolshevik Revolution nor Stalin's crimes could destroy; these figures are present in the sketches from the collection *Upiory rewolucji* (Ghosts of the Revolution) published in Paris in 1969, partially published in Poland in the volume *Godzina cieni* (An Hour of Shadow, 1991).

BIBLIOGRAPHY

English

The Island, Three Tales, translated by Ronald Strom, Cleveland and New York: World Publishing, 1967.

A World Apart (Inny świat), translated by Joseph Marek, New York: Roy Publishers, 1951; London: Heinemann, 1951; 1986; New York: New American Library, 1952; Wesport, Connecticut: Greenwood Press, 1974; New York: Arbor House, 1951; 1986; Oxford, New York: Oxford University Press, 1951; 1987.

HERTZ, PAWEŁ (1918–1993), poet, prose and essay writer, translator, and literary editor, began his work as a poet under the auspices of the Skamander group (debut 1934 in *Wiadomości Literackie*). During the years 1935–39 he traveled to France, Austria, and Italy. He spent most of the war in the Soviet Union, in 1941–43 working in the Polish embassy. In 1945–48 he was a member of the editorial board of the Marxist weekly *Kuźnica* in Łódź. After 1949 he resided in Warsaw, working for the PIW publishing house. From 1974 to 1975 he wrote for the Catholic *Tygodnik Powszechny* (Universal Weekly). In his poetic output, which belongs to modern Neoclassicism, he went from a mood of loneliness and contemplation, punctuated by an aesthetic stance (see his collections *Nocna muzyka* [Night Music], 1935, and *Szarfa ciemności* [The Sash of Darkness], 1937), to penetrating cultural and historical reflection, in which he expressed his respect for the humanistic tradition in Poland and elsewhere and the belief in its universal epistemic and moral values, along with a critical evaluation of contemporary culture, which he accused of excessive formal experimentation, useless exclusivity, and snobbism. He published several collections of poems (*Dwie podróże* [Two Journeys], 1946, *Małe ody i treny* [Little Odes and Threnodies], 1949, *Nowy lirnik mazowiecki* [A New Mazovian Poet], 1953, *Pieśni z rynku* [Songs from the Market], 1957) and a selection of his works, *Śpiewnik podróżny i domowy, 1935–67* (A Travel and Domestic Songbook, 1935–67, 1969). In addition to Classical poetic forms, Hertz employed folk stylizations, particularly in his references to Teofil Lenartowicz. In the cycle of short stories *Sedan* (1948), he presented a metaphorical image of the decay and destruction of the world of the interwar city intelligentsia that resulted from the aggressive rise of fascism.

Hertz's traditionalist literary program was presented in his collections of sketches *Domena polska* (The Polish Domain, 1961) and *Ład i nieład* (Order and Disorder, 1964) and in *Świat i dom* (World and Home, 1977). His interest in the history of literature was reflected in his biographical story *Portret Słowackiego* (A Portrait of Słowacki, 1949) and in his study composed of documents and letters, *Słowacki: Romans Życia* (Słowacki: The Romance of Life, 1961), and his various editions of Słowacki's works with extensive commentaries. His literary acumen is best demonstrated in his studies of the poems of K. Brodziński, T. Lenartowicz,* Or-Ot, W. Gomulicki, and K. Iłłakowiczówna.* His main achievements as an editor are best seen in *Zbiór poetów polskich XIX wieku* (A Collection of Nineteenth Century Polish Poets, Volumes 1–7, 1959–75), the most comprehensive anthology of this type, in which Hertz gathered the works of little known poets from 1795 to 1918, and (together with W. Kopaliński) *Księga cytatów z polskiej literatury pięknej od XIV do XX wieku* (Book of Quotations from Polish Literature from the Fourteenth to the Twentieth Centuries, 1975). He was also creator and editor of the series *Podróże* (Travels), containing the best literary descriptions of journeys made by foreign and Polish writers. He translated the Russian classics (Tolstoy, Turgenev, Dostoevsky), French literature (Proust), and essays by Thomas Mann. He received an award of the Polish PEN Club for his translations (1970) and editorial work (1978).

HISTORIA POLSKI (The History of Poland) (see Długosz).

HŁASKO, MAREK (1934–69), a short story writer and an exceptional prose stylist, was the enfant terrible of his generation. He worked as a truck driver from 1951 to 1953; from 1955 to 1957 he was prose editor of the influential weekly *Po prostu* (Simply). He began writing in 1951, and his first works were stamped with the official literary doctrine, Socialist Realism. A greater surprise for critics and readers was his collection of stories *Pierwszy krok w chmurach* (First Step in the Clouds, 1956; second edition, 1957), considered an expression of disillusionment with hypocritical reality (particularly shocking are the brutality and authenticity of language in *Ósmy dzień tygodnia* [The Eighth Day of the Week]). The collection brought the writer immediate popularity, confirmed shortly thereafter by the award of the Polish Association of Book Editors. The decisive moment in Hłasko's biography occurred with his trip to Paris at the beginning of 1958. The interviews in the foreign press, which made him out to be a "Communist James Dean," and his contacts with the émigré monthly *Kultura* and the publishing house *Instytut Literacki* (Literary Institute)—in which his works, prohibited in Poland, appeared—cut off Hłasko's return to Poland, where the official press launched an aggressive attack on him, and the censor condemned his works to oblivion for a number of years. Deprived of his Polish passport, Hłasko resided at the beginning in Switzerland, Italy, and West Berlin; from 1959 to 1961 in Israel; next in Europe once again; and in the United States from 1966 to 1969, where he planned to work in films with Roman Polański. During these years he combined literary work with temporary jobs, mostly those that required unskilled physical labor. During his stay in California, he received his pilot's license. He died in Germany from what in all probability was an accidental overdose of sleeping pills, although until this day the possibility of suicide is not ruled out. Hłasko's work resulted from his revolt against the naively optimistic literature of the 1950s and was aimed at the brutally disillusioned image of reality. One of the characteristic motives of his work is first love, destined for disaster in its contact with the brutality of life. His young people, mostly from the social fringes, oppose grim reality with a desperate longing for a better, although unimaginable life. In time, as a result of his émigré experiences of frustration and alienation, his attitude developed into violent protest against the whole world, with the added Romantic traits of heroism and individualism. Sensitive to the tragedy of human existence, he sought models of literary expression in Dostoevsky and in contemporary American writers (especially Faulkner), whose influence was also apparent in the matter-of-fact style of his prose. His collections of stories include *Cmentarze* (Cemeteries), *Następny do raju* (The Next to Paradise, Paris, 1958), *Opowiadania* (Stories, 1963), and *Wszyscy byli odwróceni: Brudne czyny* (Everyone Was Turned Away: Dirty Deeds, 1964), based on his experiences in Israel. His novel *Sowa, córka piekarza* (Owl, the Baker's Daughter, published in 1967) conveys (as do the stories in *Cemeteries*) an atmosphere of fear and hypocrisy, into which Polish society was plunged during the times of the greatest intensification of Stalinist terror; his memoirs, *Piękni dwudziestoletni* (Beautiful Twenty Year Olds), a kind of "life's confession" suggesting a record of his personal fate and the history of his generation, appeared in 1966. Three films have been based on his stories: *Òsmy dzień tygodnia* (The Eighth Day of the Week), *Pętla* (The Loop), and *Baza ludzi umarłych* (Base of Dead People).

(See Contemporary Polish Literature.)

BIBLIOGRAPHY

Utwory wybrane (Selected Works), Warsaw: Czytelnik, 1985.

English

The Eighth Day of the Week (Òsmy dzień tygodnia), translated by Norbert Guterman, New York: Dutton, 1958; London: Allen & Unwin, 1959; Westport, Connecticut: Greenwood Press, 1975; New York: New American Library, 1959.

The Graveyard (*Cmentarze*), translated by Norbert Gutterman, New York: Dutton, 1959; Westport, Connecticut: Greenwood Press, 1975.

Next Stop—Paradise (*Następny do Raju*), translated by Norbert Gutterman, New York: Dutton, 1960.

Next Stop—Paradise and The Graveyard: Two Novels, translated by Norbert Gutterman, London: Heinemann, 1959, 1961.

HOŁUJ, TADEUSZ (born 1916), a prose writer, playwright, poet, and publicist, was active in the democratic movement of the young during the interwar period; he was coeditor of *Nasz Wyraz* (Our Expression). He took active part in the war in 1939 and later became involved with the underground. Arrested in 1942 and sent to Auschwitz, he spent the rest of the war in concentration camps. After 1945, he became a political and social activist; he was secretary of the International Auschwitz Committee until 1965. He became a member of Parliament in 1972. The recipient of numerous literary awards, he was the initiator and cofounder (1975) of the Cracow group called *Kuźnica:* Marxist intelligentsia and Party reformers were allied with the group, a pre-Solidarity experiment.

He began his literary work with collections of poetry: *Dziewczyno, płyniemy naprzód* (Girl, We Swim Forward, 1936), *Płonące ścieżki* (Burning Paths, 1938), and a volume published underground, *Marsz triumfalny* (Triumphant March, 1942). In his later works two trends are dominant: a historical approach and a personal one based on his camp experiences. In the former group we find novels based on historical sources which reconstruct the genealogy of the Polish revolutionary and Socialist movement: the process of ideological maturation of peasant participants of the November Uprising (*Próba ognia* [Trial by Fire], 1946), the rise of democratic national awareness and of utopian Socialist ideas during the period between the two uprisings (the cycle *Królestwo bez ziemi* [Kingdom Without Land],

Volumes 1–4, 1954–56; second edition, revised, Volumes 1–2, 1960), and the formative years of the organized workers' movement and its internal ideological and moral problems (a novel about Waryński, *Róża i płonący las* [The Rose and the Burning Forest], Volumes 1–2, 1971). The novel *Osoba* (The Person, 1974) is also closely related to his historical approach: a documentarylike portrait of an activist of the revolutionary leftist movement (resembling I. Fik) during the period preceding the rise of Polska Partia Robotnicza (PPR) is presented. The theme of Nazi concentration camps often appears in Hołuj's works, depicted as a traumatic spiritual experience with lasting psychological and moral consequences. According to Włodzimierz Maciąg, the themes range from humiliation and deprivation of the victims to active resistance and superhuman attempts to come to terms with a normal life. These problems are best expressed in the novel *Koniec naszego świata* (The End of Our World, 1958; film version, 1964); in the nonfiction piece *Oświęcim* (Auschwitz, 1946, with F. Friedman); in the dramas, *Dom pod Oświęcimiem* (The House near Auschwitz), published and produced in 1948 (a television production in 1962), and *Puste pole* (Empty Fields), produced in 1965 by Józef Szajna; in stories from three collections—*Jutrzeńka* (Dawn, 1956), *Marzenia* (Dreams, 1956), and *To* (This, 1964); in his poetry (*Wiersze z obozu* [Poems from Camp], 1946; *Źródło* [The Source], 1969); and in his novels—*Jeden stamtąd* (One from over There, 1962), *Drzewo rodzi owoc* (The Tree Begets Fruit, 1963), and *Raj* (Paradise, 1972), in which camp memories are intertwined with contemporary social and political problems.

BIBLIOGRAPHY

Opowiadania wybrane (Selected Stories), Warsaw, 1966.

HOMO SAPIENS (see Przybyszewski).

HOZJUSZ, STANISŁAW (Hosius) (1504–1579), a humanist and Catholic theologian, bishop of Warmia, and later cardinal, was born in Cracow and was buried in Rome. Hozjusz has the distinction of writing the first world best-seller by a Pole. Although written in Latin, his polemical tract, *Confessio fidei catholicas christionae* (Part I was published in Cracow in 1553; the entire work appeared in 1558), was soon translated into French and German. His next important work brought him renown: *De expresso Dei verbo . . . libellus* (1558) was translated into Polish in 1562 as *Księgi o jasnym a szczytnym Słowie Bożym* (Books of God's Serene and Sublime Words). It was translated into German, French, and Czech and into English by T. Stapleton. Hozjusz, according to Janusz Tazbir, was a contentious theologian who fought with his superiors and was summarily sent to Rome by the king in 1569. He was never to return to Poland and died on the outskirts of Rome. He left an enormous amount of correspondence.

Originally a follower of Erasmus of Rotterdam, Cardinal Hozjusz (Hosius) was a staunch supporter and leader of the Counter-Reformation in Poland. He was one of the most influential leaders of the Council of Trent, attempting to impose various edicts upon the king, including a strict adherence to Roman Catholicism for all candidates holding public office. He was beatified by Pope John Paul II in 1991.

BIBLIOGRAPHY

English

Of the Expresse Worde of God, translated by Thomas Stapleton, Lowanium, 1567; translated from Latin by R. Griffith, Menston, England: Scholar Press, 1971.

I

IŁŁAKOWICZÓWNA, KAZIMIERA (1889–1983), a poet and translator, was educated at the home of a distant relative, then at Oxford. She also studied Polish and English philology at the Jagiellonian University. She made her literary debut in 1905 in *Tygodnik Ilustrowany* (Illustrated Weekly), with the poem *Jabłonie* (Apple Trees). In 1911 she published her first collection of poems, *Ikarowe loty* (The Flights of Icarus). In 1915–17 she was a nurse in the Russian army; she returned to Warsaw in 1918 and worked for the Foreign Office and the Ministry of Military Affairs. For a time she was a secretary to Józef Piłsudski, who is depicted in her memoirs, *Ścieżka obok drogi* (The Path beside the Road, 1938), and in her collection of poems, *Wiersze o Marszałku Piłsudskim* 1912–35 (Poems About Marshal Piłsudski, 1912–35, 1936). In 1939 she was evacuated to Romania and spent the war years in Transylvania. In 1947 she returned to Poland and settled in Poznań. Her numerous publications include the collections *Kolędy polskiej biedy* (The Carols of Polish Poverty, 1917), *Trzy struny* (Three Strings, 1917), *Śmierć Feniksa* (The Death of Phoenix, 1922); the cycle of humorous poetic "portraits" *Obrazy imion wróżebne* (Pictures of Names of Fortunes Told, 1926), *Połów* (Fishing, 1926), *Płaczący ptak* (The Crying Bird, 1927), *Zwierciadło nocy* (The Mirror of Night, 1928), *Popiół i perły* (Ashes and Pearls, 1930), *Ballady bohaterskie* (Heroic Ballads, 1934), and *Słowik litewski* (Lithuanian Nightingale, 1936); in her postwar collections, *Poezje 1940–1954* (Poetry, 1940–1954, 1954), *Lekkomyślne serce* (Lighthearted Heart, 1959), *Szeptem* (With a Whisper, 1966); and in selections from her works—*Wiersze wybrane 1912–1947* (Selected Poems, 1912–1947, 1949), *Wybór wierszy* (A Selection of Poems, 1956), *Poezje wybrane* (Selected Poetry, 1968), *Liście i posągi* (Leaves and Sculptures, 1968), *Odejście w tło* (Exit into the Background, 1976), and *Sługi nieu żyteczne* (Useless Servants, 1977). She was the recipient of numerous literary awards, among others, the PEN Club award for her work as a translator and the State Award in 1935 and 1976; she received an honorary doctorate from the Adam Mickiewicz University in Poznań.

Iłłakowiczówna's lyrics are varied in genre—personal, reflexive, influenced by the landscape and contemporary events. According to Ryszard Matuszewski, her output occupies a special position in Polish poetry. It freely combines elements of traditional poetry, especially the Romantic and modernist (ballad or tale style, use of folk fantasy, etc.) with formal novelties antagonistic to traditional structure, best exemplified in her use of prosaicism, lyrical anecdote, ironical and humorous elements, and straightforward psychological and social observations. Closely connected in this respect to the poets of the Skamander group, she differs from them in her stronger and more traditional poetic feeling, and in her use of religious motives taken from the Bible, the Gospels, and carols. Her personal beliefs are further expressed in her selections of poems *Wiersze religijne 1912–1954* (Religious Poems, 1912–1954, 1955) and *Ta jedna nić: Wiersze religijne* (This One Thread: Religious Poems, 1967). Iłakowiczówna's poetry is also characterized by her wide use of a variety of original forms of verse (consider the characteristic sentence-intonation verse) and a specific form of stylization, somewhat primitive and naive, which refers to medieval and folk beliefs. She also wrote stories and poems for children: *Rymy dziecięce* (Children's Rhymes, 1923) and *Wiersze dziecięce* (Children's Poems, 1959). She published a volume of poetic prose, *Z rozbitego fotoplastikonu* (From Shattered Photoplastic, 1957); collections of sketches and memories—*Niewczesne wynurzenia* (Untimely Outpourings, 1958) and *Trazymeński zając* (The Hare of Trazymen, 1968, 1975); and several plays, *Rzeczy sceniczne* (Stage Works, 1969). She also translated literary works from German (Schiller, Goethe), Russian, Hungarian, and English.

BIBLIOGRAPHY

Wiersze 1912–1959 (Poems, 1912–1959), edited by Paweł Hertz, Warsaw, 1964.
Wiersze zebrane (Collected Poems), Volumes 1–2, Warsaw, 1971.

English

Five Songs for Female Voice and Piano (Pięć Pieśni), translated by Ann and Adam Czerniawski, Celle: Hermann Moeck, 1963.

INNY ŚWIAT (A World Apart) (see Herling-Grudziński).

IREDYŃSKI, IRENEUSZ (1939–86), a playwright, prose writer, and poet, began his literary career with poetry which was aesthetically and morally provocative (*Wszystko jest obok* [Everything Is Alongside], 1959; *Moment bitwy* [The Moment of Battle], 1961; and *Muzyka konkretna* [Concrete Music], 1971). His prose was similar in character: novelettes and short stories—*Dzień oszusta* (The Day of the Swindler, 1962), *Ukryty w słońcu* (Hidden in the Sun, definitive edition, 1973), *Związki uczuciowe* (Sentimental Ties, 1962), *Człowiek epoki* (The Man of His Epoch, 1971), and *Manipulacja* (Manipulation, 1974). His technique includes employing a behaviorist description of gestures and reflexes to portray characters living on the fringes of society, in a moral vacuum. His heroes and heroines feel that their existence is not authentic (see, especially, *Dzień oszusta,* which some critics regard as a manifesto of anarchical cynicism and nihilism). In his work as a playwright, he experimented with a psychological analysis of various cases of mythomania and make believing, complexes and frustrations (*Męczeństwo z przymiarką* [Suffering with Measure], produced in 1960, and *Ostatni odcinek drogi* [The Last Stage of the Road], produced in 1962), in order to create dramas that would reveal the mechanisms of psychological and physical violence, cruelty, and humiliation. He presented model situations, metaphorical and grotesque projections of the reality of a concentration camp in *Zejście do piekła* (Descent into Hell), produced in 1964; *Jasełka-moderne* (Christmas [Play—Moderne]) in *Dialog,* 1962, produced in 1965; *Trzecia pierś* (Third Breast) in *Dialog,* 1973, produced in Zurich in 1973 and in Poland in 1975. He was the first Polish playwright to depict a terrorist underground movement in *Żegnaj Judaszu* (Farewell Judas, in *Dialog,* 1965, produced in Zurich in 1968 and in Poland in 1971). He employed the metaphor of a quarantined hospital for blind and incurable patients in *Dobroczyńca* (Benefactor, produced in 1971) and in *Sama Słodycz* (Pure Sweetness, in *Dialog,* 1971; produced in 1973). Iredyński's last play, *Ołtarz wzniesiony sobie* (An Altar to Himself, *Dialog,* 1981, number 6) is a violent attack on the destructive influence of the Stalinist period, which shatters the character of the main hero, who commits suicide, as did his father, a political prisoner. According to Andrzej Konkowski, Iredyński's view of life is a ruthless struggle and never-ending game in which no one wins, in which a man is reduced to the role of an actor who accepts any role or mask imposed on him by a given situation. He wrote several psychological monodramas, including *Czysta miłość* (Pure Love, in *Dialog,* 1972) and *Maria* (Mary, in *Dialog,* 1974; produced jointly in 1975). He was also the author of numerous radio plays and film scenarios.

(See Contemporary Polish Literature.)

BIBLIOGRAPHY

Sytuacje teatralne (Theatrical Situations) (a selection of plays) Warsaw, 1974.

English

An Altar to Himself (Ołtarz wzniesiony sobie) (a play), translated by Michał Kobiałka, New York: Institute for Contemporary Eastern European Drama and Theater, 1982.

Farewell Judas (*Żegnaj Judaszu*) (a play in 3 acts), New York: Center for Advanced Study in Theater Arts, 1983.

IRYDION (see Krasiński).

IRZYKOWSKI, KAROL (1873–1944), a novelist and literary critic, specialized in German literature at the University of Lvov (1889–93). Although he began his career as a poet, Irzykowski soon turned to prose. His novel *Pałuba* (Make-Believe or Palubism), published together with the symbolic-grotesque novelette *Sny Marii Dunin* (The Dreams of Maria Dunin) in 1903, when he was only thirty years old, established him as an innovator, a compelling force in Polish belles lettres. Probably more discussed than read today, *Pałuba* nonetheless deserves the attention of anyone interested in the history of the modern novel. The work is amazing in its structure: it is not only a novel within a novel but a commentary by the author about the putative author writing about characters invented by Irzykowski. *Sny Marii Dunin,* although a separate work, is structurally bound to *Pałuba.* Irzykowski often refers to the shorter work during the course of the narration. In fact, he dissociates himself from the authorship of *Dreams* by informing the reader in the "notes" to *Pałuba* that the author of *Dreams* had recently died. The question arises, Who is the putative author of *Pałuba?* Is it Irzykowski or another "author" who is creating his analytical novel? Does the author really believe that there is a "spiritual world" alongside our material one which continues after our earthly journey? The point of view is highly complex: the putative author of *Pałuba* is omniscient; he is also judgmental. Strumieński is the quintessential antihero, who creates his own tragic world, a make-believe playground where "spirits" cavort—Angelika and Ola, the eloquent phantom Maria Dunin, Paulina, Ksenia, and so on. *Pałuba,* in all its structural and thematic complexity, prefigures the work of later Polish innovators (e.g., Gombrowicz, Witkacy, and Schulz), and also the experimentations in the area of point of view of Henry James, Joseph Conrad, Jean-Paul Sartre (the novel within a novel), and Robbes-Grillet (the antinovel or nonnovel).

Pałuba, like *Don Quixote* or *The Brothers Karamazow,* is, in a word, inimitable. It is a great literary work, written by a young man who wanted to create something monumental. Unfortunately, his remaining works are not of similar high quality. A member of *Młoda Polska,* Irzykowski often engaged in polemics with various poets and critics. Scattered throughout various journals, his critical articles were collected in the volume *Czyn i słowo* (An Art and a Word, 1912), which became an important event in the intellectual life of the early twentieth century, as an attempt to underscore the aesthetic experiences of the literature of Young Poland in confrontation with the Revolution of 1905. Irzykowski's basic ideas were ultimately given shape during the war years. Irzykowski's "clericism" (derived from the French *clerc,* an intellectual) was based on the acknowledgment of intellectual culture as an autonomous area only indirectly linked to political action and practical life.

During the period 1918–39, Irzykowski was one of the most active and influential literary critics of that period. He was interested in theory and the literary practices of formism, futurism, and expressionism. He carried on polemics with writers of the avant-garde as a spokesman aware of the duties of literature, its philosophic and psychological explorations. *Dziesiąta Muza* (The Tenth Muse, 1924), characterized by penetrating observations, is a lengthy discourse dedicated to the aesthetics of film. A significant part of his book *Walka o treść* (The Battle for Contents, 1929) was a polemic with the Theory of Pure Form of S. I. Witkiewicz.*

In 1933 Irzykowski became a member of the Polish Academy of Literature (*PAL*). During the Nazi occupation he supported himself as a teacher of stenography, which for many years had been his main profession. He also took active part in underground cultural life. Wounded during the Warsaw Uprising, he died shortly thereafter in a hospital. It is *Pałuba,* however, that gives Irzykowski a secure place in world literature. A seminal work, charting the development of the author's later interests, it is, on the whole, a sustained literary masterpiece. Palubism is a many-layered metaphor, encompassing everything: "a curtain, the deck of a ship, and an old, spiteful hag." But, in essence, it involves the area of make-believe, the inner, psychological world that man creates for himself despite himself. Irzykowski admitted, perhaps with a sly wink, that "that which is unlike anything else ought to have a name unlike anything else" (*Pałuba,* p. 483).

(See *Młoda Polska.*)

BIBLIOGRAPHY

"Pałuba i Sny Marii Dunin" (Make-Believe: The Dreams of Maria Dunin), in *Pisma,* Cracow: Wydawnictwo Literackie, 1976.

Pałuba, edited and with an introduction by A. Budrecka, Wrocław, 1981.

Pałuba, introduction by K. Wyka, Cracow, 1948.

Pisma (Writings), Volumes 1–7, edited by A. Lam, Cracow, 1975–82.

Wybór pism krytyczno-literackich (Selected Critical Writings), edited and with an introduction by W. Głowala, Wrocław, 1975.

IWASZKIEWICZ, JAROSŁAW (pseudonym Eleuter) (1894–1980), a prose writer, poet, playwright, essay writer, and translator, was born into a gentry intelligentsia family near Kiev which cherished patriotic and cultural tradition. He was brought up in a cultural milieu which was Polish, as well as Russian and Ukrainian. His literary and artistic interests, which awakened quite early, were influenced by his friendship with Karol Szymanowski, which later brought them together to work on various artistic undertakings (for example, Iwaszkiewicz wrote the libretto to Szymanowski's opera *Król Roger* [King Roger]). He went to school in Elizavetgrad and then Kiev, where he also began studying law and music and he wrote his first works (a digressive poem *Młodość pana Twardowskiego* [Mr. Twardowski's Youth], written during the period 1912–15 and published in 1979). He made his debut in 1915 with the poem *Lilith* (published in the first and only issue of *Pióro* [Pen]). In 1918 he went to Warsaw and joined a group of young poets gathered around the magazine *Pro arte et studio* and the cabaret *Pod Pikadorem* (Under the Picador); later the entire group joined *Skamander.* For a short time he worked for the expressionist magazine *Zdrój* (Spring). He accepted various positions: with *Kurier Polski* (Polish Courier, 1920–23), in the Foreign Office, and with the diplomatic corps (Copenhagen, Brussels). All his life he traveled a great deal throughout Europe. In 1928 he settled in Stawisko near Warsaw, where he lived during the period of the war and the occupation, giving shelter to many artists and writers. After the war he worked actively for *ZLP* (Union of Polish Writers), taking on the duties of union president (1945–46, 1947–49, and after 1959); he tried with variable success to defend the interests of the writers' community, subjected to the supervision of the political powers and the censor; he himself, nonetheless, did not lose anything by accepting dubious honors; for example, as the leader of the pro-Soviet movement of "the defenders of peace" during the years 1953–57, or recipient of the International Lenin Prize (1970). He was editor of several journals: *Życie Literackie* (Literary Life, 1945–46), *Nowiny Literackie* (Literary News, 1947–48), and the monthly *Twórczość* (Creativity), beginning in 1955. He became a member of Parliament in 1952. He held two honorary doctorates: from the University of Warsaw (where he lectured on literature) and the Jagiellonian University. He was the recipient of several important literary awards, including Premio Mondello in 1979. His home in Stawisko is now a museum devoted to his memory.

Iwaszkiewicz's prose is strongly connected with both literary tradition and recent trends in contemporary literature, but he cannot in any way be assigned to any one twentieth century trend. His early works, written in the exotic, fablelike convention of the poetic novel (*Zenobia Palmura,* 1920; *Ucieczka do Bagdadu* [Escape to Baghdad], 1923; and *Wieczór u Abdona* [Evening at Abdon's], 1923), are dominated by the modernist tradition, but at the same time deviate from the trend in their attempt to depict the opposition of art to life. The same motive appears in the novels, which are stylized autobiographies—*Hilary, syn buchaltera* (Hilary, the Bookkeeper's Son, 1923) and *Księżyc wschodzi* (The Moon Rises, 1925), where the solution is resolved in the deheroization of the two members of the opposition. Beginning with the novel *Zmowa mężczyzn* (The Men's Conspiracy, 1930) the writer creates his own, original view of the world, which reaches its full expression in the stories *Panny z Wilka* (Ladies from Wilk), *Brzezina* (Birch Grove, published jointly in 1933), *Młyn nad Utratą* (The Mill over

Utrata, 1936), and in the novels *Czerwone tarcze* (Red Shields, 1934) and *Pasje błędomierskie* (Błędomierz Passions, 1938), which characterized the artistic and ideological beliefs of the Polish intelligentsia in relation to the crisis of contemporary culture. According to Janusz Rohoziński, Iwaszkiewicz's mature works are based on oppositions (life-death, love-hatred, attempt-achievement, memory-time, biologism-spiritualism), which are presented philosophically; they offer a generalization of the lives of characters, who are clearly delineated, sensitive, and living a rich spiritual life, rooted in a world which is drawn with precision and which offers a number of sensual charms. His heroes, entangled in the antinomies, are almost invariably haunted with tragic thoughts, which arise from the cruelty of the laws of nature (e.g., a frequent motive of premature death) or from the defeat of the individual in confrontation with the historical process. The tragical gains a wider dimension in the works arising from the experiences of the war and the occupation: *Kongres we Florencji* (Congress in Florence), in *Nowele włoskie* (Italian Novels, 1947); *Bitwa na równinie Sedgemoor* (Battle on Sedgemoor Plain) and *Matka Joanna od Aniołów* (Mother Joan of the Angels), in the collection *Nowa miłość* (New Love, 1946); *Stara cegielnia* (The Old Brick Factory) and *Młyn nad Lutynią* (The Mill on the Lutynia), published jointly in 1946; *Kwartet Mendelssohna* (Mendlessohn Quartette), in *Opowieści zasłyszane* (Overhead Stories, 1954); *Kościół w Skaryszewie* (Church in Skaryszew), in the collection *O psach, kotach i diabłach* (About Dogs, Cats and Devils, 1968); and the epiclike novel about the Polish intelligentsia during the first half of this century *Sława i chwała* (Glory and Praise, Volumes 1–3, 1956–62). The humanistic values of Iwaszkiewicz's prose arise, however, not only from intellectual and moral anxiety, but also from the belief in human nature, in the capability of man to make the right ethical choice, and in the existence of a connection between the tragic experience and the specific intensity of aesthetic and sensual experiences (e.g., *Tatarak* [Sweet Flag], 1960; *Kochankowie z Marony* [Lovers from Marona], 1961; *Sny: Ogrody: Serenite* [Dreams: Gardens: Serenity], 1974; *Noc czerwcowa: Zarudzie: Heydenreich* [June Night: Zarudzie: Heydenreich], 1976). Consciously exploiting an entire gamut of styles and literary conventions, Iwaszkiewicz developed and modernized the form of the short story, gave new shape to the historical novel, and enlivened epic narrative, enriching it with lyrical and reflective elements.

As a poet Iwaszkiewicz was the least typical representative of the Skamander group. What made him different from other members were his cultural background, broader literary and philosophical interests, and internal complexity: these factors account for the specifically polar structure of his poetry, with oppositions such as East and West, aestheticism and public spirit, a "personal" and "cultural" point of view, a passion for life and fascination with death. According to Jerzy Kwiatkowski the most characteristic and permanent features of his poetry include a great perceptive sensitivity (which allowed him to picture the beauty of the world with unusual intensity), his cult of art (which is one of the main themes of his poetry), and, finally, "the resignation motive" (his awareness of the impossibility of attaining happiness, a motive which is strongly emphasized in his poetry and which is illuminated in his final aesthetic effect). In Iwaszkiewicz's prewar poetry one can note his penchant for employing contrast and contradiction. After his sophisticatedly aesthetic *Oktostychy* (Octostichs, 1919), a series of poems which are ingeniously stylized, his next collection *Dionizje* (Dionysuses, 1922) was astonishing in its markedly different, expressionistic tone. The search for beauty was here replaced with a search for the power of expression; harmony accompanied dissonance. After two more collections dominated by a personal tone of quiet philosophical resignation (*Kasydy zakończone siedmioma wierszami* [Cassidas Ending with Seven Verses], 1925, and *Księga dnia i księga nocy* [The Book of Day and the Book of Night], 1929), Iwaszkiewicz published *Powrót do Europy* [Return to Europe], 1931, which introduced historical, philosophical themes; a polemic tone; and elements of pathos into his work. And finally, after *Lato 1932* (Summer 1932, 1933), a cycle of poems employing the symbols of a nocturnal landscape to project internal anxiety and metaphysical fear, Iwaszkiewicz composed *Inne życie* (Other Life, 1938), a work dominated by the poetry of culture, that is, poetic "translations" of great paintings. Iwaszkiewicz's lyrics of the period are far from innovative; they tend toward a more classical orientation. In his postwar poetry this trend is continued in *Ody olimpijskie* (Olympic Odes, 1946). Basically, however, his poetry developed in a different direction: toward rejection of traditional rules, toward "bare poetry." After several collections marking a transitional period (*Warkocz jesieni* [The Braid of Autumn], 1954; the elegiac cycle *Plejady* [The Pleiades], and *Ciemne ścieżki* [Dark Paths], 1957; the cycle *Album tatrzański* [Tatra Album], revised edition, 1976) a decisive turn came with the collection *Jutro żniwa* (Tomorrow the Harvest, 1963). It affirmed the renaissance of Iwaszkiewicz's poetry, which continued in the collections *Krągły rok* (The Year Round, 1967), *Xenie i elegie* (Xenie and Elegies, 1970), and *Śpiewnik włoski* (The Italian Song Book, 1974). With their modern, ascetic language the poems first and foremost deal with the terminal, crucial problems of human life. Perhaps Iwaszkiewicz's greatest poetic achievements are the collection *Mapa pogody* (Weather Map, 1977) and his last poems, in which he returned to a rich means of expression, to a broad historical and cultural perspective, and attained poetic mastery in the art of bidding farewell to the world.

Iwaszkiewicz's dramas center around artistic motives drawn directly from literature (e.g., his view of the tragedy of Romeo and Juliet as presented in *Kochankowie z Werony* [Lovers from Verona], 1928, a polemic with Shakespeare), or from biographies of great artists: Chopin in *Lato w Nohant* (Summer in Nohant, 1936), Pushkin in *Maskarada* (Masquerade,

1938), and Balzac in *Wesele pana Balzaca* [The Wedding of Mr. Balzac], 1959). These plays provide an insight into the psyche of an artist and reconstruct the moral conflicts in which he is involved. The conflicts stem from the clash with bourgeois mentality, from restrictions imposed on the artist's freedom, from the impossibility of reconciling the universal aspects of art with the concrete requirements of life. The main characters of the plays are unheroic; Iwaszkiewicz frees them from the pompous decorum imposed on historic personages.

Iwaszkiewicz's essays and journalistic pieces reflect his broad knowledge and cultural horizons and are valuable biographical and artistic comments on his own work. They reveal three areas of interest. The first one concerns music and theater: these include monographic studies on *Chopin* (1938; revised edition, 1949) and *Bach* (1951), reminiscences regarding Szymanowski (*Spotkania z Szymanowskim* [Meeting with Szymanowski], 1947) and sketches about the Polish composer (*Harnasie,* 1964), and studies on Stanisława Wysocka's theater in Kiev (1963) and on *Teatr Polski* in Warsaw (1971). The second group includes reminiscences on the author's youth (*Książka moich wspomnień* [Book of My Recollections], 1957, third edition, 1975) and from his travels (*Pejzaże sentymentalne* [Sentimental Landscapes], 1926; *Listy z podróży do Ameryki Południowej* [Letters from a Journey to South America], 1954; *Książka o Sycylii* [A Book About Sicily], 1956; and *Gniazdo łabędzi: Szkice z Danii* [The Nest of Swans: Sketches from Denmark], 1962), enriched with his reflections on the cultural tradition of the groups he describes (e.g., *Podróże do Włoch* [Journeys to Italy], 1977, and *Podróże do Polski* [Journeys to Poland], 1977). The third trend is concerned with literature: these include numerous reviews, articles, sketches, and studies, only a few of which were published in book form (*Gawędy o książkach i czytelnikach* [Tales About Books and Readers], 1959; *Rozmowy o ksiązkach* [Conversations About Books], Volumes 1–2, 1961–68; and *Ludzie i książki* [People and Books], 1971); he also composed a series of sketches on Polish and Russian writers (Petersburg, 1976) and sketches on Scandinavian literature. After his death his memoirs, *Aleja przyjaciół* (An Alley of Friends, 1984), appeared. He translated widely from several languages: Rimbaud, Claudel, Gide, Girodoux, Shakespeare, Tolstoy, Chekhov, Andersen, and Kierkegaard. Some of his works were made into films by Jerzy Kawalerowicz (*Matka Joanna od Aniołów* [Mother Joan of the Angels], 1961) and Andrzej Wajda (*Brzezina* [Birch wood], 1970, and *Panny z Wilka,* [the Girls from Wilk], 1979).

(See Contemporary Polish Literature.)

BIBLIOGRAPHY

Dzieła (Works), Volumes 1–10, Warsaw, 1958–59.
Wiersze zebrane (Collected Poems), Warsaw, 1968.

Opowiadania zebrane (Collected Stories), Volumes 1–3, Warsaw, 1969.
Dzieła (Works), Warsaw, 1975.

English

Summer at Nohant (Lato w Nohant) (a play in three acts), translated by Celina Wieniewska, London: Minerva, 1942.

Gathering Time: Five Modern Polish Elegies, translated by Andrzej Busza and Bogdan Czaykowski, Mission, British Columbia: C and J Elsted at Barbarian Press, 1983.

The Wedding of Balzac (Wesele pana Balzaca), translator anonymous, *Dialog,* Number 1, 1959; translator anonymous, Act II only published in Poland, July 1959.

J

JAGIELLONIAN UNIVERSITY IN CRACOW (*UJ*), one of the oldest institutions of higher education in Europe, was founded in 1364 by Kazimierz the Great and modeled after the University of Bologna. At the beginning there were only three faculties: law, medicine, and philosophy. It was reconstructed by Jagiełło and Jadwiga (1397–1400) and reorganized on the model of the University of Paris. It became the scholarly and cultural center of Poland in the fifteenth century, touching on every aspect of life in Poland, including Silesia. In the fifteenth century the Jagiellonian Library was also inaugurated. Thanks to outstanding professors, the university was soon internationally recognized. Its alumni from the fifteenth to the seventeenth century included great politicians and men of letters: Z. Oleśnicki, J. Długosz,* A. Frycz Modrzewski,* S. Hozjusz,* J. Kochanowski,* M. Kromer, Sz. Szymonowic,* J. Zamoski, Sz. Starowolski, and A. Fredro.* In the midsixteenth century the university began to lose its prestige, standing aloof from the humanistic and reform currents; nevertheless, it remained a center of education until the eighteenth century. It was thoroughly reformed by Hugo K. Kołłątaj,* changed its name to the Main State School, and employed Polish, not Latin as its main language. After the loss of independence the Jagiellonian University also suffered from repressive measures imposed upon it. In 1815, however, on the basis of the Treaty of Vienna, it received the official name Jagiellonian University and remained an autonomous school, open to all youths from all the Poland's partitions. Germanized in 1847–48, then again in 1854, it was re-Polonized in 1870—this time for good—becoming a national center of science. It was shut down by the Nazis in 1939; its 183 professors were arrested and sent to the concentration camp in Sachsenhausen.

During the nineteenth and twentieth centuries Jagiellonian scholars contributed greatly to the development of the Polish humanities: the Cracow

School of History was represented by J. Szujski, M. Bobrzyński, S. Smolka; later by W. Czermak, K. Potkański, S. Kutrzeba, W. Sobieski, W. Tokarz, W. Konopczyński, J. Feldman, M. Kukiel, O. Halecki, and R. Grodecki; Ethnology by J. S. Bystroń, K. Moszyński; Classical Philology by K. Morawski, T. Sinko, R. Gansiniec, W. Madyda, M. Plezia; Oriental Studies by T. Pobożniak and W. Zajączkowski; Roman Philology by S. Wędkiewicz, W. Folkierski, S. Stroński, C. Czerny, and M. Strzałkowa; English Philology by R. Dyboski and P. Mroczkowski; German Philology by A. Kleczkowski; Russian and Ukrainian Philology by J. Tretiak, M. Zdziechowski, W. Lednicki, R. Łużny; General Linguistics by J. Baudouin de Courtenay, J. Kuryłowicz, and T. Milewski; Indo-European Linguistics by J. Safarewicz and A. Heinz; Slavic and Polish Philology by J. M. Rozwadowski, J. Łoś, K. Nitsch, T. Lehr-Spławiński, W. Taszycki, Z. Klemensiewicz, S. Urbańczyk; Aesthetics by R. Ingarden; History of Art by K. Estreicher, J. Szablowski, and M. Porębski; and Bibliography by the Estreicher family.

According to Jan Wojnowski, Polish Literature and Language Studies became an independent branch of the Jagiellonian in the late eighteenth century, but the traditions really began much earlier: Jakub Parkoszowic developed Polish spelling in the fifteenth century. Initially, literature and language were taught jointly; they were separated in the early nineteenth century. An important period in the development of this area occurred when S. Tarnowski (1871–1910) assumed the chair. It was then that the history of literature gained an independent position. The teaching syllabus was made much more specific; educational methods were modernized, and the methodology of philological studies was given appropriate attention. On the other hand, Tarnowski's conservatism and his critical attitude toward the Young Poland movement did not win the approval of many students. The subsequent head of the chair, Ignacy Chrzanowski, was far more in tune with the times. His tenure ran 1910–31. Among the professors who went to Sachsenhausen concentration camp were Chrzanowski (who died in the camp), Pigoń, and Kołaczkowski. After the war, some of the greatest authorities in their fields became members of the faculty; among others, S. Pigoń, J. Kleiner, K. Wyka, H. Markiewicz, and J. Błoński. In 1970 the chair was reorganized into an Institute of Polish Philology, with independent sections devoted to language, theory of literature, history of literature, theater, and film. The publications of the institute appear in two series: *Zeszyty Naukowe* (Scholarly Notebooks of Jagiellonian University: Historio-Literary Works) and *Rozprawy i studia* (Dissertations and Studies).

BIBLIOGRAPHY

K. Morawski, *Historia Uniwersytetu Jagiellońskiego* (The History of Jagiellonian University), Volumes 1–2, Cracow, 1900.

Historia nauki polskiej (The History of Polish Education), edited by B. Suchodolski, Volumes 1–3, Wrocław, 1970–77.

JASIENICA, PAWEŁ (1890–1970), whose real name was Leon Lech Beynar, was a historical writer and journalist. An alumnus of Vilnius University, where he studied history in 1928–32, he published several papers before 1939 about the history of the Grand Duchy of Lithuania. He participated in the Polish-German war in 1939; during the occupation he belonged to the underground unit of *Armia Krajowa* (Home Army), which conducted resistance activities in the Vilnius area. Threatened by the impending Soviet army in 1944, after his arrest and escape from prison, he remained until 1945 in a forest unit of Armia Krajowa. After the war he settled incognito in Cracow, beginning work for the Catholic periodical *Tygodnik Powszechny* (The Universal Weekly). He was imprisoned in 1948 and freed after a proregime, nationalist-Catholic group, *PAX*, interceded on his behalf. He worked as a journalist and a reporter. Later he started to participate in political activities; in 1968 he publicly condemned the harassment of students by the Communist officials and the abuses of authority exercised by censorship officials (he was punished for this by harassment and a ban on publishing).

Jasienica's most important work, which has brought him broad and permanent readership, is his multivolume synthesis of Poland's history: *Polska Piastów* (Poland During the Piast Dynasty, 1960); *Polska Jagiellonów* (Poland During the Jagiellon Dynasty, 1963); *Rzeczpospolita Obojga Narodów* (The Republic of Both Nations—Part 1, *Srebrny wiek* [The Silver Age], 1967; Part 2, *Calamitatis regnum* 1967; Part 3, *Dzieje agonii* [History of Agony], 1972). The history of the multinational Polish state, from the Piast Dynasty beginnings through the Union with Lithuania, until the decline and collapse in the eighteenth century, were comprehensively drawn up by Jasienica as a history of the centers of political power, of society, of wars, diplomacy, spiritual and temporal culture, as well as the individual dilemmas faced by the rulers and politicians shaping the face of one of the greatest powers in the history of Europe. He presented the whole as a colorful, essayistic tale, not devoid of references to contemporary times. The modernizing approach to history also characterized other books by Jasienica, such as *Rozważania o wojnie domowej* (Thoughts About the Civil War, published in 1978 by the underground publisher *NOWA** and officially in 1985), in which, using the example of the rural uprising in Wandea (1793–96), he showed the process of transformation undergone by the revolutionary movement, directed by the Jacobin ideologists of freedom and equality, as it changed into a terrorist dictatorship bringing the masses suffering and death. He also paid a great deal of attention (especially in the beginning of his writing career) to the prehistory and early history of Poland (*Słowiański rodowód* [The Slavic Origins], 1961, *Myśli o dawnej Polsce* [The Thoughts About Early Poland], 1960) and to the

January Uprising of 1863 *(Dwie drogi* [The Two Roads], 1960). In the collection of essays *Polska anarchia* (The Polish Anarchy) he argued with the thesis assigning Poles a special propensity toward anarchistic behavior. He also wrote memoirs of his youth, among other aspects, as a witness of the revolution in Russia, *Pamiętnik* (Diary, 1986).

JASIEŃSKI, BRUNO (originally Wiktor Bruno Zysman) (1901–39), was a poet, prose writer, and playwright. During the period 1914–18 he resided with his parents in Moscow, where he completed a Polish secondary school and became acquainted with the revolutionary literary avant-garde. After 1918 he moved to Cracow. He was one of the main initiators of Polish futurism, as a cofounder of the Club *Katarynka* (Hurdy-Gurdy, 1919) and as the author of several manifestos, including *Do narodu polskiego manifest w sprawie natychmiastowej futuryzacji życia* (A Manifesto to the Polish Nation Concerning the Immediate Futurization of Life) and *Manifest w sprawie poezji futurystycznej* (Manifesto Concerning Futuristic Poetry in *Jednodniówka futurystów* [One Day Publication of the Futurists], 1921). He was cofounder of the famous one-day paper *Nuż w bzuhu* (Knife in the Stomach, 1921) and actively engaged with two avant-garde papers, *Zwrotnica* (Turning Point) and *Almanach Nowej Sztuki* (Almanac of New Art). In 1923 he became involved with the Communist movement and contributed to *Trybuna Robotnicza* (The Worker's Tribune), published in Lvov, and to *Nowa Kultura* (New Culture). Persecuted by the police and the censorship, in 1925 he left for France, where he was active in the French Communist Party. Expelled by the French authorities, he went to the Soviet Union, where he settled down and started writing in Russian. He accepted Russian citizenship, joined the Soviet Communist Party, worked as a journalist, and was active in the Union of Soviet Writers. In 1937 during the period of the great Stalinist purge he was arrested and sentenced to fifteen years in a labor camp. He died near Vladivostok, after a serious illness, on his way to the place of his imprisonment. He was rehabilitated in 1955.

In Jasieński's early lyrics (the collection *But w butonierce* [Boot in the Boutonniere], 1921), which claimed a kinship to Russian egofuturism (Severjanin), he combined a sentimental decadent pose with a fascination with the products of urban, technical civilization and provocative moral and aesthetic antitraditionalism. In his later works (the poem *Pieśń o głodzie* [Song About Hunger], 1922, and the collection *Ziemia na lewo* [The Earth on the Left], 1924) the influence of Mayakovsky can be discerned, while his anarchical and at the same time pacifist views developed into a philosophy which advocated a social revolution. According to Helena Karwacka, his poetic style, which early included a skillful imitation of traditional versification forms and the use of eccentric metaphors, developed later into his penchant for employing brutal aesthetic dissonance and hyperbolic imagery, as well as in his attempts, characteristic of futurism, to adapt non-literary forms of expression—film narration, journalistic reports, and a telegraphic style. Jasieński made great use of the poetics of folk songs, whose mastery he made excellent use of in the poem *Słowo o Jakubie Szeli* (A Word About Jacob Szela, Paris, 1926), woven around the vicissitudes of the hero, the leader of the peasant rebellion in Galicja during the second half of the nineteenth century. The ideological premises of the poem stirred and still stir strong objections (the apotheosis of Jacob Szela, in which the author wishes to see a precursor of the social revolution, and which in reality was an agent of the invading Austrian powers who fought against the nobleman's independence movement); on the other hand, the originality of the form of the work is praised: "the skillful blending of folk stylization with a prestidigitator's versification and rhyme" (J. Kwiatkowski). As a prose writer he was the author of a micronovel, *Nogi Izoldy Morgan* (The Legs of Isolde Morgan, 1923), which included an introduction presenting his views on avant-garde prose, and of the famous antiutopian novel *Palę Paryż* (I Burn Paris, 1929). In his prose writings he developed the form which combined fantastic grotesque and expressionist-catastrophic elements. Jasieński's writings in Russian include the play *Bal manekinów* (The Ball of Mannequins, 1931, produced in Poland, 1957); short stories (e.g., *Nos* [The Nose], *Męstwo* [Manhood], *Główny winowajca* [The Main Culprit]); and the novel *Człowiek zmienia skórę* (Man Changes Skin), 1932–33, Polish edition, 1934), a kind of agitprop-reportage from Central Asia, in which the author attempted to paint a majestic "picture of cultural and economic blossoming in a former tsarist colony under the conditions of proletariat dictatorship"; his last novel *Zmowa obojętnych* (The Conspiracy of the Indifferent) was unfinished.

Palę Paryż (I Burn Paris), written in Paris, was initially published in French in *L'Humanité* (1928, definitive edition in Polish, 1929; new edition 1974, with an introduction by A. Stern). Written with polemic intent, as a response to P. Morand's pamphlet-short story *Palę Moskwę* (I Burn Moscow), 1926, published in Poland in 1927, it presents a fantastic vision of the destruction of Paris—a symbol of the capitalist world. A plague, purposely caused by a young unemployed worker, has enveloped the city. Paris is cut off from the rest of the country and divided into separatist states-republics. It is slowly dying as a result of famine and internal conflicts. Only one "state" survives the cataclysm: an international proletarian republic, which takes over the entire city when the epidemic ends and becomes the source of world revolution. The novel has the character of a sensational report with poetic and grotesque elements; it is also a political manifesto and a work of propaganda. There are references to catastrophic science fiction, but it differs from other catastrophic works in its optimistic faith in the revolutionary change coming to the world. The book gained success both as a literary and a political event (the author was expelled from France because of it). Its evaluation by leftist circles was not entirely unanimous; for example, Polish critics in the Soviet Union accused it of spreading an "apocalyptic-moralizing ideology," alien to the proletariat.

BIBLIOGRAPHY

Nogi Izoldy Morgan i inne utwory (The Legs of Isolde Morgan and Other Works), edited by G. Lasota, Warsaw, 1966.

Utwory poetyckie, manifesty, szkice (Poetic Works, Manifestos, Sketches), selected and with an introduction by E. Balcerzan, Wrocław, 1972.

English

Man Changes His Skin, translated from Russian by H. G. Scott, Moscow: Co-Operative Publishing Society of Foreign Workers in the U.S.S.R., 1935.

JASTRUN, MIECZYSŁAW (1903–83), a poet, prose writer, essayist, and translator, studied Polish and German philology and philosophy at the Jagiellonian University. Early in his career he worked as a teacher of Polish. He published his first poems in 1924, and made his debut in *Skamander* in 1925. From 1945 he was a member of the Communist Party; he resigned from it in 1956; in later years he took part in various protests against the restraint of free speech. Among others, in 1964 he was one of the signers of the Letter of 34. His wife, Mieczysława Buczkówna, is also a fine poet, like their son, Tomasz Jastrun. During the war he lived in Lvov and in Warsaw, working for the underground schools and for Communist publications. In 1945–49 he was a member of the editorial staff of the Marxist Weekly *Kuźnica* (The Forge) in Łódź, then moved to Warsaw. In 1970–71 he taught poetry at the University of Warsaw.

Jastrun's meditative lyrics occupy a separate position in contemporary Polish poetry, not associated with any of the dominant trends, but closer to older literature (the great Romantics, e.g., Norwid) and to the phenomena in European literature of the early twentieth century (symbolism, Rilke, Pasternak). His early works (the collections *Spotkanie w czasie* [A Meeting in Time], 1929; *Inna młodość* [Another Youth], 1933; *Dzieje nieostygłe* [Uncooled History], 1935; and *Strumień i milczenie* [The Stream and Silence], 1937), consciously restricted to intimate contemplation, are characterized by a dominance of philosophical-existential reflection, and later, by a growing catastrophic premonition of the coming war. In his works written during the occupation and during the postwar period (the collections *Godzina strzeżona* [The Guarded Hour], 1944; *Rzecz ludzka* [A Human Matter], 1946; and *Sezon w Alpach* [A Season in the Alps], 1948), which reflect the experiences of the Nazi terror, Jastrun turned to the tradition of Polish Romanticism and advocated a closer relation of poetry to historical reality and the experiences of the nation. According to Ryszard Matuszewski, Jastrun abandoned the allusive poetics of symbolism and searched for a new means of expression in public rhetoric and colloquial language. His wish to provide still stronger ties between his own poetry on the one hand and current social and cultural problems as well as national tradition on the other was reflected in the collections *Rok urodzaju* (The Year of Plenty, 1950), *Barwy ziemi* (The Colors of the Earth, 1952), and *Poemat o mowie polskiej* (Poem on Polish Speech, 1952). In his later works (*Poezja i prawda* [Poetry and Truth], 1955; *Gorący popiół* [Hot Ashes], 1956) Jastrun voiced his protest, widely felt at the time, against deformations of the idea of Socialism and the crimes of Stalin. His later lyrics, in the collections *Genezy* (Origins, 1959), *Większe od życia* (Larger Than Life, 1960), *Intonacje* (Intonations, 1962), *Strefa owoców* (The Region of Fruits, 1964), *W biały dzień* (In the Light of Day, 1967), *Godła pamięci* (Emblems of Memory, 1969), *Wyspa* (The Island, 1973), *Błysk obrazu* (The Flash of the Picture, 1975), and *Scena obrotowa* (Revolving Stage, 1977), a more general moral reflection, concerning the direction in which contemporary civilization was developing, can be discerned. At the same time, Jastrun returned to the themes of his early works—time, death, consciousness, and memory. In his collection of poems *Z innego świata światło* (Light from Another World, 1987) religious accents appeared.

Jastrun wrote a number of biographical essays: *Mickiewicz* (1949, twelfth edition, 1974); *Poeta i dworzanin: Rzecz o Janie Kochanowskim* (Poet and Courtier: About Jan Kochanowski, 1954), a story from Słowacki's life; *Spotkanie z Salomeą* (Meeting with Salomea, 1951); thoughts on poets and poetry (*Dzienniki i wspomnienia* [Journals and Recollections], 1955; *Wizerunki* [Images], 1956; *Między słowem a milczeniem* [Between Word and Silence], 1960; and *Poezja i rzeczywistość* [Poetry and Reality], 1965); about European and Polish culture (*Mit śródziemnomorski* [Mediterranean Myth], 1962; *Wolność wyboru* [Freedom of Choice], 1969; *Historia Fausta* [The Story of Faust] in the collection *Eseje* [Essays, 1973]; *Podróż do Grecji* [Journey to Greece], 1978); and a series of sketches on Norwid, *Gwiaździsty diament* (Starry Diamond, 1971). He also wrote a semiautobiographical prose tale, *Piękna choroba* (Beautiful Illness, 1961), an analysis of the formation of a creative personality. He translated poetry from Russian, French, and German and edited several anthologies of poetry. He was the recipient of numerous literary awards, including the State Award in 1950 and 1955, and the PEN Club Award for his translations.

(See Contemporary Polish Literature.)

BIBLIOGRAPHY

Wiersze zebrane (Collected Poetry), Warsaw, 1956.
Poezje zebrane (Collected Poems), Warsaw, 1975.

English

Adam Mickiewicz, Warsaw: Polonia, 1955.

JEZIORO BODEŃSKIE (Lake Boden) (see Dygat).

K

KADEN-BANDROWSKI, JULIUSZ (whose real name was J. Bandrowski and whose pseudonym was Juliusz Kaden) (1885–1944), was a prose writer and publicist. He came from a family with artistic traditions; he began his career in music, but had to give up his studies as a musician, after having broken his arm twice. During his studies in Brussels he began sending articles to Polish papers on cultural life in Belgium; he also joined an independence organization of the young. In 1914 he enrolled in the Polish Legions: as a soldier he reached the rank of a captain and was Piłsudski's aide-de-camp. During the years 1918–20 he was in charge of the press division of the main headquarters and published a newspaper, *Żołnierz Polski* (Polish Soldier). Settling down in Warsaw, he devoted his energy, organizational talents, and political position to strengthening the union of Polish writers, of which he was president from 1923 to 1926. After 1926 he worked as a journalist. In 1933 he became Secretary General of the newly established Polish Academy of Literature. He was cofounder (with A. Szyfman) of a society for supporting the theater; in 1935 he was elected to the foreign affairs committee of PEN Club. He spent the period of the German occupation in Warsaw. Arrested and investigated by the Gestapo, he died of wounds inflicted during the uprising. Both his sons died as soldiers of the Home Army.

Kaden-Bandrowski was considered the successor to Żeromski, although his writings are much more violent and brutal. His early novels were written in the modernist tradition (*Niezguła* [The Bungler], 1911, and *Proch* [Powder], 1913), based on his experiences during his short stay in the Caucasus and his studies in Brussels. His first attempt to break away from Neo-Romanticism was the collection *Zawody* (Occupations, 1911), in which basic human occupations were described with expressionistic dynamism and elevating pathos. His works, published during the war years, journalistic and documentary in character, created the legend of Piłsudski and the First Brigade: *Piłsudczycy* (Piłsudski's Men, 1915), *Iskry* (Sparks, 1915), *Mogiły* (Graves, 1916), and others. This theme is expressed more artistically in the collection of novelettes *Przymierze serc* (Alliance of Hearts, 1924). He followed the naturalists' example and spent time before each of his works involved in a thorough study of the problem. He had planned a cycle of novels modeled after Balzac and Zola. According to Artur Hutnikiewicz, the most mature and ambitious period of his work began with the novel *Łuk* (The Bow, 1919), a satirical, critical view of the conservative and loyalist stance of the Cracow middle classes during the time of the war; first and foremost, the novel is a study of the psychological and moral evolution of a young woman whose difficult, brutal experiences stimulate her metamorphosis into an independent, free person. He returned to the idea later, treating the problem as his contribution in the "struggle for a new woman." Kaden-Bandrowski's finest political novel is *Generał Barcz* (1922–23). His subsequent two novels, *Lenora* and *Tadeusz,* in the cycle *Czarne skrzydła* (Black Wings, 1928–29), presented political and social conflicts in the Silesian (*Śląsk*) mining region, which was the center of confrontation between the interests of the capitalists and those of the working class. He completed *Mateusz Bigda* in 1933 (Volumes 1–3). The novel paints a brilliant portrait of the leader of a peasant movement, whose ruthless political manipulations serve only one end—his own career. Each of the novels had a vivid response and met with passionate, violent criticism. Kaden-Bandrowski was accused of being libelous and not presenting an objective picture of reality; critics claimed that his characters represented authentic personages from political life. In fact, the "personal interpretation" was superfluous, since Kaden-Bandrowski constructed his characters out of both authentic and fictitious elements, creating personalities much different from their alleged real life counterparts. He was interested in typical attitudes, temperaments, and political or social actions. Contrary to the critics' accusations of one-sidedness and pamphletlike intentions, the novels were true to facts, precise, and deep-reaching in their analysis of the life of the various social groups. The last novel in the cycle was entitled *Białe skrzydła* (White Wings), completed in 1942, but preserved only in fragments.

Kaden-Bandrowski's style was based primarily on his adaptation to the naturalistic and expressionistic method, characterized, above all, by literary behaviorism, that is, observing man almost exclusively through his physiological, almost animal, reflexes. A character's inner life was depicted through his somatic reactions, emphasized by Kaden-Bandrowski's unique style: rough, concrete, ranging from pathos or Neo-Romantic lyricism to brutal colloquialisms; it was a typically expressionist style, based on contrast and dissonance, elliptical forms, and the constant changes in the pace of the narration. He created images which were violent, dynamic, expressive, but also inflated, close to caricature and the grotesque.

Kaden-Bandrowski's style and tone are surprisingly different in his two volumes of lyrical memories: *Miasto mojej matki* (My Mother's City, 1925) and *W cieniu zapomnianej olszyny* (In the Shadow of Forgotten Alderwood, 1926), for which he received the State Award in 1928. These are reminiscences about the author's childhood, in which he praises the wisdom of his father and the heart of his mother, simultaneously offering a brilliant study of the psychology of childhood and adolescence. He also published several volumes of essays, travel diaries, and reports: *Europa zbiera siano* (Europe Gathers Hay, 1927), *Stefan Żeromski, prorok niepodległości* (Stefan Żeromski, Prophet of Independence, 1930), *Pióro, miłość i kobieta* (The Pen, Love and Woman, 1931), *Za stołem i na rynku* (At the Table and at the Market, 1932), *Wspomnienia i nadzieje* (Memories and Hopes, 1938), and *Życie Chopina* (The Life of Chopin, 1938).

Generał Barcz, a novel published in *Kurier Polski* in 1922–23 (published in book form in 1923, in Warsaw; revised, Lvov, 1930), is a literary chronicle of the political events in Poland just before the restoration of independence (October 1918–autumn 1919). The novel presents in brief fragments and more developed episodes the major political processes of the time: the breakup of occupied countries and their disarmament, the rise of the Polish state administration, the war in the East, and the struggle for power between the National Democrats and the so-called Belvedere camp (in reality, embodied by Józef Piłsudski; in the novel, by General Barcz). The novel is not, however, a mere naturalistic copy of real events; the author freely manipulates the sequence of actions and creates new original characters (although he gives them some features of the real politicians of his time). Thus Barcz bears some resemblance to Piłsudski and Sosnkowski, Dąbrowa to the folk radical B. Roja, Krywult (Barcz's main antagonist) to Dowbór-Muśnicki and Haller, Pyc (the protagonist's friend and adviser) to A. Koc, and the writer Rasiński to Kaden-Bandrowski himself. The novel aroused much interest when first published; it was treated by most critics as political diatribe. But neither the historical events themselves nor their contemporary interpretation was the writer's real interest. The novel offers a study of the rise and formation of a state and its structure, and as such it can be treated independently of the historical facts. In keeping with his naturalistic point of view, Kaden-Bandrowski sees the process as a ruthless struggle of contradictory goals, ambitions, and group interests (of parties, social classes, and individuals); as a series of compromise agreements and deals, in which a man, his honor, and his dignity invariably have to give in to the "higher" interests of the state, while the individual propelled to the role of leader is sentenced to total loneliness and self-destruction. The aim of this struggle, of the sacrifice and unbearable psychological and moral burden, is the "scrap heap" of everyday existence, minor comforts which make people in the entire country live better and easier. "The joy over the regained scrap heap"—the words of one of the characters, which also sum up the first months of independence—in a way underscores the ideological essence of the novel: independent Poland is no longer an abstract idea and a myth; it is embodied in common everyday effort, a thing that must be done, the expectation of hard work; it is the reality of a free and self-governing people.

Generał Barcz is a remarkable example of the changes in understanding the role of a writer in an independent country: Romantic myths are no longer needed; the period of "strengthening the hearts" (see Sienkiewicz) is gone. The living country needed the truth, ruthless and severe though it might be, for only truth could set it on a path to real renaissance. *Generał Barcz* is the first novel by Kaden-Bandrowski in which his writing techniques found full expression: naturalistic and expressionistic style, the Baroque-like language, the rich metaphors, brutal imagery, and penchant for dissonance. The novel clearly defines his idea of "somatism," presenting a man not through his psychological states, but through violent physiological reactions, through hyperactivity and anxious, incessant work. The novel was adapted for the stage and for television.

BIBLIOGRAPHY

Dzieła wybrane (Selected Works), edited by M. Sprusiński, Cracow, 1981.
Generał Barcz, edited and with an introduction by M. Sprusiński, Wrocław, 1975.

English

Call to the Cuckoo (W cieniu Zapomnianej Olszyny), translated by Hans Lunn Altrincham and J. Sherratt, Altrincham: J. Sherratt and Son, 1948.
The Battle on the Vistula, translated by Harriet E. Kennedy, New York: AMS Press, 1972.

KAPŁAN I BŁAZEN (The Priest and the Jester) (see Kołakowski).

KARPIŃSKI, FRANCISZEK (1741–1825), a poet, was the son of a poor nobleman. He began working in aristocratic homes as a teacher, always hoping to find a sponsor or to get close to the king in order to gain his support. He worked for several major magnate families (the Czartoryskis, the Sanguszkos) and was introduced to the king; meanwhile, he became acquainted with the school in Puławy. However, he was never able to attain his goal. After 1773 he decided to live in the country; in 1818 he became owner of the village of Chorowszczyzna.

Karpiński's works, published in subsequent volumes of *Zabawki wierszem i prozą* (Trifles in Verse and Prose, Volumes 1–7, 1782–87), are the best examples of sentimentalism in Polish literature of the eighteenth century. He is also the author of the best theoretical study of the aesthetic and philosophical assumptions of the trend (*O wymowie w prozie albo w wier-*

szu [On Pronunciation in Prose or in Verse], 1782; *O szczęściu człowieka: List do Rozyny* [On the Happiness of Man: A Letter to Rozyna, 1783]). The main works of his first period (until 1780) are idylls. Hoping to express his personal feelings about love, Karpiński used the traditional idyll, but subjected it to changes resulting from his own understanding of poetry. Consequently, he created a cycle of works, a number of which show various ways of breaking the idyllic convention (e.g., *Laura i Filon*), while others go far beyond the idyll form to become personal lyrics of the type new to the poetry of the Enlightenment (e.g., *Do Justyny: Tęskność na wiosnę* [To Justine: A Yearning During Spring]). Even though personal lyrics prevail in this first period, Karpiński was not indifferent to the important events of the time (see the elegy *Tęskność do kraju* [Longing for One's Country], written after the Confederacy of Bar, and *Pieśń dziada Sokalskiego w kordonie cesarskim* [Grandfather Sokalski's Song in the Imperial Cordon], written after the first partition of Poland). A follower of Rousseau's philosophy, Karpiński also expressed his criticism of contemporary times and his admiration of "the state of nature." In the early phase of the second period, 1780–94, Karpiński continued to employ the main themes and improved his model of poetry through further individualization of the lyrical subject and transformation of monologue into direct confession (see the elegy *Powrót z Warszawy na wieś* [Return from Warsaw to the Countryside], 1784). Karpiński maintained his interest in folk poetry, which inspired many of his erotic poems. These works are folk paraphrases or stylizations; he employed some of the formal elements and themes, as well as the mood of folk poetry (consider *Pieśni światowe* [Worldly Songs], *Przypomnienie dawnej miłości* [A Remembrance of Old Love], and *Pieśń pasterska do Zosi* [A Pastoral Song to Sophie]). Similar tendencies can be seen in *Duma Lukierdy* (The Ballad of Lukierda), *Żebrak przy drodze* (Beggar by the Road), and *Pieśń mazurska* (Mazovian Song). In these Karpiński transformed original folk songs in a manner that predates the Romantic treatment of folk themes. The latter two works also express a morally based criticism of the magnates and the feudal system. According to Roman Sobol, Karpiński's best work in folk adaptations is contained in his collection of religious songs, *Pieśni nabożne* (Religious Songs); in this collection are songs sung to this day: *Kiedy ranne* (When the morning . . .), *Wszystkie nasze dzienne sprawy* (All our daily affairs), and the celebrating hymn *Bóg się rodzi* (God is born), all in the rhythm of a polonaise. During this second period Karpiński's poetry was enriched with public problems (the culmination came in 1788–92); the author appears here as the supporter of the reformist wing (*Czynsz* [Rent], *Bolesław III*). Karpiński also wrote didactic and moralizing pieces, but they do not present any concrete program and are based on the abstract and eclectic concept of "virtue." After the partitions of Poland, Karpiński practically became silent as a poet, and concentrated on prose writings of a didactic character (*Rozmowy Platona z uczniami swoimi* [Conversations Between Plato and His Pupils], 1802), memoirs, and translations.

Karpiński created a new model of lyrical poetry in which, contrary to Classical rules, emphasis is placed on feelings and personal experience. The artistic form is also different (rejection of rhetoric and mythology, naturalness and simplicity of language). His output, however, is not uniform stylistically or ideologically: sentimental elements and pre-Romantic tendencies appear alongside Classical patterns of the Enlightenment and Polish literary traditions of the sixteenth and seventeenth centuries. Karpiński's works were immensely popular during his time; many of them are still well known today; some have even been absorbed into folklore.

Laura i Filon, an idyll written during the period 1772–80, is in the form of a dialogue between two lovers. The plot develops according to the rules of opera. A representative of its genre, the idyll shows some innovative elements (individualization of the lyrical subject, a concrete situation, a realistic background, and colloquial language). This most famous of idylls (the favorite of Mickiewicz) soon was absorbed into folklore. It is still sung today (especially by the folk ensemble Mazowsze) and has acquired almost proverbial status.

(See Enlightenment.)

BIBLIOGRAPHY

Wiersze wybrane (Selected Poetry), edited by Jan Kott, Warsaw, 1966.
Poezje wybrane, edited by A. K. Guzek, Warsaw, 1972.

KARPOWICZ, TYMOTEUSZ (born 1921), a poet and playwright, made his debut under the Soviet occupation in *Prawda Wileńska* (Vilnius Truth) in 1941. After the war he moved to Szczecin, where he published *Legendy pomorskie* (Legends of Pomerania, 1948) and his collection of poems *Żywe wymiary* (Live Dimensions, 1948). He studied Polish philology and was president of the Wrocław division of the Union of Polish Writers (1957–61) and coeditor of *Nowe Sygnały* (New Signals), *Odra* (Oder, 1958–74), and *Poezja* (Poetry). Since 1974 he has lived abroad. He was a professor of Polish Studies at the university in West Berlin and in Munich and is currently a professor at the Chicago Center of the University of Illinois. Influenced by the Cracow avant-garde, in particular Julian Przyboś, he created his own type of lyrical expression within so-called linguistic poetry. He is deeply concerned with social and political problems and approaches them from a moral perspective (*Gorzkie źródła* [Bitter Sources], 1957; *Kamienna muzyka* [Stone Music], 1958). Karpowicz has always been concerned with philosophical and cultural ideas (*Znaki równania* [Equation Signs], 1960; *W imię znaczenia* [In the Name of Meaning], 1962;

Trudny las [Difficult Forest], 1964; and *Odwrócone światło* [The Light Turned Around], 1972). According to Jacek Łukasiewicz, his poetics during the early period of his career follow the model of one voice and one sense (poems of a polemic character); they aim at revealing the imperfection of language canons and the complexity and multidimensionality of language. Karpowicz transferred his linguistic creativity into the sphere of the language of the stage, creating his own type of poetic theater which aims at reaching into the human psyche and the creative abilities of man. His technique is based on that of a radio play, on the foundations of balladry and fairy tale. Karpowicz is also not averse to introducing sensational plots, elements of the grotesque, and science fiction: *Wracamy późno do domu* (We Return Home Late, in *Dialog*, 1958), *Zielone rękawice* (Green Gloves, in *Dialog*, 1960, produced in 1961), *Dziwny pasażer* (The Strange Passenger, in *Dialog*, 1964, produced by the Slavic Cultural Center in New York in 1974), and *Charon od świtu do świtu* (Charon from Dawn to Dawn, produced in 1972). He has also worked on the theory of poetry: *Poezja niemożliwa: Modele Leśmianowskiej wyobraźni* ([Impossible Poetry: Model of Leśmian's Imagination], 1975). Since his emigration Karpowicz has remained quite active as a writer. During the 1980s he published fragments of a "polyphonic poem," *Rozwiązywanie przestrzeni* (Resolving Space), and a lengthy study on the motif of the wanderer in Polish émigré literature, *Homo viator*. According to Daniel Weissbort, Karpowicz's latest poems (often described as "linguistic") are "listening poetry, meditative and alert."

(See Contemporary Polish Literature.)

BIBLIOGRAPHY

Wiersze wybrane (Selected Poems), Wrocław, 1969.

Dramaty zebrane (Collected Dramas), introduction by Andrzej Falkiewicz, Wrocław, 1975.

"Homo viator," *Archipelago 87*, Numbers 4, 5/6.

English

The Strange Passenger (Dziwny pasażer) (a full-length play), translated by E. J. Czerwiński, *Drama and Theater*, Volume 7, Number 2, 116–40, Winter 1968–69.

Three Slavic Poets, translated by Jan Darowski, Chicago: Elpenor Books, 1975.

Tymoteusz Karpowicz (The Poetry of Survival), edited by Daniel Weissbort, New York: St. Martin's Press, 1991, 185–89.

Stranger at the Door (Kiedy ktoś zapuka), translated by Haline Carroll, 1967, Polish Radio.

KARTOTEKA (The Card-Index) (see Różewicz).

KASPROWICZ, JAN (1860–1926), a poet, playwright, critic, and translator, son of a simple peasant from the Kujawy region, made his debut in 1882 in *Kłosy* (Ears of Corn). He worked for various daily papers (*Kurier Lwowski* [Lvov Courier], *Słowo Polskie* [Polish Word]) as literary editor and theatrical reviewer. He joined the Socialist movement in 1884, when he was a student in Leipzig, and later studied in Warsaw. He published several articles in the Geneva newspapers of the proletariat; in 1887 he was arrested twice and sentenced to six months of imprisonment. During World War I he was connected with the National Democracy movement. He received his doctorate from the University in Lwów, on the basis of his dissertation on Teofil Lenartowicz. He then held the chair of comparative literary studies in Lvov. In 1921–22 he was the rector of Lvov University. He was married three times, for the third time to a Russian woman, Maria Bunin, who left a set of memories, *W naszym górskim domu* (In Our Mountain Home, 1969). After 1924 he lived permanently in Harenda near Poronin na Podhalu (in the Tatra Highlands), where he died.

Kasprowicz began writing early, while still at school, under the influence of the Romantics. During his stay in Leipzig (1884) he became fascinated with the current cultural trends in Germany, namely naturalism, and with the philosophical views of A. Schopenhauer and E. Hartmann, as well as with monism. Germany was then under the spell of P. B. Shelley, in poetry as well as ideology. These ideas inspired Kasprowicz to write his long poem *Giordano Bruno* (1884) and the dramatic poem (with certain features of a mystery play) *Aryman i Oromaz* (Aryman and Oromaz, 1884 or 1885). Soon, however, Kasprowicz entered a purely naturalistic period in his work, which lasted until 1891. He was then mostly concerned with the peasant class, although he also wrote a few poems about the city proletariat. The poems, mostly narrative or descriptive, are an original and unique attempt at creating naturalistic poetry; they introduce many innovations in composition, imagery, and versification (Kasprowicz experimented with unrhymed verse, distant rhyme, free verse, etc.). The following cycles belong to this period: *Obrazki natury* (Pictures of Nature), *Ze Śląska* (From Silesia), *Z chałupy* (From the Peasant's Hut), *Obrazy i obrazki chłopskie* (Peasant Pictures and Paintings), *Obrazy, gawędy i opowiadania* (Pictures, Tales and Stories), *Z swojskiej flory* (From Native Flora); he also wrote a volume of tales, *Z chłopskiego zagonu* (From the Peasant's Field, 1891). A characteristic feature of these works is the concept of the narrator as a character within the community described. During the same period Kasprowicz also wrote a cycle of sonnets, *Z więzienia* (From Prison), which reflects his ideological crisis and his turning away from Socialism; a cycle of poems on biblical themes; and a number of publicistic poems-manifestos. The majority of works from this period appeared in the collections *Poezje* (Poems, 1888) and *Anima lachrymans i inne nowe poezje* (Anima Lachrymans and Other New Poems, 1884). Among the naturalistic works by Kasprowicz are a drama, *Świat się kończy* (The Word Is Ending, 1891), dealing with the collapse of the traditional rural ethos in relation to the advent of capitalism, and a religious epic, *Chrystus* (Christ, 1890), the first signal of Kasprowicz's turn to metaphysical and ethical problems.

After 1891 Kasprowicz's poetry shows a turn to modernist trends: *Miłość* (Love), 1895, which contains the third part of the trilogy of the same title (the earlier two parts are naturalistic); three longer poems under the title *Z gór* (From Mountains); and *Krzak dzikiej róży* (The Wild Rose Bush, 1898). In 1899 he published the "dramatic poem" *Bunt Napierskiego* (The Napierski's Rebellion), a tragedy about the defeat of a social revolution as a result of the immaturity of the masses and moral imperfection of the leader. As early as 1897 Kasprowicz published several works which marked the expressionist stage in his modernist output. The finest achievements of that period are two collections of hymns—*Ginącemu światu* (To a Dying World, 1902) and *Salve Regina* (1902). The period came to a close with the dramatic poem *Uczta Herodiady* (The Feast of Herodias, 1905), based on the motive of Salome, a very popular figure in modernism, and a volume of poetic prose, *O bohaterskim koniu i walącym się domu* (About a Heroic Horse and a House Falling Down, 1906). After the hymns a new tendency—primitivism—can be discerned in Kasprowicz's poetry: a reaching out to rural folklore and tradition, to the cult of ordinary man and his everyday problems, and to a naive means of artistic expression. During this period, Kasprowicz also wrote ballads, based on authentic folk motives (*Ballada o słoneczniku* [A Ballad About a Sunflower], 1908), and prose adaptations of folk tales (*Bajki, klechdy i baśnie* [Fables, Tales and Fairy Tales], 1902). After 1906 the dominant tone of his lyrics is the acceptance of the world of the simple folk (the highlanders from Podhale), Franciscanism, and faith in a personal God, a view resembling Catholic personalism. These beliefs are reflected in three subsequent collections of poems: *Chwile* (Moments, 1911), *Księga ubogich* (The Book of the Poor, 1916), and *Mój świat* (My World, 1926). The primitivist tendency appears again in his drama *Marcholt gruby a sprośny* (Marcholt, the Fat and the Bawdy, completed in 1913 and published in 1920). Mention should also be made of his drama *Sita* (Sita, 1917), which, like some of his earlier poems, is based on Indian motives.

Kasprowicz was also very productive as a journalist and publicist, writing political and social articles, historical brochures, literary reviews, and sketches. He translated many important works from Greek, Latin, English, German, French, Norwegian, and Dutch.

Księga ubogich (The Book of the Poor), a collection of lyrical poems, was first published in *Kurier Poznański* in 1915, then in Lvov in 1916. According to Jan Józef Lipski, the new tendencies in Karpowicz's poetry take final shape in this collection: acceptance of the world, which appears after his Promethean revolt in *Hymny,* taking the stand adumbrated by

Catholic personalism, mainly reflected in the new concept of the harmony between bodily and spiritual factors in a man's personality, as well as in the understanding of nature (the region of the Tatry and Podhale) as evidence of the existence of a personal God. The ethical nature of this volume (the cult of naturalness, of the simple man) is a basic reflection of Franciscanism in Polish literature. It can also be seen in the origin of the title: the name *Biblia pauperum* was used in the Middle Ages to refer to an illustrated version of the Bible for simple folk.

(See *Młoda Polska.*)

BIBLIOGRAPHY

Dzieła (Works), edited by S. Kołaczkowski, Volumes 1–22, Warsaw, 1930.

Jan Józef Lipski, *Twórczość Jana Kasprowicza,* Volumes 1–2, Warsaw, 1967–75.

KAZANIA ŚWIĘTOKRZYSKIE (The Sermons of the Holy Cross) (see Medieval Literature).

KISIELEWSKI, STEFAN (1911–91) (pseudonyms Kisiel, Teodor Klon, and Tomasz Staliński), a prose writer, political essayist, journalist, music composer, and critic, came from a family with rich literary and artistic traditions (his uncle, Jan August, was a well-known playwright; his father, Zygmunt, was a man of letters and a journalist). He started his journalistic career in 1932, while still a student of music at the Warsaw Conservatory (he received degrees in theory of music, composition, and piano). He also studied Polish philology at Warsaw University. From 1938 he worked with the conservative periodical *Bunt Młodych* (Youth's Rebellion), edited by Jerzy Giedroyc (who later, as the director of the émigré Literary Institute in Paris and editor-in-chief of the monthly *Kultura* [Culture], became the publisher of the majority of Kisielewski's works). A participant in the Polish-German war in 1939, he took part in the underground literary life during the occupation and, in 1944, fought in the Warsaw Uprising as a soldier of the *Armia Krajowa.* After 1945 he settled in Cracow, where he became a longtime contributing editor to the Catholic periodical *Tygodnik Powszechny* (The Universal Weekly), writing feuilletons under the pseudonym "Kisiel" until 1989. He also lectured at the Music College, from which he was expelled in 1949 by the Communist authorities. Taking advantage of the possibilities opened up by the limited liberalization after Stalin's death, Kisielewski made an attempt at independent political activity as a member of the Parliament (1957–1965) as a delegate of a small Catholic group, *Znak* (The Sign). After his return from Warsaw in 1965, he was active in campaigns for the defense of citizens' rights; in 1968, as a result of his criticizing censorship and the government's cultural policy, he was punished by a ban on his publishing activities. At the beginning of the 1970s he published his works in émigré periodicals and publishing houses (in Paris, London, Chicago), and later in the underground publications in Poland. In the last years of his life he, after the collapse of the Communist system, became a member of a newly created, liberal conservative party, *Unia Polityki Realnej* (Union of Realistic Policy).

Kisielewski's work, including both literary and journalistic writings, is one of the strongest testimonials to the existence of independent Polish thought: he took on the challenge of Communism and opposed Marxist dogmatism with an individual view of the world based on common sense, rationalism, and skepticism, as well as traditional values, shaped by Christian philosophy and moderate European liberalism. His immense collection of feuilletons ran for almost a half-century in *Tygodnik Powszechny*, in a series entitled, respectively, *Pod Włos* (Rubbing the Wrong Way), *Łopatą do głowy* (In the Simplest Terms), *Gwoździe w mózgu* (Nails in the Brain), *Głową w ściany* (Beating One's Head Against the Walls), *Wołanie na puszczy* (Into Deaf Ears), *Widziane inaczej* (Seen Differently), *Bez dogmatu* (Without Dogma), and *Sam sobie celem . . .* (A Goal unto Himself. . .). It became for the Polish intelligentsia a school of political education which was free of any dogmas and was able to pass independent judgment and to criticize any authority, from the official Communist ideology to the social teachings of the Catholic Church. The attractiveness of Kisielewski's feuilletons was augmented by the zesty style of his disputes, his brilliant humor, his ability to utilize the art of irony and innuendo (useful at navigating the obstacle course of censorship), and his excellent command of the Polish language, voicing Kisielewski's fierce objection to the invasion of Communist "Newspeak." Selected feuilletons and essays on various topics (i.e., music) were published in the collections *Polityka i sztuka* (Politics and Art, 1949), *Rzeczy małe* (The Small Things, 1956), *Z muzyką przez lata* (With Music Throughout the Years, 1957), *Opowiadania i Podróże* (Tales and Travels, 1959), *Z muzycznej międzyepoki* (From the Musical Inter-Epoch, 1966), *Muzyka i mózg* (Music and the Brain, 1974), *Z literackiego lamusa* (From the Literary Junkroom, 1979), and in collections published abroad, *100 razy głową w ściany* (100 Times Beating One's Head Against the Wall, Paris, 1972), *Materii pomieszanie* (The Confusion of Matter, London, 1973), *Moje dzwony trzydziestolecia* (My Bells on the Thirtieth Anniversary, Chicago, 1978). He published the essay *Na czym polega socjalizm* (What Socialism Is All About), which unveils the absurdities of Socialist economics, mostly with the Western reader in mind. Kisielewski treated his novels as a useful means of conveying his views, enabling him to reach any group of readers, through the broadness and attractiveness of the genre of fiction (he often used the form of a thriller). Besides the psychological novel *Sprżysiężenie* (The Conspiracy, 1949), and several books dealing with customs and morality published under the pseudonym "Teodor Klon" (e.g., *Miałem tylko jedno życie* [I Only Had One Life, 1958]), he published a whole series of political novels under the pseudonym "Tomasz Staliński": *Widziane z góry* (Seen from Above, Paris, 1967), *Cienie w pieczarze* (Shadows in the Cavern, Paris, 1971), *Romans zimowy* (The Winter Romance), *Śledztwo* (The Investigation, Paris, 1974), *Przygoda w Warszawie* (The Adventure in Warsaw, Paris, 1976), *Ludzie w akwarium* (People in the Aquarium, Paris, 1976), *Podróż w czasie* (Journey in Time), and *Widziane Inaczej* (Seen Differently, Paris, 1986). The novels make up a full record of Polish life under postwar Sovietization, rich in moral, social, and political facts. The novels present the various forms in which Communist totalitarianism functions in daily life and how it infiltrates people's consciousness and behavior. They show both the dangerous and destructive and the grotesquely absurd aspects of the system brought into existence by Communism. The last book by Kisielewski is also the most widely read: *Abecadło Kisiela* (Kisiel's Alphabet, 1990) is a series of 250 miniature portraits of personages of Polish political and cultural life personally known to him, painted with good-natured irony.

KNIAŹNIN, FRANCISZEK DIONIZY (1749–1807), a poet and playwright, entered a monastery and in 1770 became a teacher in a Jesuit college in Warsaw, thus participating in the life of the intellectual elite of his time. After 1773, when the monastery was dispersed, his life became linked with the V.A.K. Czartoryski family, teaching literature and acting as the prince's secretary, literary adviser, and court poet. In 1792 he began displaying signs of insanity; he was still able to work in 1796, but the defeat of Kościuszko's Uprising in 1794 and the destruction of the Czartoryski's famous family estate in Puławy led him into complete loss of control. He spent his late years with Franciszek Zabłocki, who took care of him.

Kniaźnin wrote his first poems in Latin while in school and made his literary debut in 1774. In 1766 he published a volume of fables based on the model of La Fontaine. His most characteristic collection, *Erotyki* (Erotica, Volumes 1–2), appeared in 1779 and contains some of Kniaźnin's best work, such as his famous *Oda do Wąsów* (Ode to Whiskers), as well as translations and adaptations of ancient and contemporary poets. The works show some Rococo inclinations: Kniaźnin maintained that the main role of literature was to express joy of life, together with exploring sentimental themes which expressed the poet's personal experiences and thoughts. These poems display the author's linguistic skill but also show that the poet kept his distance from the literary conventions that he was realizing. In 1783 Kniaźnin published another collection, *Wiersze* (Poems), in which some of his earlier poems were adapted to the more "tender" norms of sentimentalism. During the period spent in Puławy (after 1783), the poet's interests were centered on conventional themes, the life of the court and current political events. In his collection *Poezje* (Poetry) (Volumes

1–3, 1787–88) Kniaźnin rejected all of his earlier achievements, and the few works he selected were adapted to the official moralizing tone of the poetry written during the reign of King Stanisław August. Kniaźnin referred to the works of this period as odes, employing some of the features of the Classicist ode, but creating his own variety of the genre. The themes of his odes were patriotic (e.g., *Matka Obywatelka, Do Zgody, Do Ojczyzny* [Mother Citizen, To Agreeing, To the Homeland], reflective or personal (e.g., *Do lutni, Do nocy* [To a Lute, To Night]). The system of values that his poems reflect, in which goodness, happiness, friendship, and virtue share the highest position, reflects an ideal moral order; the same values are underscored in his numerous religious poems and paraphrases of the Psalms. He also continued writing idylls and humorous pieces. His works connected with court life are lengthy poems, such as *Balon* (The Sphere) and *Rozmaryn* (Rosemary)(written during 1784–85), and foremost, dramas written for the Puławy Court Theater to give an air of glamour to the various celebrations or to support current political views of his sponsor. In addition Kniaźnin composed dramatic idylls (e.g., *Trzy gody* [Three Festivities], 1790); an opera-buffo opera, *Cyganie* (The Gypsies); patriotic operas (e.g., *Matka Spartanka* [A Spartan Mother]); a tragedy, *Hektor* (1792–93), in which he depicted the tragic situation of his dying homeland. Kniaźnin translated many works from Classical literature (Horace, Anacreon), as well as McPherson's *The Songs of Ossian.* According to Teresa Kostkiewiczowa, Kniaźnin's works were shaped by the aesthetic standards of his epoch and the demands of the court in Puławy. They are, however, highly original and give evidence that Kniaźnin was one of the greatest poets of the Enlightenment. His poetry was admired by his contemporaries, and his appearance—an ever-present moustache and traditional Polish clothes—as well as his personal life (especially his affection for one of the daughters of Prince Czartoryski) made him a theme of a literary legend and the subject of numerous poetic works.

(See Enlightenment.)

BIBLIOGRAPHY

Wybór poezji (Selected Poetry), edited by W. Borowy, Wrocław, 1948.
Utwory dramatyczne: Wybór (Dramatic Works: A Selection), edited by A. Jendrysik, Warsaw, 1958.

KOCHANOWSKI, JAN (Joannes Cochanovius) (1530–84), a poet, was the greatest representative of humanistic national poetry of the Polish Renaissance and the most outstanding poetic personality of the Slavic countries between the Middle Ages and Romanticism. He came from a Małopolska (Little Poland) noble family of moderate means, with six brothers and five sisters. After 1544, when he enrolled in the Cracow Academy, he lived the life of a student and a peripatetic intellectual for over fifteen years. The Cracow period was interrupted several times by family problems which prevented Kochanowski from earning his degree. During his peregrinations Kochanowski stopped at Królewiec (Koenigsberg, 1551–52 and 1555–56). The decisive period of his studies came with his stays in Padua (1552–59), with interruptions: the first stay, 1552–55, interrupted through the plague, after which lectures were suspended; the second 1556–57, the third 1558–59. He managed to earn his degree, then traveled to France, and returned to Poland in 1559.

The affair with his brothers and sisters concerning the division of parental inheritance inaugurated the court period in Kochanowski's life, which lasted fifteen years. At first he worked for various magnate families in Małopolska; in late 1563 or early 1564 he became secretary and courtier at the Royal Castle of Wawel. These years marked the most comprehensive development of his talent, undoubtedly under the influence of the intellectual atmosphere of the king's residence, and of Cracow in general, then the most important center of literary life and humanistic thought in Eastern Europe. He also became interested in various ideological trends of the period (the Reformation and Counter-Reformation), and the political life of the state, especially in the area of legal reform. In 1567 Kochanowski accompanied the king to Lithuania; in 1569 to Lublin, where Kochanowski witnessed the session of the *Sejm* which decided upon the union of Poland and Lithuania. Supposedly after 1571 his links with the court were weakened, and he spent much of his time at his estate in Czarnolas. He returned to political life after the death of King Zygmunt August; he took active part in the election of Henryk Valois (1573). Soon, however, deeply disappointed, he broke his contacts with the court and settled down in the country, around 1575, having earlier married Dorota Podlodowska. His marriage and stay in Czarnolas opened the third period of his life and works, typical of the Polish noble landowners of the Renaissance. These were the years of family bliss and contemplative, peaceful writing. However, he did not totally cut himself off from political life, as can be seen in his writings, and despite the disappointment he was able to recognize the political talent of Stefan Batory. After 1579 the peace of his family life was profoundly affected by the unexpected death of his beloved daughter Orszula, whom he mourned in his masterpiece, *Treny* (Threnodies). A few years later his daughter Hanna died. These traumatic experiences, along with failing health and recurring thoughts of death, cast a deep shadow on his literary work. At the same time he became concerned with the poetic output of his life. He did not live to see the publication of a complete edition of his works (*Jan Kochanowski,* Cracow, 1585–86): he died unexpectedly, of a heart attack, during a convocation in Lublin.

We know practically nothing about Kochanowski's early poetic attempts, except that he had started very early (e.g., a Latin epigram in 1552 and

Pieśń o potopie [Song About the Flood]); his published works appeared much later. In Padua he wrote poetry in Latin, mainly elegies, epigrams, and odes. His student years also witnessed a number of works in Polish, among others the famous hymn *Czego chcesz od nas, Panie* (What Do You Want of Us, Lord), which praises the order and beauty of the world and God as the creator of the abundance of life and the harmony of nature. During his early years Kochanowski primarily wrote epics, considerably varied in their themes and forms: storytelling—*Zuzanna* (Susanna, 1562), humorous—*Szachy* (Chess, between 1564 and 1566), commemorative paeans—*O śmierci Jana Tarnowskiego* (On the Death of Jan Tarnowski, 1561), and, above all, political and ideological epics—for example, *Zgoda* (Agreement, written perhaps in 1562 and published in 1564) and *Satyr, albo Dziki Mąż* (Satyr, or The Wild Husband, around 1564). The latter two works inaugurated the poet's career at the royal court. In time, however, his interests shifted almost totally to lyrical writings in Polish, which best suited the poet's psychological inclinations and artistic talent. His first attempts included *Pieśni* (Songs), based on Horace and Petrarch, patriotic and philosophical in their themes, which created a foundation for modern poetic language and provided an artistic form for Polish lyrical writings. *Fraszki* (Trifles), written throughout the poet's lifetime, sometimes jocular, often serious, contained epic elements intertwined with a lyrical and personal tone. Some time later Kochanowski turned to composing Latin odes, mostly political and commemorative, contained in the collection *Lyricorum libellus* (1580). His most important work during this period was a translation, or rather, a verse paraphrase, of *Psałterz Dawidowy* (The Psalms of David), based on the Latin models of George Buchanan, Jan Campensis, and C. Marot. Among other significant works during the court period are the following: a humorous work, *Broda* (The Beard); a poetic manifesto, *Muza* (The Muse, written around 1567); an epic, *Proporzec albo Hołd pruski* (The Pennant or The Prussian Tribute, written in 1569); political dialogues; translations from Greek; and a Renaissance tragedy written in the Classical style, *Odprawa posłów greckich* (The Dismissal of The Greek Envoys, staged in 1578).

The Czarnolas period of Kochanowski's life includes works based on earlier themes, although these new works are now enriched with an idyllic tone best seen in some of the songs. New elements were introduced in his famous cycle *Treny* (Threnodies) and in a little prose treatise on Slavic mythology, *O Czechu i Lechu* (About Czech and Lech, left unfinished).

Kochanowski was truly a great poet. He enriched Polish literature by introducing a modern poetic language, with a variety of new literary forms in various genres, a personal style, and original versification. According to Tadeusz Ulewicz, he gave a firm footing to syllabic verse, making it fluent, varied in rhythm and stanzaic forms, enabling it to express a wide spectrum of moods—from an anecdote appropriate to be told at a dinner table and the intimate atmosphere of a love confession to the serious tone of a prayer, the pathos of a catastrophic warning, and elegiac grief and despair. He was the first poet to add a special dimension to the universe of man's personal inner life; at the same time, he remained a keen observer of outside reality—everyday life, public affairs, and especially national problems. He was also deeply concerned about reforming the political system and raising cultural standards. His personality was formed by the prevailing intellectual atmosphere of the era, the influence of humanism and the Renaissance. In Poland he was the chief representative, the embodiment of these ideals. From Classical tradition he drew upon the Epicurean attitude of Horatio and the stoicism of Seneca. He expressed a faith in the harmony of the world, in the laws of nature, in the capability of the human mind, its capacity to go beyond religious dogma. He considered virtue, especially service to one's country, to be a superior value. He was fond of the heroic myths concerning Hercules and Orpheus and believed that poetry brought immortal fame. He was widely considered the greatest poet among Poles and Slavs. Even in his early court period he was considered "the love of his century." He remained admired, loved, and respected for generations, praised by poets, depicted with love and admiration in literature and in painting. His works were translated into other languages as early as the seventeenth century.

Fraszki (Trifles), a collection of short poetic works written throughout Kochanowski's life, was published in Cracow in 1584, shortly before the author's death. It is an important literary document, unfolding the intellectual attitude of a poet during his personal experiences and thoughts. An admirer of Classical writers, Kochanowski included in his *Fraszki* a number of translations of Anacreontic Greek poems, as well as the works of Sappho and the Roman poet Martial. He created a perfect artistic form for his observations of the life around him—at court, in town, and in the country. In the concise epigrammatic form he portrayed various contemporaries whom he met at the king's court: officials, bishops, as well as the famous king's jester Stańczyk. When he left the court, he devoted himself to farming and expressed in poetic form his admiration for country life, often spent in the shadow of his beloved linden tree. This collection, containing over three hundred works, represents the values which the poet appreciated most: the warmth of friendship, the courtly admiration of a woman, and the high regard of a writer's profession. Kochanowski repeatedly enunciated his conviction about the lasting value of his work and defended his right to see and present the world in his own way.

Pieśni (Songs), a collection of lyrical poems, written in the spirit of humanism and the Renaissance, was basically modeled on Horatio, sometimes on Petrarch. Basically the collection contains forty-nine poems in two books; the publisher, however, added *Pieśń świętojańska o Sobótce* (St. John's Eve) and a much older work, *Czego chcesz od nas, Panie* (What Do

You Want of Us, Lord). *Pieśni* were composed over a period of more than twenty years, mainly during the court period of Kochanowski's life, but also during his stay in Czarnolas. The poet continued polishing and correcting these works throughout his life. They were published in 1586, after his death. Even before publication, the collection circulated in manuscript and was widely known and admired.

The collection marks a major step in Kochanowski's work on the Polish poetic language, in which he introduced new forms in stanza and verse, revealing new horizons for poetic expression in Polish. They are quite varied in their themes: love, philosophical and religious reflection, picturesque history and honest patriotism, current themes, and poems for social occasions.

Treny (Threnodies), a cycle of nineteen lyrical poems written after the death of the poet's daughter, Orszula Kochanowska, closed with *Epitafium Hannie Kochanowskiej* (Epitaph for Hanna Kochanowska), who soon followed her sister in death. Published in Cracow in 1580, *Treny* is the last and the most mature and the most uniform collection in the output of the poet, summing up his creative experiences and his earlier reflection on the sense of human existence and the universe around him, governed by laws of reason. While other collections by Kochanowski were created over several years or even decades, *Treny* was written in just a few months. It was associated with just one event which shook the foundations of the poet's attitude toward life—the death of his beloved daughter, two and a half years old, who was beginning her life and at the same time saying farewell to it. The structure of the cycle, which ends on a note of consolation in *Tren XIX, albo Sen* (Threnody XIX, or Dream), has certain features of a complete poem, even though individual poems can be read as separate lyrics. The author intended that *Treny* would be a literary monument erected to his lost child, a fact which shocked a number of sixteenth century readers. Comparing Orszula to the Greek poetess Sappho, endowing the child with unusual, adult characteristics, Kochanowski acted against the rules of the poetics of his time, which reserved the term *personae graves* (serious literary persons) for adults and people with certain merits: Kochanowski felt that for a father a lost daughter cannot be considered an unimportant person (*persona levis*); the father's grief made her great, equal to Classical heroines. The main character of *Treny,* however, is not Orszula, but her mourning father, a man of the Renaissance, whose carefully erected edifice of ideals of wisdom and virtue falls apart as a result of the cruel turn of fate. In the moment of trial of the father, these ideals appeared to be empty formulae, consistent and sophisticated, and yet counteracted by his experience. The main theme of *Treny* is the great philosophical crisis of a man of the Renaissance and his attempts, eventually successful, at overcoming the crisis and finding firm ground. In *Tren XIX, albo Sen,* the tormented father regains his inner balance with the thought that a man of reason has to act with reason and dignity during moments of joy, as well as moments of despair; he has to bear his human fate as a human being. The conclusion, certainly free of cheap optimism, is thoroughly humanistic in nature.

Treny is also a work of the Renaissance in regard to form—in composition and style it refers to Classical models, as well as to contemporary funeral cycles by Petrarch, Pontano, Ronsard, and others. Classical in its uniformity, in the modesty of ornamentation, varied and sophisticated in verse, *Treny* is a highly innovative and original work. Translated into various languages, it has provided inspiration for thousands of poets.

(See Renaissance.)

BIBLIOGRAPHY

Dzieła wszystkie (Complete Works), The Parliament (Sejmowe) Edition, Volumes 1–4, Warsaw, 1983.

Dzieła polskie (Polish Works), tenth edition, edited by Julian Krzyżanowski, Warsaw: Państwowy Instytut Wydawniczy, 1980.

Janusz Pelc, *Jan Kochanowski: Szczyt renesansu w literaturze polskiej* (Jan Kochanowski: The Height of the Renaissance in Polish Literature), Warsaw, 1980.

Wiktor Weintraub, *Rzecz czarnoleska* (The Czarnolas Matter), Cracow: Wydawnictwo Literackie, 1977.

English

Poems, translated by D. P. Radin, M. B. Peacock, G. R. Noyes, and others, Berkeley: University of California Press, 1928.

Poems, translated by D. P. Radin, New York: AMS Press, 1978.

Odprawa posłów greckich:

The Dismissal of the Grecian Envoys, translated by George Rapall Noyes, Berkeley: University of California Press, 1918.

Treny:

Laments, translated by D. P. Radin, Berkeley: University of California Press, 1920.

Pieśni świętojańskie:

St. John's Eve, translated by G. R. Noyes and M. B. Peacock, *Slavonic Review VI,* 1927.

KOLBERG, (HENRYK) OSKAR (1814–80), an ethnographer, folklorist, musician, and composer, was the son of a university professor in Warsaw. He was closely connected with representatives of the scientific and artistic milieu of Warsaw. He studied economy and music and worked as a teacher of music, and later as an accountant. He wrote several entries on music and musicology for Orgelbrand's encyclopedia.

In 1839 Kolberg began collecting folk songs from the Warsaw region. As a folklorist, he had the aim of determining the character of Slavic music; as a composer, he developed folk motives in the shorter forms (*kujawiak, mazurek*) and one-act folk plays (e.g., *Janek spod Ojcowa* [Johnny from Ojcow] by J. K. Gregorowicz and *Król pasterzy* [King of the Shepherds] by T. Lenartowicz). In his research work on musical folklore he updated methods of recording materials and the form for publishing his findings. In his publication of *Pieśni ludu polskiego* (Songs of the Polish People, 1842, and later in 1846–47 in the periodical *Przyjaciel Ludu* [Friend of the People]) he censored the material by omitting songs containing obscenities and superstitions; in the collection *O pieśniach litewskich* (About Lithuanian Songs), published in 1846 in *Dzwon Literacki* (Literary Bell), he gave the texts in Polish and Lithuanian, providing a comparative analysis and tracing Scandinavian, Latvian, and German influences. His collection *Pieśni czeskie i słowackie* (Czech and Slovak Songs) (also published in *Dzwon Literacki,* 1846) is primarily source material. He supplied all the songs he published with a piano accompaniment. Unlike many other Romantic folklorists, he did not halt his research after 1848. His main publication is *Pieśni ludu polskiego* (Volumes 1–12, 1856–57), the most substantial and most varied work of this type in existence (with 910 sources), complete with folk texts in their authentic form. He hoped that this collection would lay the foundation for future historical and comparative studies. He also traveled to the south of Europe; as a result of his travels he published the collection *Obrazy Słowiańszczyzny południowej* (A Picture of South Slavic Lands), which appeared in *Gazeta Polska* (The Polish Gazette) in 1871–72, an unprecedentedly broad and well-documented description of the social structure and material culture of the ethnic groups of Slovenia, Croatia, Serbia, and Montenegro. In 1865 he revised his original concept of *Pieśni* (Songs) and decided to include additional materials and change the title to *Lud: Jego zwyczaje, sposób życia, mowa, podania, przysłowia, obrzędy, gusła, zabawy, pieśni, muzyka i tańce* (The People: Their Customs, Way of Life, Speech, Legends, Proverbs, Ceremonies, Sorcery, Games, Songs, Music and Dance, Volumes 1–23, including the *Pieśni* of 1857 and 1890). According to Ryszard Górski, this monumental work was meant to outline the picture of folk life and culture in the nineteenth century through ethnographic monographs of individual regions, distinguished on the basis of administrative divisions. The source materials come from his own collection and from manuscripts offered by other folklorists; some were found in old manuscripts, in publications, in calendars and literature. The materials gathered together in Kolberg's major publications contain 12,500 songs, over 550 folk tales, and 2,710 proverbs. A great deal of material exists in manuscript form. Kolberg's extraordinary work (unfinished) was highly appreciated by his contemporaries as well as by future generations.

BIBLIOGRAPHY

Dzieła wszystkie (Complete Works), Volumes 1–68, introduction by Julian Krzy żanowski, edited by J. Burszta, J. Krzyżanowski, and after 1977 by G. Łabuda, Wrocław-Poznań: Towarzystwo Ludoznawcze, 1961–1990.

KOŁAKOWSKI, LESZEK (born 1927), a philosopher, dramatist, essayist, journalist, and prose writer, has been labeled "The Polish Socialist Hus." From 1953 to 1955 Kołakowski taught Marxist Philosophy at a Communist Party school, the Institute for the Training of Scientific Workers, and became a lecturer at Warsaw University. In 1959 he was appointed Professor of Modern Philosophy; he was also a professor at the Institute of Philosophy and Sociology of the Polish Academy of Sciences.

In 1955 Kołakowski joined the editorial staff of the maverick weekly *Po prostu* (In Plain Words), which was a presage of the Polish October, 1956, during which time the Poles rebelled against censorship and political abuse. Wladystaw Gomuzka came into power. The authorities disbanded the group in 1957, but the tides demanding reform were unleashed. Kołakowski became the philosophical spokesman for the movement which the Communist authorities considered revisionist. In 1966 he was deprived of his Party membership and later lost his chair at Warsaw University. In 1968 he left Poland and settled in England, where he became a professor at Oxford University (Fellow of All Souls College). He took active part in several political, cultural, and scientific initiatives, supporting the struggle against Communist totalitarianism, in Poland (he was an active member of *KOR*) as well as on the international scene. He is a member of the British Academy, the American Academy of Arts and Sciences, the International Institute of Philosophy, a laureate of several prestigious awards, among others, the Peace Prize of German Booksellers (1977) and *Prix Europeen D'Essai* (1980). Kołakowski's scholarly works encompass a wide circle of issues from the field of cultural philosophy, philosophy and history of religion, history of modern and contemporary philosophy, ethics, and philosophy of politics. His studies in these fields have been translated into almost all the European languages, and Japanese and Korean as well. His views underwent a significant evolution, as with many twentieth century intellectuals, from "institutional Marxism" and Communism, from delusive hopes of the renewal of the road cutting off totalitarianism and dogmatic Stalinist legacy (so-called revisionism), up to a deep and comprehensively justified criticism of Marxism, which he designated as "the greatest fantasy of the twentieth century," and, at the same time, the basis of a system of mass crime and terror (his fundamental synthetic work, *Główne nurty marksizmu* [Main Currents of Marxism, Volumes 1–3], published in Paris, 1976–79).

Kołakowski's most important works include *Świadomość religijna i więź kościelna: Studia nad Chrześcijaństwem bezwyznaniowym XVII wieku* (Religious Awareness and Church Ties: A Study of Nondenominational Christianity of the Seventeenth Century, 1965), *Kultura i fetysze* (Culture and Fetishes, 1967), *Obecność mitu* (The Presence of Myth, Paris, 1972), and *Religia* (Religion, 1983). In addition to these are numerous studies published in German.

Parallel with his scholarly work, Kołakowski engages in essayistic studies, and at times in purely literary work. In 1959 he published his most influential essay, *Kapłan i błazen* (The Priest and Jester), which beyond actual political references also had meaning for literature, and literally inaugurated the Polish theater of the absurd. His stricture directed to all artists and society at large called for "a negative vigilance in the face of any absolute." For the next decade the Jester-Priest metaphor became a staple of Polish theater and drama, from Mrożek and Różewicz to Iredyński and Broszkiewicz.

He published several collections, including essays on various themes, *Czy diabeł może być Zbawiony i 27 innych kazań* (Can the Devil Be Saved and 27 Other Sermons, 1982). As a prose writer he is the author of perverse philosophical tales, *Klucz niebieski albo Opowieści budujące z historii świętej zebrane ku pouczeniu i przestrodze* (A Heavenly Key or Edifying Stories from Holy History Gathered for Instruction and Admonition, 1957), *13 bajek z królestwa Lailonii dla dużych i małych* (13 Fairy Tales from the Kingdom of Lailonia for Big and Small, 1963), and *Rozmowy z diabłem* (The Devil and Scripture, 1965). As a dramatist, Kołakowski wrote the comic farce *System księdza Jensena albo wejście i wyjście* (Father Jensen's System or Entrance and Exit, *Dialog,* 1965), *Żebrak i ładna dziewczyna* (The Beggar and the Beautiful Girl), as well as the film scenario, *Wygnanie z raju* (Banishment from Paradise, *Dialog,* 1961). These works are humorous but have a philosophic base, namely the concept of Kołakowski's Jester-Priest metaphor.

BIBLIOGRAPHY

English

The Devil and Scripture, London: Oxford University Press, 1973.

Main Currents of Marxism, two volumes, London: Oxford University Press, 1978.

Marxism and Beyond: An Historical Understanding and Individual Responsibility, London, 1969.

E. J. Czerwiński, "*Kołakowski and the Jester-Priest Metaphor,*" *The Polish Review,* Summer, 1968, 62–71.

KOŁŁĄTAJ, HUGO (1750–1812), political activist and writer, theoretician of science and organizer of educational reforms, historian, and philosopher, was the youngest son in a noble family of modest means. A clergyman from 1775, he studied in Cracow, Vienna, and Rome, where he became acquainted with the philosophical and scientific ideas of the Enlightenment. He devoted his life to developing these ideals and putting them into practice. His public activity was mostly devoted to the Commission for National Education. As the rector of the Cracow Academy (1783–86), he changed this scholastic, anachronous university into a modern center of academic education and research.

In 1786 he settled in Warsaw, where he soon began a brilliant political career: in 1791 he was raised to the rank of a minister. He soon developed into one of the nation's leaders during the period 1789–94, adapting a more and more radical, though still well-tempered program of "benign revolution." He wanted to transform feudal society, then dominated by the magnates, into a modern bourgeois state, though maintaining monarchical status, in which the rich nobility and middle class would be dominant forces, governed by a permanent parliament. He actively supported the middle class in its struggle for political rights. He ran a campaign for this cause in his political writings, *Listy Anonima* (Letters from Anonymous, 1788–89) and *Ostatnia przestroga dla Polski* (The Last Warning for Poland, 1790), and gathered around him other men of letters (the so-called *Kuźnica Kołłątajowska*). He was one of the authors of the Constitution of the Third of May but considered it to be merely a stage in his conception of far-reaching reform.

According to Zofia Lewinówna, Kołłątaj—a daring reformer in his program, a realist in his actions—lacked the strength of character that future events demanded: after the catastrophe of 1792 (the perfidious Confederacy of Targowica) he assumed a conformist position, advising the king to join the confederacy; he himself went abroad. He was still politically active as an émigré, becoming more and more radical in his views. In Leipzig in 1793 he published (together with Ignacy Potocki and Franciszek K. Dmochowski) a tract, *O ustanowieniu i upadku Konstytucji polskiej 3 maja 1791* (About the Rise and Fall of the Polish Constitution of the Third of May 1791). He was a coauthor of the daring *Uniwersał Połaniecki,* an unquestionable leader of the left, and a protector of the Jacobins.

Arrested by the Austrian police in 1794, he was imprisoned until 1802. He continued to work while incarcerated, seeking some consolation in writing poetry (e.g., *Smutki* [Sorrows] and *Jobiada* [Jobiad]. He gathered research materials and planned his future work, which aimed at a synthesis of Polish history, which for the first time would include economic and cultural history. Upon his release he settled down on an estate in Wołyń (Volhynia). In spite of seemingly favorable circumstances and his repeated attempts, he was unable to return to political life, principally because of Napoleon's anti-Jacobin attitude.

He was also unable to attain fame as a researcher. Of the enormous work planned and constantly developed, he was able to publish only one, *Porządek fizyczno-moralny* (Physical-Moral Order, 1810), an outline of philosophical anthropology. Two more works appeared after his death: *Stan oświecenia w Polszcze* (The State of Education in Poland, 1841) and *Rozbiór krytyczny zasad historii początkowej wszystkich ludów* (A Critical Analysis of the Laws of History of the Beginning of All Peoples, Volumes 1–3, 1842). It is only recently that Kołłątaj's work has gained the high regard that it deserves.

One of the most outstanding personalities in modern Polish history, he always raised controversial issues—idolized by some, detested by others. In the history of Polish literature his position as a creator of modern argumentative prose is quite secure. In his works clarity and consistency of thought are accompanied with clarity and flexibility of linguistic expression.

BIBLIOGRAPHY

Wybór pism politycznych (Selected Political Writings), edited and with an introduction by B. Leśnodorski, Wrocław, 1951.

Wybór pism naukowych (A Selection of Scholarly Writings), edited and with an introduction by K. Opałek, Warsaw, 1953.

KOMPLEKS POLSKI (The Polish Complex) (see Konwicki).

KONOPNICKA, MARIA (family name Wasiłowska; pseudonyms Marko, Jan Sawa, Jan Waręż) (1842–1910), was a poet, short story writer, author of children's literature, literary critic, publicist, and translator. Her husband was threatened with Russian repressive measures in 1863 after the Uprising; thus she and her family left for Dresden. She returned two years later in order to raise her six children and to continue her self-education. She made her debut as a poet in Kaliszanin in 1870. A few years later she published a cycle of poems, *W górach* (In the Mountains), in *Tygodnik Ilustrowany* (The Illustrated Weekly, 1876). In 1877 she moved to Warsaw, where she continued her literary work and also became a private teacher. After 1878 she took part in all official and underground actions to help political and criminal prisoners. She also worked in educational institutions for women and lower class people. In 1884–86 she was the editor of a women's magazine, *Świt* (Dawn), but her radical program was opposed by the censors and conservative circles. After 1890 she lived abroad but remained in close contact with the country, above all with publishers, the press, and social organizations. She helped organize protests against repressive actions of the Prussian government against Polish children in Września in 1901–2 and championed causes against other forms of discrimination by the authorities in Poland during the period of Poland's partitions. In 1903 during the twenty-fifth anniversary of her literary and social work, she was offered a house in Żarnowiec as a gift from the nation; in 1905–7 she was able to make her way to Warsaw surreptitiously, in order to organize help for imprisoned people and their families.

During the first decade of Konopnicka's literary activity she was best known as a poet and her works gave rise to heated ideological discussion: three volumes of *Poezje* (Poems, 1881, 1883, 1887, with the cycle *Obrazki* [Pictures] included in two of the volumes and a long poem, *Imagina* [Imagination], which was published in fragments in 1886, and later in 1913). These works were influenced by Romantic radical ideas and were faithful to the poetics of Romanticism and the antifeudal ideals of positivism: they gave a dramatic image of society, torn by internal conflicts and deprived of its own state. The unique character of Konopnicka's poetry, which appeared almost from the start, consists of an often incongruous combination of elements which are usually separate: a Romantic revolt against the ties imposed upon an individual and his society, an ambitious view of poetry as a Promethean expression, a cult of imagination, and a very intense appraisal of the poetic value of folklore. Alongside these themes is a persuasive and educational tone, woven together with a journalistic faithfulness to realistic detail. According to Alina Brodzka, Konopnicka's poetic personality can best be appreciated in her poems in the style of folk songs, which appeared mainly in Volumes 2 and 3 of *Poezje* (the cycles *Wieczorne pieśni* [Night Songs], *Na fujarce* [On Pan's Pipe], *Z łąk i pól* [From Meadows and Fields], *Łzy i pieśni* [Tears and Songs], *Piosenki i pieśni* [Ditties and Songs], *Po rosie* [After the Dew], and *Pieśni bez echa* [Songs Without Echo]). In her later works Konopnicka employed syllabotonic versification, although solely syllabic forms appear quite often. After 1890 Konopnicka's poetry became enriched with new motives, particularly references to the European cultural tradition; new ways of referring to biblical and Romantic traditions; and employment of the poetics of symbolism and Parnassism (the cycle *Z mojej Biblii, Poezje* [From My Bible, Poems], Volume 4, 1896; the collection *Italia* [Italy], 1901). She returned to folk stylizations in the collection *Nowe pieśni* (New Songs, 1905). She continued her didactic and incidental works (published under the pseudonym "Jan Sawa") and tried her hand at writing an epic: *Przez głębinę* (Through the Depths, 1907, under the pseudonym "Jan Waręż") and an epic poem about peasant emigration, *Pan Balcer w Brazylii* (Mr. Balcer in Brazil, 1910).

After 1892 Konopnicka wrote a number of short stories: *Cztery nowele* (Four Novelettes, 1888), *Moi znajomi* (My Acquaintances, 1890), *Na drodze* (Along the Way, 1893), and her best known stories, *Nasza szkapa* (Our Mare) and *Mendel Gdański* (A Gdansk Fifteen), *Nowele* (Novelettes, 1897), *Ludzie i rzeczy* (People and Things, 1898), and *Na normandzkim brzegu* (On Normandy's Shore, 1904). She was mostly interested in contemporary themes and remained faithful to the poetics of realism, but her stories are varied in genre: sketches, reminiscences, psychological studies, stories characterized by complex plot, and a broad description of social groups. She created a type of narration which foreshadowed future changes in prose; she employed authentic dialogues in which the narrator, the eyewitness, converses with another character, who is often a person from the lower class but a character integral to the story.

Her writings for children, composed after 1884, were a revelation to contemporary readers. They were free of importunate didacticism; they awakened the reader's aesthetic sensitivity by combining authentic themes with fantasy, jocular with serious moods. They represent new models in individual genres, creating an artistic autonomy in this area of literature: *O krasnoludkach i sierotce Marysi* (About Munchkins and the Orphan Marysia, 1896), *O Janku Wędrowniczku* (About Wandering John, 1893), and *Na jagody* (Berry Picking, 1903).

After 1881 she worked as a literary critic and social publicist, publishing her essays in *Kłosy* (Spikes), *Świt* (Dawn), *Gazeta Polska* (Polish Gazette), and many other journals. Until 1890 she mostly wrote reviews on contemporary Polish and foreign texts. After 1890 she published sketches on contemporary Polish and world literature: *O Adamie Asnyku słów kilka* (A Few Words About Adam Asnyk, 1897) and *O komedii bohaterskiej Edmunda Rostanda i "Krzyżakach" Sienkiewicza* (About the Heroic Comedy of Edmund Rostand and Sienkiewicz's *The Teutonic Knights,* 1900). She also published several important works on the Romantics (Mickiewicz, Słowacki, Lenartowicz, Zaleski). She made a major contribution as a translator from German, Italian, English, Czech, and other languages.

Obrazki (Pictures), a narrative-poetic work, combines the elements of epic, lyric, and persuasive rhetoric. The author employed the title to refer to a group of poems which appeared in several collections: *Co pocznie?* (What Will He Do?), *Sobotni wieczór* (Saturday Night), *Wolny najmita* (A Free Mercenary), *Z wiejskiej szkółki* (From a Village School), *Bez dachu* (Homeless), *Przed sądem* (Before the Court), *Jaś nie doczekał* (Johnny Did Not Live to See), *Dwie wiosny* (Two Springs), *Na dnie przepaści* (On the Bottom of the Precipice), *Czy zginie* (Will She Die?), *Chłopskie serce* (Peasant's Heart), and *W piwnicznej izbie* (In a Basement Room). The material of the stories related in poetic form encompasses contemporary reality, the tragedy of homelessness, and the poverty of the pariah classes in a middle-class society. The poems have quite similar structures, resembling a novelette, with a heavy emphasis on an aphoristic culminating point. However, both the epic and the sentimentally lyrical elements are weakened by the author's commentaries, often expounded as sententious dicta or rhetorical questions. Nonetheless, *Obrazki,* daring in its social diagnosis, innovative in the choice of characters, played an important role in the literary culture of the time.

Nasza szkapa (Our Mare), a short story, was first printed in *Przegląd*

Literacki (Literary Review) in 1890, then in the collection *Na drodze* (On the Way, Cracow, 1893). The story is written in the form of memories of a teenager, who is both a witness and participant in the events. It presents the common tragedy of poverty and death which often became the fate of a plebeian family of the time. The story is woven around common everyday problems, which are dramatized through the childlike sensitivity of the main characters.

(See Positivism.)

BIBLIOGRAPHY

Poezje (Poetry), Volumes 1–8, 10, edited by J. Czubek, introduction by Henryk Sienkiewicz, Cracow, 1916 and 1925.

Pisma wybrane (Selected Writings), edited by Irena Śliwińska and S.R. Dobrowolski, Volumes 107; Warsaw, 1951–1952.

Poezje, edited by A. Brodska, Warsaw, 1963.

Nowele, edited by A. Brodska, T. 1–2, Warsaw, 1962.

English

O krasnoludkach:

The Brownie Scouts, translated by Kate Zuk-Skarszewska, London, Warsaw: M. Arct, 1929.

Jak to ze lnem było:

The Golden Seed: A Legend of Old Poland, translated by Margaret Sperry, Copenhagen: Golden Mill Press, 1958.

A gdy poszedł król na wojnę:

When the King Went Forth to War (song score), London: J. & W. Chester, 1920.

KONWICKI, TADEUSZ (born 1926), a prose writer and film director, was born in Nowa Wilejka near Wilno (Vilnius), a region to which he remained nostalgically faithful for the rest of his life. He went to school in Wilno; in 1944–45 he fought in the Wilno division of the Home Army (*Armia Krajowa* [*AK*]). He participated in the struggle against both the German occupiers and the Soviet Army, which, encroaching on these territories, together with the NKVD (Soviet Secret Police), liquidated all Polish organizations in Lithuania and deported the soldiers of the *AK* to labor camps. After the war he studied Polish philology in Cracow. He worked for various cultural magazines, including *Odrodzenie* (Rebirth) and *Nowa Kultura* (New Culture). He also wrote screenplays and became a film director. He started his literary work with the novel *Rojsty,* based on remembrances of his partisan struggles in Vilnius, which were revealed in his coverage, written in 1948 and published in 1956. A member of the Communist Party from 1950, he made his debut with works which supported the Party's then current political aims: *Przy budowie* (By the Construction), 1950; a novel *Władza* (Power), 1954; in the psychological short story *Godzina smutku* (An Hour of Sadness, 1954), he abandoned this direction; in time he left the Communist Party (in 1966), and in the 1970s he became associated with the democratic opposition.

In the novel *Z oblężonego miasta* (From a Besieged City, 1956) he turned to the dominating motive of his works: the cruel experiences of the war and their influence on the consciousness and life of people, especially those living in the northeastern regions of Poland, the young generation confused by the turn of historical events and starting their lives with feelings of guilt and personal defeat. The wounds of the past, made more painful because of one's involvement in the political and ideological conflicts of the postwar period, give the writer the feeling that his current life is unstable and alien to him. The past recurs in sensually concrete images, dense with symbolic meanings; it becomes an obsession. Contemporary reality, on the other hand, takes on a strange, dreamy atmosphere as if being grotesquely unreal, a situation which pushes Konwicki's heroes into emotional and psychological inertia. These problems are best presented in *Sennik współczesny* (A Dreambook for Our Time, 1963), *Wniebowstąpienie* (The Assumption into Heaven, 1967), *Nic albo nic* (Nothing or Nothing, 1971), *Kompleks Polski* (The Polish Complex, 1977), and *Mała apokalipsa* (A Minor Apocalypse, 1979), first published underground, after Konwicki became involved with the Committee for the Workers Defense (*KOR*). In this grim, grotesque exaggerated portrait of contemporary society Konwicki portrays the country sunk in inertia and torn by dramatic conflicts. These are juxtaposed with tragic episodes in Polish history and a catastrophic vision of the near future. These dramatic accounts are contrasted with and complemented by elegiac memories of the author's youth, a lyrical vision of a child's mental and emotional life and a young man's initiation into love and life. These themes and motives are repeated and developed in *Dziura w niebie* (A Hole in the Heavens, 1959), *Zwierzoczłekoupiór* (The Anthropos-Spectre-Beast, 1969), and *Kronika wypadków miłosnych* (A Chronicle of Love Affairs, 1974). His pseudodiary *Kalendarz i klepsydra* (Calendar and the Hourglass, 1976), purportedly a true account of the author's biographical and literary experiences, is full of digressions—lyrical, reflective, ironic, satirical and anecdotal. He maintained a similar form in the novels *Wschody i zachody księżyca* (Moonrise, Moonset)—published in 1982 in the underground press. His works published underground also include a novel, *Rzeka podziemna, podziemne ptaki* (Underground River, Underground Birds, 1985). *Nowy Świat i okolice* (Nowy Świat Street and Its Neighborhood Environs, 1987), a continuation of *Calendar and the Hourglass* (1976), as well as the novel *Bohin* (1987), which takes place at the end of the nineteenth century, have all already appeared in the official press. He directed a number of excellent films, based on his own screenplays, among others, *Ostatni dzień lata* (The Last Day of Summer, 1971); *Dolina Issy* (The Issa Valley, based on Czesław Miłosz's novel); and most recently, *Lawa* (Lava, 1989), based on Mickiewicz's *Dziady* (Forefathers' Eve). His novel *Kronika wypadków miłosnych* (A Chronicle of Love Affairs) was made into a film by Andrzej Wajda. He has received several literary awards. His books have been translated into numerous languages.

Sennik współczesny (A Dreambook for Our Time) presents the vicissitudes of Paweł (the narrator), who arrives in a small village hidden in the woods. The reason for his arrival is an attempt to settle accounts with the past (World War II). As a member of a partisan unit in Wileńszczyzna, Paweł was to kill a man sentenced by the underground army: the possibility exists that the man still lives in the village. The story is set in a valley, full of relics symbolic of bygone days. The valley is to be flooded by the water needed to supply the electric plant under construction. The characters are life's bankrupts of all sorts, including a former teacher and Communist, now a leader of a religious sect; a former officer of the secret police, now a railway worker; a party activist, now dying of tuberculosis; a rightist partisan; and a count trying to conceal his aristocratic origin. This gallery of complex personalities allows the author to present astonishing contrasts of attitudes and experiences, characteristic of the war and postwar fate of Polish society. Against this background Paweł is trying to settle his own moral accounts, hoping to liberate himself from the heavy burden of memories concerning the suffering he experienced and inflicted upon others. The narration is constructed like a crossword puzzle, with the war years of the main character gradually appearing out of the numerous reminiscences, supplying an explanation for his neurotic behavior. The novel is marked by a keen psychological insight into the lives of these characters and by a highly sophisticated style. The feverish visionary aspect of the novel and the sensual description of events heighten the merits of this unusual work.

Kompleks polski—one of Konwicki's best novels—had to wait twelve years to be published officially. Written in 1976, submitted to the state publishing house and then withdrawn as a result of censorship, it was one of the first prose publications in the Second Circulation (alternative press) in 1979 and only in 1989 published in the official press. The title of the novel has a number of meanings. The Polish complex is the complex of Polish-Russian conflicts; the Polish complex is the battle over freedom; it is also the Western complex concerning Poland, a country misunderstood in its resistance to the Soviet Union; and the Polish complex, of a country betrayed by the Allied nations, in relation to the West; it also involves complexes of people, injured and deceived by history and corrupted by the Soviets. It appeared when Poles sought explanations: it immediately became famous, not only because it gave an accurate diagnosis of Poland's reality and revealed the political mechanisms governing it, but rather, because *Kompleks polski,* like the coming *Mała apokalipsa,* was above all a record of the state of the nation's collective consciousness. It registered the country's subconscious fears and longings. The first episode from the 1863 Uprising in *Kompleks polski* ends with the well-known question "Was it worth it?" The hero of the second episode, Romuald Traugutt, a commander of the uprising against the Russian Empire, when asked, "Did it make sense to stand up against such power?" answers, "I do not know if it made sense; I know we had to." This brief statement seems to carry the message of Konwicki's novel. The novel is a warning against social apathy, against growing accustomed to the reality of "transparent" enslavement.

The novel is synonymous with the syndrome of being Polish, in short, about the experience of being Polish, or rather, the experience of "never having completed" being Polish. It repeats the similar biographies of past generations, the manifestation of a contagious vision of a free, noble, and wise Poland, which inspires the same fear of a cockeyed "logic" of history. Konwicki himself often refers in the novel to the tradition of Romanticism, recalling Romantic symbols and stereotypes. The episodes of the January Uprising are here contrasted with scenes from contemporary reality (e.g., the symbolic line in front of the jewelry store to buy Russian gold). *The Polish Complex* is constructed like many of Konwicki's earlier works: the narrator is a writer endowed with elements of the author's biography; individual elements and episodes are loosely tied in and consecutive fragments of the work are divided into essayistic reflections. The story takes place on two levels: contemporary and historical. The reality of *Kompleks polski* is not as grotesque as the reality of *Mała apokalipsa*. But it is the same world, uprooted from its past, the world of collapsing values and unbearable existence, and of the never dying hope for a reassuring miracle.

Mała apokalipsa, on the other hand, is a vision of the reality of "the Polish Soviet Republic" at the end of the twentieth century, a vision which is catastrophic and grotesque, drawn from the author's fears and intuitions. It is a picture of a small, enslaved country of polluted rivers and land turning into a desert, of ruined cities with patchworks of posters in Polish and Russian proclaiming the absurd: "We have built Socialism!" It is a picture of a society in which all values and rules have been distorted, where good is mixed with evil, where conformism has the appearance of revolt, where any form of behavior seems ambiguous. It is also a story of the slow agony of a nation which "no longer works," which disappears into nothingness to the accompaniment of empty rituals carried out by the regime and the meaningless actions of the opposition. The story takes place in Warsaw, on the day of the beginning of the Party Congress, which hosts a party secretary from a neighboring superpower. The hero and narrator is a writer who is charged by his colleagues-oppositionists with the mission of burning himself in front of the main Warsaw edifice, a nightmare, Stalin's "gift" to Poland—the Palace of Culture (Konwicki's favorite symbol). The act is supposed to shock the passive nation; on the other hand, it is the last argument in the opposition's battle with the powers that be: If Czechoslovakia's Jan Palach could not effect a change, how could an ineffectual Pole hope to accomplish the impossible?

An important aspect of Konwicki's philosophy is the motive of collapse as a result of erosion—of values, buildings, people's minds, and the debased "real Socialist" system with its apparatus of terror. Nothing works because of people's apathy and gradual decay. After the events of 1980 and 1989 and the triumph of October 1989, Konwicki may yet have to alter his terrifying anticipations and diagnoses. In 1993 Konwicki published an anthology of movie scripts, *Salto* (Somersault).

(See Contemporary Polish Literature.)

BIBLIOGRAPHY

English

The Anthropos-Spectre-Beast (Zwierzoczłekoupiór), translated by George and Audry Korwin-Rodziszewski, New York: S. Phillips, 1977; New York: Oxford University Press, 1977.

A Dreambook for Our Time (Sennik współczesny), translated by David Welsh, Cambridge, Massachusetts: M.I.T. Press, 1969; introduction by Leszek Kołakowski, New York: Penguin Books, 1976, 1983.

A Minor Apocalypse (Mała apokalipsa), London: Faber and Faber, 1983, 1988; New York: Farrar, Straus, Giroux, 1983; New York: Vintage Books, 1984.

Moonrise, Moonset, (Wschody i zachody księżyca), New York: Farrar, Straus, Giroux, 1987; London: Faber, 1988.

The Polish Complex (Kompleks polski), New York: Farrar, Straus, Giroux, 1981, 1982; Harmondsworth, England: Penguin, 1982, 1984.

KORCZAK, JANUSZ (Henryk Goldszmit) (1878 [or 1879]–1942), came from a Polonized Jewish family. A prose writer, publicist, author of works on pedagogy, and writer of children's literature, Korczak was a doctor by profession, a pedagogue and psychologist by vocation. He devoted all his life to defending the rights of children. As cofounder and manager of two orphanages (for Jewish children 1912–42; for Polish children 1919–36), he introduced his own system of upbringing, which included, among other elements, various forms of social activity for the child. He worked for many charitable institutions; he was also a lecturer. He contributed to and was associated with many journals and magazines devoted to pedagogy. He was also the author of a popular radio show for children (collected, among others, in the volume *Pedagogika żartobliwa* [Joyful Pedagogy], 1939). He was killed in a Nazi extermination camp in Treblinka on August 5, 1942, having voluntarily accompanied his wards from his orphanage, who were earlier transported from the Warsaw ghetto, where he had been incarcerated since 1940.

Korczak's writings are primarily connected with his practical work as a pedagogue. Original in their content and form, they combine humanitarianism and a thorough knowledge of the psychology of a child with lyricism, imagination, and humor. Several works stand on the border of a literary essay (*Momenty wychowawcze* [Educational Moments], 1919, *Jak kochać dzieci* [How to Love Children], Parts 1–3, 1920, and *Prawo dziecka do szacunku* [The Right of a Child to Be Respected], 1929); a psychological study written in the form of a story (*Bobo*, 1914 and *Kiedy znów będę mały* [When I'm Young Again], 1925); or a diary (*Spowiedź motyla* [Confessions of a Butterfly], 1914). He also wrote fiction: the novel *Dzieci ulicy* (Children of the Street, 1901), a naturalistic, sensational-didactic novel, and the autobiographical novel written in the form of a diary *Dziecko salonu* (Child of the Salon, 1906), which combines various narrative techniques, including personal subject matter. The works specifically meant for children are *Sława* (Fame, 1913), *Kajtuś czarodziej* (The Little Magician, 1934), *Bankructwo małego Dżeka* (Big Business Billy, 1924). His best known work is *Król Maciuś Pierwszy* (King Matthew the First, 1923), made into a film by Wanda Jakubowska in 1958, a fantastic story about the little king-reformer, and its sequel, *Król Maciuś na wyspie bezludnej* (King Matthew on the Deserted Island, 1923). Its adventurous plot, easily comprehended by children, contains underlayers of serious philosophical reflection on life, people, and power. Thus it can be only fully appreciated by adults. Korczak also wrote a grotesque-metaphorical play, *Senat szaleńców* (A Senate of Madmen, staged in 1931). Especially important is his diary, written in 1942 while he was interned in the ghetto, published in selected writings. Korczak's works have been translated into many languages. He has also been portrayed in numerous literary works (by L. S. Liciński, H. Mortkowicz-Olczakowa, and I. Newerly). The centenary of his birth was celebrated all over the world. He has become a symbol of courage, self-sacrifice, and the finest aspects of humanity.

BIBLIOGRAPHY

Wybór pism pedagogicznych (A Selection of Pedagogical Writings), Volumes 1–2, edited by E. Frydman, Warsaw, 1957–58.

Wybór pism (Selected Writings), Volumes 1–4, edited and with an introduction by I. Newerly, Warsaw, 1957–58.

English

Ghetto Diary, New York: Holocaust Library, 1978.

Selected Works of Janusz Korczak, translated by Jerzy Bacharach Washington, published for the National Science Foundation by the Scientific Publications Foreign Cooperation Center of the Central Institute for Scientific, Technical and Economic Information, Washington, D.C., 1967.

Big Business Billy (Bankructwo małego Dżeka), translated by Cyrus Brooks, London, 1939.

The Warsaw Ghetto Memoirs of Janusz Korczak (Pamiętnik z getta), translated by E. P. Kulowiec, Washington D.C.: University Press of America, 1978, 1979.
The Ghetto Years: 1939–1942 (Pamiętnik z getta), Tel Aviv: Ghetto Fighters House and Hakibbutz Hameuchad, 1980, 1983.

KORDIAN (see Słowacki).

KORDIAN I CHAM (Kordian and the Boor) (see Kruczkowski).

KORZENIOWSKI, JÓZEF (1797–1863), a novelist, playwright, and pedagogue, studied at the secondary school in Krzemieniec, where he also made his debut while still in school and later (1823) lectured on rhetoric and poetry. He was a member of *TPN* (Society of Friends of Science). His early writings were influenced by Classical models and by readings in sentimental literature. They are characterized by aesthetic eclecticism, slavish devotion to foreign models, and the abstractness of a moralistic tone. These are mainly Classical odes, poetic letters and tragedies, sentimental poems, and dramas influenced by the pre-Romantic tradition. After the Polish school in Krzemieniec was closed down (1832), Korzeniowski became a professor at the University of Kiev, and later the headmaster of a high school in Kharkov.

During the Kharkov period Korzeniowski turned more and more to realism, basing his observations on cultural and social phenomena. The dominant genres during this period were contemporary comedies, short stories, and novels. The breakthrough came with the drama *Karpaccy górale* (Carpathian Mountaineers, 1843), in which the clichétic convention of "brigand drama" and Schiller-style conflict between an individual and the law are enlivened by setting the action in a folk environment. For the first time in Polish drama the folk theme is given a social dimension within the dramatic conflict and presented a noble image of peasant characters. A bitter satire on the aristocracy, the "high comedy" *Żydzi* (Jews, 1843) could have easily been understood as severe social criticism. But Korzeniowski's political caution, together with his policy of conciliation, did not allow him to attack the foundation of the system but merely to criticize the functioning mechanism of repression. In the comedies of this period Korzeniowski chastises middle-class occupations (*Doktor medycyny* [Doctor of Medicine], staged in 1845), mildly criticizes aristocratic pride (*Pani kasztelanowa* [The Castellan's Wife], written in 1844, staged in 1846), ridicules the industrial ambitions of the gentry (*Fabrykant* [The Factory Owner], staged in 1844) and the heroines of the emancipation (*Młoda wdowa* [The Young Widow], written in 1843, staged in 1846). The novels of the Kharkov period (*Spekulant* [The Speculator], 1846, and *Kollokacja* [Collocation], 1847) played an important role in the development of nineteenth century realism. *Spekulant* is a novel of manners from the life of the nobility, whose actions are tied in with the adventures of a fortune hunter. *Kollokacja,* a term for a village distributed among small owners, is the first novel in Polish literature that gives a social and economic picture of the differentiation of the nobility as well as a Balzacian portrait of a gentry speculator.

After 1846 Korzeniowski lived in Warsaw. He continued writing for the theater (these works were published in 1853). These comedies, however, were not very ambitious, based loosely on motives from family and social life: *Majster i czeladnik* (Master and Journeyman, 1847) and *Majątek albo imię* (Wealth or Good Name, 1860). At the same time, Korzeniowski wrote a number of narrative works, turning to the novel, a genre he felt would take over the role of poetry and drama. According to Maria Żmigrodzka, the works written after the events of 1846–48 are generally less significant than his earlier works. An interesting combination of Romantic plot and positivist didacticism can be found in *Nowe wędrówki oryginała* (New Travels of an Original, written in 1848, published in 1851). It was followed by *Emeryt* (The Pensioner, written in 1849, published in 1850), *Tadeusz bezimienny* (Thadeus Anonymous, written in 1850, published in 1852), *Garbaty* (Hunch-Backed, written in 1851, published in 1853), and *Wdowiec* (Widower, written in 1854, published in 1856), which are typical of the so-called Biedermeier trend, the moralistic program which aimed at creating a man reduced to the narrow area of family duties. His interest in public life reappears in the novel *Krewni* (Relatives, written in 1855).

During the period of Wielopolski's reforms Korzeniowski was the director of the Department of Education and was responsible for the reconstruction of the system of education. In 1863 he left for Dresden, where he wrote his only patriotic work, *Nasza prawda: Scena z życia Polski z roku 1863* (Our Truth: A Scene from Polish Life from the Year 1863, published in 1898).

(See Positivism.)

BIBLIOGRAPHY

Dzieła (Works), Volumes 1–12, Warsaw, 1871–73.
Dzieła wybrane, Volumes 1–8, Cracow, 1954.

KOSSAK, ZOFIA (Kossak-Szczucki and Kossak-Szatkowski) (primo voto, secundo voto) (1890–1968), a novelist and publicist, was the granddaughter of the famous painter Juliusz Kossak. She studied art in Warsaw and Geneva and made her literary debut in 1913 with the story *Bulli zaginął* (Bulli Disappeared) in *Wieś polska* (Polish Village). After 1909 she spent more time in Wołyń (Volhynia), where her family had earlier moved. After her marriage she settled down in Wołyń and lived there during the time of the revolution in Russia, whose cruelties she presented in her stirring memories *Pożoga* (The Blaze, 1922). After her husband's death in 1922 she moved to Górki Wielkie in Beskid Śląski. In 1925 she married again. For some time she was connected with the local literary group Czartak. As a publicist she cooperated mainly with the Catholic press. In 1932 she received the Silesian Literary Award, in 1936 the Golden Wreath of PAL, and the award of the Readers of *Wiadomości Literackie* (Literary News). She was generally considered the successor of Kraszewski and Sienkiewicz in the area of the historical novel. During the Nazi occupation she became involved with the underground press (*Polska żyje* [Poland Lives], *Prawda* [Truth]); she was cofounder of the underground organization of the Polish Catholic intelligentsia. She also took part in the activities of the underground Council for Aiding Jews and wrote protests against the extermination of Jews. Arrested in 1943 under a false name, she was sent to Auschwitz, then transferred to Pawiak in Warsaw and sentenced to death. She was released in July 1944 as a result of the intervention of the underground authorities and subsequently took part in the Warsaw Uprising, writing for the press. In August 1945 she was sent to London on a Red Cross mission and remained in England until 1957, farming with her husband and writing. Upon her return she settled permanently in Górki Wielkie.

The major part of Kossak's output was in the area of historical novels. The first, *Beatum scelus* (1924), is concerned with the religious, moral, and political problems of Poland during the time of the Reformation. A new version of the novel, *Błogosławiona wina* (Blessed Guilt), was published in London in 1953, and in Poland in 1958. *Złota wolność* (Golden Freedom, 1928) takes place at the turn of the sixteenth and seventeenth centuries and tells a story of an Aryan family, set against the panorama of the time. Religious themes are prominent in the story of Saint Stanislaus Kostka, *Z miłości* (With Love, 1926), and a collection of legends, *Szaleńcy Boży* (God's Madmen, 1929); they also dominate the novel *Legnickie pole* (The Battlefield of Legnica, 1930), presenting the conflict of the Christian world and the Mongolian East. The novel also demonstrated the writer's interest in Silesia. The history and struggle of persecuted Poles were often presented in her stories, chronicles, and tales: *Wielcy i mali* (The Great and the Small, 1927); *Nieznany kraj* (The Unknown Country, 1932); *Z dziejów Śląska* (From the History of Silesia, 1933); *Skarb Śląski* (Silesian Treasure, 1937); and *Na Śląsku* (In Silesia, 1939). The theme also appears in the series of novels about the history of the Crusades published during a six-year period; she traveled to Jerusalem and described her trip in the book *Pątniczym szlakiem* (Pilgrim's Way, 1933). Kossak returned to the problems of seventeenth century Poland in her *Trembowla*, (1939), based on the war with the Turks under Jan Sobieski, and in *Suknia Dejaniry* (Dejanira's Dress, 1939), a travesty of the old Polish story about K. Korsak, who, like Saint Alex, chose to live in poverty. Kossak's experiences in Auschwitz were reflected in *Z otchłani: Wspomnienia z lagru* (From the Abyss: Reminiscences of the Camp, 1946). According to Małgorzata Czermińska, the book aroused a heated discussion, provoked by an article by Tadeusz Borowski, *Alicja w krainie czarów* (Alice in Wonderland, 1947), in which the author attacks the philosophical interpretation of the phenomenon of concentration camps and the moral message of the book. In England Kossak wrote a novel based on biblical motives, *Przymierze* (The Covenant, London, 1952; published in Poland, 1957); a book about Polish customs and landscape, *Rok polski* (The Polish Year, London, 1955; in Poland, 1958); the first part of the trilogy *Dziedzictwo* (Heritage, Part 1); *Juliusz i Zofia* (Julius and Sophia, London, 1956; in Poland, 1961); and a saga of the Kossak family. She continued writing the work in Poland (Part 2, 1964; Part 3, together with her husband, Z. Szatkowski, 1967). *Troja Północy* (Northern Troy, 1960), a book based on the early medieval history of the Slavs who lived on the Laba and fought with the Germans, was also a joint work with her husband. For young people and children Kossak wrote works based mainly on historical themes: *Puszkarz Orbano* (Orbano the Gunsmith, 1936), an episode in the siege of Constantinople by the Turks in the fifteenth century; *Bursztyny* (Amber, 1936), glimpses of Polish history from the times of the Piasts to the Great Emigration; *Gród nad jeziorem* (Castle on the Lake, 1938); *Warna* (1939); *Topsy i Lupus* (Topsy and Lupus, 1931), and a folktale, *Kłopoty Kacperka, góreckiego skrzata* (The Troubles of Kacperek, Mountain Gnome, 1926).

Crusaders, a historical novel, was published in Poznań in 1935, Volumes 1–4: *Bóg tak chce* (God Wants It That Way), *Fides graeca; Wieża trzech sióstr* (The Tower of the Three Sisters), and *Jerozolima wyzwolona* (Jerusalem Delivered). A monumental epic, devoted to the First Crusade at the turn of the eleventh and twelfth centuries, the story begins in 1095 in Poland, when Silesian knights, named *Strzegonie,* set off on a pilgrimage to Provence and joined the Crusade. The novel presents a broad historical background of the Crusade (the role of Peter of Amiens, the Council of Clermont) and the tragic fate of the earlier folk Crusade. The story is filled with dramatic events: battles, the horror of experiences in the desert, famine, diseases, the difficult sieges of Nicea and Antioch, and, finally, the capture of Jerusalem and the election of King Gotfried of Lorraine. The epilogue takes us back to Silesia, with the knights' return.

The novel continues the tradition of the great historical epic of the nineteenth century. The complex plot, often sensational and adventurous, is set against an overall image of the epoch, portrayed with a thorough knowledge of political events and social relations and embroidered with rich detail. The characters (and there are several, leading critics to speak of a collective hero) are often reduced to one characteristic feature (a greedy Greek man, a brave knight, or a proud princess). Realistic motivation of events is intertwined with fantasy and legend. The story is thus rich in miraculous events, resulting from the Christian philosophy on which Kossak based her historiosophical view of the Crusades. She believed that events were the creation of God, and, at the same time, of man. The socioeconomic and political origin of the events is combined with a mystical and religious background: its historical importance is linked closely with its metaphysical foundation. The author expressed her personal credo in the words of Pope Urban in the epilogue, adding a symbolic interpretation of the Crusades, which Kossak referred to as "a terrifying shortcut in the history of mankind." The novel, together with two other works on the same theme, received a great deal of attention, went through several editions, and was translated into over twenty languages.

(See Contemporary Polish Literature.)

BIBLIOGRAPHY

English

The Blaze-Reminiscences of Volhynia, 1917–1919, (Pożoga), New York: Polish Book, 1927; London: G. Allen and Unwin, 1927.

The Troubles of Gnome, translated by Monica M. Gardner, London: A. and C. Black, 1928.

Blessed Are the Meek (Bez oręża), translated by Lurka Langer, New York: Roy, 1944; London, New York: Hutchinson, 1944; New York: Grosset and Dunlap, 1944.

The Leper King (Król Trędowaty), London: Hutchinson, 1945; translated by F. S. Placzek, New York: Roy, 1945.

The Covenant (Przymierze), translated by H. C. Stevens, London: New York Wingate, 1951; New York: Roy, 1951.

Angels in the Dust (Krzyżowcy), London, New York: Hutchinson, 1951; New York: Roy, 1947.

The Gift of Nessus, London, New York: Hutchinson, 1948.

The Meek Shall Inherit, translated by Maurice Michael, New York: Roy, 1948.

KOTT, JAN (born 1914) is a critic, essay writer, literary historian, and translator. During his studies of law in Warsaw he cofounded an artistic club called "S" (1933) and began writing poetry. His collection *Podwojony świat* (A Duplicated World) appeared in 1936. After 1939 he lived in Lvov; in the fall of 1941 he moved to Warsaw, active in the circles of leftist intelligentsia; he was also a member of the underground People's Army organized by the Communist Party (*PPR*). In 1945 he cofounded and until 1948 was coeditor of the Marxist weekly *Kuźnica* (Ironworks). In 1949–52 he assumed a position as a professor of Polish Philology at Wrocław University and in 1953–68 at Warsaw University. In 1953–61 he wrote theatrical reviews for *Przegląd Kulturalny* (Cultural Review). During the period of political upheaval in 1956, he sided with the movement known as "revisionists" and shortly resigned from the Communist Party (he described his ideological and political peripeteia in his memoirs, *Przyczynek* *do biografii* [A Contribution to Biography], 1990). In 1966 he left Poland for the United States. In 1968 he became professor of Comparative Literature at SUNY Stony Brook. He is now a Professor Emeritus.

According to his journalistic writings in the forties he propagated the secularization of life, the realization of a program of cultural revolution and ideological changes in literature (a collection of feuilletons, *Po prostu* [In Plain Words], appeared in 1946; a selection written during the period 1945–56, *Postęp i głupstwo* [Progress and Stupidity], was published in 1957). He was a radical propagator of "greater realism": these ideas developed from his views regarding the contrast between the illusions and pretenses of the avant-garde and of literature in general advocating abstract moral stands, on the one hand, and "the time of contempt" and the experiences of the war, on the other (the essays *Mitologia i realizm* [Mythology and Realism], 1946, written in 1943–44). He attempted to reevaluate the tradition of realism, both foreign (*Szkoła klasyków* [School of the Classics], 1949; third enlarged edition in 1955) and Polish (an attempt at a Marxist analysis in the sketch *O "Lalce" Bolesława Prusa* [About Prus's "The Doll"], 1948). Together with Tadeusz Mikulski he initiated studies on the writers and the theater of the Enlightenment: he published essays on Trembecki, Bohomolec, and Krasicki; a book, *Warszawa wieku oświecenia* (Warsaw During the Enlightenment, 1954, with S. Lorentz); and a now somewhat outdated anthology, *Poezja polskiego oświecenia* (Poetry During Poland's Enlightenment, 1954). He was the driving force and editor of the series *Teatr Polskiego Oświecenia* (Polish Theater of the Enlightenment) and the collection *Teatr Narodowy* (The National Theater, 1765–94), published in 1967. During the midfifties he became a propagator of avant-garde ideas, clearly seen in his attitude toward the theater. He published numerous reviews which gave a picture of the changes in the traditions and tastes of the period (*Jak wam się podoba* [As You Like It], 1955; *Poskromienie złośników* [Taming of the Shrews], 1957; *Miarka za miarkę* [Measure for Measure], 1962; *Aloes* [Aloe], 1967) and a selection in English, *Theatre Notebook 1947–1967* (1968). His *Szkice o Szekspirze* (Sketches on Shakespeare, 1961, third edition, revised and published as *Szekspir współczesny* [Shakespeare Our Contemporary]) appeared in 1965. This volume that climaxed Kott's career has been translated into almost every major language in the world. His essays on Greek tragedy, *The Eating of the Gods* (1973, the revised edition in French, *Manger les Dieux,* appeared in 1975), were an attempt (like *Shakespeare Our Contemporary*) to view Classical drama through the experiences of contemporary theater and history. His other works include a comedy, *Nowy Świętoszek* (The New Tartuffe, 1950, with Stanisław Dygat); a travesty of Moliere's *Misanthrope* (1967); an anthology, *Wiersze, które lubimy* (Poetry Which We Like, 1961, with Adam Wazyk); translations from the French, among others Diderot, Rimbaud, Apollinaire, Elurad, Aragon, and plays by Sartre and Ionesco. He received a State Award in 1955, and the International Herder's Award in 1964.

BIBLIOGRAPHY

English

"Leszek Kołakowski and Jan Kott: The Jester-Priest Metaphor," in *Contemporary Polish Theater and Drama,* 1956–1984, edited by E. J. Czerwiński, New York: Greenwood Press, 1988, 21–33.

The Eating of the Gods: An Interpretation of Greek Tragedy, translated by Bolesław Taborski and Edward J. Czerwiński, New York: Vintage Books, 1974; New York: Random House, 1973; London: Eyre Metheum, 1974; Evanston, Illinois: Northwestern University Press, 1987.

Shakespeare Our Contemporary (Szkice o Szekspirze), translated by Bolesław Taborski, Garden City, New York: Doubleday, 1964; Norton, 1964; 1974; London: Methuen, 1965; Garden City, New York: Anchor Books, 1966; London: Methuen, 1967.

The Theater of Essence and Other Essays, Evanston, Illinois: Northwestern University Press, 1984.

Theater Notebook 1947–1967, translated by Bolesław Taborski, Garden City, New York: Doubleday, 1968; London: Methuen, 1968.

Four Decades of Polish Essays, edited and with an introduction by Jan Kott, Evanston, Illinois: Northwestern University Press, 1990.

The Memory of the Body: Essays on Theater and Death, translated by Jadwiga Kosicka, Evanston, Illinois: Northwestern University Press, 1992.

KRASICKI, IGNACY (1735–1801), a poet, prose writer, publicist, and author of comedies, was the greatest representative of the literature of the Polish Enlightenment. He was called "the prince among poets" by his contemporaries. The difficult financial situation of his family forced him into the career of a clergyman. During his studies at a religious seminary in Warsaw (1751–54), he became acquainted with the milieu of the early Enlightenment and through his readings became familiar with French Classicism of the seventeenth century and with the ideas of the European Enlightenment. Through family ties he was connected with the Conservative magnate circle, which opposed the Czartoryski family and its program of reform. His relatives helped him obtain lucrative posts within the Church and were instrumental in dispatching him to Rome to pursue his studies (1759–61). He changed his orientation during the interregnum, and soon after the elections he became one of the closest aides to King Stanisław August and helped the king with his cultural reforms. He was the founder and coeditor of the journal *Monitor,* the most important periodical of the Polish Enlightenment, modeled on the English *The Spectator.* In 1766 he was consecrated as bishop of Warmia and his visits to Warsaw became rather rare, but he remained in contact with the court through letters. He also sent all his works to Warsaw, to be published by Michał Groll. In Heilsberg (now Lidzbark Warmiński) he created a court with high cultural ambitions, collecting books, paintings, and medals. He was constantly in financial straits: his debt grew throughout his life.

The period 1775–86 witnessed Krasicki's greatest literary activity: *Myszeis* (Mouseiad), 1775; *Mikołaja Doświadczyńskiego przypadki* (The Fortunes of Mikołaj Doświadczyński), 1776; *Monachomachia,* 1778; *Pan Podstoli* (Mr. Podstoli) Part 1, 1778; *Bajki i przypowieści* (Fables and Parables), 1779; *Satyry* (Satires), 1779; *Historia* (History), 1779; *Antymonachomachia* (Antimonachomania), 1779; *Wojna chocimska* (The Chocim War), 1780; and three comedies written for the Court Theater in Heilsberg: *Solenizant* (Nameday Celebrant), *Łgarz* (The Liar), and *Statysta* (Supernumerary), 1780. During this period he also composed an encyclopedia, *Zbiór najpotrzebniejszych wiadomości* (A Collection of Most Useful Information, Volumes 1–2, 1781–83), and published *Wiersze X. B. W.* (Poems X. B. W., 1784), the second part of *Satyry* (Satires); a new cycle of fables, *Bajki nowe* (New Fables); a collection of novels, *Powieści wschodnie* (Eastern Novels); and a translation of *The Songs of Ossian* (1792–93), then considered to be authentic old Celtic poems.

Krasicki supported King Stanisław's reforms in his works, but he never took active part in political life. During the Bar Confederacy he assumed an ambiguous position, thus losing the king's trust. In spite of his patriotic works (*Hymn do miłości ojczyzny* [Hymn to Love of Homeland], 1774; *Pieśń na dzień 3 maja* [A Song on the Day of the Third of May], 1792; and *Powieść prawdziwa o narożnej kamienicy w Kukurowcach* [A True Story of a Corner Tenament House in Kukurowiec], 1794), he easily accepted being subjugated to Prussian authority as a result of the dismemberment of Poland (although he never gave up arguing with authorities over financial problems). He visited the courts in Berlin and Potsdam and was received by Frederick II and Frederick Wilhelm II, who made him archbishop of Gniezno. He rarely concerned himself with his diocese, but rather devoted his time and energy to making new gardens; publishing the weekly *Co tydzień* (Each Week), which he practically wrote himself; and preparing his writings with a complete edition in mind. His works did appear after his death (*Dzieła* [Works], Volumes 1–10, 1803–4), with over half never published during the author's lifetime (among them dialogues modeled on Lucian and biographies based on Plutarch).

Krasicki's work played an important role during the renaissance of Polish literature during the epoch of King Stanisław August. The main characteristics of his genius include an accuracy of perception, clarity and precision of language, a mastery in containing important thought within aphoristic form and in employing humor, irony, mockery, and parody. These features, along with his unusual intelligence and intellectual and artistic talents, undoubtedly aided him in presenting his idea of literature as a tool of social education. However, his artistic program reflects the weaknesses, illusions, and disappointments of the policies of the supporters of the king.

The main point in the program during the king's early years was to overcome the tradition of *Sarmatism* and to spread the ideas of the age of the Enlightenment. However, the painful lessons learned during the Confederacies of Radom and Bar and the first partition revealed the necessity to take into consideration the deep-rooted ideals of the nobility; thus, the program was modified in the direction of compromise. Krasicki continued his criticism of *Sarmatism* but changed his point of reference, agreeing more strongly with the better educated representatives of the nobility who directed attention to the valuable elements of the national traditions in contrast to the superficial beauty of foreign culture, especially French. The positive model Krasicki advocated was based on the ideas of Jean Jacques Rousseau, who argued for a society like that of the "Golden Age," not demoralized by civilization, and governed by reason. He presented an exaggerated model of such a utopian society in *Mikołaja Doświadczyńskiego Przypadki* (The Fortunes of Nicholas Doświadczyński), and a more realistic one in his novel-treatise, *Pan Podstoli.* The most important feature of the ideal society was to live according to real, not apparent values: the struggle of appearances versus genuine values is ever-present in Krasicki's works.

An interesting feature of Krasicki's output is the variety of literary genres he wrote in: lyrics, fables, satires, poetic letters, mock-heroic poems, historical epics, comedies, publicist prose, philosophical tales, literary criticism, dialogues and biographies based on ancient models, an encyclopedia, and a supplement to an armorial. The model for his poetry was French Classicism, without reference to the Polish literary tradition; the model of his prose writings were the European novels of the Enlightenment (social, adventurous, utopian, educational); he decidedly rejected the "tender" (sentimental) romance. In terms of literary genres with a Classical tradition, Krasicki's works are great achievements—masterpieces (especially his fables and satires). From another perspective he is an innovator in Polish literature, especially in the area of publicist writings and the novel. In his writings for the theater he deserves credit for stimulating the development of the young National Theater; his own comedies, however, are not among the greatest achievements of Polish literature.

He began his career by writing pieces of journalism. He made his poetic debut with his mock-heroic poem *Myszeis* (The Mouseiad), but the mastery in poetic technique present in the work would indicate that it was a debut in print, not in writing. Later his talent for composing fine lyrics led him to reach for higher levels—the epic. His *Wojna Chocimska* (The Chocim War) proved, however, that the serious epic was not his domain, and that his poetic gift could be better appreciated in parody.

Krasicki is among those writers whose greatness was appreciated by their contemporaries and never seriously questioned by later generations. On the other hand, he aroused less and less interest among readers after the period of Romanticism; he became the writer of a school, rather than a favorite of the reading public, with one exception—the fables, often mistakenly considered to be appropriate only for children. The first attempts at a synthesis of his achievements were undertaken soon after his death (by F. K. Dmochowski and S. K. Potocki). The first monograph on Krasicki was published in 1879 by Kraszewski. In spite of the great number of works devoted to Krasicki, we still lack a comprehensive modern summing up of the research done thus far.

His best work, *Bajki i przypowieści* (Fables and Parables), a cycle of 106 fables written between 1774–75 and 1778, was published in Warsaw in 1779. The preserved manuscript version contains eleven more fables, which did not appear in the first printing, but were published in 1906 by A. Kurpiel. Krasicki found plots for his fables in various sources (e.g., Oriental stories), or composed original stories, often traditionally based on animal motives. He created his own variety of epigrammatic fable, which is characterized by extreme brevity, a differentiation of the length of the poem in direct respect to the theme, a precision of plot construction based on the principle of symmetry, and a philosophical perspective in formulating the general statement. The fables are characterized by a specific rhythm (referred to as the rhythm of Krasicki's fables) which emphasizes the main elements of the story: these effects are achieved by means of *13 zgłoskowy* (thirteen-syllable) verse, a device with great semantic capacity; rhyming lines in pairs, allowing the reader to distinguish various areas of plot construction; maximally reducing the detail imposed by the rigor of epigrammatic poetics; choosing key words (often abstract in meaning); and paying special attention to syntactic parallelism, inversion, and the interaction of sentence intonation with the verse form. By emphasizing the contrast between the beginning and the end, and, in the majority of cases, between major characters, Krasicki emphasized the antitheses which were so typical of his fables: truth and falsity, good and bad, strength and weakness, and hope and disappointment. The reaching for the truth—expressed in the making of a point, in an ironic aphorism, a maxim (many of which became proverbs)—usually springs from the dramatic situation, culminating in the defeat of the weaker party or of the character who has miscalculated the situation.

The world of Krasicki's fables was seen as "the country of fools" (Juliusz Kleiner), governed by the brutal laws of violence. The universal character of these fables was also emphasized, although some poems (e.g., *Ptaszki w klatce* [Birds in a Cage]) were understood as allusions to the contemporary situation. Krasicki's philosophy, however, escapes uniform interpretation, somewhere between skepticism and the ethics of common sense, with an emphasis on maxims that praise modesty and skepticism.

His mock-heroic epic, *Monachomachia, czyli wojna mnichów* (Monochomachia, or War of the Monks), written most probably in Berlin between the end of 1776 and the spring of 1777, was published anonymously and contained numerous errors. An edited text, with corrections, appeared in Volume 1 of *Dzieła* (Works) in 1803. The poem tells the story of the conflict stirred up by the Witch of Discord between two monasteries in a city in which there are three taverns, four ruined gates, nine monasteries, and a few houses. The public theological dispute, in which Dominican friars challenge the Carmelites, soon turns into a battle fought with fists, beer mugs, and books, happily terminated by raising a huge glass of wine—*vitrum gloriosum*. The talent for parody which Krasicki revealed earlier in *Myszeis* (Mouseiad) reaches utmost mastery; however, parody is not a goal here: it is a satire of anti-*Sarmatism* aimed at the excessive number of monasteries in the country, especially the mendicant orders—uneducated, idle, given to drinking—which were partly to blame for the low economic and cultural level of provincial Poland. The author refers to the tradition of literary genres, but he is mostly concerned with concrete reality in Poland. Although the tone of the poem is ironic and mocking, giving it an appearance of being unimportant and playful, it created a great storm among Krasicki's contemporaries when it was discovered that he was the author of the work. Krasicki reacted to the versified "responses" with another poem, *Antymonachomachia* (1780), in which he appeared to withdraw the accusations, but in fact ridiculed both the monks and their defenders.

The poem was received enthusiastically during the Enlightenment, neglected by the Romantics, appreciated by the positivists; conservative clerical circles were outraged by it. The final evaluation of the poem is still subject to controversy, in regard not to its unquestionable artistic value, but to the circumstances of its publication. It is alleged that *Monachomachia* is associated with a conflict between several bishops and various religious orders not under their jurisdiction.

(See Enlightenment.)

BIBLIOGRAPHY

Pisma wybrane (Selected Writings), Volumes 1–4, edited by T. Mikulski, augmented by Z. Goliński, M. Klimowicz, and R. Wołoszyński, Warsaw, 1954.

Pisma wybrane (Selected Works), Volumes 1–4, edited by Tadeusz Mikulski, Warsaw: Państwowy Instytut Wydawniczy, 1954; Volumes 1–4, Polska Akademia Nauk, Instytut Badań Literackich.

Pisma poetyckie, Volumes 1–2, edited by Z. Goliński, Warsaw, 1976.

KRASIŃSKI, (NAPOLEON STANISŁAW ADAM LUDWIK) ZYGMUNT (1812–59), a poet, playwright, novelist, and philosopher, according to the traditional Romantic canon, was one of the "three national poets." On the one hand, he was deeply influenced by his aristocratic origin, and on the other hand, by the personality of his father, Wincenty, a Napoleonic general, who represented extreme loyalism to the tsar in politics and "the Classical wing" in literature. He studied law in Warsaw, but had to leave the university in 1829 because of the abusive behavior of fellow students toward him after he refused to participate in a patriotic demonstration; at the time he had given in to his father's extreme pressure. Before leaving for Switzerland that year, his first literary attempts were already behind him. These included several not very original historical novels (*Grób rodziny Reichstalów* [The Family Plot of the Reichstals], 1828, and *Władysław Herman i dwór jego* [Władysław Herman and His Court], 1830), written under the influence of the Gothic novel, the historical novels of Sir Walter Scott, the then-fashionable Byronism, and the "frenzied" historical French novel. Young Krasiński learned about Romanticism from French sources, and his interest in the novel coincided with the early stages of French Romanticism. At the same time, in his early works he showed interest in the problems which would later recur in the best of his works. One of the themes involves a hero devoted to one idea of "terrible vengeance," "vindictive betrayal," a demoniacal rebel and unhappy avenger of his own personal defeat. He also attempted to create in Polish the equivalent of the French Romantic "frenetic" prose: the results of this stylistic experiment can be seen in *Agaj-Han* (1833); *Nie-Boska Komedia* (The Undivine Comedy, 1835), especially in the scenes presenting the camp of the revolution; and in *Irydion* (1836).

His stay in Geneva appeared to be very important for Krasiński. His ruthlessly critical evaluation of his own early works went still further in 1830, after he met Mickiewicz. The great poet demanded "an idea" from the young colleague. At the same time, Krasiński developed a very close relationship with a young Englishman, Henry Reeve, under whose influence he developed the historiosophical stand he developed in *Nie-Boska Komedia* and *Irydion*. The process is documented in Krasiński's letters to Reeve and in the mostly unpublished pieces of poetic prose. In these writings the reader can see how Krasiński arrived at a new understanding of Romanticism through the generalization of his personal experiences. Krasiński discovered in Reeve a man of the Romantic Age, and also raised himself to the rank of literary hero. In the historiosophical considerations Krasiński undertook in Geneva, he was inspired by the French historians of the Restoration period: from Ballanche he took the idea of sacrifice as a necessary condition of progress in the advancement of the human spirit; from de Maistre, the motive of inevitable catastrophe threatening mankind; from Michelet, the vision of mankind's progress. Krasiński's historiosophical views constantly oscillated between optimism and catastrophism, between progressivism and traditionalism. His principal view, however, is providentialism (God's influence over history, the limits of human activity, and the relationship between freedom and necessity). The providentialism of the Romantics is linked with modern historicism through the concepts developed by G. Vico and I. G. Herder, that is, "historical providence"—which, as embodied in history, constituted its immanent law. Even though God governs the world, man is given the possibility of acting freely. From this point of view both *Nie-Boska Komedia* and *Irydion* are "providentialist dramas."

Krasiński did not take part in the November Uprising, again under heavy pressure from his father, who was a decided opponent of the uprising. The loyalty cost the poet a great deal, since he forever suffered the moral consequences of having violated the laws of honor. He often thereafter had to choose between his father and his country, and if he invariably chose the father, if he was unable to oppose him, it was not merely out of his wish to remain a loving and obedient son, for he often rejected his father's arguments and formulated his own views in the spirit of modern nineteenth century patriotism. Rather, his views were not quite free of feudal elements, since Krasiński's national conscience remained forever torn between seeing his homeland as the inheritance of all Poles and identifying it with the interests of the great aristocratic families. In his evaluation of this reality, however, he remained faithful to Romantic historiosophy, and for this reason he retains a firm position in Polish literature.

In 1832 his father summoned Krasiński back to Poland, then took him to Petersburg, where he was introduced to the tsar. His father urged him to follow a diplomatic career, but Krasiński opposed these plans and, using an eye disease as a pretext, went abroad again. He remained in Europe (mainly Italy and France) until the end of his life, returning only occasionally for brief periods. His conflicts with his father did not end. His father interfered in his son's most private problems (he was responsible for a breach between Krasiński and Joanna Bobrowa, to whom he had dedicated *Nie-Boska Komedia*). In 1843 his father forced Krasiński to marry Eliza Branicka, knowing full well that his son was then having an affair with Delfina Potocka, whom, according to rumor, he loved "fantastically."

With the publication of *Nie-Boska Komedia* (1835) and *Irydion* (1836), the young poet (not yet twenty-five) had his major works behind him. His views became more and more conservative. By the end of the thirties, Krasiński moved from progressive traditionalism to an organicistic theory of social progress. He combined these ideas with messianism and a distorted interpretation of Hegel's theories. He rejected Hegel's pantheistic concept of God, advocating a belief in a God who was at the same time transcendent and immanent. His idea of God and man, assuming the priority of religion and illumination, together with the idea of pure intuition as a tool of cognition, made him closer to the later writings of Schelling.

These new ideas are first expressed in *Trzy myśli pozostałe po ś. p. Henryku Ligenzie* (Three Thoughts Remaining After Henry Ligenza, 1840). They were also explicitly formulated in a treatise, *O stanowisku Polski z Bożych i ludzkich względów* (About the Position of Poland from the Point of View of God and Men), not published until 1912, as a result of the intervention of Catholic orthodox circles. According to Maria Janion, the most representative work of the period is a prophetic poem, *Przedświt* (Daybreak, 1843). Frightened by the growing revolutionary atmosphere in the country, he published *Psalmy przyszłości* (Psalms of the Future, 1845, with an enlarged edition in 1848), which provoked a response by Słowacki, *Odpowiedź na "Psalmy przyszłości"* (An Answer to Psalms of the Future). In the works of this period Krasiński revealed his conservative views: giving priority to the feudal tradition in the history of the nation, repudiating violence as the source of evil, and championing a specific, antirevolutionary concept of "action" as a component in the program of organic evolution. Krasiński opposed all revolutionary movements and argued for the separation of the struggle for independence from any revolutionary action. He felt that Poland would be saved by "God's will" and went so far as to condemn the struggle for independence.

Throughout his life Krasiński corresponded with numerous people. His letters are preserved for the most part; they contain many interesting views on literature, art, and philosophy. Jan Kott called the letters "the greatest novel of Polish Romanticism," for they are, in fact, the writer's diary, "the memoirs of the soul" of a great Romantic. Critics consider the letters to be Krasiński's greatest and most interesting achievement. This attitude reflects the change in the evaluation of the poet's work. Their artistic and ideological values have been questioned in a way in which those of neither of the other two great Romantic poets was ever criticized. The literary worth of Krasiński's work, especially his lyrical poems, was undermined. Krasiński was condemned as a "morally bound" man, as a conservative and an aristocratic reactionary. Regardless of the criticism, the high quality of *Nie-Boska Komedia* is unquestionable, and, on the basis of this work alone, Krasiński will hold his position in Polish literature as a writer who combined Christianity and historicism.

Nie-Boska Komedia, a drama, written in 1833, was published anonymously in Paris in 1835. The author's name was first revealed in Volume 1 of *Poezje* (Poetry, 1863) in Leipzig. It was first staged in Cracow on November 29, 1902. The title refers to the poem by Dante and can be understood in two ways: either it is a story of the nondivine (i.e., of people), or the "comedy" is directed against God and in spite of him.

Krasiński himself said in a letter to the poet Konstanty Gaszyński that the leading theme of *Komedia* was social and political conflict. The main hero, Count Henryk, leads a normal family life before getting involved in the social conflict. Thus the drama can be divided into two sections: Parts 1 and 2 present Henryk's private life; Parts 3 and 4, his participation in the history of the society. Originally, the drama was to be entitled *Mąż* (Husband; in fact, that is how Henryk is referred to in the dramatis personae), and the ambiguity of the word ("husband" or "man") corresponds to the personality of the hero as presented in Parts 1 and 2 (a bad husband and father); in Parts 3 and 4, he is depicted as the leader of the feudal party. In Part 1 the husband, who is a poet, is tempted by the phantoms of "false" poetry, the infernal demons of rebellious Romanticism representing absolute love, pride and contempt for the common people, the utopian dreams of happy life within the bosom of nature. Misled by these visions, the "false" poet neglects his duties as a husband and a father, thus driving his wife into insanity. He is criticized for his typically Romantic attitude toward life; he appears to be a heartless man, unable to see the moral beauty of family life, who tries to make poetry of reality, and is thus punished through both, the madness and death of his wife and the loss of eyesight of his son Orcio. Orcio is also a poet, but a genuine, prophetic one; he is thus sentenced to premature death.

In Part 2 the fate of Orcio is revealed: he bears the sign of damnation awaiting all prophets, and the unhappy father realizes that the only road to salvation is to love "poor people": evangelical morality is a cure for bitter Byronists and high-flown individualists. Nevertheless, fame remains the main goal of Henryk's life: He thus embodies Krasiński's dilemmas and is never totally condemned but is rather presented in tragic dimensions.

In Part 3 Henryk appears as the leader of the aristocrats opposing the victorious revolution of "the poor and the hungry," led by Pankracy. Henryk visits the enemy camp in disguise, watching the blasphemous rituals of the new revolutionary faith and the cruel revenge of the crowd. In the famous conversation with Pankracy, in which the new world confronts the old, he evaluates the revolution as "the old crimes of humanity, only dressed up anew." The agreement between the two camps is impossible, and in Part 4 the final battle takes place. Count Henryk's adherents, the aristocrats, appear to be weak, cowardly, and mean; he himself is condemned for loving no one but himself. Orcio is shot to death, and Count Henryk commits suicide, crying out, "Poetry, be damned!" Pankracy, the leader of the triumphant revolution, dreams of building a new happy future but is overcome by anxiety and doubt when a vision of Christ the Avenger appears before him. He dies, crying "Galilee, vicisti!" (You have won, man of Galilee!).

In the image of the great battle between the "aristocracy" and "democracy"—whose artistic power is exceptional in the literature of the world—Krasiński brought into play his knowledge of the Jacobins and the French Revolution, and of the Saint-Simonists. Such a view of the revolution, as well as Krasiński's awareness of the class conflicts of contemporary society and his foreboding about the coming social revolution—all these ideas were intellectually and artistically organized in terms of historicism and tragedy. For Krasiński the world of human history was nondivine: only Providence could give the world its goals and sense—as occurs at the end of the drama—although doubt lingers whether the vision of Christ brings death or rebirth of the world. Krasiński did not deprive the world of autonomy of action, but denied its having power of renascence; for whatever man might be able to do on the historical plane is relative and subjected to the final will of God. Such a vision of reality is given ideological unity regarding the concepts of the tragedy, understood in the spirit of Goethe and Hegel, as a necessity to destroy extreme, partial reasons in view of universal truth (for Krasiński, God's truth). The ideological structure of *Komedia,* which reflects the constant conflict between divine laws and the laws of human history, is based on contemporary historical providentialism, combined with catastrophism, which is characteristic of Krasiński's intellectual style. The structure of the drama emphasizes the same conflict by contrasting the medieval morality play, in which good and bad spirits fight for the sinner's soul, with contemporary drama regarding the world of history. These two different motivations tend to give the impression of ambiguity in the drama and account for its having received so many different, and often contradictory interpretations. Along with Goethe's *Faust,* Byron's *Manfred,* and Mickiewicz's *Dziady,* Part III, it is regarded as a Romantic "metaphysical drama," in which divine logic and human vulnerability, supernatural and earthly forces, interact in the spiritual life of the hero, a suffering, rebellious man, seeking the sense of his own existence between the earth and the heavens.

Krasiński intended to continue *Komedia.* He sketched a trilogy under the same title and completed Part I, in which the main character is a young man, led by Aligier (Dante) through the "inferno of the present day." The work was never completed. What remains lacks the artistic power of *Komedia.*

Nie-Boska Komedia was staged numerous times (since its first production in 1902) by some of Poland's greatest directors (Swinarski in 1965, Hanuszkiewicz in 1969). Great composers have written musical accompaniments to various productions (Różycki, Maklakiewicz, Bacewicz, and Penderecki). The part of Count Henryk was played by some of Poland's best actors. Its universal message also made it popular beyond Poland's borders: in the nineteenth century it was translated into German, French, Serbo-Croatian, Russian, and English; in the twentieth, into Swedish, Finnish, Danish, Italian, Hungarian, Spanish, and Arabic.

(See Romanticism.)

BIBLIOGRAPHY

Pisma (Writings), Volumes 1–8, edited by J. Czubek, Cracow, 1912.

Dzieła (Works), Volumes 1–12, edited by L. Piwiński, introduction by Manfred Kridl, Warsaw, 1931.

J. Kleiner, *Zygmunt Krasiński: Dzieje myśli* (Zygmunt Krasiński: History of Thought), T. 1–2, Lvov, 1912.

M. Janion. *Zygmunt Krasiński: Debiut dojrzałości* (Zygmunt Krasiński: Mature Debut), Warsaw, 1962.

English

Polish Romantic Drama, (three plays) translated by Harold B. Segel, Ithaca, New York: Cornell University Press, 1977; Contains translations of *Forefathers' Eve,* Part III, by Adam Mickiewicz; *The Un-Divine Comedy,* by Zygmunt Krasiński; and *Fantazy,* by Juliusz Słowacki.

Iridion, edited by George Rapall Noyes, translated by Florence Noyes, London: Oxford University Press, 1927; Westport, Connecticut: Greenwood, 1975.

The Undivine Comedy (Nie-Boska komedija), translated by Harriette E. Kennedy and Zofia Umińska, preface by G. K. Chesterton, London: G. G. Harrap, 1924; Warsaw: Ksiązn, Polska, 1924; Westport, Connecticut: Greenwood Press, 1976.

Zygmunt Krasiński, Romantic Universalist: An International Tribute, edited by Wacław Lednicki, New York: Polish Institute of Arts and Sciences in America, 1964.

KRASZEWSKI, JÓZEF IGNACY (pseudonym B. Bolesławita) (1812–87), was a novelist, poet, literary critic, publicist, journalist, editor, and social and political activist. He came from a *szlachta* (gentry) family. In 1829 he began his study of literature in Vilnius. Arrested in 1830 for being a member of a secret youth organization, he was released in 1832. In 1837–53 he led the life of a gentryman. He made his debut in 1829 and published his first stories in 1830, and his first novels in Vilnius during 1831–33. In 1837–50 he contributed to *Tygodnik Petersburski* (The Petersburg Weekly). During 1841–51 he was the editor of *Athenaeum* in Vilnius; during 1851–59 he worked as a columnist for *Gazeta Warszawska* (The Warsaw Gazette). In 1853 he settled down in Żytomierz, but in 1858–59 he became involved in various conflicts with the local *szlachta* (gentry), who considered him "a dangerous utopist" because of his views concerning the peasants. Having visited Western Europe for several months and discouraged from living among the *szlachta,* he accepted the proposal of L. Kronenberg and became chief editor of *Gazeta Codzienna* (The Daily Gazette) in Warsaw; in 1861 he changed the title of the newspaper to *Gazeta Polska* (The Polish Gazette) and published it until 1862. Kraszewski's contacts with Kronenberg, a representative of the bourgeoisie, helped him overcome his traditional views. Before the January Uprising (1863) he did not belong to those who favored armed resistance, and advocated peaceful development of the country, but he never accepted Wielopolski's policy favoring an attempt at independence from Russia and eventually had to leave Warsaw. In 1863 he settled in Dresden (though he had first attempted to remain in Galicia), but he maintained contacts with the country through letters, writing for the press in all three partitions and publishing books. In 1864–76 he was a publicist and political activist. Linked to bourgeois-democratic groups, he opposed the conservatists in his writings. He also joined the liberals in their polemics regarding the dogma of the pope's infallibility. After 1876 he devoted himself totally to literature. In 1883 he was arrested in Berlin and accused of being a French spy. His guilt was not fully confirmed (although his contacts with the French intelligence were beyond any doubt): he was sentenced to three and a half years of imprisonment in Magdeburg. He never stopped writing, and, upon release on bail for six months in order to receive medical treatment, he left Germany in 1885. He spent the rest of his life in Italy and Switzerland.

Kraszewski's output is indeed unique, and not only in Poland: Few writers have produced such an enormous number of works and with such great variety. However, he was chiefly a novelist. Beginning with *Poeta i świat* (The Poet and the World, 1839) he formulated his program (1830–32) advocating a "faithful picture" of social life. In the cycle which included *Historia Sawki* (The History of Sawka, 1842), *Ulana* (1843), *Budnik* (written in 1847), *Ostap Bondarczuk* (1847), *Chata za wsią* (Hut Beyond the Village, written in 1852), *Jermoła* (written in 1855), and *Historia kołka w płocie* (History of a Peg in the Fence, 1860), he raised the character of the peasantry to the rank of a literary theme, presenting characters as fully developed personalities—passionate, righteous, eager to learn, capable of sacrifice, and artistically gifted. This noble view of the peasant was an important addition to the Polish novel and was a clear indictment of the system, even though Kraszewski himself placed the onus on the dishonesty of individual officials. *Latarnia czarnoksięska* (A Magic Lantern, 1843–44) presented a much broader view of the peasant class and began a series of novels which attacked the moral decay of the *szlachta,* especially of the aristocracy: *Komedianci* (The Comedians, 1851), *Interesa familijne* (Family Interests, 1853), and *Dwa światy* (Two Worlds, 1856). The period of the forties marked Kraszewski's growing interest in philosophy, regarding human existence: *Pamiętniki nieznajomego* (The Diaries of a Stranger, 1846), *Sfinks* (The Sphinx, 1847), *Tomko Prawdzic* (1850), *Powieść bez tytułu* (A Novel Without a Title, 1855), and *Metamorfozy* (Metamorphosis, 1859). The characters in these novels, based on Kraszewski's own observations, rarely attain what they dream about and have to accept social conditions as they are. These pessimistic conclusions, that human life invariably ends in defeat, did not suggest, however, the rejection of all activity. Kraszewski valued work and regarded it as a moral necessity.

Besides historical novels, Kraszewski published his theoretical views on the subject of the novel. He advocated a tight relationship between plot and history; he felt that ideally the novel should be free of fictitious elements. His attempts to put these principles into practice in *Kościół świętomichalski w Wilnie* (St. Michael's Church in Vilnius, 1833) and*Żacy krakowscy w r. 1549* (Students of Cracow in 1549, published in 1845) were not artistically successful: Only when Kraszewski combined elements of the documentary novel and historical romance did he succeed, especially in his most artistic historical novel before 1863, *Zygmuntowskie czasy* (The Times of Zygmunt, 1846).

The Dresden period opened with a cycle (published as *Bolesławita*) in which he tried to portray the events of 1860–64, specifically the people involved in the struggle for independence. The term "pictures from nature" emphasized the documentary character of the works. The subsequent novels of the cycle reflected the change of the author's attitude toward the January Uprising of 1863, which ranged from feelings of enthusiasm and solidarity to questioning of the sense of such a struggle and his advocacy of a peaceful solution—in effect, a spiritual revolution which included utilizing moral pressure. Consequently, Bolesławita's "pictures" can be divided into three groups: novels written during the course of the struggle, 1863–64: *Dziecię Starego Miasta* (Child of the Old Town, 1863), *Szpieg* (Spy, 1864), and *Para czerwona* (Red Steam, 1865); novels composed near the end of the Uprising and after the defeat, 1864–66: *My i oni* (We and They), *Moskal* (Moscowite), and *Żyd* (The Jew); and, finally, novels connected with later polemics and evaluations of the Uprising: *Dziadunio* (Grandpa, 1869) and *Zagadki* (Riddles, 1870–73). The Uprising also made Kraszewski reevaluate the role of individual social groups. In his view the nobility lost its leadership, and the intelligentsia and young tradesmen proved superior in their patriotism.

In his subsequent novels he maintained that over the centuries of idleness the *szlachta* became biologically and psychologically depraved: *Morituri* (1874) and *Niebieskie migdały* (Blue Almonds, 1876). He also did not trust the middle class, whom he accused of concentrating on their own business and clothing their actions with beautiful clichés: *Złoty Jasieńko* (Golden Johnny, 1869), *Roboty i prace* (Labor and Work, 1875), *Ładny chłopiec* (Handsome Youth, 1879). Among the most interesting novels of the period are those connected with the writer's debates with the conservatives: *Pałac i folwark* (The Mansion and the Grange, 1871), *Ramultowie* (Ramultows, 1872), *Wielki nieznajomy* (The Great Stranger, 1871–72), *Pamiętnik panicza* (Memoir of the Young Master, 1875), and *Dziennik Serafiny* (Seraphine's Diary, 1876).

The third period of Kraszewski's work is associated with the development of the historical novel. He made use of his earlier historical studies and initiated a major work on popularizing Polish history in the form of novels. The first attempts were connected with the political atmosphere after the defeat of the Uprising: *Rzym za Nerona* (Rome During Nero's Reign, written in 1964) and *Tułacze* (The Exiles, 1868–70). After 1870 Kraszewski moved to the eighteenth century as the background of the majority of his works: at this time he wrote the so-called Saxon Trilogy: *Hrabina Cosel* (The Countess Cosel, 1874), *Bruehl*, 1865, and *Z siedmioletniej wojny* (From the Seven-Year War, 1876). His other novels from this period include *Macocha* (The Stepmother, 1873), *Warszawa w 1794 roku* (Warsaw in the Year 1794, 1873), *Historia o Janaszu Korczaku i pięknej miecznikównie* (History of Janasz Korczak and the Beautiful Swordbearer's Daughter, 1875), and *Krzyżacy 1410* (The Teutonic Knights 1410, published in 1874). These works emphasized a broader interest in history.

In 1876 Kraszewski started publishing a huge cycle of historical novels (twenty-nine novels in seventy-nine volumes), covering the history of Poland from legendary times (*Stara baśń* [The Old Legend]) through the eighteenth century (*Saskie ostatki* [The Last Saxon Judgment], written in 1886, published after the author's death in 1889). The main idea of the cycle is the constant threat of Germany to Polish national existence. The work was stimulated by the publication of the cycle *Die Ahnen* by G. Freytag, in which the author praised German victories over "the savage Slavs." In regard to internal problems, Kraszewski emphasized the struggle for power, blaming the magnates for many of the misfortunes of the Polish state and sympathizing with the oppressed peasants and townsmen. He questioned the myth of Poland as a power and revealed the sources of the state's destruction in the eighteenth century. He was careful, however, to balance fiction with historical sources. His "history in novels" was a type of handbook of national history and was available in the three partitions of Poland. The novels differ in artistic value. The outstanding ones include *Stara baśń* (The Old Legend), *Masław* (1877), *Król chłopów* (King of the Peasants, 1881), and *Banita* (1885).

According to Stanisław Burkot, Kraszewski's work made a breakthrough in the development of the Polish novel. A disciple of the realists, he introduced their achievements into Polish literature, creating models of plot construction, characterization of social groups, and dialogue. Regarding the task of the novelist as watching and representing reality, not in creating new worlds, he gave the picture of the society of his times and his own view of the history of the nation in his 223 novels. He never wrote a masterpiece, but the Polish novel during the second half of the nineteenth century grew on the foundation of his work.

As a poet and playwright Kraszewski left little of permanent value to Polish literature. His poetic works, contained in the two volumes of *Poezje* (Poems, 1838), as well as his national Lithuanian epic *Anafielas* (1840–45), are merely imitations of Romanticism. His poem *Dziad i baba* (The Old Man and the Old Woman) became widely popular. His best poems are to be found in *Hymny boleści* (Hymns of Pain, 1857). Of his twenty plays, only his *kontusz* comedies (comedies ridiculing the nobility)—*Miód kasztelański* (Castle Honey, 1860) and *Panie kochanku* (My Dear, 1867)—are worth mentioning. Kraszewski was much more interesting as a writer of sketches of his travels in Poland and abroad, as a historian and editor of historical sources, old Polish literature, and Shakespeare's dramas. His publicistic pieces, as well as literary criticism, are also of major importance.

Apart from literature, Kraszewski contributed to art and music: he painted and sketched, collected paintings, composed music, and was a music critic. He also left behind an enormous number of letters.

Kraszewski's work still awaits a just evaluation, but one thing can be said beyond doubt—he created a Polish novel for the popular reader. During the Dresden period he became the ideological leader of the nation. Appropriately referred to as "an institution," he created a monumental amount of work in the domain of culture, far beyond the capabilities of any single individual.

Stara baśń (The Old Legend: A Novel from the Ninth Century), the first in the cycle of novels based on Polish history, was published in 1876. It presents, according to contemporary research, the process of the formation of the Polish state and the legendary Piasts' rise to power. The conflicts in which the fictitious characters of the novel are involved are set against the background of the disintegration of the tribal community and the German expansion into the lands of Polanie (the Polan tribe). With epic impetus Kraszewski recreated the everyday life, customs, and traditions of the Slavs, presenting an artistically convincing vision of pre-Christian Poland. In the construction of the plot Kraszewski employed the legends about the death of King Popiel (that he was eaten by mice) and the ritual hair clippings of Ziemowit, Piast's son, presenting rational interpretations of these myths. It is Kraszewski's most popular novel.

(See Positivism.)

BIBLIOGRAPHY

Cykl powieści historycznych obejmujących dzieje Polski (A Cycle of Historical Novels Encompassing Polish History), Volumes 1–29, Warsaw, 1958–63.

Dzieła: Powieści obyczajowe (Works: Novels of Customs and Manners), Cracow, after 1959.

Dzieła: Powieści historyczne (Works: Historical Novels), Warsaw, after 1961.

W. Danek, *Józef Ignacy Kraszewski,* Warsaw, 1973.

English

The Princess and the Jew, translated by Meta De Vere, New York: G. Munro, 1889.

The Countess Cosel (Hrabina Cosel), translated by S. C. de Soissons, London: Downey, 1901; New York: Brentano's, 1902.

Count Bruehl (Bruehl), translated by S. C. de Soissons, London: Greening, 1911; New York, 1922.

Jermoła, translated by M. Carey, New York, 1891.

The Jew (Żyd), translated by Linda de Kowalewski, New York, 1893; London: Heinemann, 1893, with an introduction by Edmund Gosse.

KRONIKA POLSKA (Polish Chronicles) (see Medieval Literature).

KRONIKA WIELKOPOLSKA (The Greater Poland Chronicle) (see Medieval Literature).

KRÓL-DUCH (King-Spirit) (see Słowacki).

KRUCZKOWSKI, LEON (1900–1962), a playwright, prose writer, and publicist, graduated from the chemistry department of a technical school. He later worked in industry and a vocational school. In 1926–33 he lived in the coal-mining region Zagłębie Dąbrowskie and worked for the local press and the Cracow newspaper *Gazeta Literacka* (Literary Gazette). Upon his return to Cracow he became an activist for leftist social and cultural organizations and worked as a publicist for many leftist papers. He also published several journalistic brochures. An officer in the campaign of 1939, he was detained for the rest of the war and occupation in German camps, where he organized and ran a theater, staging works of Polish classics. After the war he held many important posts in the Communist Party and in administration (e.g., member of the Central Committee, member of the *Sejm* and State Council, and Vice-Minister of Culture). He was active in the Union of Polish Writers, becoming its president in 1949–56. During the period of his political activity he published several collections of publicistic pieces (e.g., *Spotkania i konfrontacje* [Meetings and Confrontations], 1950, and *Wśród swoich i obcych* [Among One's Own and Others, 1954]). He received the International Lenin Award in 1953 for "cementing peaceful co-existence among nations."

His literary career began with poetry; he made his debut in 1919 in the magazine *Maski* (Masks). Ten years later he published his only collection, *Młoty nad światem* (Hammers over the World, 1928). His poetry gives expression to radical philosophical and social ideas concerning the class struggle, which seem to sum up his experiences in Zagłębie. In its artistic form Kruczkowski refers to the models of Romantic poetry but also points to Żeromski as his spiritual patron. His early stories have the same ideological base: they are Neo-Romantic in form, but present the author as a keen observer of social phenomena. In 1930, after reading the memoirs of K. Deczyński, Kruczkowski wrote his best novel, *Kordian i cham* (Kordian and the Boor, 1932), which revised the Romantic myths which were deeply rooted in the national consciousness, and presented an interpretation of the November Uprising of 1830 from the Marxist point of view. His next novel, *Pawie pióra* (Peacock's Feathers, 1935), presented an accurate analysis of social and political relations in rural Galicia before World War I. The novel *Sidła* (Snares, 1937) is a psychological portrait of the contemporary intelligentsia. His work on two subsequent novels was interrupted by the war. In 1954–57 he wrote several stories presenting the ideological and moral dilemmas Communists had to face during those years (published posthumously in 1963 in the volume *Szkice z piekła uczciwych* [Sketches from the Hell of Honest People]).

As a playwright, Kruczkowski made his first attempts shortly before the war; after the war, drama became the dominant genre in his writings. In some plays he presents the political conflicts and dilemmas encountered during the first years of the new rule in a rather traditional form (*Odwety* [Retaliations], 1948, *Odwiedziny* [The Visits], 1955), but he also turns to universal moral and ideological problems, casting them in the form of an intellectual drama. In this convention he wrote *Niemcy* (The Germans, 1949), which presents the various moral stands taken by Germans during the war; *Juliusz i Ethel* (1954), which depicts the story of the trial of the Rosenbergs, condemned to death in the United States for spying for the Soviet Union, which he depicted as the tragedy of allegedly innocent people condemned by ungrounded accusations; *Pierwszy dzień wolności* (First Day of Freedom, 1959), which underscored the problem of the conflict between human freedom and social duty; and his last play, *Śmierć gubernatora* (The Death of the Governor, 1961), which depicted the moral defeat of power based on violence.

According to Janusz Rohoziński, *Niemcy* (The Germans) was one of Kruczkowski's most effective plays. The author's main preoccupation is the moral motivation of "honest Germans" under the Nazi rule and the reasons for which the Nazi system could be imposed upon a nation with such high cultural and humanistic traditions. The embodiment of such values is Professor Sonnenbruch, who condemns Nazi ideology morally and politically but refuses to face it. Sonnenbruch's jubilee brings all members of his family home (among others, his son, an SS officer; his daughter-in-law, who lost her husband and children during the war; and his daughter Ruth, a pianist touring Europe). The conflict centers around Joachim Peters, a German anti-Nazi and Communist activist, formerly Sonnenbruch's colleague and friend, now escaped from a concentration camp and seeking help. He makes the professor realize the moral falsity of his stand and the illusiveness of personal freedom in a situation which demands active political choice. Eventually, only Ruth decides to help Joachim, driven by her instinctive rebellion against injustice. The professor discovers that the results of his research are used in creating new arms and is left with the tragic feeling of isolation and moral crisis. The drama is very accurate in its presentation of reality; it depicts German society of the time, its ideological conflicts, and the atmosphere of fanatic hatred, fear, and terror. Going beyond realistic-psychological convention, the drama reaches the rank of a universal intellectual morality play.

(See Contemporary Polish Literature.)

BIBLIOGRAPHY

Leon Kruczkowski, *Dramaty* (Dramas), Warsaw, 1962.

English

E. J. Czerwiński, "Leon Kruczkowski: A Search for Universality," in *Contemporary Polish Theater and Drama (1956–1984)*, New York: Greenwood Press, 1988.

The First Day of Freedom (Pierwszy dzień wolności), translated by Floryan Sobieniowski and John Coates, Warsaw: Authors Agency, no date.

The Germans (Niemcy), translated by M. Michatosko and J. Radker, Warsaw: Authors Agency, no date.

KRZYSZTOŃ, JERZY (1931–82), a prose writer and playwright, spent the war years in Kazakhstan, where he had been deported together with his family in 1940, then in Iran, India, and East Africa. He returned to Poland in 1948 and completed his degree in English philology at the Catholic University of Lublin. After 1960 he worked for Polish Radio in Warsaw. He was also a member of the editorial board of a Catholic monthly, *Więź* (Bond). Constrained by intensified psychological depression, he committed suicide. In his writings, semiautobiographical and moralistic in character, he touched upon social and psychological problems, depicting the conflict between the war and postwar generations and analyzing the mythology of war from the perspective of the new reality. He combined moral elements with metaphoric and symbolic ones; he also employed black humor. He published several collections of stories: *Opowiadania indyjskie* (Indian Stories, 1953); *Sekret i inne opowiadania* (The Secret and Other Stories, 1956); *Złote gody* (Golden Years, 1965); *Panna radosna* (A Joyful Maiden, 1969); *Cyrograf dojrzałości* (A Pledge of Maturity, 1975). He also published the novels *Kamienne niebo* (A Stone Heaven, 1958), made into a film in 1959, about the Warsaw Uprising, and *Wielbłąd na stepie* (A Camel on the Steppes, 1978), memories of his childhood spent during the war in the Soviet Union; he included a continuation of his memoirs in *Krzyż Południa* (Southern Cross, 1983). According to Jacek Łukasiewicz, his main novel, *Obłęd* (Madness, 1980), is highly ambiguous: it is based on the political reality of contemporary times, but it is also a parable of the myth of Odysseus. It is a literary description of insanity arising from the chaos of the contemporary world and, at the same time, is a personal commitment to find a balance of values. He wrote of his impressions of the United States in *Skok do Eldorado* (A Jump into Eldorado, 1967). He also wrote several plays for radio and was a translator from English. He received a PEN Club award in 1971.

BIBLIOGRAPHY

The Boys from Verdun (Chłopcy spod Verdun), translated by Krzysztof Klinger, Warsaw: Authors Agency, no date.

KRZYŻACY (Knights of the Cross) (see Sienkiewicz).

KRZYŻANOWSKI, JULIAN (1892–1976), literary historian, folklorist, and editor, studied Polish philology from 1911 to 1914 at the Jagiellonian University. He made his debut in 1913 in *Pamiętnik Literacki* (Literary Diary). As an Austrian subject during World War I he was sent to an internment camp in Siberia by the Russian authorities. He returned in 1920, continued his studies, then worked as a teacher and a lecturer at the Catholic University of Lublin. In 1927–30 he lectured at the School of Slavonic and East European Studies in London and from 1930 to 1934 at the Latvian University in Riga. In 1934 he became professor of history of Polish literature at Warsaw University, where he remained until 1962. During the occupation he was one of the organizers and an active participant of the underground university. He was editor of several journals: *Nauka i Sztuka* (Education and Art), *Pamiętnik Literacki* (Literary Diary), and *Literatura Ludowa* (Folk Literature). In 1957–58 he lectured on Polish literature at Columbia University in New York. He was a member of the Polish Academy of Sciences and president of many scholarly organizations. He received honorary doctorates from Jagiellonian University (1964) and Wrocław University (1972).

As a historian of Polish literature Krzyżanowski developed a synthetic approach, both in his general works and in his monographs. *Historia literatury polskiej: Alegoryzm-preromantyzm* (A History of Polish Literature: From Allegorism to Pre-Romanticism, 1939; sixth edition, 1979) covers the period through Romanticism (the remainder of the manuscript was destroyed in 1939). The preserved materials helped him write *Neoromantyzm polski 1890–1918* (Polish Neo-Romanticism, 1890–1918, 1963; third edition, 1980). He next published a complete edition of *Dzieje literatury polskiej, od początków do czasów najnowszych* (A History of Polish Literature, From Its Beginnings to Modern Times, 1969, third edition, revised, 1979; translated into English in 1978). He also wrote in English: *Polish Romantic Literature* (1938, 1968). His views on literature and its scientific analysis were expressed in *Nauka o literaturze* (The Science of Literature, 1966, 2nd edition, revised, 1969) and in the popular work *Sztuka słowa: Rzecz o zjawiskach literackich* (Art of the Word: A Matter of Literary Phenomena, 1972, second edition, 1973). He worked mainly in the area of old Polish literature, for example, in his studies *Bogurodzica* (Mother of God) and *Kazania świętokrzyskie* (The Holy Cross Gospels); the Renaissance and the Baroque, as in *Romans pseudohistoryczny w Polsce wieku XVI* (The Pseudohistoric Romance in Poland in the Sixteenth Century, 1926) and *Romans polski wieku XVI* (The Polish Romance in the Sixteenth Century, 1934); and in the collections *Od średniowiecza do baroku* (From the Middle Ages to the Baroque, 1938) and *W wieku Reja i Stańczyka* (In the Century of Rej and Stańczyk, 1958). The later epochs, from Romanticism to the literature between the wars, are presented in the collections *W świecie romantycznym* (In the Romantic World, 1961) and *W kręgu wielkich realistów* (In the Circle of Great Realists, 1962). He was particularly interested in Sienkiewicz's work: he devoted three books and a number of papers to the Nobel Prize winner. He also wrote a monograph on Reymont and a sketch on Orkan.

Krzyżanowski was the founder of the Polish school of folklore studies and the country's most outstanding folklorist. He included the Polish fable and tale in the international system of Aarne-Thompson and published a fundamental work, *Polska bajka ludowa w układzie systematycznym* (The Polish Folk Tale in a Systematic Order, two volumes, 1947; second edition, revised, 1962–63). He expanded upon 500 Polish proverbs in the two parts of the collection, *Mądrej głowie dość dwie słowie* (Two Words Are Enough for Someone Smart, 1958–60; third edition, revised, 1975). The overlap area between literature and the spoken tradition is presented in *Paralele: Studia porównawcze z pogranicza literatury i folkloru* (Parallels: A Comparative Study on the Borders of Literature and Folklore, 1935; third edition, revised, 1977). Other works on the subject are gathered in three volumes: *Szkice folklorystyczne* (Folklore Sketches, 1980). He was also a coeditor of and major contributor to *Nowa księga przysłów i wyrażeń przysłowiowych polskich* (A New Volume of Proverbs and Polish Proverbial Expressions, Volumes 1–4, 1969–78), *Słownik folkloru polskiego* (A Dictionary of Polish Folklore, 1965), and *Dzieje folklorystyki polskiej* (A History of Polish Folklore, Volume 1, 1970). He was also an outstanding editor of the works of Kochanowski, Słowacki, Sienkiewicz, Orzeszkowa, Mickiewicz, Kraszewski and Kolberg; of Kochowski, Rej, Tetmajer and Sęp-Szarzyński.

Krzyżanowski was an outstanding researcher and theorist of literature. He enriched his works with his knowledge of folklore, sociology of literary life, and comparative studies. He wrote in a lively personal style that attracted even nonprofessional readers. Opposed to the metaphysical and moralizing tendencies of the humanities of previous years, he regarded the task of literary studies as predominantly cognitive.

(See Baroque.)

BIBLIOGRAPHY

A History of Polish Literature (Historia Literatury Polskiej), translated by Doris Ronowicz, Warsaw, PWN—Polish Scientific, 1978.

English

Polish Romantic Literature, London: G. Allen and Unwin, 1930; New York: Dutton, 1931; Freeport, New York: Books for Libraries Press, 1968.

KSIĘGA UBOGICH (The Book of the Poor) (see Kasprowicz).

KUNCEWICZOWA, MARIA (née Szczepańska) (1899–1989), a prose writer, was brought up in a patriotic family whose traditions included championing the national struggle for independence. Her father was a headmaster; her mother, a violinist. The family lived in Russia until 1899 (she was born in Samara). She studied French philology in Nancy, Polish philology in Cracow and Warsaw, and voice at the musical conservatories in Warsaw and Paris. She published her first stories in *Pro arte et studio* and *Bluszcz* (Ivy); after 1924 she worked for the Polish section of PEN Club (in 1939 she became vice president). During World War II she lived in France and England; during 1940–55 she ran the Polish section of PEN Club in exile in London. In 1956 she left for the United States: from 1963 to 1971 she taught Polish literature at the University of Chicago. During her visits to Poland she lived in Kazimierz on Vistula, where she spent her last years. She received numerous awards, among others the Golden Wreath of the Polish Academy of Literature in 1938 and a medal from the Kościuszko Foundation in 1971.

Kuncewiczowa is a representative of Polish contemporary psychological prose. Her works include journalistic reports, articles, literary studies, sketches, and translations. Her early works consist of stories which appeared in the collection *Przymierze z dzieckiem* (An Alliance with a Child, 1927) and the novelette *Twarz mężczyzny* (The Face of a Man, 1928), published in the volume *Twarz mężczyzny i trzy nowele* (The Face of a Man and Three Novels, 1969). She wrote of the personal experiences of a woman—marriage, love, maternity—using a naturalistic style, but also employing subtle humor and lyricism. She constantly returned to these themes. Basing her analysis on her own experiences, she revealed the complexes resulting from a lack of inner balance and analyzed the emotional states of a woman from her teens to old age; her novel *Cudzoziemka* (The Foreign Woman) is a psychological study on these themes. In the collection of stories *Dwa księżyce* (Two Moons, 1933, 1960), written under the influence of her first impressions of Kazimierz in 1930, Kuncewiczowa portrayed the contrasting milieus of the little resort town. Poland's social problems between the wars were explored in the stories in the volumes *Serce kraju* (The Heart of the Country, 1939) and *W domu i w Polsce* (At Home and in Poland, 1939), and the literary sketches *Dyliżans warszawski* (Warsaw Stagecoach, 1935; revised edition, 1958), which portrayed the atmosphere of everyday life in a great city. According to Danuta Knysz-Rudzka, she created the first serial for radio in Poland, *Dni powszednie państwa Kowalskich* (The Ordinary Days of the Kowalskis, 1938, 1960) and *Kowalscy się odnaleźli* (The Kowalskis Have Returned, 1938). She published her notes from a trip to Palestine in *Miasto Heroda* (Herod's City, 1939). The problems of the war and the fate of Poles are captured in her diary of 1939, *Klucze* (The Keys; published in London in 1943; Warsaw, 1948), and the novel *Zmowa nieobecnych* (A Conspiracy of the Absent; published in London, 1946; Munich, 1950; Warsaw, 1957). She portrayed the influence of history on the formation of an individual's character and depicted patriotic feelings in the novel *Leśnik* (The Forester; published in Paris, 1952; Warsaw, 1957), in which she questioned established literary traditions and revised the concepts of the nation, of one's homeland, of being Polish. Critics considered the novel to be the most mature among her works. Human lives disturbed by World War II formed the basis of her novel *Gaj oliwny* (Olive Grove, 1961), which presented reality through the eyes of a child. *Tristan 1946* (1967, which was also adapted for television) juxtaposes the story of Tristan and Isolde with the generation of survivors. The sketches from her trip to Spain, *Don Kichot i niańki* (Don Quixote and the Nursemaids, 1965), combine the elements of journalism, history, and culture with an intimately personal diary. Kuncewiczowa's prose presents man in conflict with his environment, his social duties, and his own past. The essence of her work is its autobiographic character, which is revealed in the diptych *Fantomy* (Phantoms, 1971) and in *Natura* (Nature, 1975). Kuncewiczowa also edited two anthologies of contemporary Polish literature: *Modern Polish Prose* (1945) and *The Modern Polish Mind* (1962). Her works were very popular in Poland and abroad and were translated into a number of languages.

Cudzoziemka (The Foreign Woman), a novel, was first published in *Kurier Poranny* (Morning Courier) in 1935; the definitive edition was published in Warsaw in 1936. The plot is enclosed within the period of one day and presents the thoughts and experiences of the main character, Róża Żabczyńska, who sums up her unsuccessful life on the threshold of death. She is searching for the causes of her personal defeat by analyzing her own psyche. The daughter of a Polish emigrant, she was born in Russia. The feeling of political and ethnic alienation accompanied her to Poland, where she returned at the age of sixteen. The gap between Róża and her environment is widened by her unhappy love for Michał Badski and the necessity to give up her career as a violinist. The lack of erotic and artistic fulfillment results in her constant dissatisfaction and the need to torment others. The dreams to which Róża escapes from reality are masochistic in character. Critics emphasized the psychoanalytic interpretation of the personality of the main heroine, the artistic perfection of the novel, and the originality of its structure, which resembles that of a dream or a musical piece. The importance of music and the analysis of love and psychological loneliness are characteristic themes in Kuncewiczowa's works. Another fundamental feature is her reliance on autobiographical material (*Cudzoziemka* is a transposition of the biography of the writer's mother). The novel is considered one of the most outstanding achievements of psychologism between the wars. It ran through more than twenty editions and has been translated into every major language.

(See Contemporary Polish Literature.)

BIBLIOGRAPHY

English

The Conspiracy of the Absent: A Novel (Zmowa Nieobecnych), translated by Maurice Michael and Harry Stevens, New York: Roy, 1950; London, New York: Hutchinson, 1950.

The Forester: A Novel (Leśnik), translated by H. C. Stevens, New York: Roy, 1954; London, New York: Hutchinson, 1954.

The Keys: A Journey through Europe at War, London, New York: Hutchinson, 1945.

The Olive Grove (Gaj oliwny), New York: Walker, 1963.

The Stranger: A Novel (Cudzoziemka), translated by B.W.A. Massey, New York: L. B. Fischer, 1945; London, New York: Hutchinson, 1947.

The Modern Polish Mind, Boston: Little, Brown, 1962; London: Secker and Warburg, 1962, 1963; New York: Grosset and Dunlap, 1963.

Modern Polish Prose, Birkenhead, England: Polish Publications Committee, 1945.

Polish Millstones, translated by Stephen Garry, London: P. S. King and Staples, 1942.

Tristan, New York: G. Braziller, 1974.

Werewolves (Wijuny), translated by Kaut-Howson, in *Plays and Players,* November/December, London, 1978.

KWIATY POLSKIE (Polish Flowers) (see Tuwim).

L

LALKA (The Doll) (see Prus).

LAM, JAN (1838–86), a journalist, novelist, and satirist, was born the son of an Austrian official. He chose to be a Pole; he later fought in the January Uprising (1863) and opposed in his writings the Germanization of Polish literature. He started publishing satires while still a student of law in Lvov. His early works were full of polemics and scandals which were recorded in the press. These formed the essence of his works. He was on the board of *Gazeta Narodowa* (The National Gazette) and *Dziennik Polski* (The Polish Daily). He became famous with his *Kroniki Lwowskie* (Lvov Chronicles), in which he supported the policies of A. Gołuchowski, who as a supporter of Galicia championed the guaranteeing of autonomy for the region (within the boundaries of the Czech Republic and Austria). He became still more daring in his criticism of political, social, and cultural life, and his popularity among readers began to grow. He ridiculed conservatism, both of the nobility and of the petit bourgeois. He fought against clericalism, the policy of conciliation, but was also opposed to flashy displays of patriotism. He exploited the poetics of the pamphlet genre, using authentic facts as pretext for his story. The fictitious scenes and conversations in which authentic personages take part, as well as the absurdly exaggerated causes of real events, had their logical motivation in a thorough and ruthless analysis of the contemporary social scene. According to Stanisław Frybes, the unifying feature of these works is their humor, based on daring and astonishing intellectual associations. Lam's depiction of Galicia's "high society" presented a grotesque vision of the world, monstrous and senseless, in which people were funny and pathetic puppets. Lam's works, always based on authentic events and people, require extensive historical commentaries to be understood by contemporary readers.

His first novels, both written in 1869—*Wielki świat Capowic* (Capowice's Great World) and *Koroniarz w Galicji* (The Crowner in Galicia)—stem from his work as a journalist and are interspersed with journalistic pieces. They are grotesque, ironic, and parodistic in style, reflected in the point of view of the omniscient narrator, in the functional treatment of the plot, and in the conscious, caricaturelike simplification of the psychological presentation of characters. Referring to the techniques of the philosophical tale, Lam created highly original and humorous pieces, unpretentious and artistically consistent. In *Głowy do pozłoty* (Addleheaded, 1873) he attempted to give a satirical but epiclike quality to the society of Galicia after the January Uprising. With this novel, Lam began to draw from the tradition of Dickens and Thackeray. He gave up omniscient narration in favor of satirical thrust. However, neither in this novel nor in *Idealiści* (The Idealists, 1876) was he able to carry the realistically outlined themes to their logical conclusion. He resorted to motives of "fortuitous coincidence" and sensational elements.

Lam's works include novels and stories, *Dziwne kariery* (Strange Careers, 1880) and *Pan komisarz wojenny* (Martial Commissar, 1863), and the collections *Rozmaitości i powiastki* (Variety and Tales, 1878) and *Humoreski* (Humoresques, 1883). Near the end of his life the writer was weakened by illness and the attacks of his opponents. He became much milder in his satirical criticism. Critics disagree over the merits of Lam's works: he was attacked by conservatists, but highly estimated by writers like Bolesław Prus. Critics of literature appreciate much of his work and value his role in the development of Polish satire.

BIBLIOGRAPHY

Pisma (Writings), Volumes 1–5, Anniversary Edition, 1838–1938, edited by S. Lam, introduction by Julian Krzyżanowski, Warsaw, 1938.

Dzieła literackie (Literary Works), Volumes 1–4, edited and with an introduction by S. Frybes, Warsaw, 1956–57.

LANGE, ANTONI (pseudonyms Napierski and A. Wrzesień) (1861–1929), was a poet, novelist, short story writer, playwright, critic, and translator. He came from a Jewish family with patriotic Polish traditions (his father took part in the November Uprising). He studied at the University of Warsaw but was soon expelled for participating in a student demonstration and for a time worked as a private teacher. In 1886–90 he studied Oriental languages, philosophy, and literature in Paris. During this period he sent reviews of French literature to the Warsaw papers; he also worked for the Paris Socialist paper *Pobudka* (Reveille). In 1890 he returned to Warsaw and became the literary editor of the Warsaw journal *Życie* (Life,

1887–91). In 1907 he was imprisoned in connection with a press trial; from 1909 to 1912 he lived in Paris.

Lange's early poetry is rhetorical, devoted to revolutionary, social, political, and patriotic themes. His preoccupation with the poetry of Romanticism is reflected in *Pogrzeb Shelleya* (Shelley's Funeral, 1890) and poems from *Pobudka* (Reveille) gathered in the volumes *Pogrobowcom* (To the Inheritors, 1901) and *Pierwszy dzień stworzenia: Pieśni społeczne* (First Day of Creation: Social Songs, 1907). Lange was one of the first poets whose works expressed the motives of the "young generation"—feelings of decadence and pessimism as in *Poezje* (Poems, 1895–98). His poems also expressed his interests in cosmogonic hypotheses, mythology, esotericism, and the social sciences. The intellectual atmosphere and erudition of Lange's poetry, his use of the Mediterranean tradition and of exotic cultures (Polynesian and Mexican legends, and religions of the East), together with his formal sophistication, are factors which relate Lange to Parnassism. He was apparently the first Polish poet to use assonance; he exploited rare and intricate poetic forms such as *pantun,* the French ballad, *stornella,* and *rondeletto.* In the later period the dominant trend in his poetry was reflective intellectual lyrics, published in the volume *Rozmyślania* (Meditations, 1906). The collection *XXVII sonetów* (XXVII Sonnets, 1914, unsigned, 110 copies) continued this trend and revealed Classical tendencies. The collection *Trzeci dzień* (The Third Day, 1925) referred in its idea and form to the mystic messianism of Romanticism. As a critic Lange wrote objective literary analyses of new trends in European literature: *Studia z literatury francuskiej* (Studies of French Literature, 1897) and *Studia i wrażenia* (Studies and Impressions, 1900). He also published sketches on contemporary Polish literature, *Pochodnie w mroku: Żeromski—Reymont—Kasprowicz* (Torches in the Dusk: Żeromski, Reymont, Kasprowicz, 1927). He is the author of numerous short stories, among them an interesting collection of science fiction, *W czwartym wymiarze* (In the Fourth Dimension, 1922); two novels, *Stypa* (Funeral Banquet, 1911) and *Miranda* (1924); tragedies, *Atylla* (Attilla, 1898) and *Wenedzi* (The Wenedians, 1908); and a dramatic poem, *Malczewski* (1931) in *Ostatni zbiór poezji, Part 3* (The Last Collection of Poems, Part 3). He was also an editor and translator (translating, among other things, contemporary French literature, Old English, and Sanskrit).

(See *Młoda Polska.*)

BIBLIOGRAPHY

Rozmyślania i inne Wiersze (Reflections and Other Poems), wybór i wstęp (edited and with an introduction) J. Poradecki, Warsaw, 1979.

LEC, STANISŁAW JERZY (de Tusch-lec) (1909–66), poet, satirist, and aphorist, was educated in Vienna and Lvov (from 1927 to 1933 he studied law and Polish philology at the local university). During the interwar years he was associated with the Communist left and contributed his work to the antigovernment satirical weekly *Szpilki* (Needles and Pins). During the war he was imprisoned in a German concentration camp; after escaping he participated in the Communist resistance movement. From 1946 to 1950 he served as the press attaché of the Polish mission in Vienna, then lived in Israel, from which he returned to Poland in 1952. Disillusioned with Communism, he did not participate in politics during the later years of his life.

He created satirical and meditative poetry, which was characterized by epigrammatic conciseness and a predilection toward sophisticated linguistic concepts. These poems were collected in the volumes *Spacer cynika* (Cynical Man Takes a Walk, 1946), *Kpię i pytam o drogę* (I Jeer and I Ask for Directions, 1959), *Do Abla i Kaina* (To Abel and Cain, 1961), *Fraszkobranie* (Harvesting Epigrams, 1966), and others. He gained popular acclaim and a permanent place in Polish letters as an aphorist, the author of a series of maxims entitled *Myśli nieuczesane* (The Unkempt Thoughts) published in periodicals from 1954 and, after 1957, in separate collections (i.e., the two-volume publication in 1977). Drawing on the Classical traditions of the European aphorism, Lec dealt with both the universal theme of the permanent nature of man and current and circumstantial problems. With relish he tracked down and unveiled the stereotypes and conventions of contemporary customs and fashions in all spheres of life: the intellectual-artistic, social, and erotic. The most esteemed motif of *Myśli nieuczesane* is the penetrating study of the mechanisms of power and politics, especially of the totalitarian kind represented by fascism and Communism. Lec's observations, because of censorship expressed by means of innuendo and metaphor, were a dissenting voice against fossilized and dogmatic Marxist thought, against the collectivism threatening the individual's right to free and natural development, against the falseness of propaganda, and, above all, against the illegitimate government whose only raison d'être is producing terror and fear in its subjects. Multiplicity of tones ranging from jeering, mocking, ironic, and skeptical to melancholy and mastery in employing various stylistic figures (paradox, word-play, absurdity, perfidious reversing of common sayings, proverbs, ideological slogans) strengthened the power of expression contained in *Myśli nieuczesane,* ensuring its popularity not only in Poland but also abroad (translations have been made into a number of foreign languages, among others, several publications in German).

BIBLIOGRAPHY

Wybór wierszy (Selected Poems), wstęp J. Śpiewak, Warsaw, 1968.
Utwory wybrane (Selected Works), T. 1–2, wstęp i wybór J. Łukasiewicz, Cracow, 1977.

LECHOŃ, JAN (Leszek Serafinowicz) (1899–1956), who was primarily a poet, studied Polish philology at the University of Warsaw and simultaneously assumed duties as coeditor of *Pro arte et studio*. Cofounder (1918) of the literary cabaret *Pod Picadorem* (Under the Picador) and the poetic group Skamander (1920), he also worked for *Pamiętnik Warszawski* (The Warsaw Diary) and the satirical weekly *Cyrulik Warszawski* (The Warsaw Barber). In 1930 he left for Paris as cultural attaché. After the outbreak of World War II, he made his way from Portugal to Brazil; in 1941 he settled in the United States, in New York. In 1943–46 he was coeditor of *Tygodnik Polski* (The Polish Weekly); he also published in the London-based *Wiadomości Polskie* (Polish News); and his poetry, written during the war, was widely known among Polish émigré circles and army units. He remained an exile after the war; he worked with Voice of America and Radio Free Europe. He was cofounder of the Polish Research Institute and was also a lecturer. Afflicted from his early youth by periods of psychic depression, he committed suicide.

He made his poetic debut at the age of fourteen with two collections: *Na złotym polu* (On a Gold Field, 1913) and *Po ró żnych ścieżkach* (Along Various Paths, 1914). In 1916 his one-act dramatic "nocturne" *W pałacu Stanisława Augusta* (In the Palace of Stanisław Augustus) was staged in the former royal residence Łazienki. During the period 1917–20 he contributed to the satirical weekly *Sowizdrzał* (The Rogue), composing pamphlets and satirical poems, which he later published in the collections *Królewsko-polski kabaret* (The Royal-Polish Cabaret, 1918, unsigned), *Facecje republikańskie* (The Republican Anecdotes, 1919, with Antoni Słonimski), and *Rzeczpospolita babińska: Śpiewy historyczne* (Sixteenth Century Humorists: Historical Songs, 1920). In 1920 he also published his first mature collection, *Karmazynowy poemat* (The Crimson Poem), containing seven miniature masterpieces which make a historiosophical reference to personages and events which have permanent positions in Polish culture, history, and mythology. They reveal the author's preoccupation with national history and tradition, but also his rebellion against their power. Written before Poland regained independence (except for two poems, *Mochracki* and *Piłsudski*), the poems express the author's anxiety about Poland's ability to liberate herself from the fatalism of national defeats and the paralyzing charm of "the poetry of graves."

Lechoń's next collection, *Srebrne i czarne* (Silver and Black, 1924), was radically different in its content and mood; his new themes became death and love. These are poems about loneliness, the sorrow of life and the elusiveness of happiness, about one's tragic involvement in lies and illusions behind which there is nothing but emptiness. The distinct artistic form of these poems also deserves attention, shaped by Classical and Baroque traditions. The two volumes brought Lechoń immediate success, but his artistic power was paralyzed by both his own expectations and those of the public. He published nothing until the beginning of World War II, which apparently reawakened the poet in him: *Lutnia po Bekwarku* (The Lute Along Bekwark, 1942), *Aria z kurantem* (An Aria with Chimes, New York, 1945), and *Marmur i róża* (Marble and a Rose) in *Poezje zebrane* (Collected Poems, 1954). The collections contain patriotic lyrics, with the nostalgic memories of an emigrant and a protest against the postwar control of Poland by the Soviet powers (e.g., the poem *Reytan* and other works withheld by the censor in the volumes published in Poland). His later themes include artistic reflections, impressions of the landscape, and, finally, grave and allusive personal contemplations. According to Artur Hutnikiewicz, Lechoń's poetry is, on the one hand, deeply rooted in national history, mythology, and tradition, and, on the other, saturated with intimate personal experiences related to the tragedy of human fate. His poetry is that of allusions: Lechoń consciously refers to the great names and achievements in art and literature. The poet treats them as symbols and metaphorical short-cuts which evoke the desired thoughts and emotions. With its traditional versification and style, Lechoń's poetry has the broadness of imagery which reaches the reader by means of not logical straightforwardness but mood and allusions.

Lechoń is also the author of numerous essays. During the period 1930–38 he published several critical sketches and reviews in *Gazeta Polska* (Polish Gazette). In 1940 he gave a series of lectures on Polish literature in Paris. He wrote on Słowacki and Mickiewicz and published a series of sketches about America and its culture, *Aut Caesar aut nihil* (London, 1955). Observations on literature and art can be found in his *Dziennik* (Diary), written from 1949 through June 1956 (Volumes 1–3; London, 1967–73). *Dziennik* is also an interesting personal document and a "self-creation"; it was also written for psychotherapeutic reasons, suggested by a psychoanalyst. He planned to publish various dramatic pieces and a novel, but only a few fragments appeared. He also translated plays and poetry.

BIBLIOGRAPHY

Poezje zebrane, 1916–1953 (Collected Poetry), London, 1954.

Poezje (Poetry), selected and with an introduction by M. Toporowski, Warsaw, 1957.

Poezje, selected by W. Nowakowska, afterword by R. Matuszewski, Warsaw, 1979.

Poezje, selected and with an introduction by R. Loth, Wrocław, 1990.

English

American Transformations, New York: Voyages Press, 1959.
(English translation of *Aut Caesar aut nihil*)

Justice for the Jews (three articles), New York: Genevieve Tabouis, 1943.

LELEWEL, JOACHIM (1786–1861), a historian and political activist, was the son of a gentryman and lawyer. He studied at the university in Vilnius and in 1815–18 taught general history there. In 1815–16 he was the editor of *Tygodnik Wileński* (The Wilno Weekly). Regarding his chances of becoming a professor at Vilnius University as very slim, he accepted a position as a librarian and lecturer on bibliography at the university in Warsaw. As a result he published *Bibliograficznych ksiąg dwoje* (Two Bibliographical Volumes, 1823–26), a fundamental work on bibliography and bibliology. In 1818 he became a member of the Society of Friends of Science (TPN). In 1820 he earned his doctorate at the Jagiellonian University and was offered the history chair at the university in Vilnius, enthusiastically endorsed by the students. Expelled after the trial of the Filarets, he settled in Warsaw and devoted himself to research; by 1830 he had published over 150 works on history, historical geography, and so on, among them a pioneering work on methodology, *Historyka* (Historiography, 1915); *Dzieje bibliotek* (The History of Libraries) appeared in *Dziennik Warszawski* (The Warsaw Daily) in 1827–28; *Dzieje Polski . . . potocznym sposobem opowiedział* (The History of Poland . . . Related in a Colloquial Way) was published in 1829. Member of the Parliament in the Duchy of Warsaw, he was also a member of the opposition in 1830. During the uprising (1830–31), he was a member of the national government and simultaneously president of the Patriotic Society.

He continued his political activity in Paris, where he arrived in the fall of 1831. He was expelled from the capital in December 1832, and from France in September 1833. He settled in Brussels, where he devoted himself to research: *Numismatique du Moyen Age* (Volumes 1–3, Paris, 1835), *Porównanie dwu powstań polskich, 1794 i 1830–1831* (A Comparison of the Two Polish Uprisings, 1794 and 1830–1831, Paris, 1840), *Polska wieków średnich* (The Polish Middle Ages, Poznań, 1846–51), and *Stracone obywatelstwo stanu kmiecego w Polsce* (The Lost Citizenship of the Serfs in Poland, Brussels, 1846). In 1855–59 the Poznań publisher J. K. Żupański published seven volumes of Lelewel's collected works, entitled *Polska, dzieje i rzeczy jej* (Poland, Its History and Affairs). In 1863–68 he published an enlarged edition under the same title (Volumes 1–13 and 16–20: volumes 14 and 15 did not appear). According to Jarosław Maciejewski, Lelewel took active part in the political life of the emigration, hoping to consolidate its various groups around a unified program—republican and moderately democratic. Throughout his stay in Brussels, he popularized democratic ideas with his publications and speeches on current topics, as well as on Polish history, the reasons for Poland's destruction, and conditions for revival. He believed that the democratic ideas of freedom and equality were part of the Polish "national element," which created the power of the state in the fifteenth and sixteenth centuries, while the subsequent collapse was brought about by the disturbance of the national element under foreign influences.

Lelewel's links with literature are varied. As a young man he was a collector of Polish folk songs, a translator and critic of Scandinavian literature. He also participated in the controversy involving the Classicists and the Romantics, advocating the ideas of Romanticism. His lectures and essays had a fundamental influence on the intellectual development of many of the Romantics. He was related to the Filomats, particularly to Mickiewicz, who welcomed him back to Vilnius with a poem, *Do Joachima Lelewela* (To Joachim Lelewel, 1822). Lelewel also represented the poet in financial matters in Warsaw, and, finally, helped publish Mickiewicz's works in Poznań and Paris. The historian's name is mentioned in *Dziady* (Forefathers' Eve). His influence can be discerned in *Księgi narodu i pielgrzymstwa polskiego* (The Book of the Polish Nation and Polish Pilgrimage) and in *Pan Tadeusz.* Słowacki, on the other hand, was critical of Lelewel's political and historical views; he ridiculed them in private letters and some of his works and argued against Lelewel's understanding of Polish history in *Balladyna* and *Lilla Weneda.* After 1840, however, Słowacki seemed to come closer to Lelewel's historiosophy, which was most apparent in his final poetic work, *Król-Duch* (Spirit-King). Lelewel's views influenced many other writers, among others Berwiński, Kraszewski, Lenartowicz, and Siemieński. His impact waned in the second half of the nineteenth century. He appeared again as a literary character in Wyspiański's plays.

BIBLIOGRAPHY

Dzieła (Works), Volumes 1–4, 6–8, 10, Warsaw, 1957–69.

LEM, STANISŁAW (born 1921), a prose and essay writer, studied medicine in Lvov and received his degree at the Jagiellonian University in Cracow, where he settled after the war. At first he published medical papers and scientific reviews in journals, and occasional short stories and poems. He made his debut in 1946 in a Katowice weekly, *Nowy Świat Przygód* (The New World of Adventures), with the novel *Człowiek z Marsa* (Man from Mars). He published his first book, the novel *Astronauci* (The Astronauts), in 1951. Subsequent works made him the most outstanding representative of Polish science fiction. He also earned international fame as a writer of futurologist essays, and, above all, as a reformer of the subject matter and stylistic conventions of science fiction. His works have been translated into over twenty-five languages. He is a member of the Science Fiction Research Association and Science Fiction Writers of America. He has received numerous prestigious awards in Poland. He lived abroad from 1982 to 1988, at first in West Berlin and later in Vienna.

Lem's interests center around science, scientific study, and the possibilities and the future of science. His imagination and unusual inventiveness in creating and naming new worlds, phenomena, and physical and biological laws—these help shape the substance of his works, that is, man confronted with his own learning capacities. Lem generously introduces problems from other areas—morality, erotic life, social rules—but the area that stimulates his imagination most is the confrontation of reason with the material world. Science fiction for Lem is a backdrop on which problems of this type can be enriched and developed in terms of the imagined progress in science and technology: that is, they are intensified by the achievements of human reason which the writer freely designs. According to Włodzimierz Maciąg, his broad erudition and thorough knowledge of science and philosophy have allowed Lem gradually to broaden his field of interest. His unusual, often astounding imagination has become more and more of a pretext for formulating humanistic problems connected with a man as a partner of those forces hidden in nonhuman matter, that is, in posing questions about the essence of being human.

In the first period of his work—the novels *Astronauci* (Astronauts, 1951), *Obłok Magellana* (The Magellan Meteor, 1955), *Eden* (1959), *Powrót z gwiazd* (Return from the Stars, 1961)—these issues were treated rather cautiously; Lem's imagination was stimulated more powerfully by the vision of technical possibilities, and the trip into space, into the technological future which formed the main basis of his plots. In Lem's early novels there also appeared certain characteristics of the Socialist Realism of the period—practical motives, employed by the writer to satisfy his poetics (for example, a Communist vision of the future presented as an actual fact). The space journeys encompassed expectations and hopes, but also prejudices and anxieties connected with the progress of our civilization. Gradually, these anxieties and warnings came to the fore as material of fantasies. Man threatened by the forces he himself liberated is a motive that recurs in many variants, for example, in his humorous-grotesque pieces, stylized in his allegorical tales, chivalrous epics, and philosophical tales: the cycles of stories *Dzienniki gwiazdowe* (Star Diaries, 1957), *Księga robotów* (The Book of Robots, 1961), *Bajki robotów* (Fairy Tales of Robots, 1964), *Cyberiada* (1965), and *Opowieści o pilocie Pirxie* (The Tales About Pirxie the Pilot, 1968). The development of high technology questions the Classical values of humanism and seems to negate human integrity. Questions concerning man in his new technological situation, his immunity to its psychological consequences, the possibility of existence of and contact with other, nonhuman forms of conscious life, especially in *Niezwyciężony* (The Invincible, 1964) and *Maska* (The Mask, 1976), are eschatological questions concerning the ontological basis of being human. Humanity is not a value which can be technologically reproduced: the important aspects of human life are its fragility and brevity. There are limits to man's ability to adapt; he cannot exist in different psychological realities, for his identity is then destroyed. Mankind, according to Lem, is alone and is building its spiritual universe upon loneliness. Lem's warnings are addressed to the reader in his novels *Solaris* (1961), *Pamiętnik znaleziony w wannie* (Memoirs Found in a Bathtub, 1961), and *Głos Pana* (His Master's Voice, 1968).

Apart from novels and short stories Lem has also written discursive prose developing similar ideas. In his collections of sketches *Dialogi* (Dialogues, 1957; revised edition, 1972), *Wejście na orbitę* (Going into Orbit, 1962), *Summa technologiae* (1964, second edition, enlarged, 1967), Lem explored the relationships between high-tech civilization and the evolution of man as a biological species, the limits of human learning, never allowing the reader to forget the ethical and cultural threats associated with the advance of science and technology. In the midsixties a new theme emerged: literature as a means of studying and creating another reality. These works made up the volume *Filozofia przypadku: Literatura w świetle empirii* (Philosophy of Chance: Literature in Light of Empiricism, 1968). This new theme also appears in his collections *Fantastyka i futurologia* (The Fantastic and Futurology, Volumes 1–2, 1970) and *Rozprawy i szkice* (Discourses and Sketches, 1975). Lem's polemics in these works are directed against the existing theories of fiction (especially structuralism and semiotics) and reveal the areas of indeterminacy and cognitive insufficiency of these theories. At the same time, the writer's imagination explores other forms of literary expression. In a willful, humorous manner he creates fictitious works: a series of parodies and pastiche pieces, *Doskonała próżnia* (A Perfect Vacuum, 1971), and reviews of nonexisting books, *Wielkość urojona* (Imaginary Magnitude, 1973). The science-fiction novel was merely a stage in Lem's work: he opened totally new perspectives for the genre, enriched it with new problems, and enlivened it with humor and grotesquery. He became faithful, however, to the main issue, to the question regarding the value of human life, and arrived at the conclusion that whatever man would do, whatever worlds he would create and explore, he himself, his nature, his spiritual powers, would remain his model and his ideal.

He also published a cycle of novels, *Czas nieutracony* (Unforfeited Time, 1955), part 1 of which, *Szpital Przemienienia* (A Hospital of the Transfiguration), had separate printings: the cycle is a metaphorical diagnosis of the ideological stands of the intelligentsia at the beginning of the war (a film version by E. Żebrowski appeared in 1978). An autobiographical novel, *Wysoki Zamek* (High Castle), was published in 1966, and *Wiersze młodzieńcze* (Youthful Poetry) appeared in 1975. He also wrote two works which combined sensational plot with elements of science fiction: *Śledztwo* (The Investigation, 1959) and *Katar* (The Chain of Chance, 1976). In the Soviet Union Andrej Tarkowski directed a film based on *Solaris* in 1973.

His recent publications include *Pokój na ziemi* (Peace on Earth, 1987), *Golem XIV* (1981), and *Fiasko* (Fiasco, 1987). Lem is undoubtedly the best known Polish contemporary writer.

(See Contemporary Polish Literature.)

BIBLIOGRAPHY

English

R. E. Ziegfeld, *Stanislaus Lem,* New York: Ungar Books, 1985.

The Chain of Chance (Katar), translated by Louis Iribarne, New York: Harcourt, Brace, Jovanovich, A Helen and Kurt Wolff Book, 1975, 1978, 1984; London: Secker and Warburg, 1978; New York: Jove, 1979.

The Cosmic Carnival of Stanislaw Lem: An Anthology of Entertaining Stories by the Modern Master of Science Fiction, edited and compiled by Michael Kandel, New York: Continuum, 1981.

The Cyberiad: Fables for the Cybernetic Age (Cyberiada), translated by Michael Kandel, New York: Seabury Press, 1974; London: Secker and Warburg, 1975; New York: Avon, 1976, 1980.

The Futurological Congress (from the Memories of Ijon Tichy), translated by Michael Kandel, London: Secker and Warburg, 1975; New York: Avon Books, 1976, 1981; London: Futura, 1977; San Diego: Harcourt, 1985; New York: Seabury Press, 1974.

The Investigation (Śledztwo), translated by Adele Milch, New York: Seabury Press, 1974; New York: Avon Books, 1976; San Diego: Harcourt, 1986.

The Invincible (Niezwyciężony), translated from German by Wendayne Ackerman, New York: Seabury Press, 1973; New York: Ace Books, 1973, 1975; New York: Penguin Books, 1976; London: Sidgwich and Jackson, 1973.

Memoirs Found in a Bathtub (Pamiętnik znaleziony w wannie), translated by Michael Kandel and Christine Rose, New York: Seabury Press, 1973; New York: Avon Books, 1976; San Diego: Harcourt, 1986.

Mortal Engines, translated and with an introduction by Michael Kandel, New York: Seabury Press, 1977; New York: Avon, 1982.

More Tales of Perix the Pilot, translated by Louis Iribarne, New York, London: Harcourt Brace Jovanovich, A Helen and Kurt Wolff Book, 1982; San Diego: Harcourt, 1982–83; London: Secker and Warburg, 1983.

A Perfect Vacuum (Doskonała próżnia), translated by Michael Kandel, Mount Kisco, New York: Futura Publications, 1978; New York: Harcourt, Brace, Jovanovich, 1979, 1980; London: Secker and Warburg, 1979.

Return from the Stars (Powrót z gwiazd), translated by Barbara Marszal and Frank Simpson, New York: Harcourt Brace Jovanovich, 1980; London: Secker and Warburg, 1980; New York: Avon, 1980.

Solaris, translated from French by Joanna Kilmartin and Steve Cox, New York: Walker, 1970; London: Faber and Faber, 1971; Harmondsworth, England: Penguin, 1981; Berkeley: University of California, 1961; Berkeley Books, 1970, 1971.

The Star Diaries (Dzienniki gwiazdowe), translated by Michael Kandel, New York: Seabury Press, 1976; London: Secker and Warburg, 1976; New York: Avon Books, 1977; London: Futura, 1978.

Tales of Perxie the Pilot (Opowieści o Pilocie Pirxie), edited by Helen Wolff, translated by Louis Iribarne, New York: Harcourt Brace Jovanovich, 1979; London: Secker and Warburg, 1980.

Imaginary Magnitude (Wielkość urojona), translated by Marc E. Heine, New York:

Harcourt, 1981; San Diego: Harcourt, 1984–85; London: Secker and Warburg, 1985.

Memoirs of a Space Traveler (Dzienniki Gwiazdowe), New York: Harcourt, Brace, Jovanovich, 1982; San Diego: Harcourt, 1983–85.

His Master's Voice (Głos Pana), translated by Michael Kandel, San Diego: Harcourt, 1983–84; London: Secker and Warburg, 1983.

Microworlds, San Diego: Harcourt, 1984–86; London: Secker and Warburg, 1986.

One Human Minute, translated by Catherine S. Leach, London: Deutsch, 1985, 1986; San Diego: Harcourt, 1985.

Hospital of the Transfiguration (Szpital Przemienienia), translated by William Brand, London: Deutsch, 1989; San Diego: Harcourt, 1988.

Fiasco, translated by Michael Kandel, London: Deutsch, 1987; San Diego: Harcourt, 1987; 1988.

LEMAŃSKI, JAN (cryptonyms J. Lem, J. Leman; pseudonym Tredecim) (1866–1933), a writer of fables, a poet, a satirist, a prose writer, and a translator, first worked on the railroad after graduating with a degree in law. He was connected with *Chimera*. His unhappy marriage and its violent ending (Lemański attempted to shoot his wife and himself because of jealousy) cast a shadow on all his life and work. After the war, he worked as a censor. His growing melancholy led him to another suicide attempt, and soon after he died.

Lemański was a reviver of the Classical fable. In *Bajki* (Fables, 1902), *Proza ironiczna* (Ironic Prose, 1904), and *Colloquia, albo Rozmowy* (Colloquium, or Conversations, 1905), he deliberately freed the genre of its cheap moralizing tone and imbued the fables with new ideas which reflected the spirit of the time: antiutilitarianism, an attack on the petit bourgeois, and an apotheosis of an artist. On the one hand, he brought the fable closer to lyrical poetry; on the other hand, he consciously annihilated the patterns on which the fable was based for centuries. According to Jerzy Kwiatkowski, he basically followed the program of *Chimera,* but he departed from it in his own writings by introducing realistic observations, using a language which was free of pathos and contained elements of everyday speech. During the years 1902–5, Lemański's best poems appeared: *Stracony kwiat* (A Discarded Flower) and *Mur* (Wall). During this period he also published a satirical-fantastic novel, *Ofiara królewny* (The Sacrifice of the King's Daughter, 1906), a kind of ideological summing up, an expression of his struggle against utilitarianism and hedonism in the name of the freedom of art and spiritual values. However, artistic realization did not match his daring ideas and broad horizons. In Lemański's subsequent works (collections of satirical poems, fables, and lyrical pieces, volumes of prose writings) his attacks on the narrow-minded petit bourgeois evolved into anticapitalist satire. At the same time, the author's philosophical position was slowly being transformed into a dangerous tendency to be enslaved by idées fixes (one of which was clearly related to his growing misogynism). His language became more complex, full of boring pseudoetymological speculations. Mechanical, monotonous, obsessive, tedious—these features of Lemański's language are clearly seen in *Jasełka* (Nativity Play, 1911) and *Zwierzyniec* (The Zoo, 1912), and his later works, a collection of stories, *Prawo mężczyzny* (The Right of a Man, 1922), and *Toast: Bajki powojenne* (A Toast: Post-War Fables, 1923) disappointed most critics.

BIBLIOGRAPHY

Wybór bajek (A Selection of Fables), selected and with an introduction by A. Frybesowa, Warsaw, 1956.

Poezje wybrane (Selected Poetry), selected and with an introduction by J. Zacharska, Warsaw 1973.

LENARTOWICZ, TEOFIL (1822–93), a poet and sculptor, whose father died early, had a rather difficult childhood in the house of his stepfather. In 1834 he traveled to Warsaw, finished school, and found a job. In 1840 he became acquainted with groups of *Boheme* (Pseudo-Gypsies), associated with a number of men of letters, and continued his self-education. His first poems were set to music and were sung at social gatherings, and published after 1841 in various publications of the young generation of writers and artists in Warsaw. Threatened with arrest, he left for Poznań, where he became acquainted with leftist circles. After returning to Warsaw he mingled with the milieu of *Biblioteka Warszawska* (Warsaw Library) and *Dzwon literacki* (Literary Bell). In 1848 he had to leave Warsaw again and went to Cracow, where he began his career as an agitator, pedagogue, and writer. He staged his dramatic dialogue *Wskrzeszenie* (Revival) and a monodrama *Tyrteusz* (Tyrteus), published in his first collection of poems, *Polska ziemia w obrazkach* (The Polish Land in Pictures, Cracow, 1948). He later settled in Dresden, Wrocław, Brussels, and, finally, Paris (1852–55), where he met Mickiewicz, Norwid, and Zaleski. His fully mature collections, published in 1855, *Lirenka* (Lyrene), *Zachwycenie* (Ecstasies), and *Z błogosławioną* (With the Blessed), confirmed his already established reputation.

He moved to Italy, where he lived in Rome and in Florence. He married Zofia Szymanowska, a relative of Mickiewicz's wife. However, the nostalgia for his country, his difficult financial situation (in spite of his success as a sculptor), and finally the death of his only son (1864) and his wife (1870) cast a shadow on this period of his life: his depression was deepened by conflicts with critics and with the disappointment brought on by his trip to Cracow, where conservative influence predominated. Lenartowicz remained faithful to the freedom-fighting ideals of Romanticism; he reacted by composing patriotic poems dedicated to the national tragedy of 1861–

64. He glorified the popular uprising in *Bitwa Racławicka* (The Battle of Racławice, 1859). These tendencies continued in his subsequent collections: *Poezje* (Poems, 1858), *Nowa lirenka* (The New Lyrene, 1859), *Poezje* (Poems, 1863), *Echa nadwiślańskie* (Echoes Beyond the Vistula, 1872), *Wybór poezji* (Collected Poems, 1876), and *Poezje* (Poems, 1895, published after his death). The collections *Album włoski* (Italian Album, 1870) and *Ze starych zbroic* (From Old Arms, 1870) broadened his themes and means of expression, an argument against claims by critics that Lenartowicz's work was petrified in the manner of a folk song. During the period 1879–83 Lenartowicz lectured in Bologna on Polish and Slavic literature, but the lectures were interrupted as a result of the voices raised by some critics and the intrigues of Lenartowicz's compatriots.

According to Jan Nowakowski, Lenartowicz's remaining output, which includes epic and dramatic works, is not as valuable as his lyrical pieces, in which he presents himself as an independent personality, a creator of an original view of folklore and folk motives in literature. For Lenartowicz folk culture was a reservoir of aesthetic, moral, and national values. Simplicity, brevity, discrete lyricism, and artistic concentration were the main ingredients of Lenartowicz's best poems. In his poetry, the landscape motives are accompanied by patriotic themes and a prevailing religious tone. His poetry is widely popular; many of his works entered the repertory of songs or poems for children. Critics, on the other hand, have treated him rather ruthlessly, attacking his works as models of post-Romantic epigonism, primitivism, and sentimentalism. He was greatly appreciated, however, by writers such as Kraszewski, Konopnicka, Kasprowicz, Żeromski, and Pawlikowska-Jasnorzewska. Paweł Hertz attempted to revive his reputation by editing his *Poezje wybrane* (Selected Poetry) in 1954.

BIBLIOGRAPHY

Wybór poezyj (Selected Poetry), edited and with an introduction by J. Nowakowski, Fourth edition, Wrocław, 1972.

J. Nowakowski, . . . *a ślad po mnie pieśń złota: Teofil Lenartowicz* (. . . Left After Him Songs of Gold: Teofil Lenartowicz), Warsaw, 1973.

LEŚMIAN, BOLESŁAW (Bolesław Lesman) (1877–1937), a poet, prose and essay writer, and translator, came from a Polonized Jewish family. He spent his early years in Ukraine and studied law in Kiev. Having moved to Warsaw, he was introduced into its literary life by his uncle, Antoni Lange. In 1911 he was cofounder and director of *Teatr Artystyczny* (Artistic Theater) in Warsaw. He also spent several years in France. During World War I he lived in Łódź, where he became literary manager of *Teatr Polski* (Polish Theater). Later after many years he lived in a provincial town (Hrubieszów, Zamość), making a living as a notary and continuing his poetic activities.

In 1933 he was elected a member of the Polish Academy of Literature *(PAL)*. He made his debut in 1895. A friend of Zenon "Miriam" Przesmycki, he began to contribute to *Chimera* in 1901. In his youth he also wrote in Russian, *Wiersze rosyjskie* ([Russian Poems], London, 1961, translated by M. Pankowski). Leśmian's early work developed under the influence of Neo-Romanticism, but even his first collection, *Sad rozstajny* (Crossroads Orchard, 1912), violated Neo-Romantic conventions; it was a manifestation of the poet's own artistic credo. Leśmian ignored contemporary reality, simultaneously advocating an active attitude toward life and the cult of spiritual adventure, whose philosophical background can be found in Nietzsche and Bergson. The poet allegorized intellectual stands, best seen in the motive of the return to nature, which is understood literally, philosophically, and symbolically. During the period of Young Poland Leśmian became a literary critic and essayist; his works were collected in *Szkice literackie* (Literary Sketches, 1959). These works determined his poetic program to a large extent. He also wrote stylized prose tales, based on Oriental motives, *Klechdy sezamowe* (Sesame Folk Tales, 1913), *Przygody Sindbada Żeglarza* (Adventures of Sindbad the Sailor, 1913), and tales based on Polish folklore: *Klechdy polskie* (Polish Folktales, London, 1956; in Poland, 1959). He translated several short stories by Edgar Allan Poe. His poetic talent reached its full development in the second collection of poems, *Łąka* (The Meadow, 1920), with its philosophical view of nature and references to folklore. A number of Leśmian's poems were in the form of "philosophical ballads," such as *Dusiołek* and *Świdryga i Midryga;* some were lyrical, combining visionary and reflective elements with an artful observation of reality. In this collection Leśmian proved himself a master of erotic poetry, sublime and at the same time very daring. All these poems are characterized by a specific richness of linguistic expression. The collection was highly regarded by critics, but undervalued by readers. His popularity began to grow in the thirties and became more firm after his last two collections appeared: *Napój cienisty* (A Shadowy Drink, 1936) and *Dziejba leśna* (A Forest Fable, 1938). New motives appeared in these collections: emptiness, death, and a mood that could be referred to as existential. According to Jacek Trznadel, his view of man was dictated by existential and tragic humanism: man himself appears to be man's main problem. Leśmian's symbolism was also transmitted: a symbol is mortal like man; it is an empty mask, without any transcendent quality hidden behind it. Elegiac tones were intensified, and Leśmian's humor, ribald and lively in his earlier works, was transformed into a dark and gloomy mood, presented in the style of bitter grotesque.

Leśmian's poetic output, otherwise quite individualistic, is related in a variety of ways to Slavic folklore and Polish literary tradition, which can be detected in his language, full of neologisms and neosemanticisms of Old Polish and folk origin. His poetic style is both visionary and realistic, combining fairy tale and grotesque elements with a sensual perception of detail, above all in the world of nature. He was also innovative in his work, reviving traditional forms of elegiac, erotic, and personal lyricism, creating a new type of stylized folk ballad and philosophical poem with elements of the fairy tale. His popularity had steadily grown since the end of World War II. According to Czesław Miłosz, certain features of Leśmian's poetry contain a distant affinity with the works of W. B. Yeats.

(See *Młoda Polska.*)

BIBLIOGRAPHY

Z pism B.L. (From the Writings of B.L.), Volumes 1–3, *Szkice literackie, Utwory rozproszone—Listy, Poezje* (Literary Sketches, Scattered Works—Letters, Poetry), edited by J. Trznadel, Warsaw, 1959–65.

Poezje wybrane (Selected Poetry), edited and with an introduction by J. Trznadel, Wrocław, 1974.

English

Mythematics and Entropy (selected poems), translated by Sandra Celt, Stevens Point, Wisconsin: A. R. Poray, 1984.

Carpenter, Bogdana, *The Polish Avant-Garde in Poland, 1918–1939,* Seattle: University of Washington Press, 1983.

LIPSKA, EWA (born 1945), a poet, studied art in Cracow and made her debut in the literary press in 1961. Her collections include *Wiersze* (Poems, 1967), *Drugi zbiór wierszy* (A Second Collection of Verses, 1970), *Trzeci zbiór wierszy* (A Third Collection of Verses, 1972), *Czwarty zbiór wierszy* (A Fourth Collection of Verses, 1974), *Piąty zbiór wierszy* (A Fifth Collection of Verses, 1978), and a selection of her poems, *Dom spokojnej młodości* (Home of Peaceful Youth, 1979), in addition to the volume *Nie o śmierć tutaj chodzi, lecz o biały kordonek* (Not a Matter Here of Death, but of a White Purl, 1982) and the experiment in poetic prose *Żywa śmierć* (Living Death, 1978). Lipska's moralist poems are characterized by a critical attitude toward the contemporary world. She centers her attention on the involvement of a sensitive individual within the story of a generation, its present and past. Her penetrating image of the world is developed in all of her collections and makes of them a disturbing whole. She received the PEN Club award of the Robert Graves Foundation in 1979.

BIBLIOGRAPHY

English

Such Times (selected poems), translated by Robert Colombo and Wacław Iwaniuk, Toronto: Hounslaw Press, 1981.

Shifting Borders: East European Poetry of the Eighties, Rutherford, New Jersey: Fairleigh Dickinson University Press, 1993, 288–89.

Spoiling Cannibals' Fun: Polish Poetry of the Last Two Decades of Communist Rule, edited by Stanisław Barańczak, Evanston, Illinois: Northwestern University Press, 1991, 146–52.

M

MACKIEWICZ, JÓZEF (1902–85), a novelist, short-story writer, and publicist, was born in Petersburg but in 1907 settled in Vilnius. He served as a volunteer in the Polish-Russian War (1919–20). He completed his studies in the natural sciences at the University of Warsaw and returned to Vilnius, where he worked as a reporter for the conservative daily *Słowo* (The Word), edited by his brother, the well-known journalist and politician Stanisław Cata-Mackiewicz. Connected to the traditions of the old multinational Great Kingdom of Lithuania, he criticized the Polonization politics of the Polish government in the northeastern areas (his news coverage was published in *Bunt rojstów* [The Revolt of the Marshes], 1938). After the fall of the Polish government (1939), he presented his views in the Vilnius presses, which were under the control of the Lithuanian authorities, and later of the German occupation. For his activities he was accused of collaborating with the enemy and sentenced to death in 1943 by the underground court of the *AK* (Home Army). In spite of the fact that the sentence was revoked by the local commander of the *AK,* the Mackiewicz affair to this day is a matter of polemics and opposing opinions. As a witness to German and Russian atrocities in the territories of Lithuania and Belorus, he has left a wide range of documented materials concerning the extermination of the Jewish and Polish population. In 1943 he was one of the many Polish "observers" of the exhumation of graves of Polish war prisoners in Katyń, murdered in 1940 by the Russian Secret Police (in 1949 he was one of the witnesses before the special commission of the United States Congress, leading to an investigation of this affair). In 1944 he left Vilnius for Warsaw; a year later he left for Italy, and then for London, choosing the status of emigrant. From 1954 he lived in Munich. As one who constantly unmasked Soviet and international Communism, he belonged to that group of writers whose work was completely banned in postwar Poland. He published in the émigré press in London; he also published a number of works in the Paris-based Literary Institute. His works became available in Poland in the eighties, thanks to the underground press, and were officially published only after the lifting of censorship in 1990.

Mackiewicz was a writer of realism, uniting a political and historical approach with the posture of a moralist. He combined a traditional epic narrative with a rich and sensational plot (often based on autobiographical elements) and a distinct description of nature, together with documentary-chronicle, publicistic material. His heroes were confrontations with authentic events of history—two world wars, the Bolshevik Revolution, the expansion of Communism into Russia and Eastern Europe. In his novel *Droga do nikąd* (The Road to Nowhere, 1955), he revealed the comprehensive manifestations of Sovietization against the background of the occupation by the Red Army from 1939 to 1941: the political terror, the mass deportations, the extreme poverty, the destruction of the social life caused by universal fear, the mendacity, and the paralyzing apathy following every attempt at resistance. *Kontra* (Against, 1957) describes the tragic history of the Russians, the Cossacks, and the members of other nationalities living in the Soviet Union, who in their fight against Communism searched for support in the Third Reich and who after the war, together with their families, were thrown into the hands of the Secret Police by Western lovers. *Lewa wolna* (O.K. on the Left, 1965), whose action takes place during the Polish-Bolshevik war (1919–20), is a great polemic with the political-strategic conceptions of Marshal Piłsudski who, motivated by animosity toward the Russian contrarevolutionary camp, missed the chance, according to Mackiewicz, to effect a final defeat of Soviet Russia. The main theme of his next novel, *Nie trzeba głośno mówić* (No Need to Talk Loudly, 1969), is the tragic consequence of the Polish-Lithuanian-Belorus quarrels during World War II; the Anglo-Soviet Alliance, which also included the Polish underground government and its army (*AK*), made it easier for Stalin to annex these lands (this thesis, in agreement with the legend of the Polish anti-Hitler conspiracy, provoked violent responses from émigré combatant circles). Other novels were also based on authentic events: *Karierowicz* (The Careerist, 1955) and *Śpiewa żona pułkownika Miasojedowa* (The Wife of Colonel Miasojedow Sings, 1962), the latter, based on the notorious "Russian Dreyfus affair," takes place during World War I. His short stories and commentaries from the collections *Fakty, przyroda i ludzie* (Facts, Nature and People, 1984) and *Droga Pani* (Dear Madam, 1984, written with his wife, Barbara Toporska), contained material previously published, regarding the Katyń murders and the extermination of the Jews of Vilnius during the German occupation.

Called "the writer of perpetual protest," Mackiewicz as a publicist voiced an independent, often isolated point of view (among others, in the sketches contained in the following collections: *Zwycięstwo prowokacji* [The Victory of Provocation], 1962, *W cieniu krzyża: Kabel Opatrzności* [In the Shadow of the Cross: Cable of Providence], 1972, and *Watykan w cieniu czerwonej gwiazdy* [The Vatican in the Shadow of the Red Star], 1975). He carried on polemics about the Soviet Union and world Communism with the political strategy of the West, criticizing the Eastern politics of the Catholic Church, with the revisionist and dissident illusions of those who advocated waiting for an evolutionary change of the Communist system, which he considered the main evil threatening civilization (Nazism was, in his opinion, nothing short of a "secondary imitation"). Many of Mackiewicz's views turned out to be convergent with the precursory to the theses of contemporary Sovietology and the works of Alexander Solzhenitsyn.

BIBLIOGRAPHY

Road to Nowhere, translated by Lew Sapieha, London: Collins and Harvill Press, 1963.

MALEWSKA, HANNA (1911–83), a novelist, short-story writer, and publicist, studied history at the Catholic University of Lublin. From 1935 she worked as a teacher in various Warsaw schools. During World War II, she worked with the underground, among others, with the Main Command of the Home Army (*AK*). In 1944 she took part in the Warsaw Uprising. After the war she settled in Cracow, where for many years she contributed and was the editor of the Catholic periodical *Tygodnik Powszechny* (The Universal Weekly) and the monthly *Znak* (The Sign), which she edited from 1960 to 1976.

She engaged in writing historical prose with moral-historiosophic aspirations, inspired by a personal Catholic belief and concerned with the violent political and societal transformations in Poland and Europe in the first half of the twentieth century. She was particularly interested in the confrontation of individual consciousness with the pace of historical events and the problems of moral choice in a situation where the previous system of values has disintegrated. In her main work, *Przemija postać świata* (Fleeting Is the Shape of the World, Vols. 1–2, 1954), she delineated a comprehensive picture of the fall of Rome, the war with Byzantium and the Franks and Lombards, and the beginnings of European Christian culture (the character of Saint Benedict). The destinies of the historical and fictional heroes were here densely woven into the action of the novel: the clash of different cultures and historical forces, the rivalry concerning the meaning of civilization and the spiritual Roman heritage. Her collections of short stories, *Wiosna grecka* (Greek Spring, 1933) and *Opowieść o siedmiu mędrcach* (The Story of the Seven Wise Men, 1959), deal with ancient Greece.

Her novel *Żelazna korona* (The Iron Crown, Vols. 1–2, 1936) deals with the epoch of medieval universalism and is based on the biography of Charles V. *Kamienie wołać będą* (The Stones Will Bear Witness, 1946) concerns the building of the cathedral in Beauvais; *Sir Tomasz More odmawia* (Sir Thomas More Refuses, 1956) is a collection of short stories on the same subject. Malewska was also interested in Polish history; her novel *Panowie Leszczyńscy* (The Leszczyńskis, 1961) is a personal account of Polish culture in the seventeenth century, quite at odds with Sienkiewicz's vision in his *Trilogy.* In her chronicle-novel *Apokryf rodzinny* (A Family Apocrypha, 1965), she paints a genealogy of the intelligentsia descended from the nobility. In her novel *Żniwo na sierpie* (Harvest on the Sickle, 1947), she paints a fictionalized biography of the great poet Cyprian Kamil Norwid. In later life she attempted to write metaphysical novels: *LLW, czyli co się może wydarzyć jutro* (LLW, or What Can Happen Tomorrow, 1970), published together with a fairy tale based on ancient times, *Labirynt* (Labyrinth). At times she wrote publicistic prose: *O odpowiedzialności i inne szkice* (About Responsibility and Other Sketches, 1987). The famous sketch of the book's title was a camouflaged polemic with the ideas in Czesław Miłosz's *The Captive Mind.*

BIBLIOGRAPHY

J. Ziomek, "Hanna Malewska: Księgi Kronik" (Hanna Malewska: Books of Chronicles) in *Wizerunki polskich pisarzy katolickich* (Portraits of Polish Catholic Writers), Poznań, 1963.

MAŁA APOKALIPSA (A Minor Apocalypse) (see Konwicki).

MARIA CURIE-SKŁODOWSKA UNIVERSITY IN LUBLIN (*UMCS*), established in 1944 as the first state institution of higher education in the Polish People's Republic, possessed five faculties in 1945. A sixth, the Faculty of the Humanities, was established in 1952. Its outstanding graduates include A. Kersten, H. Zins (history), N. Łubnicki (philosophy), and A. Gardawski (archeology).

The chair of Polish Studies was set up in 1953 and became part of the Faculty of Humanities in 1954. In 1971 it was reorganized into the Institute of Polish Philology (headed by Skubalanka, during 1972–73 and after 1975). The research interests are mostly concerned with more recent literature, beginning with the Enlightenment. The Department of Polish Language conducts broad research on the dialects of the Lublin region.

BIBLIOGRAPHY

Narodziny pierwszego uniwersytetu Polski Ludowej (The Anniversary of the First University of the Polish People's Republic), edited by S. Flaneżewska and Z. Kowalski, Lublin, 1979.

MATKA JOANNA OD ANIOŁÓW (Mother Joan of the Angels) (see Iwaszkiewicz).

MĄŻ I ŻONA (Husband and Wife) (see Fredro).

MEDIEVAL LITERATURE The term "Middle Ages" (or "medieval") is usually used in reference to a period in European history spanning the fourth through the fourteenth centuries A.D. Roughly speaking, the beginning of the Middle Ages is associated with the fall of the Western Roman Empire (476 A.D.), whereas the close is usually dated somewhere during the second half of the fifteenth century, either 1453, the fall of Constantinople, or 1492, the discovery of the New World by Columbus. Dates and major historical events aside, the Middle Ages is considered to be the era between antiquity and modern times.

During the span of ten centuries changes took place which definitively influenced the direction of European culture. Both the spread of Christianity and the birth of the feudal economic system and the modern monarchy played a monumental role in shaping the societies of the times. Christendom's rapid expansion was accompanied by the expansion of Latin as an official state language as well as the language of the well-educated throughout Europe. Christianity and its Latin influences tended toward unification and homogenization of European culture. At the same time, beginning with the Romance languages, the gradual emergence of the vernacular languages on a Latin foundation can be observed.

After the collapse of the Western Roman Empire, Western medieval culture was initially centered in Alexandria and only later returned to Rome. Although the spiritual and cultural heart remained in Rome, the Holy Roman Empire held a vast amount of political power and played the role of a secondary center throughout the Middle Ages.

Medieval thought was in many ways directly descendant from antiquity and accepted most of the ancient aesthetic ideals with the difference that they were made directly subservient to Church doctrine. The Fathers of the Church mapped out the philosophical and cultural principles of Christianity. The world was conceived as a closed hierarchical system on top of which was God, below God, man; and, on the very bottom, material matter.

The role of the poet was strictly defined as an explorer of divine truths. Art was supposed to expose the essence of existence and the world we live in as well as promote and develop Christian role models. Literature was intended mainly to be a tool in sculpting the ideal man, in installing Christian ideals, and in encouraging sacrifice and suffering with the hope of achieving salvation in the afterlife.

Written poetry in Latin was in direct opposition to the ancient oral traditions. Most genres were either used directly in religious services or served a religious purpose, for example, hymns, church dramas, morality plays, or lives of the saints. The secular poetry that did exist consisted mainly of epigrams and panegyrics.

In the tenth century, as a result of the stabilization of feudal monarchies, the appearance of literature in the vernacular can be observed, mainly in the courts of the wealthy landowners, which were to become the birthplace of chivalric culture. The heroic epic was one of the more popular genres, for example, the Germanic epic *The Legend of the Nibelungen* or Chaucer's *The Canterbury Tales.* In medieval literature the epic romance, also well represented, is in many ways related to the ancient epics but at the same time makes use of various local legends and traditions, an outstanding example of which is the legend of King Arthur. Well into the eleventh century many Latin authors made use of local tradition, but in the twelfth century, with the development of institutions of higher education, there was a tendency toward the uniformization of European culture and away from that which was not considered of a universal nature.

Medieval folk culture, although quite different from its feudal, chivalric, or Church counterparts, was widespread and extremely diversified; however, it was mainly oral and could best be studied in various rituals, religious practices, and observances of folk holidays. Folk culture very often contained a specific kind of grotesque humor and comic attacks on the existing social hierarchy and the trends prevalent in official culture. Depending on the country, most or all of the elements of traditional folk culture were either at best forgotten or at worst consciously eradicated.

The Middle Ages reached Poland relatively late. The tribes inhabiting what would later become Polish lands began to unite during the late ninth century and entered the community of European states with the christening of their ruler (and consequently his subjects) in 966. Until that time the pagan state possessed only oral traditions, which, on the basis of what can be deduced from scraps of evidence, were reasonably well developed. Unfortunately pagan relics were not spared during the induction of Poland into Christendom. The only people capable of recording the traditional folk heritage (the clergy) were precisely those with the least interest in doing so. What is more, well into the twelfth century the Church was dominated by non-Poles, who were even less interested in or capable of preserving the native cultural heritage. What has survived from medieval times is a mere fragment of the literature of the period. Not only was the cultural output of medieval Poland subject to destruction during war and times of unrest, of which there was never a lack in Poland, but, in addition, medieval literary works were considered of little value, and next to no effort was exerted to save what had been written for future generations. An outstanding example of this tendency is *The Sermons of the Holy Cross* (Kazania świętokrzyskie), which, cut into strips, was used as reinforcement for the binding of another manuscript from the late fifteenth century.

With the introduction of Latin as the official state language, which remained until the sixteenth century, Poland entered European history. The first works of Polish literature, as well as the majority of medieval writings from Poland, were written in Latin. The Polish language had two main functions: it was used in religious literature for those who did not know Latin (nuns, other semieducated women, and lay people) and acted as a second language in legal documents, as well as an aid for non–Latin speakers. Literary Polish developed relatively slowly for several reasons: first and foremost, all teachers were members of the clergy and occupied with the mission of preparing others to become priests; second, education spread slowly as a result of wars, the Tartar invasions, and the feudal fragmentation; third, in the thirteenth century intense colonization by German settlers Germanicized Polish cities, churches, and educational institutions to such an extent that Polish returned as the dominant tongue only late in the fifteenth century. It should be remembered that native literary traditions had been either completely forgotten or destroyed and when the time came for the emergence of Polish as a literary language there was nothing save the Latin base to build on.

The Middle Ages in Poland can be divided into two phases. The first phase was from 966 to 1400, during which, culturally and politically, Poland was still an underdeveloped state preoccupied with catching up to the rest of Europe. The second stage is marked by Poland's emergence into the ranks of European states, as a country which played an active role in European affairs. This role change was possible only as a result of two major events in Poland: the restructurization of the University of Cracow (founded in 1364) in 1400 and the definitive victory over the Teutonic Knights in 1410. Poland, having recovered from the period of feudal fragmentation, equipped with a thriving institution of higher learning and rid of its most troublesome enemy, stepped into the fifteenth century well prepared to participate in European cultural life.

The earliest written works in Poland were annals (*Roczniki*), which were initiated during the reign of Mieszko I. These registers containing brief notes of the most important events were written in Latin. Of the many annals (some researchers are of the opinion that the tradition remained late into the fifteenth century) only a few have survived. The most well known are *Rocznik kapitulny krakowski* (Cracow's Capitulary Annal, from the first half of the twelfth century), *Rocznik świętokrzyski* (Holy Cross Annal, from the twelfth century), and *Rocznik miechowski* (The Miechow Annal, from the fourteenth century). The annals were of considerable importance for the earliest Polish accounts of the beginnings of Polish history on these laconic sources.

Chronicles and sundry hagiographic works were the first full-blown literary forms to appear in Poland, and not surprisingly the authors were foreigners. The lives of the earliest Polish saints, St. Adalbert and St. Kinga, were recorded by visitors to Poland as early as the tenth century.

The first chronicle, *Kronika Polska* (Polish Chronicle, 1112–13), was written by an anonymous monk of foreign extraction who later came to be known as Gallus Anonymous. His origins remain somewhat a mystery, though he is considered to have most likely come from France, to have been quite well educated and well informed as to current trends in the written Latin of the times, and to have spent a good deal of time in Hungary. Gallus Anonymous gathered information from various annals and from numerous discussions with learned men of the times. In *Kronika Polska,* the historical chain of events is interspersed with various fictional or semifictional anecdotes, legends, speeches, and letters, as well as poems and songs. *Kronika Polska* is considered a curious literary work as well as an invaluable, if biased toward Gallus Anonymous's benefactor (Bolesław Krzywousty [Wry-Mouth]), historical work. In it we find the first mention of many of the most important Polish legends, such as the legends of Popiel and Piast. Some of the legends containing elements of the mysterious with suggestions that the Piast dynasty enjoyed the patronage of God incorporate epic tones.

The next chronicle, known as *Chronica Polonorum,* written by a Pole, Wincenty Kadłubek (1159–1223), was radically different. The exact dates when Kadłubek wrote his chronicle are unknown; however, we know that it covers Polish history from its beginnings to the year 1202. *Chronica Polonorum* is made up of four separate books. The first three are composed of a dialogue between two individuals, Mateusz and Jan: the former narrates the tale of Polish history while the latter interjects commentary from a moral and legal standpoint. The fourth book, containing the history of the years during which Kadłubek lived, is written in a continuous narrative. *Chronica Polonorum,* though quite popular during the Middle Ages and even used as a textbook by Professor Jan Dąbrowski (at the University of Cracow, where he lectured on Polish history), is of questionable historical value. Kadłubek's intentions for writing were largely panegyric and didactic, leading him to conjure up or slightly alter large parts of history to suit his aims. Nonetheless, Kadłubek's chronicle played a major role in elevating the status of Polish history to the ranks of other subjects worthy of deeper study and served as an outstanding example of eloquence and practiced style in Latin. What is more, it marked the beginning of a Polish takeover of Latin-Polish literature; all subsequent major works were the products of Polish writers.

Another noteworthy chronicle is the thirteenth century *Kronika wielkopolska* (The Greater Poland Chronicle), whose authorship is usually attributed to Godzisław Baszko, although in many sources Janko of Czarnków is mentioned as well. Baszko's chronicle is of lesser importance than the previous two except for the fact that it contains the remainder of the great Polish legends not recorded by Gallus or Kadłubek: the legend of the three Slavic brothers Czech, Lech, and Rus and the legend of Walgier Udały and his traitorous wife, Heligunda. Another reason The Greater Poland Chronicle may be of interest is that it is the first Polish chronicle to take notice of social problems and includes peasants and townspeople in a literary form reserved for state history and the history of the clergy and the knighthood.

The most voluminous (twelve tomes in all) and historical of the chronicles was written by Poland's first modern historian, Jan Długosz (1415–80). Secretary and assistant to the bishop of Cracow, Zbigniew Oleśnicki; tutor to the sons of Kazimierz Jagiellończyk and later the archbishop of Lvov, Długosz dedicated practically twenty-five years of his life (1455–80) to compiling *Annales Poloniae,* which he completed only shortly before his death. Długosz not only knew how to use sources which he meticulously gathered and critically evaluated, but reached for reference materials outside Poland as well, for example, Czech and German chronicles, the Eastern Slavic *Letopisi* (Yearbooks), and the works of other non-Polish medieval historians. Though somewhat more conscious of his historical importance, Długosz was motivated to write for reasons similar to those of his predecessors: in order to pass on the history of Poland and its neighbors to future generations and to teach others how the state should be organized and governed. For Długosz history was the "mother of virtue," and he did his best to preserve that which he considered virtuous on paper. Długosz's Latin was considerably better that that of the earlier Polish chroniclers: in places, however, he can be rather long-winded, and sometimes his lengthier diversions are difficult to follow. This can be explained partly by Długosz's desire to follow in the footsteps of the great Roman historians, whom he greatly admired. In comparison to the chronicles previously mentioned, Długosz's work can be considered objective, although it is not free of personal biases and attacks on ideological enemies.

With the entrance of Poland into the arena of European affairs, Polish writers began to deal with political and legal problems of the day. A great deal of the political writing was connected with the various "public relations" campaigns conducted in an attempt to win the Vatican's favor in the dispute with the Teutonic Knights. One of the main reasons for the refurbishing of the University of Cracow was to enhance the university's abilities to educate specialists in legal and diplomatic affairs. Along with Poland's growing importance in Europe the demand for educated people increased. Until the fifteenth century, for the most part, only candidates for the clergy received an education. This shortage and the desire to enhance the university's ability to educate specialists in legal and diplomatic matters were among the main reasons for the refurbishing of the University of Cracow in 1400.

Jan Ostroróg (1436–1501) was the most outstanding of Polish political writers, and his *Monumentum pro Respublicae Ordinatione* (On the Organization of the State) earned him the title of Poland's first lay writer. A member of the royal court and a diplomatic emissary to Rome, Ostroróg favored strengthening the powers of the sovereign and a concomitant strong central government, independent of Church interference. In his writings Ostroróg strongly promoted the Polish language and argued that anyone who wished to live in Poland had to go through the trouble of mastering the native tongue.

Alongside medieval Latin prose, Latin language poetry also existed. Much verse can be found in the chronicles: Gall and Kadłubek recorded numerous poems, songs, and lyrical compositions, mostly of anonymous authorship. The Latin-Polish poetry written in Poland during the Middle Ages, or at least what we know of it, was not terribly interesting nor written in large amounts. The most widely practiced genre, epitaphs to the most famous personalities of the times, were often very long texts, at times including extensive episodes from the life of the deceased. In his *Annales,* Jan Długosz recorded several epitaphs written by Adam Świnka: one to Queen Jadwiga and another to the renowned knight Zawisza Czarny. The most talented Latin poet was a notary from the chancellery of King Władysław Jagiełło, Stanisław Ciołek (1382–1437). His best known poem, *Laus Cracoviae* (In Praise of Cracow), is a panegyric addressed to the then current rulers and their dynasty. Toward the close of the fifteenth century lesser poets attempted to preserve some passing thoughts or feelings in Latin verse. The best examples are those of love poetry, most likely the work of young, amorous Cracovian schoolboys.

The earliest vestiges of Polish literature in Polish are rather sparse and in many cases represent fragments of the original works. The first sentence written in Polish (in 1270) can be found in the *Księga henrykowska* (Henrykow Book), a ledger book containing the history and records of a monastery in Henryków. The sentence, for whatever reason written down, records a peasant's telling his wife to give him the grinder so she can take a rest. Other fragments of Polish can be found in the form of notes for difficult-to-translate passages on the margins of Latin sermons, which were usually translated simultaneously for the non-Latin-speaking believers.

Although only copies from the fifteenth century have survived, the first full-blown work of Polish literature in Polish is a hymn most likely composed in the early thirteenth century entitled *Bogurodzica** (Mary Who Gave Birth to God), which for several centuries served as a national anthem of sorts. Throughout Polish history many legends have attempted to attribute authorship of *Bogurodzica* to various great individuals (St. Adalbert, Władysław Jagiełło), but the fact is that the author remains unknown. A possible source in Latin has never been found. There is a good possibility that *Bogurodzica** has its roots in an Old Church Slavonic equivalent which could have reached Poland via a Czech translation, as proposed by Roman Jakobson. Byzantine motifs present in the hymn and very intense Eastern influences during the reign of Władysław Jagiellonńczyk seem to support Jakobson's thesis. Whatever the case, the first two stanzas, which are the oldest, with their well developed poetics, suggest that other such hymns may have existed but have since been destroyed.

The Sermons of the Holy Cross (*Kazania Świętokrzyskie*), considered the oldest example of Polish prose, are original sermons (at the time most sermons were translations) written most likely near the turn of the thirteenth and fourteenth centuries. Used in the binding of a fifteenth century manuscript, the sermons were discovered by Aleksander Brueckner in 1890. Unfortunately, only one sermon is intact, whereas of the remaining five mere fragments have survived. The sermons are mainly of interest as linguistic relics of Old Polish.

Many religious and legal texts were translated for the benefit of women (who usually did not receive a Latin education) and others who knew no Latin. During the fourteenth century religious texts intended for individual readers and not just for the clergy to use during church services began to appear. The Book of Psalms was first translated for Queen Jadwiga at the end of the fourteenth century and is thus known as *Psałterz Jadwigi* (Jadwiga's Psalm Book, sometimes referred to as *Psałterz Floriański*). The original manuscript has been preserved to this day. Considered the oldest Polish book in existence, it is also the largest single piece of Old Polish writing to date. In the midfifteenth century, as a fruit of the labors of several translators under the guidance of Father Jędrzej from Jaszowice, the Bible was translated into Polish for the widow of King Władysław Jagiełło and since has come to be known as Queen Zofia's Bible, or the Sarospatak Bible (after the town in Hungary where the Bible was kept until the end of World War II).

In comparison with the fourteenth century the fifteenth century represents a relative boom in Polish religious literature, as well as the introduction of secular themes into poetry. Jakub Parkoszowic composed the first guide to Polish orthography, *Obiecado czyli Wierszowany alfabet* (The ABC's or the Alphabet in Verse), which was the first serious step toward the uniformization of Polish spelling as well as an invaluable aid to those wishing to write in proper Polish. Polish began to be heard increasingly often in churches, and along with Latin hymns translated en masse into Polish, new translations from German as well as Polish originals turned up in Poland. Translations played a very important role, not only because they aided the introduction of Christian culture but also because the translators, while translating, laid the foundations of literary Polish; versification and syntax were heavily borrowed from the Latin originals; new expressions were invented or borrowed directly, later to become permanent elements of literary Polish. The translators, most often monks, did their best to translate into Polish while observing the existing norms in medieval poetics.

One example of such a translation is the *Conversation of Master Polycarp with Death* (*Rozmowa mistrza Polikarpa ze Śmiercią*) from the late fifteenth century, which is a Polish adaptation of a Latin original presenting a versified dialogue between death and a learned man. The Polish version, a loose translation, includes many local elements and is more than a translation and one of the most interesting relics of Polish medieval literature. The *Conversation* is a classic piece of medieval didactic literature showing the transitory nature of our existence and is quite indicative of the fascination with death in medieval art. As in the danse-macabre, death is personified as a decaying corpse with scythe in hand who waits for all, for the young and the old, the rich and the poor, the pious and the sinful. Two other noteworthy examples of Polish medieval poetry, *The Lament of a Dying Man* (*Skarga człowieka umierającego*) as well as *The Legend of St. Alexis* (*Legenda o św. Aleksym*), present two totally different heroes but the message is the same: do not neglect the soul, worldly possessions only pollute and weigh down the soul, abandon all and surrender yourself to the service of God and to your fellow man.

During the time when poetry of a religious nature was occupied with its moralizing mission, secular poetry, often containing satirical social commentary, was in abundance. However, it seems that most such verse either was destroyed by the censors or faded into nonexistence because of the critical tendencies toward the ruling classes (i.e., the nobility and the clergy). Though some more neutral texts have survived, such as *On Good Behavior at the Table* (*O zachowaniu się przy stole*), the majority of those preserved tend to reflect the interests of the upper classes. A Song About the Killing of Andrzej Tęczyński (*Pieśń o zabiciu Andrzeja Tęczyńskiego*), about the death of a noble at the hands of the burghers of Cracow after the nobleman slapped an armorer for not completing a suit of armor in time, and A Satire on Lazy Peasants (*Satyra na leniwych chłopów*) are both good examples of this tendency.

Apocrypha, texts of a religious nature dealing with biblical themes but not belonging to Church canon, were very well represented in medieval literature. Their popularity grew as the Bible itself was not always able to satisfy the curiosity of its readers and the apocrypha came to serve as supplemental material to various biblical themes. During the Middle Ages many apocrypha based on the New Testament were translated into Polish; however, those based on motifs from the Old Testament were never very popular in Poland. Of the Polish apocrypha the best examples are *Rozmyślanie o żywocie Pana Jezusa* (Meditations on the Life of Jesus Christ, ca. 1500, also known as *Rozmyślanie Przemyskie* [Przemys Meditations]), and *Rozmyślania dominikańskie* (The Dominican Meditations, 1532).

BIBLIOGRAPHY

Ignacy Chrzanowski, *Historia literatury niepodleglej Polski* (History of Literature of Independent Poland), Warsaw: Państwowy Instytut Wydawniczy, 1983.

Słownik literatury staropolskiej (Dictionary of Old Polish Literature), Redaktor T. Michałowska, Wroclaw, 1990.

Juliusz Kleiner, and Włodzimierz Maciąg, *Zarys dziejów literatury polskiej* (Outline of the History of Polish Literature), Wrocław: Zakład Narodowy imienia Ossolińskich, 1985.

Julian Krzyżanowski, *Dzieje literatury polskiej* (History of Polish Literature), Warsaw: Państwowe Wydawnictwo Naukowe, 1969.

Julian Krzyżanowski, and Czesław Hernas, *Literatura Polska: Przewodnik Encyklopedyczny* (Polish Literature: Encyclopedic Handbook), Warsaw: Państwowe Wydawnictwo Naukowe, 1984.

Zdzisława Libera, Jadwiga Pietrusiewiczowa, and Jadwiga Rytel, *Literatura Polska: Od średniowiecza do oświecenia* (Polish Literature: From the Middle Ages to the Enlightenment, Warsaw: Państwowe Wydawnictwo Naukowe, 1988.

Henryk Samsonowicz, *Złota jesień polskiego średniowiecza* (The Golden Autumn of the Polish Middle Ages), Warsaw: Państwowe Wydawnictwo Naukowe, 1971.

T. Witczak, *Literatura średniowiecza* (Medieval Literature), Warsaw, 1990.

Jerzy Woronczak, *Polskość i europejskość literatury naszego średniowiecza* (Polish and European Traits in our Middle Ages), Problemy Literatury Staropolskiej: Seria I, Wrocław: Zakład Narodowy imienia Ossolińskich, 1971.

English

Norman Davies, *God's Playground: A History of Poland,* New York, Columbia University Press, 1982.

MEIR EZOFOWICZ (see Orzeszkowa).

MICIŃSKI, TADEUSZ (1873–1918), a poet, playwright, prose writer, and journalist, studied history in Cracow, and philosophy in Leipzig and Berlin. As a student he belonged to various radical youth organizations. His journey to Spain (1897–98) aroused his interest in Spanish and Polish mysticism (Towiańszczyzna) and in Plato and Fichte. He knew Stanisław Przybyszewski, Witold Lutosławski, and Stanisław Ignacy Witkiewicz. From 1915 to 1918 he lived in Moscow, Petersburg, and Belarus, writing for Polish and Russian papers. He was killed on his way back to Poland.

Miciński made his debut in 1896 with the poem *Łazarze* (Beggars). His drama, *Marcin Luba,* was staged the same year. In 1902 he published the collection of poems *W mroku gwiazd* (In the Shade of the Stars). His later publications include fragments of the drama *Noc Rabinowa* (A Rabbi's Night), published in Ateneum in 1903–4; the drama *Kniaź Patiomkin* (Prince Potomkin, 1906); the prose-poem *Niedokonany* (The Imperfect, written in 1907 and published in 1931); the political poem *Życie nowe* (A New Life, 1907); the poetic political treatise *Widmo Wallenroda* (Wallenrod's Ghost, 1908); the drama *W mrokach złotego pałacu, czyli Bazylissa Teofanu* (In the Shadow of the Golden Palace, or Bazylissa Teofanu, Tragedy from the History of Byzantium of the Tenth Century, 1909); the novel *Nietota* (Club-Moss, The Mystery Book of the Tatra Mountains, 1910); the collection of stories *Dęby czarnobylskie* (Chernobyl Oaks, 1911); the novel *Xiądz Faust* (The Priest Faust, 1913); a fragment of a fantasy prose work, *Mene-Mene-Thekel-Upharisim!* (written in 1913–14, published in 1931); *Termopile polskie: Misterium na tle życia i śmierci ks. Józefa Poniatowskiego* (The Polish Thermopylae: A Mysterium Based on the Life and Death of Prince Joseph Poniatowski), published in *Krytyka* (Criticism) in 1914, then in the volume *Warownia* (The Fortress, 1916, staged in 1970); and the novel *Wita*, published in 1926. Many of his works remain in manuscript. He was also an active publicist: a number of his articles and literary studies appeared in the volume *Do źródeł duszy polskiej* (To the Source of the Polish Soul, 1906).

In the poetry of Young Poland Miciński's lyrics occupy a special position: in his major achievements, especially the collection *W mroku gwiazd* (In the Shade of the Stars), he went beyond the impressionistic tendencies of early Neo-Romantic Polish poetry: he combined elements of symbolism with new wave surrealism. The metaphoric pathos and wordiness characteristic of poetry of the period were blurred with unusual associations, loose logical ties between subsequent images, that is, what appeared to be the main achievement of the poetry of the twentieth century. According to Bożena Wojnowska, the best poems are constructed as sequences of images which aim at revealing complex and strange psychological experiences. They introduce the motive of a dream in the modern, almost Freudian sense; they present characteristic combinations of mysticism, sadism, and eroticism. The collection is considered Miciński's finest work.

In his dramas Miciński is a follower of expressionist trends. He began with the poetics of dreams and arrived at the formula of drama as a sort of philosophical and social mystery play: it is a drama of ideas and a political tribunal at the same time. Viewing the world as a place of struggle between good and evil, he presented the problem both in the universal, and in the national and social senses. He introduced motives of messianism and Pan-Slavism. He made use of symbol, allegory, and political grotesquery; he mixed realistic scenes with fantastic ones, tragic with grotesque; and employed the technique of a dream, giving theatrical form to subconscious states of mind. He ranks with such reformers of the theater as Gordon Craig, Adolph Appia, and Stanisław Wyspiański.

His novels are also innovative, although artistically not quite successful. They employ symbolic and expressionist techniques, introduce a historiosophical synthesis, and make use of myths, symbols, and tales. The novels present the metaphysical drama of man and demand freedom and internal changes for the individual as well as the nation and the world. In their disagreement with existing reality and the presence of catastrophic motives, they resemble the literature between the wars.

(See *Młoda Polska.*)

BIBLIOGRAPHY

Poezje wybrane (Selected Poetry), edited and with an introduction by P. Kuncewicz, Warsaw, 1976.

Utwory dramatyczne (Dramatic Works), Volumes 2–4, selected and edited by T. Wróblewska, Cracow, 1979–84.

Poezje (Poetry), edited by J. Prokop, Cracow, 1980.

MICKIEWICZ, ADAM (1798–1855), the greatest Polish poet, came from a minor *szlachta* (nobility) family, went to school in Nowogródek, and studied literature in Vilnius. In 1819–23 he taught literature, history, and law in a school in Kowno. His studies gave him a thorough knowledge of Classical philology, history, and theory of poetry and rhetoric. One of the founders of the secret *Towarzystwo Filomatów* (Society of Filomats, 1817), he was also one of its most active members. Mickiewicz's early works are written in the eighteenth century tradition. These include translations and adaptions of Voltaire; the mock-heroic *Kartofla* (Potatoes), left unfinished; *Warcaby* (Checkers, 1819; definitive version 1821–22), published in 1822; his first printed poem, *Zima miejska* (Urban Winter), in the *Tygodnik Wileński* (Vilnius Weekly, 1818); the so-called iambs, a number of jocular poems for his Filomat friends (written 1818–19, published for the most part in 1910); and, finally, programmatic poems, mainly Classical in form: *Już się z pogodnych niebios* (Already from the Sunny Skies, 1818, published in 1866); *Pieśń filaretów* (Songs of the Filarets, written in 1820, published unsigned in 1828); a convivial students' song, patriotic in theme, *Do Joachima Lelewela* (To Joachim Lelewel, published unsigned in 1822), his glorifying view of history; and his famous *Oda do młodości* (Ode to Youth, written in Kowno 1820, published in the collection of poetry *Polihymnia* [Polyhymnia], Lvov, 1827), which reflects the evolutionary change in the views of the Filomats and Mickiewicz's role in the movement. The poem is deeply rooted in the Enlightenment tradition, both ideologically and formally, but it is at the same time a passionately enthusiastic call for revolutionary changes and an apotheosis of youth as the moving force of the metamorphosis; this duality accounts for the radically different interpretations the poem has received.

The period spent in Kowno brought Mickiewicz a series of disappointments and personal problems; he confronted his educational ideals as a Filomat with bitter reality: his mother died in 1820, and in 1821 his beloved Maryla Wereszczakówna married Count Puttkamer. Mickiewicz's affection for her is reflected in many of his works: *Dziady Part IV* (Forefathers' Eve, Part IV), *Upiór* (Ghost), lyrical poems *Do M**** (To M***, written in 1823; published in 1826), *Na Alpach w Spluegen* (In the Alps of Spluegen, written in 1829); published in *Poezje* (Poems, Volume 3, 1833). In 1822 he published Volume 1 of *Poezje* (Poems), containing some varied poems and, above all, the cycle *Ballady i romanse* (Ballads and Romances). The date of the publication of the cycle is widely considered the date of the Romantic breakthrough in Polish literature. It contains the programmatic ballad *Romantyczność* (Romanticism), which presents folklore not as a literary ornament, but as an attitude toward the world and concentrates on the reality which cannot be reached through reason alone but is dependent on intuition. Other ballads—*Świteź* (Water Sprite), *Świtezianka* (Water Nymph), *Pani Twardowska,* and *Lilie* (Lilies), to mention just a few of the most famous, are innovative in their use of the tradition of Polish *duma* (elegy), and in their reference to English and German ballads, which combine epic, lyrical, and dramatic elements. In 1823 Mickiewicz published Volume 2 of *Poezje,* containing *Grażyna* (written in 1822), a poetic novel about a Lithuanian heroine, patriotic in spirit; he also composed *Dziady* (Forefathers' Eve), Parts 2 and 4, during this period.

Arrested as a result of the investigations of the secret youth organizations, Mickiewicz was imprisoned from November 4, 1823, to May 3, 1824. He was later sent into exile deep within the Russian Empire. After three months in Petersburg, where he met the future Decembrists Rylyeyev and Bestuzhev, he was sent to Odessa. From Odessa he made his way to Crimea. These experiences inspired his *Sonety odeskie* (Odessa Sonnets) and *Sonety krymskie* (Crimean Sonnets), published jointly in 1826. These works were received with indignation by Warsaw Classicists. Between December 1825 and April 1828 he lived in Moscow; he was already a recognized poet and mingled with the Russian intellectual élite (Pushkin, Polevoy, and Vyazemskij). At this time he wrote *Konrad Wallenrod,* a poetic novel. The poem relates the story of a Prussian knight, virtuous and brave, but often for some reason rather agitated. The mystery is gradually revealed: the man was kidnapped as a child and brought up by Teutonic Knights. He was later able to return to Lithuania but chose rather to abandon his home and his family to sacrifice himself for his country. He fulfills his duty and takes revenge by leading the Prussian army to defeat. His betrayal, however, is too heavy a burden, and he commits suicide. The character of Konrad has provoked controversy among critics, including contemporary critics: some condemn the idea of the poem as immoral; others defend its so-called Wallenrodism, claiming that the love of one's country justifies any action undertaken in its defense. According to Maria Janion, it would appear, however, that the main idea of the poem is not an apotheosis of betrayal, but rather the tragedy of any unethical action undertaken to preserve higher values. *Konrad Wallenrod* supposedly provided inspiration for the November Uprising, and its hero remained an embodiment of the fate of those who started their struggle conscious of inevitable tragic consequences.

In May 1829 Mickiewicz left Russia and began his year-and-a-half-long trip through Europe. He met countless personages of his time (among others, he met Goethe in Weimar and listened to the lectures of Hegel) and visited Germany, Switzerland, Italy. In Rome he met H. E. Ankwiczówna, whom he wanted to marry, but her parents refused to give their consent: she is the model for Ewa in *Dziady, Part III* and Ewa Horeszkówna in *Pan Tadeusz.* She is also the persona of the poems *Do mego cziczerona* (To My Cicero, published in 1860), *Do H**** (To H***), and *Wezwanie do Neapolu* (A Summons to Naples), all published in *Poezje* (Poems), Volume 3, 1833). Having visited Naples, Mickiewicz left for Geneva with A. E. Odyniec, toured Switzerland with Zygmunt Krasiński, and returned to Rome alone, only to receive news about the outbreak of the uprising.

Mickiewicz planned to return to Poland, but for some unknown reason the departure was continually delayed. He arrived in Paris in June 1831, and from there, with a forged passport, he made his way to Greater Poland through Leipzig and Dresden. He allegedly planned to get into the Polish Kingdom, but he gave up, since the defeat of the uprising was predictable by that time. During the months spent in the manors of Wielkopolska, he wrote the ballad *Ucieczka* (Flight, published in 1832) and poems about the uprising: *Śmierć pułkownika* (The Death of the Colonel, published in 1833), *Nocleg* (Night's Lodging, published in 1852), and *Reduta Ordona* (Ordon's Redoubt), a short descriptive-reflective poem, creating a patriotic picture of a soldier dying heroically under the ruins of the position he refused to surrender to the enemy (written in 1832; published in 1833). In March 1832 he traveled to Dresden; the three months he spent there brought many important works: *Dziady, Part III* (Forefathers' Eve, Part III), several poems, and part of the translation of Byron's *Giaur.* In July 1832 Mickiewicz returned to Paris.

With occasional interruptions, Mickiewicz decided to spend the rest of his life in Paris but adapted to France with difficulty. He knew the intellectual milieu of Paris, but never became part of it. He never joined any of the emigrant groups. His views on the role of emigration are contained in *Księgi narodu polskiego i pielgrzymstwa polskiego* (Books of the Polish People and Polish Pilgrimage) and in his articles in *Pielgrzym Polski* (Polish Pilgrim), of which he was chief editor from April through June 1833. He believed in the coming changes in Europe and equated the freedom of Poland with the freedom of other nations; he argued for the necessity of all emigrant groups to remain steadfast and forever ready to do military duty. At the same time he completed the translation of *Giaur* and began work on *Pan Tadeusz.* Disappointed, he turned away from public life to religious and mystic literature. In July 1834 he married Celina Szymanowska; they had six children (born between 1835 and 1850). Their financial situation was becoming more and more difficult. The poet tried to write dramas in French, without much success. His poetic output came practically to a close with *Pan Tadeusz.* Subsequently he composed a few poems called the lyrics of Lousanne, and two fables, published in 1880. He wrote parts of the history of Poland that he had earlier planned. After November 1839 he began lecturing on Latin literature in Lousanne. In spite of his success, he returned to Paris to teach Slavic literature at the College de France.

His lectures aroused a great deal of interest and controversy but because of their political orientation and propaganda regarding the messianic views of Andrzej Towiański, and because of the demonstrations by the students that his lectures provoked, severe criticism appeared in the press and in May 1844 Mickiewicz was relieved of his position as a professor. Mickiewicz met Towiański in 1841, at a difficult moment in his life: he was exhausted from his hopeless existence as an emigrant and tormented because of his wife's mental illness. He became a follower of "the master's" views, even after Towiański himself was expelled from France.

Arriving in Rome in February 1848, he tried to convince the pope to become the leader of the popular movement in Europe called the "Spring of the Peoples." He overcame many obstacles to gather a group of volunteers who became the core of his legion; he formulated its ideological goals (doling land to the farmers, gaining equality for women and Jews, and promoting democratic reform) in *Skład zasad* (A Body of Laws, in Italian, 1848; in Polish, 1875). The Legion left for Milan and was accepted to fight as a Polish unit for the freedom of Lombardy; they remained in combat until July 1849. Back in Paris, he started a daily, *La Tribune des Peuples,* in cooperation with French leftists and emigrants of various nationalities. The paper advocated a radical program, closely alligned to French Socialism, especially an espousal of the Napoleonic idea, with which few members of the board agreed. The paper was soon suspended. Mickiewicz was removed from the board after Russian intervention. In 1851 he was put under police surveillance and was forbidden to lecture. Mickiewicz's hopes regarding Napoleon the Third were revived after France joined the Crimean War. In the fall of 1855 he left for Istanbul to help organize Polish legions for battle against Russia. He was soon in conflict with Władysław Zamoyski, whose plan was to have all Polish units under his control, that is, under the control of the conciliatory policy of the conservative Hotel Lambert. The poet's sudden death under these circumstances raised suspicions that he had been poisoned; most probably, however, he died of cholera.

According to Zofia Stefanowska, Mickiewicz's contemporaries considered him a genius, and even though only a few could comprehend his personality, they were able to appreciate his ability to influence opinions in Poland and on the international scene. Various emigrant groups tried to claim him as espousing their views, but, since his political philosophy could not be contained within the limits of any one political program, he was constantly under attack. He was accused of blasphemy, of revolutionary anarchism, of conservatism, of nationalism, and of supporting Russia. The arguments regarding his ideological heritage have never ceased: each political group has attempted to make his ideas their own, shaping them to fit the size of its own program. At the same time, few could distance themselves from him, for the work and life of Adam Mickiewicz, even today, are inalienable parts of the Polish collective consciousness. Basic individual and social problems, moral issues, patriotism, the concept of the nation, the vision of the Polish landscape, and especially his language, with myriad quotations absorbed into colloquial speech—all these have remained in the memory of generations. He has had and still has a decisive influence on Polish literature, on its language and its poetic imagination.

Dziady (Forefathers' Eve), a dramatic cycle written in verse, is composed of two earlier parts, the *Dziady of Kowno and Vilnius* (1820–23, published in 1823), the unfinished Part I (first published after Mickiewicz's death), and Part III, called *Dziady of Dresden,* which was written in the spring of 1832, published in Paris, 1832, in Volume 4, *Poezji* (Poems).

In Part II spirits of the dead appear before a group of peasants, summoned by *Guślarz* (Sorcerer). They admit their guilt, give warning to the living, and disappear, except for the last Phantom, who silently follows a shepherdess and disregards the warning of *Guślarz.* In Part IV an unexpected guest, Gustaw, comes to visit the priest, his former teacher, on All Souls' Day. He talks about his suffering (his beloved married another, a richer man): the monologues have great emotional power, but the simple priest tends to treat Gustaw as a madman. In a fit of despair, Gustaw stabs himself with a knife, but no wound appears. We do not know whether he is a ghost or a living man; perhaps his words about suicide are to be understood metaphorically, as the killing of an individual who very well could be a member of society. We can surmise that the Phantom from Part II and Gustaw are the same person, though there is no strict connection between the two scenes: the loose structure of *Dziady* is a use of Romantic fragmentarism; the two parts of the cycle violate sequential rules. The preserved fragments of Part I lead one to believe that it would involve the story of the love that destroyed Gustaw's life. Mickiewicz left Part I unfinished and proceeded to Parts II and IV, including the ballad *Upiór* (Ghost), about a man who killed himself for his love. The two parts of *Dziady* are the first examples of the Romantic attitude toward folklore, containing not only poetic, but moral and social inspiration.

Part III is composed of dramatic scenes under the subtitle *Litwa* (Lithuania), and the epic part, *Ustęp* (Passage). The core of the drama revolves around the trial of the Filomats (1823–24), its dramatis personae mostly made up of authentic personages. Part III was written after the defeat of the uprising. Mickiewicz endeavored to endow the Vilnius repressions with a contemporary interpretation, treating them as an example of the occupiers' crimes, but, more generally, the historical struggle between freedom and despotism, between good and evil. The parties in the metaphysical conflict are not only patriots and servants of the czar (Russian or Polish), but supernatural forces: The battleground is the human conscience. The scenes written in the style of historical realism adjoin parts written as mystery plays.

According to Zofia Stefanowska, the main character is Konrad, formerly Gustaw, now an imprisoned poet—the change of the name symbolizes the shift between private life and public cause. In the scene of the Great Improvisation Konrad demands that God bestow on him some of his power, for he believes that he could create, as he does poetry, a new happy life on earth for his country. Accusing God of cold rationalism, he reaches the border of blasphemy; his pride leads him into the realm of the devil. Konrad is a poet and confronts God as creator to creator. He is saved by the poor friar Piotr (Peter): Konrad sinned in the name of reason but was forced into it because of his love for the people. In the vision of Father Piotr we see the destruction of Poland and its coming resurrection—Poland is the Messiah of nations. The symbolic form of the vision is modeled after the biblical Apocalypse of Saint John, with various mystic symbols whose meaning cannot be fully explained. In subsequent scenes (Salon Warszawski) the governing elite loyal to the czar are bitterly ridiculed; some of those people are representatives of Neo-Classical and sentimental literature. They are contrasted with the young patriots, who demand that literature treat current national problems. They present the truth regarding the persecution of Poles by the Russian government. This scene together with the scene at the hall in the senator's residence in Vilnius presents a synthetic contrast between the conforming part of society and the battling persecuted patriots.

Dziady Part III dramatizes the conflict of conscience of a Polish patriot in view of the national defeat, about his obligation to believe in the power of the nation and its future revival, guaranteed by the providential order of history. The cycle is innovative in its theme and in its form: in its loose structure, with fragmentary presentation of the plot, in the mixture of literary genres, in its language—studded with colloquialisms—Part III has gained the stature of a manifesto of patriotism, a testimony of the nation's love of freedom. In the past, several productions have signaled a change in Poland's political structure. Poles have rallied around these productions during moments when the nation's existence seemed threatened.

Pan Tadeusz, czyli ostatni zajazd na Litwie (Pan Tadeusz, or the Last Foray in Lithuania), a poem written between the fall of 1832 and February 1834, was published in Paris in 1834. Mickiewicz's life in exile made him choose the topic: memories of his homeland, its nature, and its inhabitants. Situating the plot in the past gave Mickiewicz the opportunity to present human types and customs, linking them to historical events—the opportunity to complete the epic with the vision of a free Lithuania. The action takes place over several days in the late summer of 1811, and one night and day in the spring of 1812, near Nowogródek, in Soplicowo, the estate of a wealthy *szlachcic* (nobleman), Judge Soplica. The most important character of the poem is the clergyman, Father Robak: from his final confession we learn that he is in fact the Judge's brother, Jacek. He had, at one time, planned to marry the daughter of the magnate Horeszko, but the magnate refused, and the desperate Jacek killed him; he was consequently condemned as a national traitor and was banished from the country. He returned years later as a monk and a Napoleonic emissary, hoping to put an end to the conflict between the families of Soplica and Horeszko. The story is made more complex because of its many minor plots and digressions, but eventually Robak's aim is attained: all conflicting parties are united when faced with a common enemy. The poem concludes with a burst of optimism and with the belief in the success of Napoleon.

According to Zofia Stefanowska, history is present everywhere in the poem: the fate of Robak, with his metamorphosis from a rebellious gentryman into a nameless servant espousing the national cause, is a synthesis of the fate of all Poles. The narration, which varies between humor and lyricism, the seriousness of the storyteller and the attitude toward exotic "Sarmatism," allows the poet to portray the mentality and everyday life of the provincial *szlachta,* with their virtues (patriotism, bravado) and their vices (self-centeredness, pride, narrow intellectual horizons). Mickiewicz approaches the latter group as a humorist rather than a satirist and is aware that they are passing away into history. The characters are psychologically convincing and highly individualized; the descriptions of the landscape mirror the peaceful existence in this well-organized world. The language is often colloquial, with a variety of dialectal and obsolete expressions; the versification pattern, *13-zgłoskowiec* (thirteen-syllable verse) is used in a variety of syntactic and accentual patterns, with unusual ease and fluency.

The poem had a major influence on the national consciousness of the Poles, implanting the image of the Polish national character and landscape. It is a truly national and, one might even venture to say, an international epic that deserves greater critical attention.

(See Romanticism.)

BIBLIOGRAPHY

Dzieła (Works), Volumes 1–16, Warsaw, 1948–55.

English

Adam Mickiewicz, 1798–1855: Selected Poems, edited by Clark Mills, New York: Noonday Press, 1956.

Poems, edited by George Rapall Noyes, New York: Herald Square Press, 1944; translated by Jack Lindsay, London, Sylvan Press, 1957.

Selected Poems, edited by Clark Mills, translations by W. H. Auden and others, New York: Voyages Press, 1957; New York: Noonday Press, 1956.

Polish Romantic Drama, by Harold B. Segel, Ithaca, New York: Cornell University Press, 1977 (translations of *Forefathers' Eve,* Part III, by Adam Mickiewicz; *The Un-Divine Comedy,* by Zygmunt Krasiński; and *Fantazy,* by Juliusz Słowacki).

Forefathers' Eve, Parts 1 and 2 (Dziady), translated by Władysław Potocki, London: Polish Cultural Foundation, 1944, 1968; London: The Right Review, 1944; Oraguignan: Royal Polish Cultural Foundation, 1970.

Grażyna, translated by D. P. Radin, *Poet Lore,* Volume LVI, 1940.

Konrad Wallenrod and Other Writings, edited by George R. Noyes and translated by Jewell Parish, Westport, Connecticut: Greenwood Press, 1975; Berkeley: University of California Press, 1925; London: M. I. Kolin, 1943.

Pan Tadeusz, or The Last Foray in Lithuania: A Story of Life Among Polish Gentlefolk in the Years 1811 and 1812, translated by G. R. Noyes, London and Toronto: J. M. Dent and Sons, 1917; New York: E. P. Dutton, Everyman's Library, 1930, 1917; London: Dent, 1916, 1917, 1943.

Pan Tadeusz, or the Last Foray in Lithuania, translated by Watson Kirk Connell, annotated by Harold B. Segel, New York: Polish Institute of Arts and Sciences in America, 1962, 1981; Toronto: University of Toronto Press, 1962; London: Polish Cultural Foundation, 1964, 1986.

Pan Tadeusz, or the Last Foray in Lithuania, translated by Kenneth Mackenzie, London: Polish Cultural Foundation, 1964; London: J. M. Dent, 1966; New York: Dutton, Everyman's Library, 1966.

The Poetry of Adam Mickiewicz, The Hague: Mouton, Slavistic Printings and Reprintings, No. 2, 1954.

Improvisation, translated by Walter J. Hochlowski, Ann Arbor, Michigan: University of Michigan, n.d.

Sonnets From the Crimea, translated by Edna Worthley Underwood, San Francisco, California: P. Edler, 1917.

Forefathers' Eve, translated by Dorothea Prall Rodin, London: School of Slavonic Studies, University of London, Kings College, 1925.

Gems of Polish Poetry, translated by Frank H. Fortey, Warsaw: Polish Editorial Agency, 1923.

Abdication of the Sun (excerpts from *Forefathers' Eve*), London: Right Review, 1938.

Poems by Adam Mickiewicz, New York: Polish Institute of Arts and Sciences in America, 1944.

The Books of Our Pilgrimage, translated by T. K. Tautmyla, Chicago: Draugas Press, 1950; New York: Dutton, 1949; New York: The Polish Institute of Arts and Sciences in America, 1962.

Mickiewicz Art Exhibition—Certain Poems, Washington, D.C.: Mickiewicz Centenary Committee, 1955.

Selected Poetry and Prose, translated by Stanisław Helsztyński, Warsaw: Polonia Publishing House, 1955.

Adam Mickiewicz (selected poems), New York: Noonday Press, 1956.

The Concert of Concerts, translated by Aaron Kramer, New York, reprint from *The Polish Review,* vol. 1, no. 4, 1956.

The Great Improvisation, translated by Louise Varese, New York: Voyages Press, 1956.
New Selected Poems, translated by Louis Bogan, New York: Voyages Press, 1957, 1979.
Adam Mickiewicz, Poet of Poland, New York: Greenwood Press, 1969.
Zosia and Thaddeus or an Ancient Feud Ended, Cheshire, Connecticut: Cherry Hill Books, 1974.
Mickiewicz, Adam, *Konrad Wallenrod and Grażyna,* translated by Irene Suboczewski, Lanham, Maryland: University Press of America, 1989.
Wiktor Weintraub, *Literature as Prophecy: Scholarship and Martinist Poetics in Mickiewicz's Parisian Lectures,* The Hague: Mouton, 1959.
David Welsh, *Adam Mickiewicz,* New York: Twayne, World Authors Series, 1966.

MIĘDZYRZECKI, ARTUR (born 1922), a poet, prose writer, essayist, and translator, spent the years 1940–42 in forced labor camps in the Soviet Union, later in the Near East with the army of General Anders. He also took part in the battle of Monte Cassino. In 1946–49 he studied journalism in Paris; in 1950 he returned to Poland and worked for numerous magazines (*Świat* [World], *Nowa Kultura* [New Culture], *Poezja* [Poetry]). Long an active member of the Polish PEN Club, he has been president since 1991. He has published a number of collections of poems, including *Namiot z Kanady* (A Tent from Canada, Jerozolima, 1943), *Strony przydrożne* (Wayside Parts, Paris, 1949), *Noc darowana* (Gift Night, 1960), *Piękne zmęczenia* (A Beautiful Weariness, 1962), *Selekcje* (Selections, 1964), *Zamówienia* (Witchcraft, 1968), *Wygnanie do rymu* (Banishment to Rhyme, 1977). In addition he has published *Wojna Nerwów* (War of Nerves, 1983), in which he sublimates the collective anxieties regarding Martial Law in Poland, as well as *Koniec gry* (The End of the Game, 1987). His collections of short stories include *Opowieści mieszkańca namiotów* (Stories of a Tenant of Tents, 1957); *Powrót do Sorrento* (A Return to Sorrento, 1959), based on his memoirs *Wiek mentorów* (Age of Mentors, 1979); the grotesque-fantasy *Śmierć Robinsona* (The Death of Robinson, 1963); and the novel *Złota papuga* (Golden Parrot, 1970). He has also published a number of volumes of literary sketches, including *Poezja dzisiaj* (Poetry Today, 1964) and *Dialogi i sąsiedztwa* (Dialogues and Environs, 1970). In his early works Międzyrzecki's main concerns were his war experiences and the social problems of his generation. According to Ryszard Matuszewski, his later works have been characterized by a growing reflective-ironic distance from the memories of his youth, with ironic criticism of the stereotypes of contemporary politics and culture, in both its avant-garde and traditional forms. Międzyrzecki based his lyrics on free imagination, mixing styles and conventions, advocating "open" poetry. He is also an editor and translator of French literature, as well as a translator of Mandelshtam, Lundkvist, Cummings, and Auden. In the 1970s Międzyrzecki and his wife, Julia Hartwig, were on the faculty at SUNY Stony

Brook, New York. At the time both writers took an active part in the literary life of New York City and have written a number of poems and essays concerning their experiences in the United States.

BIBLIOGRAPHY

Poezje (Poems), introduction by J. M. Rymkiewicz, Warsaw, 1980.

English

Focus on Poland (sound recording), Washington, D.C.: National Public Radio, 1982.

14 Poems, translated by the author, Iowa City: Windhover Press, University of Iowa, 1972.

Spoiling Cannibals' Fun: Polish Poetry of the Last Two Decades of Communist Rule, edited and translated by Stanisław Barańczak and Clare Cavanagh, foreword by Helen Vendler, Evanston, Illinois: Northwestern University Press, 1991.

MIKOŁAJ KOPERNIK UNIVERSITY (University of Toruń) was established in 1945. At first most of its faculty members were from the universities in Vilnius and Lvov. The two original faculties soon grew into six. Its organizer and first rector was L. Kolankowski; the first Dean of the Humanities was Konrad Górski. The faculty had twenty-eight chairs.

The Polish Studies section was originally divided into the chairs of the Theory of Literature, Comparative Literature, History of Polish Literature, the Polish Language, and Slavic Languages and Literatures. In 1952, as a result of the reorganization of the university and the death of several excellent professors (Zawodziński, Kucharski, Makowiecki), the section was reduced to only two chairs: Polish Literature (headed by B. Nadolski) and Polish Language (headed by Turska). Several members of the faculty left the university at this time. In 1956 the setting up of a new chair was discussed. Only in 1970 was the suggestion realized and the Institute of Polish Philology was established with six sections; Nadolski and A. Hutnikiewicz (after 1973) were its directors. The research interests of the institute are varied; the works by Górski are the most comprehensive: Arian Literature, Romanticism, artistic expression, and the language of Mickiewicz.

MIŁOSZ, CZESŁAW (born 1911), a poet, essayist, translator, and literary historian, was awarded the Nobel Prize in literature in 1980. He spent his youth in Vilnius (Wilno); at the time of his studies in the Department of Law (1929–34), he was cofounder of the literary group *Żagary* and coeditor of its newspaper. Miłosz made his debut in 1930 in a university paper; in 1933 he published the first collection of his own poetry, *Peomat o czasie zastygłym* (A Poem About a Set Time) and *Antologia poezji społecznej* (An Anthology of Social Poetry), which he edited with Zbigniew

Folejewski. In 1934 he received an award from the Vilnius section of the Union of Writers. He visited Paris twice (1931, 1934–35) and came into contact with his distant relative, Oscar Miłosz. In 1936 he worked for Polish Radio, first in Vilnius, then in Warsaw from 1937. During the occupation he participated in the underground cultural life, publishing in 1940 a collection, *Wiersze* (Poems, signed Jan Syruc), and in 1942 a poetic anthology, *Pieśń niepodległa* (Songs of Independence), and a translation, with his own commentaries of Maritain's sketch against collaboration with the Nazis, *Drogami klęski* (By Roads of Defeat). He also translated Shakespeare's *As You Like It* (staged in 1946).

After the war he lived in Cracow for a short time. In late 1945 he went into diplomatic service, working as a cultural officer in the United States. In 1949 he left for Paris. During this period he continued to publish in Poland. In 1951 he refused to return to Poland and remained in Paris. After this decision, his works (his prewar output as well) were forbidden by the Communist censor, and his sole publisher became the émigré Literary Institute in Paris. From the moment of the founding of *Drugi obieg** (alternative press) in Poland, the underground presses began to make Miłosz's works available to the public, and the possibility of being published by the official press opened up in 1980: the Nobel Prize and the birth of Solidarity, which led to the curtailment of all-powerful censorship. In 1960 he was invited by the University of California at Berkeley to lecture on Polish literature, and in 1961 he settled in Berkeley as a professor of Slavic literature and languages. He published mainly in the United States and Paris. Well known in Western countries, first as an essayist, then as a poet, he received a Guggenheim Fellowship in 1976, the Neustadt International Prize for Literature in 1978, and the Nobel Prize in Literature in 1980. In the same year he received an honorary doctorate from the Catholic University in Lublin, and in 1989 from the Jagiellonian University in Cracow.

Miłosz's early works *Poemat o czasie zastygłym* (A Poem About a Set Time, 1933) and the collection *Trzy zimy* (Three Winters, 1936) have often been described as a reflection of catastrophism. This appellation, however, cannot encompass the characteristic antinomies of his poetry: the constant fluctuation between the longing for Arcadia and a foreboding of the Apocalypse, between the need for the affirmation of life and a fascination with the beauty of nature, with the expectation of a catastrophe for our civilization and of the unavoidable end of the world as he then perceived it. Aware of a crisis in culture, Miłosz composed his poetry not only with a feeling of awe but with one of guilt and shared responsibility. His persona took a heroic and stoical stand, as reflected in his conception of the fate of the poet and society in eschatological and metaphysical terms. Some of Miłosz's prewar poems were published in the collection *Ocalenie* (Salvation, 1945), together with his output from the period of the Nazi occupation. He explained the meaning of the title in the preface: it refers to the "salvation aspect" of poetry, which brings knowledge and purification. According to Irena Sławińska, the collection is considered to be an accurate representation of the nation's war experiences, containing poems which are thoroughly moving, although a somewhat withdrawn testimony of the time. The collection includes poems which give expression of foreboding to the coming catastrophe. *Ocalenie* was considered a tribute to the tragic fate of Warsaw—the occupation, the uprising, and the tragedy of the ghetto. The poems also contemplate the role of poetry and the duties of the poet in view of total destruction. They explore the painful dilemma of being torn between the longing for pure joyful art and the obligations to others. The early poems and those of the war period shaped the main features of Miłosz's poetic style, its visionary character and Classical discipline. From the very beginning his poetry was characterized by a tendency to objectify lyrical emotions, to combine them with contemplative and discursive elements, to overcome seriousness and prophetic pathos with irony and distance, and, finally, to look for a synthesis of human experience in inner dialogues and arguments. Miłosz's lyrical poetry violates the rigors of literary genres: he is modest in use of metaphor and stylistic form; he employs sequential poetic images and the phraseology of natural, contemporary, spoken language and, at the same time, makes widespread references to literary and linguistic traditions, both Polish and foreign.

The next stage in Miłosz's poetic development is "the period of anger," in the spirit of Jonathan Swift. It opened with poems written in the United States (1946–47), among others *Dziecię Europy* (A Child of Europe) and *Traktat moralny* (A Moral Treatise), published in *Twórczość* (Creativity) in 1948, a poem which is a peculiar combination of irony and sarcasm, humor and a moral message, which explores the intellectual as well as social and political situation of Poland and the world after the war and gives a warning of the coming totalitarian epoch. A very sharp tone of indignation could also be heard in the poem *Który skrzywdziłeś człowieka prostego* (Who Harmed the Simple Man). These works are contained in his first collection published abroad, *Światło dzienne* (Day Light, 1953). He explored the mechanisms of manipulation and self-mystification leading to the degradation of literature and its constraints by Communist ideology in his parabolic story of several Polish writers referred to as Alfa, Beta, Delta, and Gamma, in *Zniewolony umysł* (The Captive Mind, written in 1951; published in 1953, translated into a number of languages and republished several times). His novel in French *La prise du pouvoir,* written in 1952 and published in Polish as *Zdobycie władzy* (The Seizure of Power, 1953), had similar intentions. It is a roman à clef, widely translated and awarded the Prix Litteraire in 1953. His novel *Dolina Issy* (The Issa Valley, published in 1955) had obvious autobiographical features: it is the story of the growing up of a boy, Tomasz, who lives with his grandparents in a Polish country house in Lithuania. The setting of the story is the amazingly uncivilized beauty of the wild lands of the lakes region, overrun with swamps and forests, where Tomasz is initiated into the life of nature and takes his first steps as a hunter. The boy is surrounded by strange and extraordinary people, living in the world of traditional superstitions, old customs, songs, and beliefs. They all share a common destiny made up of mystery and suffering. Their intertwined, tragic lives give rise to philosophical reflection on the mystery of being ("living is too little") and the awe regarding ubiquitous death.

In his later years Miłosz published collections: *Traktat poetycki* (A Poetic Treatise, 1957), *Król Popiel i inne wiersze* (King Popiel and Other Poems, 1962), *Gucio zaczarowany* (The Enchanted Gucio, 1965), *Miasto bez imienia* (A Town Without a Name, 1969), *Gdzie wschodzi słońce i kędy zapada* (Where the Sun Rises and Whither It Falls, 1974), *Hymn o perle* (Hymn About a Pearl, 1982), *Nieobjęta ziemia* (Unembraced Earth, 1984), *Kroniki* (Chronicles, 1987). The poems became more and more concise, more and more disciplined; at the same time they were free of formal divisions and genre categories. *Traktat poetycki* gave a passionate and sarcastic picture of the genealogy of contemporary Polish poetry, portraying its representatives in aphoristically brief critical formulae. The American period brought philosophical and historiosophical contemplations on the passing of time and the laws governing it, on the impossibility of naming things and giving expression to the repetitiousness of human existence. The characteristic motives of the period were connected with Vilnius and its atmosphere, with the memories of Miłosz's youth, with the Polish language as the "preserved homeland of an exile," with Miłosz's readings, his historical reminiscences, and the recurring questions concerning the role of poetry and the obligations of the poet. The volumes *Miasto bez imienia* (A Town Without a Name) and *Gdzie wschodzi słońce* (Where the Sun Rises) also contain some religious poems, which mark Miłosz's preoccupation with the Bible and the beginning of his work as a translator.

Translation for Miłosz is directly connected with his own original work, for he considers translating to be part and parcel of his poetic search for "new diction," an opportunity to penetrate the specificity of one's own language and consciousness. He first began translating from French: prose (Simone Weil) and poetry (Oscar Miłosz); later from and into English. He translated authors from the great Anglo-Saxon tradition: John Milton, William Blake, W. B. Yeats, and, above all, T. S. Eliot. His translations of Polish contemporary poets are contained in his anthology *Postwar Polish Poetry* (1965, 1970). He devoted separate volumes to Zbigniew Herbert (1968) and Aleksander Wat (1977). He received an award from the Polish PEN Club in 1973 for these works. In the 1970s Miłosz began his work on the translation of the Bible, publishing *The Gospel According to Saint Mark, The Book of Ecclesiastes, The Book of Psalms, Jeremiah's Laments,* and *The Book of Job.* The work, done in cooperation with the Reverend

J. Sadzik and based on Miłosz's own biblical and linguistic studies (Hebrew, Greek), was intended to give a modern, yet "high and liturgic" version of the Bible to contemporary Polish culture.

Miłosz has written essays in both Polish and English. The sketches written during the war and soon after (on Browning, Milton, and Oscar Miłosz) are contained in the volume *Kontynenty* (Continents, 1958), together with *Wprowadzenie w Amerykanów* (An Introduction to American Writers) and a study of Saint-John Perse's poetry. The same duality of translation and research can be seen in his later books, mainly *Prywatne obowiązki* (Private Obligations, 1972) and *Ogród nauk* (A Garden of Sciences, 1979), on the linguistic and poetic aspects of the work of his intellectual mentors (Mickiewicz, Blake, Oscar Miłosz, and Eliot), as well as contemporary Polish writers (S. I. Witkiewicz* and W. Gombrowicz*). He also wrote a book about Stanisław Brzozowski,* *Człowiek wśród skorpionów* (A Man Among Scorpions, 1962). *Rodzinna Europa* (Native Realm, 1959) resulted from a trip into the poet's past, generalized as an experience of an East European; on the other hand, *Widzenia nad zatoką San Francisco* (Visions from San Francisco Bay, 1969) referred to Miłosz's American experiences and to contemporary American culture. All these motives are combined in *Ziemia Ulro* (The Land of Ulro, 1977). A volume of his essays in English (*Emperor of the Earth: Modes of Eccentric Vision*) appeared in 1977; it contains his works on Dostoevsky and other writers and on Manichaean motives in European thought and culture. Further critical studies and essays appeared in *Świadectwo poezji: Część wykładów o dotkliwościach naszego wieku* (The Witness of Poetry: Six Lectures on the Severity of Our Century, 1983), *Zaczynając od moich ulic* (Beginning from My Streets, 1985), and the diary *Rok myśliwego* (The Year of the Hunter, 1990). Miłosz also wrote *The History of Polish Literature* (1969). His works have been translated into every major language.

(See Contemporary Polish Literature.)

BIBLIOGRAPHY

Dzieła zbiorowe (Collected Works), Volumes 1–12, Paris: Instytut Literacki, 1980–85.

Utwory poetyckie (Poems), Ann Arbor, Michigan: Michigan Slavic Publications, 1977; 1976 (in English and Polish, with an introduction by A. M. Schenker).

Poezje (Poems), Warsaw, 1981.

Wiersze (Poems), Volumes 1–2, Cracow, 1984.

English

Leonard Nathan and Arthur Quinn, *The Poet's Work: An Introduction to Czesław Miłosz,* Cambridge, Massachusetts: Harvard University Press, 1991.

Bells in Winter (poems), translated by the author and Lillian Vallee, New York: Ecco Press, 1974; 1978; London: Carcanet, 1980; 1986.

The Captive Mind (Zniewolony umysł), translated by Jane Zielonko, New York: A. A. Knopf, 1953; New York: Vintage Books, 1953; 1955; 1959; 1964; 1981; New York: Random House, 1981; London: Secker and Warburg, 1953; New York: Penguin, 1980; New York: Octagon Books, 1981; New York: Limited Editions Club, 1983.

Emperor of the Earth: Modes of Eccentric Vision (essays), Berkeley: University of California Press, 1977; 1981.

The Issa Valley (Dolina Issy), translated by Louis Iribarne, London: Sidgwick and Jackson, 1981; New York: Farrar, Straus & Giroux, 1981; London: Abacus, 1984.

Native Realm: A Search for Self-Definition (Rodzinna Europa), translated by Catherine S. Leach, Garden City, New York: Doubleday, 1968; Berkeley: University of California Press, 1981; London: Carcanet, 1981; London: Sidgwick and Jackson, 1981.

The Seizure of Power (Zdobycie władzy), translated by Celina Wieniewska, New York: Criterion Books, 1955; New York: Farrar, Straus & Giroux, 1982.

Selected Poems, translated by the author and Peter Dale Scott, New York: Ecco Press, 1981; 1986; Harmondsworth, England: Penguin, 1968; New York: Continuum, 1981; Manchester: Carcanet, 1985.

The Usurpers (The Seizure of Power) (Zdobycie władzy), translated by Celina Wieniewska, London: Faber and Faber, 1955; London: Abacus, 1985.

Visions from San Francisco Bay (Widzenia nad Zatoką San Francisco), translated by Richard Lourie, New York: Farrar, Straus & Giroux, 1982; Manchester: Carcanet, 1982.

Post-War Polish Poetry, edited and translated by Czesław Miłosz, Baltimore: Penguin Books, 1970; New York: Doubleday, 1965.

Incantation (Poem), Berkeley, California: Black Oak Books, 1983.

The Land of Ulro (*Ziemia Ulro*), translated by Louis Iribarne, New York: Farrar, Straus and Giroux, 1984; Manchester: Carcanet, 1985.

The Separate Notebook (Osobny zeszyt), translated by Robert Hass and Robert Pinsky, New York: Ecco Press, 1984.

Happy as a Dog'd Tail, translated by the author and Leonard Nathan, San Diego: Harcourt, Brace, Jovanovich, 1985.

Re-Thinking Our Human Environment for the 21st Century, Barre, Vermont: Northlight Studio Press, 1986.

Unattainable Earth (Nieobjęta ziemia), translated by Robert Hass, New York: Ecco Press, 1986.

The Witness of Poetry (Świadectwo poezji), Cambridge, Massachusetts: Harvard University Press, 1983

Czesław Miłosz: An International Bibliography, 1930–1980, preface by S. Barańczak, Ann Arbor: University of Michigan, 1983.

The Mature Laurel: Essays on Modern Polish Poetry, edited by Adam Czerniawski, Chester Springs, Pennsylvania: Dufour Editions, 1991.

MŁODA POLSKA (Young Poland), a literary period which lasted roughly from 1890 to 1918, followed Polish positivism and preceded the interwar period. It is one of the more complex periods of Polish literature, since there are differences of opinion regarding almost every aspect of the movement, ranging from the exact time of its existence to the name it should take. Modernism (*Moderna*), decadentism, Neo-Romanticism are terms that from time to time designated the movement. *Młoda Polska* is the broadest term that takes into account all literary trends followed by the writers of that time. It also parallels other European movements (Young Germany, Young Scandinavia) which had roots in the same kind of social aura. The entire Western world was undergoing a deep spiritual crisis at the end of the nineteenth century. The failure of the previous system of values, which relied on scientific progress, evolutionism, and development of industry, was apparent. Science which undermined religion did not provide an alternative nor an acceptable value system. It also failed to provide a practical basis for existence: on the contrary, it led to increasing social conflict.

The young generation reacted to this by what was termed an "antipositivist breakthrough." They rebelled against the positivist mentality of organic work and gradual improvement and proclaimed the positivist philosophy a fraud. Positivism* was blamed for the ideology of adaptation and minimalism which manifested itself on several levels. It revealed itself in its pedestrian mentality, resignation from a broad philosophical quest, and shunning of the metaphysical in favor of the practical. In the political sphere it led to an acquiescence to a lack of independence and the "triple loyalty" toward the partitioning powers. On social grounds positivism was accused of covering up class conflict and following a program of individual enrichment under the pretense of supporting the growth of Poland's economic potential. In art it marked a lowering of standards due to didactic and ideological functions which it was required to take on. Such a negative view of the previous generation's program led to the younger generation's total abolition of the fundamental elements of positivism. Instead, they turned to romantic ideals of independence and revolution. *Młoda Polska,* however, drew more inspiration from European Romanticism than from Polish Romanticism, which was burdened with national-social duty. For this reason Słowacki* with his mysticism and individualism and Norwid* with his status as a "damned poet" were *Młoda Polska*'s main Polish Romantic influences.

After the provincial and highly local sphere of literary interest manifested during positivism, *Młoda Polska* opened Polish literature to all kinds of international influences. The young generation's ambition was to bring Polish literature up to par with European literature, to make it more universal and cosmopolitan. This intense interest in foreign writings enormously enriched *Młoda Polska*'s mentality. The writers drew on many resources. The French lyric had a foremost inspirational role. Charles Baudelaire was a Romantic forerunner of many literary trends. Both European and Polish modernism drew inspiration from him, particularly, his mastery of form, his predilection for themes of death, his emphasis on decay, his preoccupation with evil and sin, and his escape into eroticism and perversion. Polish poets were also inspired by the French Parnassians, such as de Lisle, Prudhomme, and his patron and predecessor, Gautier, as well as symbolists such as Verlaine, Rimbaud, and Mallarmé. *Młoda Polska*'s drama was influenced by the two main European theatrical trends: naturalism represented by Ibsen and Strindberg and symbolism based mainly on Maeterlinck. Polish prose drew its inspiration from such various sources as Huysmans, Poe, Kipling, Conrad, d'Annunzio, Hamsun, and Dostoyevsky. However, *Młoda Polska*'s creative force was not merely fueled by literary fashions. The crisis in the world outlook and value system caused the young to search for answers and inspiration not only in foreign literature but also in philosophical and religious systems. The ideas of Arthur Schopenhauer enjoyed a period of renaissance during *Młoda Polska:* human fate was determined by blind forces. Man ought to separate himself from society and forefeit any will to live. Happiness was unreachable since people are always dissatisfied and unable to realize all their hopes. Values that give one a feeling of contentment are creations of the spirit and mind. Contemplation of these values can give life meaning and protect one from the blind forces of nature. Besides this generally pessimistic outlook, *Młoda Polska* also adopted Schopenhauer's views on the role of art and the artist. These ideas were mostly assimilated through Nietzsche, who in his philosophy provided an attempt to overcome the ideological crisis. Worship of man as a strong individual who realized Dionysian ideas, who also was a superhuman redeemer of decayed culture, were elements of Nietzchean philosophy absorbed by *Młoda Polska.* Other philosophical ideas were drawn from Max Steiner, who emphasized the self unburdened by any social duties, and Edward von Hartman with his stress on the unconscious. Later the ideas of Henri Bergson and Soren Kierkegaard were also much debated.

Multiplicity of inspirational sources, literary as well as philosophical, led to a greatly complex and heterogeneous output from members of *Młoda Polska.* Unlike in other European countries, where literary trends were usually practiced in a pure form and in chronological order, in Poland many tendencies coexisted during this period. Different views, ideas, opinions, and artistic conventions converged and intertwined and many Polish artists developed in this climate. Elements of many literary trends appeared, but it is difficult to assign them exclusively to one writer or group of writers. The leading writers of positivism were still active and some of them were only now publishing their best works: *Bez dogmatu* (Without Dogma) and *Krzyżacy* (The Teutonic Knights) by Henryk Sienkiewicz*; *Emancypantki* (The Emancipated Ladies) and *Faraon* (The Pharoah) by Bolesław Prus*; *Gloria victis* and *Ad astra* by Eliza Orzeszkowa.* Although they were not a part of *Młoda Polska,* their criticism of and ongoing discussion with the new generation helped to form the epoch's consciousness. Parnassianism was a movement, even though not fully developed on Polish ground, which found its way into the main literary programs of the time. Zenon "Miriam" Przesmycki and Antoni Lange* were considered typical Polish Parnassians, chiefly because they practiced a meticulous attentiveness to form. Some elements of this trend were utilized by almost every poet associated with *Młoda Polska.* It was especially apparent in choice of theme and topic (antiquity and native nature studies), and in attempts at perfecting form. Symbolism as a trend did not exist in its pure form in Poland but was an element of the multileveled structure of *Młoda Polska* literature.

The creators of French symbolism, as already pointed out, were the inspiration for the young generation: fragments of their literary technique and spiritual ideology were readily incorporated into the works of most young writers. Jan Kasprowicz,* Leopold Staff,* Kazimierz Przerwa-Tetmajer,* and Bolesław Leśmian* incorporated certain elements of symbolism into their works. Impressionism was also employed along with symbolism. Materialistic impressionism, of course, ran contrary to spiritualistic symbolism, but as a technique it effectively expressed symbolic content. This combination was so popular that it is difficult today to separate one from the other. Przybyszewski,* Berent,* Irzykowski,* and Żeromski* absorbed impressionism into their works to a greater or lesser degree.

Naturalism, too, had a remarkable success with adherents of *Młoda Polska.* The movement was the connecting element between positivism and modernism, and within modernism cohabited with the contradictory assumptions of Parnassianism, symbolism, impressionism, and even expressionism. The materialistic foundations of some of these trends rarely collided with the more extreme idealistic theories of *Młoda Polska.* On the one hand, its cult of instinct and biologization of emotions, and, on the other hand, its tendency to expose social injustice appealed to various literary orientations. Naturalism was multifaceted and had many internal contradictions which enabled it to coexist and intertwine with the sometimes totally contrary and seemingly incompatible literary currents. For example, the idea of art as a tool of cognition and knowledge as well as the sacralization of the laws of nature, the longing for the absolute, brought naturalism closer to the literary programs of *Młoda Polska.* Naturalism sanctioned the artist's right to a personal, subjective interpretation of the truth, which brought the artist closer to impressionism. Both these trends recreated and recorded pictures and scenes in their autonomous form; they were characterized by a withholding of any judgment. Naturalism, in amalgamation with other techniques, was used by Zapolska, Reymont, Żeromski, and others.

In the latter phase of modernism another current marked its existence as a part of *Młoda Polska:* Expressionism is considered by some literary historians as the most significant style of the epoch. Expressionist practice took place even in the early phases of modernism. In its fully mature form it can be observed in Wyspiański's *Wesele** (The Wedding) and *Wyzwolenie* (Liberation), Berent's *Ozimina** (Winter Corn) and *Żywe kamienie* (Living Stones), Miciński's* *Nietota* (Club Moss), Kasprowicz's* *Hymny* (Hymns), and Leśmian's poetry. Expressionist style was practiced in Poland before the formulation of a theoretical program for the movement. It was only in 1917, however, that an expressionist periodical was established. Expressionism attempted a synthesis of all parallel trends.

The various contemporary literary debates, discussions, and polemics, as well as literary programs, were published by several literary periodicals, such as *Życie* (Life, published in Warsaw, 1887–91), *Życie* (Life, published in Cracow, 1897–1900), *Chimera* (published in Warsaw, 1901–7), *Krytyka* (Criticism, published in Cracow, 1896–1914), *Lamus* (published in Lvov, 1908–13), and *Museion* (published in Cracow, 1911–13). Some of these periodicals strongly urged certain views of the shape *Młoda Polska* should be taking. They were propagated by the writers associated with these periodicals. The greatest controversy involving *Młoda Polska* raged between the advocates of autonomous art for art's sake and those who thought art should serve public interests and fulfill social obligations. Literature in Poland had for a long time been forced to serve the national cause, as a result of the country's loss of independence. It was from social obligation that Przybyszewski and Miriam tried to liberate literature. Both writer-editors proclaimed that art had no other aim but to propagate art, which brought man closer to metaphysical values and the essence of the universe. Artur Górski, who coined the term "Young Poland," was more moderate. He considered art only a value, and promoted individualism and earnestness, but he shunned extreme aestheticism. He propagated the Romantic tradition and synthesized views on the moral redemption of the individual as a condition to social and national development. Ludwik Krzywicki felt that art should face up to its moral obligation. He was convinced that art was dependent on social and economic processes which caused social change which, in some way, should be reflected in art. He did not accept psychological explanations of literary processes. The value of a literary work for him was judged on the basis of how well it served the social and national interests. He was quintessentially an advocate of art as a propagator of moral, national, and scientific values. There were other variations on these themes, some more radical and extreme, some more liberal. The main conflict, however, was between these two camps.

Młoda Polska was an epoch which witnessed intensive development of poetry. It is in poetry that the specific features of the era are most apparent. The new, modernist poetry made its debut much earlier than prose or drama of that period. Poetry during the positivist era had greatly depreciated. It ceased to be the most popular or most honored genre. Within the convention of realistic literature, directed toward cognitive goals and fulfilling social obligations, poetry played a secondary role. After 1890, new forms and new spiritual content were decisive elements in the development of literature. Symbolist content and impressionistic forms marked the new achievements of modernism. Poetry was a most compatible genre for expressing symbolist mysticism; impressionism seemed the best technique for achieving these results. Language was freed from the scheme of everyday use. Experimentation with language and creation of new words (neologisms) and new meanings for words already existing were quite common during this period. The goal of many poets was to evoke certain feelings and emotions in a reader indirectly, without explicitly revealing their source. The technique of free associations or correspondences was used to convey a feeling of moodiness. The favorite themes and motifs, often overused by writers of the epoch, included the following: hopelessness, pessimism, existential despair, an escape from the feelings of fatalism into sensuality, eroticism, nirvana, and oblivion. These were accompanied by a penchant for regarding art as the only value in the decayed world of ideals; the artist was regarded as a bearer of absolute truths. These conventions of *Młoda Polska* were expressed both in outright declarations as well as in symbols and allegories of good, evil, love, and death, represented most often by female figures who were repulsive and alluring at the same time. Anticivilization sentiments, as derivatives of the nineteenth century crisis of consciousness, took form in the glorification of the Tatra Mountains and Oriental scenery, village landscape, native nature, and the simple life of the peasant, idealized as a merger of spiritual culture undefiled by urban civilization and of the vital force (peasantmania). The more pedestrian work of *Młoda Polska* often contains some or all of these elements. Combined with abuse of freedom of form and a schematized use of neologisms and archaisms, some of *Młoda Polska*'s works epitomized bad taste. But it is precisely the use of these very same elements by talented writers that produced the most moving Polish poetry.

Prose made its debut later than poetry during the period of *Młoda Polska*. Its heterogeneity has its root in the fact that two tendencies were dominant: naturalism and impressionism. From the naturalist doctrine *Młoda Polska* assimilated components of the declining phase of positivism: a pessimistic interpretation of determinism, the idea of struggle for survival, the conflict between nature and civilization, and the alienation of man from urban existence. *Młoda Polska* prose was strongly influenced by the theories of Przybyszewski.* Przybyszewski emphasized the dark side of human nature and the ruthless search for truth, constrained by neither moral nor didactic limitations. These modernist elements had naturalistic origins. From impressionism, on the other hand, the writers emphasized the subjective presentation of reality and the "psychization" of nature, that is, they endowed nature with a spiritual quality but hedged on the subject of the existence of God. The subjective presentation of reality corresponded with the method of presenting heroes: a stress on the distinctiveness and uniqueness of individual experience and the presentation of fleeting emotional states. The ideological content of experiences and thought was often presented through emotional reactions rather than intellectual ponderings.

As a result of the assimilation of both naturalistic and impressionistic elements, a unique prose model was created. Various combinations of elements of naturalism and impressionism or a balance of both were employed by prose writers. Certain common elements exist in the majority of works and are recognizable as typical of the *Młoda Polska* style. A stress on subjective experience over the recording of facts is a dominant trait. Worldview becomes the sum total of subjective cognitions of reality. Stress is on the subject. The spiritual biography of the hero becomes primary, considered more substantial than his exterior ups and downs. Distrust of the external world and "objective reality" results in the emphasis on the inner life of the hero. The consequence of this is that the choice of topics favors psychological analysis and detailed investigation of all spiritual experiences. This concentration on the individual caused a major change in the selection of main themes. An aversion to portraying social problems gave way to an intensified interest in the individual. *Młoda Polska* preferred the ethos of individuality to the positivist ethos of collectivity. The phenomenon known as autothematism originated from this shift. A large body of works on the topic of the artist, so-called prose about the artist, was created at this time.

Drama during the era of *Młoda Polska* developed well beyond the scope of positivism. The sheer number of dramatic works created attests to the fact; almost all writers of the era were at the same time playwrights. Three styles emerged: naturalistic, symbolistic, and expressionistic. Naturalist drama appeared relatively early. The emphasis was on character, social diagnosis, and spiritual content. A wide body of symbolist drama can be further divided into drama of mood and symbolic Neo-Romanticism revolving around moral, spiritual, and metaphysical content in the realm of national consciousness. Symbolist technique was used to express romantic content. Expressionist drama became the most avant-garde trend during the period of *Młoda Polska*. The trend reached its maturity during the interwar period.

Młoda Polska was, above all, a period of literary revolution. Many of its trends were continued and developed by following generations, and many of its leading artists were active well into the next epoch. Some critics consider *Młoda Polska* the beginning of Polish contemporary literature. Leaders of *Młoda Polska* included Stanisław Przybyszewski and Zenon "Miriam" Przesmycki. Among the leading poets were Antoni Lange,* Wacław Rolicz-Lieder, Tetmajer,* Jan Kasprowicz, Tadeusz Miciński,* Jerzy Żuławski, Maria Komornicka, Bronisława Ostrowska, Leopold Staff,* and Bolesław Leśmian.* The leading novelists included Stefan Żeromski,* Władysław Reymont,* and Wacław Berent.* The chief critics of *Młoda Polska* were Stanisław Brzozowski, Tadeusz "Boy" Żeleński,* Karol Irzykowski,* and Ignacy Matuszewski. The most important playwrights were Stanisław Wyspiański,* Jan August Kisielewski, Karol Hubert Rostworowski, Włodzimierz Perzyński, and Gabriela Zapolska.*

BIBLIOGRAPHY

M. Podraża-Kwiatkowska, *Literatura Młodej Polski* (The Literature of Young Poland), Warsaw, 1992.

MONACHOMACHIA, CZYLI WOJNA MNICHÓW (Monachomachia, or War of the Monks) (see Krasicki).

MORALNOŚĆ PANI DULSKIEJ (The Morality of Mrs. Dulski) (see Zapolska).

MORSTIN, LUDWIK HIERONIM (1886–1966), a playwright, poet, novelist, and translator, studied philosophy, psychology, and classical philology in Munich, Berlin, Leipzig, and Paris. He was coeditor of the monthly *Museion.* During World War I he fought in the Polish Legions; he later became a diplomat in Paris and Rome. From 1926 he lived in his family manor in Plewowice, which he made into a literary meeting place. In 1930–31 he was editor of *Pamiętnik Warszawski* (The Warsaw Diary). During the Nazi occupation he was active in the underground. After the war he spent a number of years in Zakopane and was literary manager of the theaters in Katowice and Cracow. He was awarded a Golden Wreath from the Polish Academy of Literature (*PAL*) in 1936, as well as awards from the City of Cracow in 1938, and the PEN Club in 1952.

In his output Morstin gave expression to his love of ancient civilization, philosophy, and art. He also reached into the sixteenth and seventeenth centuries, at the same time dealing with the problems of contemporary society. He wrote in both prose and verse, paying special attention to the setting (especially architecture and landscape), to the charm and lightness of the dialogue, and to the color and flavor of the epoch. In his portrayal of historical personages he defied established legends and common opinions. According to Lesław Eustachiewicz, his dramas are characterized by a multitude of forms, often employed as a pastiche. His youthful works include lyrical poems (*Pieśni* [Songs], 1907), dramatic pictures (*Na racławickim błoniu* [On the Field of Racławice], published and staged in 1906), a dramatized version of Mickiewicz's ballad (*Lilie* [The Lilies], published and staged in 1912), a drama (*Szlakiem legionów* [Tracking the Legions], staged in 1913), and a dramatic poem (*Rzeczpospolita poetów* [The Republic of Poets], written in 1933; published in 1934), an Aristophanean satire on the Platonic idea of the participation of poets in social and political life; and the famous *Obrona Ksantypy* (Defense of Xanthippe, published and staged in 1939), a comedy which is an apologia for Socrates' wife. Ancient times are again explored in *Panteja* (Panthea, 1937); *Penelopa* (Penelope, staged in 1945); and *Kleopatra* (Cleopatra, staged in 1960). Motives from Polish history are used in *Zakon krzyżowy* (Teutonic Order, staged in 1948); a comedy about Rej, *Polacy nie gęsi* (Poles Are Not Geese, staged in 1953); a comedy about Queen Jadwiga, *Jaskółka* (The Swallow, 1960; staged in 1961); *Burmistrz z Wieliczki* (Mayor of Wieliczka, 1963), and a novel about Copernicus, *Kłos Panny* (A Virgo's Ear of Corn, 1929). In his comedies on contemporary themes, such as *Taniec księżniczki* (The Dance of the Princess, staged in 1947) and *Przygoda florencka* (Florentine Adventure, staged in 1957), he wrote in the style of Flers and Caillavet, and Pirandello. He was the translator of Sophocles, Horace, Lope de Vega, Calderón, and Goethe. He was also the author of numerous literary essays and memoirs.

(See Contemporary Polish Literature.)

BIBLIOGRAPHY

Z pism Ludwika Hieronima Morstina (From the Writings of Ludwik Hieronim Morstin), Volumes 1–4, Cracow, 1959–67.

MORSZTYN, JAN ANDRZEJ (1621–93), a poet, was descended from a wealthy family. From birth he was linked with the court of the Lubomirski family, later with the king's court. He held a number of important state positions. He was an advocate of the pro-French political position, and, as a result, after King Jan III chose Austria as an ally, he had to escape to France, where he spent the rest of his life.

Morsztyn's poetry (during his lifetime circulated in manuscript) is the best specimen of Baroque court poetry in Poland. It combines sophisticated taste and exquisite knowledge of literature with skill and unfailing technique. It is polished, because of Morsztyn's masterful use of language, and melodious, because of its fluent rhythm and phrase. Morsztyn modeled many of his works on examples from Latin and Romance literature, but he transformed the originals to a large extent by shifting the point of gravity from intellect to emotion. Morsztyn's poems are mainly about love and social life, especially in his best known collections, *Lutnia* (The Lyre) and *Kanikuła* (Dog Days). *Lutnia* contains poems from the years 1638–60 (in manuscript 1661, first published in 1874). The collection mostly includes love poems, several jocular epigrams on themes from social life, and poetic letters to relatives, sponsors, and friends. According to Leszek Kukulski, most of the works are translations or imitations, often based on the works of Marino. *Kanikuła* (written in 1647, published in 1844) is a series of thirty-one poems on the star mentioned in the title. The volume *Fraszki* (Trifles, written around 1645) contains frivolous epigrams, not meant for the general public. Many incidental poems commemorate contemporary social and political events; some of his religious poems are inspired by the Calvinist religion (he became a Catholic in 1655). In *Pieśni* (Songs, written around 1658) he used some interesting experimental forms of verse. Morsztyn is the author of three important translations: Tasso's *Amintas* (written before 1650; published in 1840); a fragment of Marino's *Adone,* entitled *Psyche* (written circa 1661; published in 1696–98); and Corneille's *Cyd, albo Roderyk* (Le Cid, or Roderick, written circa 1660; published in 1696–98).

(See Baroque.)

BIBLIOGRAPHY

Utwory zebrane (Collected Works), edited by L. Kukulski, Warsaw, 1971.

MORSZTYN, ZBIGNIEW (Zbigneus Morstinus) (1627–1689), a poet, came from a Socinian family with literary traditions. He was a soldier and courtier to the Lithuanian hetman Janusz Radziwiłł, but during the Swedish invasion (1656) remained faithful to the Polish king, fighting against the attackers. In 1662 he left the territory of Poland because of religious repressions against the Aryans and lived in East Prussia, again under the protection of the Radziwiłłs.

Morsztyn wrote mostly lyrical poems. In 1671 he published *Pieśń w ucisku* (A Song in Oppression), a document listing the repressions against Aryans. In 1674 he published *Sławna wiktoryja nad Turkami* (A Famous Victory over the Turks), a poem praising the victory of Chocim. Around 1675 he wrote *Wiersze polskie* (Polish Poems, published in J. T. Trembecki's *Wirydarz poetycki* (The Poetic Pleasure Garden). In 1676–80 he wrote the major part of his collection *Muza domowa* (House Muse). Several more works were added in 1681–84; however, the collection was first published only in 1954. Morsztyn explained the title in the preface to the volume by claiming that his poetry was different from the work of his famous relative Jan Andrzej, and that his works were for the home, rather than for the court. In his poetry he gives a deeply moving picture of the dehumanizing role of war; he describes the life of a soldier and combines patriotic feelings with his defense of the freedom of conscience, his dreams of the idyllic life with the apotheosis of meditative thought, reaching beyond all barriers of human cognition. His style also reconciles simplicity with Baroque ornamentation.

(See Baroque.)

BIBLIOGRAPHY

Muza domowa (Home Muse), Volumes 1–2, edited by and with an introduction by J. Durr-Durski, Warsaw, 1954.

Wybór wierszy (Selected Poems), edited and with an introduction by J. Pelc, Wrocław, 1975.

MÓJ WIEK (My Century) (see Wat).

MROŻEK, SŁAWOMIR (born 1930), a playwright, prose writer, and satirist, made his debut in 1950 in a popular weekly, *Przekrój* (Crosscut). He was associated with the experimental Bim-Bom Theater in Gdańsk, and the *Piwnica pod Baranami* (Cellar Under the Rams) Cabaret in Cracow, and subsequently contributed to various papers and magazines, writing a satirical column entitled *Postępowiec* (Progressive). Associated with Cracow already as a well-known writer, he decided to move to Italy in 1963 and then to Paris in 1968. From 1969 to 1971 his works were forbidden to be popularized in Poland because of the protest which he lodged in 1969 after the aggressive assault of the Communist countries against Czechoslovakia. He lived in the United States and West Germany and after December 1981 expressed his displeasure against the declaration of Martial Law in Poland. In 1987 he married a Mexican, Susana Ocorio Rosas, and in 1990—after a farewell festival in Cracow in his honor—left Europe and settled in Mexico.

Mrożek's work is grotesque in its concept. It consists of a reportorial-like content, but also contains artistic generalizations concerned, above all, with the relationship between an individual and the group. It depicts a deformed and absurd world, which corresponds to the false consciousness motivated by contemporary mythological idealizations; it also confronts anachronous relics of history, particularly Polish Romanticism. Mrożek's social satire, with an obvious moralistic bent, is directed against the schematization of life, intellectual primitivism, the paradoxes of civilization, and crude didacticism. The comical effect, often in the style of a cabaret, unmasks the power of cliché over meaning and is achieved through parodies of various styles—colloquial and formal language, school jargon, journalese, literary style (for example, of the nineteenth century moralizing literature for children and contemporary Socialist Realist novels *à these*). He gains effects through pastiche and combinations of contradictory conventions.

Mrożek's dramatic works, largely because of the obvious conventionality of staged events, resemble morality plays or philosophical tales. Mrożek creates theoretical models of extreme situations and then proves by logical means that man is not capable of transcending his own view of reality. He introduces two patterns—that of a hero and that of the hostile world of unintelligible and hierarchical forms. He unmasks the anachronous forms-ideas by arbitrarily giving them absolute value. The characters, often caricaturelike to an extreme, embody mental, moral, conceptual stereotypical traits, imposed upon them by society and its institutions. According to Ewa Zuberbier, the typology of characters has social, ethical, and existential motivation: they can be divided into intellectual puppets, conscious creators of masks, and thoughtless "boors." In *Policja* (The Police, 1958, staged in 1958) Mrożek illustrates the absurdity of the idea of "policehood" in a utopian state system. He presents the individual as the victim of the outrageous expectations of society in *Męczeństwo Piotra Oheya* (The Martyrdom of Peter Ohey, 1959, staged in 1959). In his one-act pieces, published in *Dialog*, the monthly devoted to the dramatic arts, Mrożek dramatized a situational anecdote and parody to create a metaphor about the process of mythologization and mystification of everyday life, which endeavors to hide aggression, conformism, lack of tolerance, and especially fear, fear which arises in the atmosphere of a threatening situation: *Na pełnym morzu* (At Sea, 1961), *Karol* (1961), and *Striptease* (1961), staged as a triptych in 1961. Mrożek also ridiculed the contemporary perception and common understanding of Romanticism: *Indyk* (The Turkey, 1960; staged in 1961) is a satire on contemporary society during the "little stabilization" and at the same time shows the degradation of Romantic ideas through the dramatization of collective impotence and lack of authenticity. In *Śmierć porucznika* (Death of the Lieutenant, 1963; staged in 1963) he questioned the Romantic myth of heroism; in *Zabawa* (The Party, 1962; staged in 1963), a paraphrase of Wyspiański's *Wesele,* he revealed the contradiction between the idea of action and its nonsensical embodiment. The broadest and most ambiguous interpretation of social and political processes was dramatized in Mrożek's finest play, *Tango* (1964; staged in 1965). The play was written in the characteristic convention of the grotesque, at the same time both surrealist and realistic. The play explores the role and place of an intellectual in the contemporary world. The setting is the family home of Stomił, an unproductive artist. The characters live on the historical garbage heap piled in their apartment, in a state of inertia which they cannot and do not want to overcome. All the old conventions and forms have been discarded: there is nothing to fight against, everything is allowed, and, as a result, there is no freedom. Arthur, Stomił's son, attempts artificially to impose old forms onto the family. He fails since form is shaped from petrified contents and neither content nor ideas exist in this world. Arthur is killed by Edek, a primitive, aggressive individual, who becomes a dictator in the house and demands obedience. In the final scene Edek forces the old uncle to dance a tango with him, and the entire family watch the grotesque display. The characters and the idea of the play are in the tradition of Witkacy, while the ending suggests the finale of Wyspiański's *Wesele* (The Wedding). The play is a warning against conformism, but also against nihilism and anarchy, and totalitarianism arising out of blind rebellion.

Szczęśliwe wydarzenie (Happy Event, published and staged in 1973) strikes a similar chord, this time, the various youth movements in the West. In *Krawiec* (The Tailor, written in 1964 and published in 1977) Mrożek, like Gombrowicz in *Operetta,* explores the areas of culture and fashion, conventional values, which somehow impose a social and individual identity onto individuals. In his radio play, *Rzeźnia* (Slaughterhouse, written in 1973 and staged in 1975), Mrożek questioned both the mystic role of art and the deformed concept of returning to nature and to cruelty in the name of truth.

His subsequent dramas are quite different in style; his characters are no longer stereotypical and Mrożek's main preoccupation centers around the tragedy of man, who cannot liberate himself from the imperatives imposed on him by nature and history. In *Emigranci* (The Emigrés, published in 1974 and staged in 1975) Mrożek dramatizes the tragedy of the dispossessed, the dialogue between an intellectual and a worker. Mrożek explores the national and social alienation of these two dissimilar men, revealing the characteristic ambivalence of their attitudes, which range from primitive carelessness to tragic helplessness, from affirmation of complete freedom to an understanding of the necessity to hold on to social ties. Some critics consider *Emigrés* Mrożek's best work.

Mrożek continues to write, but his latest works seem somehow divorced from Polish soil. *Garbus* (The Hunchback, written in 1975 and staged in 1976) projects a world headed for annihilation. The dubious ideas and speculations are contrasted with the permanence of nature and with a realistic approach. *Vatzlav* (staged in 1979) presents a bitterly mocking view of man's utopian drive to search for basic values, in spite of the relativity of all action. In Mrożek's later plays—*Ambasador* (The Ambassador), *Portret* (The Portrait), and *Pieszo* (On Foot), produced in 1983–84 and published in the collection *Dramaty* (Dramas, 1990)—references to concrete situations and experiences are presented; as a whole they become more transparently readable, and in the hero of the drama *Alfa* (Alpha), published in Paris in 1984, one easily recognized Lech Wałęsa, imprisoned after the declaration of Martial Law.

In his prose, which is quite analogous to his dramatic works, Mrożek moved from the caricature of social phenomena to the penetration of the inner world of his characters. In his cycle of satirical drawings and sketches *Polska w obrazach* (Poland in Pictures, 1957), *Przez okulary S.M.* (Through S.M.'s Glasses), sketches which appeared in *Przekrój* (Crosscut or Section) from 1953 to 1968 and published in a collection in 1968; in his stories *Półpancerze praktyczne* (Practical Half-Armor, 1953), *Słoń* (The Elephant, 1957), *Wesele w Atomicach* (A Wedding in Atomice, 1959); and in his novels, *Maleńkie lato* (A Little Summer, 1956) and *Ucieczka na południe* (A Flight South, 1961), he presented the clash between provincial mentality and progress utilizing absurd humor. In the stories from the volumes *Deszcz* (Rain, 1962) and *Dwa listy* (Two Letters, Paris, 1970, 1974), Mrożek employed a parabolic and symbolic language to express his views on the impossibility of penetrating the human psyche and finding order in the conventional world (for example, the short story *Moniza Clavier*—a bravura tragicomic satire about a Pole who arrives from a Sovietized province in East Europe and who becomes a temporary social star of a film festival in Venice). His feuilletons were published in the collection *Małe listy* (Little Letters, 1982), and his satirical pieces in *Donosy* (Delations) were published in London in 1982. They enjoyed great popularity in Poland during Martial Law, disseminated widely by the underground press.

His plays have an established position in theaters both in Poland and abroad. They have been translated into almost every language and have been adapted for television in a number of countries. Unfortunately, since his absence from Poland, Mrożek has not been able to capture the spirit of the times of his country. *Emigrés,* however, was his finest work since leaving Poland because the play explored the problems of the dispossessed—Mrożek's personal dilemma. Like Czechoslovakia's Milan Kundera's works written since leaving his country, Mrożek's plays seem to have a different setting, a different orientation, a foreign tone.

(See Contemporary Polish Literature.)

BIBLIOGRAPHY

Opowiadania, (Short Stories), Cracow, 1964; enlarged edition, 1974.

Utwory sceniczne, Volumes 1–2, Cracow, 1973.

Utwory sceniczne nowe, Cracow, 1975.

Wybór dramatów i opowiadań, Cracow, 1978.

Utwory Sławomira Mrożka na scenach polskich i zagranicznych Wykaz bibliograficzny, (Sławomir Mrożek's Works on the Polish and Foreign Stages: A Bibliographical Listing), Cracow, 1990.

English

At Sea (Na pełnym morzu), translated by Ewa Markowska, *East Europe,* Volume X, October 1961.

The Elephant (Słoń), translated by Konrad Syrop, illustrated by Daniel Mroz, New York: Grove Press, 1963; 1965; 1984; London: MacDonold, 1962.

Six Plays (*The Police, The Martyrdom of Peter Ohey, Out at Sea, Charlie, The Party, Enchanted Night*), translated by Nicholas Bethell, New York: Grove Press, 1967; London: Cape, 1967–68.

Striptease, Repeat Performance, and Three Prophets: Three Plays, New York: Grove Press, 1972; *Striptease,* translated by I. A. Langnos and Robert O'Brien, *Odyssey Review,* Volume 3, Number 2, June 1963; translated by Edward Rothert; *Polish Perspectives,* Number 10, 53–72, 1965; and *Tulane Drama Review,* Volume 11, Number 3, Spring 1967.

Tango: A Play in Three Acts, translated by Ralph Manheim and Teresa Dzieduszycka, New York: Grove Press, 1968; translated by Nicholas Bethell, London: Cape, 1968.

The Ugupu Bird, translated by Konrad Syrop, London: MacDonald, 1968.

Vatzlav: A Play in 77 Scenes, translated by Ralph Manheim, New York: Grove Press, 1970; London: Cape, 1972.

The Ambassador (Ambasador), translated by the author and Ralph Manheim, New York: Institute for Contemporary Eastern European Drama and Theater, 1984.

The Emigrants (Emigranci), translated by Henry Beissel, Westport, New York, and London: French, 1984.
The Police (movie), New York: Grove Press Film Division, 1973.
The Prophets, New York: Samuel French, n.d.
Three European Plays, Harmondsworth, England: Penguin, 1970; New York: Grove Press, 1972.
Party (Zabawa), translated by Nicholas Bethell, New York: Grove Press, 1967.
Home on the Border (Dom na granicy), translated by Edward Rothert, *Polish Perspectives,* Number 8–9, 1967.

MYŚLIWSKI, WIESŁAW (born 1932), a playwright and novelist, graduated with a degree in Polish Philology from the Catholic University in Lublin. In 1975 he became editor of the quarterly *Regiony* (Regions). According to Antoni Chojnacki, Myśliwski writes about life in the country, but his innovative presentation of the theme gives Myśliwski a secure place in the literary tradition. He employs historical, social, cultural, and psychological reality as well as folk dialect in order to create a major metaphor that attempts to capture the psychological consequences of the processes of the great social migration. Through the form of a diary (the novel *Nagi sad* [Naked Garden], 1967; adapted for television), he describes the means by which social consciousness is formed: he places the burden on the many centuries of "enslavement," on the impossibility of assimilating into the new culture, and on the strength of family ties. Employing symbolic, poetic images (the novel *Pałac* [Palace], 1970), he expresses the power of passions and dreams in transforming the world, and the defeat of the main character, a shepherd, who tries to absorb the values of the higher culture of the landlords, which are alien to him. The characters of his dramas have certain features of "social types." He explores the problems brought about by distributing land to farmers (*Klucznik* [Gatekeeper], published in *Dialog,* 1978, staged in 1978) and the theme of moral values in relation to the occupation, where he takes into consideration the *subjectivity* of examining human behavior (*Złodziej* [Thief], published in *Dialog,* 1973, staged in 1974). His novel *Kamień na kamieniu* (Stone upon Stone, 1984) is considered one of the best portraits of the peasant social class written in Polish contemporary literature.

BIBLIOGRAPHY

R. Sulima, "Scalanie wartości" ("Union of Value"), in *Folklor i literatura* (Folklore and Literature), Warsaw, 1976.

N

NA SKALNYM PODHALU (In the Rocky Tatra Mountains) (see Tetmajer).

NA WSI WESELE (A Village Wedding) (see Dąbrowska).

NAD NIEMNEM (On the Banks of the Niemen) (see Orzeszkowa).

NAŁKOWSKA, ZOFIA (1884–1954) (husbands' names Rygier and Gorzechowski), a novelist, playwright, and publicist, made her debut in 1898 with a poem. At this time she also published her first short story and a novel, serialized in various magazines. She resided in a number of cities of Poland, with her first husband and later her second, whom she divorced in 1929. She was an active member of the Union of Writers, the PEN Club, and later the Academy of Literature. Under the Nazi occupation she took part in the underground literary life and later accepted a seat in the postwar parliament. She worked for various organizations: the Committee for the Investigation of Nazi Crimes and the Committee for the Defenders of Peace. She received both the State Award and the PAL Award.

Nałkowska's views were formed under the influence of both her father, an esteemed scientist and publicist, and of a revolutionary activist struggling for social and national liberation with whom she became acquainted. She championed the program of philosophical modernism in literature and regarded the French moralists of the eighteenth century and Stendhal, Flaubert, Dostoyevsky, Brzozowski,* and Irzykowski* as her mentors. In her youthful novels *Kobiety* (Women, 1906), *Książę* (The Prince, 1907), *Rówieśnice* (Contemporaries, 1909), *Narcyza* (Narcissa, 1910), and *Węże i róże* (Serpents and Roses, 1915) and the collections of stories *Koteczka, czyli białe tulipany* (Pussycat, or the White Tulips, 1909) and *Lustra* (Mirrors, 1913) she analyzed the psyche of a woman, basing her model on both the women in the works of Oscar Wilde and Nietzschean individualism, against a historical background. She tried to discover the mechanisms of personality, searching for them in the competition between nature and culture. The search for a philosophical hypothesis and a generalizing formula became a characteristic theme in her prose. After 1918, she turned to the phenomena of human life which appeared common and thus universal. She began to analyze the cultural conventions of human consciousness and behavior and their mystifications, in such works as *Charaktery* (Characters, 1922), analyzing how a man was formed by the realia of life, his social role, his interaction with others, and the evaluation of these factors. She explored the variability of personality in time and history in such novels as *Romans Teresy Hennert* (Teresa Hennert's Romance, 1924), *Niedobra miłość* (A Bad Love, 1928), and the drama *Dom kobiet* (A House of Women, 1930). She contrasted the consciousness of an individual with the patterns of collective consciousness, the cruelty of which were revealed during the time of war in her novel *Hrabia Emil* (Count Emil, 1920). *Romans* (Romance) also conveyed her criticism of and disappointment with the reality of independent Poland.

According to Hanna Kirchner, the changes apparent in Nałkowska's subsequent stories are part of the overall evolution of the novel between the wars. Apart from changes in language and the character of the hero, her novels explore everyday life, the cult of authenticity, and the nobilization of nonfiction prose; hence the autobiographism and the presence of simple folk in *Dom nad łąkami* (The House Beyond the Meadows, 1925) and the nonfiction character of the novel *Choucas* (1927), a protest against all forms of nationalism and militarism. Autobiographical elements can also be found in the stories in the collection *Ściany świata* (The Walls of the World, 1931). Nałkowska delved into the darker corners of society and explored the problem of crime, its social and existential roots. One of these problems, the potential crime hidden in every man, is also developed in her second drama, *Dzień jego powrotu* (The Day of His Return, 1931). The culmination of Nałkowska's exploration of man and society is reached in her best novel and her ideological manifesto, *Granica* (The Border, 1935). Her philosophical views on the existential nature of an individual are contained in her innovative novel *Niecierpliwi* (The Impatient Ones, 1939). She also published several volumes of stories: *Moje zwierzęta* (My Animals, 1915); *Tajemnice krwi* (The Secrets of the Blood, 1917); *Między zwierzętami* (Among Animals, 1934), a radio play; and *Wspomnienia o sprawie Brzozowskiego* (Recollection Regarding the Brzozowski's Affair, 1936). In 1939 Nałkowska published *Węzły życia* (The Nooses of Life, 1948), which dramatized the decline and catastrophic end of the governing circles of Poland between the wars. Her first book published after the war was a small collection of stories, *Medaliony* (The Medallions, 1946), a masterpiece of anti-Nazi literature. After the war she also wrote some biographical pieces, among others the book for young readers *Mój ojciec* (My Father, 1953) and *Charaktery dawne i ostatnie* (Old and Last Characters, 1958); a volume of essays and sketches, *Widzenie bliskie i dalekie* (A Close and Far View, 1957), was published after her death. An important event marked the publication of her diary: from the time of the war (1970); then from the years 1899–1905 (1975), 1909–17 (1976), 1918–29 (1980), 1930–39 (1988); and from World War II (1970). This document of intellectual self-awareness, introspection, and psychological observation is also an artistic self-comment, revealing the sources and techniques of the writer's output. Nałkowska was not only a woman of letters, but also a famous person—her home was perhaps the last literary salon, a gathering for the most outstanding personages of the time.

A novel, *Granica* (Border), considered one of her best works, relates the story of Zenon Ziembiewicz, first as a radical student, then as an official of *Sanacja* (Piłsudski's followers after 1929), governor of the city, responsible for shooting the workers marching in protest. A series of moral concessions leads to his catastrophe, both in public and in private life, where he becomes a victim of the revenge of a poor woman, Justyna Bogutówna, whom he had earlier seduced and abandoned. The novel is an accusation against the social reality in Poland under the rule of *sanacja*. The title refers not only to the social "border" between the characters, but also to the moral borders which the mechanisms of power force Ziembiewicz to cross again and again, and to the antinomy between the conscience of an individual and the social effects of his or her actions. A man's personality is determined by what Nałkowska referred to as schemata—conventions, cultural stereotypes, social roles, class divisions. In her words, "You are like the place where you are." These problems are accompanied by a discussion between materialistic and theological ontology—thus involving the question of the limits (borders) of our knowledge of the world. Nałkowska was also concerned with the role of time, which changes both a man and the way he is perceived, reflected in the structure of the novel, with its reversal of chronological order. The novel ran through a number of editions and has been translated into several languages.

(See Contemporary Polish Literature.)

BIBLIOGRAPHY

Dzieła (Works), Volumes 1–14, Warsaw, 1976–86.

English

Women (Kobiety), translated by Michael Henry Dziewicki, New York, London: G. P. Putnam's Sons, 1920.

NARUSZEWICZ, ADAM (1733–96), a poet, historian, and translator, was descended from an impoverished magnate family. He became a Jesuit, later teaching rhetoric, history, and French at the Jesuit College in Warsaw. Around 1770 he became closely associated with King Stanisław August, acting as both his adviser in political and cultural matters and his court poet. He often accompanied the king, assuming various important offices, until Targowica, when he withdrew from political life.

Naruszewicz made his debut in the fifties with Latin poetry, but the main bulk of his poetic output, published in *Dzieła* (Works, Volumes 1–4, 1778), was written in 1770–74 and first published in *Zabawy przyjemne i pożyteczne* (Pleasant and Useful Playthings). He began working on *Historia narodu polskiego* (A History of the Polish Nation) in 1775. The work covered Poland's inception through 1386 (Volumes 2–7, published in 1780–86; Volume 1 in 1824). During the years 1781–92 he continued collecting source materials for the early history of Poland through 1763. He also published *Historia Jana Karola Chodkiewicza* (The History of Jan Karol Chodkiewicz, Volumes 1–2, 1781). He wrote odes, satires, idylls, fables, epigrams, and two tragedies: *Gwido, hrabia Blezu* (Guido, Count Blez, probably during 1767–70) and *Tankred* (Tancred, written in 1772–73, but lost). He translated and paraphrased Latin poetry (Horace, Sarbiewski), seventeenth and eighteenth century French poetry (La Fontaine, Rousseau, Voltaire), and the complete writings of Tacitus.

According to Julian Platt, Naruszewicz's works are characterized by a variety of tendencies and patterns: Classical and sentimental elements coexist with Baroque. He derived his predilection—for individualization, for dynamic images, for expressive characterization, for extreme and paradoxical forms of expression, for violent, sometimes insulting criticism—from the Baroque. His language is also Baroque in nature: rich, colloquial, down-to-earth. Naruszewicz also crossed the border into Classicism, introducing satirical elements into his idylls. His Jesuit background accounted for his penchant for rhetoric, especially formal speech in the letter genre, and a certain pompousness of style. Naruszewicz's personal lyrics are free of these vices, expressing educational views or discussing current problems in the spirit of the epoch. Naruszewicz advocated the ideas of the Enlightenment; he is a ruthless critic of fanaticism and the lack of education, and, above all, of the egoism of the magnates.

Naruszewicz's poetry was so influential that it generated a "poetic school," whose members were T. K. Węgierski, F. Zabłocki,* J. K. Świętorzecki. Held in high esteem by his contemporaries, he was severely criticized by the Classicists of the post-Stanislaus period. The Romantics appreciated the vernacular character of his works, but rejected the rhetoric and artificiality. Contemporary critics have assigned Naruszewicz a high position, especially in regard to his ability to absorb the Renaissance and Baroque traditions into the poetry of his own epoch.

(See Enlightenment.)

BIBLIOGRAPHY

Wybór poezyj (Selected Poetry), edited and with an introduction by P. Chmielowski, Warsaw, 1882.

Satyry (Satires), edited by S. Grzeszczuk, Wrocław: Ossolineum, 1962.

NEO-ROMANTICISM (see *Młoda Polska*).

NIE-BOSKA KOMEDIA (The Undivine Comedy) (see Krasiński).

NIEMCEWICZ, JULIAN URSYN (1758–1841), a poet, satirist, playwright, novelist, author of memoirs, and political and cultural activist, was the son of a nobleman who was linked with the Czartoryski family. He became A. K. Czartoryski's aide-de-camp and courtier. In 1778 he began his public career, which was to last half a century. A member of parliament, he supported the views of the reform party, both by means of his activity and in his writings. He published polemical articles in the party's paper, but also wrote literary works whose themes included political struggle, such as the tragedy *Władysław pod Warną* (Władysław Below Warna, written in 1787–88, published in 1803), a warning against signing a treaty with Russia. He also composed a comedy, *Powrót posła* (The Return of the Envoy, 1791), a historical drama *Kazimierz Wielki* (Casimir the Great, 1792), and fables, circulated in manuscript. The fables are different from those by Krasicki or Trembecki; universal generalization is substituted for current political goals, formal perfection and clarity and unambiguousness of the "moral."

When political struggle took more violent forms, Niemcewicz resorted to composing political pamphlets in which he showed a talent for parody and travesty. Some of the pamphlets, like *Forma prawdziwego wolnego rządu przez konfederację targowicką ułożona* (A Form of a Truly Free Government Drafted by the Confederacy of Targowice), were written in 1792, while he was still in Poland. Others, like *Fragment Biblie Targowickiej: Księgi Szczęsnowe* (A Fragment of the Bible of Targowice: Szczęsny's Volumes), were smuggled into Poland (1792–93) from Vienna, where Niemcewicz escaped after the king joined Targowica. He returned in 1794, having received the news of the Kościuszko Insurrection. He became Kościuszko's secretary, then, wounded and captured, was imprisoned for two years in Petropavlovsk, where he wrote some twenty fables, patriotic elegies, and a translation of Pope's *The Rape of the Lock* and Racine's *Atalia.*

Freed by Tsar Paul II, he left in 1796 for America with Kościuszko, at the latter's request. There he met George Washington and Thomas Jefferson; he married and settled down in Elizabethtown. His literary output during the early years of the nineteenth century was published in *Pisma różne wierszem i prozą* (Various Writings in Poetry and Prose, Volumes 1–

2, 1803–5): fables, translations, *dumy* (which laid the ground for Romantic ballads), two long poems—*Puławy* (fragments published in 1855) and *Cztery pory życia człowieka* (Four Seasons of Man's Life, fragments published in 1811, and in its entirety in 1973).

In 1807, summoned by S. Małachowski, he returned to Poland, in an attempt to use his popularity to moderate conflicts and prevent intrigues. He held many important posts: with his moderate, anti-Jacobin views, he was critical of Napoleon, whom he considered a tyrant; in 1812, however, he was swept up in the universal enthusiasm for Napoleon. He expressed his hopes in *Pieśń wojenna* (A Martial Song) and *Oda z okoliczności ogłoszenia Polski* (Ode Coincidental with the Proclamation of Poland).

At the time of the kingdom he took active part in its social and cultural life, above all, in the Society for the Promotion of Science (e.g., he published the continuation of Naruszewicz's history of Poland). He wrote a treatise on the fable and in 1816 published *Śpiewy historyczne* (Historical Songs), containing a series of poems popularizing Polish history, rather mediocre on the artistic level. In 1815–25 Niemcewicz published three novels: *Dwaj panowie Sieciechowie* (The Two Gentlemen Sieciechow), *Lejbe i Siora,* and *Jan z Tęczyna* (John of Tęczyn). He also published *Bajki i opowieści* (Fables and Short Stories, 1817; enlarged edition, 1820). After 1808 Niemcewicz began to stage his dramatic pieces on national themes. They were mostly accompanied by the music of K. Kurpiński: *Jadwiga, królowa polska* (Jadwiga, Queen of Poland, 1814), *Jan Kochanowski w Czarnym Lesie* (Jan Kochanowski in the Czarnolas, 1817), and *Zbigniew* (1819). He also wrote satirical comedies: *Samolub* (The Egoist, 1811) and *Pan Nowina* (Mr. News, 1815); *Podejrzliwy* (The Suspicious One), written in 1819 or 1823 and staged and published only in 1831 for political reasons, caricatured Prince Konstanty and Novosilcov. According to Zofia Lewinówna, although wielding little influence on political life, he was still "the moral dictator of Warsaw." Strongly opposed to the occupying forces, he felt the only fair solution involved a legal struggle for defense of constitutional rights and condemned all forms of conspiracy and underground activity (he is the model for the character of Prezes in Słowacki's *Kordian*). In spite of his beliefs, after the outbreak of the uprising in 1830, he returned to the political arena. In 1833 he settled in Paris, published in the emigrant press, and wrote his memoirs.

Niemcewicz's work is of particular interest for the critic of literature: he reflected the ideas and techniques of the late Enlightenment, with an admixture of pre-Romantic tendencies. Niemcewicz's openness to new ideas allowed him to oppose orthodox views on literature and champion the cause of the young. His own artistic ambitions were subordinated to the political purpose of his writings, and his moral authority and unique position among his contemporaries overshadowed his literary talents.

On the other hand, his reputation as a memoirist has grown, especially due to his synthetically enclosed *Pamiętniki czasów moich* (Memoirs of My Time, published 1848). *Powrót posła* (The Return of the Envoy), a comedy dedicated to S. Małachowski, produced and published in 1791, involves trivial intrigue (two lovers, who are unable to receive their parents' permission to marry, but with a happy ending) but carries important political content, connected with the work of the reform party in the Four Year's Diet. There is little action on the stage, but the characters speak a great deal, confronting the program of political reform with the old gentry opposition. Niemcewicz ridicules conservatism, but also the parrotlike imitation of foreign cultural models. The play gives the impression of being somewhat hastily written. It is also didactic and lacks psychological motivation in the presentation of characters, but it shows that Niemcewicz had a great talent for parody and satire. The play is the first Polish political comedy—in the strict sense of the term.

Niemcewicz also wrote what can be considered to be the first biography of the first president of the United States, George Washington, based on personal interviews: *Krótka wiadomość o życiu i sprawach generała Washington* (Brief Information on the Life and Activities of General Washington), published in various periodicals, Volume 1, 1803).

(See Enlightenment.)

BIBLIOGRAPHY

Dzieła poetyczne wierszem i prozą (Poetic Works in Verse and Prose), Volumes 1–12, Leipzig, 1838–40.

Dzieła, Volume 1–5, Cracow, 1883–86.

Pamiętniki czasów moich, Volumes 1–2, edited by J. Dihm and L. Lewinówna, Warsaw: PIW, 1957.

English

Under Their Vine and Fig Tree: Travels Through America in 1797–1799, 1805, with Some Further Account of Life in New Jersey, edited and translated by Metchie J. E. Budka, preface by W. Weintraub, Newark, New Jersey: New Jersey Historical Society, 1965.

Julian Ursyn Niemcewicz and America, New York: Polish Institute of Arts and Sciences in America, 1961.

Notes of My Captivity in Russia in the Years 1794–1796, translated by Alexander Laski, Edinburgh: W. Tait, 1844.

Levi and Sarah, the Jewish Lovers: A Polish Tale (Lejbe i Siora), translated by Jacob, London, 1830.

NIEMCY (The Germans) (see Kruczkowski).

NOCE I DNIE (Nights and Days) (see Dąbrowska).

NORWID, CYPRIAN KAMIL (1821–83), a poet, playwright, and prose writer, was also proficient in sculpture, painting, drawing, and engraving. He spent his youth in Warsaw, attended high school but never graduated. He then studied painting and in 1840 published several poems. In these poems he identifies himself with the generation which grew up after the defeat of the November Uprising. In 1842 he left Warsaw and, after visiting Cracow and Germany, left for Italy to study sculpture. In 1846 while in Berlin, he was accused by the Prussian government of revolutionary activity in preparing the uprising in Greater Poland and was imprisoned for a month. He left prison with impaired hearing. Soon he accepted the status of an émigré. During the Spring of Nations he was in Rome, where he met Krasiński;* in 1849 he arrived in Paris, beginning, or rather reinstating, his contacts with famous émigrés (Mickiewicz,* Słowacki,* Chopin, Zaleski,* etc.). His interpretation of the Spring of Nations in 1848 brought about a series of literary works and articles presenting Norwid's ideological and artistic program. One should mention here his cycle of poetic treatises: *Wigilia* (Christmas Eve, Paris, 1848), *Pieśni społecznej cztery strony* (Four Sides of a Social Song, Poznań, 1849), *Niewola* (Bondage, written in 1848–49, published in Leipzig, 1864), *Psalmów-psalm* (Psalm of Psalms, written in 1850, published in 1933 in *Wiadomości Literackie* [Literary News]). He also composed a drama, *Zwolon,* the relation of his generation to the revolutionary fight (written in 1848–49, published in Poznań, 1851); a poetic treatise about art, *Promethidion* (written in 1848–50, published in Paris, 1851); and a cycle of articles, *Listy o emigracji* (Letters About Emigration, in *Dziennik Polski* [Polish Daily], 1849). The outstanding work of the period is *Promethidion,* composed of two dialogues in verse. In it Norwid sees art as the basic factor in a social and national renaissance. He argues for the need of national fine arts, including applied arts (for the first time), and points to folk art as the life-giving source of art in general. The poem is one of the works which later established his reputation as an intellectual precursor. His ideas were further explored by Witkiewicz Senior* and Stanisław Brzozowski.* Norwid's artistic program presented in the preceding works complements Romanticism, initiating its new phase; he emphasized the meaning and greatness of Romantic poetry, but, at the same time, questioned the need for its continuation, especially in the spirit of Mickiewicz. He was under the influence of Krasiński and Mochnacki and the philosophy of Cieszkowski and Trentowski: in particular, Norwid's postulate of new art and literature ("the literature of action"), which argued against the Romantic departure from reality and everyday life, was largely inspired by Cieszkowski. These works provoked a great deal of misunderstanding between the poet and his readers: Norwid was accused of "obfuscation of thought, image and expression."

Norwid's lack of success, in personal life as well (his unrequited love for Maria Kalergis, "the great lady"), and his financial problems explain his decision to leave for America in 1852. He lived in New York, earning a living by selling his drawings and sculptures, always struggling with nostalgia. In 1854 he returned to Paris. There he made another attempt at formulating his ideas, this time more consistently and conspicuously manifested in his works. During 1855–57 he wrote a major poem based on ancient times, *Quidam,* in which he created a new type of hero, in opposition to the Romantic individualists. During 1856–57 he published several works of poetic prose, among them *Czarne kwiaty* (Black Flowers) and *Białe kwiaty* (White Flowers), achieving a readership, thanks especially to a straightforward, personal relating of the last meetings of the poet with, among others, Chopin, Słowacki, and Mickiewicz. In 1858 he wrote a study, *O sztuce dla Polaków* (About Art—For Poles), and in 1860 he delivered a series of lectures, *O Juliuszu Słowackim* (On Juliusz Słowacki), published in 1861. In these publications he presented his aesthetic and literary credo and stated in blunt language his attitude toward his poetic predecessors. In 1863 the F. A. Brockhaus Publishing House printed his *Poezje* (Poems), the only selection of Norwid's works published during his lifetime. The edition contained several poetic treatises—*Pięć zarysów* (Five Outlines, written during 1847–62); *Rozmowa umarłych* (Dialogues of the Dead, written probably in 1857); *O sztuce* (About Art); several poetic and narrative prose pieces, including *Garstka piasku* (A Handful of Sand, written in 1858–59), *Bransoletka* (The Bracelet), and *Cywilizacja* (Civilization); a mystery play, *Krakus;* the poems—"parables," *Quidam* and *Epimenides,* written in 1854; and several lyrical poems. However, like *Niewola* (Slavery) and *Fulminant* published earlier, the book passed unnoticed. After further negotiations with Brockhaus, who later withdrew from the contract, Norwid, during 1865–66, began to prepare his best and most original collection of poetry, a cycle of lyrics, *Vade-mecum,* containing, among other great poems, the famous *Fortepian Szopena* (Chopin's Piano) and *Klaskaniem mając obrzękłe prawice* (With Applause Having Swollen Hands). This collection was, however, published only during the period of Young Poland by Lenon Przesmycki (Miriam) from 1903 to 1933 (fragments), and in its entirety by Wacław Borowy in 1947. Clearly opposed to contemporary national literature, *Vade-mecum* is simultaneously a program for a renascence of Polish poetry and its realization. Norwid's polemical views concern three aspects of poetry: its ideology, form, and social function in a given situation. The poet accuses the great Romantics of misunderstanding the relationship between an individual and society, the nation and humanity, of being one-sided in their concentration on the rights of the nation and their evaluation of current political events, and of neglecting universal moral problems. He severely criticizes post-Romantic epigones, who passively continued Mickiewicz's "world of the spirit," while the demands of the new epoch were only faced by the world of thought. He demands intellectual poetry and creates it himself. He remained close to Romanticism in his views on the role of art, which he regarded as an autonomous power capable of reviving man and society. The poems are largely critical of messianistic ideas, the narrow-mindedness of "local nationalism," and the intellectual void of the salon. Moral issues appear in the context of history and civilization, but always from the point of view of the individual. According to Elżbieta Feliksiak, in his Christian beliefs Norwid is a precursor of personalism. In opposition to bland and regular verse, he posits poems, characterized by considerable freedom and variety in the use of versification; in contrast to the "talkativeness" of descriptive poetry his style is maximally condensed, synthetic, accurate, manifested either in explicit inferences or in symbols and metaphors. The metaphors in *Vade-mecum* evoke not only images, but also concepts; poetic vision becomes simultaneously intellectual vision—philosophy can be read in the images. Symbols, on the other hand, are complex, "double": a sign is not only an image symbol, but also a thing corresponding to the image. Descriptiveness is substituted by dramatic elements, best seen in Norwid's characteristic intellectual "short-cuts." As a cycle, *Vade-mecum* is a highly organized whole, in spite of its generic variety: the unifying principle is the poetic program, while internal links are based on thematic criteria. *Vade-mecum* remains an object of critical speculation.

Norwid failed in his numerous attempts to publish *Vade-mecum*. From 1865 to 1883 he was able to publish only twenty-one poems and the poetic treatise *Rzecz o wolności słowa* (A Matter of Freedom of the Word, Paris, 1869). He was unable to stage any of his great dramas, which develop his views on the theater, reflected in *Noc tysiączna druga* (The One Thousand and Second Night, 1859, published 1907), *Wanda* (1851, published 1901), and *Krakus* (1851, published 1908). His achievement as a writer of contemporary "high comedy" can be discerned in *Aktor* (Actor, 1862, published 1937), *Za kulisami* (Behind the Scenes, 1865–66, published 1912), and *Pierścień wielkiej damy* (The Great Lady's Ring, 1872, published 1933). He also wrote a historical tragedy, *Kleopatra* (Cleopatra, 1872–79, published 1904). Some of his work during this period remained in manuscript: *Assunta* (1870, published 1907) and *A Dorio ad Phrygium* (1872, published 1915); the stories *Tajemnica lorda Singleworth* (Lord Singleworth's Secret, 1872, published 1902), *Stygmat* (Stigma, 1883, published 1901), and *Ad leones* (1882, published 1904); a philosophical treatise, *Milczenie* (Silence, 1882, published 1902), and his final dramatic attempt, the comedy *Miłość czysta u kąpieli morskich* (Pure Love in Sea-Baths, 1874, published 1933).

Norwid's lack of success in literature is the main motive of his biography and is often the subject of his reflections. He also failed in his numerous attempts to become part of the life of the nation. He was highly regarded as a speaker and orator. He made his living on drawing and painting, but this did not provide sufficient compensation. Living in poverty and loneliness, he was greatly admired for his original intellect (by Lenartowicz,* Cieszkowski, and the painters Scheffer and Delaroche). After 1877 he lived in a charity home for orphans and veterans, and that added to his isolation.

According to Zofia Trojanowicz, Norwid was one of the most original and versatile of Polish writers and thinkers. His imposing literary output is characterized by a variety of genres, philosophical reflections, and innovations. His position in the history of Polish literature is influenced by the fact that he appeared after the three "national poets" of Romanticism. He wrote against the background of late Romanticism and emerging positivism. As one of the great Romantics himself, he wanted to create a new model of Romanticism and accused his predecessors of concentrating on the nation and its martyrdom, at the expense of regarding man and his duties; on extraordinary emotions at the expense of thought and art. Norwid's program aimed to eradicate these flaws and change the collective consciousness. Some of the new motives which appeared in Norwid's works are imposed by the violent development of capitalism, and hence resemble positivist claims, but the similarity is superficial, since Norwid's proposals always remain subordinated to the Romantic view of the world.

The center of Norwid's interest is man and the reality he creates. He looked at human existence from various perspectives. He perceived reality, whether that of minor details or that of major events, as having symbolic sense, "the invisible content," but tried to reach this essence through showing man conditioned by historical and contemporary factors of a cultural, social, and national nature. He wrote a number of poems about outstanding personalities (General Bem, John Brown), in which he praises them as those who were able to free themselves from the pressure of circumstances and surge ahead of others, supporting Providence and consciously shaping history in their own way. The modes of expression most often employed by Norwid (varieties of irony, understatement, parable, allusion, contrast) augmented his vision of the world but were subordinated to his peculiar form of didacticism, whereby the reader is forced to look for the meaning hidden in his poetry and reach the truth himself. Norwid's lyrical works are mostly contemplative poems, reserved in their expression of emotions, lacking lyrical mood and descriptiveness. The starting point is usually a minor observation, a detail sketched briefly and accurately, but in a way which reveals unexpected meanings, enriching the symbolic sense, pointing to a certain general truth, often phrased as an aphorism or merely suggested in the poem. The texts are dense with meanings, written in a language full of archaic forms and neologisms, as well as colloquial expressions. This, in connection with his intellectual abstractness and complexity, demands active imaginative and intellectual effort of the reader and perhaps explains Norwid's lack of popularity at a time when literature was perceived through the works of Mickiewicz and the invasion of positivist fiction.

Since the beginning of the twentieth century Norwid's work has commanded a great deal of interest. Raised from oblivion by his "discoverer" and commentator Z. "Miriam" Przesmycki, Norwid was seen as a precursor of modernism, and Neo-Romantics emphasized his tragic "fate of a genius." The period between the wars witnessed a growing interest in his dramatic output. His lyrics were given a special position in his output and have exerted a strong and persistent influence on Polish poetry. A number of his lyrical poems are reminiscent of those of his reclusive contemporary, Emily Dickinson. Similarities in style, diction, innovation in technique, and aphoristic tendencies abound.

(See Romanticism.)

BIBLIOGRAPHY

Pisma wszystkie (Complete Writings), Volumes 1–11, edited by J. W. Gomulicki, Warsaw: PIN, 1971–76.

English

Krakus and the Dragon (Krakus), paraphrased by Victorie Ogrynska, Frankfurt am Main: Office of the Bauersche Giesserei, 1929.

Twelve Poems (Vade-mecum), translated by Christine Brooke-Rose, Rome: The Polish Committee in Rome, 1958.

Letters (Listy), translated by J. Peterkiewicz, Rome: The Polish Committee in Rome, 1958.

Lord Singleworth's Secret (Tajemnica Lorda Singleworth), translated by Olga Scherer-Virski, Hague: The Modern Polish Short Story, 1955.

NOWA, the oldest independent publishing house in Poland, was established in 1977 by a group of members of *KOR*. Since its inception, *NOWA* has published over four hundred books, with a circulation ranging between several hundred and several thousand copies.

NOWA does not represent any specific political orientation; it is also not restricted to any field of interest or literary form. It has always tried to respond to various creative initiatives. It has published poetry, drama, and prose by both Polish and foreign authors. Its list also includes essays and publicistic pieces, historical monographs, philosophical works, and collections of documents. From the very beginning *NOWA*'s goal was to give the Polish reader an opportunity to become acquainted with the most interesting and valuable writings in Poland and abroad, especially works prohibited by Polish censorship.

Among the authors published by *NOWA* one can find almost all of the most outstanding Polish writers: Miłosz* (the first Polish edition), Gombrowicz,* Herling-Grudziński,* Hłasko,* Józef Mackiewicz,* Andrzejewski,* Nowakowski,* Rymkiewicz,* and Janusz Głowacki.*

Many of *NOWA*'s publications are translations of Russian, Czech, and German literature; dramas by Václav Havel; poetry by Jozef Brodski and Anna Akhmatova; the prose of Solzhenitsyn and Hrabal; stories by Shalamov; and novels by Kundera, Grass, Orwell, and Vonnegut.

NOWA is the main publisher of *Kwartalnik Polityczny* (The Political Quarterly), *Krytyka* (Criticism), and the series *Biblioteka Krytyki* (A Critical Library), in which works by Popper, Weber, Podhoretz, and Jaspers have appeared. A number of books on contemporary Polish history and that of other Communist countries have also been published.

NOWA is also one of the initiators of *Archiwum Solidarności* (The Solidarity Archives). The group in charge of this section has prepared over twenty monographs and studies on the history of the Solidarity Trade Union and other independent social initiatives and have presented them for publication to various independent publishing houses.

NOWA is also involved in other activities: *Nowakaseta* (New Cassettes) has produced almost forty audiocassettes, among them recitals, musical concerts, publicistic programs, cabaret shows, and radio plays; *VideoNowa* (New Video) circulates videocassettes of censored films and original publicistic and documentary programs; and *FotoNowa* (New Photo) publishes sets of photographs. It has continued to function since the lifting of censorship in 1990.

(See *Drugi obieg.*)

NOWAK, TADEUSZ (b. 1930), a poet and prose writer, studied Polish philology in Cracow and published his first poems in magazines. He has received many literary awards.

According to Stefan Lichański, Nowak has no predecessors in Polish literature: certain analogies link him solely with post-Romanticism in his treatment of rural themes. He created his own vision of the countryside as a form of social existence, determined by tribal and social myths, shaping people's moral and national consciousness. According priority to elements of the ballad and fairy tale, but not to the idyll, he has created a form of poetic expression which is more expressive and dramatic than that of Lenartowicz,* allowing him an outlet for his anxiety and rebellion, precipitated by the experiences of living in a contemporary urban civilization which is alien to him. He utilizes rural images from folk songs; in his prose he presents the experiences of an individual, the family, the community. By combining a realistic approach with elements of Slavic and Christian mythology, with symbolism and the poetics of a dream, he has achieved a rarely encountered harmony of meaning and artistic expression. The poems also contain publicistic and didactic elements, for instance, *Uczę się mówić* (I'm Learning to Speak, 1953) and *Prorocy już odchodzą* (Prophets Are

Already Leaving, 1956): in their poetics they refer to the conventions of folk songs, the carol and ballad. They contain a rich layer of metaphor and elements of the grotesque. They are lyrical reflections of the poet's experiences, based on the recurring motive of going back into the realm of childhood: *Jasełkowe niebiosa* (Christmas Play Heavens, 1957), *Ślepe koła wyobraźni* (The Blind Wheels of the Imagination, 1958), *Psalmy na użytek domowy* (Psalms for Home Use, 1959), *Kolędy stręczyciela* (Carols of a Pimp, 1962), and *Pacierze i paciorki* (Prayers and Beads, 1988). Humanistic philosophical reflection is emphasized in the poems *Ziarenko trawy* (A Grain of Grass, 1964), *W jutrzni* (In Morning Service, 1966), *Bielsze nad śnieg* (Whiter Than Snow, 1973), and *Psalmy wszystkie* (All the Psalms, 1980).

Nowak's prose is written in the spirit of a tale from olden times; it is marked by a fragmentary structure and poetic stylization. His prose includes the stories *Przebudzenia* (The Awakening, 1962); *W puchu alleluja* (In a Fluffy Alleluja, 1965); a tale, *Obcoplemienna ballada* (A Foreign Tribe's Ballad, 1963); the collection *Półbaśnie* (Half-Fairy Tale, 1976), which gives a unified, intellectual view of folk culture; and the novels *Takie większe wesele* (Such a Bigger Wedding, 1966); *A jak królem, a jak katem będziesz* (And When You'll Be King, and When You'll Be a Hangman, 1968, adapted for the stage in 1973), based on motives of the maturation of the hero in the shadow of the cruelties of war; *Diabły* (Devils, 1971); *Dwunastu* (The Twelve, 1974); and *Prorok* (Prophet, 1977), depicting the impossibility for one born in a village to accustom himself to village conditions.

(See Contemporary Polish Literature.)

BIBLIOGRAPHY

Poezje wybrane (Selected Poetry), edited by Tadeusz Nowak, Cracow, 1967.
Wybór wierszy (Selected Poetry), with an introduction by S. Balbus, Cracow, 1973.

O

ODA DO MŁODOŚCI (Ode to Youth) (see Mickiewicz).

ODOJEWSKI, WŁODZIMIERZ (born 1930), a novelist and short story writer, was born in western Poland (Poznań). Most of his works are concerned with the war and its aftermath in the southeastern sections of Poland (Podole), which he knew from his childhood. He made his literary debut in 1948 during his studies in sociology at the University of Poznań. In 1960 he moved to Warsaw, where he began working closely with the youth-oriented literary periodical *Współczesność* (Contemporary Times) and with Polish Radio. Persecuted by the censor, he published a number of his works under dangerous circumstances and uncertain variations. During the seventies and eighties he published abroad. In 1971 he left for West Berlin on a grant from the Akademie der Kunste; he remained abroad and settled in Munich as an émigré. He worked with the Paris publishing house *Kultura* (Culture); he is also editor of the Polish cultural-literary section of Radio Free Europe.

Early in his career he was mainly known as the author of psychological works which analyzed the phenomena of time transference and the mechanisms of memory: the novels *Miejsca nawiedzone* (Stricken Places, 1959), *Czas odwrócony* (Time Turned Around, 1965), and a collection of short stories *Kwarantanna* (Quarantine, 1960). He achieved greater acclaim with his works evoking the dramatic tangle of conflicts which during World War II touched the southeastern parts of Poland and brought annihilation to the multiethnic and multireligious society that inhabited these lands for ages. In his novels *Wyspa ocalenia* (Island of Salvation, written in 1950 and published in 1964), *Zasypie wszystko, zawieje . . .* (Everything Will Be Filled Up, Covered Up . . . , published partially in *Twórczość* [Creativity], 1967–69, published in its entirety in Paris in 1973), and *Zapomniane, nieuśmierzone* (Forgotten, Not Assuaged, Berlin, 1987). In the cycle of short stories *Zmierzch świata* (The Decline of the World, 1962, emended and published in 1966) and *Zabezpieczanie śladów* (The Protection of One's Traces, Paris, 1984), the subsequent episodes of the drama were written: the Soviet occupation, the deportation of Poles into the heart of the Soviet Union and the Katyn murders, the extermination of the Jews during the German occupation, and, lastly, the slaughter of Poles perpetrated after 1942 by Ukrainian nationalists, which led to the outbreak of the fraternal Polish-Ukrainian War, conducted under the cruelest conditions of a civil war. The many-layered character of the conflict, whose background was both ethnic and social (the Polish gentry and the Ukrainian village in greater part), a matter of religious beliefs (the Polish Roman Catholics and the Greek Orthodox Ukrainians, closer to the Byzantine traditions), and historically motivated (the Cossack rebellions of the seventeenth and eighteenth centuries), was depicted by Odojewski ingeniously by portraying the entangled destinies of the local society, families, and individuals.

The heroes in *Zasypie wszystko*, considered to be Odojewski's finest novel, are two brothers: one fights with the Polish partisans in the war against Hitler; the other is attached to the Ukrainian division, S. S. Galizien. The subtly developed catastrophe, which envelops the moral and civilized world and which the Polish-Ukrainian borders succumb to, is used by the writer as a form of narration (conducted frequently from the point of view of a youthful witness who was part of the action) and composed of a Faulknerian style, with a frequent time mixture of retrospection by means of inner monologue. Also interesting is the similarity of Odojewski's work to the traditions of the Polish Baroque and Romanticism (the Ukrainian School) as well as the Russian epic (e.g., Boris Pasternak's *Doctor Zhivago*).

ODPRAWA POSŁÓW GRECKICH (The Dismissal of the Greek Envoys) (see Kochanowski).

OFICYNA LITERACKA (Literary Publishing House) (see *Drugi obieg*).

OGNIEM I MIECZEM (With Fire and Sword) (see Sienkiewicz).

ORKAN, WŁADYSŁAW (Franciszek Smreczyński) (1875–1930), a novelist, playwright, poet, and publicist, came from a poor family of highlanders from the Gorce Mountains. He experienced all the frustration typical of the first generation of the rural intelligentsia: he had to overcome financial and social barriers, to seek support in the family, to remain faithful to the place of his birth. He was a farmer in Poręba until the end of his life, but he remained in close contact with the artistic milieu in Cracow, especially in Zakopane. He was ideologically connected with the peasants' movement in Galicia, but also associated with members of the left. He defended Brzozowski* and Lenin when he was imprisoned by the Austrian authorities after the outbreak of World War I, but his main interest was regionalism, in which he developed and modified the ideas of Witkiewicz Senior.* During the war he was an officer of the Polish Legion; he was buried in Zakopane.

Orkan made his debut with an elegiac-patriotic poem, *Nad grobem Matki* (Over Mother's Grave, 1896), and several satirical poems and prose sketches followed. Most valued as a prose writer, Orkan gave expression to his experiences in the Podhale region in all his writings. His early works include two volumes of stories, *Nowele* (Short Novels, 1898) and *Nad urwiskiem* (Over the Precipice, 1900); the novel *Komornicy* (Village Tenants, 1900); the plays *Postronni* (The Outsiders, written in 1897) and *Skąpany świat* (Bathed World, written in 1899; staged in 1902; published in 1903); and a collection of poems, *Z tej smutnej ziemi* (From This Sad Earth, 1903). They give a depressing image of poverty and its moral and social consequences. Contrary to his predecessors, Orkan did not concentrate on the conflict between landowner and peasant, but emphasized the internal problems of the community. His works are ethnographically accurate in the image they create and are based on the cult of facts, akin to naturalism. His early lyrics, impressive in mood, are filled with realistic detail. Orkan's outspokenness and his uncompromising criticism brought him violent attacks from conservative and clerical circles, but he was enthusiastically received by the progressive circles of society.

Orkan's astute observations about class divisions in the rural community demonstrate his talent for generalization. Hoping to arrive at a synthetic view of his class, he used both realistic and modernist means of expression. His novel *W roztokach* (In the Glen, 1903) described a vision of the new country community, governed collectively according to the rules of justice. The hero fails, however, because of his individualism and lack of support from the community. In his subsequent works Orkan tried to find a solution to the ideological and artistic problems arising as a consequence of such a represented defeat, but he never reached comparable clarity of thought or effectiveness of technique.

Orkan made several more attempts at presenting the character of a peasant reformer. In the play *Franek Rakoczy* (1908), he reintroduced the hero of *W roztokach* and criticized him severely in the spirit of Maxim Gorky. Rakoczy has several replicas in the stories from the volumes *Herkules nowożytny i inne wesołe rzeczy* (A Modern Hercules and Other Merry Things, 1905) and *Wesele Prometeusza* (Prometheus's Wedding, 1920), but they are ridiculed in these grotesque and satirical parables. The ironic tone is dominant in Orkan's later stories.

In Orkan's works nature and man are presented in dramatic, even tragic terms as rivals. In the novel *Pomór* (The Plague, 1910) he depicted the biological extermination of a village plagued by famine and epidemic; the destructive aggressiveness of nature has a catastrophic interpretation in this work. Despair and disbelief in humanistic values also permeate his lyrics in the volume *Z martwej roztoki* (From a Dead Glen, 1912). In his novel *Drzewiej* (In the Past, 1912), he presented the existential drama of man, confronted by the rhythm of life in nature. Orkan also evinced interest in the historical tradition, for instance, his drama *Ofiara* (Sacrifice, 1905; written in 1899) and the novel *Kostka Napierski* (Kostka Napierski, 1925, written after 1904). His main interests also included national and patriotic themes (e.g., *Pieśni czasu* [The Songs of Time], a collection of hymns and poetic appeals, published in Piotrków in 1915; and a piece of nonfiction, *Droga Czwartaków* [Czwartaks' Road], 1916).

During 1918–30 he outlined several literary works, but only a few were completed; the lyrical cycle *Pochwała życia* (Praise of Life); a visionary drama, *Widma* (Ghosts, written during 1917–27); and the novel *Czantoria,* written in 1928–29. These works were published after Orkan's death. The most valuable part of Orkan's output in his late years is the collection of letters *Listy ze wsi* (Letters from the Village, 1925–27), which gives a psychological characterization of a contemporary peasant, analyzes his historical and current situation, emphasizes the culture-forming and public values of the class, and formulates a program for the rural intelligentsia.

After his death Orkan became the object of a cult in Podhale. In the history of Polish literature he remains a writer with unusual broadness of vision concerning matters of the Polish village.

BIBLIOGRAPHY

Dzieła (Works), Volumes 1–14, edited by S. Pigoń, Cracow, 1960–72.

ORZESZKOWA, ELIZA (née Pawłowska) (second husband's name Nahorski) (1841–1910), a novelist, publicist, and social activist, married P. Orzeszko. The years 1859–63, which she spent on his estate of Ludwinów, near Brest, Belarus, played an important role in the formation of the writer's personality. She conducted educational work among the simple folk. She offered help to the January Uprising of 1863, hiding R. Traugutt and transporting him to the border. In 1869 her marriage was invalidated and she settled in Grodno, where she got to know city life, which was later reflected in her works.

Orzeszkowa's output can be divided into three periods: 1866–76, 1877–91, 1892–1910. According to Mieczysława Romankówna, the linking motive is the emotional attitude toward the January Uprising. In the first period Orzeszkowa formulated her positivist views and wrote her *roman á these.* Her determinism of the time was shaped mainly under the influence of Buckle; she also absorbed Spencer's evolutionism and agnosticism, abandoning her former materialism. She expressed her theoretical literary program in several articles: *Kilka uwag nad powieścią* (A Number of Points Concerning the Novel, 1866), *O przekładach* (About Translations, 1872), *Listy o literaturze* (Letters About Literature, 1873), *O powieściach T. T. Jeża* (About the Novels of T. T. Jeż, 1879), and *Drugie dziesięciolecie 1840–1850* (The Second Decade: 1840–1850) in *Książka Jubileuszowa . . . Józef I. Kraszewski* (The Jubilee Edition . . . Józef I. Kraszewski, 1880). She opposed Romanticism, demanding that literature bear a resemblance to real life. She considered the novel to be the leading literary genre and emphasized the intellectual dependence of a writer on society and his responsibility for the collective fate. She made her debut with the story *Obrazek z lat głodowych* (A Picture from the Hungry Years, 1866). She followed this with several narrative works: *Początek powieści* (The Beginning of a Novel) in *Zbiór oryginalnych powiastek i gawęd* (A Collection of Original Stories and Tales, 1866), *Ostatnia miłość* (Last Love, 1868), *Z życia realisty* (From the Life of a Realist, 1868), *Na prowincji* (In the Provinces, 1870), *W klatce* (In a Cage, 1870), *Cnotliwi* (The Virtuous, 1871), and *Pamiętnik Wacławy* (Wacława's Diary, 1871); *Pan Graba* (Mr. Graba, 1872), the first work to receive critical approval, was followed by *Na dnie sumienia* (At the Bottom of Conscience, 1873), *Marta* (1873), *Eli Makower* (1875), *Rodzina Brochwiczów* (The Brochwiczows Family, 1876), *Pompalińscy* (The Pompalińskis, 1876), and *Maria* (1877). Most of these stories and novels are not of high quality. They are rich with autobiographical elements and display the writer's interest in the emancipation of women (which she also promulgated in the press). She discussed women's education and their upbringing, love, marriage, family life, divorce, the situation of the unmarried woman, women's work, and illegitimate children. From this point of view she is quite close to other writer-feminists of Western Europe, like Charlotte Brontë, E. Gaskell, and others. A new hero appeared in her novels: doctors, engineers, scholars—idealistic, totally devoted to public service. All the novels of this period, except *Marta,* also contain typical love stories. Third person narration prevails, but Orzeszkowa also attempted a memoiristic structure *(Pamiętnik Wacławy)* and epistolary novel (*Maria*). In the earlier works the narrator is also an observer, a commentator, and a judge, sometimes a character: he often treats the reader as a confidant in his observations and thoughts. Her texts are filled with addresses to the reader and dialogues with him.

The novel *Meir Ezofowicz* (1878) marked the period of Orzeszkowa's mature work. She published *Widma* (Ghosts, 1881), *Sylwek Cmentarnik* (1882), *Zygmunt Ławicz i jego koledzy* (Zygmunt Ławicz and His Colleagues, 1882), *Bańka mydlana* (Soap Bubbles, 1882–83), *Pierwotni* (The Primitive Ones, 1884), *Niziny* (The Underdogs, 1885), *Dziurdziowie* (Dziurdzia Family, 1885), *Mirtala* (1886), *Nad Niemnem* (Beyond the Niemen, 1888), *Cham* (The Boor, 1888), *Czciciel potęgi* (The Worshipper of

Power, 1891), *Jędza* (The Shrew, 1891), *Bene nati* (1891), *Westalka* (The Vestal Virgin, 1891), and several collections of stories: *Z różnych sfer* (From Various Spheres, 1879–82), *Panna Antonina* (Miss Antonina, 1888), *W zimowy wieczór* (On a Winter Eve, 1888), as well as several treatises (e.g., *Patriotyzm i kosmopolityzm* [Patriotism and Cosmopolitanism], 1880, *O Żydach i kwestii żydowskiej* [On Jews and the Jewish Question], 1882) and a study, *Ernest Renan* (1886). During this period Orzeszkowa wrote realistic novels with broad social and democratic horizons. The main themes of the novels are social and national conflicts; a number of plots evolve around the Jewish question, life in the country, and an interest in ancient times. Her pantheon of characters include low rank craftsmen, tradesmen, and poor people. She revealed the face of the city that the reader had not known before, seeking inspiration in courtrooms, city streets, basements, and attics. In spite of her disappointment with the positivist ideals, she still believed in the power of education. Her language was enriched with various dialects and expressions marking social status. The position of the narrator was strengthened: he dominated the reader and the characters with his universal knowledge. The characters are presented in these later works with psychological motivations, especially in her first psychological novel, *Cham* (The Boor).

In the final period of her work Orzeszkowa turned to religious and ethical problems, abandoning atheism and anticlericalism. More and more she concentrated on the inner life of the individual, his or her attitude toward the world. A positivist writer, she accepted the techniques of naturalism and modernism. The works of this period are also her major achievements in terms of language and style—they are lyrical, written in beautiful poetic prose. She saw her main ideological enemies in modernism and decadence. She voiced her concerns in *Dwa bieguny* (Two Extremes, 1893), her collection of stories *Melancholicy* (The Melancholy Ones, 1896), *Ad astra,* (1904), and *I pieśń niech zapłacze* (And Let the Song Cry Out, 1905). She blamed the modernists for "argonautism," that is, seeking careers abroad, in *Argonauci* (The Argonauts, 1900), *Australczyk* (The Southerner, 1896), and in a collection of stories, *Iskry* (Sparks, 1898). Above all, however, the January Uprising shaped her artistic personality—she gathered her personal memories in the collection of stories *Gloria victis* (1910).

Meir Ezofowicz, a novel which appeared in 1878, according to Czesław Miłosz, is something of a poetic "saga" about a small Jewish town, in which the representatives of an enlightened, reform-minded family of Ezofowicz descended from the sixteenth century battle about the assimilation and close relations of Jews living in Poland to Polish society. These ideas from the eighteenth century take on the name of Jewish Enlightenment (*Haskala*). The young Meir, a lone fighter in the style of the heroes of Romantic literature, attempts to oppose the fanatically orthodox Rabbi Todros and the ignorant, backward society of the town. He indeed loses the battle and, after the tragic death of his loved one, Golda, is forced to leave the town, but his ideas do not die. In this novel Orzeszkowa displayed an excellent knowledge of history, customs, and Jewish culture, masterfully painting a picture of a miserable life, cut off from the world. The novel was loudly acclaimed among its contemporaries. It has been translated into twelve languages.

Nad Niemnem (On the Banks of the Niemen) was originally entitled *Mezalians* (Misalliance). The new title reflects the broadening of the work's horizons and its epic character, suggesting the tradition of *Pan Tadeusz*. The novel presents a broad picture of society, with the January Uprising as one of the main motives. It appeared in retrospect, since the censors would have prevented more explicit mention of the problem. The story takes place in the eighties, on the estate of the Korczyński family and the neighboring *zaścianek* (worker's settlement) of the Bohatyrowicz family. The two families are in conflict for economic reasons, made more acute by the social gap that exists between them. The young Korczyński, a representative of his generation, wants to resolve the conflict and bridge the gap, highly critical of the ideological minimalism of early positivism represented by his father. The antinomy is also mirrored in the theme of love between Justyna Korczyńska and Jan Bohatyrowicz. The conflict is resolved, and Justyna and Jan are engaged. The novel presents a gallery of characters, each embodying a social type or problem.

The novel is constructed on a double temporal plane. The past appears in the memories of the characters and in the information provided by the narrator: it reveals motivations and lays the grounds for evaluation of the characters' actions in the present. In the novel Orzeszkowa made full use of her ethnographic studies around the area of Grodno and her contacts with the local people, who served as models for some of the characters. *Nad Niemnem* presents folk traditions, tales, legends, and the beauty of the landscape, described in detail and with love and admiration. It portrays the fight of the Polish landed gentry in the eastern territories of former Poland concerning the keeping of land in Polish hands. The novel is generally considered a masterpiece by most critics. It has been translated into numerous languages, including a collection of her works in twenty volumes in Swedish.

(See *Młoda Polska* and Positivism.)

BIBLIOGRAPHY

Pisma (Writings), Volumes 1–25, introduction by A. Drogoszewski, Warsaw, 1912–28.

Pisma zebrane, Volumes 1–52, edited by J. Krzyżanowski, Warsaw, 1947–53.

Letters, Volumes 1–9, edited by E. Jankowski, Wrocław, 1959–81.

English

The Argonauts, translated by Jeremiah Curtin, New York: Scribner's, 1901, 1988.

An Obscure Apostle (Meir Ezofowicz), translated by S. C. de Soissous, London, 1899.

The Forsaken (Niziny), translated by Edward Koenigsberger, Bournemouth, England: Delaware, 1980.

OZIMINA (Winter Corn) (see Berent).

ÓSMY DZIEŃ TYGODNIA (The Eighth Day of the Week) (see Hłasko).

OSTRORÓG, JAN (see Medieval Literature and Renaissance).

P

PALĘ PARYŻ (I Burn Paris) (see Jasieński).

PAŁUBA (Make-Believe or Palubism) (see Irzykowski).

PAN COGITO (see Herbert).

PAN TADEUSZ (see Mickiewicz).

PARANDOWSKI, JAN (1895–1978), a prose and essay writer and translator, made his debut in 1913 with a literary-philosophical sketch, *Rousseau.* He began his studies in Classical philology and archeology and traveled to France, Greece, and Italy. He early published reviews in Warsaw and Lvov publications, collected in *Kiedy byłem recenzentem* (When I Was a Reviewer, 1963). During 1933–78 he was the president of the Polish PEN Club. In 1962 he was elected vice president of the International PEN Club. He received an honorary doctorate from the Catholic University in Lublin in 1976.

He studied and admired Greek and Roman culture, popularizing it and giving it artistic expression. In Classical Greco-Roman civilization he sought harmony and order which would reconcile nature and culture, life and art, Dionysian vitalism and a contemplative approach. He was also particularly interested in the artistic and intellectual trends of Classical origin (humanism, Parnassism, and late modernism). As a writer he advocated ideas associated with these traditions, which included a reverence toward the cultural achievements of humanity, the cult of art appreciation, acceptance of the moral authority of literature, and defense of the Classical rules of clarity of style and thought. Parandowski's main works skate the border between fiction and essay. The best known are those which popularize the knowledge of ancient times. His *Mitologia* (Mythology, 1924) has been the main source of information for younger readers for more than half a century. The same can be said of his popular adaptations of two epics by Homer, *Wojna trojańska* (The Trojan War, 1927) and *Przygody Odyseusza* (The Adventures of Odysseus, 1935). The collection *Eros na Olimpie* (Eros on Olympus, 1924), stylized somewhat humorously, was addressed to older readers. The book *Dysk olimpijski* (The Olympic Disc, 1933) was awarded a bronze medal at the Eleventh Olympic Games in Berlin in 1936: the historical reconstruction of the ancient games first held in 476 B.C. gave grounds for a more general humanistic reflection. The themes of Greek and Roman traditions also appear in his travel reports *Rzym czarodziejski* (Magical Rome, 1924), *Dwie wiosny* (Two Springs, 1927), and *Mój Rzym* (My Rome, 1959; enlarged edition, 1970); his stories for young people in the volume *Trzy znaki Zodiaku* (Three Signs of the Zodiac, 1938); the sketches *Z antycznego świata* (From an Ancient World, 1958); various albums, *Grecja* (Greece, 1962) and *Rzym* (Rome, 1968, edited with Z. Parandowski); and his only drama, *Medea* (1961; staged in 1964).

According to Ryszard Matuszewski, Parandowski was also interested in the personalities of great writers and the psychology of artistic production, presented in the form of "fictionized biographies." He devoted the novel *Król życia* (The King of Life, 1930) to Oscar Wilde, emphasizing the motive of the artist's rebellion against the mentality of Victorian England and his ultimate defeat. Another biography, *Petrarka* (Petrarch, 1956), presents the Italian poet's life as a realization of Renaissance ideals. The collection of sketches *Alchemia słowa* (Alchemy of Words, 1951; enlarged edition, 1956) introduced the reader to the mysteries and peculiarities of the writing techniques of artists from various epochs. Some autobiographical elements can be found in the novel *Niebo w płomieniach* (The Sky in Flames, 1936), which presents a religious crisis and intellectual breakthrough in the life of a young man. The same character reappears as an adult in the novel *Powrót do życia* (A Return to Life, 1961). He also reminisces on his youth in Lvov in the cycle *Zegar słoneczny* (Sundial, 1953; enlarged edition, 1959). Contemplation and reminiscences are also present in the collections of essays, stories, and autobiographical notes *Godzina śródziemnomorska* (Mediterranean Hour, 1949; enlarged edition, 1956), *Wrześniowa noc* (September Night, 1962), *Luźne kartki* (Loose Cards, 1965), *Akacja* (Acacia, 1967), and *Pod zamkniętymi drzwiami czasu* (Behind the Closed Doors of Time, 1975); reports from travels and congresses of PEN Club, *Podróże literackie* (Literary Travels, 1958, enlarged edition, 1968); and portraits of outstanding writers and scholars in the volumes *Odwiedziny i spotkania* (Visits and Meetings, 1934) and *Wspomnienia i sylwety* (Reminiscences and Profiles, 1960). Parandowski was also a translator. His translations include a prose version of Odysseus (*Odysea,* 1953), of Daphne and Chloe by Longos

(*Dafnis i Chloe,* 1925), and About Civil War (*O wojnie domowej,* 1951), based on the writings of Caesar. He also wrote on the theory of translation. (See Contemporary Polish Literature.)

BIBLIOGRAPHY

Pisma wybrane (Selected Writings), Warsaw, 1955.
Dzieła wybrane (Selected Works), Volumes 1–3, Warsaw, 1957.

English

The Olympic Discus (Dysk olimpijski), translated by S. A. Walewski and A. M. Malecka, London: Minerva, 1939, New York: Ungar, 1964.
Olympic Athletes (Olimpijczycy), Warsaw: Sport i Turystyka, 1960.

PARNICKI, TEODOR (1908–88), a novelist born in Berlin into a family of mixed parentage (his father was a Pole, his mother, a Jew from Kiev), spent his childhood in Russia, then in 1920 found himself in Manchuria, where he made his debut in 1928 with an article on Henryk Sienkiewicz and Alexander Dumas. Upon his return to Poland he studied Polish, Oriental, and English philology in Lvov. He worked for various papers and magazines in Lvov, writing historical short stories, reviews and studies, and finally his first novel, *Trzy minuty po trzeciej* (Three Minutes After Three, 1929–30). In 1934 he staged his drama *Mandżukuo: Walka o wschód* (The Manchurian: Battle of the East) and wrote his first historical novel, *Hrabia Julian i król Roderyk* (Count Julian and King Roderick, published in 1976). In 1940 he was arrested after the occupation of Lvov by the Red Army; he was in various Soviet prisons until 1941, when amnesty for Poles was declared. He worked in the Polish Embassy; in 1943—after diplomatic relations with the Polish émigré government were broken—he went to Teheran together with the embassy personnel; from there he traveled from Iraq, Syria, and Lebanon to Jerusalem. In 1944 he found himself in London, where he worked for the Polish diplomatic service in Mexico. After 1945 he began to devote all of his time to writing. He returned to Poland permanently in 1967.

Parnicki's novels cover two thousand years of history and take place almost all over the world. They are grouped around two cycles: *Twarz księżyca* (The Face of the Moon) and *Nowa baśń* (The New Fairy Tale). The trilogy *Twarz księżyca* (Volumes 1–2, 1961, Volume 3, 1967) presents the relationships between the cultures of Asia and the Latin countries at the time of the decline of the Roman Empire and of increasing Christian influences on Greco-Roman civilization. The works associated with the trilogy include *Aecjusz ostatni Rzymianin* (Aesius, the Last Roman, 1937), Parnicki's first published historical novel, and its sequel *Śmierć Aecjusza* (The Death of Aesius, 1966), which related the story of the public and military career of the defender of Rome against the attacks of the barbarians. His other works include *Koniec "Zgody Narodów"* (The End of the "Concord of Nations," Paris, 1955; Poland, 1957), whose plot was later complemented in *Koła na piasku* (Wheels on Sand, 1966), a study of the history of the fall of Hellenistic culture in Asia. His historical novel *Słowo i ciało* (Word and Flesh, 1959) dramatizes the story of a man of Greek and Partian origin living in Egypt in the early third century. The works connected with the six volume cycle *Nowa baśń* (The New Fairy Tale, 1962–70), which cover one thousand years of history of the Old and New World, and of Poland from Chrobry to contemporary times, include the following: *Srebrne orły* (Silver Eagles, 1944), *Tylko Beatrycze* (Only Beatrice, 1962, adapted for television in 1975), and *I u możnych dziwny* (And Strange with the Powerful, 1965). Both cycles are given a common base in *Zabij Kleopatrę* (Kill Cleopatra, 1968), in which historical facts are a pretext for presenting the author's own reflections on writing, which include the most fantastic suppositions about the course of history. The latter traits can also be found in subsequent novels, in which the themes from *Nowa baśń* predominate: *Inne życie Kleopatry* (Cleopatra's Different Life, 1969), *Tożsamość* (Identity, 1970), *Muza dalekich podróży* (The Muse of Distant Travels, 1970), *Przeobrażenie* (Transformation, 1973), *Staliśmy jak dwa sny* (We Stood Like Two Dreams, 1973), and *Sam wyjdę bezbronny* (I Myself Will Leave Unarmed, 1976). Parnicki's biographical and artistic comments are offered in *Rodowód literacki* (Literary Origin, 1974). The enlarged edition was entitled *Historia w literaturę przekuwana* (History Reforged in Literature, 1980), a transcript of the writer's lectures delivered at the University of Warsaw during 1972–73.

According to Małgorzata Czermińska, the main themes of Parnicki's early works are connected with great historical breakthroughs, the struggle for political power, and especially the rise of new civilizations as a result of the competition between and mutual influence of independent cultures. The philosophical and historiosophical reflections concentrate on the repetitiousness of historical cycles, the determinism of the laws of history, the role of outstanding individuals in history, and the very possibility of getting to know the course and sense of historical events. The motive of "half-breeds," people of complex ethnic and social origin who play a special role in shaping the course of history, is specifically important in the novels written in the 1950s and the 1960s. In his later works the "half-breed" is seen as an intellectual and an artist, leading the writer to reflect on his own biography and on his entire output. His work appears to be a uniform creation, both in the area of events and people and in narrative structure. The narrator appears to be common to all texts, stylized as the writer himself. Contrary to the descriptive and storytelling tradition of the historical novel, Parnicki operates almost exclusively with indirect narration, which consists of dialogues and monologues, long speculative fragments, confessions, fragments of letters and diaries. He often constructs the plot according to the rules of conjectural prosecution, questioning not only the identity of characters and the factuality of events but also the authenticity of the text itself.

Srebrne orły (Silver Eagles) was published in Jerusalem in 1944 and in Wrocław in 1949. It presents the formation of the Polish state at the turn of the tenth and eleventh centuries from the perspective of the changes taking place throughout Europe, and especially in the Holy Roman Empire of the German nation. Otto III wants to raise the empire to its former prosperity and sees Bolesław Chrobry as capable of realizing the idea. The plot is subordinated to the experiences and thoughts of Aron, a monk from Ireland, whose travels and secret missions introduce the reader to the conflicts of the time. Aron tries to understand the arguments of Chrobry, who wants to free himself of the domination of the emperor and refuses to accept the "silver eagles"—the symbol of the patrician of the empire. The world of the novel is presented through the inner life of the characters; the use of devices from the contemporary psychological novel, especially in narration and in the presentation of time and characters, greatly enhances the view of history espoused by the novel: Parnicki does not pretend to offer a complete knowledge of facts, but rather presents a critical cognition of the historical process. The novel is considered to be the major achievement among his works, in which Parnicki undertook to depict the beginnings of the Polish state.

BIBLIOGRAPHY

T. Cieślikowska, *Pisarstwo Teodora Parnickiego* (The Writings of Teodor Parnicki), Warsaw, 1965.

W. Sadkowski, *Parnicki,* Warsaw, 1970.

PAWLIKOWSKA-JASNORZEWSKA, MARIA (née Kossak; husbands' names Bżowski, Pawlikowski, and Jasnorzewski) (1891–1945), the daughter of a famous painter, Wojciech Kossak; granddaughter of Julius, who was also a painter; and sister of the writer Magdalena Samozwaniec; was a poet and playwright. She owed her intellectual growth largely to a thorough education received at home. She never attended any school or university, except for a short period as a volunteer at the Academy of Fine Arts. Among her friends were the poets from the Skamander* group, Witkacy, and members of the formist group from Cracow. She traveled a great deal in France, Italy, Turkey, northern Africa, and Greece. In 1935 she received the Golden Wreath of *PAL* (The Polish Academy of Literature). After the outbreak of World War II, she moved to Paris and from there (with her pilot husband) to England, where she spent the last years of her life.

She made her debut in 1922 with the collection *Niebieskie migdały* (Blue Almonds). She also published the collections *Różowa magia* (Rose Magic, 1924), *Pocałunki* (Kisses, 1926), *Dansing* (Dancing, 1927), *Wachlarz* (The Fan, 1927), *Cisza leśna* (Forest Silence, 1928), *Paryż* (Paris, 1929), *Profil białej damy* (A Profile of a White Lady, 1930), *Surowy jedwab* (Raw Silk, 1932), *Śpiąca załoga* (A Sleeping Crew, 1933), *Balet powojów* (A Ballet of Bindweed, 1935), *Krystalizacje* (Crystallization, 1937), and *Szkicownik poetycki* (A Poetic Sketchbook, 1939). She was a true poet of love, presenting it in a new way, direct and natural. At the same time, like the poets of the Skamander group, she filled her poems with the atmosphere and the reality of everyday life. The genre which was most characteristic of her, in which she achieved mastery, was the miniature poem which ended with an unexpected point. In the first period of her work, until around 1927, her poetry was mostly light in tone, at times joyful and jocular. The following years, beginning with the collection *Cisza leśna* (Forest Silence), brought a change. She was more and more fascinated with the passing of time, aging, and death. From the poet of love she changed into a poet of nature, rebelling against it, but also somehow enchanted. Her poems from the thirties reveal a thorough knowledge of current works in science (Fabre, Maeterlinck) and philosophy (Schopenhauer, Nietzsche, Bergson), and also the field of occultism. Her interests in spiritualism and magic led her to Indian beliefs, such as palingenesis and a direct relationship to nature. According to Jerzy Kwiatkowski, during this period she also moved away from formal rigor, aiming at greater simplicity and "transparency" in her means of expression, introducing the poetics of brevity and fragments (*Krystalizacje*). The process led her (in *Szkicownik poetycki* [A Poetic Sketchbook]) to a rejection of versification canons and an acceptance of poetic prose. The year 1939 marked a breakthrough in both her private and artistic life. The war and her absence from Poland had a traumatic influence on her. Her poetry began to express antiwar, catastrophic motives, with the painful longing for home. At this time she published two volumes: *Róża i lasy płonące* (The Rose and the Burning Forests, 1940) and *Gołąb ofiarny* (Sacrificial Dove, 1941). The third collection she planned, *Bagienne niezapominajki* (Swampy Forget-Me-Nots), was lost by her publisher; the poems were included in her collection *Ostatnie utwory* (The Last Works), published in 1956 by T. Terlecki.

Only a few of her plays were published; most of the works remain in manuscript. They repeat the main motives of her poetry. The most interesting among them are her metaphorical dramas, *Kochanek Sybilli Thompson* (Sybil Thompson's Lover, staged in 1926), with elements of fantasy and futurology; *Mrówki* (Ants, staged in 1936), with allegorical and fairy tale elements; and the grotesque *Baba-Dziwo* (Crazy Old Hag, staged in 1938; published in *Dialog*, 1966), a satire on totalitarian power.

BIBLIOGRAPHY

Poezje (Poetry), Volumes 1–2; edited by M. Wiśniewska, introduction by A. Mauersberger, second edition, Warsaw, 1974; first edition, 1958.

Wybór poezji (A Selection of Poetry), fourth edition, selected and with an introduction by J. Kwiatkowski, Wrocław, 1980.

Dramaty (Dramatic Works), Volumes 1–2, second edition, edited by A. Bolecka, introduction by S. Treugutt, Lublin, 1988.

PEIPER, TADEUSZ (1891–1969), a poet, prose writer, playwright, literary and theatrical critic, studied philosophy and law in Cracow, Berlin, and Paris. In 1914–20 he lived in Spain; after his return, he became editor of *Zwrotnica* (Switch, 1922–23, 1926–27), in which he expressed his aesthetic views. His articles had a decisive influence on the poetic program of the Cracow avant-garde. He was associated with the avant-garde throughout the 1930s, developing and defending his views in leftist papers. In 1939, after the outbreak of World War II, he found himself in Lvov, and shortly thereafter was taken by the Red Army. In 1940 he was arrested by the Soviet Secret Police (NKVD) and sent into the heart of the Soviet Union. Released as a result of amnesty, which the émigré Polish government had negotiated with the Soviet authorities, he began to work with Polish Communist circles in Russia. After his return in 1944 he worked mainly as a theater critic. Soon thereafter, however, he withdrew from literary life as a result of psychological disorders.

He expressed his theoretical views in the sketches and articles published in the collection *Tędy* (That Way, 1930). They are grounded in the belief that the development of art is associated with the changes in the social consciousness resulting from the advance of modern civilization: the growth of great cities, democratic changes in cultural traditions, the increasing restrictions imposed on the individual, the stronger laws of economics, and the greater independence from one's natural environment. Peiper demanded a new art which would support that evolution, not directly, however, but through artistic form, imprinting intellectual and emotional patterns in the social subconscious. He shared with the futurist movement enthusiasm for technology, but he opposed its undisciplined tendencies, advocating a rigorous, purposeful, logical artistic structure. His views are best expressed in the sketch *Nowe usta* (New Mouths, 1925), in which he opposed Romantic expression of the poet's personality—the cult of poetic craftsmanship, the style of prose which referred to things by their realistic names—the style of poetry which substituted the "name" with a poetic "pseudonym"; rather than expressing emotion directly, poetry, according to Peiper, ought to use poetic equivalents, to qualify it with extended paraphrases, in which the emotions of the artist are encoded. He espoused the idea of the "blooming pattern"—defining an object or a situation through a series of more and more complex sentence structures.

According to Stanisław Jaworski, Peiper's poetry is intellectual and conceptual; his astonishing metaphors are always subjected to rigorous syntactic structure. Its characteristic feature is the opposition between the fascination with sensual beauty of the world and the desire to control it; between erotic obsession and physiology—and working for the advancement of a new world. His collections include *A* (1924), *Żywe linie* (Living Lines, 1924), and *Raz* (Once, 1929), in which longer lyrical forms appear. His political poem *Na przykład* (For Example, 1931) was confiscated by the censors; the same fate was accorded his collection *Poematy* (Poems, 1935). Peiper's novels are of much lesser importance. They include *Ma lat 22* (He's 22 Years Old, 1936) and *Krzysztof Kolumb odkrywca* (Christopher Columbus the Discoverer, 1949). His plays only recently have aroused some interest: *Szósta! Szósta!* (Sixth! Sixth!, 1925; staged in 1974), *Skoro go nie ma* (Since He's Not Here, 1933; staged in 1973). His last publication in his lifetime was the translation of *Pies ogrodnika* (The Gardener's Dog) by Lope de Vega (1956). Peiper assumed a major role in Polish art as a theoretician of the avant-garde.

BIBLIOGRAPHY

Pisma (Writings), Volumes 1–4, introduction and commentaries by S. Jaworski, edited by T. Podoska, Cracow, 1972–79.

Pisma wybrane (Selected Writings), selected and with an introduction by S. Jaworski, Wrocław, 1979.

Carpenter, Bogdana, *The Poetic Avant-Garde in Poland, 1918–1939,* Seattle: University of Washington Press, 1983.

PIGOŃ, STANISŁAW (1885–1968), a literary historian, editor, and memoir writer, studied Polish philology in Cracow, mainly under the guidance of Ignacy Chrzanowski.* He made his debut with a sketch, *Słowacki w dobie przełomu* (Słowacki During the Time of Change, 1908). In 1911 he published a treatise, *O "Księgach narodu i pielgrzymstwa polskiego" Adama Mickiewicza* (About "The Book of the Nation and Polish Pilgrimage" by Adam Mickiewicz). He presented his moral and social views in *Do podstaw wychowania narodowego* (To the Foundations of a National Education, 1917; second edition in 1920). He was given a professorship in Vilnius in 1921. After 1931 he was a professor at the Jagiellonian University in Cracow until 1960; from 1939 to 1940 he was imprisoned by the Nazis, together with other professors of the university. After being freed, he returned to Cracow, where he took part in the secret university. After the war he became a member of the Polish Academy of Sciences.

Having worked in the entire area of Polish literature, he became mainly interested in Romanticism, and in Mickiewicz's life and work in particular. During the time spent in Vilnius he studied the background of the poet's young years: *Głosy sprzed wieku: Szkice z dziejów procesu filareckiego*

(Voices from the Last Century: Sketches from the History of the Filaret Affair, 1924) and *Z dawnego Wilna: Szkice obyczajowe i literackie* (From Old Vilnius: Moral and Literary Sketches, 1929). He wrote a study of *Pan Tadeusz,* which he published in 1925 with detailed comments. His research was crowned with a monograph, *"Pan Tadeusz": wzrost, wielkość i sława* (Pan Tadeusz: Its Growth, Greatness, and Fame, 1934), a classic by today's standards. He prepared a new edition of Mickiewicz's poetry and participated in the monumental "Parliament" Edition of his *Dzieła wszystkie* (Complete Works). He also contributed to the National and Anniversary Editions, among other activities, gathering for the first time all of Mickiewicz's correspondence. He also worked on Fredro and almost completed the edition of all of his works. He was also editor of letters by the great Romantics: Goszczyński,* Trentowski, Norwid,* and Krasiński.* Pigoń was the editor of Żeromski's* and Orkan's* complete works. He published a monograph, *Władysław Orkan: Twórca i dzieło* (Władysław Orkan: Author and Works), in 1958. He was also the editor of the scholarly works of K. M. Górski (1913), S. Tarnowski (1922), I. Chrzanowski* (1946), and S. Kołaczkowski.

The results of his research on texts, sources, and interpretations—mainly in Romantic and Neo-Romantic literature—are presented in the volumes *Na wyżynach romantyzmu* (On the Summit of Romanticism, 1936), *Wśród twórców* (Among Authors, 1947), *Studia literackie* (Literary Studies, 1951), *Zawsze o Nim: Studia i odczyty o Mickiewiczu* (Always About Him: Studies and Lectures on Mickiewicz, 1960), *Z ogniw życia i literatury* (From Links of Life and Literature, 1961), *Miłe życia drobiazgi* (Pleasant Odds and Ends of Life, 1964), *Drzewiej i wczoraj* (Then and Today, 1966), and *Wiązanka historycznoliteracka* (Historo-Literary Bouquet, 1969). He was also interested in folk culture, publishing a pioneering work, *Zarys nowszej literatury ludowej* (An Outline of the New Folk Literature, 1946); an anthology, *Wybór pisarzy ludowych* (An Anthology of Folk Writers, 1947–48); and a volume of sketches, *Na drogach i manowcach kultury ludowej* (On the Roads and Byroads of Folk Cultures, 1939). He also wrote his memoirs of his early years, *Z Komborni w świat* (From Komborna to the World, 1946; fourth edition, 1957), depicting the vicissitudes of a son of a peasant who attains the summit of national culture. He also related his experiences as a soldier, scholar, and prisoner in *Z przędziwa pamięci: Urywki wspomnień* (From the Yarn of Memory: Fragments of Memories, 1968).

According to Zbigniew Jerzy Nowak, Pigoń never formulated his methodology explicitly. It is inherent, however, in his work. It is determined, on the one hand, by the philological tradition which treated literature as a reflection of life (hence the view that one has to know life first to understand literature); and, on the other hand, by the aesthetics of Romanticism, which required that the work be analyzed in its growth and in connection with its creator. The latter tendency was strengthened by the so-called Cracow personalism, also espoused by Ignacy Chrzanowski and Kazimierz Wyka,* which can best be summarized in the view that the writer's creative personality must be considered. Pigoń will be remembered as a scholar and as a writer of reminiscences and letters. His unique style, slightly archaic and dialectal, drawing metaphors and imagery from rural, biological, and military spheres, was an expression of his rich and fascinating personality.

BIBLIOGRAPHY

Księga pamiątkowa ku czci Stanisława Pigońa (A Commemorative Album in Honor of Stanisława Pigoń), Cracow, 1961.

POLOWANIE NA KARALUCHY (Hunting Cockroaches) (see Głowacki).

POPIÓŁ I DIAMENT (Ashes and Diamonds) (see Andrzejewski).

POPIOŁY (Ashes) (see Żeromski).

PORNOGRAFIA (see Gombrowicz).

POSITIVISM (*Pozytywizm*), or Warsaw positivism, was a period in the area of Polish literature which chronologically occupies the development of the literary talents of writers who attended the *Szkoła Główna Warszawska* (Warsaw's Main School, 1862–69). This was the generation who grew up after the abortive January Uprising of 1863 and was influenced by the multifarious complications of its outcome.

The term "positivism" was borrowed from the reigning current in philosophy, with its roots in the Enlightenment and which dominated European thought from the 1840s, beginning with Comte and continuing in France with E. Littre, and in England with H. Taine, J. S. Mill, H. Spencer, H. T. Buckle, and Charles Darwin. Positivism stood in opposition to metaphysics. Knowledge of the world was based on the examination of facts accessible to the mind, verified by empiricism. With faith in science (scientism) and in the laws of nature discovered by man, social institutions could be erected (determinism and evolution). This generation of Poles, maturing after the abortive January Uprising, sought support and a theoretical base in positivism for the programs they put forward under the new political situation, aimed at rebuilding a social-economic structure for the nation. They attempted to direct the nation toward a democratic bourgeoisie and to strengthen and modernize the country's economy. The philosophy of positivism was developed in spite of the fact that conditions in the kingdom were less than auspicious. A. Świętochowski was the first to liquidate old habits of thoughts. J. Ochorowicz, with the courage of youth, tried to continue, and even improve upon, the work of Comte (*Wstęp i pogląd ogólny na filozofię pozytywną* [A Foreword and Overall View of Positive Philosophy], 1872). Polish views of positivism were marked by agnosticism and anticlericalism, a sweeping understanding of liberalism and utilitarianism, and a desire to attain happiness through the cult of work and knowledge, which became the basis for the development of education. The emancipation of women was also part of the program. Contact with Europe was an essential element in the development of a new model of a Pole, active socially and within the economic sphere. Literature took an active part in the process.

Concerning the term "positivism" unanimity of opinion does not exist, even though its social profile is distinct and despite the fact that the movement is precisely localized (the Polish Kingdom) and its dating from the Uprising of 1863 is unchallenged. The term presents certain complications, since the development of literature in Europe differs from the Polish current. Its dominant trends (realism and naturalism in prose, Parnassism in poetry) did not exist in Poland. The first to employ the term was W. Feldman* in his handbooks published between the two world wars. After 1945, Kazimierz Wyka* argued for the use of the term and proved that the movement was strictly Polish and did not appear in other countries. It is true that some of the writers involved in the movement (P. Chmielowski and B. Prus) began to employ the term "realistic literature" in the latter phase of its development. Today's critics (Kulczycka-Saloni, Ładyka, Markiewicz, etc.) have returned to the use of the term "positivism."

Although the date for its beginnings has not been questioned, the ending of the period presents some problems. Most young scholars would agree with Feldman that the movement ended in 1881, with the collapse of social and political programs. Some argue that the latter phase of the movement coincides with the beginning of *Młoda Polska* (Young Poland)—1890, and the beginning of modernism.

J. Supiński, the founder of the Polish School of Economics, is considered the leading theorist of the movement. In literature, J. I. Kraszewski* was one of the chief precursors of positivism. T. T. Jeż and, to a lesser degree, J. Korzeniowski* also introduced themes in their works that would be later developed by the positivists.

According to Janina Kulczycka-Saloni, during the early phase of the movement few writers appeared. Most of the members of the movement were theorists, publicists, and activists. In their ideological declarations these young people showed an interest in Western European literature but concentrated more on the philosophical currents of positivism. They were more interested in building a social-national program than a literary one. This included modernizing agriculture, introducing industrialization and urbanization, and blaming the nobility and gentry for the backwardness of the country. They demanded the supremacy of the common man and failed to see that a new day was dawning, that of class conflicts among the capitalists and workers that unfolded in the late nineteenth century.

A number of studies appeared defining the new literature: A. Wyślicki's *Groch na ścianę* (Peas on the Wall, 1868), E. Orzeszkowa's* *Kilka uwag nad powieścią* (A Few Comments on the Novel, 1866) and *Listy o literaturze* (Letters About Literature, 1873), P. Chmielowski's* *Nienormalność w literaturze* (Abnormality in Literature, 1872) and *Utylitaryzm w literaturze* (Utilitarianism in Literature, 1872). The new hero of this literature, instead of being a Romantic, lonely eccentric, was going to be a workingman. The writers of these early novels concentrated on the idea of "a healthy mind" (*zdrowa myśl*). This utilitarian literature served a function of educating society in the ways of the new social order. The novel, considered to be the ideal instrument to carry out this program, became the prime means of expressing the positivists' views. The young writers avoided drama and poetry, not appreciating the propagandistic value of these genres. In fact, the young writers went so far as to attack lyric poets. Their literary program was narrow and tendentious, in both prose and poetry.

Disenchantment with this sort of literature became manifest in the seventies and the eighties, with the development of French naturalism (Emil Zola), Scandinavian literature (Ibsen), and Russian realism (Turgenev, Dostoevsky, Tolstoy, and Saltykov-Schedrin). The older and more mature generation of positivists began to shape a new social and literary program. Unfortunately, the new social program was merely an attempt to fuse old ideas onto changing conditions. On the other hand, the new literary program, outlined in numerous articles and speeches by Orzeszkowa,* Prus,* Sygietyński, and Stanisław Witkiewicz,* endeavored both to generalize the experiences of the writers and to offer postulates for the future of literature. A thin line existed between the writer and the scholar. The work of the writer was often identified with the work of the scholar, as it was in France with Taine and the Goncourt brothers. Two stages of the writer's process were differentiated: the intellectual preparation in general and the gathering of material through observation and incorporation of it into the basic structure of the novel (Prus fashioned a theory based on these stages).

In practice the writers sought historical themes, although historical writing was frowned upon, since, according to the theorists, it was impossible to paint a true and accurate picture of the past. Orzeszkowa* became interested in Jewish themes (*Mirtala,* 1886), and Prus* attempted to capture the past of Egypt in *Faraon* (The Pharaoh, 1895). Opposing the theories of the positivists, Henryk Sienkiewicz* attacked scientism in novels in his works, *Listy o Zoli* (Letters About Zola, 1893) and *O naturaliźmie w powieści* (About Naturalism in the Novel, 1881). His advice to Polish writers was to "climb upward" (*pieli się wzwyż*) "in their not inconsiderable labor for strengthening hearts" (*w trudzie niemałym dla pokrzepienia serc*).

The positivists' attitude toward the past is an area not quite clearly delineated. It involves their views of the Enlightenment and their relationship toward their fathers (Romanticism) and their grandfathers (invoking the ideas of Staszic and Śniadecki). The most difficult area of controversy involved the positivists' attitude toward the great Romantics. They first criticized the poetry of the three great national poets: Mickiewicz,* Słowacki,* and Krasiński.* Their first program was antithetical toward Romanticism. Their ideas were never clearly stated, and their program failed because of their own subjectivity and because of censorship. After the revolution of 1905–7, the positivists confessed their debt to the great Romantics: Prus* to Mickiewicz,* Sienkiewicz* to Słowacki,* and Orzeszkowa* to Krasiński.*

The most important representatives of the theories of positivism were Świętochowski and Chmielowski. The panoply of poets and writers is impressive: Prus, Orzeszkowa,* Sienkiewicz,* Asnyk,* Konopnicka,* W. Gomulicki, A. Dygasiński,* and A. Sygietyński. They were all associated with Warsaw, although some, like Orzeszkowa, lived elsewhere (Grodno). Nevertheless, their works were all published in Warsaw. They published widely in weeklies (*Niwa* [Soil]) and monthlies (*Ateneum*). A number of them published in the weekly *Kraj* (Country), which first appeared in Petersburg in 1882, aimed at Poles living in Russia. Other areas of Poland had representatives of positivism, for example, J. Lam* in Lvov, I. Gumplowicz in Cracow, and E. Callier and W. Olendzki in Poznań.

A number of other writers were connected with positivism. During the latter phase of the movement the young began to attack their elders. Sienkiewicz* was bitterly attacked by S. Brzozowski,* S. Przybyszewski,* and W. Nałkowski. Prus was unfairly vilified by C. Jellent and L. Winiarski.

It is true that the optimism and vigor of their early programs were somewhat toned down in the later writing of the positivists; nonetheless, the basic tenets of the program can be detected in these writings. The heroes in Prus's* *Lalka* (The Doll) and Orzeszkowa's* *Nad Niemnen* (On the Bank of the Niemen) do not possess the uncomplicated optimism of the young positivists; however, they hold on to their belief in progress—the work of man armed with modern learning and the future of the nation assured through results of labor consciously executed to attain desired results in the social, economic, and cultural spheres.

Although almost all areas of literature were represented by the positivists, including the lyrical epic (Konopnicka) and philosophical lyricism (Asnyk), it is in the novel that the positivists triumphed. Sienkiewicz, Prus, and Orzeszkowa gained world renown. Their works share a permanent place in Polish and world literature. It is to them that almost every Polish novelist owes a debt.

BIBLIOGRAPHY

Dramat mieszczański epoki pozytywizmu warszawskiego (Bourgeois Drama During the Epoch of Warsaw Positivism), edited by T. Sivert, Wrocław, 1953.

W. Feldman, *Współczesna literatura polska (1864–1907)* (Contemporary Polish Literature 1864–1907), Warsaw, 1919.
J. Krzyżanowski, *W kręgu wielkich realistów* (In the Circle of Great Realists), Cracow, 1962.
J. Kulczycka-Saloni, *Pozytywizm* (Positivism), Warsaw, 1971.

POTOCKI, JAN (1761–1815), a historian, traveler, and prose writer, wrote exclusively in French. Descended from a magnate family, brought up in Switzerland and France, he absorbed the ideas of the French Enlightenment. When he returned to Poland, he became a member of the Four Years Diet (1888–92) and the founder of a publishing firm, which published religious writings of a publicistic nature. Known for his extravagant life-style, he once flew in a balloon with Blanchard in 1790. He traveled throughout Germany, Turkey, Egypt, Holland, Morocco, the Caucassus, and Mongolia. He studied the early history of the Slavs, arguing for the first time for the indigenous origin of the Slavonic tribes. He also worked on the chronology of the oldest epochs in general history. All of his writings were published in French. In literature he is known for his travel reports and his one-act play *Recueil de Parades* (*Parady* [Parades], staged in 1792; published in 1793; Polish translation in *Dialog,* 1958). According to Leszek Kukulski, these ironic, grotesque, and parodistic pieces introduced motives and characters from comedia dell'arte. His novel *Manuscript trouve à Saragosse* (A Manuscript Discovered in Saragossa, written during 1803–15; published during 1805–14; Polish translation in 1847) resembles the stories in *A Thousand and One Nights* with its Eastern flavor and structure. It contains a number of stories, which occur at various times and in exotic places; they are linked together in a very complex manner. The story takes place in 1739 in the mountains of Andalusia, where the hero is involved in the mysterious affairs of the Maur family of Gomelez. The novel contains elements of the Gothic and picaresque novels, but it is also a fictionized presentation of philosophical views. Potocki presents himself as a student of the French "Encyclopedists," arguing against an illuminative view of religion, and for cognitive sensualism, ontological materialism, and hedonist ethics. Even with its intellectual complexity, the novel has remained attractive to readers. It has been translated into numerous languages and was made into a film by Wojciech Has in 1965.

BIBLIOGRAPHY

Rękopis znaleziony w Saragossie (A Manuscript Found in Saragossa), edited by Leszek Kukulski, Warsaw: Czytelnik, 1965.
Podróże (Travels), edited by Leszek Kukulski, Warsaw: Czytelnik, 1959.

English

The Saragossa Manuscript: A Collection of Weird Tales, edited by Roger Caillois, translated from French by Elisabeth Abbott, New York: Orion Press, 1960; New York: Avon, 1960; London: Cassell, 1962; London: Icon Books, 1966.

New Decameron (Further Tales of the Saragossa Manuscript), translated by Elisabeth Abbott, New York: Orion Press, Grossman, 1966.

POTOCKI, WACŁAW (1621–96), a poet, was descended from an Aryan family and spent all his life farming on his family estate, at times holding various local offices.

According to Leszek Kukulski, he started writing under the inspiration of the Aryan brotherhood, utilizing their favorite genres: didactic poems, religious songs, and versified tales based on biblical and historical themes (e.g., *Judyta* [Judith], written in 1652, and *Wirginia* [Virginia], written in 1652). Both works were published in 1911. After the Aryans were banished from Poland in 1658, he was forced to become a Catholic and continued his literary work in solitude. He developed his epic output, writing long romances in verse: *Syloret, albo Prawdziwy abrys po ciężkim straconych synów żalu . . . wesela* (A True Sketch of Grief After the Heavy Loss of Sons . . . of a Wedding, written in 1674–91; published in 1764) and *Historia o Argenidzie, królewnie sycylijskiej* (The History of Argenida, the Sicilian Princess, published in 1697), both based on foreign sources (adapted from a work by J. Barclay). After the abdication of King Jan Kazimierz, he returned to public life, seeking salvation for his country in the old knightly virtues of the *szlachta* (nobility) during the Renaissance. He expressed these ideas in his greatest heroic epic, *Transakcja wojny chocimskiej* (Transactions of the Chocim War), written in 1670 on the fiftieth anniversary of the victory over the Turks in the battle of Chocim in 1621. It is almost a chronicle of the war; the author's comments and ideas are expounded in numerous digressions. The poem is deeply patriotic and praises former Polish bravado, especially that of the commander of the army, J. K. Chodkiewicz. A continuation of these themes can be found in a series of publicistic poems written during the period 1672–78 which commemorate the virtues and military successes of Jan Sobieski. In the seventies his home in Łużna became the center of social life, reflected in numerous convivial poems written during this period and later included in the collection *Ogród fraszek* (Garden of Trifles). He also wrote a number of poems commemorating local holidays, and a few lengthy romances in verse, based on Neo-Latin texts, for example, *Historia Florydana z Lidią* (The History of Floridan and Lidie, published in 1953). In subsequent years he wrote mostly religious works, most of which have been lost. He also mourned the death of his two sons and a daughter in a series of poems. Near the end of his life he was working on two major collections: *Ogród fraszek* (Garden of Trifles), first published in its entirety in 1907, which presents a unique colorful image of everyday life, language, and traditions of the nobility. A work of a somewhat different character is *Moralia,* published during the period 1915–18. Modeling his work on Erasmus of Rotterdam's *Adagrach,* Potocki here created a collection of poetic and moral reflections (the titles of several works are maxims or proverbs). In this collection he transmits his own genealogical life experiences; he views the fate of his country with patriotic concern; with a severe, mythic gaze, he embraces the entire gentry society. The work provides a link between the Renaissance and the Enlightenment traditions regarding social criticism.

Potocki's enormous literary output, which generally remained unpublished during his lifetime and appeared in print only in the nineteenth and twentieth centuries, gives him a significant position in the literature of the Baroque, as an admirer and also a critic of the traditions of the *szlachta*.

(See Baroque.)

BIBLIOGRAPHY

Dzieła (Works), Volumes 1–3, edited by Leszek Kukulski, introduction by Barbara Otwinowska, Warsaw, 1987.

POTOP (The Deluge) (see Sienkiewicz).

POWRÓT POSŁA (The Return of the Envoy) (see Niemcewicz).

POWRÓT Z GWIAZD (Return from the Stars) (see Lem).

POŻEGNANIE Z MARIA (Farewell to Maria) (see Borowski).

PROFESSOR TUTKA (see Szaniawski).

PRÓCHNO (Dry Rot) (see Berent).

PRUS, BOLESŁAW (Aleksander Głowacki) (1847–1912), a novelist, short story writer, and publicist, early became an orphan and was brought up by his relatives in Puławy, later in Lublin. He took part in the January Uprising of 1863, was wounded, and found himself in a hospital and, subsequently, in prison. Later he entered *Szkoła Główna* (the Warsaw Main School), but never completed his education, although he continued studying on his own and never stopped dreaming about working in the sciences.

He made his literary debut with a series of letters (1864), humorous pieces (1866), and a popular treatise on electricity (1872). In 1872 he began signing his "unimportant" works with the pseudonym "Bolesław Prus." He continued writing for the press, the ill-famed *Mucha* (Fly), *Kolce* (Thorns), and *Niwa* (Soil), for which he wrote as a feuilletonist. In 1874 he published the first part of his *Szkice warszawskie* (Warsaw Sketches) in *Kurier Warszawski* (The Warsaw Courier). On March 23, 1875, he began his cycle of sketches *Kroniki* (Chronicles) in *The Warsaw Courier*, which made him one of the best publicists in Poland. He wrote continuously through 1887 (with a break of ten months in 1882–83). He also wrote for *Ateneum* and

Nowiny (Newsbits). He became the chief editor of the latter in 1882 and attempted to make the paper into a center of knowledge for contemporary Polish society. He wanted to use scientific, not journalistic, methods but did not succeed, and *Nowiny* went bankrupt a year later. Prus returned to the *Courier* and postponed his literary plans. During this period he developed his own theory of literature, in particular the novel (his views are scattered in various writings). He considered the main task of the novelist to discover new human types and draw attention to important sociological processes. For Prus, the novelist's mission was to observe and systematize factual knowledge and also design "plans," which relied on the writer's intuition. In 1882 he became a regular visitor to the spa Nałęczów, where he had earlier started a novel in 1880, *Nasza Placówka* (Our Outpost). During his years as a publicist he composed a number of short stories and made several attempts at writing a novel, for example, *Dusze w niewoli* (Souls in Bondage, 1877). Among his first "independent" pieces are humorous stories—*To i owo* (This and That, 1873); *Kłopoty babuni* (Granny's Worries, 1874); his first story on social themes, *Lokator poddasza* (The Attic's Lodger, 1875), which already reveals the main features of Prus's writings—an interest in the "simple man," a belief in his moral values, and the ability to move the reader. In the same year he also published *Pałac i rudera* (The Palace and the Hovel). *Sieroca dola* (An Orphan's Fate) and *Sukienka balowa* (A Ball Dress) were published in 1876. These works were influenced by the masters of the European novel, above all, Dickens.

According to Janina Kulczycka-Saloni, Prus came to maturity with *Przygoda Stasia* (Stanley's Adventure, 1879) and *Anielka* (Angela, 1880). His nonconformist view of social conflicts was adumbrated in *Powracająca fala* (A Returning Wave, 1880). These were quickly followed by *Michałko* (1880), *Nawrócony* (The Reformed One, 1881), *Katarynka* (Hurdy-Gurdy, 1881), *Antek* (1881), *Kamizelka* (The Vest, 1882), and the short story *On* (He, 1882), portraying Bismarck and his political games with masterful accuracy. In 1883 he published *Milknące głosy* (Hushed Voices), one of very few patriotic texts, and a little masterpiece, *Grzechy dzieciństwa* (Sins of Childhood, 1883). He became aware that his work as a journalist interfered with his artistic plans, and he tried to keep within certain limits. He continued writing *Kroniki* (Chronicles), not only for the *Courier* but for other papers. In the fall of 1884 he met Witkiewicz Senior* and, thanks to his efforts, became involved with the weekly *Wędrowiec* (The Rover), a periodical advocating naturalism in art. His new contacts greatly influenced Prus's aesthetic views. His short novels, *Przy księżycu* (By the Moon) and *Podwójny człowiek* (A Double Man) and *Placówka* (The Outpost), his first naturalistic novel, were all published in *The Rover*. His short novels and short stories were gathered in the volumes *Pierwsze opowiadania* (First Stories, 1881) and *Szkice i obrazki* (Sketches and Pictures, 1885). He remained a lively and, at times, an offensive publicist. He also published *Szkic* *programowy w warunkach obecnego rozwoju społeczeństwa* (A Programmatic Sketch Under the Conditions of Present Development of Society, 1883), in which he presented a program that adapted the sociology of Spencer to the situation in Poland.

The period between 1885 and 1897 marked the zenith of Prus's literary achievement. In 1885 he published *Cienie* (Shadows) and a study about Farys, followed by his four great novels, *Placówka* (The Outpost, 1886), which appeared to be a revelation in its presentation of the Polish peasant—objective and without idealization, but with respect for his instinctive patriotism and moral standard; *Lalka* (The Doll, 1890); *Emancypantki* (Emancipated Women, 1894), a novel about the role of women in social and professional life in the 1880s, set against a realistic picture of Warsaw and the provinces; and *Faraon* (The Pharaoh, 1897), his only historical novel, which presented a comprehensive image of ancient Egypt, the mechanics of power, and the struggle to change a system. These novels are major achievements in the history of the realistic novel in Poland.

In 1895 Prus traveled to Germany, Switzerland, and France. Upon his return he assumed work as a publicist but had more and more problems reaching his readers. At the turn of the century he devoted much of his time to social work. He wrote very little and was less successful: *Widzenie* (Vision, 1900), *Ze wspomnień cyklisty* (From the Remembrances of a Cyclist, 1903), and *Wojna i praca* (War and Work, 1907). In 1901 he published *Najogólniejsze ideały życiowe* (The Most General Living Ideals), his only attempt at giving a synthesis of his theoretical views, but the book was received rather coldly. His temperament as a publicist reawakened as a result of the Russian-Japanese War and the Revolution of 1905–7. In his novel *Dzieci* (Children), set against the background of the 1905 Russian Revolution, he returned to his earlier views of the young generation—their vivid political interests and feeble social awareness. His work on the novel *Przemiany* (Metamorphoses) was interrupted by his death.

Prus determined the path of the development of one of the main trends in Polish literature—realism; being sensitive to social problems, he inspired the interests of Żeromski,* Reymont,* and Dąbrowska.* He will also remain respected for his passionate social activism.

Lalka (definitive edition, 1890) was defined by Prus as giving an accurate picture of "Polish idealists against the background of social decay." The setting of *Lalka* is Warsaw. The plot is constructed on two levels: the events during the years 1878–79 describe the unhappy love of a Warsaw merchant of *szlachta* (noble) origin, Stanisław Wokulski, for the impoverished aristocrat Izabela Łęcka, his struggle to become rich in order to win her, his engagement, his loss of illusions and attempted suicide, and, finally, his ambiguous disappearance. The theme is presented from the point of view of a putative author (perhaps Prus himself)—objective, but full of inner tension. The second level contains the memoirs of the old salesman, a Romantic, a soldier with a love of Napoleon, Ignacy Rzecki, Wokulski's friend. His story seems only chaotically related, but in fact the good-hearted chatter and naive philosophy of the old soldier serve an important function, that of recounting the social and political roots of the two heroes (especially Wokulski's participation in the January Uprising), enriching the sociological portrait of Warsaw and revealing the essence of Wokulski's tragedy. The fragments involving Napoleon's Hungarian campaign are considered a masterpiece of descriptions of battle scenes. Because of the double narrative structure, Prus achieved an in-depth temporal perspective and a comprehensive view of the social background. The two heroes are not only highly individualized personalities but representatives of their social environment. Prus was able to overcome the earlier patterns of the positivist novel: Wokulski and Rzecki are people who were formed during the period of Romanticism but live in the new epoch.

The characters of *Lalka* represent a broad picture of Poland's social classes: the aristocracy and the *szlachta*—selfish, morally empty, dull, and degenerate; the middle class, soaked in inertia; and the simple folk dying in poverty. A separate group includes the Jewish middle class; the image is supplemented by portraits of the first Polish Socialists. The novel depicts the anachronous social structure, which blocks the development of the young; it signals the helplessness of the positivist program, of creative individuals, who are made impotent by the enslavement of the nation and the idleness and selfishness of its leaders. Such a view is characteristic of the feelings of disappointment which appeared in the works of most of the outstanding positivists after the period of youthful enthusiasm (referred to as critical realism). *Lalka* combines the features of both the social and the psychological novel and is regarded as a classic in both genres. An important role, however, is also attributed to other elements of this bittersweet story; satire, its historical background, and even echoes of science fiction. One of its characteristic features is its humor, in the spirit of Dickens.

The novel was first received without a great deal of enthusiasm. It was recognized as a classic by the younger generation of critics (e.g., Nałkowska*). It is now considered a masterpiece, the best Polish novel in its artistic perfection and intellectual depth, the most European of Polish novels. It has been translated into every major language, adapted for the theater, filmed, and made into a television series.

(See Positivism and *Młoda Polska*.)

BIBLIOGRAPHY

Pisma (Writings), Volumes 1–29, Warsaw, 1948–52, I. Chrzanowski and Z. Szweykowski.

Z. Szweykowski, *Twórczość Bolesława Prusa*, second edition, Warsaw, 1972.

English

The Doll (Lalka), translated by David Welsh, New York: Twayne Publishers, 1972; New York: Hippocrene, 1972.

Pharaoh (Faraon), translated by Mary de Mankowski, New York: Abbey Press, 1901 (abridged).
The Pharaoh and the Priest: A Historical Novel of Ancient Egypt, translated by Jeremiah Curtin, Boston: Little, Brown, 1902; London: Samson Low, Maraton, 1910.
Ten Morgs of Land (Placówka), translated by Christine Rockover Eastus, Austin, Texas: Castus Publishers, 1957.

PRUSZYŃSKI, KSAWERY (1907–50), a prose writer and journalist, studied law at the Jagiellonian University, then worked as a journalist. He was a war correspondent in the Spanish Civil War in 1936 (coverage published in *W Czerwonej Hiszpanii* [In Red Spain], 1937). During World War II he fought at Narvik and Falaise; he spent 1941–42 in Moscow, as the cultural attaché of the Polish Embassy. After his return in 1945 he remained with the diplomatic service (Washington, The Hague) and also worked for the journal *Odrodzenie* (Rebirth). He lost his life in an automobile accident. Having been brought up in the cultural tradition of the gentry, he gradually evolved from conservative views toward political and social radicalism, assuming an original and critical position, displaying political realism, a journalistic temper, and erudite tendencies. His best known collections of journalistic pieces are the following: *Sarajewo, Szanghaj, Gdańsk* (Sarajevo, 1914; Shanghai, 1932; Gdańsk, 1932); *Palestyna po raz trzeci* (Palestine for the Third Time, 1933) and *Podróż po Polsce* (Travels Through Poland, 1937). In his polemic writings *Księga ponurych niedopowiedzeń* (A Book of Gloomy Unfinished Conversations, 1941) and *1000 mil od prawdy* (1000 Miles from the Truth, 1941) he opposed the version of the campaign of September 1939 which was circulated among emigrant circles. He also published two brochures in English, *Poland Fights Back* (1941) and *The Polish Invasion* (1941), and a cycle of articles, *The Russian Year* (1944).

He began his literary work during the war. His writings combine fiction and fact, characterized by narrative vigor and vivid, beautiful language. Contrary to the sober tone of his journalistic pieces, his literary works were inspired by history in which he sought consolation and attempted to reassure the reader. Among his writings are a novel, *Droga wiodła przez Narvik* (The Road Led Through Narvik, 1941), published in Poland in 1945, and collections of stories, *Trzynaście opowieści* (Thirteen Stories, 1946) and *Karabela z Meschedu* (The Curved Sword from Mesched, 1948), in which he depicted the fate of Polish soldiers who fought outside their country during World War II.

BIBLIOGRAPHY

Wybór pism publicystycznych (A Selection of Publicist Writings), Volumes 1–2, introduction by Kazimierz Wyka, Cracow, 1966.

English

Adam Mickiewicz, The Life Story of the Greatest Polish Poet, London: Fore, 1950; London: Polish Cultural Institute, 1955.
Poland Fights Back, translated by Peter Jordan, London: Hodder and Stoughton, 1941; New York: Roy, 1944.
Polish Invasion, London: Minerva, 1941.
Russian Year, New York: Roy, 1944.

PRZEDWIOŚNIE (Early Spring) (see Żeromski).

PRZESMYCKI, Z. ("Miriam") (see Norwid and *Młoda Polska*).

PRZYBOŚ, JULIAN (1901–70), a poet and essay writer, served as a foot soldier in the Polish-Soviet War in 1920, studied Polish philology at the Jagiellonian University, then later worked as a teacher. His stay in France (1937–39) acquainted him with European art. During the war he first lived in Lvov; then, after being arrested and released, he hid in his native village, Gwoźnica, and lived as a farmer. After the war he worked for the weekly *Odrodzenie* (Rebirth). He was a member of the first National Council, president of the Polish Writers' Union *(ZLP),* and later director of the Jagiellonian Library in Cracow. From 1945 he was a member of the Communist Party, from which he resigned in 1958. After 1955 he worked for *Przegląd Kulturalny* (The Cultural Review), *Poezja* (Poetry), and *Miesięcznik Literacki* (The Literary Monthly). He received numerous literary awards during his career.

His early poetry dates back to 1916, but he considered his real debut the poem *Cieśle* (Carpenters), published in 1922 in *Skamander.* He soon became one of the most outstanding representatives of the Cracow avant-garde, publishing to 1922 numerous polemic and programmatic articles in *Zwrotnica* (Switch) and *Linia* (Line). During 1929–30 he contributed to *L'Art contemporain* in Paris. During the period 1930–35 he worked with W. Strzemiński and was associated with the Łódź group "*a.r.*" (revolutionary artists). His first two collections *Śruby* (Screws, 1925) and *Oburącz* (With Both Hands, 1926) praised the modern way of life, called for a collective effort, and vividly portrayed the heroes of the "new world" (workers, pilots). He saw his role as that of a worker sweating over words. He wanted to derive modern poetry from modern technology, employing principles of economy and functionalism (departure from traditional meter, ellipsis and metaphor, motives of the wheel, electric current, and motion).

According to Stanisław Jaworski, Przyboś's poetic development can be traced to two overlapping phases: 1930–50 and 1940–70. The volumes *Z ponad* (From the Beyond, 1930) and *W głąb lasu* (In the Depth of the Forest, 1932) inaugurated his artistic maturity. He became obsessed with nature, the landscape, and eroticism, disappointed with urban civilization and social reality. His poetic ego was in opposition to the world and his creative will. He achieved his goal through the so-called creative trope, which presented objects as if created within the difficult process of visual perception. His recurring theme is an exploration of the present emotional attitude of the ego in relation to past experiences. External dynamism was transformed into internal activity. The principles of functionalism make him exploit the ambiguity of words (which later inspired his so-called linguistic poetry). His collection *Równanie serca* (Equation of the Heart, 1938) introduced a social perspective: the conviction of the inevitable collapse of the current order, the belief in a better future, contrasting the values of Western civilization with the labor and values of a simple man. In the collections published in the thirties, Przyboś's poetic style evolved its final form: based on ellipsis and metaphor, characterized by the so-called explosive trope, emphasizing the energy potentially present in objects and phenomena (e.g., "the unexploded roar of the stones"). Przyboś's position in literature was further confirmed by the collections *Póki my żyjemy* (So Long As We Live, 1944) and *Miejsce na ziemi* (A Place on Earth, 1945), which are manifestos of the inner independence of a man and an artist against the background of the horrors of war. In the postwar years Przyboś seemed to accept a new poetics—his poetry became more communicative, more in the form of "narrative": his rebellious stand evolved into a more affirmative and didactic position. He returned to the theme of work in *Najmniej słów* (The Fewest Words, 1955). In his later works (*Narzędzie ze światła* [Instruments of Light], 1958; *Próba całości* [Test of the Whole], 1961; *Więcej o manifest* [More About the Manifesto], 1963; *Na znak* [On the Mark], 1965; and *Kwiat nieznany* [Unknown Flower], 1968), he emphasized the theme of his own identity and individuality, against the background of his childhood memories, employing versified polemics on current topics.

Along with his poetic writings, Przyboś also published articles and essays on poetry and other forms of art, commentaries on his own works, and polemic texts. In the period between the wars he formulated the theory of functionalism and developed the categories of image and vision. After the war (*Linia i gwar* [Line and Chatter], 1963; *Sens poetycki* [Poetic Sense], 1967) he was mainly concerned with justifying the call for innovativeness in art, at the same time reinterpreting various motives from the Polish cultural tradition, mainly that of Romanticism (*Czytając Mickiewicza* [Reading Mickiewicz], 1950; enlarged edition, 1956). He was interested in literary folklore and provided materials concerning his own biography and work. He also worked on the theory of Polish twentieth century lyrical writings and literature. He was a reviewer and critic (he coined the term "turpism": see Grochowiak), as well as a translator of over a dozen languages.

(See Contemporary Polish Literature.)

BIBLIOGRAPHY

Poezje zebrane (Collected Poetry), Warsaw, 1959.

Pisma zebrane (Collected Works), Volume 1, *Utwory poetyckie* (Poetical Works), introduction by J. Kwiatkowski, Cracow, 1984.

PRZYBYSZEWSKA, STANISŁAWA (pseudonym Andree Lynee) (1901–35), was chiefly a playwright. A teacher by education, she worked in a school while studying philosophy. She moved in 1922 to Warsaw, where she became involved with the Communist Party of Poland and was arrested because of her connections with the group. Released in 1923, she moved to Gdańsk. Her interests were completely centered on literature and painting. She lived in isolation, expressing her thoughts in letters that she wrote during her lifetime (*Listy* [Letters], edited by T. Lewandowski, 1978). She published a few articles and fragments of her plays. She was chiefly interested in political and social problems. Her works, an original style combining dramatic chronicle with intellectual discussion in which the different arguments of the heroes collide, present historical processes and the lives of outstanding personalities who shape the course of history. Certain analogies link Przybyszewska's dramas with late German Romanticism (G. Buechner) and stage works of Romain Rolland. The French Revolution absorbed her almost exclusively. She presented the theme, pondering over the sense and mechanism of revolution in her finest drama: *Dziewięćdziesiąty trzeci* (The Ninety-Third), adapted for television in 1969, presents a family disaster caused by the revolution; *Sprawa Dantona* (The Danton Affair), fragments of which appeared in 1929 and 1930, was staged in 1931, and later in 1961. Translated into German, English, Russian, and Italian, the play was made into a film by Andrzej Wajda in 1982. A remarkable piece of writing, it is devoted to the political struggle within the revolutionary party. *Thermidor,* originally written in German and translated into Polish by S. Helsztyński, was first staged in 1971. The play explores the collapse of a dictatorship as a result of a clash between political principles and social changes. Her novelette, *Ostatnie noce Ventose'a* (The Final Nights of Ventose, 1958), which is constructed in great part as an inner monologue of Robespierre, complements *Sprawa Dantona.* In her prose writings she emphasized the economic and social problems of the twentieth century against the background of melodramatic plots. She wrote several novels (e.g., *Twórczość Gerarda Gasztowta* [The Creative Works of Gerard Gasztowt]), several short novels, and short stories. Her works can be found in the archives of the Polish Academy of Sciences in Poznań. They were practically unknown during her lifetime. Contemporary criticism accords Przybyszewska a higher place in literature than her famous father, Stanisław Przybyszewski. Her life was spent in "absolute solitude." Addicted to morphine, she sketched her tragic life in her letters—some of the saddest moments recorded by a human heart. The last years of her life were simply a living hell. She lived in a bare cell—without heat, without any human comforts. Jerzy Krasowski, the director responsible for reviving Przybyszewska's works, also produced a play based on Przybyszewska's life and letters.

BIBLIOGRAPHY

Dramaty (Dramas), edited by Roman Taborski, commentary by Jerzy Krasowski, Gdańsk, 1975.

English

The Danton Case; Thermidor (Two Plays), translated by Bolesław Taborski, introduction by Daniel Gerould, Evanston, Illinois: Northwestern University Press, 1989.

Jadwiga Kosicka and Daniel Gerould, *A Life of Solitude: Stanisława Przybyszewska: a Biographical Study with Selected Letters,* Evanston, Illinois: Northwestern University Press, 1989.

PRZYBYSZEWSKI, STANISŁAW (1868–1927), a playwright, novelist, writer of essays and prose poems, attended a German school in Toruń, then left for Berlin to study architecture and medicine. During 1892–93 he edited a Socialist paper for Polish emigrants in Berlin. His philosophical essays in German gained him a reputation in Berlin, and he soon became a friend of R. Dehmel, A. Strindberg, and E. Muench. He married a Norwegian, Dagny Juel. His name soon became well known in Germany and elsewhere in Europe. In 1898 he returned to Cracow, where he was enthusiastically received by young Polish artists. He was the editor of the leading Young Poland paper, *Życie** (Life), until 1900, when the magazine stopped appearing. The writer lived in a heightened atmosphere of scandal, due to his shocking life-style, to the profligate artists and pseudo-artists gathered around him, and to his relationship with the wife of Jan Kasprowicz,* which led to the couple's eventual separation. His heavy drinking and daring approach to eroticism in his writings were also stimuli for attacks on his character. He lived in various cities (Warsaw, Munich, Poznań, Gdańsk); in Poznań he exerted a strong influence on the expressionist group gathered around *Zdrój* (The Spring) in which he published his programmatic work *Ekspresjonizm, Słowacki i "Genesis z Ducha"* (Expressionism, Słowacki and The Genesis of "King Spirit," 1918). In his late years he worked on his memoirs, combining a self-created profile of the writer and man with interesting characteristics of the Bohemian milieu of Berlin at the end of the nineteenth century and the outstanding personalities of European literary and artistic life of this epoch.

Przybyszewski was the most militant follower and propagator of extreme modernist aestheticism, expressed in the phrase "art for art's sake." His views were primarily formed in Germany and later repeated in his manifesto *Confiteor* (1899) and other articles published in *Życie* and later gathered in the volume *Na drogach Duszy* (On the Roads of the Soul, 1900). Przybyszewski based his philosophy and artistic convictions concerning the tragic nature of man on the dichotomy of two elements: the higher one—the soul—and the lower one—the brain. The aim of a real artist was to reach the "bare soul," liberated from the ties of rationalism and sensualism. Gaining his knowledge was possible through the analysis of sex and pathological states, domains not controlled by man's consciousness. In his view, sex was the main cosmic element ("First there was desire"—*Requiem aeternam).* Przybyszewski's deterministic philosophy was largely an adaptation of Schopenhauer's views, from which he derived extremely pessimistic conclusions. He was also under the influence of Nietzsche in his individualism, in his rejection of any moral or social obligations for an artist. He radically opposed old naturalistic "cerebral" art with modernist art—an aim in itself. His contemporaries valued Przybyszewski's prose poems: *Totenmesse* (1893, published in Polish as *Requiem aeternam* in 1904), *Vigilien* (1895, published in Polish as *z cyklu Wigilii* [From the Christmas Eve Cycle,] 1899), *De profundis* (1895, published in Polish in 1900), *Nad morzem* (Beyond the Sea, 1899), and *Androgyne* (1900). The main theme in these works is eroticism, viewed both metaphysically, as a cosmic power, and pathologically, as psychic states. In accordance with the poetics of the genre, Przybyszewski employed an elevated, exalted style, modeled after the poetic prose of Zygmunt Krasiński,* which distracted the reader with the exaggeration and artificiality of the chaos of words.

Przybyszewski's novels gained considerable popularity: the trilogy *Homo sapiens* (The German version in 1895–96; the Polish version in 1901); *Satans Kinder* (1897, published in Polish as *Dzieci Szatana* [The Children of Satan], 1899); the trilogies *Synowie ziemi* (Sons of the Earth, 1904–11), *Mocny człowiek* (Mighty Man, 1912–13), and *Dzieci nędzy* (Children of Poverty, 1913–14); and *Krzyk* (The Cry, 1917). The novels revolve around the conflict between a creative individual and his environment and the destructive forces within the individual's personality. The setting is usually the life-style of the *boheme*. His novels contributed to some extent to the development of the psychological novel in Poland; however, his works never attained a permanent position in Polish literature: the language of his prose suffered from the same faults as his prose poems.

Przybyszewski also wrote numerous dramas: *Das grosse Glueck* (1897, published in Polish as *Dla szczęścia* [For the Sake of Happiness], staged in Prague in 1898 and in Cracow in 1899, published in 1900); *Złote runo* (The Golden Fleece, 1901); *Goście* (The Guests), staged in 1901 and published in 1902; *Matka* (The Mother), staged in 1902 and published in 1903; *Śnieg* (Snow), staged and published in 1903; *Odwieczna baśń* (Everlasting Fable), staged and published in 1906; *Śluby* (Marriages), staged and published in 1906; *Gody życia* (Feast of Life), staged in 1909 and published in 1910; *Topiel* (Deep Water), staged and published in 1912; *Miasto* (The City, 1914); and *Mściciel* (The Avenger), staged and published in 1927. The major conflict of the dramas is the tragic clash between eroticism and ethical standards. Przybyszewski helped overcome the restrictions on what was permissible in literature at the time. He also introduced the innovative techniques of Ibsen, Strindberg, and Maeterlinck, thus contributing greatly to the development of Polish drama. Przybyszewski summed up his experiences as a playwright in the treatise *O dramacie i scenie* (About Drama and the Stage, 1905).

Przybyszewski, the embodiment of modernistic rebellion and provocation, played an important role in the cultural life of Europe. He aroused much less interest later, but his influential role is duly recognized.

(See Positivism and *Młoda Polska*.)

BIBLIOGRAPHY

Wybór pism (Selected Writings), edited and with an introduction by Roman Taborski, Wrocław, 1966.

English

Homo-sapiens, translated by Thomas Seltzer, New York: AMS Press, 1970; New York: Alfred Knopf, 1915.

Snow (Śnieg) (play in four acts), New York: N. L. Brown, 1920.

For Happiness (Dla szczęścia) (drama in three acts), translated by Lucille Baron, *Poet Love* (a monthly magazine devoted to Shakespeare, Browning and the Comparative Study of Literature) Volume XXIII, 81–110, Boston: R. G. Badger, 1912.

The Work of Edvard Muench (four essays), Translated by Hanna Marks, Berlin: S. Fischer, 1894.

PSAŁTERZ FLORIAŃSKI (see *Psałterz Jadwigi*).

PSAŁTERZ JADWIGI or ***PSAŁTERZ FLORIAŃSKI*** (Jadwiga's Psalm Book) (see Medieval Literature).

PUŁAPKA (The Trap) (see Różewicz).

PUTRAMENT, JERZY (1910–86), a prose writer, poet, and publicist, was actively involved in the literary life of Vilnius (mainly with the group *Żagary*) during his studies of Polish philology at the University of Vilnius. He began his literary work in poetry closely linked to the avant-garde (e.g., his collection *Wczoraj powrót* [Yesterday the Return], 1935), sporadically returning to it later in *Wojna i wiosna* (War and Spring, 1944) and *Wiersze wybrane 1932–1949* (Selected Poems, 1932–49, published in 1951). During his student years he was associated with the leftist movement and the Communist Party. Having worked for various Communist papers, he was accused of disseminating Communist propaganda in the famous trial of the Dembiński group. During the war he found himself in the Soviet Union, where he was politically active as an officer of the Polish army and a journalist. After the war he became a diplomat, and the organizer of literary life. He was secretary of the Writers' Union, a member of parliament, and a member of the Politburo. He was the recipient of numerous state awards.

His main interest in literature was political—the mechanisms and objective limitations of politics and the motives of those individuals engaged in the historical process. According to T. Bujnicki, the characteristic feature of his prose is the coexistence of an empiricist stand (authenticity, autobiographism) with grotesque, caricaturelike, even brutal overemphasis on the portrayal of characters. His first novel, *Rzeczywistość* (Reality, 1947), is mostly autobiographical, based on the political trial of the young people of Vilnius. His novel *Wrzesień* (September, 1950) is a panorama of the Polish-German war of 1939 and an attempt to unmask the political background of Poland's defeat. A deeper analysis of people's behavior in light of the catastrophe of war can be found in *Święta kulo* (O, Holy Sphere, 1946). Similar motives appear in the stories published in the collections *Wypadek w Krasnymstawie* (An Accident in Krasnystav, 1957), *Puste oczy* (Empty Eyes, 1967), *Wybór opowiadań* (A Collection of Short Stories, 1972), and *Początek eposu* (The Beginning of an Epic, 1974).

Putrament devoted several works to the political changes and conflicts in contemporary Poland: *Rozstaje* (Crossroads, 1954), *Pasierbowie* (The Stepsons, 1963), *Małowierni* (Those of Little Faith, 1967), and *Bołdyn* (1969). Closely connected with these novels are those presenting the "behind the scenes" of international politics of the period during the cold war: *Arka Noego* (Noah's Ark, 1961) and *Akropol* (Acropolis, 1975); the documentary report of Hitler's assassination, *20 lipca* (20 July, 1974); and the psychological novels, *Odyniec* (The Boar, 1964) and *Puszcza* (The Wilderness, 1966), in which politics dramatize the personal lives of the characters. Putrament's publicistic writings are also an important part of his output: *Na literackim froncie* (On the Literary Front, 1953), *Notatki polemiczne* (Polemical Notes, 1956), *Kronika obyczajów* (The Chronicle of Customs, 1959), *Kącik laika* (A Layman's Corner, 1964), *Być sobą* (A Good Man, 1968), and *W stylu dowolnym* (In a Free Style, 1971). He also published reports of his travels: *Notatnik chiński* (Chinese Notes, 1952), *Dwa łyki Ameryki* (Two Gulps of America, 1956), and *Na drogach Indii* (On the Road to India, 1967). These are complemented by stories displaying the writer's love of nature, his affection for the Mazurian district, and his passion for fishing: *Trzynasty z Wesołka* (Thirteen from Wesołek, 1957), *Arkadia* (Arcadia, 1961), *Z wędką przez trzy kontynenty* (With a Fishing Pole Across Three Continents, 1968), *Krajobrazy* (Landscapes,

1968), and *Balet boleni* (Ballet of Pain, 1974). His memoirs, *Pół wieku* (A Half-Century, Parts 1–7, 1961–80), provide an interesting personal commentary on his life and his literary works.

Bołdyn, a novel, takes place during the Nazi occupation, within a Communist guerrilla group in northeast Poland. The hardships of life and the struggles in the forest form the background of this study of the human psyche overburdened with power and responsibility. The nature and results of the burden are determined by the character of the main hero—Roman Bołdyn, a simple man, who has attained his high position through his courage and talent. He eventually becomes the hero of folk legends. His success, however, is also the root of his defeat. Insecure in his position and less certain of judgment, he becomes alienated, distrustful, and suspicious. His personality affects the entire group, who are caught up in a net of lies and false pretenses, which almost result in catastrophe. Bołdyn is killed in combat, but his legend survives as an independent entity.

(See Contemporary Polish Literature.)

BIBLIOGRAPHY

Pisma (Works), Warsaw, 1979.

Q

QUO VADIS? (see Sienkiewicz).

R

REDLIŃSKI, EDWARD (see Contemporary Polish Literature).

REJ, MIKOŁAJ, OF NAGŁOWICE (pseudonyms including Ambroży Korczbork Rożek) (1505–69), a poet, prose writer, and translator, was the first outstanding representative of Renaissance literature in Poland. He was descended from a noble family. He attended schools in Skalmierz and Lvov and spent a year as a student in Cracow. His life is known to us through the biography added to *Zwierciadło* (The Looking Glass), supposedly written by A. Trzecieski, who presented Rej as an advocate of the Reformation, championing the principles of Renaissance ethics. In the minds of generations that followed, however, the image of Rej as a simpleminded man, without an education, more of a rebel than a serious statesman, grew into a myth. However, as a courtier in the magnate family of Tęczyński, he certainly must have acquired great culture and knowledge, even through self-education.

An excellent farmer, he amassed a substantial estate (he was a founder of two small towns, Rejowiec and Oksza). He was also a political man, a member of parliament and a highly respected one, often repaid for his work by the king in the form of new villages and estates. In his political views he sided with the "executionists," who argued for limiting the rights of the magnates and the clergy and for developing a more democratic *szlachta* (nobility) society. Refusing to accept local offices, he was a religious activist of the Reformation movement, founder of new Calvinist schools and churches, writer of sermons (*Postylla Pańska,* 1557 [Postilla], 1557) and of numerous nonreligious texts ridiculing the Roman Catholic Church. His Catholic opponents repaid him in kind, presenting him as a monstrous glutton and heavy drinker. Rej is still referred to as the "father of Polish literature"; he certainly deserves the epithet, if only for the broadness of his talent. He had an innate love of knowledge of the world and of all people; he read texts in Latin and then shared his knowledge with others in the vernacular, adapting the texts he had read to his didactic purpose, seldom giving credit to writers or heeding the law of copyright. A gallery of great humanists and Classical writers appear in the works "adapted" by Rej. He freely moved from one literary genre to another, modernizing old medieval genres like the mystery play (*Żywot Józefa* [The Life of Joseph], 1545) and the morality play (*Kupiec* [The Merchant], 1549).

Rej's literary program emphasized those political views that espoused changing Poland into a *szlachta*-based republic with a king as its leader. He continuously propagated his program, from his best early work, *Krótka rozprawa*... (A Short Debate..., 1543), to *Zwierciadło* (The Looking Glass, 1568), following the path blazed earlier by Frycz-Modrzewski.

Rej's finest work is undoubtedly *Wizerunek własny żywota człowieka poczciwego* (A Self-Portrait of the Life of an Honest Man, 1558), an adaptation of a treatise by the humanist from Ferrara, Palingenius. It was the first attempt in Polish literature to present one's beliefs from a secular point of view. The Renaissance love of life and the writer's sensitivity to the beauty of the world found their most appealing expression in his most popular work, the prose piece *Żywot człowieka poczciwego* (The Life of an Honest Man), part of the volume *Zwierciadło*. Here Rej summed up his experiences and his observation of rural everyday life, looking at man and his vicissitudes with the wise and understanding smile of a humorist.

According to Julian Krzyżanowski, Rej's output makes up a unique colorful encyclopedia of the times of King Zygmunt the Old and his son, King Zygmunt August: a wide spectrum of literary genres (dialogue, morality play, mystery play, drama, epigram, *fraszka* [trifles], moralistic poems, and prose treatise). Rej proved that Polish was not the "language of geese," a contemptible jargon, but a language capable of expressing the same content as scholarly and elegant Latin. Rej's artistic language is expressive and varied, from ribald and vulgar jokes of *Figliki* (Pranks) to the elevated prose of *Spólne narzekanie wszej korony na porządną niedbałość naszą* (A Common Complaint of the Entire Crown on Our Systematic Neglect).

Krótka rozprawa między trzema osobami, panem, wójtem a plebanem (A Short Debate Among Three People—a Lord, a Bailiff Officer and a Priest) is a versified dialogue with twenty-one hundred verses. Rej's first outstanding work is a political treatise in its content, developing the political program of the *szlachta* democracy, which demanded restrictions on the rule of the magnates, the clergy, and the king and gave priority to the *szlachta*. All these problems are touched upon in the conversation among the representatives of the three classes living in the country. The lord accuses the priest of greediness and debauchery; the priest in turn blames the lord for abuse in the courts; while the chief officer concludes that the other two will somehow communicate with one another in the end, but the peasants will remain poor, since they pay the greatest tax and are victims of greedy soldiers and have no civil rights. The discussion contains excellent pictures of everyday life. The allegorical conclusion has Poland accusing all social classes of selfishness and indifference to the needs of the state. Aside from its political ideas, the dialogue possesses great artistic value.

(See Renaissance.)

BIBLIOGRAPHY

Dzieła wszystkie (Complete Works), Wrocław, 1953 (edition not completed).

Pisma wierszem (Works in Verse), edited and with an introduction by Julian Krzyżanowski, Wrocław, 1954.

Wybór pism (Selected Writings), edited by Jan Śląski, Warsaw, 1975.

RENAISSANCE (*Renesans*) The social and economic changes marking the end of the Middle Ages were manifested early and strongly in Italy. In the fourteenth century Italy consisted of a number of city-states, some of which, like Genoa and Venice, were competing for trade with the East, and others that were developing industrial centers, like Milan and Florence. The rich middle class of northern and central Italy were powerful enough to take political power into their own hands. In so doing, they created a new political form: the republic. The powerful banking and manufacturing families were the patrons of scholars, artists, and poets. This resulted in a quite lively cultural development in the city-states. In contrast to the theocentric Middle Ages, the focus of interest was on humanity and its worldly affairs.

In Italy there was widespread desire to unite the country as well as to return to Italy the glory and the power which were once Rome's. Intellectual life of the period, following the models of antiquity, concentrated on the fresh discovery of ancient art, literature, sculpture, and architecture. The masterpieces of Greece and Rome became the source of inspiration for all creative activities. From this came a new view of humanity and of the world. This new cultural model is known by the name "Renaissance." The word was first used by Giorgio Vasari (1511–74) in his study *Lives of Eminent Artists.* The word means "rebirth" and is most often used in opposition to "Dark Ages" as a term of derision for the Middle Ages, when cultural life was supposed to have been in "decline."

There is a good deal of disagreement concerning the content and referent of this word. It is used to denote a number of differing tendencies, including, above all, whether the "Renaissance" was the general awakening of antiquity or the dawn of Italian art and culture. There is also the question whether the term should be used in a narrow sense to denote a period in the history of Italy, or in a more general sense to refer to a period in the history of European art and culture as a whole.

Italy of the fourteenth century was the birthplace of the Renaissance, from which it spread to the rest of Europe. In Italy the Renaissance lasted from the end of the fourteenth century to the middle of the sixteenth century. In the rest of Europe it lasted from the end of the fifteenth century to the end of the sixteenth century. Of the many intellectual and religious movements of the period, the two most important are humanism and the Reformation.

Within the intellectual milieu of the humanists, and often because of powerful patrons, Renaissance art and literature first blossomed in Italy, later in France, Spain, England, Poland, and other nations. Paradoxically, simultaneously with this new interest in antiquity, the various national languages were being fashioned into literary languages. There were many theoretical works dedicated to the problems of these languages, which also laid the foundations of modern literary criticism. The general formula for these works was the imitation of nature, the beautiful, and a high esteem for Horace and Aristotle.

The handbooks of poetics written at this time presupposed a familiarity with the rules and forms of poetic expression, the perfection of which would lead to the attainment of artistic perfection. But, equally important, they also added to the requirement of competence, that of the gift of inspiration. The stylistic ideal was clarity and purity of language. In this respect, the Renaissance ideal alluded to the Ciceronian ideal, which "preferred" an explicit recognition of poetic means and figures.

The problems of poetic language and recognition of its characteristics were the subject of numerous discussions and polemics in which the various views were expressed. These conceptions were continually developing and changing aesthetic theories. Many writers of the Renaissance wrote in Classical Latin; at the same time, however, literature started to develop in a lively fashion in the various "national" languages, for example, in the works of Petrarch, Boccaccio, and Ronsard.

Poets cultivated the literary forms recognized by the ancients: Homeric epic, tragedy, comedy, lyrical poetry, elegies of a reflective and philosophical nature, hymns, and shorter poetic forms, such as epigrams and anacreontic verses. Arcadian and pastoral literature also enjoyed great popularity. Didactic poetry and literature, which were coupled with the pedagogic ambition to form and shape the Renaissance model of humanity and social practice, took the form of dialogues and tractates.

At this time a variety of new forms of fiction came into being: novels of manners and picaresque and pastoral novels. There was also an abundance of publications and writings involving reformist discussions of theology and politics. The Renaissance was a general European phenomenon with essential differences appearing in its development in different countries, with the most pronounced differences in Northern and Southern Europe.

In Italian literature heroic poems (Berni and Folengo) appeared, as well as novelistic prose, comedies of manners, and pastoral comedies which developed into commedia dell'arte. In the realm of lyric poetry Petrarchism was represented by Michelangelo. Didactic prose was represented by Machiavelli (*The Prince*) and Castiglione (*The Courtesan*). In Portugal (de Camoes) and Spain (Lope de Vega and Cervantes) drama developed widely, as did pastoral romances, for example, de Montemayor's *Diana*.

In France the theoretical-programmatic and literary activity of a group of poets known as the Pleiad was most prominent. The most important prose writers were Rabelais and de Montaigne. In England the most perfect expression was attained in the dramas of Marlowe, Lyly, and Shakespeare. Renaissance tendencies are also to be found in the poetry of Edmund Spenser.

The Renaissance found expression in the German-speaking lands in the poetry of the Meistersingers, the most important of whom was Hans Sachs. A tradition of a didactic and static nature was developed from popular traditions. It was connected with the Reformation's stream of religious polemics, which were highly critical of the clergy. These mostly took the form of dialogues, satires, and pamphlets.

The Renaissance in Poland (in Polish, *Odrodzenie*) began in the sixteenth century as it did in the rest of Europe, although signs and traits characteristic of the Renaissance were already apparent in the second half of the fifteenth century. The high point in Poland was under the reign of Zygmunt August and Stefan Batory. This "Golden Age" (in Polish, *Złoty Wiek*) lasted from 1543 to 1584, from the publication of Mikołaj Rej's* *Krótka Rozprawa* (A Short Debate) to the death of Jan Kochanowski.* The end of the Renaissance falls between the last years of the sixteenth century and the beginning of the seventeenth. The generally agreed upon date is 1620, after which the Baroque begins.

In the early centuries of the Christian era the cultural legacy of Greece and Rome was neglected and largely forgotten because it was pagan and, as such, was a source of competition for the Church. However, as the Church grew stronger and was no longer threatened by pagan religions and thought, its relationship to the pagan legacy of antiquity was fundamentally altered. Beginning in the ninth century there were successive periods of rising and declining interest in the culture of antiquity. After the reign of Charlemagne, there was an awakening in the institutions and practices of the Roman Empire. During the twelfth and thirteenth centuries, there was a lively interest in the works of Plato and Aristotle, although chiefly among Jewish, Christian, and Islamic theologians. But the broadest and most powerful interest in antiquity existed during the Renaissance. During this time the literary and artistic legacy of antiquity began to exert a powerful influence on the views of humanity and the world.

In the fifteenth century the culture of Rome and of Greece began to be studied more or less systematically. Against the background of constant wars and unresolved social conflicts, the study of antiquity resulted in a cult of the individual, in a love of beauty, in patriotism, and in a break with the formalistic constraints of medieval cultural life. This enthusiasm for antiquity almost resulted in its complete assimilation and a return to paganism.

This tendency, whose supreme goal was the overall development of the individual personality through the study of antiquity and the use of antiquity as a model to imitate in behavior and in creative endeavors, came to be known as humanism. In order to differentiate this tendency from others similar to it, it is often referred to as "Renaissance humanism." It determined the essential character of the period. It placed a great value on human dignity and in the belief in the possibilities of human reason. It overthrew the theological authorities which reigned up to this time, and in their place put the knowledge of humanity and of the laws regulating natural phenomena as the essential subject matter of scholarly and scientific endeavors.

Poles first came into contact with Italian art and literature through the numerous trips of the gentry to study at Italian universities and through the cultural activities of foreigners staying in Poland. Classical Latin was used and its precedents were sought in antiquity (A. Krzycki and J. Dantyszek). Scientific and scholarly works written in Latin were reprinted abroad (Copernicus and Frycz Modrzewski's *De republica emendanda*); historical works were also important (Maciej from Miechów's *Chronica Polonorum* and *De duabus Sarmatiis* and M. Kromer's *De origine et rebus gestis Polonorum*).

Humanism first came to Poland in the second half of the fifteenth century. Evidence of this can be found not only in Jan Długosz's* *Historia Polski* (History of Poland) but also in several other works of the period. Jan z Ludziska, a professor at the Cracow Academy, received his doctorate from the university in Padua in 1433. He was both an official of the academy and a famous lecturer on Roman oratory and the writers of antiquity.

Grzegorz of Sanoka (1407?–77) was a patron of the arts and himself a humanist poet and historian. He lectured on Virgil's poetics at the Cracow Academy. Having become the archbishop of Lvov, he modeled his court on the Italian model and surrounded himself with humanist scholars. Among these was Phillip Kallimachus, who, in gratitude for his protection and friendship, wrote an extensive biography of the archbishop.

The first secular writer to earn his doctorate in Bologna was Jan Ostroróg* (1436–1501). In his *Memoriale w sprawie uporządkowania Rzeczypospolitej* (Memorials Regarding the Settlement of the Republic) the credo of the humanists of the Renaissance can be found: "Show in your words and deeds that you love your country more than yourself and public matters more than private."

Not only Poles propagated humanist ideas in Poland; so did two foreigners who particularly deserve attention: Kallimachus, already mentioned, and the German Konrad Celtis.

At the beginning of the fifteenth century, literature was written in Polish for the first time with the result that Polish became a modern literary language. Literature and scholarly works of the Polish Renaissance reflected the changing sociopolitical and cultural relations taking place within Poland during this period.

Alongside the court and Church dignitaries, there appeared not only representatives of the wealthy and middle gentry (Rej), but also writers living in the cities (Biernat of Lublin, S. Gąsiorek-Kleryka, and Jan of Koszyczek) and the lyric poet K. Janicki, who was the son of a peasant. Didactic works were also quite common (see Rej).

Various forms of writings which showed concern for the social problems of the day were produced (Modrzewski* and Orzechowski). There were also sermons and exhortations (for example, *Kazania sejmowe* [The Sejm Sermons] by Piotr Skarga). Historical and historiographic writings developed alongside the memoirs of Latin writers. The best examples of this genre are works by M. Bielski (*Kronika wszystkiego świata* [Chronicle of the Whole World] and *Kronika Polska* [The Polish Chronicle]) and the works of Paprocki and Stryjkowski.

The beginnings of Polish narrative prose fall within this period, founded mainly on the work of schoolmasters and writers of an urban background who composed popular tales of the Middle Ages and antiquity, notably *Marcholt* and *Poncjan,* translated by Jan of Koszyczek, and *Etiopki* (The Ethiopian Women) by Heliodorus, translated by A. Zacharzewski.

The most lasting achievements of the Polish Renaissance are to be found in the works of Kochanowski,* Szymonowic,* and Sęp-Szarzyński*—poets with ties to the Baroque. Kochanowski was the author of poetry of a didactic character and of a satirical-political nature (*Zgoda* [Harmony] and *Satyr* [Satire]). However, the greatest of his achievements is the creation of lyrics in Polish in the style of Horace. These include poetry of a reflective and philosophical nature, light verse (*Fraszki* [Trifles]) and *Treny* (Threnodies), a cycle of lamentations in the form of elegies. These *Treny* were the most perfect poetical expression of Renaissance individualism in Poland, which emphasized interest in the particulars of everyday life and in the philosophical aspects of human existence. In Kochanowski's lyrical poetry syllabic verse in Polish was perfected.

Poets of the Polish Renaissance also cultivated pastoral and bucolic poetry. Examples of this genre are Kochanowski's *Pieśń świętojańska o sobótce* (Saint John's Song About Midsummer Bonfires) and Szymonowic's *Sielanki* (Pastorals). These enriched the Classical standards of antiquity with elements of native folklore.

According to Julian Krzyżanowski,* Klonowic introduced the form of a descriptive poetic epic—*Roxolania, Flis, Worek Judaszów* (A Bag of Judases)—which portrayed the various social strata of the period. Kochanowski undertook the creation of Renaissance drama, based on the examples of antiquity—*Odprawa posłów greckich* (The Dismissal of the Greek Envoys). The writers of the Renaissance also aided in the assimilation of a number of important foreign works: *Psałterz Dawidów* (David's Psalter), translated by Kochanowski; the works of Ovid, Virgil, Plutarch, and Heliodorus and paraphrases of Horace's lyrical poetry. Polish literature creatively undertook the development of the most essential ideas of the European Renaissance, the formation of modern literary Polish, and the fundamentals of the further development of the national literature.

The Reformation was a socioreligious movement which threw Europe into convulsions in the sixteenth century and resulted in the breakup of the former unity of organized religion. It had its roots deep in the Middle Ages, reaching back even to the founding of the Franciscan Order in the eighth century, and later with the Hussites, who called for the rebirth and reform of the individual and a correction of the relations between the rulers and the ruled in the Church. The growing social conflicts in the cities and sporadic peasant rebellions were also contributing factors in the development and genesis of the Reformation.

At the time of the Renaissance these aspirations arose on a wave of an increase in critical and independent thought and were coupled with a decline in the morality of the clergy. This became more pronounced in the fifteenth century and certainly aided in the reception of the reformers' pronouncements and declarations.

This religious controversy was started by the monk, preacher, and theologian Martin Luther. He was a professor at the University of Wittenburg; in 1517 he published his ninety-five theses condemning the church's trade in indulgences. Luther declared that one could find all the essentials of the Christian faith in the Gospels and protested against the pronouncements of the papacy and the Church councils, which were treated by the Church as dogma.

In addition to Luther, the Frenchman John Calvin was also a prominent reformer and a contemporary of Luther. He advocated even more radical reforms and criticism of the Catholic Church. He was a monk, preacher, and theologian. The center of his activity was in Geneva.

The calls of the reformers fell on the receptive ground of troubled social and political relations among the mass of peasants, who were hoping for an improvement in their situation. The calls of the reformers also fell in line with the desires of rulers and princes, who were desirous of greater independence from the papacy.

The Reformation released an enormous amount of energy which was expended in vehement quarrels and polemics on dogma and on the persistent religious and social conflicts of the period. In Germany there was a bloody suppression of a peasants' rebellion in 1525, while religious wars raged in other parts of Europe.

The Catholic Church, deeply threatened by the Reformation, worked out a program of internal reforms at the Council of Trent (1545–63). The result was the Counter-Reformation, led by the Jesuits, an order founded in 1534 with the express purpose of fighting heresy on a theological basis.

In Poland the calls of the reformers also found fertile ground. The Church enjoyed a privileged position and was the largest landowner. In addition to this, it levied payments for Rome and for the support of the clergy, whose moral state was frequently criticized.

The Reformation appealed to the nobility for other reasons: it brought a greater independence from clerical courts and a limitation of the political role of the clergy. Apart from this was the temptation of the Church's landholdings. For these reasons the new religions spread quickly in Poland, which then became heterogeneous in religious matters. This attrition from the ranks of the Catholic Church did not lead to religious wars as it did in the West, where there were constant ongoing bloody religious conflicts. The Polish Republic took pride in its broad tolerance in religious matters; because of this, dogmatic religious attitudes found their expression in polemical exchanges.

Peace in religious matters was ultimately guaranteed by the resolution of the *Sejm* in 1573, the so-called Warsaw Confederation. It ensured complete freedom of conscience and equality of treatment of the gentry without regard to religious confession. This was the first legal act of its kind in Europe, guaranteeing freedom of religion.

The Reformation was a major force in the development of national languages and literature. Because the reformers regarded the Bible as the single legitimate source of religious instruction, it was translated into the various national languages. The Bible was translated, songs were composed, propagandistic brochures were written, polemics were exchanged—all in one's mother tongue. The reformers, thus, became pioneers in the development and genesis of national literatures. Luther's translation of the Bible determined which German dialect would become the literary language of Germany. In Poland Mikołaj Rej,* a fervent Calvinist, raised Polish to the level of a literary language: "A niechaj narodowie wżdy postronni znają, / Iż Polacy nie gęsi, iż swój język mają. (And to nations on all sides let this be known, / Poles—no geese—possess a language of their own.) He was faithful to this credo throughout his life.

Of the variants of Protestantism in Poland, Lutheranism took root mainly in the cities, and Calvinism among the gentry. The Arians, or Polish Brethren, were a sect apart. Their sect came about as a result of divisions among Polish Calvinists. This sect was quite progressive for its time. The head of its radical wing, Marcin Czechowic, was against the shedding of blood, and thus opposed not only war but capital punishment. He also called for the elimination of the papacy and subjection of the peasantry. In the internal conflicts of the Polish Brethren, a more moderate faction won out. It was headed by Szymon Budny and condemned predatory and aggressive warfare and called for the humane treatment of the peasantry by the gentry.

The Arians valued education very highly. Their schools were of the highest quality and their academy in Raków enjoyed fame throughout Europe. They not only valued education but also placed a great emphasis on moral and civic responsibility. They also demonstrated their concern for the Polish language and its purity. They were advocates of religious tolerance and defended variant views, as well as the principle of not answering evil with evil. The Polish Brethren had many opponents even in the camp of the reformers; thus, they remained an isolated group. The Czech Brethren, Calvinists, and Lutherans were included in the Sandomierz Agreement of 1570, but the Polish Brethren were not.

BIBLIOGRAPHY

J. Ziomek, *Renesans* (Renaissance), *Historia literatury polskiej,* pod redakcja Kazimierza Wyki, wyd. 4, Warsaw, 1980; wydanie 1, 1973.

J. Krzyżanowski, *W wieku Reja i Stańczyka* (During the Era of Rej and Stańczyk), Warsaw, 1958.

Słownik literatury staropolskiej (A Dictionary of Old Polish Literature), redakcja T. Michałowska, Wrocław, 1990.

REYMONT, WŁADYSŁAW STANISŁAW (1867–1925), a novelist and short story writer and Nobel Prize winner in 1924, was born and brought up in the country. After 1880 he moved to Warsaw, where he learned to be a tailor. He later worked as an actor in a vagabond group and as a minor railway employee and railroad switchman. In 1890 he became acquainted with spiritualism, which influenced his life and his writings. After 1893 he concentrated fully on his literary work. He also worked as a journalist: the report of his pilgrimage to Częstochowa brought him fame and success. He traveled a great deal and visited various countries and places (Italy, Berlin, Brussels, London, Brittany). In 1920 he fell victim to a railway crash near Warsaw, which undermined his health but improved his financial situation. He was the president of the union of journalists and one of the founders of the Polish Academy of Literature. In 1924 he received the Nobel Prize for his novel *Chłopi* (The Peasants).

In 1882 Reymont wrote poems based on his work in a tailor's shop. During 1888–95 he began to make detailed notes on his life and artistic ideas. He made his literary debut in 1892 as a journalist and short story writer (*Wigilia Bożego Narodzenia* [Christmas Eve], in *Myśl* [Idea]). During 1892–94 he wrote seventeen short stories, based on various experiences of his life (life in the country and in the city, railway work, life of actors). All these themes were later developed in his more mature works. The stories are characterized by a combination of realistic plot and naturalistic observation, of impressionistic technique and expressionist dynamism.

During 1891–1896 he devoted a series of works to the world of actors (*Franek* [Frankie], *Adeptka* [Apprentice], *Komediantka* [Comedienne], *Lili* [Lilacs], *Fermenty* [Ferments]), which presented the conflict between the artist and society. These were among the first "milieu" novels in Polish literature. During 1895–99 he worked on *Ziemia obiecana* (Promised Land), based on his experiences in Łódź, presenting for the first time in Polish literature a Moloch-city, the process of becoming rich during the early stages of capitalism, and the social and psychological consequences of the process. The novel was made into a movie, directed by Andrzej Wajda, in 1975. His antiurban views were connected with his philosophy of nature. He considered rural life to be natural, authentic, and, consequently, positive, while life in the city seemed unnatural, inauthentic, and, consequently, negative.

During 1899–1908 he devoted his time chiefly to *Chłopi* (The Peasants). The work on his most famous novel was preceded by "experimental" short stories. In 1900 he wrote *Sielanka* (Idyll), the first work on the revolution. In the cycle connected with the revolution of 1905 (*Z konstytucyjnych dni* [From Constitutional Days], *Czekam* [I'm Waiting], *Na krawędzi* [On the Brink], *Zabiłem* [I Killed]), he passed through a phase during which he first approved of the revolutionary struggle then grew to fear the revolution and its social consequences. In 1906 he wrote a short story, *Sąd* (The Trial), regarded as a supplement to *Chłopi*, in which he presented the morality of a rural community and described the collective lynching of several thieves. In the story *Ave Patria* (1907) he wrote an apology for the struggle of independence when confronted by a revolution. In his works from 1904 to 1908, a clear dichotomy of themes was developed: realistic prose appears alongside works presenting the realm of visions and parapsychological phenomena.

During 1904–7 Reymont wrote several short stories based on his stay in Brittany: *Burza* (The Storm), *Tęsknota* (Longing), *Ostatni* (The Last), *Powrót* (The Return). In the following year (1908) he again returned to his experiences as a railway worker in the story *Marzyciel* (The Dreamer). Undoubtedly influenced by Dostoyevsky, Reymont illuminates a gallery of fascinating characters. However, in his subsequent stories, *Senne marzenia* (Sleepy Dreams, 1908) and *Dziwna opowieść* (A Strange Story, 1908), Reymont again returned to dreams and parapsychological phenomena. His next novel *Wampir* (Vampire, 1911), filled with hallucinatory images, was not a success, nor was his drama *Przegrana* (Lost), published almost simultaneously. During 1913–18 he published his historical trilogy, *Rok 1794* (The Year 1794), intended as the first part of a major historical work linking the past with the present. Reymont's views changed during the process of writing, but the final shape of the trilogy was influenced by World War I. The final results were nonfiction, rather than fiction, chiefly because of the writer's thorough knowledge of the epoch.

During World War I Reymont wrote several short stories, *Orka* (Tillage) and *Dola* (Fate) in 1917, and *Echa* (Echo) in 1918, from the volume *Za frontem* (Beyond the Front, 1919), in which he presented the experiences of Polish civilians and soldiers during the war in the country; the naturalistic images reveal the most traumatic aspects of the war. The novels and short stories written during 1921–24 present Reymont's impressions of America and give the first evaluation of the early postwar years: *Księżniczka* (The Princess), *Powrót* (The Return), *Spowiedź* (The Confession) in 1921–23, and *Bunt* (Riot) in 1924. Reymont's works of his later years lack artistic and ideological merit. The collection of stories published after his death, *Krosnowa i świat* (Krosnowa and the World, 1928), primarily consisted of his early works never published before.

Reymont's literary output was quite voluminous and thematically varied, but not entirely meritorious. According to Józef Rurowski, he undoubtedly contributed a great deal to the cultural tradition in Poland and his reputation abroad placed him in the front ranks of more writers. But his works are not uniformly of high quality.

Chłopi (The Peasants) is a novel cycle. The definitive edition was published in Warsaw: Volumes 1–2, 1904; Volume 3, 1906, and Volume 4, 1909. The story takes place in an authentic village of Lipce, in the south of the former Księstwo Łowickie. The action takes place during ten months of one year, beginning in early fall and ending after the harvest during the following year. The plot consists of three lines: the first presents the main characters and the entire community of Lipce, highly varied in terms of both human types and their psychological makeup. A rich peasant, Maciej Boryna, a widower, marries a young and temperamental beauty, Jagna, against the wishes of his children. The marriage leads to a conflict with his eldest son, Antek, who had hoped to inherit his father's wealth and improve the life of his family but now must leave the family home. The conflict becomes more acute as Antek becomes Jagna's lover; the husband learns of Jagna's infidelity. During early spring the community becomes involved in a conflict with the local manor over a piece of forest, which they feel they have a right to use. A violent fight ensues; Antek defends his father and is imprisoned, along with several other young men. Maciej is injured in the fight, paralyzed as a result; he dies later that spring. In the summer the imprisoned people return to the village. The community, outraged by Jagna's numerous love affairs, force her out of the village by throwing stones at her. Subsequent parts of the cycle were to take place in America; some of his characters were to emigrate.

The fate of Maciej Boryna thus takes place from the time of his wedding and his death to the funeral banquet. The action makes up the second line of the plot, which dramatizes the year as a series of ritual religious and social events. Reymont learned about these customs from Church calendars and ancient folk beliefs. It was his intention here to suggest the subordination of the individual to the rules and morality of the community.

The third line of the cycle is determined by the flow of time, expressed through the invariable repeated rhythms of the seasons of the year, the subsequent months, and the work in the fields. The writer presents time mainly through elaborate descriptions of nature, which provide a framework for the affairs of people. The three lines of the plot give the novel its epic dimensions; the fate of an individual is dependent on the community and the work it has to do, and this in turn depends on nature, on time and biological phenomena, ever present in human existence.

Reymont received the Nobel Prize for *Chłopi*. Even though Polish critics thought that Żeromski deserved it more, the decision was later evaluated as appropriate. Foreign critics considered the novel to be a truthful epic of rural life, a model of the genre.

BIBLIOGRAPHY

Pisma: Wydanie zbiorowe zupełne (Works: Complete Collected Edition), Volumes 1–20, introduction by A. Grzymała-Siedlecki, Warsaw, 1920–25.

English

The Peasants: A Tale of Our Own Times, Four volumes, translated by Michael H. Dziewicki, New York: A. A. Knopf, 1925; 1942.

More Tales by Polish Authors: The Trial (Sąd), New York: Longmans, Green, 1916.

The Promised Land (Ziemia Obiecana), translated by M. H. Dziewicki, New York: Alfred Knopf, 1927.

Polish Folklore Stories, English-Polish Publication Committee, 1944.

Burek: The Dog That Followed the Lord, English-Polish Publication Committee, 1944.

RĘKOPIS ZNALEZIONY W SARAGOSSIE (A Manuscript Found in Saragossa) (see Potocki).

RITTNER, TADEUSZ (pseudonym Tomasz Czaszka) (1873–1921), a playwright and prose writer, studied in Vienna after 1884 and received a doctorate in law. He learned German as a second language but knew it well enough to write in it. He began writing in 1893, but success came much later. During the period 1904–20 he staged eleven plays in Vienna. In 1898 he began to contribute to various Austrian and German journals and soon thereafter wrote novels in German. He considered himself Polish, and in 1894 he made his Polish literary debut with the novelette *Lulu* published in the journal *Czas* (Time). During the subsequent twenty years he published several collections of modernist novelettes (*Przebudzenie* [The Awakening], 1905; *Nowele* [Novels], 1907; *W obcym mieście* [In a Strange City], 1912; and *Powrót* [The Return], 1915), all basically psychological in character. He also staged eleven plays in Poland, mostly translations of his German plays, with few exceptions: for example, his best known play, *W małym domku* (In a Small Home), was originally written in Polish. In his dramatic output he experimented within all categories, from modernism (e.g., *Sąsiadka* [The Lady Next Door]), to realism in his best plays: *W małym domku,* staged in 1904, and *Głupi Jakub* (Crazy Jacob) staged in 1910. He returned to modernistic poetics later: *Don Juan,* written in German in 1909, translated into Polish by Z. Rittnerowa and staged in 1922, and *Dzieci ziemi* (Children of the Earth), staged in German in 1915, published in 1919, and staged in Polish in 1922, with a translation by Z. Rittnerowa. *Don Juan* was a turning point in Rittner's work: after it satire and irony started to play important roles in his works and became the dominant themes in his fiction: *Człowiek z budki suflera* (The Man from the Prompter's Box), published in German in 1912, staged in German and Polish in 1913, and published in Polish in 1930; *Lato* (Summer), published in German in 1912 and staged in both languages in 1913; and *Wilki w nocy* (Wolves in the Night), staged in 1916.

In 1911 he published an article, *Komedia* (Comedy), in which he presented his view on drama. He claimed that tragic drama could not appear in the twentieth century, because critics force dramatists to look for the simple and funny in the most elevated of phenomena. The task of the writer was to show that chaos, that admixture of high and ridiculous elements. Such a picture of life was close to reality, and relating this aspect of the truth gave relief to man. Rittner followed these criteria in his best plays, which he called comedies. According to Zbigniew Raszewski, they indeed do have comic elements, but they all end with the defeat of the hero: his comedy is laced with pessimism.

He wrote several novels, the Polish versions of which were published after his death: *Duchy w mieście* (Ghosts in the City), 1921; *Między nocą a brzaskiem* (Between Night and Daybreak), 1921; *Drzwi zamknięte* (Closed Doors), 1922; and *Most* (The Bridge), 1926.

W małym domku (In a Small House), a drama in three acts, written and staged in 1904, was published in Warsaw in 1907. A young doctor marries a simple girl he has seduced. He thinks that the marriage has ruined his career and treats his wife with contempt. She betrays him, and he kills her but is declared innocent by the jury. However, he cannot bear the guilt and social boycott and commits suicide. The play is reminiscent of Dostoyevsky's *The Idiot.* Rittner explores the milieu of a small town's intelligentsia in Galicia, presenting the most accurate portrayal of the class ever created in Polish drama.

BIBLIOGRAPHY

Nowele (Novels), Warsaw, 1960.
Dramaty (Dramas), Volumes 1–2, edited and with an introduction by Z. Raszewski, Warsaw, 1966.

ROMANOWICZOWA, ZOFIA (née Górska) (born 1922), a novelist, poet, and translator, fought in the Home Army during the Nazi occupation. She was arrested in 1941, and during the period 1942–45 she was moved to several concentration camps. Poems written in the camps were published in the collection *Ravensbrueck: Wiersze obozowe* (Ravensbrueck: Concentration Camp Poems, 1961). After the war she traveled to Italy and France; she made her debut in 1945 in *Orzeł biały* (The White Eagle) in Rome with the story *Tomuś* (Tommy). She studied Romance philology in Paris, where she made her home with her husband, Kazimierz Romanowicz, founder and director of the Polish Publishing House Libella and the Lambert Gallery on the Island of Saint Ludwig. Her first major success was the novel *Baśka i Barbara* (Barb and Barbara), published in Paris in 1956 and in Poland in 1958. The novel explores the plight of a Polish child brought up in an alien environment—the problems of bilingualism, the inner struggle of the mother who attempts to awaken the daughter to her ethnic identity, at the same time protecting her against the complexes associated with alienation in a foreign society. The problem recurs in her later works, especially in the novel *Groby Napoleona* (The Graves of Napoleon, London, 1972) and *Na Wyspie* (On the Island, Paris, 1983). According to Halina Urbas, Romanowiczowa's war and concentration camp experiences, as well as her disappointment about the postwar situation in Poland, are reflected in all her novels: *Przejście przez Morze Czerwone* (Passage Through the Red Sea, Paris, 1960, published in Poland in 1961), *Słońce dziesięciu linii* (The Sun of Ten Lines, Paris, 1963), *Szklana kula* (A Glass Sphere, Paris, 1964), *Łagodne oko błękitu* (The Gentle Eye of Blue, Paris, 1968), and the collection of stories *Próby i zamiary* (Trials and Designs, London, 1965). Romanowiczowa is the author of the highly praised Polish translation of old Provençal lyrics *Brewiarz miłości* (Breviary of Love, 1963).

BIBLIOGRAPHY

English

Passage Through the Red Sea (Przejście przez Morze Czerwone), translated by Virgilia Peterson, New York: Harcourt, Brace and World, 1962.

ROMANTICISM (*Romantyzm*) was an ideological, literary, and artistic current, which in Europe occupied the period between the French Revolution and *Wiosna Ludów* (The Spring of Nations, 1848). In Poland Romanticism began with the publication of Volume 1 of Adam Mickiewicz's anthology *Poezje* (Poems) in 1822 and ended with the January Uprising in 1863. Romantic tendencies, however, can be discerned as early as the loss of Poland's independence at the end of the eighteenth century. The work of these writers is often referred to as examples of pre-Romanticism.

France led the way in declaring "the rights of man," which led to the development of individualism as a basic tenet, both in the social arena and in philosophy. The courtly-feudal culture was placed in opposition to the new European culture, a flowering of the bourgeoisie. The basic dilemmas arising from the new order were the opposition of "nature" and "culture," "feeling" and "reasoning," "life" and "lifelessness"—or simply, genuineness versus artificiality. "The return to nature" was understood as a protest against courtly artificiality. Napoleon was a personification of an optimistic democracy, bourgeoisie, and nation, and at the same time was the embodiment of the myth of progress, especially concerning the magnificence of individualism. He was considered the greatest genius of modern times by the Romantics, not necessarily for his intellectual acumen but for his charismatic character. The Polish Romantics propagated the Napoleonic legend (Mickiewicz was one of the greatest of his supporters). For many, Napoleon united within himself all the Romantic ideas: freedom of the nation and its people, the potential might of the individual, a noble and unrelenting fight for the highest ideals. This heroic-Romantic interpretation of events also served to encourage the legends of heroes in Poland, especially involving Kościuszko and Poniatowski.

The Spring of Nations in a sense closed the process which had begun with the French Revolution. It signaled the culmination of the European national movement. The Romantics championed the idea of a utopian socialism, based on a Christian revolution. Romantic political thought was nourished on the idea of unbreakable ties between religion and freedom, particularly between true Christianity and the new world of justice for all who were oppressed (Mickiewicz's* *Księgi narodu polskiego i pielgrzymstwa polskiego* [Books of the Polish Nation and Polish Pilgrimage]). What is apparent here, above all, is the difference between Romanticism and the ideas of the Enlightenment and the French Revolution. The revolutionary and Romantic activists rejected the previously held view of the indispensable ties between the revolution and materialism; they attacked the platitudinous and prosaic practical mind of the bourgeoisie as being antirevolutionary. They also declared themselves against intellectual elitism and rationalism. Emotionalism became an important aspect of Romanticism, as a deciding basis for interpreting reality in which "living truths" were of greatest importance. Intuition and looking at life "through the eyes of the soul" were the tools of Romanticism; in the latter phase, mysticism (especially in the works of Słowacki*) became an important aspect of Romanticism. Resurrection of a new life was attained through sacrifice, suffering, and death. The road to moral regeneration gave the greatest sense to the existence of the individual and nation.

The Romantic hero is a mutinous man, torn asunder; he has had to search for sense in his life between heaven and earth, to maintain an uninterrupted dialogue with God. Earthly reasoning was inadequate to understand human history. Prometheus and Christ fascinated them. They considered their loneliness both a privilege and a curse. Time became a real Romantic obsession, made up of "eternity" and an "instant," with the cosmos representing, above all, eternity. They considered it an unfinished whole, in which secret ties linked the minerals deep in the earth with the stars in the heavens. Evidence of cosmic unity was for them the harmonious correspondence of heavenly bodies, minerals, and parts of human anatomy. Man occupied a privileged position in the chain of being: his soul was a vital and separate part of the world's soul. Without man the spirit present in nature could not attain consciousness of self.

Mysticism of a universal nature explains the deep ties between Romantic theory and the theory of the cosmos. Romantic poetry and aesthetics were shaped within the circle of beliefs about the primordiality and indivisibility of the life of nature, which could be penetrated not by the mind but by the imagination, employing symbols. The basic shape of Romantic symbolism became the descent into the depths, a penetration into the inside of existence and discovery of "the inner man," in whom truth lives, understood also as "a conscious man," "an archetypal man," "the human abyss," because it represented "the night side" of one man and of all humanity, revealing itself in dreams, myth, desire, rites, the language of children, and folk poetry. The two realities, the seen and the unseen, came closer and closer together, revealing their indissoluble unity.

For the Romantics, poetry became both a form of individual expression as well as a monologue of the individual or his dialogue with God and Nature, as a means of "acknowledging the nation in his being" (M. Mochnacki) or "actualizing the idea of love of the entire nation" (E. Dembowski). Poetry exposed the truth revealed only to the creator-prophet, but it also revealed the collective truth, still indistinct in the essence of the collective consciousness.

Polish Romanticism is one of the most original among European forms of the movement. The loss of independence, the most important event in the modern history of Polish consciousness, was the decisive factor in formulating a completely different understanding of the nation and the individual, society and the state, as well as the destiny and function of culture, above all, literature. The young Polish Romantics, convinced of the might of the spirit as a deciding force for change, were certain that reason and spiritual value should stand in opposition to empirical constraint and to insipid reality. They considered opposition—revolt—an obligation of the young. They regarded revolt and covert acts as the only means of effecting a complete independent life for the nation.

The first study of Romanticism was a description of German Romanticism by K. Brodziński* (*O klasyczności i romantyczności* [About Classicism and Romanticism], 1818). It was actually a polemic against Jan Śniadecki's study of pre-Romantic aspects of Classical literature (*O pismach klasycznych i romantycznych* [About Classical and Romantic Writings]). Śniadecki considered Romanticism a cult of barbarian medieval violence. He abhorred the frenzy of expression, the wildness and deviation from the norm, the Gothic and fantastic. The young Romantics searched for support for themselves in that which they considered distinct, individual, characterized by authentic and primordial experience, untainted by the refinement of civilization, which they found within themselves (*we wnętrzu*), as well as in their own region, provinces, the nature and folklore of their native land. Mickiewicz embodied these concepts in his early poetry.

The first works of Mickiewicz* (*Ballady i romanse* [Ballads and Romances], Volume 1 of *Poezje* [Poems] and *Dziady* [Forefathers' Eve], Parts I and II, Volume 2, 1823) marked the beginning of the Romantic movement in Poland. In his foreword to *Poezje* (Poems), Mickiewicz stated that there were two cultures, the folk-national and the gentry culture of the magnates. This general idea Mickiewicz adumbrated in Part II of *Dziady* (Forefathers' Eve), within the world of folk ceremonies. Mickiewicz's people represented inexorable universal truth, with which the justification of the individual, the justification for suffering, loneliness, despair, and revolt—the justification of Gustav, the hero, the individual—had to come in conflict with the collective. In *Konrad Wallenrod* (1828), Mickiewicz presented the conflict of the individual and the nation, the two embodiments of freedom, the Arcadian innocence of nature, and the violence of historical necessity.

A different view was presented by A. Malczewski in *Maria* (1825). Into the knightly past of seventeenth century Poland the poet transplants an ideal Romantic hero, human values in conflict with the cruelty of laws governing the world. The heroine of the poem is for Malczewski a metaphysical image of the world. Earth (nature and history) represents merely a temporary abode for the "exile," on the road to eternity, and the inimitable sadness of the Ukrainian steppes underscores the magnitude of the journey.

A different Ukraine, less "philosophical," more primordial and folkish, appeared in the works of S. Goszczyński,* especially in his *Zamek kaniowski* (Kaniowski Castle, 1828). Highly praised by Romantic critics (M. Mochnacki), the novel was received with indignation and disgust by traditionalists and advocates of the idyllic model of national literature. For Mickiewicz, Goszczyński's Ukrainian experiences were an organic and harmonious representation of Romantic folk poetry, free of artistic stylization.

In this work the people appeared as a part of nature, and their eighteenth century revolt represented an uncontrollable element.

A great change in Polish literature was effected by the early Romantics. New poetic forms (ballad, poetic novel, drama) were created. In them the writers expressed all the most important matters of their times: the idea of history and the idea of nature, freedom of the individual and freedom of the nation, the idea of creation and the idea of poetry, and the discovery of "historic man" and "subconscious man." To these ends poetry served as an infinite creative power, breaking the cramped barriers defined by man's reason: Romantic imagination knew no boundaries; it wanted to define modern man to the very end.

Mickiewicz's *Oda do młodości* (Ode to Youth, written in 1820) became a symbol of the battle between Classical and Romantic thought. The Romantics called for a heroic moral responsibility for the fate of the nation and its people. They toppled down the partitions in the areas of literature and life, and the literary revolution became transformed into a political battle between the Romantics and the Classicists. The end came with the November Uprising, which was considered the result and the culminating point of the Romantic revolution.

The failure of the uprising became the critical moment in the history of the Poles and greatly affected the changes in Romanticism. Polish society was divided into two parts: "the emigration," which was located largely in France (therefore, in the midst of European thought), and "the country" (above all, the Kingdom of Poland). The exchange of ideas between the emigrants and the country continued uninterruptedly. There was unanimity of spirit among both camps which never waned.

The central figure in Polish Romanticism was Adam Mickiewicz, before and after the November Uprising. This poet-prophet was regarded as the leader of the nation. He attained this status largely through Part III of *Dziady* (Forefathers' Eve), in which was encompassed the entire Romantic dialectic. The transformation of Gustaw, the "private" man, into Konrad, the "social" man, the suffering Prometheus of the nation, became the basic moral and ideological symbol in Polish Romanticism. Poland began to be regarded as the "Christ of Nations." "The psychology of the abyss" gave birth to Polish messianism.

The living truth for Mickiewicz was the truth of freedom, the truth of freeing man: for this reason messianism and revolution were not alien to one another in his philosophy. In fact, they were wed, "an impulse of the spirit to a better life." Mickiewicz seems the most representative figure among European advocates of so-called Romantic Socialism, as well as of social Romanticism. The myth of resurrection and rebirth that was present in Part III of *Forefathers' Eve* Mickiewicz further developed in *Pan Tadeusz* (1834). It became the Romantic epos of the nation. The "history of the nobility" was related in this poem in the full brilliance of past greatness.

Alongside Mickiewicz's Romantic messianism and revolution belong another version of Romantic historicism and a different interpretation of Christianity espoused by Zygmunt Krasiński.* His drama, *Nie-Boska komedia* (The Undivine Comedy, 1835), is the first Polish modern tragedy. It is the first modern tragedy to present the class war. Krasiński felt that the future of the nation was in the hands of God and only God could lead man to perfection.

The credit for forming a modern idiom in Polish poetry is largely given to Juliusz Słowacki,* about whom the great poet and critic of Romanticism Cyprian Norwid* once wrote: "In a single lyric . . . he had all the languages of the ages, the times, the social institutions, types, and sexes." *Kordian* (1834) was one of the most admired of his works among the young Romantics because it seemed to be a Romantic confession, a biography of the young revolutionaries. *Balladyna* (1839), the "political fairy tale," is one of the finest examples of tragic irony in Polish literature. *Beniowski* (1841) presents a different "new language," in which the narrator becomes part of the dramatic action. The unfinished *Król-Duch* (King-Spirit, 1847), called by Norwid "a phenomenological epos," is perhaps Słowacki's greatest creation.

In the great shadow of the Romantic émigrés, the second and third generations of Romantics created a revolutionary poetry in their country, often referred to as *tyrtejski* (Tyrtesian), poetry which constantly acknowledged Gustaw's transformation into Konrad. The role of Tyrteus and prophet was played out by K. Ujejski in the Kingdom of Poland. Folk poetry found an eminent representative in T. Lenartowicz,* who was able artistically to create the tone of folk poetry. In 1865, in his foreword to *Vade-mecum,* Norwid* spoke of the "critical moment" at which Polish poetry had arrived. He felt that the time had come when art should be responsible for itself and that "a necessary turn be made in Polish poetry." Norwid effected the change himself, creating a modern, intellectual poetry.

After Poland lost its independence, Polish Romanticism created a picture of the world that encompassed the New World. The Romantic poets created a new poetry. They accomplished this completely in their own way, in the vanguard of European Romanticism, leaving an inexhaustible heritage.

BIBLIOGRAPHY

J. Ujejski, *Romantycy* (The Romantics), Warsaw, 1963.

J. Krzyżanowski, *W romantycznym świecie* (In a Romantic World), Cracow, 1961.

M. Janion, *Gorączka romantyczna* (Romantic Fever), Warsaw, 1975.

M. Piwińska, *Legenda romantyczna i szydercy* (Romantic Legend and Scoffers), Warsaw, 1973.

RÓŻEWICZ, TADEUSZ (born 1921) (pseudonym Satyr), a poet, playwright, and prose writer, made his debut as a poet in 1938. During the occupation he fought in the Home Army, contributed to the underground press, and published a collection of poetry and short stories, *Echa leśne* (Forest Echoes), under the pseudonym "Satyr." After the war he studied history; in 1946 he published a collection of prose and verse satires, *Włyżce wody* (In a Spoonful of Water).

Różewicz's first volume of poetry, *Niepokój* (Anxiety, 1947), which according to Mieczysław Dąbrowski contained almost all the features that can be found in his later works, was highly praised by most critics. The typical themes of postwar poetry—the alienation felt among the survivors, the desire to liberate oneself from fears and obsessive memories, to rebuild basic human values—found a new form of expression: simple and withdrawn, free of ornamentation and metaphor, alien to the traditional forms of poetry, and closer to the coarseness of everyday language, framed within the form of free verse and a rhetorical, though highly disciplined monologue. In the next decade he published the collections *Czerwona rękawiczka* (The Red Glove, 1948) and *Poemat otwarty* (Open Narrative Poem, 1956). In these early poems, Różewicz employed both catastrophic and Arcadian motives; he emphasized his belief in the impossibility of communication among people, his protest against cruelty, violence, and indifference. But he also expressed his longing for a world of simple feelings, words, and meanings. With the publication of the volume *Formy* (Forms, 1958) Różewicz's range of themes and problems broadened and became more complex from a philosophical point of view. According to Daniel Weissbort, the "new realism" which Różewicz introduced to poetry after the Holocaust was an attempt "to identify the psycho-physiological conditions of survival." Różewicz was the quintessential poet who raised his voice to the highest decibel in a postapocalyptic world. The poems *Et in Arcadia ego* from the volume *Głos Anonima* (The Voice of an Anonymous Person, 1961) and *Spadanie* (The Falling) and *Non-Stop Show* from the volume *Twarz trzecia* (A Third Face, 1968), and those from the collections *Rozmowa z księciem* (A Conversation with a Prince, 1960), *Nic w płaszczu Prospera* (Nothing in Prospero's Cloak, 1962), and *Twarz* (Face, 1964) contained a severe and critical attitude, presenting a reality in which all values were relative, in which man was an object dominated by high-tech civilization and its products, or by biology, caught up in the kaleidoscope of changing fashions and styles. The description of this world, which contained moral warnings, was given in his longer poems, building metaphorical images from naturalistic observations, using elements of the grotesque, combining various styles and genres to create a seemingly incoherent whole: *Świat 1906* (The World 1906)—a collage from the volume *Zielona róża* (The Green Rose, 1961); the "poem with prose" *Złowiony* (The Catch), from the volume *Regio* (1969); *Duszyczka* (Little Soul, 1977) and *Płaskorzeźba* (Bas-Relief, 1991).

In time Różewicz's reputation may rest not on his poetic output but on his dramatic works. There is no doubt that he was "the father of postwar poetry" (at least in its main trend) and that his contributions as an innovator both in poetry and in drama remain unchallenged. But his drama captured a moment of Polish history and culture, and it was Różewicz who gave voice to the changes that were taking place in the fifties and sixties. The plays have an open structure, usually with little or no plot or temporal sequence, presenting anonymous, multifaceted characters. The themes that recur are usually related to Różewicz's poetry: the bitter experiences of the war generation (*Kartoteka* [The Card Index], staged in 1960), grotesque and apocalyptic visions of dehumanized civilization (*Stara kobieta wysiaduje* [The Old Lady Broods], staged in 1969), a society dominated by consumer ideals (*Świadkowie, albo nasza mała stabilizacja* [The Witnesses, or Our Tiny Stabilization], staged in 1964, and man's obsession with anachronous, false aestheticism (*Grupa Laokoona* [The Laocoon Group], staged in 1962). Różewicz also ridicules sentimental-Romantic heroic ideals (*Spaghetti i miecz* [Spaghetti and Sword], staged in 1967) and lofty thoughts on the role of the artist (*Na czworakach* [On All Fours], staged in 1972). He is also capable of presenting tragic-comical portraits of average citizens, who attempt to find their role in the world (*Śmieszny staruszek* [The Funny Old Man], staged in 1965, and in New York's Józef Szajna Theater in 1972; *Wyszedł z domu* [He Left Home], staged in 1965). In *Białe małżeństwo* (White Marriage), staged in 1975 and in New York's Józef Szajna Theater in 1976, Różewicz seemed obsessed with the motive of erotic behavior. But his real obsession was with a play that he began writing in 1948 and finally completed in 1972. *Do piachu . . .* (Dead and Buried) cleared the censor in 1978 and was produced and directed by the brilliant actor-director Tadeusz Łomnicki. The antiheroic picture of the Polish partisans angered those who participated in Poland's war with the Nazis. Różewicz's naive hero, Waluś, is reminiscent of Herman Melville's Billy Budd. The realistic treatment of the subject matter seems labored and amateurish. One tends to agree with Halina Filipowicz, who felt that "any cathartic quality is missing in the play."

Różewicz's subsequent plays are based on literary figures or texts and owe much to biographical materials. Even *Pogrzeb po polsku* (A Funeral Polish Style, 1971) seems a parody of some of Różewicz's other plays (e.g., *The Card-File* and *He Left Home*). Even the hero—Kowalski—is a familiar Różewiczian Everyman. Unfortunately, Różewicz is unable to decide what to do with him.

Różewicz's last two plays, inspired by or based on Franz Kafka's life and works, have had an excellent response from foreign critics. *Odejście Głodomora* (Departure of the Hunger Artist, 1976) received a noteworthy production in Buffalo, New York, directed by Kazimierz Braun in 1987.

Pułapka (The Trap, 1981) has also been produced abroad, most notably in Sweden. Spanning over twenty years, the play primarily explores the relationship between Franz and his father. Różewicz was frustrated with the ending and changed it several times. He finished writing the prologue to *The Trap* in 1990, entitled *Przerwana rozmowa* (An Interrupted Conversation). His own views on drama and theater are contained in his Shaw-like comments and didascalia (e.g., in the dramatic essay or treatise *Akt przerywany* [The Interrupted Act], staged in 1970), in his sketches, outlines, and scenarios published in the collection *Teatr niekonsekwencji* (Inconsistent or Inconsequential Theater, 1970).

Różewicz deserves a special position in Polish literature for his prose writings, stories based on his guerrilla experiences (*Opadły liście z drzew* [Leaves Fell from the Trees], 1955), and especially his brilliant attempt to find the philosophical sense of war and life in general in *Przerwany egzamin* (The Interrupted Exam, 1960) and *Wycieczka do muzeum* (A Trip to a Museum, 1966). The drama of human alienation in the contemporary world found its expression in the story *Moja córeczka* (My Little Daughter, adapted for the stage in 1968) and in the monologue *Śmierć w starych dekoracjach* (Death Among Old Settings, 1970). The collection *Przygotowanie do wieczoru autorskiego* (A Preparation for an Author's Evening, 1971) contains his commentaries, memories, sketches of other writers, literary fragments, and notes. He is the editor of several collections of poetry and author of numerous screenplays for his brother, Stanisław. Różewicz has been translated into over twenty languages.

Kartoteka (The Card-Index) is Różewicz's most popular play. The main character is Hero, a former guerrilla fighter in the war. Unrelated scenes, which have multimetaphoric significance, present his life: realistic scenes (the permanent setting is a room or a corner of a street) alternate with surrealistic action, in keeping with the poetics of a dream (the Hero lies in bed; the room is subsequently a street, a café, an office, etc.). Confrontations with other characters (relatives, friends, strangers) circumscribe the main character as a faceless and nameless person in the crowd (he has numerous names), with no exact age (varying from seven to thirty-eight and forty), with no profession—he is nobody. He has lost the innocence of childhood, the faith in love, the respect for tradition; he hates the existence of a simple clerk. Values have become stereotypes and clichés. The experiences of the war have made Hero empty inside, unable to communicate, helpless, and disillusioned. He defends his personality with self-irony. He personalizes the fate of the author's generation but also is the inheritor of the Polish tradition of Romanticism. One of the meanings of the title of the play refers to the way in which the Hero's life is presented: fragmentary facts, events, encounters, conversations, questionnaires, interviews, and appendices. The stream of scenes represents the stream of consciousness. The reality presented is grotesque, a parody, sometimes a symbol. The Choir of Old Men, referring to Classical tragedy, comments on the appropriateness and accuracy of the scenes being presented, but also becomes involved in the plot, murdered by the Hero while trying to make him take a more active role. The ironic statements of the Old Men show the uselessness of traditional forms of theater and drama: the drama unfolds the hidden reality and presents a character with an indeterminate personality. *The Card Index* is open drama at its peak, open to a number of interpretations. The open structure explores the metaphor of the moral position of man in the contemporary world. Różewicz reached his zenith in this peculiarly Polish and universal work.

His subsequent plays merely underscored his theatrical genius. One tends to agree with Czesław Miłosz that Różewicz is still in the process of evolving.

(See Contemporary Polish Literature.)

BIBLIOGRAPHY

Utwory dramatyczne (Dramatic Works), Cracow, 1966.

Wiersze i poematy (Poems and Narrative Poems), selected and with an introduction by H. Michalski, Warsaw, 1967.

Poezje zebrane (Collected Poems), second edition, Wrocław, 1976.

Tadeusz Drewnowski, *Walka o oddech: O pisarstwie Tadeusza Różewicza* (A Battle for Breath: About the Writings of Tadeusz Różewicz), Warsaw, 1990.

ENGLISH

The Card Index, and Other Plays, translated by Adam Czerniawski, London: Calder & Boyars, 1969; New York: Grove Press, 1970.

Faces of Anxiety: Poems, translated by Adam Czerniawski, Chicago: Swallow Press, 1969; London: Rapp and Whiting, 1969.

Selected Poems of Tadeusz Różewicz, translated and with an introduction by Adam Czerniawski, Harmondsworth, England, Baltimore: Penguin, 1976.

"The Survivor" and Other Poems, translated and with an introduction by Magnus J. Kryński and Robert A. Maguire, Princeton, New Jersey: Princeton University Press, 1976.

Unease, translated by Victor Contoski, St. Paul, Minnesota: New Rivers Press, 1980; Kensington, California: Small Press Distribution, 1980.

The Witnesses and Other Plays, translated by Adam Czerniawski, London: Calder & Boyars, 1970, 1984.

Three Poems by Tadeusz Różewicz, translated by E. J. Czerwiński, *Mr. Cogito,* Volume IX, Number 1, Winter 1989.

The Trap (Pułapka), translated by Adam Czerniawski, New York: Institute for Contemporary East European Drama and Theater, 1984.

Marriage Blanc and the Hunger Artist Departs (two plays), translated by Adam Czerniawski, London and New York: Marion Boyars, 1983.

Green Rose (poems), translated by Geoffrey Thurley, Melbourne, Australia: John Michael Group of Publishers, 1982.

Conversation with the Prince and Other Poems, translated by Adam Czerniawski, London: Anvil Press Poetry, 1982.

Boobsie Tootsie or Romantic Love Is Already Waiting and Three Short Plays,

translated by E. J. Czerwiński, in *Pieces of Poland: Four Polish Dramatists, Slavic and East European Arts,* Volume 1, Number 2, Spring 1983.
Halina Filipowicz, *A Laboratory of Impure Forms,* Westport, Connecticut: Greenwood Press, 1991.
Tadeusz Różewicz's Bas-Relief and Other Poems, selected, translated, and with an introduction by E. J. Czerwiński, *Slavic and East European Arts,* Volume 7, Number 2, Winter–Spring 1992.
"Tadeusz Różewicz," in *The Poetry of Survival,* edited by Daniel Weissbort, New York: St. Martin's Press, 1991, 257–72.
The Mature Laurel: Essays on Modern Polish Poetry, edited by Adam Czerniawski, Chester Springs, Pennsylvania: Dufour Editions, 1991.

RYDEL, LUCJAN (1870–1918), a poet, playwright, prose writer, and translator, studied law, history, and history of art. After spending a short period in Warsaw, he left for Paris. After his return, he settled down in Cracow. On November 20, 1900, he married Jadwiga Mikołajczykówna, the daughter of a peasant from near the village of Bronowice: this marriage became an important event in the literary-artistic milieu of Young Poland and provided the background for Wyspiański's* *Wesele* (The Wedding), in which Rydel became the prototype of the bridegroom. His home in Bronowice was the center of cultural life in the country: he established reading rooms, gave talks, organized amateur theater, and staged, among other works, his own play, *Betlejem polskie* (The Polish Bethlehem), in 1904. A lover of Classical art, he traveled to Greece; he also lectured on Greek art at the Cracow Academy of Fine Arts until the end of his life. During 1915–16 he was the director of the Słowacki Theatre in Cracow.

Rydel's poetry is mostly lyrical in nature, especially his collection *Poezje* (Poems, 1899, enlarged editions in 1901 and 1909), which contains both folk motives and Classical themes. His cycle of sonnets *Mitologie greckie* (Greek Mythologies) illustrates scenes from Classical Greek mythology. He began work as a playwright with one-act pieces, for example, his Maeterlinck-style drama *Matka* (Mother, 1893), his fantasy-mystery play *Dies irae* (1893), and *Na marne* (In Vain), staged in 1895 and later published in the anthology *Utwory dramatyczne* (Dramatic Works, Volumes 1–2, 1902). He became known as a playwright with the staging (1899) of his dramatic fairy tale *Zaczarowane koło* (The Enchanted Wheel). His position as a playwright was later confirmed with *Betlejem polskie* (The Polish Bethlehem) and the historical trilogy *Zygmunt August* (1913). His other plays, containing strong moralizing tendencies, were much less popular. Rydel was also the author of several fairy tales in verse (*Bajka o Kasi i królewiczu* [The Fable of Kathy and the Royal Prince], 1903; *Pan Twardowski* [Mr. Twardowski], 1906; and *Madejowe łoże* [The Bed of Ruffian Madey], 1909) based on the ancient fable; Classical stories from the times of ancient Greece (*Ferenike i Pejsidoros* [Pherenike and Peisidoros], 1909); and historical sketches (e.g., *Królowa Jadwiga* [Queen Jadwiga], 1910). He was also a translator of ancient literature. His satirically overemphasized portrait in Wyspiański's *Wesele* (The Wedding) and in *Plotka o Weselu* (Gossip About "The Wedding") by Tadeusz Żeleński–Boy created a one-sided portrait of Rydel which only now is being challenged by modern critics.

Betlejem polskie is a dramatized Nativity play in three acts with several interludes. It was the outcome of the writer's social work and his dream of creating "a rural theater of the future." The plot is based on the Bethlehem Christmas story, incorporated into the landscape of villages around Cracow and into Polish historical reality. Rydel revived the old glory of Poland and made various characters symbolize the suffering of the nation, painting a patriotic fresco of Polish history. The play is still often staged at Christmastime.

(See *Młoda Polska*.)

BIBLIOGRAPHY

Poezje (Poems), enlarged third edition, Cracow, 1909.

English

Polish Bethlehem (Betlejem polskie), translated by Viola Wojnarski-Piszorek, Wilkes-Barre, Pennsylvania: Wilkes College Publishers, 1957.

RYMKIEWICZ, JAROSŁAW MAREK (born 1935), a poet, translator, playwright, literary historian, and critic, graduated from the Department of Polish Philology in Łódź. He continued his research at the university and later at the Polish Academy of Sciences in Warsaw, from which he was repressively removed in 1985 because of his political opposition; he also worked for various cultural magazines and for the theater. He was a representative and theoretician of contemporary Neo-Classicism in Poland. He presented his view of poetry in the collection of sketches *Czym jest klasycyzm: Manifesty poetyckie* (What Is Classicism: Poetic Manifestos, 1967) and in the treatises *Czym jest klasycyzm (w teatrze)* (What Is Classicism [in the Theater], published in *Dialog* in 1970) and *Co to jest imitacja* (What Is Imitation, in *Dialog* in 1971). In his theory he cited T. S. Eliot (and Ezra Pound), accepting their concept of time and their assumptions on the unity and continuity of art and culture. Rymkiewicz revived old forms of rhythm and imagery (hence stylization, imitation, pastiche); he sought archetypes and myths of European art in Mediterranean models. He cited poets of the seventeenth and early eighteenth centuries and the poets of the Polish Baroque, who were concerned with metaphysical and existential problems. He employed poetic symbols of dream and reality, the technique of loose associations, and contrasting oppositions. His poetic volumes included the following: *Konwencje* (Conventions, 1957), *Człowiek z głową jastrzębia* (A Man with the Head of a Hawk, 1960), *Metafizyka* (Metaphysics, 1963),

Animula (1964), *Anatomia* (Anatomy, 1970), *Co to jest drozd* (What Is a Thrush, 1973), *Thema regium* (1978), and *Srebrny jeleń* (Silver Stag, 1979). In his later works, *Ulica Mandelsztama* (Mandelshtam Street, 1983) and *Mogiła Ordona* (Ordon's Tomb, 1984), published in underground presses, the poet turned to the Polish Romantic tradition. Revealed here were catastrophic motives, connected with historical Polish experiences, in particular the fate of the nation, its manners, and spiritual identity threatened by the Russian powers in its past and contemporary embodiment.

Rymkiewicz is a translator of English, American, Russian, and Spanish poetry (e.g., Shakespeare's sonnets, T. S. Eliot, Mandelshtam, and Lorca). He wrote imitations of Calderón's plays (*Życie jest snem* [Life Is a Dream], staged in 1969, and *Księżniczka na opak wywrócona* [The Princess Turned Inside Out], published in 1973), regarding them as archetypes of comedy. His other plays, based on Classical patterns and drawing inspiration from Calderón, include the following: *Król Mięsopust* (King Carnival), published in *Dialog* in 1970; *Porwanie Europy* (The Rape of Europe), published in 1971; *Kochankowie piekła* (Lovers of Hell), published in 1972; and *Niebiańskie bliźnięta* (Heavenly Twins), staged in 1973. He turned to Polish Romantic tradition in his "serious comedies": *Ułani* (The Uhlans), staged in 1975, and *Dwór nad Narwią* (The Manor on the Narwia), staged in 1979. As a researcher, he concentrated on the Mediterranean topos of paradise gardens (*Myśli różne o ogrodach* [Various Thoughts About Gardens], 1968). In time he achieved an original synthesis of his research and literary interests, creating a type of novel that combines characteristics of scholarly treatises and biographical essays, philological inquiry with a fictional subject and psychological speculation. The following works were written in this convention: on Alexander Fredro* (1977), on Juliusz Słowacki* (1982), and on Adam Mickiewicz* and the country of his youth, Lithuania (*Żmut* [Ball of Yarn, 1987] and *Baket* [Basket, 1990]). A similar distance is maintained in his major literary works, books dedicated to contemporary themes: *Rozmowy polskie latem 1983* (Polish Conversations During the Summer of 1983, Paris, 1984), revealing characteristic Polish attitudes during Martial Law 1981–83, laying open people's fears and hopes regarding the changes in the fate of the nation, and *Umschlagplatz* (Paris, 1988), a record of the author's personal inquiries and reflections, in which he tries to reconstruct circumstances of the riddle of the Warsaw Ghetto during the German occupation and the complicated history of Polish-Jewish relations.

BIBLIOGRAPHY

J. Błoński, *Czym był, czym mógł być klasycyzm* (What Was, What Could Be Classicism), *Odmarsz* (Marching Off), Cracow, 1978.

RZEWUSKI, HENRYK (1791–1866), a prose writer and publicist, was perhaps the greatest representative of extreme conservatism and loyalism during the years between the two uprisings, 1830 and 1863. The son of a violent opponent of Enlightenment reforms and a nephew of one of the founders of Targowica, he was brought up to worship old *szlachta* (nobility) ideals. His early literary work was influenced by his meeting with Mickiewicz* in 1825. Mickiewicz is said to have inspired Rzewuski to set down those tales from the recent past that he related in Rome. His cycle of stories, published in Paris from 1839 to 1841, became known as *Pamiątki Soplicy* (Souvenirs of Soplica). He was responsible for initiating a new literary genre—*gawęda szlachecka* (nobleman's chatter). Rzewuski tried to make light of his book, since its contents were not in accord with his political program.

In his political views he often cited the philosophical works of de Maistre. According to Zofia Lewinówna, Rzewuski considered religion to be the only basis on which to base life in a society. Each nation had its role to play, determined by Providence; history thus consisted not in the process of development, but in the preservation of unchanged tradition. Nations passed through different periods, once realizing their mission, abandoning it. The latter could often lead to the collapse of a nation—as the Enlightenment reforms led to the partitions. Romantic literature, according to Rzewuski, had no national character and led the country to its demise. Rzewuski presented these views in his publicistic writings in *Tygodnik Petersburski* (The Petersburg Weekly) and *Mieszaniny obyczajowe* (Moral Varieties, 1841–43). In 1851 he established *Dziennik Warszawski* (The Warsaw Daily), which seemed to be quite a fine publication, the first of its kind to include a permanent section for publishing novels. The initial success, however, was soon undermined by Rzewuski's programmatic article *Cywilizacja i religia* (Civilization and Religion).

Rzewuski wrote several historical novels: *Listopad* (November, 1845–46), *Zamek krakowski* (The Cracow Castle, Volumes 1–3, 1847–48), *Adam Śmigielski* (Volumes 1–2, 1851), *Zaporożec* (Man from Zaporożec, Volumes 1–4, 1854), *Rycerz Lizdejko* (The Knight Lizdejko, Volumes 1–3, 1851–52). He also wrote several short stories. Many of his works have remained in manuscript.

Pamiątki Soplicy (Souvenirs of Soplica, 1830–32, published in Paris, 1839–41), a series of twenty-five stories, was an attempt to re-create the authentic atmosphere, views, beliefs, life-style, and customs of the provincial *szlachta* before the fall of the Polish Republic. Rzewuski managed to employ "overheard," discretely stylized language and, above all, create an original narrator, an ideally typical personality, with an equally typical biography. By distancing himself from his hero Soplica and by treating the character with mild irony, he achieved a superb artistic and cognitive effect, presenting the world of the *szlachta* as if from within. The artistic effect results not only from what Soplica says but from how he relates the story and comments on it—the seemingly distracting digressions appear to be indispensable. The structure of the series is rather loose, but consistency is achieved through the narrator, the setting, the method of narration, and the emphasis on one person—the most "Sarmatian" of the magnates, *Radziwiłł Panie Kochanku*—and on one event—the Confederacy of Bar.

BIBLIOGRAPHY

Henryk Rzewuski, *Dzieła* (Works). Seria I. *Powieści historyczne* (Historical Novels), Warsaw, 1877–84.

S

SANATORIUM POD KLEPSYDRĄ (The Sanatorium Under the Sign of the Hourglass) (see Schulz).

SARBIEWSKI, MACIEJ KAZIMIERZ (1595–1640), a Polish-Latin poet and literary theoretician, was born in Sarbiewo. From 1635 he was a preacher in the court of Władysław IV. He studied at the Academy in Wilno (Vilnius) and at the college in Braniewo. He became a Jesuit in 1612 and received his doctorates in philosophy and religion in 1632 and 1636, respectively. Earlier he studied in Rome (1622–25), at the same time formulating his aesthetic theories. A friend of the erudite Pope Urban VIII, he was crowned poet laureate and became one of the most popular Neo-Latinist poets of the period. His works represented Jesuit Classicism: in his odes and epodes (four volumes of odes, one of epodes, and one of epigrams—*Lyricorum libri IV: Epodon liber unus alterque epigrammatum,* the best edition published in Antwerp in 1634). His works were translated into various languages, including English, German, and French. His poems were known as "parodies of Horace" in language, style, and metrics. He was able to enunciate Christian themes through the use of antique forms (he was called the Christian Horace). Sarbiewski's poetry is characterized by Baroque elements (especially in his verses dedicated to the cult of Mary, with its description of stars, the moon, lilies, full of radiance and azure, expressing the anxiety and longing for a heavenly home, which was characteristic of the period). His poetry also enunciated resignation in the face of the changes of fortune (under the influence of Christian stoicism adumbrated by J. Lipsius, whom Sarbiewski greatly admired). The ease with which he wrote in Latin gave him the opportunity to hide the inner turmoil he felt under the guise of Classicism. This inner turmoil was characteristic of Neo-Latin poetry written by the Renaissance humanists, who often paraphrased biblical themes. Influenced by Kochanowski,* whom he eagerly imitated (*Lyricorum liber IV 5, 6*), Sarbiewski often dedicated a great deal of space to a description of his country's landscape (among other things, praise of the river Bug, published in *Opera posthuma* by S. Lubienski in 1643, as well as a description of the River Narwa, *Lyricorum liber II 15*). He also wrote of public matters that interested him.

In his book of 265 epigrams, Sarbiewski almost duplicated the success of one of the finest epigrammatists of the period, the Scot-Latin poet J. Owen. Although Sarbiewski's epigrams are not devoid of irony, they are far from the satirical tone of Martial, since the Polish poet emphasizes form and avoids social criticism.

Sarbiewski was also the author of epic poems, published posthumously (among them, fragments of *Lechias,* as well as numerous panegyric poems). By order of the king, he created *Silviludia poetica.* As a teacher, he has left behind numerous theoretical treatises, *De perfecta poesi* and *Praecepta poetica,* the basis of his poetical genius.

Sarbiewski's poetry became a model for works written in Polish, as well as in Latin, until the end of the eighteenth century, among others, the works of A. Naruszewicz,* published in Wilno (Vilnius) in 1757. His works were translated into Polish in the nineteenth century by W. Syrokomla, who gave the poems a Romantic tone which is not present in the original. In the twentieth century T. Karyłowski published a number of translations in various periodicals.

BIBLIOGRAPHY

Poemata omnia, edited by T. Wall, Stara Wieś, 1892; second edition, containing a bibliography, 1911.

Liryki oraz Droga rzymska i fragmenty: Lechiady (Lyrics and the Roman Way and Fragments: Lechiady), translated by T. Karyłowski, edited by M. Korołko and J. Okoń, Warsaw, 1980.

English

Monumenta Polonica: The First Four Centuries of Polish Poetry: A Bilingual Anthology, edited by Bogdana Carpenter, Ann Arbor: Michigan Slavic Publications, 1989.

SCHULZ, BRUNO (1892–1942), a prose writer, literary critic, and graphic artist, came from a Polish-speaking Jewish family. He also knew German from his childhood. He studied architecture and painting, then taught drawing in a school in his birthplace, Drohobycz, a moderately sized provincial town in southeastern Poland. He died of a gunshot wound inflicted while he was in the Drohobycz ghetto during the Nazi occupation.

He began writing in 1925–26. His first known work, *Noc lipcowa* (July Night), was written in 1928, but published only in 1936. Through

Nałkowska's* efforts, he made his debut with a collection, a cycle of stories, *Sklepy cynamonowe* (Cinnamon Shops, 1933), originally written as postscripts in letters to his friend, Debora Voegel. The success of the book generated his friendship with writers like Gombrowicz,* S. I. Witkiewicz,* T. Breza,* Nowaczyński,* Słonimski,* and Tuwim,* who nominated the book for the award of the weekly *Wiadomości Literackie* (Literary News). Schulz's second book, *Sanatorium Pod Klepsydrą* (The Sanatorium Under the Sign of the Hourglass, 1936), was chiefly made up of works written earlier than those published in *Sklepy cynamonowe.* Both collections are written in a lyrical poetic prose, in which the plot is of secondary importance. They are poetic, partly fantastic, but readily recognizable transformations of reality in a small town in Galicia before World War I. *Sklepy cynamonowe* seems a more unified collection, with a unity of setting, a putative narrator, and the main characters (father, mother, Adela). The internal links throughout the stories create a loose structure resembling an avant-garde novel. The stories in *Sanatorium Pod Klepsydrą* contain fantastic plots which play an important role in the overall structure (e.g., *Wiosna* [Spring]). The title story resembles a dream sequence. In 1934 Schulz began working on a novel, *Mesjasz* (The Messiah), whose theme was the arrival of a contemporary Savior. Two fragments of the book (*Genialna epoka* [The Magnificent Epoch] and *Księga* [The Book]) were included in *Sanatorium Pod Klepsydrą* as separate stories. The rest of the novel (probably never completed) has been lost. His other preserved works include four published prose pieces and about a hundred letters, highly informative and containing artistic merit.

As a literary critic Schulz wrote over twenty reviews and sketches published in various literary magazines. In the essay *Mityzacja rzeczywistości* (A Mythicization of Reality, 1936) he presented a brief outline of his theory of poetry, which he saw as a revival of primitive myths in words. Words incessantly aim at reconstructing the original sense, lost in everyday use. He also published an enthusiastic review of Gombrowicz's *Ferdydurke* and wrote about Nałkowska, Kuncewiczowa,* Breza, Wierzyński,* Mauriac, Bernanos, Huxley, Aragon, and Kafka (he translated *Proces* [The Trial]). His paintings are lost; the only works preserved are drawings and prints, among them, the series *Xięga bałwochwalcza* (The Book of Idolatrous Veneration) containing expressionist elements related in spirit to Schulz's later writings.

Schulz employed a variety of expressionistic and modernistic elements in his prose, characteristic of the decadent era of the Austrian-Hungarian empire (Rilke, Kafka, Musil). According to Jan Józef Lipski, Schulz attempted to treat fundamental existential problems with the language of myths and symbols which referred to the subconscious. Schulz viewed myth as the main principle, which in the case of an individual was a Freudian return to childhood and its mythology, return to the original sense of words, which ultimately would result in the identity of the mechanism of poetic language and the mechanism of the world. Metaphor described the world as it was seen by the narrator: dynamic, ever-changing, kaleidoscopic. This approach, along with the use of grotesque elements and self-irony, is what differentiated Schulz's prose from earlier attempts. He wrote in a highly lyrical manner, contrasted by frequent stylization for a lecture or a treatise and accompanied by the introduction of foreign and sophisticated words: all these elements produced a Baroque effect. Erotic symbols also played an important role, symbols of guilt, of dreams. Schulz was highly appreciated as a writer during the period between the wars, but only since the 1957 edition of his works has he begun to receive the attention he deserved in the literature of the twentieth century. The numerous translations of his works into numerous languages also hastened his acceptance in the literary world.

(See Contemporary Polish Literature.)

BIBLIOGRAPHY

Proza (Prose), introduction by Arthur Sandauer, *Rzeczywistość zdegradowana: Rzecz o Brunonie Schulzu* (Degraded Reality: Concerning Bruno Schulz), first edition, 1956, with letters edited by J. Ficowski, Cracow, 1964; second enlarged edition, Cracow, 1973.

English

The Street of Crocodiles, translated by Celina Wieniewska, New York: Walker, 1963; New York: Penguin Books, 1977.

Cinnamon Shops (Sklepy cynamonowe), translated by Celina Wieniewska, London: MacGibbon and Kee, 1963.

The Wild Ricer's Guide, Berkeley, California, Appleseed Press, 1979.

Sanatorium Under the Sign of the Hourglass (Sanatorium Pod Klepsydrą), translated by Celina Wieniewska, New York: Walker, 1978.

SENNIK WSPÓŁCZESNY (A Dreambook of Our Time) (see Konwicki).

SĘP-SZARZYŃSKI, MIKOŁAJ (ca. 1550–81), unknown during his lifetime, is considered the first poet of the Polish Baroque period. Metaphysical, intellectual, and difficult to understand, his poetry was rediscovered in the twentieth century. Born into a family of the nobility, Sęp-Szarzyński studied in Lvov, Wittenberg, and Leipzig. After a journey to Italy, he changed his religion from Protestant to Catholic. His poetry expressed his anxiety about man's failure to recognize and accept the true metaphysical values of a fleeting earthly world and the eternal world, and somehow incorporate these values into his everyday life. He believed that man's life was merely a brief episode leading to eternal salvation. Twenty years after his death, his brother, at the insistence of the poet's closest friends, published a small volume, *Rytmy abo wiersze polskie* (Rhythms or Polish Poetry, 1601), containing all the extant poems. The high quality of his verse and innovative techniques give him a secure place in Polish literature. His verse forms include epigrams, sonnets, songs, epitaphs, and paraphrases of the Psalms.

(See Renaissance.)

BIBLIOGRAPHY

Rytmy abo wiersze polskie oraz cykl erotyków (Rhythms or Polish Poetry as Well as a Cycle of Eroticism), edited by J. Krzyżanowski, Wrocław: Ossolineum, 1973.

Jan Błoński, *Mikołaj Sęp Szarzyński a początki polskiego baroku* (Mikołaj Sęp Szarzyński and the Beginnings of Polish Baroque), Cracow, 1967.

English

Richard Sokoloski, *The Poetry of Mikołaj Sęp Szarzyński,* 1988, Ottawa, Canada: Ottawa University.

SHAKESPEARE OUR CONTEMPORARY (see Kott).

SIEDLECKI, ADAM GRZYMAŁA (pseudonyms Quis, Mus, Franciszek Wierzbiński, and Jan z Marnowa) (1876–1967), was a literary and theater critic, playwright, and prose writer. His father took part in the January Uprising of 1863. Siedlecki himself participated in various underground patriotic activities, for which he was arrested. He studied in Cracow and in Italy and made his debut in Cracow with the comedy *Niewolnicy krwi* (Slaves of Blood, 1899). He published in a number of cultural and literary magazines and was a lecturer (at the People's University and at a drama school in Bydgoszcz). He was director or literary director of many theaters in Cracow and Warsaw. He was the recipient of the Golden Wreath of the Polish Academy of Literature (PAL) and many other awards.

Siedlecki was deeply interested in social phenomena and scholarly and literary innovations. His patriotic, somewhat nationalistic views are also expressed in his work: he actually considered criticism and literature as functions which emphasized and strengthened the independence of Polish culture, which he further claimed was based on chivalrous and gentry ideals. He appreciated Romanticism for its national value, but his social programs were closer to positivism. Fascinated with Roman culture, he stressed its assimilation into Polish culture with the reign of Kazimierz (Casimir) the Great. On the other hand, he argued for the separation of German and Russian models in respect to the Polish tradition. He preferred the poetics of Neo-Classicism and realism. His critical writings are very personal, often based on intuition, not only on research, and bear a relationship to both subjective-impressionistic and positivist trends. He advocated Taine's theory of environment and race and supported the ideas of Sainte-Beuve, that is, a psychobiographical analysis of the writer's creative personality in all its complexities. Siedlecki wrote several outstanding works on Wyspiański, for example, *Wyspiański: Cechy i elementy twórczości* (Wyspiański: Features and Elements of his Creative Works, 1909; reissued edition, *O twórczości Wyspiańskiego* [About Wyspiański's Creative Works], 1970) which Wyka considered one of the exceptional books of the epoch. Siedlecki also wrote monographs on Fredro,* Dygasiński,* Reymont,* J. A. Kisielewski,* and Staff.* Portraits of outstanding personalities of positivism and Young Poland are gathered in his collection *Niepospolici ludzie w dniu swoim powszednim* (Extraordinary People in Their Daily Life, 1961) and *Nie pożegnani* (Those Not Bid a Farewell, 1972), which is especially important, since it commemorates those writers and scholars who died during the Nazi occupation. Siedlecki rejected the ideological and artistic claims of modernism, though later his view, for example, of Berent,* was somewhat modified.

He worked in a variety of genres (review, feuilleton, sketch, essay). He did not reject anecdotes or personal memories and employed irony and satire, lightened somewhat by his compassion for human frailties. He made major contributions to the history of Polish theater: *Świat aktorski moich czasów* (The Actor's World During My Time, 1957) and *Tadeusz Pawlikowski i jego krakowscy aktorzy* (Tadeusz Pawlikowski and His Cracow Actors, 1971). His reviews appeared in *Z teatrów warszawskich 1926–1939* (From the Warsaw Theaters, 1926–1939, 1972). He also wrote several short stories, including *Galeria moich bliźnich* (A Gallery of My Close Friends, 1911); novels, including *Samosęki* (1924); and some farcical plays. He translated the plays of Gorky, Gogol, and Chekhov.

BIBLIOGRAPHY

J. Konieczny, *Twórczość krytycznoliteracka Adama Grzymały Siedlickiego* (Critical-Literary Works of Adam Gryzmała Siedlecki), Poznań, 1976.

SIELANKI (Idylls) (see Szymonowic).

SIENKIEWICZ, HENRYK (pseudonym Litwos) (1846–1916), a novelist and short story writer, was awarded the Nobel Prize in 1905. He was from an impoverished gentry family in Warsaw. He studied law and the humanities. He began his career as a reporter and columnist in Warsaw. He was founder and co-owner of *Niwa* (Soil) and then editor of a mildly conservative daily newspaper, *Słowo* (The Word).

He spent the years 1876–78 in America, as a correspondent for *Gazeta Polska* (The Polish Gazette). In 1879 he visited Western Europe: after 1880 he went abroad every year to heal his wife, who suffered from tuberculosis. An avid traveler, he visited Constantinople, Athens, Naples, Rome, Spain, and Zanzibar. He wrote of his travels, publishing his articles, stories, and novels in magazines in various cities of Poland. He soon became the most popular writer in Poland. In honor of his twenty-fifth anniversary as a writer, in 1906 he was awarded the estate in Oblęgorek by the Anniversary Committee, as a gift from the Polish nation and in honor of his receiving the Nobel Prize in Literature.

After the outbreak of World War I, Sienkiewicz left for Vevey in Switzerland, organizing (with Ignacy Paderewski) a committee to help the victims of the war. According to Julian Krzyżanowski, he continuously was engaged in social and political activity, initiating the fund for erecting Mickiewicz's* monument in Warsaw, for building a nursing home for children and a church in Zakopane, providing fellowships for young writers (among the awardees were Konopnicka,* Przybyszewski,* Daniłowski, and Przerwa-Tetmajer*). He wrote letters protesting the anti-Polish actions of the Prussian government, published articles demanding autonomy for the Kingdom of Poland, and fought for "national unification." His support for the National Democratic Party (directed mainly against Socialism) was manipulated into a political game by various factions.

Sienkiewicz's broad publicistic interests are best reflected in his feuilletons: *Bez tytułu* (Without a Title, 1873) and *Chwila obecna* (The Present Moment, 1875) in *Gazeta Polska* (The Polish Gazette); *Sprawy Bieżące* (Current Affairs, 1874–75, in *Niwa* [Soil]) and *Wiadomości bieżące* (Current News, 1880–81) in *Gazeta Polska* (The Polish Gazette); and, most importantly, his reports written during his travels, *Listy z podróży do Ameryki* (Letters from Travels to America, 1876–78) and *Listy z Afryki* (Letters from Africa, 1891–92). The American series presented a very broad and thorough analysis of social life in America. It also provided a bridge between Sienkiewicz's journalistic writings and his novels. The echo of his American themes are found in his historical novels like *Ogniem i mieczem* (With Fire and Sword) and *Wiry* (Whirlpools). His magazine articles include literary criticism: reviews (e.g., of Chmielowski's *Zarys literatury polskiej* [An Outline of Polish Literature]), original studies (e.g., on Sęp-Szarzyński), and theoretical criticism (e.g., the lectures *O naturaliźmie w powieści* [On Naturalism in Novels], 1880, and *O powieści historycznej* [About the Historical Novel], 1889). Sienkiewicz declared himself to be an advocate of realism, supported by a writer's knowledge and intuition.

Sienkiewicz predominantly wrote novelettes and short stories during the first decade of his literary career. In these works he explored then current positivist problems (*Humoreski z teki Worszyłły* [Humoresques from Worszyłła's Portfolio], 1872), the plight of the peasant, education, forced military service by the occupant army, and emigration: *Szkice węglem* (Charcoal Sketches, 1880), *Bartek Zwycięzca* (Bartek the Conqueror, 1882), *Za chlebem* (In Search of Bread, 1880), *Janko Muzykant* (Johnny the Musician, 1880), and *Jamioł* (Angel, 1882). His "American" stories form a separate group; life in America, a condemnation of the extermination of the Indians, and a depiction of the so-called old emigration: *Orso* (1880), *Przez stepy* (Through the Steppes, 1880), *Sachem* (1889), *Latarnik* (The Light-House Keeper, 1882), and *Wspomnienie z Maripozy* (Thoughts from Mariposa, 1889). Among those are also several humorous stories, such as *Ta trzecia* (This Third Woman, 1889). In these works Sienkiewicz seems sensitive to the problems which animated his social consciousness; they also reveal his knowledge of the human psyche and his skill in dramatizing a situation. He always seems master of the genre: brevity and suspense are upheld throughout. He wrote over forty novelettes and contributed significantly to the development of the genre in the late nineteenth century. Some of these works have become classics of the genre.

Ten years after his first novel *Na marne* (In Vain, 1872), Sienkiewicz began working on *Ogniem i mieczem* (With Fire and Sword, published in *Słowo* [Word] in 1883–84; definitive edition in 1884) and on the next two novels in the series, *Potop* (The Flood, 1886) and *Pan Wołodyjowski* (Mister Wołodyjowski, 1888). The three novels became known as *Trylogia* (The Trilogy), which almost instantly became the most popular novels both in Poland and abroad. The popularity of *Trylogia* did not rescue it from harsh criticism. Several critics argued that the depiction of the past did not agree with the historical view of events, especially as presented by the Cracow historical school. The novel was also attacked because of its psychological drawbacks. Smarting from these critical remarks, Sienkiewicz began work on a psychological novel, *Bez dogmatu* (Without Dogma, 1891), the memoirs of a decadent man, an elegant social parasite, suffering from a chronic lack of willpower—the Polish Oblomov. Although critical of his hero, Sienkiewicz was, for some reason, unable to maintain appropriate artistic distance. A similar artistic deficiency can be discerned in *Rodzina Połanieckich* (The Połaniecki Family, 1895), which contained insightful observations about the bourgeois gentry, but failed as an artistic whole. The novel was received as an apology of the petit bourgeois rather than as a condemnation of bourgeois values.

These contemporary novels are considered by most critics as "lesser Sienkiewicz"; his métier lay in the historical novel. His best known achievement in the genre was *Quo vadis* (1896), a depiction of Nero's Rome and the rise of Christianity. Before *Quo vadis* Sienkiewicz had written a novelette, *Pójdźmy za Nim* (Let's Follow Him, 1893), based on a similar theme. Some Polish critics consider *Krzyżacy* (The Teutonic Knights, 1900) his greatest achievement. The historical perspective in this work is certainly much broader then in any of his earlier works. The epoch of Jadwiga and Jagiełło, the historical breakthrough and the rise of the Polish national identity, are explored in this work. The symbolic ending, the victorious battle of Grunwald in which the power of the Teutonic Knights is destroyed, gave the entire novel a contemporary political interpretation, which later proved to be almost prophetic. His next historical novels, *Na polu chwały* (On the

Field of Glory, published in *Biesiada Literacka* [Literary Banquet], in 1903–4; definitive edition in 1906) and the unfinished *Legiony* (The Legions, 1913; definitive edition in 1918), show a diminution of Sienkiewicz's art. His last novel, the story for young readers *W pustyni i w puszczy* (In the Desert and the Wilderness, 1911), gained great popularity and has become a classic in its field.

Sienkiewicz is still one of the most popular writers in the world. A century after his death, arguments regarding his merits have not diminished.

Quo vadis is a novel whose setting is the time of Nero. The idea of the novel arose from nineteenth century interest in ancient times and early Christianity. It was also inspired by paintings by H. Siemiradzki. According to legend, "Quo vadis, Domine?" is the question Peter asked Jesus: Peter was then escaping from Rome; Jesus was on his way to Rome. Hearing Christ's answer, Peter returned to Rome to die for his faith.

Sienkiewicz's intention in the novel was an ambitious one: to show the mutual relationship between the pagan-Roman and Judeo-Christian cultures. The picture of Christianity, however, is far from convincing, as several critics have noted. It is all the more obvious in contrast to the rich and exhaustive portrait of life in Rome: of common citizens, the caesar, the intellectual elite. An astute critic, I. Matuszewski, saw the reason for this in Sienkiewicz's temperament, that made him more "a prophet of the body" than of the soul. Like Milton's Devil, Sienkiewicz's villains fare better than his adversaries; hence, excellent portraits of Petronius, Nero, Chilon Chilonides, while the apostles Peter and Paul seem two-dimensional and lacklustre.

The plot of *Quo vadis* is quite traditional: a young officer from a patrician family, Vinicius, meets a girl, Ligia, a Christian, who escapes from his obsessive affection for her through the protection of her Christian community; he wins her only when he becomes a Christian himself. The character of Ligia, who is a Slavic hostage brought up in the family of a Roman commander, is introduced to provide a link between the Slavic and Roman-Christian cultures. The novel has a symbolic ending, when Ligia's servant, Ursus, breaks the neck of a Teutonic aurochs. These subtleties, which at first escaped the attention of Polish readers and which have never been noted by foreign readers, hardly affect the artistic message of the novel, which is the conflict of two cultures, the aristocratic, powerful rulers and the plebeian, weaker subjugated majority. The weak win in the end.

Trylogia (The Trilogy) contains three historical novels: *Ogniem i mieczem* (With Fire and Sword), which describes the war with the Cossacks, culminating in Poland's victory in 1651; *Potop* (The Flood), which involves the Swedish invasion in 1656; and *Pan Wołodyjowski* (Mister Wołodyjowski), which depicts the beginning of the war with Turkey, the loss of Kamieniec Podolski, and Sobieski's ultimate victory at Chocim in 1672.

The three novels have a number of features in common. In each a broad and detailed historical background is skillfully combined with the plot; the historical events are usually connected with battles and the siege of fortresses, such as Zbaraż, Częstochowa, and Kamieniec Podolski, which in turn are accompanied by diplomatic negotiations. Against this background Sienkiewicz presents his characters, fictitious and authentic, handled with care and detail. The historical personages include King Jan Kazimierz; the great hetmans and commanders, J. Wiśniowiecki, S. Czarniecki, P. J. Sapieha; and the prospective king, Jan Sobieski. The enemies of Poland include Bohdan Chmielnicki, the leader of the Ukrainian Revolution; the Swedish king, Karol Gustav; and a fictitious Tartar, Azja Tuhajbejowicz. Two Radziwiłł brothers who take the side of the Swedes are also vividly portrayed. The fictitious characters, who have remote historical predecessors and possess authentic names, are the brave soldiers Skrzetuski, Kmicic, and Wołodyjowski. Zagłoba, one of the main characters in all three of the novels, should also be singled out; he is something of a Polish Sancho Panza.

The plots of the three novels are based on a similar pattern, but so individualized that repetition seldom occurs. The pattern consists of a love affair that meets with serious obstacles, provoked by the course of history: Skrzetuski, Helena, and Bohun; Kmicic, Oleńka, and Bogusław Radziwiłł; Wołodyjowski, Basia, and Azja—these shape the three triangles in which the girl, loved by a Polish officer, falls into the hands of his rival and political enemy. She is able to defend herself and a happy ending is ensured. Sienkiewicz himself once ridiculed the scheme, but in *The Trilogy* he was able each time to give it a varied and attractive form so that an impression of freshness is created. During the period when *Trylogia* was being composed, adventure novels were decidedly out of fashion, but Sienkiewicz's unfailing intuition selected the maligned old epic genre and he unfailingly proved its eternal fascination. In the choice of the setting he was guided by the Slavic Romantic tradition, which always admired the beauty of Ukraine. *Potop,* on the other hand, takes place throughout all Poland. The never ending chain of adventures is presented similarly to those in the Homeric epic: the superhuman martial deeds of the heroes, their ability to extract themselves from hopeless situations, and their willingness to sacrifice their lives (Podbipięta, Wołodyjowski) for the good and honor of their country. The heroic aspect does not make them any less human: never avoiding pathos, Sienkiewicz, a great humorist himself and admirer of Shakespeare, made one of the main characters a comic one—Zagłoba, an unmistakable successor to Ulysses and Falstaff, to Stańczyk and Sancho Panza. He is also an embodiment of Polish Sarmatism. He plays a crucial role in all of the novels, accompanied by characters like Rzędzian or Roch Kowalski, who bring humor into the serious story of Poland's trials. Sienkiewicz's companion was Homer, before and during the composition of *Trylogia,* which has traces of the Greek epic style.

The publication of *Trylogia* was an artistic event, received critically by contemporary writers and enthusiastically by the readers. The success was certainly due to the patriotic tone of the novel, the belief in the survival of the nation. During the period when historiography presented Poland's past so critically, the picture of past glory achieved through courage was certainly a consolation to Polish readers. For the foreign reader, *Trylogia*'s artistic and aesthetic values—its pathos, tragedy, humor, and picturesque nature—had great appeal. *Ogniem i mieczem* has been translated into twenty-six languages, *Potop* into twenty-three, *Pan Wołodyjowski* into twenty. *Ogniem i mieczem* was made into a film in Italy in 1962: *Potop* and *Pan Wołodyjowski* were filmed by Jerzy Hoffman in Poland; the former was nominated for an Oscar, the latter made into a television series.

(See Positivism and *Młoda Polska.*)

BIBLIOGRAPHY

Dzieła (Works), sixty volumes, edited by Julian Krzyżanowski, Warsaw: Państwowy Instytut Wydawniczy, 1948–55.

J. Krzyżanowski, *Henryka Sienkiewicza żywot i sprawy* (Henryk Sienkiewicz's Life and Affairs), Warsaw, 1966.

J. Krzyżanowski, *Twórczość Henryka Sienkiewicza* (The Creativity of Henryk Sienkiewicz), Warsaw, 1970.

English

"Henryk Sienkiewicz," in *America Through Polish Eyes: Selected and with Commentaries by Bogdan Grzeloński,* translated by E. J. Czerwiński, Warsaw: Interpress, 1988.

The Deluge: An Historical Novel of Poland, Sweden and Russia (A Sequel to *With Fire and Sword*), translated by Jeremiah Curtin, Boston: Little, Brown, 1891; 1892; 1894; 1897; 1898; 1928; St. Clair Shore, Michigan: Scholarly Press, 1970; New York: AMS Press, 1971.

Hania, translated by Jeremiah Curtin, Philadelphia: H. Altemus, 1896; 1898; London: J. M. Dent, 1897; Boston: Little, Brown, 1897; Chicago: Donohue, Henneberry, 1898; Plainview, New York: Books for Libraries, 1973.

Pan Michael: An Historical Novel of Poland, the Ukraine, and Turkey (A Sequel to *With Fire and Sword* and *The Deluge*), translated by Jeremiah Curtin, Boston: Little, Brown, 1896; 1897; London: J. M. Dent, 1901; Westport, Connecticut: Greenwood, 1968.

Portrait of America: Letters (Listy z podróży do Ameryki), edited and translated by Charles Morley, New York: Columbia University Press, 1959.

Selected Tales, Miami: American Institute of Polish Culture, 1975.

Tales, edited by Monica Mary Gardner, London: J. M. Dent, 1946; New York: E. P. Dutton, 1946.

The Teutonic Knights: An Historical Novel, Edinburgh: A. Tyszkiewicz, 1943.

Western Septet: Seven Stories of the American West, edited and translated by Marion Moore Coleman, Cheshire, Connecticut: Cherry Hill, 1963.

With Fire and Sword: An Historical Novel of Poland and Russia (Trylogia: Ogniem i mieczem), translated by Jeremiah Curtin, Boston: Little, Brown, 1890; 1892; 1895; 1898.

Children of the Soil, translated by Jeremiah Curtin, Boston: Little, Brown, 1895; 1898.

Without Dogma (Bez dogmatu), translated by Iza Young, Boston: Little, Brown, 1893.

After Bread (Za chlebem), translated by Vatslaf Hlasko and Thomas Bullick, New York: H. M. Caldwell, 1897; New York: R. F. Fenno, 1897.

An Excursion to Athens, New York: H. M. Caldwell, 1897; New York: R. F. Fenno, 1897.

For Daily Bread and Other Stories, translated by Iza Young, Philadelphia: H. Altemus, 1896.

Knights of the Cross (Krzyżacy), translated by S. C. de Soissons, New York: R. F. Renno, 1897; Boston: Little, Brown, 1899.

Let Us Follow Him, translated by Jeremiah Curtin, Boston: Little, Brown, 1897; New York: H. M. Caldwell, 1897; New York: R. F. Fenno, 1897; Philadelphia: Altemus, 1989.

On The Sunny Shore, translated by S. C. de Soissons, New York: R. F. Fenno, 1897; Philadelphia: Altemus, 1898.

Quo Vadis? translated by Jeremiah Curtin and Samuel Augustus Binion, London, New York: Nelson, 1896; Boston: Little, Brown, 1897; H. Altemus, 1897; New York: Hurst, 1897; 1898; Philadelphia: Altemus, 1897; Boston: Little, Brown, 1896; 1897; 1898; New York: Book League of America, 1897; New York: Grosset and Dunlap, 1897; Toronto: George N. Morang, 1897; London: J. M. Dent, 1897; New York: Lupton, 1897; London: Aldor, 1896; London: G. Routledge, 1897.

Quo Vadis? (an Opera adapted by Henri Coin from the novel of H. Sienkiewicz), English libretto by A. St. John Brenon, London: Enoch & Sons, 1911.

Quo Vadis? translated by C. J. Hogarth, adapted for radio in ten parts by Felix Felton and Susan Ashman, BBC, July 4, 1965, to July 17, 1966.

Quo Vadis? translated by Stanley F. Conrad, New York: Hippocrene Books, 1992.

Dust and Ashes, translated by J. Christian Bay, New York: F. T. Nelly, 1899.

Her Tragic Fate, translated by J. Christian Bay, New York: F. T. Nelly, 1899.

In Vain (Na marne), translated by Jeremiah Curtin, Boston: Little, Brown, 1899; London: J. M. Dent, 1899.

The New Soldier or Nature and Life, translated by Christian Bay, New York: F. T. Nelly, 1899.

On the Bright Shore (Na jasnym brzegu), translated by Jeremiah Curtin, Boston: Little, Brown, 1898.

On a Single Cord, translated by Jeremiah Curtin, London: Sielenks, 1898.

Whose Fault (Czyja wina), translated by Jeremiah Curtin, London: Sielenks, 1898.

I Must Take a Rest, translation anonymous, *Current Literature,* Volume XVI, July 1906.

SIEROSZEWSKI, WACŁAW (pseudonym Wacław Sirko) (1858–1945) lost both parents early in his life. He joined his first underground patriotic organization as a youth. A self-educated man, he became closely associated with the Socialist movement. Arrested in 1878, he became coeditor of the underground prison periodical *Głos Więźnia* (The Voice of a Convict). He also wrote a revolutionary poem at this time, *Czegóz chcą?* (What Do They Want?). Sent to Siberia for disobedience, he later described his ordeal in *Ciupasem na Syberię* (Under Police Escort to Siberia, 1926). After finally settling down near Yakuck, he secretly dispatched his stories to the Warsaw *Głos* (the Voice). During this period he also wrote a novel, *Na kresach lasów* (On The Borders of the Forests, 1894). After his period of exile came to an end, he wrote an ethnographic study, *Dwanaście lat w kraju Jakutów* (Twelve Years in the Land of the Yakuts, 1900). After a time he received permission to return to Poland, and eventually settled in Warsaw, establishing contacts with the literary milieu (e.g., Żeromski) and with the Polish Socialist Party. He published his early stories under the title *W matni* (In a Noose, 1897). His later stories are included in the collection *Dno nędzy* (The Depths of Indigence, 1900). He began writing for young readers with the story *Latorośle* (The Sprouts) and an adventure novel, *Risztau* (1899). He drew material for his works mainly from his own biography (the story *Powrót* [The Return], 1903; the novel *Ucieczka* [The Escape], 1904). This period of his literary activity was highly regarded by critics, largely because of the Siberian themes, practically unknown in Polish literature. Sieroszewski's open attitude toward foreign cultures, his expressive descriptions of nature, his well-described characters, his dramatic plots which presented heroic struggles against adverse circumstances, human life in direct relation with living conditions—these were elements most valued by contemporary critics. These features brought his work closer to naturalism, though still strongly influenced by Romantic and patriotic ideals.

Arrested again in 1900 for participating in a patriotic rally, he was sent back to Irkuck. However, because of the intervention of the Russian Geographical Society he was able to visit the Japanese islands, Korea, and China. He then returned to Warsaw in 1904 through Ceylon, Egypt, and Italy. After his journey he wrote a series of reports (*Na Daleki Wschód* [In the Far East], 1904); a study on Korea (*Korea,* 1906); a story about the tragic fate of a Korean dancer (*Ol-Soni Kisan,* 1906); and stories with Oriental themes (*Z fali na falę* [From Wave to Wave], 1910). During the revolution of 1905 he was imprisoned; he later moved to Galicia, then lived in Zakopane and Cracow, retaining contacts with the Socialist-Independent movement. His works began to lose their rugged authenticity; they gradually became more and more a *roman à these* (e.g., *W szponach* [In the Clutches], 1918; and *Łańcuchy* [Chains], 1919). He also started writing fairy tales which gained great popularity, for example, *Dary wiatru północnego* (Gifts of the North Wind) and *Bajka o Żelaznym Wilku* (A

Fable About the Iron Wolf). In Paris, where he lived during the period 1910–14, he joined *Związek Strzelecki* (Rifle Club); then he fought in World War I in Polish legions and remained a faithful admirer of Marshal Piłsudski. In liberated Poland he became a senator and president of the Writers' Union and the Polish Academy of Literature (*PAL*). In his later years he began writing his memoirs and nonfiction; however, he still managed to write three novels (*Dalaj Lama,* 1927; *Miłość samuraja* [The Love of a Samurai], 1926; and *Pan Twardowski, czarnoksiężnik polski* [Master Twardowski, the Sorcerer of Poland], 1930). He also tried writing dramas and screenplays. He remained a very popular personality, as a result of his exotic writings and his legend as a Socialist, an exile, a traveler, and a soldier.

BIBLIOGRAPHY

Dzieła (Works), Volumes 1–20, edited by A. Lam and J. Skornicki, introduction by A. Lam, Cracow, 1958–63.

SKAMANDER, MIESIĘCZNIK POETYCKI (Skamander, a Monthly Devoted to Poetry), a literary magazine published in Warsaw from 1920 to 1928 (irregularly) and from 1935 to 1939, was first edited by W. Zawistowski, and after 1922 by M. Grydzewski. During its early period, the magazine was, in fact, edited collectively by the five main poets of the Skamander group: Jarosław Iwaszkiewicz,* Jan Lechoń,* Antoni Słonimski,* Julian Tuwim,* and Kazimierz Wierzyński,* who made up the editorial board. Later the board also included E. Breiter, W. Horzyca, K. Irzykowski,* and W. Rzymowski. The title of the magazine comes from the fragment of Wyspiański's* *Akropolis—Skamander połyska, wiślaną świetlący się falą.* (The Skamander River Glitters, Emblazoned by Vistula's Wave . . .). The magazine was meant to be eclectic: in the early period it was in fact a tribune for the poets gathered around it. The magazine defended their collective interests, spoke in opposition to other literary groups, and popularized the work of the leading Skamandrites and their young disciples. In addition to literary sketches, critical reviews (of literature, theater, the graphic arts, music, and film) were also published. After 1935 the collective character seemed to disappear: writers of other orientations were included. At the same time the magazine also changed its profile, becoming a specialized literary monthly, publishing papers on history and the theory of literature. Fragments of prose were also accepted (e.g., Kaden-Bandrowski's* *Generał Barcz* and Zegadłowicz's *Zmory* [Nightmares]), as were dramas (e.g., Witkiewicz's* *Wariat i zakonnica* [The Madman and the Nun] and Gombrowicz's* *Iwona, księżniczka Burgunda* [Yvonne, Princess of Burgundy]). The magazine invited leftist writers and critics as well; its translation section was dominated by Classical literature and the poetry of Russian and French symbolism.

The Skamander group basically included five poets: Iwaszkiewicz,* Lechoń,* Słonimski,* Tuwim,* and Wierzyński.* In a broader sense the group also included poets who published their works together with the Skamandrites and shared their aesthetic beliefs—F. Przysiecki, S. Baliński, L. Okołów-Podhorski, M. Braun, Z. Karski, M. G. Karski, J. Tuwim,* J. Brzechwa—and the younger generation: J. Paczkowski, S. Karpiński, and J. Minkiewicz. The following poets also had loose ties to the group: K. Iłłakowiczówna,* M. Pawlikowska-Jasnorzewska,* J. Wittlin,* and J. Liebert. The Skamandrites considered Leopold Staff* their main patron; their leading critic was W. W. Zawodziński. The group initially formed around the magazine *Pro arte et studio* (1916–19); its first gathering place was the café *Pod Picadorem* (Under the Picador). They were also identified as a group socially, often visiting the *Ziemiańska* café.

According to Janusz Stradecki, the Skamandrites were the most popular and influential literary group between the wars. All other poetic programs of the period were formed in opposition to it. The group held steadfast to their own individual creative temperaments and never formulated a common theoretical program. Its postulates were quite general: the linking of poetry to current reality, the free development of individual talent, the exaltation of all aspects of existence in its biological ripeness and vitality. Even though each member of the group had a different canon of poetics, some elements were common, an attribute which helped implant an original model of the group in the minds of other artists and of readers. The characteristic features of the group appeared particularly during the period 1917–26 and resulted from the reaction to it created by *Młoda Polska* (Young Poland) and from a different understanding of the role of a poet: instead of the Romantic model of "prophetic poet" and the modernist idea of "the poet beyond this world," they proposed the idea of the poet-participant. Hence, they abandoned the post-Romantic canon of pathos and didacticism, which was connected to martyrological themes; some statements (e.g., by Lechoń in *Herostrates*) demanded the liberation of poetry from its traditional civic obligations. Thus the new lyrical hero is in every man; the themes explore everyday life in a contemporary city. This is also reflected in the poetic language: colloquial, conversational, or even jargonlike, combined with lyrical elements, satire, irony, humor, and even cabaretlike literary devices. At the same time the Skamandrites consciously referred to literary heritage, preserving traditional means of expression (e.g., forms of verse). In its later stages their poetry became more and more Classical in nature. It was influenced by Balmont, Briusov, Baudelaire, and Rimbaud. After 1922 the poets tried to link poetry with the current political life, especially in their satirical writings (Tuwim, Słonimski). They expressed pacifist and liberal ideas and were violently attacked by conservative and nationalistic circles. On the artistic level they were criticized by Irzykowski and Peiper and other protagonists of avant-garde trends.

BIBLIOGRAPHY

K. W. Zawodziński, "Jubileusz Skamandra" (Skamander's Jubilee), in *Wsród poetów* (Among the Poets), Cracow, 1964.

SKARBEK, FRYDERYK (1792–1866), an economist, social activist, novelist, and writer of comedies, was a Professor of Economics. During the period 1820–24 he mainly published works in his field. He devoted his life to social work, working in various hospitals, prisons, and charity institutions. An advocate of conciliatory politics, he held various offices in the Kingdom of Poland.

According to Izabela Jarosińska, his literary activity was not in the mainstream, but was unusually varied. After 1829 he began writing comedies, comic operas, and short pieces on social themes. His novels *Tarlo* (Spawning Time, Volumes 1–3, 1827) and *Damian Ruszczyc* (Volumes 1–3, 1827–28) are good examples of historical novels in the style of Sir Walter Scott. *Życie i przypadki Faustyna Dodosińskiego* (Life and Fortunes of Faustyn Dodosiński, 1–2, 1838) gives an authentic image of Saxon times in Poland, based primarily on Kitowicz's *Opis obyczajów* (A Description of Customs). His most interesting works are modeled upon the sentimentalism of Laurence Sterne: *Pan Antoni* (Mr. Anthony), 1824; *Pan Starosta* (Mr. Foreman, Volumes 1–2, 1826; and *Pamiętniki Seglasa* (Diary of Seglas), 1845. Interestingly, the primary characters are modeled after those in Sterne's novels, but the secondary ones are typical of the Enlightenment, especially in their satirical tone. Thus, Skarbek's Sterne-like characters live side by side with personages taken from Krasicki's satires.

BIBLIOGRAPHY

Powieści i pisma humorystyczne (Novels and Humorous Works), Volumes 1–7, Wrocław, 1840–47.

SKARGA, PIOTR (see Renaissance).

SKLEPY CYNAMONOWE (Cinnamon Shops) (see Schulz).

SŁOŃ (The Elephant) (see Mrożek).

SŁONIMSKI, ANTONI (pseudonym: Pro-rok) (1895–1976), a poet, satirist, publicist, playwright, prose writer, and theater critic, came from an assimilated Jewish family, esteemed for services rendered in the social and intellectual life of Warsaw. He studied the fine arts and practiced painting, the graphic arts, and drawing in his youth. He made his debut in 1913 with *Wiersz o poecie* (A Poem About a Poet). His first cycle, *Sonety* (Sonnets), was published in 1918. During 1917–19 he worked for the monthly *Pro arte et studio;* in 1918 he was the founder and member of the literary cabaret *Pod Picadorem* (Under the Picador); and in 1920 he was one of the founders and main representatives of the Skamander group. After 1924 he contributed to *Wiadomości Literackie* (Literary News) (reviews and feuilletons), but worked for other magazines as well. He spent the war years in Paris and (after 1940) in London, where from 1942 to 1946 he edited the monthly *Nowa Polska* (New Poland), and later worked for UNESCO and was the director of the Institute of Polish Culture in London. In 1951 he moved to Warsaw. After his return to Poland he took part, in the beginning, in the official literary life and expressed himself in the obligatory political spirit of the time (for example, he attacked Czesław Miłosz vehemently when the latter decided to remain abroad); later—after 1956—he became one of the leaders of the intellectual movement which contested Communist repression, censorship, and violations of the rights of man (among other things, he was the initiator of the first protest against those who prohibited freedom of speech—*List 34* [Letter 34]), and in 1968 was the coorganizer of the protest that attacked the writers' community after the censorship of Mickiewicz's *Dziady* (Forefathers' Eve) at the *Narodowy* (National) Theater in Warsaw. From 1956 to 1959 he was president of the Writers' Union; in 1971 he came into contact with the Catholic paper *Tygodnik Powszechny* (Universal Weekly).

According to Stefan Lichański, the conflict in Słonimski's lyrics is Romantic in nature: a feeling of exaltation, a search for free expression, and Classical reticence, a striving for rigor, order, and moderation. This conflict resulted in the poet's acceptance of Parnassism, which consisted mainly in borrowing of rhythmic, metric, and stanzaic patterns. Direct references to Jose Maria de Heredia (1842–1905) can be found in Słonimski's early sonnets (*Sonety* [Sonnets], 1918, and *Harmonia* [Harmony], 1919), and in *Czarna wiosna* (Black Spring, 1919), a poem once confiscated because of its anarchistic tone. Parnassism provided the "cold, iron molds of form" which restricted the emotions in its content. However, Słonimski's poetry is related to Romanticism and Neo-Romanticism. The combination of these elements is given particular expressiveness in the collections *Godzina poezji* (The Hour of Poetry, 1923), *Droga na Wschód* (Road to the East, 1924), and *Z dalekiej podróży* (From a Distant Journey, 1926). Słonimski makes direct references to Mickiewicz, creating his own variety of ballad form, endowing it with dynamic brevity of expression and expressionist imagery. Poems "of everyday life," postulated by the Skamandrites, are also among his works. Żeromski's influence, especially in the collection *Okno bez krat* (A Window Without Bars, 1935), can be discerned, particularly in its concern about the fate of Poland and European culture in view of the Nazi threat. His collection *Alarm* (London, 1940), which became widely known, describes his experiences during the first years of the war. His war poems speak of nostalgia, human solidarity in the struggle with the Nazis, his tribute to the victims of terror, and his dreams of a free world. His later poems (*Nowe wiersze* [New Poems], 1959, and *Wiersze, 1958–63* [Poems, 1958–63], 1963) are dominated by themes calling for the moral and civic obligations of poetry and for the reconstruction of poetry's preeminence.

As a writer of feuilletons, Słonimski chose Prus* as his model. He proved to be an outstanding satirist, humorist, and polemicist. Rational and skeptical, he fought against conservatism, intolerance, fanaticism, and totalitarianism (of both Nazi and Bolshevik provenance) with ruthless mockery. His publicistic pieces also reveal the conflict between the optimistic utopia of progress and the growing onset of catastrophism. His collections of publicistic pieces include *Moje walki nad Bzdurą* (My Battles with Nonsense, 1932) and *Heretyk na ambonie* (Heretic in the Pulpit, 1934). His postwar pieces in *Szpilki* (Needles) and *Tygodnik Powszechny* (The Universal Weekly) and his collections *Artykuły pierwszej potrzeby* (Articles of Primary Use, 1959), *Załatwione odmownie* (Settled Negatively, Volumes I–II, 1962–64), and *Obecność* (Presence, 1973) include attacks on conformism, snobbism, and the extreme avant-garde. Before the war he also wrote several pieces for the stage, mainly satirical comedies modeled on the plays of G. B. Shaw. He was also the author of two science fiction novels (*Torpeda czasu* [Torpedo of Time], 1924, and *Dwa końce świata* [Two Ends of the World], 1937), in which he presented a catastrophic vision of the subjugation of Europe by dictatorial regimes—fascistic and Communistic. As a humorist, he was fond of puns, parody, and pure nonsense and published a collection of humorous pieces with Julian Tuwim, *W oparach absurdu* (In the Clouds of the Absurd, 1958).

BIBLIOGRAPHY

Poezje zebrane (Collected Poetry), Warsaw, 1964; second edition, 1970.

SŁOWACKI, JULIUSZ (1809–49), a poet and playwright, was the creator of his own original Romantic cosmogony and messianistic historiography and is traditionally acknowledged as one of the three national poets (with Mickiewicz* and Krasiński*). After his father's death in 1814, he was brought up by his mother, Salomea, who married Dr. August Bécu. He grew up among the intellectual elite of Krzemieniec and Vilnius. In 1829 he left for Warsaw, where he was employed in various state offices.

During his Warsaw period he fully developed his poetic talent. Although he started writing in 1825, he actually made his debut in 1830 with a poetic novel, *Hugo*. His views crystallized under the influence of the November

Uprising; he gained some popularity with his patriotic poems written at the time and published in the underground press. In March 1831, he left Warsaw for Dresden; from there he left for Paris as a diplomatic messenger, and, having completed his mission, settled there.

In 1832 he published two volumes of *Poezje* (Poems), containing mostly poetic novels written in Warsaw (Żmija [Viper], *Jan Bielecki, Hugo, Mnich* [The Monk], and *Arab*) and the tragedies *Mindowe* and *Maria Stuart*. The works, clearly Romantic in spirit, did not arouse much interest among the émigrés, who were preoccupied with the defeat of the Uprising. Mickiewicz considered the poems "a beautiful edifice," an elevated church, but without God inside: Mickiewicz's criticism naturally affected the reception of Słowacki's works negatively for the next ten years.

Between December 1832 and February 1836 Słowacki lived in Geneva; he left with feelings of bitterness, after Mickiewicz presented Doctor Bécu as Doktor in *Dziady* (Forefathers' Eve), Part III. The Alpine region influenced Słowacki's new ideas of aestheticism, reflected in his poem *W Szwajcarii* (In Switzerland), inspired by young Maria Wodzińska, and also detected in some of his lyrical poems (e.g., *Rozłączenie* [Parting], *Rzym* [Rome], and *Sumienie* [Conscience]). His reflection on national history, the current situation, and the role of literature found expression in his great dramas: *Kordian* (1834), *Balladyna* (1839), *Horsztyński* (written in 1835), which realized his program for national poetry as outlined in Volume III of *Poezje* (Poems, 1833). The volume contained the poetic novel *Lambro*, the poem *Godzina myśli* (The Hour of Thoughts), lyrics devoted to the Uprising, and the poems *Paryż* (Paris) and *Duma o Wacławie Rzewuskim* (Elegy Regarding Wacław Rzewuski). The works of his Swiss period deal with important national problems as explored in his artistically innovative dramas. They open a new stage in Słowacki's work and in Polish Romanticism in general.

During his stay in Rome Słowacki met Krasiński, the first critic with insight who offered Słowacki understanding and respect: the friendship, however, ended in 1845 because of the ideological and political conflict which erupted over Krasiński's *Psalmy przyszłości* (The Psalms of the Future). Słowacki traveled to Greece, Egypt, and Palestine; the journey inspired him to write such lyrics as *Hymn o zachodzie słońca* (A Hymn About the Setting of the Sun, published in 1839); a digressive poem, *Podróż do Ziemi Świętej z Neapolu* (A Trip to the Holy Land from Napoli, written during 1836–39); and Song VIII, which became known as *Grób Agamemnona* (Agamemnon's Grave), one of the best examples of patriotic narrative verse. The poem contrasts two views of Poland: a passionately critical evaluation and an idealized description. Reading the poem as violent criticism and a call for military action, critics attacked the work unfairly, mainly for "slander of sacred values." In the spring of 1837 Słowacki composed his poem *Anhelli*, his opinion of the emigration, quite different from Mickiewicz's views presented in *Księgi pielgrzymstwa* (Books of a Pilgrimage). His stay in Florence inspired him to write several works influenced by Dante about suffering and death, for example, *Ojciec zadżumionych* (Father of the Plague-Stricken) and *Wacław* (both published in 1839).

In December 1838 Słowacki returned to Paris, where he spent the rest of his life. He wrote two tragedies, *Mazepa* and *Lilla Weneda* (both in 1840), and several more poems, among them his well known *Testament mój* (My Testament, 1857). The works did not evoke much interest, so different were they from the poetry of other Romantics, especially Mickiewicz and Krasiński.

Słowacki answered the indifference of readers and attacks of critics with an article in *Młoda Polska* (Young Poland). He also added fuel to his criticism in his digressive poem *Beniowski* (Songs 1–5, published in 1841), in which he achieved the peak of his artistic skills. *Beniowski* made an impression among émigré circles. *Fantazy* (published in 1866) was also an ironic-satirical drama in the spirit of *Beniowski.* Along with the lyrics (*Do pani Joanny Bobrowej* [To Joanna Bobrowa] and *W pamiętniku Zofii Bobrówny* [In the Diary of Zofia Bobrówna]), these works are a monument to Słowacki's last great love—Joanna Bobrowa.

Earlier in July 1842, Słowacki was introduced to Towiański. Even though the friendship was short-lived as a result of differences in their views on politics and literature, the clash with Towiański's ideas helped him formulate his own philosophical system. The system was presented in the poetic treatise *Genezis z Ducha* (The Genesis of the Spirit, written in the summer of 1844) and later developed in an unfinished work which publishers titled *Dzieło filozoficzne* (Philosophic Work) and in poetic fragments which researchers have published as *Poemat filozoficzny* (Philosophic Narrative Poem).

According to Stanisław Makowski, Słowacki's doctrine of genesis assumed the spiritual nature of all things and their progressive development based on metapsychosis. On the basis of rational logic and the support of evidence from science, Słowacki's theory explained the nature and sense of things with universal laws. The cosmos and man are in a state of constant development, the source of which is the opposition between the spirit aiming for greater and greater perfection, and material form created by the spirit, which seems to resist these efforts. There is no development without painful sacrifice of destroying old forms, in order to create new ones. Progress consists in the activity of the spirit, that is, in the revolutionary change of one form into another. Spirits on a similar level of perfection act collectively; nations are also groups of spirits run by the most perfect models. The messianistic assumption consisted in the belief that the spirits of the Polish nation have gone through the greatest number of incarnations; thus, they are the most perfect. The defeats and suffering experienced by the Polish nation are explained through the social pressure administered by an Absolute God, who thus has forced the perfect nation to aim for the final goal, that is, reaching the form of light. These ideas find their poetic realization in the drama *Samuel Zborowski* (written in 1845), in the historical epic *Król Duch* (King Spirit, written during 1845–49), and in *Odpowiedź na "Psalmy przyszłości"* (An Answer to The Psalms of the Future, 1848), which present the Spirit as the moving power of history.

The process of forming and verbalizing the system inspired Słowacki's poetic imagination, enriching it with surrealist imagery. His poetic power was sustained in *Król Duch,* in several lyrics, and in a series of dramas: *Ksiądz Marek* (Father Marek, 1843), *Sen srebrny Salomei* (The Silver Dream of Salome, 1844), *Agezylausz* (Agezylaus, written in 1844 and published in 1884), and *Zawisza Czarny* (Black Zawisza, written in 1844–45 and published in 1908). The characters presented in these dramas bear a striking resemblance to the hero in Calderón's play *Książę niezłomny* (The Steadfast Prince), which Słowacki paraphrased (1844).

Słowacki's historiosophical views also intensified his sensitivity to contemporary events in Poland and Europe, which he commented upon in the spirit of progress, political revolution, and national reason. His optimism is directly related to his ideas regarding permanent progress. The great and tragic nation that had once lost its freedom was ultimately politically revived, the chief requirement of the logic of progress.

In 1845–46 he addressed himself directly to émigré circles, in *Do emigracji o potrzebie idei* (To the Emigration About the Necessity of Ideas, 1848) and in the two letters to Czartoryski. He was able to gather around him a group of followers—Feliński, Niewiarowski, Norwid,* and Ujejski—and hoped to make the group the ideological and political center of the entire Polish emigration. At the news of the uprising in Wielkopolska (1848), which he considered to be a realization of his ideas, he organized a confederacy and left for Poznań with a group of friends. The police demanded that he leave and he went to Wrocław, then back to Paris. He died of tuberculosis, leaving many of his works in manuscript form.

Słowacki's ideological and artistic innovativeness accounts for the fact that his contemporaries found his works difficult and could not properly estimate his poetry. But his influence kept increasing and became very important during the period before the January Uprising. He became the poet of the patriotic leftist movement, an embodiment of the idea of the uncompromising struggle for independence, a stand criticized in clerical and conservative circles.

Beniowski is a digressive poem, composed of ten songs. The unifying factor of the piece lies in the character of Maurycy Beniowski, a *szlachcic* (nobleman) from Podole, who, after participating in the Confederacy of Bar, changes from a lighthearted youth into a conscious patriot. The historical Beniowski was a Hungarian and was merely a remote prototype for the character in the poem. Other characters in the work also have historical predecessors in the epoch of Bar or in Słowacki's circle.

The main character is not Beniowski, however, but the narrator (who can be identified with Słowacki). He is a Romantic poet, who maintains an ironic distance from the materials in the poem and himself, piling up problems and difficulties only to show his brilliance and mastery in solving them. Objective plot and subjective digression are indistinguishable. Everything is subjective but important to the events presented. The richness and originality of *Beniowski* transcend the limits of the genre.

The themes are considerably varied: self-comments on the writing of the poem, personal remarks on the fate of an émigré poet, and, above all, polemic pieces commenting on the old-fashioned tastes of the readers and on incompetent critics. It is a humorous defense of the writer's right to be innovative, and a proposal for a new model of a national poet—one to compete with Mickiewicz.

The polemic character of *Beniowski* is associated with its "conversational" character: the author addresses the reader directly or makes him a witness of his polemics or confessions. The work is innovative in all of its aspects: the concept of the hero, the open structure, the broad temporal and spatial perspective, its poetic and political program, its unusually rich imagination. Słowacki reached his artistic peak in this work, astonishing both readers and critics. *Beniowski* is one of the most important works in Polish Romanticism and in Polish literature as a whole. Even though saturated with Polish problems, the work has a universal quality and should be better known.

Kordian, Part I of a planned trilogy of dramas, was written in 1833, after Mickiewicz published *Dziady* (Forefathers' Eve), Part III, in which he depicted Doctor Bécu, Słowacki's father-in-law, as a collaborator with Poland's enemy. *Kordian* was meant as a challenge to Mickiewicz; the battle for prime position as national poet had begun.

It begins with *Przygotowania* (Preparation), in the spirit of the witch scene in Macbeth, where infernal forces create the leaders of the oncoming uprising. It is followed by a *Prolog* (Prologue), in which Słowacki outlines the role of poetry in the life of the nation and clearly suggests a rivalry with Mickiewicz. In act I Kordian experiences his first disappointment in love and attempts to commit suicide. In act II he travels to foreign countries and experiences more disappointments (with women and religion). The monologue delivered on the peak of Mont Blanc closes act III and parallels the Great Improvization in *Dziady* (Forefathers' Eve), Part III, announcing the hero's return to Poland, to political activity, and introduces the famous phrase "Poland, Winkelried of the nations," suggesting that the reason for the uprising of 1830 was to prevent Russian intervention in France and Belgium. Act III takes place in Warsaw, during the coronation of Nicholas I as King of Poland in 1829. Kordian fails to organize a conspiracy against the tsar; his individual attempt to assassinate Nicholas is also unsuccessful, and Kordian is imprisoned. The crucial scene in the lunatic asylum presents the hero as being torn between contemporary philosophical theories and the actual problems of Poland, which philosophy alone can solve.

But it is *Anhelli* that Słowacki cherished most. According to Krasiński, the words Słowacki wanted as his epitaph were the following: *Autorowi Anhellego* (For the author of Anhelli). The poem, symbolic in character, relates the fate of the nation, exiles impaled on the background of white-silver-black Siberia. A shaman, Anhelli's guide through the land of suffering, knows the meaning of sacrifice and imparts his wisdom to Anhelli. He becomes, in a sense, the redeemeer of his people. Anhelli dies at the hour of the universal revolution. His death brings no immediate solace to his people, but his sacrifice seems necessary for a future regeneration.

(See Romanticism.)

BIBLIOGRAPHY

Dzieła wszystkie (Complete Works), Volumes 1–7, edited by Juliusz Kleiner and W. Floryan, Wrocław, 1952–76.

Dzieła (Works), Volumes 1–14, third edition, edited by Julian Krzyżanowski, Wrocław: Zakład Ossolineum, 1959.

English

Polish Romantic Drama, Ithaca, New York: Cornell University Press, 1977 (translations of *Forefathers' Eve,* Part III, by Adam Mickiewicz; *The Un-Divine Comedy,* by Zygmunt Krasiński; and *Fantazy,* by Juliusz Słowacki).

Anhelli, translated by Dorothea Prall Radin, edited by George Rapall Noyes, London: Allen & Unwin, Select Library of Polish Authors, 1930.

Balladyna, translated by Marion Moore Coleman and Walter Twardowski, Cambridge Springs, Pennsylvania: Alliance College Publishers, 1960.

Fantazy, translated by Harold B. Segel, *Polish Romantic Drama,* Ithaca, New York: Cornell University Press.

"The Father of the Plague-Stricken at El-Arish," translated by J. P. Wachowski, *Free Poland* Number 13, 1915; translated by William J. Rose, in *Julius Słowacki: 1809–1849: Centenary Volume,* London 1951.

Genesis of the Spirit, translated by Kazimierz Chodkiewicz, London: Chodkiewicz, 1966.

In Switzerland (W Szwajcarii), translated by Kenneth Mackenzie, London: Eyre and Spottiswoode, 1953.

Mary Stuart (Maria Stuart), translated by A. P. Coleman and Marion M. Coleman, Cambridge Springs, Pennsylvania: Alliance College Publishers, 1937.

Mazeppa (Mazepa), translated by Carolen Dolenge Wells and Carlton F. Wells, Ann Arbor: Alumni Press, University of Michigan, 1929; translated by Marion Moore Coleman, Cheshire, Connecticut: Cherry Hill Books, 1966.

SOLARIS (see Lem).

SÓL ZIEMI (Salt of the Earth) (see Wittlin).

SPRAWA DANTONA (The Danton Case) (see Przybyszewska).

STAFF, LEOPOLD (1878–1957), a poet, playwright, and translator, studied law, philosophy, and Latin philology at Lvov University. He broadened his education while visiting Italy and Paris. Editor of the Symposion Philosophical Series, coeditor of the monthly *Nowy Przegląd Literatury i Sztuki* (A New Review of Literature and Art), he became a member of the Polish Academy of Literature (*PAL*) and was the recipient of numerous awards (state as well as those granted by various cities). He was highly regarded during the years between the wars and was considered a patron of the young generation of poets gathered around the journal *Skamander.** He also received the PEN Club award for translations. The University of Warsaw and the Jagiellonian University awarded him honorary doctorates.

Staff started as a modernist, although even in his first volume of poetry (*Sny o potędze* [Dreams of Power], 1901) he seems to have attempted to overcome modernist decadentism. The collection immediately placed him among Poland's best poets of the twentieth century. The basic features of his poetics were also formed during this period. He modified his views later on, assimilating the achievements of twentieth century poetry, but he always preserved his individual style. His collections include *Sny o potędze* (Dreams of Power, 1901); *Dzień duszy* (A Day of the Soul, 1903); *Ptakom niebieskim* (To the Celestial Birds, 1905); *Gałąż kwitnąca* (The Blossoming Bough, 1908); *Uśmiechy godzin* (Smiles of the Hours, 1910); *W cieniu miecza* (In the Shadow of the Sword, 1911); *Łabędź i Lira* (The Swan and the Lyre, 1914); *Siew doli* (Sowing of Fate, 1916); *Ścieżki polne* (Forest Paths, 1919); *Ucho igielne* (Needle's Eye, 1927); *Wysokie drzewa* (High Trees, 1932); *Barwa miodu* (The Color of Honey, 1936); *Martwa pogoda* (Dead Weather, 1946); *Wiklina* (Willow, 1954); *Dziewięć muz* (Nine Muses, 1958); the poem *Mistrz Twardowski* (Master Twardowski, 1902); the dramas *Skarb* (Treasure, 1904), *Godiwa* (Lady Godiva, 1906), *Igrzysko* (Athletic Games, 1909), *Wawrzyny* (Laurels), *To samo* (The Same, 1912), and *Południca* (The Noonday Ghost, 1920); and a monograph, *Michał Anioł* (Michelangelo, 1934).

Staff was influenced by Nietzscheanism and Romanticism: according to his own admission, of permanent value was an active pursuit of unattainable happiness and truth. In his dramas he explored the problem of truth, which he viewed relativistically and pragmatically. Arguing for the relativity of truth and for its necessity, Staff defended dreams and myths—not only religious myths, but, above all, secular ones. He saw the humanistic role of poetry as the creation of such myths.

Staff was the most outstanding representative of Classicism in twentieth century Polish poetry. He understood Classicism not only as poetics but as a philosophy of order and the approbation of life, an integration of various trends of European culture, ancient as well as Christian, especially those based on the traditions of Saint Francis. On this basis Staff created a model of man beautiful and good, joyful, but cognizant of and accepting the role of suffering. Before World War I the collections most characteristic of such a view of Classicism were *Gałąź kwitnąca* (The Blossoming Bough) and *Uśmiechy godzin* (Smiles of the Hours); between the wars, *Wysokie drzewa* (High Trees) and *Barwa miodu* (The Color of Honey). The latter collections finally overcame the restrictive poetic conventions of Young Poland and tightened the relationship of the Polish landscape and Polish culture. The most drastic change in his poetics and view of the world are found in *Wiklina* (Willow) and *Dziewięć muz* (Nine Muses). In these volumes the poet overcame the traditional systems of meter, modernized his imagery, and created a less harmonious, self-ironic vision of the world.

Staff translated poetry, novels, philosophical writings, ancient classics, medieval and Renaissance works, Diderot, Goethe, Nietzsche, Roland, and Tagore. His output of translated works is indeed rich and varied.

(See *Młoda Polska.*)

BIBLIOGRAPHY

Pisma (Works), Volumes 1–19, Warsaw, Cracow, 1931–34.

Wiersze zebrane (Collected Poems), Volumes 1–5, Warsaw, 1955.

Wybór poezji (Selected Poetry), edited and with an introduction by M. Jastrun, Wrocław, 1963.

English

Bogdana Carpenter, *The Poetic Avant-Garde in Poland, 1918–1939,* Seattle: University of Washington Press, 1983.

STARA BAŚŃ (The Old Legend) (see Kraszewski).

STEMPOWSKI, JERZY (pseudonym Paweł Hostowiec) (1894–1969), an essay writer and literary critic, descended from a wealthy gentry family who had settled for generations in Ukraine, studied philosophy, medicine, and the history of literature in Cracow, Munich, and Zurich. After 1918 he became a correspondent for the Polish Press in Paris, Geneva, and Berlin; he later assumed duties as an official and a lecturer. After war broke out in 1939, he found himself in Hungary; from there he made his way to Switzerland; from 1952 he lived in Bern, where he lived until the end of his life, cooperating with the Paris publishing house *Instytut Literacki* (Literary Institute) and its monthly, *Kultura* (Culture), in which he regularly published from 1954 a series of essays, *Notatnik niespiesznego przechodnia* (Notes of a Leisurely Passer-by) and the London *Wiadomości* (News).

Stempowski was already a recognized authority in his field during the period between the wars. His brilliant imagination and erudition were legendary. A foremost master of the literary essay in Poland (together with Boy Żeleński and Miciński), Stempowski developed the genre with his original approach to essay writing, that is, as an analytic, distant observer.

His education and wide experiences made him sensitive to the crisis and variability of forms in the European way of life. Critical of a traditional upbringing and a humanistic education (*O współczesnej formacji humanistycznej* [Concerning a Contemporary Humanistic Formation]) and ruthlessly critical of the Polish Sarmatian tradition (*Pan Jowialski i jego spadkobiercy* [Mr. Jowialski and His Heirs], 1931), he also opposed the uniformity and lack of insight that a more democratic way of life and culture brought about. He recognized the opposition of the increasing "chaos" between discipline and the unlimited resources of the human intellect. According to Jerzy Jackl, in literature, Stempowski was mainly interested in its cultural, even its economic background, and the variability of tastes and styles (*Klimat życia i klimat literatury* [The Climate of Life and the Climate of Literature]). An admirer of the classics, he considered the ancients a model of intellectual discipline. He expressed critical views on naturalism and so-called fact literature (*Graniczne punkty sztuki u naturalistów* [Limited Points of Art Among the Naturalists]). He also denigrated the twentieth century avant-garde, which he nevertheless analyzed with unusual insight (*Chimera jako zwierzę pociągowe* [Chimera as a Draft Animal], 1933). He was decidedly hostile toward literature inspired by existentialism, especially Sartre, Beckett, and the nouveau roman. He could never understand or appreciate the new tendencies that appeared in literature after World War II, although he acknowledged the need for a new style and a new language to express the experiences of the postwar generation.

Stempowski occupies a special position among his contemporaries: in spite of sharing some views with other critics, he was the most outstanding representative of modern Classicism.

He also wrote memoirs (*Dzieci Warszawy w początkach XX stulecia* [The Children of Warsaw at the Beginning of the Twentieth Century] and *Wronia i Sienna* [Wronia and Sienna Streets]) and sketches from his travels (*Pielgrzym* [Pilgrim], 1924, and *Dziennik podróży do Austrii i Niemiec* [Diary of Travels to Austria and Germany], 1946). His collections of essays include *Eseje dla Kassandry* (Essays for Cassandra, Paris, 1961), *Od Berdyczowa do Rzymu* (From Berdyczow to Rome, Paris, 1971), *Listy z ziemi berneńskiej* (Letters from Land of Bern, London, 1974), and those published in Poland: *Eseje* (Essays, 1984) and *Szkice literackie* (Literary Sketches, Volumes 1–2, 1988).

STERN, ANATOL (1899–1968), a poet, prose writer, comedy writer, film and literary critic, screenplay writer, and translator, was cofounder of Polish futurism. He took active part in scandalous polemics in the press (in 1920 he was imprisoned for blasphemy and released after a protest was lodged by several writers). He was also a coauthor and editor of futurist one-day papers and manifestos published in 1920–21. During World War

II he remained in Lvov; he was captured by the Red Army in 1939. He was arrested by the Soviet Secret Police (NKVD) and was sent deep inside the Soviet Union; he was released in 1941 as a result of the amnesty signed by the Polish government in exile and the Soviet authorities; then he enlisted in General Anders's army. He saw combat in the Near East. He made his home in Palestine until 1948 and then returned to Poland.

Stern's early poetry (*Futuryzacje* [Futurization], 1919, and the poem *Nagi człowiek w śródmieściu* [The Naked Man Downtown], 1919) is strikingly dynamic and brutal in its form of expression. Saturated with youthful buffoonery and a mocking sense of humor, the poems are an excellent example of futurist biologism and optimism. The hero is a man liberated from the chains of tradition and convention, driven by natural instincts, leading a free life within an urban modern landscape. According to Jan Wojnowski, his later poems express anarchistic revolt and radical protest, especially the volume, written with Jasieński, *Ziemia na lewo* (Earth on the Left, 1924), the poem *Piłsudski* (1934), and the collections *Anielski cham* (Angelic Boor, 1924) and *Bieg do bieguna* (A Run to the Pole, 1927). After publishing the collection *Rozmowa z Apollinem* (Conversation with Apollo, 1938), a gloomy and depressing view of life, Stern turned toward traditional descriptive-reflective lyrics (*Wiersze i poematy* [Poems and Narrative Poems], 1956, and *Wiersze dawne i nowe* [Old and New Poems], 1957). His former fascination with life was replaced by "dead plains of the past" in *Widzialne i niewidzialne* (Visible and Invisible, 1964) and *Alarm nocny* (Night Alarm, 1970).

Stern also wrote two parabolic novels, *Namiętny pielgrzym* (The Passionate Pilgrim, 1933) and *Ludzie i syrena* (People and the Siren, 1944; published in Poland in 1955). His short stories include *Zabawa w piekło* (A Party Called Hell, 1959), comedies, and literature for children. He was also the author of sketches and memoirs on futurism: *Poezja zbuntowana* (Mutinous Poetry, 1964), *Legendy naszych dni* (Legends of Our Days, 1969), and *Głód jednoznaczności* (Hunger of Clarity, 1972). He devoted special attention to Bruno Jasieński,* Mayakovsky, and Apollinaire.

(See Contemporary Polish Literature.)

BIBLIOGRAPHY

Poezje: 1918–1968 (Poems: 1918–1968), introduction by Kazimierz Wyka, Warsaw, 1969.

STRYJKOWSKI, JULIAN (Julian Stark) (born 1905), a novelist, was descended from an assimilated Jewish family that resided in Stryj, in the southeastern part of what was then Poland. After completing a degree in Polish studies at the University of Jan Kazimierz in Lvov (1932), he worked as a teacher. In 1935–36 he was arrested for participating in Communist activities (he was a member of the illegal Communist Party); in 1941 he was active in Polish Communist circles in the Soviet Union, among other things, on the editorial boards of the periodicals *Czerwony Sztandar* (The Red Banner) and *Wolna Polska* (Free Poland). In 1946 he returned to Poland; from 1949 he was a press correspondent in Rome, from which he was expelled in 1952 for publishing a propagandistic novel about the Italian Communist Party, *Bieg do Fragala* (Race to Fragala, 1951). From 1954 he was a member of the editorial board of the monthly *Twórczość* (Creativity); in later years he joined with centers of the democratic opposition, publishing in the underground press (*Drugi obieg*), alongside Isaac Bashevis Singer.

Stryjkowski's works are among the best examples of the now nonexistent cultural and social life of Polish Jews. His main works are the following: *Głosy w ciemności* (Voices in the Darkness, written in 1943–46 and published in 1956), *Austeria* (The Inn, 1966), and *Sen Azrila* (The Dream of Azril, 1975). The novels form a trilogy whose action takes place in an Orthodox, Hasidic milieu in various small towns in eastern Galicia before World War I. Stryjkowski's heroes live in a closed world, ossified by the conservative traditions of its religious and social life and, at the same time, decaying under the pressure of unavoidable changes. They are forced to choose, but each one of them is marked for tragedy: they are forced to reject one set of values for another. Their attempts to free themselves from the restraints of Orthodox society and the assimilation of a secularized world bring on the pains of isolation and the loss of identity, a loyalty to the orders of the Law and tradition—isolation in a reality suffering the hectic changes of civilization. Stryjkowski does not postulate any ethnic or psychological stance, and his narrative is free of authorial commentary, made up, for the most part, of monologues and dialogues of the characters. The Jewish problem is also present in his historical novel, depicting the history of the fifteenth century Spanish Inquisition, *Przybysz z Narbony* (The New Arrival from Narbona, 1978); in his short stories *Imię własne* (My Own Name, 1962) and *Na wierzbach . . . nasze skrzypce* (On the Willows . . . Our Violin, 1974); in his novel *Echo* (1988); and in the continuation of certain plots in *Głosów w ciemności* (Voices in the Dark). A number of novels paraphrase biblical episodes and form a separate group: *Król Dawid żyje* (King David Lives! 1984) and *Juda Makabi* (Judas Maccabaeus, 1986). The novel *Czarna róża* (Black Rose, 1962) is an autobiographical account with psychological overtones of the writer's youthful Communist experiences. A critical settling of accounts of that time is presented in *Wielki strach* (The Great Fear, published conspiratorially in 1979, emended and published in London in 1980, and officially published in Poland in 1990), which re-creates the atmosphere in Lvov during the Soviet occupation from 1939–41. An interesting biographical document, especially in light of the fate of the Polish-Jewish Communist intelligentsia, is the interview with P. Szewc, *Ocalony na Wschodzie* (Saved in the East, 1991).

BIBLIOGRAPHY

M. Sprusiński, Ocalenie z Sodomy (Escape from Disorder) in *Między prawdą a zmyśleniem* (Between Truth and Fabrication), Cracow, 1978.

STYL ZAKOPIAŃSKI (The Zakopane Style) (see Witkiewicz, Stanisław).

SWINARSKI, ARTUR MARYA (1900–1965), a poet, satirist, playwright, and translator, was by education a German philologist, art historian, artist, and set designer. His talent for satire and parody was revealed in his work for cabarets, and also in his brilliant literary parodies of Polish writers (*Parodie* [Parodies], 1955). His satirical writings were published in several volumes: *Karykatury poznańskie* (Poznań Caricatures, 1929), *Wielkie pranie* (A Big Laundry, 1930), *Fraszki* (Trifles, 1932), *Pamflety, parodie, paradoksy, 1926–1946* (Pamphlets, Parodies, Paradoxes, 1926–1946, published in 1946), *Satyry* (Satires, 1950), and *Satyry* (Satires, 1955).

His comedies popularizing Classical mythological themes, both ancient and biblical, were quite popular: they provided material for humorous travesties but also ironic reflection on human nature, its egoism and hidden complexes: *Achilles i panny* (Achilles and the Ladies, staged in 1955 and published in 1956), *Powrót Alcesty* (The Return of Alceste, staged and published in 1958), *Złota wieża* (The Golden Tower) and *Epilog w Egipcie* (Epilogue in Egypt), both staged in 1957 and published in the collection *Trylogia trojańska* (The Trojan Trilogy, 1958). Several of his works have yet to be staged (e.g., *Sześciu z Calais* [The Six from Calais] and *Godzina Antygony* [The Hour of Antigone]). A few plays remain in manuscript form. Swinarski's lyrical writings are of minor importance.

SYROKOMLA, WŁADYSŁAW (Ludwik Kondratowicz) (1823–62), a poet and translator, was the son of a poor nobleman who made his living leasing estates. He made his literary debut in 1844, and from that moment on literature became his main occupation. He settled with his family in the village of Załucze on the banks of the Niemen, where he leased an estate. His first major works were *Przekłady poetów polsko-łacińskich* (Translations of Polish-Latin Poets, Volumes 1–6, 1851–52), which was followed by other translations; numerous minor lyrical writings gathered in the volume *Gawędy i rymy ulotne* (Anecdotal Chats and Transitory Rhymes, 1853); a tale, *Urodzony Jan Dęboróg* (Born Jan Dęboróg, 1854); and *Zarys dziejów literatury w Polsce* (An Outline of the Works of Literature in Poland, Volumes 1–2, 1850–52). These writings brought him considerable popularity. He moved to Borejkowszczyzna near Vilnius and continued publishing "leaflet poetry" and tales "from the shores of the Niemen." His links with the literary milieu in Vilnius became stronger (he worked for an archeological committee and planned a literary magazine), and he decided to move to Vilnius, where he published his historical dramas (e.g., *Kasper*

Karliński, staged and published as *Obrona Olsztyna* [The Defense of Olsztyn], 1958). As his popularity grew, he received a warm welcome in Warsaw but on his return was imprisoned for having participated in a patriotic demonstration. He was exiled to Borejkowszczyzna for the duration of the investigation: at this time he wrote his most mature lyrics, published in the volume *Poezje ostatniej godziny* (Poetry of the Final Hour). He was given permission to return to Vilnius a few months before his death.

According to Maria Grabowska, Syrokomla's writings possess a specific approach to poetic language whose simplicity, communicativeness, and programmatic "coarseness" are linked with his conscious choice of being the poet of the simple folk, "a village singer." It also influenced his choice of genre—the rhymed tale. These are mostly folktales, but the folk aspect does not consist merely in introducing folk heroes or traditions (*Pocztylion* [The Post Boy], 1844, *Janko Cmentarnik* [Johnny Cemetery], 1856, *Chodyka*, 1848, and *Wielki Czwartek* [Holy Thursday], 1856): the folk elements are also linked with the form of narration and the emotional solidarity with the peasant class. In Syrokomla's personal lyrics his emotions are combined with self-irony, self-ridicule, and humor. He also composed satirical pieces (e.g., *Niewinnej duszyczce* [To an Innocent Little Soul] and *Nagrobek obywatelowi* [Tombstone for a Citizen]), in which he ridiculed the thoughtlessness and selfishness of the gentry. The remainder of his output includes political satire; poems on social themes, often sarcastic in tone; and several unpublished poems (e.g., *Sachar-maroz* [Sugar-Frost], 1858), bitterly anti-tsarist.

BIBLIOGRAPHY

Wybór poezji (Selected Poetry), Volumes 1–3, edited by S. Cywiński, Vilnius, 1923.

Wiersze i gawędy (Poetry and Chatter), edited by I. Korsak, introduction by J. W. Gomulicki, Warsaw, 1957.

SZANIAWSKI, JERZY (1886–1970), a playwright, prose writer, and novelist, came from a family of intelligentsia with patriotic traditions and a keen interest in the theater and literature. He studied in Switzerland and returned to Poland in 1912 to begin his literary career. After 1920 he worked with Juliusz Osterwa and the Reduta Theater. He spent most of his life in his family manor in Zegrzynek on the Narwia. He was the recipient of numerous literary awards and was a member of the Polish Academy of Literature (PAL).

Szaniawski made his literary debut as a short story writer; he also wrote humorous pieces for magazines. His main area of interest, however, was the theater and drama. The ambiguous evaluation of events and human activity seemed to challenge his curiosity. In his writings he restricted sociological and ethical aspects to simplifications and stereotypes, but he was deeply concerned with human desires and ideals associated with the beauty of the world and man's sense of the transitoriness of life. His comedies—*Murzyn* (The Negro, staged in 1917), *Papierowy kochanek* (The Paper Lover, staged in 1920), *Lekkoduch* (The Playboy, staged in 1923), and *Ptak* (The Bird, staged in 1923)—confronted both reality and the imagination and emphasized the role of poetic symbol in everyday reality. He was interested in the complex nature of human feelings, not in the analysis of human psyche: *Ewa* (Eve, staged in 1921), *Adwokat i róże* (The Lawyer and the Roses, staged in 1929), and *Dziewczyna z lasu* (The Girl from the Forest, staged in 1939). In *Żeglarz* (The Sailor, staged in 1925) he explored the mechanism of the functioning of myths in society; in *Most* (The Bridge, staged in 1933) he raised the question of the effects of a single act on a community, weighing the relativity of the concepts of good and evil; in *Fortepian* (The Grand Piano, staged in 1932) he considered the future of great art within the new social order. According to Jadwiga Jakubowska, he expressed the essence of his plays through mood and metaphor, introducing lyrical elements into the plot, maintaining an ironic distance from his characters, and revealing the ambiguity of literary conventions. He transferred his idea of drama to plays written for radio. In his first postwar drama, *Dwa teatry* (Two Theaters, staged in 1946), he summed up his experiences as a playwright. His later plays explored areas already covered in his earlier works: *Kowal, pieniądze i gwiazdy* (The Blacksmith, Money and Stars, staged in 1948) and *Chłopiec latający* (The Flying Boy, written in 1949; staged in 1958). He also wrote a novelette, *Miłość i rzeczy poważne* (Love and Important Things, 1924), and short stories, published in the volume *Łgarze pod Złotą Kotwicą* (Liars Under the Golden Anchor, 1928 and 1960). His main achievement in prose is a series of stories whose hero is Professor Tutka: *Profesor Tutka i inne opowiadania* (Professor Tutka and Other Stories, 1954) and *Profesor Tutka: Nowe opowiadania* (Professor Tutka: New Stories, 1962), adapted for television as a serial, *Klub Profesora Tutki*, 1967–69 (The Club of Professor Tutka, 1967–69). In these stories Professor Tutka relates apparently unimportant stories, under the guise of a philosophical tale, in order to provoke the reader into revising some long-established concepts.

Dwa teatry (Two Theaters) is a comedy in three acts. Two theaters are explored: the realistic *Małe Zwierciadło* (A Little Looking Glass) and *Teatr Snów* (The Theater of Dreams), based on the symbolic nature of dreams. Act I takes place backstage of *Małe Zwierciadło* prior to the fateful day—September 1939. In a series of realistic episodes the idea of a theater which rejects poetic imagination and visionary character is presented. Act II is based on the "theater within a theater" and contains two one-act pieces: *Matka* (Mother, based on the radio play *W lesie* [In the Forest]) and *Powódź* (The Flood), both staged by *Małe Zwierciadło*. Act III takes place after the war; *Teatr Snów* is presented by employing the convention of a dream. The confrontation of the two theaters takes place against the background of tragic events of the war. At first, the play was a huge success, although Marxist critics accused Szaniawski of propagating irrationalism. As a result, Szaniawski's plays were not staged for some time. In the 1960s, with the advent of the theater of the absurd, his plays were revived—an oasis of optimism and poetic realism within a desert of existential despair and self-mockery.

BIBLIOGRAPHY

Dramaty zebrane (Collected Dramatic Works), Volumes 1–3, Warsaw, 1958.
Dramaty wybrane (Selected Dramatic Works), Cracow, 1973; second edition, 1987.
W. Natanson, *Swiat Jerzego Szaniawskiego* (The World of Jerzy Szaniawski), Łódź, 1971.
K. Nastulanka, *Jerzy Szaniawski,* Warsaw, 1973.
J. Jakubowska, *Jerzy Szaniawski,* Warsaw, 1980.

SZCZEPAŃSKI, JAN JÓZEF (born 1919), a prose writer, essayist, and reporter, completed his studies as an Orientalist at the University of Jagiełło in 1947. A participant in the war against Germany, he was taken prisoner in 1939. After escaping from a camp, he joined the underground army (*AK*) and became associated with the partisans. He made his literary debut in 1943 in the conspiratorial Warsaw press. Since 1947 he has worked for *Tygodnik Powszechny* (The Universal Weekly). After 1957 he traveled a great deal, to Asia, Africa, Latin America, and the United States, and produced collections of reports and journalistic sketches. In 1980 he was elected president of the *Związek Literatów Polskich* (Union of Polish Writers). He remained in office until 1983, when the organization was dissolved by the government under Martial Law.

The main motif in Szczepański's writings is a moral tone, inspired and borrowed from the ethics of Joseph Conrad. At the beginning of his career, Szczepański utilized his experiences from the war and occupation; later he reflected deeply on the degeneration of contemporary civilization, threatened by totalitarian ideology, superficial materialism, and progressivism, losing consciousness of ties to tradition and the world of metaphysical values. Szczepański's war prose did not idealize the picture of martial life, either on the battlefront (*Polska jesień* [Polish Autumn, written 1940–49, and published in 1955], which received the Ernest Hemingway Award in 1960 as the most complete work about the war in 1939) or in conspiratorial activities (the collection of short stories *Buty* [Shoes], 1956, with the title story published in 1947; *Dzień bohatera* [Day of the Hero], 1959; and *Motyl* [Butterfly], 1962). These works depict the process of an inner maturation of the heroes, assuming the battle as an elementary, moral obligation, in spite of doubt and the possibility of a real chance at winning; a similar outlook on the theme of war is also found in the author's screenplays: *Wolne miasto* (Free City, 1958), *Westerplatte* (1967), and *Hubal* (1972). The motivation of the hero, who persists in his solitary aspiration to attain his goal in spite of every possible opposition and miscalculation, is the main theme of the second part of the biographical novel, *Ikar* (Icarus, 1966). His next novel, *Wyspa* (Island, 1968), is based on the fate of Anthony Berezowski, a Polish emigrant who was sentenced to exile for life for his attempt to assassinate Alexander II in Paris. In his later works (the collection of short stories *Rafa* [Reef, 1974], *Autograf* [Autograph, 1979], and the novelistic commentary *Kipu* [1978]), Szczepański began slowly to move away from the fictional plot to personal observation and remembrances, transforming his material into essayistic reflections, gathered around the manifestations of the moral crisis of the twentieth century. His collection of essays *Przed nieznanym trybunałem* (Before an Unknown Tribunal, 1975) is typical of this new development in his writings, where alongside citing the influence of Conrad on his generation, the writer presented the distinct contrasts of two characters: Saint Maximilian Kolbe, who saved the life of a fellow prisoner in Auschwitz by offering his own life in a hunger strike, and Charles Manson, the California killer-nihilist. A perspicacious moral assessment is also found in his documentary-memoirs *Kadencja* (Term of Office, published in the underground press in 1987; emended and published in Paris in 1988, and officially published in Poland in 1989), in which Szczepański objectively describes the moral battle waged by writers against the Communist authorities, which led to the declaration of Martial Law in 1981 that precipitated not only the liquidation of the legally elected officers of the Union of Polish Writers, but the destruction of the writers' solidarity that forced them to dissolve their organization themselves. Szczepański's works also include numerous sketches of his travels, film criticism, translations (especially from English literature: Graham Greene, Aldous Huxley), and journalistic writings (among others, *Maleńka encyklopedia totalizmu* (A Small Encyclopedia of Totalitarianism, 1990, an interesting account of the similarities between fascism and Communism).

BIBLIOGRAPHY

M. Janion, "Legenda i antylegenda wojny: Wojna i forma" (Legend and Anti-Legend of War: War and Form), in *Literatura wobec wojny i okupacji* (Literature in the Face of War and the Occupation), Wrocław, 1976.

SZEWCY (The Shoemakers) (see Witkiewicz, Stanisław Ignacy).

SZYMBORSKA, WISŁAWA (born 1923), a poet, studied Polish philology and sociology in Cracow. After 1953 she became a member of the board of the weekly *Życie Literackie* (Literary Life). She made her debut in 1945 with a poem, *Szukam słowa* (I Search for the Word), in *Dziennik Polski* (The Polish Daily). She published her first volume of poems, *Dlatego żyjemy* (That Is Why We Live), in 1952. Her collections include the following: *Pytania zadawane sobie* (Questions Asked of Oneself, 1954), *Wołanie do Yeti* (A Cry to Yeti, 1957), *Sól* (Salt, 1962), *Sto pociech* (A Hundred Consolations, 1967), *Wszelki wypadek* (Just in Case, 1972, 1975), *Wielka liczba* (A Great Number, 1976, 1977), and *Ludzie na moście* (The People on the Bridge, 1986).

Szymborska's lyrics are personal and reflective, imbued with an intellectual and moral character, centered around two motives: the existential situation of man and the relation of an individual to history. According to Barbara Gomulicka, the mystery of the sense and aim of human existence, in both the individual and the universal sense, are explored in her poetry: man is subjected to the invariable laws of nature and history, helpless and often misled by hope, constantly experiencing bitter alienation and lack of fulfillment. These complex philosophical and psychological issues find a peculiar expression in her works: solidarity with human suffering coexists with intellectual distance and shades of irony. Short lyrical forms are employed by Szymborska, brief and intricate in style, based on precisely constructed metaphors and surprising conclusions. Her poetry combines the charm of playful neologisms with a reflective mood. Her works have become very popular and have been translated into many languages. Szymborska is undoubtedly one of the greatest Polish poets of the twentieth century, once described by Stanisław Barańczak as "the premier Polish woman poet."

BIBLIOGRAPHY

Wiersze wybrane (Selected Poems), Warsaw, 1964; second edition, 1979.
Poezje (Poems), introduction by J. Kwiatkowski, Warsaw, 1977.

English

Sounds, Feelings, Thoughts: Seventy Poems, translated and with an introduction by Magnus J. Kryński and Robert A. Maguire, Princeton, New Jersey: Princeton University Press, 1981 (dual text, Polish-English).
Spoiling Cannibals' Fun: Polish Poetry of the Last Two Decades of Communist Rule, edited and translated by Stanisław Barańczak and Clare Cavanagh, foreword by Helen Vendler, Evanston, Illinois: Northwestern University Press, 1991.

SZYMONOWIC, SZYMON (pseudonym Simon Simonides) (1558–1629), is sometimes referred to as the last Polish poet of the Renaissance. An urban dweller, he studied in Cracow, then in Belgium and France. After his return to Poland, he became a member of the Court of J. Zamoyski, through whose intercession he received a coat of arms and became a nobleman.

He started writing during his student days in Cracow. In his Latin poem referring to the tradition of Pindar, *Divus Stanislaus,* he explored the evils of war, acknowledging, however, the ridiculous aspects of war in defense of country or Christianity. In his collection of songs *Flagellum livoris* (1558), he glorified Zamoyski's victory at Byczyna, while in *Aelinopaean* (1589) he developed a similar theme and added criticism of the *szlachta* (nobility). During this period he wrote a number of incidental poems and a Latin tragedy on a biblical theme, *Castus Ioseph* (1587).

During 1593–1605 Szymonowic was Zamoyski's aide in organizing the cultural institutions in Zamość (the Zamość Academy, the library, and the printing house). After his sponsor's death, he remained with the family, educating young Tomasz Zamoyski and supervising the academy. Later he withdrew to his estate Czarniecin, a gift from Zamoyski.

Devoting most of his time to the academy, he wrote only a few minor and patriotic poems at this time. In 1614, however, he published his greatest work, *Sielanki* (Idylls). During his later years he composed a Latin drama, *Pentesilea* (1618), and a few incidental poems.

According to Janusz Pelc, *Sielanki,* a collection of twenty poems, is considered the last outstanding work of Polish Renaissance literature. Based on the tradition of Greek idylls written by Theocritus and Virgil's Bucolics, *Sielanki* combines the traditional shepherd's elements and Arcadian scenery with local contemporary reality. Szymonowic was also influenced by Kochanowski's work, paraphrasing his Horatian odes, employing his phraseology and poetic rhythms.

Addressed to his own contemporaries, *Sielanki* gave expression to his keen observation and his active, moralizing attitude toward reality. The peaceful affirmation of the harmony of nature found in several poems is paralleled by the didactic criticism of manners, social life, and politics found in other poems. His critical attitude toward King Zygmunt III is combined with the glorification of the "Golden Age." The cycle also reveals Szymonowic's sensitivity to the poverty of the peasants (especially well expressed in the best idyll, *Żeńcy* [Reapers]). His sympathy is expressed in an original, personal manner. The simplicity and charm of *Kołacze* (Wedding Cakes), a description of an old Polish wedding, have not been attained by any other Polish poet.

Sielanki were written during the advent of the Baroque period: their roots are in the Renaissance in ideology and style, but the full blossoming of Baroque poetics can also be discerned.

(See Renaissance.)

BIBLIOGRAPHY

Sielanki i pozostałe wiersze polskie, edited by J. Pelc, Wrocław: Ossolineum, 1964.

T

TANGO (see Mrożek).

TETMAJER, KAZIMIERZ PRZERWA (1865–1940), a poet, novelist, short story writer, and playwright, came from a gentry family with patriotic and literary traditions. Born in the Podhale region, near the Tatra Mountains, he lived in Cracow and Zakopane. He studied philosophy, worked as a journalist, was the recipient of numerous awards. In 1934 he became an honorary member of the Polish Academy of Literature (*PAL*). In his later years he suffered from psychological disorders and lost his eyesight. Soon after the outbreak of the war, he died in a hospital.

His first important work was the volume *Poezje* (Poems, 1891, which by 1924 had already had five editions). This was followed by *Poezje: Seria II* (Poems: Series II, 1894); *Poezje: III* (Poems: III, 1898); *Poezje: IV* (Poems: IV, 1900); *Poezje: V* (Poems: V, 1905); *Poezje: VI* (Poems: VI, 1910); *Poezje: VII* (Poems: VII, 1912); and *Poezje: Seria ósma* (Poems: Series Eight, 1924). The first three of the volumes deserve special attention: there are major differences among them. Series I presents the author as a social activist, reacting vividly to the bloody suppression of strikes. These revolutionary accents were violently criticized (S. Tarnoski), and Tetmajer withdrew the poems from the second edition, publishing them separately in his collections *Hasła* (Watchwords, 1901) and *Poezje współczesne* (Contemporary Poems, 1906). Series I marked his auspicious literary debut; Series II and III became literary events, making Tetmajer one of the most popular poets of his time. He gave voice to the crucial problems of the period. He admired Schopenhauer and Nietzsche and appreciated Indian philosophy. He was the spokesman for liberal views of the decadent generation. The year 1894, when his Series II was published, is considered by most critics to be the precise point of the modernist breakthrough and the beginning of the Young Poland period. Tetmajer's view of life is presented in a most expressive way in *Hymn do nirwany* (A Hymn to Nirvana), which expresses the longing for annihilation. In Series II the appreciation of art as the major achievement in the life of an individual and society (*evviva l'arte*) appeared for the first time. The cult of art is united with the cult of love in Tetmajer's works. His unconventional erotic lyrics were considered scandalous, but they were a novelty and appreciated as such. The themes associated with the Tatra Mountains, the landscape, and the life of the highlanders were original elements in Polish literature. The world of the mountains is presented in poems interspersed with motives from folk songs (*Pieśń o Jaśku zbójniku* [The Song About Johnny the Robber]). Epic elements also appear (*Śmierć Janosika* [The Death of Janosik]), related in their mood and form to the folk "rapsodies" of Serbian poetry. Tetmajer's poems were also inspired by ancient themes. Some are also related to his travels to Italy. A number were influenced by the French Parnassists.

Tetmajer gained popularity as a prose writer with his story *Ksiądz Piotr* (Father Peter). Simultaneously with the publication of Reymont's *Chłopi* (The Peasants), he began writing the stories in *Na Skalnym Podhalu* (In the Rocky Tatra Mountains, 1903–10), in the dialect of the inhabitants of Podhale. The stories were coldly received, especially for their use of dialect, but later what was once considered its weakness by critics became its strongest point and the work is now recognized as a masterpiece. Tetmajer also wrote a historical novel, *Legenda Tatr* (The Legend of the Tatra Mountains, 1912); the novel *Koniec epopei* (The End of an Epos, Volumes 1–3, 1913–17), meant primarily to compete with Żeromski's* *Popioły* (Ashes), proved to be a failure. His remaining novels, *Anioł śmierci* (Angel of Death, 1898), *Panna Mery* (Miss Mary, 1909), *Romans Panny Opolskiej z Panem Główniakiem* (The Romance of Miss Opolska and Mister Główniak, 1912), and *Zawisza Czarny* (The Black Zawisza, 1901) were artistically inferior, as were his dramas, *Rewolucja* (Revolution, 1906) and *Judasz* (Judas, 1917).

Na Skalnym Podhalu (In the Rocky Tatra Mountains) is a series of forty short novels. Within the scenery of mountains, forests, and meadows Tetmajer presents the old culture of highland robbers, hunters, and shepherds; their adventures and passions; their love of the mountains; their natural talent for song and dance, for sculpture and storytelling. Tetmajer described the extraordinary charm and magnitude of this mountain world. His characters are heroic, but authentic, presented in songs, tales, and proverbs which the writer remembered from his childhood. Tetmajer employed these traditional motives, enriching them with literary elements and creating a harmonious whole. The consistency of poetic vision is achieved not only through the uniform view of the human psyche and traditional elements, but also through the geographical background and the stylization of language, the Tatra dialect.

(See *Młoda Polska.*)

BIBLIOGRAPHY

Wybór nowel (Selected Novels), Cracow, 1906.
Poezje: Wydanie zbiorowe (Poetry: A Collected Edition), Volumes 1–4, Warsaw, 1923–24.
Poezje wybrane (Selected Poetry), selected and with an introduction by J. Krzyżanowski, Wrocław, 1968.
Poezje (Poetry), Warsaw, 1979.

THEORY OF PURE FORM (see Witkiewicz, Stanisław Ignacy).

THIS WAY FOR THE GAS, LADIES AND GENTLEMEN AND OTHER STORIES (see Borowski).

TOWIAŃSKI, ANDRZEJ (1799–1878), a mystic and religious reformer, arrived in Paris in December 1840. He gave a speech to the Polish emigration, announcing the opening of a new, higher era of Christianity: his ideas attracted Mickiewicz,* S. Goszczyński,* Słowacki,* and others. Expelled from France in 1842 and having failed to be received by the pope, he settled in Switzerland. In his most important works *Biesiada* (Banquet, 1842) and *Wielki Period* (The Great Period), written in 1844 and published in 1922, he presented his idea of the development of the universe as a series of incarnations of spirits, who ultimately come closer and closer to God. The spirits reach perfection through "triple sacrifice"—of the spirit, the body, and the act. According to his belief, a man of unusual strength and purity of spirit has the power to disperse the dark spirits and find supernatural help for his nation, and—through the chosen nation—for all of humanity. According to Andrzej Waliski, the messianic role was to be played by the Slavic world, particularly Poland, and by France (he acknowledged Napoleon as his predecessor). In order to succeed in its mission, Poland had to be free of hatred toward Russia and abandon its revolutionary struggle. Towiański's ideas seemed indeed inspiring, especially for Mickiewicz and Słowacki.

(See Romanticism.)

BIBLIOGRAPHY

Wybór pism i nauk (Collected Writings and Studies), second enlarged edition, edited by and with an introduction by S. Pigoń, Cracow 1922.

TREMBECKI, STANISŁAW (see Enlightenment).

TRENY (Threnodies) (see Kochanowski).

TRYLOGIA (The Trilogy) (see Sienkiewicz).

TUWIM, JULIAN (1894–1953), a poet and translator, came from a white-collar Jewish family who lived in Łódź. He made his literary debut in 1913 with the poem *Prośba* (A Favor), in *Kurier Warszawski* (The Warsaw Courier). After arriving in Warsaw in 1916 he studied law and philosophy for a short time at the university; he worked for the journal *Pro arte et studio* and in 1918 was one of the coauthors of the artistic cabaret *Pod Picadorem* (Under the Picador). He was cofounder (1920) and chief representative of the Skamander group. He also worked for *Wiadomości literackie* (Literary News) and for a number of satirical magazines and various cabarets. After World War II broke out he managed to get to France by way of Romania; and later in 1942 to the United States. He worked for the émigré press, among others, *Nowa Polska* (New Poland), published from 1942 to 1946 in London by A. Słomiński. Toward the end of the war he drew closer to leftist Communist circles and to pro-Soviet political activities. He returned to Poland in 1946. He took part in the official cultural and propagandistic events organized by the Communist authorities. He became silent as a poet, however, and other than a small number of occasional poems he published only translations and his old works. He was the recipient of numerous literary awards, among them the PEN Club award for his translations of Pushkin. He was given an honorary doctorate from the University of Łódź in 1949.

Tuwim's early lyrics, published, for example, in the collections *Czyhanie na Boga* (Lurking for God, 1918) and *Sokrates tańczący* (*The Dancing Socrates,* 1920), combine a revolt against the poetry of Young Poland (mainly against the decadent moods and linguistic mannerism of the epigones) with a clear acceptance of some of the forms of the modernist movement. Accepting some of the tendencies of late modernism (e.g., the urban motives of Russian symbolists and the cult of everyday life found in Staff's* works), he also reached for the experiences of Russian futurism and German expressionism and referred often to Whitman and Rimbaud. The foundation of Tuwim's view on poetry lay in Bergson's theory, from which he extrapolated vitalism and biologism, based on a metaphysical and existential foundation. He employed colloquial language with all its vulgarisms and trivialities. He also endeavored to make lyrical poetry more common, to deprive it of its elitist character. He also undertook social themes and became more and more critical toward existing reality.

The youthful optimism is replaced by bitterness and lyrical reflection in his collection *Słowa we krwi* (Words in Blood, 1926). These tendencies are magnified later in his most mature collections: *Rzecz czarnoleska* (The Czarnoles' Case, 1929), *Biblia cygańska* (The Gypsy Bible, 1933), and *Treść gorejąca* (Burning Matter, 1936). In these works Tuwim sought Classical models, both Polish (Kochanowski,* the Romantics, Norwid*) and foreign (Horace, Pushkin). His biologism was manifested in existential anxiety. At the same time, Tuwim's formal skill, his artistic use of words and images, became the source of his own poetic philosophy: he began concentrating on the nature of a word and its relation to its meaning. According to Ryszard Matuszewski, his concern with language led to a "poeticalchemy," treated as a symbol of spiritual links with the tradition of national language. It was also a poetic response to the violent attacks of nationalistic circles and those with fascist sympathies, evoked by Tuwim's pacifist and liberal views expressed in some of his poetry (e.g., *Do prostego człowieka* [To the Simple Man], 1929). The attacks directed against him inflamed the poet's polemic talent and sharpened the edge of his satire (e.g., in the collection *Jarmark rymów* [A Market of Rhymes], 1934). Tuwim's greatest achievement in satire is the narrative poem *Bal w Operze* (Ball at the Opera, in 1936, published in 1946), which presented a grotesque, impassioned view of the elite of political power before September 1939. It was also a foreboding of the coming catastrophe. Tuwim's formal mastery and artistic innovativeness can be seen in his poems for children, the collections published in 1938, and the poems *Lokomotywa* (The Locomotive), *O panu Tralalińskim* (About Mister Tralaliński), *Słoń Trąbalski* (Trąbalski Elephant), and *Zosia Samosia.* The poems combine lyricism and humor (often pure nonsense humor); they are masterpieces in the use of language (rhythm and onomatopoeia) and have always been favorites of young people. During the war Tuwim began working on his lyric-epic poem *Kwiaty polskie* (Polish Flowers, published in 1949), reminiscent of the Romantic tradition: the poems are digressive and combine elements of various genres—memoirs, lyrical confessions, patriotic invocations, political polemics, and childhood memories. Tuwim almost stopped writing after the war, as if the traumas of the catastrophe had destroyed his memory, on which he so depended in his poems.

Tuwim's work as a translator was unusually substantial. He translated mainly from the Russian: Pushkin, Nekrasov, Gogol, Griboedov, Lermontov, Tyutchev, Balmont, Bryusov, Blok, Pasternak, Mayakovski, and Svetlov. He also translated Horatio, Longfellow, and Rimbaud. A major part of his output is associated with his passion for collecting books and with his curiosity regarding customs and traditions (*Czary i czarty polskie oraz Wypisy czarnoksięskie* [Devils and Polish Witchcraft or Witchcraft Anthology], 1923, 1960, *Polski słownik pijacki i Antologia bachiczna* [The Polish Drunk Dictionary and the Bacchus Anthology], 1935, 1959) and the three volume series *Cicer cum caule, czyli Groch z kapustą* [Cicer Cum Caule, or Peas with Cabbage, or Topsy-Turvy], 1958–63). He also edited several anthologies, collaborated with Antoni Słonimski on humorous pieces (*W oparach absurdu* [In the Clouds of the Absurd], 1958), and wrote musicals, librettos for operettas, songs, and monologues.

(See Contemporary Polish Literature.)

BIBLIOGRAPHY

Dzieła (Works), Volumes 1–5, Warsaw, 1955–64.

Wiersze wybrane (Selected Poems), fourth edition, with an introduction by M. Słowiński, Wrocław, 1986.

English

The Dancing Socrates and Other Poems (Sokrates tańczący), translated by Adam Gillon, New York: Twayne, 1971.

Bogdana Carpenter, *The Poetic Avant-Garde in Poland, 1918–1939,* Seattle: University of Washington Press, 1983.

TWARDOWSKI, JAN (born 1915), a poet, made his literary debut in 1935. In his early works, he was close to the poetics of the Skamander group. During the Nazi occupation as a soldier in the Home Army (*AK*), he participated in the Warsaw Uprising. After the war, he studied Polish philology and entered a seminary: in 1948 he was consecrated as a Catholic priest. His mature works are contained in the following collections: *Wiersze* (Poems, 1959), *Znaki ufności* (Signs of Trust, 1970), *Niebieskie okulary* (Blue Eyeglasses, 1980), *Rachunek dla dorosłego* (A Bill for an Adult, 1982), *Na ostatku* (Finally, 1986), *Sumienie ruszyło* (A Conscience Spoke Up, 1989), and *Tak ludzka* (So Human, 1990). His poems are regarded as some of the finest of contemporary religious lyrics. Twardowski's poetry rejects traditional devotional conventions and theological speculation: it is a personal, poetic confession of a poet's faith, arising out of his experience as a priest. His poetry is sensitive to and aware of the paradoxes in the psyche of contemporary man, who seems to avoid faith but instinctively feels the need for it. It is open and trusting, close to the Franciscan affirmation of the world, a solidarity with suffering of all kinds, and enchanted with the fullness and variety of life. His lyrical tone contains humor and, at times, self-irony; concrete images alternate with philosophical and ethical considerations. Father Twardowski is also the author of very popular and critically acclaimed works for children about the problems of faith and prayers (*Zeszyt w kratkę* [A Cross-Ruled Notebook], 1973). His philosophic and religious position is made perfectly clear in his poem "The World": "Love that is invisible / hides nothing."

BIBLIOGRAPHY

English

Spoiling Cannibals' Fun: Polish Poetry of the Last Two Decades of Communist Rule, edited and translated by Stanisław Barańczak and Clare Cavanagh, foreword by Helen Vendler, Evanston, Illinois: Northwestern University Press, 1991.

TWÓRCZOŚĆ (Creativity or Creative Works), a literary monthly, was first published in August 1945, first in Cracow, then after 1950 in Warsaw (from 1950 to 1956 as an organ of the Polish Writers' Union [ZLP]). The editors-in-chief included Kazimierz Wyka,* Adam Ważyk* (after 1950), Jarosław Iwaszkiewicz* (after 1955), and J. Lisowski (after 1980). *Twórczość* immediately became an all-Polish magazine, publishing the outstanding works of authors of various generations and artistic orientations, from various circles (e.g., Szaniawski's* *Dwa teatry* [Two Theaters] and Borowski's stories). The journal reflected the artistic and cultural life in Poland by publishing essays on the changes in Polish literature during the war and the postwar periods. The sketches by Kazimierz Wyka were excellent examples of the art of literary criticism. *Twórczość* always opposed suppressive attitudes toward literature. The program, if one can call it that, was to propagate "humanistic and social realism," to give equal rights to various poetic trends and literary positions. Accused of formalism in 1947, the editors of *Twórczość* began to concentrate on the history of literature. In 1949, the journal's integrity was lost completely; it became a mouthpiece of the party and faithfully published reviews and reports supporting *ZLP*. In 1953, after the death of Stalin, the editors were duly chastened for their errors of judgment. The journal regained its former prominence with Jarosław Iwaszkiewicz* as editor-in-chief. Iwaszkiewicz continued to publish literary works and essays of high quality and emphasized the literary roots of the journal by reviewing Polish and foreign literature. For a long time *Twórczość* attracted outstanding and famous writers, and talented newcomers as well. Avoiding controversies and disputes and not advocating any special program, the journal played an important role in the development of contemporary literary culture. The prominent position of *Twórczość* in Polish literary life became unsettled at the turn of the 1970s and 1980s, at the moment when the *Drugi obieg* (Second Circulation) emerged. The following journals were published underground: *Zapis* (Record), *Puls* (Pulse), *Arka* (Ark), and *Kultura Niezależna* (Independent Culture). A number of outstanding writers, who desired to free themselves from political censorship, were drawn to these journals. A similar function was effected by journals entering the country from abroad, such as the Paris-based *Kultura* (Culture) and *Zeszyty literackie* (Literary Notebooks).

BIBLIOGRAPHY

W. P. Szymański, *Kazimierz Wyka—redaktor Twórczość* (Kazimierz Wyka—Editor of *Creativity*), Cracow, 1978.

TYRMAND, LEOPOLD (1920–85), a novelist, journalist, and music critic, began studying architecture in Paris in 1938. The eruption of the war caught him in Warsaw, from which he escaped to Vilnius, which was soon overrun by the Soviet Army. Even his work with the Communist press did not protect him from arrest by the NKVD. Freed during the German offensive in 1941, he initially remained in hiding within the territory of the German occupation, then voluntarily reported to the German authorities to be sent into Germany as a laborer. Once there, he supported himself through working at many trades, all the while using a false French passport. In 1944 he enlisted as a crew member of a cargo ship from which he attempted to escape at a Norwegian port. He was arrested by the Germans and imprisoned in a concentration camp. After liberation he worked in various foreign missions of the Polish Red Cross and returned to Poland in 1946. He worked as a journalist, at first for the popular weekly *Przekrój* (Cross-Section), then for the Catholic periodical *Tygodnik Powszechny* (The Universal Weekly), in which he edited the section on music and theater reviews during the years 1950–53. After the Communist authorities shut down the paper, he remained on the outskirts of cultural and intellectual life; only the liberalization after Stalin's death enabled him to reach a wider audience (an enthusiast and an avid popularizer of jazz, he published, among others, a volume of essays entitled *U brzegów jazzu* [On the Edge of Jazz], 1957). The increasing rigors of censorship prompted him to leave the country in 1965. At first he stayed in France; then, in 1966 he moved permanently to the United States. In the years 1968–69 he taught Slavic literature at Columbia University in New York. He then became associated with the American neoconservative movement and began working with the Rockford Institute in Illinois in 1967 and became its vice president in 1981. He also served as the editor-in-chief of *Chronicles of Culture* and *The Rockford Papers,* both published by the Rockford Institute. Tyrmand was also published in American periodicals (such as *The New Yorker*) and the Polish émigré press (the London-based weekly *Wiadomości* [News] and the monthly *Kultura* [Culture], Paris).

In his literary work Tyrmand combined autobiographic motifs with themes taken from popular adventure-mystery literature. He never failed to include his own ideological or moral message. In the anthologies of short stories *Hotel Ansgar,* 1947, and *Gorzki smak czekolady Lukullus* (The Bitter Taste of Lukullus Chocolate), 1957, and in the novel *Filip* (1961), all based on wartime memories, he challenged the dominating patriotic-heroic stereotype of Polish literature. He contradicted it by representing a portrait of a levelheaded and resourceful hero fighting a cunning battle for survival amid the fascist terror. The novels *Zły* (The Evil One, 1957) and *Życie towarzyskie i uczuciowe* (The Social and Emotional Life, 1976) have brought him popular acclaim. In all of these works the action is set amid the scenery of postwar Warsaw. The first is a quick-paced romance-thriller showing the demimonde of social outcasts and the criminal underground—themes carefully avoided by official literature. The second novel is a biting satire on the conformity and hypocrisy of the official artistic milieu, in which collaboration with the Communist government is the price paid for the opportunity to have a career in one's profession. This motif was elaborated on by Tyrmand in *Dziennik 1954* (Diary, 1954, 1980); his notes very vividly and authentically portray the grim and, at the same time, grotesque world of Socialist Realism at the moment of the greatest intensity during the Stalinization of Poland. Tyrmand's diary is right on target in its analysis of the mechanisms governing the Sovietization of Polish society and its life and the devastation of culture by Communist ideology. It is also a testimonial to the independent individual's single-handed resistance against the reality imposed by an omnipotent utopia. The polemic with the system of Communist mystification also constitutes the main motif of Tyrmand's American journalism, compiled in the volumes *Notes of a Dilettante,* 1970; *The Rosa Luxemburg Contraceptives Cooperative,* 1972; and *The Ugly, Beautiful People,* 1985. In these essays Tyrmand discusses the delusions of American leftist liberalism and the youth movement of the 1960s. The direction of his journalistic activity stemmed from his personal need "to save America from itself," as the writer himself put it. Tyrmand, from an early age, had been fascinated by American civilization.

BIBLIOGRAPHY

S. Kisielewski, "Leopold Tyrmand—pisarz zapomniany" (Leopold Tyrmand—a Forgotten Writer), *Twórczość* (Creative Works), Number 4, 1962.

U

UNIVERSITY OF GDAŃSK was founded in 1970 from two institutions, *Wyższa Szkoła Pedagogiczna* (Higher School of Education, 1946) and *Wyższa Szkoła Ekonomiczna* (Higher School of Economics, 1945), in Sopot. The staff of both schools made up the majority of those employed by the new institution. The University of Gdańsk is made up of six departments, the largest of which is the Humanities Department, which includes Polish, Russian, and English Philology; the Language and Culture of the Scandinavian Countries; History; Pedagogy; and Psychology.

The Institute of Polish Philology (present director, J. Michno) has a number of sections: theory of literature, history of literature and culture of the Baltic (*Pomorze*) regions during the nineteenth and twentieth centuries (from 1973), contemporary literature (from 1978), bibliographic studies, Polish language, and methodology of Polish language and literature. Polish studies was inaugurated in 1947, first under the directorship of T. Makowiecki from the University of Nicholaus Copernicus (Toruń), then under the leadership of R. Pollak (from 1952) from the University of Adam Mickiewicz (Poznań). In 1953 a department devoted to the history of literature was established under the directorship of A. Bukowski (to 1970); B. Nadolski and M. Janion held joint appointments with the department. During this period areas of specialization became crystallized: Old Polish (Nadolski), the Enlightenment (E. Rabowicz), Romanticism (Janion), the second half of the nineteenth century and regional literature of the Baltic and the Kashubian regions (Bukowski). Other researchers joined the staff: from Wrocław, K. Głombiowski and S. Zabłocki. Others joined in the research in other areas: Old Polish Literature—Z. Rynduch, J. Kotarska, and E. Kotarski (from 1970); Polish-Latin Literature—Zabłocki and Z. Głombiowski; and the Enlightenment—Rabowicz, J. Platt, I. Kadulska, and B. Krakowski.

Other areas of specialization include the following: Vilnius from the beginning of the nineteenth century (K. Mężyński), types and systems of narration in the prose of the nineteenth and twentieth centuries (J. Bachórz, K. Chruściński, H. Cieślakowa, M. Czermińska, A. Martuszewska, and J. Michno); the literature and philosophy of *Młoda Polska* (J. Tuczyński); the theory of literature and methodology of research (S. Dąbrowski and Martuszewska); the literature for children and young people (G. Skotnicka); marine literature (Tuczyński, R. Karwacki, and Kotarski); regional literature of the Kashubian, Warmian, and Mazurian regions (Bukowski, A. Drzeżdżoń, and T. Dracki); the Baltic and Greater Poland positivism (Bukowski and J. Data); Baltic memoir-literature; folklore studies; as well as literary life in Gdańsk after 1920 and after 1945 (Bukowski).

Scandinavian studies are now a separate department (Z. Ciesielski). In 1972 a section devoted to studies in theater was established (S. Kaszyński), which also included film criticism (B. W. Lewicki, 1975–81), as well as literary criticism (Czermińska, K. Nowosielski, and S. Chwin).

Publications include the following: *Gdańskie Zeszyty Humanistyczne* (Gdańsk Humanistic Publications), *Zeszyty Naukowe Wydziała Humanistycznego* (Research Publications of the Department of the Humanities, 1958–1967), and *Zeszyty Naukowe Wydziała Humanistycznego, WSP* (Research Publications of the Department of the Humanities, Higher School of Education, 1965–69), under the editorship of Bukowski.

BIBLIOGRAPHY

A. Bukowski, "Droga do uniwersytetu w Gdańsku" (Road to the University in Gdańsk), *Litery* (Letters), Numbers 1, 3, 1970.

K. Chruściński, "Gdańska humanistyka" (Gdańsk Humanities), *Litery* (Letters), Number 3, 1971.

UNIVERSITY OF LVOV (*UJK*) was founded in 1661 by King Jan Kazimierz, by granting academic privileges to the Jesuit college which was established in 1608. As a result of the protests from the universities in Cracow and Zamość, the king's act was voted down by the *Sejm*. In 1758, King August III confirmed the university status of *UJK*, while establishing two faculty schools (Theology and Philosophy). The abolition of the Order of Jesuits in 1773 resulted in the rescinding of the act which gave *UJK* university status. Under Austrian rule it was again revived (with four faculties) but was totally subordinated to the narrow interests of the state: its language was German. Downgraded from 1805 to 1816, it returned again to academic status in 1817; its development, however, was hindered by the progress of Germanization of the country. During the period of Galicia's autonomy, conditions for the further development of the school were greatly improved. The languages employed were Polish and Ukrainian. According to Władysław Floryan, limited police control allowed for the development of faculties, such as Polish History. The Lvov Historical School was represented by T. Wojciechowski, K. Liske, O. Balzer, and Sz. Askenazy. The foremost Polish philosopher at the turn of the nineteenth and twentieth centuries was K. Twardowski, who was also associated with the university. Jan Kasprowicz became Professor of Comparative Literature.

After World War I, the name of the university was changed to that of its founder, Jan Kazimierz. The development of the humanities faculty includes such prominent names as Twardowski, K. Ajdukiewicz, R. Ingarden (Philosophy), F. Bujak, A. Szelągowski (History), W. Podlacha, M. Gebarowicz (History of Art), W. Kotwicz, Z. Smogorzewski (Oriental Studies), E. Porębowicz, and Z. Czerny (Romance Philology). The chair of Polish Language was assumed at various times by H. Ułaszyn, T. Lehr-Spławiński, H. Gaertner, and E. Taszycki; the faculty of Slavic Languages was headed by K. Nitsch, Lehr-Spławiński, Taszycki, and Z. Stieber; J. Kuryłowicz became Professor of General and Indo-European Linguistics.

After September 1939 the name of the university was changed to the Ukrainian State University of Ivan Franko and became part of the Soviet system of education. At this point T. Żelenski-Boy became Professor of French Literature. The Nazis closed the university, shot ten of its professors, and confiscated and destroyed its property. Various professors continued teaching underground. After 1945 these Polish professors assumed duties at other schools in Poland, primarily at the University of Wrocław, which continued the tradition of UJK.

The history of Polish Studies began in 1817. At the turn of the nineteenth and twentieth centuries, professors connected with the university included A. Brueckner, W. Bruchnalski, J. Kallenbach, B. Gubrynowicz, and W. Hahn. Among prominent scholars who taught at UJK before World War II were the following: J. Kleiner, S. Skwarczyńska, R. Ingarden, and L. Chwistek.

BIBLIOGRAPHY

L. Finkel and S. Starzyński, *Historia Uniwersytetu Lwowskiego* (The History of the University of Lvov), Lubów, 1894.

Historia nauki polskiej (A History of Polish Education), edited by B. Suchodolski, Volumes 1–3, Wrocław, 1970–77.

UNIVERSITY OF ŁÓDŹ (Uniwersytet Łódzki) was founded in 1945 as a continuation and development of a branch of an existing institution which was first established in 1928, *Wolna Wszechnica Polska* (Free Polish University) in Warsaw. It was meant to fulfill the needs and aspirations of Łódź and its environs. Organized by one of the university's staff, T. Viewegers, who became its first rector, the core faculty was made up of staff from various already established universities (Vilnius, Lvov, and Poznań). Subsequent rectors included T. Kotarbiński and J. Chałasiński, both from the faculty of the University of Warsaw. In 1956 the Higher School of Education became part of the University of Łódź, followed by the Higher School of Economics in 1961. The university is currently made up of six departments with various study sections attached to them. Although branches of the university work hand in hand with research centers in other cities (Kalisz, Toruń, etc.), the main center of cooperative research is the Łódź Learned Society (*Łódźkie Towarzystwo Naukowe*). The Department of Humanities has achieved great success in the areas of Philosophy, Sociology, History, Bibliographic Studies, and the history of art. The following are among its illustrious faculty: B. Baranowski, H. Brodowska, J. Dutkiewicz, N. Gąsiorowska-Grabowska, A. Kamiński, A. Kłoskowska, Z. Kuchowicz, Z. Lebiszowska, J. Muszkowski, H. Radlińska, J. Szczepański, S. Truchim, M. Wallis, and S. Zajączkowski.

The Polish Studies Department separated from the Humanities Department in 1951 and was combined with the departments of Polish Language, the History of Polish Literature, and the Theory of Literature. The first chairman of the department was S. Adamczewski (1945–50), with a faculty of the following: A. Boleski (1945–48), J. Saloni (1945–49), J. Z. Jakubowski (1949–51), and J. Durr-Durski (1954–69).

The first Polish department devoted to the Theory of Literature was chaired by S. Skwarczyńska, from 1946. In 1953, the department became part of the Polish Studies Department—Old Polish Literature, Nineteenth and Twentieth Centuries—and was successfully chaired by S. Kawyn, Durr-Durski, and Z. Skwarczyński.

Language studies were taught by the following faculty: H. Ułaszyn, Z. Stieber, K. Dejna, and S. Hrabec. The Institute of Philology was set up in 1970 under the leadership of Z. Skwarczyński and W. Śmiech (after 1979), with the following sections: the History of Old Polish Literature, the History of Modern Literature, Contemporary Literature, the History of Polish Language and Slavic Philology, Contemporary Polish Language, as well as a research center of philology and the teaching of the Polish language. An Institute of the Theory of Literature, Theater and Film was also set up under the directorship of Skwarczyńska and with a staff including B. W. Lewicki and S. Kaszyński. Other areas of research include the following: Old Polish poetry and prose (Durr-Durski and J. Starnawski), the Enlightenment* (A. Skwarcyński and W. Pusz), early Romanticism* (A. Kowalska), Positivism* and *Młoda Polska** (J. Tynecki, A. Budrecka, and T. Wróblewska), contemporary studies (Skwarczyński, H. Karwacka, J. Rzymowski, J. Poradecki, and T. Błażejewski), the theory of literature, especially sources, as well as the theory and history of literary areas of art (Skwarczyńska, T. Cieślikowska, Lewicki, Kaszyński, R. Wierzbowski, and P. Wert).

The following publications appear under the sponsorship of the university: *Polonista* (Polish Scholar, 1946–47); *Zagadnienia Literackie* (Literary Problems, 1946–48); *Prace Polonistyczne* (Polish Research, 1937–39, and continued from 1945); *Rozprawy Komisji Językowej* (Papers of the Language Commission from 1954); and the biannual *Zagadnienia Rodzajów Literackich* (Problems of Literary Types, from 1958).

BIBLIOGRAPHY

Materiały do dziejów Uniwersytetu Łódźkiego (Materials from the History of the University of Łódź), Łódź, 1962.

Uniwersytet Łódźki 1945–1980 (University of Łódź, 1945–1980), Łódź, 1980.

UNIVERSITY OF POZNAŃ whose name was changed to Adam Mickiewicz University in 1955 (*UAM*), was established in 1919, at the initiative of H. Święcicki, the first rector. Initiated with only two faculties, in 1925 it had already grown to five. During World War II, the Nazis closed it down: from 1940 it assumed status of Underground University for the Western Territories (*UZZ*) in Warsaw, with students in seventeen disciplines. After 1943 branches in Częstochowa and Kielce were also set up. Revived in 1945, it soon returned to its previous status. In addition to outstanding faculties in science and mathematics, the university had considerable achievements in such branches of the humanities as history (H. Łowmiański, G. Labuda, J. Topolski), philology (J. Berger, H. Orłowski, J. Fisiak), linguistics (S. Urbańczyk, L. Zabrocki), musicology, and sociology.

Polish Studies became a prominent discipline with the establishment of the university. Among the scholars connected with the center were the following: T. Grabowski, S. Dobrzycki, S. Pigoń, and R. Pollak. Primary research was conducted in the Methodology of Literary Studies and the History of Literary Criticism in Poland. Theses were mostly written on the cultural tradition of Wielkopolska and Pomorze, and the theory of literature and criticism. In 1969 the section was changed into the Institute of Polish Philology. Several editions of Old Polish literature have appeared. Studies connected with the cultural tradition of the region have also been central to the institute. The institute is also a center of bibliographical studies.

BIBLIOGRAPHY

J. Naciejewski, *Uniwersyteckie tradycje filologii polskiej w Poznaniu* (University Tradition of Polish Philology in Poznań), *Studia Polonistyki,* Volume 2, 1975; *Studia Polonistyki,* Volume 4, 1977.

UNIVERSITY OF SILESIA IN KATOWICE (*USI*) was established in 1968 by combining the Pedagogical College and a branch of the Jagiellonian University (established earlier in 1963). The university is especially strong in psychology (J. Pieter), history (K. Popiołek, J. Pachoski), and linguistics (K. Polański).

Polish Studies in Katowice were already developed in the Pedagogical College. In 1969 the Institute of Polish Philology was created, under the directorship of J. K. Zaremba (after 1973 by W. Lubaś). In 1977 the institute became the Institute of Polish Literature and Culture. It now has eleven chairs. The institute also houses several largely independent laboratories, whose specialties include Silesian dialects and local literary life.

BIBLIOGRAPHY

Wyższa Szkoła Pedagogiczna w Katowicach 1950–1968 (Higher School of Education in Silesia), Katowice, 1971; 1973.

UNIVERSITY OF VILNIUS (Wilno) was established in 1578 by official proclamation of King Stefan Batory. The university had earlier been a Jesuit college. Privileges were granted to the university, similar to those accorded the Academy in Cracow. Until 1780 it had three faculties. The character of the school was formed by its position on the border of various cultures. Three languages were employed: Polish, Russian, and Lithuanian. The university developed enormously until the mid-seventeenth century. The prominent faculty included the following: S. Warszewicki, P. Skarga, J. Wujek, S. Grodzicki, and M. K. Sarbiewski.* The war of 1655 and later the wars and fires of the early eighteenth century undermined the position of the university. Its revival was given impetus only during the second half of the eighteenth century, with M. Poczobut-Odlanicki as its rector and reformer, on behalf of the National Committee of Education. It was then a secular school with Polish as its language, educating teachers for high schools and with control over schools in Lithuania. After the third partition it was reorganized again and lost several of its educational prerogatives. In 1803 it rose to a higher rank again and, with greater autonomy, became the center of cultural life in Lithuania. The local press was under its control. Its curator from 1803 to 1824, A. J. Czartoryski, was able to employ foreign professors (Capelli, Saunders), who were later replaced by their disciples, among them Jan Śniadecki, rector from 1807 to 1815; S. B. Jundziłł, a scientist; and Jędrzej Śniadecki, a chemist and physician. Early in the nineteenth century the students' movement, among them the famous *filomats* (who included the poets A. Mickiewicz,* J. Czeczot, and T. Zan, and the scholars J. Jeżowski and J. Kowalewski), became quite active. In later years students included J. Słowacki,* L. Spitznagel, and J. I. Kraszewski.* The repressions of Nowosilcow, the curator after 1824, which started with the trial of the *filarets* in 1823–24, led to the collapse of the university. After the November Uprising in 1831, the university was closed down by the tsar; the medical and theological faculties became independent schools.

In independent Poland the school was reactivated and from 1919 to 1939 became the University of Stefan Batory in Vilnius (USB); it consisted of six faculties. In 1939, after the Soviets entered Vilnius, USB was changed into a Lithuanian university. Closed down by the Germans in 1943–44, it was again revived after the war as the chief university of Soviet Lithuania. In 1955 it received the name of V. Kapsukas.

According to Irena Sławińska, until the nineteenth century Polish studies were not given the status of an independent discipline, although the roots reached back far into the early years of the school, when its teachers were writers and polemicists, like P. Skarga, J. Wujek, M. Łaszcz, M. K. Sarbiewski, and A. Naruszewicz.* Polish studies proper were begun in 1919, with several prominent teachers (J. Kallenbach, S. Pigoń, and K. Kolbuszewski), graduates of UJ and UJK. S. Pigoń developed areas of study largely centered around Romanticism. The new era began with Professor M. Kridl (1932–39), who created an "aesthetic school": his disciples included K. Górski, M. R. Mayenowa, I. Sławińska, H. Turska, J. Trypućko, and Cz. Zgorzelski. The poetic group *Żagary* was created under the influence of the university.

BIBLIOGRAPHY

J. Bieliński, *Uniwersytet Wileński* (University of Vilnius, 1579–1831), Volumes 1–3, Cracow, 1899–1900.

M. Kosman, *Uniwersytet Wileński, 1579–1979,* Wrocław, 1981.

UNIVERSITY OF WARSAW (*UW*) was established in 1816–18 as the Royal University of Warsaw, on the initiative of S. K. Potocki and S. Staszic, when the Law School and Medical School were changed into faculties, and faculties of Theology, Philosophy, Science, and the Fine Arts were added. During the period preceding the November Uprising, the university played an important role in the patriotic education of the country's youth and became the center of underground student organizations. The following outstanding democratic activists are among its alumni: M. Mochnacki, J. N. Janowski, and W. Darasz. In 1831 the tsarist authorities closed down the university. In 1862, through the efforts of A. Wielopolski, the school was revived as the Main School of Warsaw, which remained thus until 1869 and exerted a great deal of influence on the formation of positivism. It was temporarily renamed the Imperial *UW,* as a result of the Russification policies of the tsar. The students' strike in 1905 began the struggle to establish a Polish university. In 1915 *UW* became a Polish school again; during 1935–39 it was renamed the University of Józef Piłsudski.

During the period between the wars, the University of Warsaw had nine faculties. Outstanding achievements were effected in many branches of the humanities, largely due to brilliant scholars: S. Arnold, W. Tokarz (History), K. Michałowski (Archeology), T. Kotarbiński, J. Łukasiewicz, W. Tatarkiewicz (Philosophy), S. Czarnowski, L. Krzywicki (Sociology), L. Petrażycki (Law), J. S. Bystroń (Ethnology), M. Brahmer (Romance Philology), J. Baudouin de Courtenay, S. Szober, and W. Doroszewski (Linguistics). During the occupation the university worked underground. However, severe losses were suffered: 44 percent of its faculty and 70 to 90 percent of its property (books, buildings, laboratories) were either confiscated, destroyed, or stolen. In 1968 a number of professors were forced to leave the university as a result of an anti-Semitic campaign (among them Leszek Kołakowski and B. Baczko). At present a number of outstanding humanists work at the university: L. Bazylow, A. Gieysztor, S. Herbst, S. Kieniewicz, B. Leśnodorski, M. Małowist, T. Manteuffel, H. Samsonowicz, J. Tazbir, A. Zahorski, A. Garlicki (History), S. Lorentz (History of Art), Z. Lissa (Musicology); T. Kotarbiński, B. Suchodolski, K. Szaniawski (Philosophy); M. and S. Ossowski, J. Szacki (Sociology), K. Kumaniecki, L. Winniczuk (Classical Philology), H. Kurkowska, A. Bogusławski, and S. Skorupka (Linguistics).

According to Zdzisław Libera, Polish Studies have been an integral part of the *UW* practically since its beginning, when K. Brodziński began teaching history of Polish literature in 1822–30. During the time of the Imperial *UW*, Polish Studies greatly weakened, but were revived again in 1915 as a Philology Section of the Philosophical Faculty. The first professors were J. Kallenbach, J. Kleiner, and B. Chlebowski. Subsequent professors included J. Ujejski, B. Gubrynowicz, J. Krzyżanowski, and W. Borowy. During the period between the wars the lecturers included M. Kridl, K. Górski, S. Adamczewski, and T. Makowiecki.

In 1940–41 the Polish Philology Section met underground. After the war a new period of its development began with W. Borowy, J. Krzyżanowski, S. Żółkiewski, and J. Z. Jakubowski. In 1968, as a result of reorganization a Faculty of Polish and Slavic Philology, which included the Institute of Polish Philology, came into existence. It was chaired by Jakubowski, then by Kulczycka-Saloni. The research interests of the institute encompass the entire history of Polish literature, from the Middle Ages to contemporary times. The institute cooperates with the Institute of Literary Studies of PAN and with the universities in Moscow, Prague, and Berlin. It also houses the Institute of the Polish Language and Culture for Foreigners *Polonicum.* It constantly invites outstanding writers to lecture to the students (J. Iwaszkiewicz,* M. Wańkowicz,* T. Parnicki,* and M. Brandys*). The publications of the institute appear in *Roczniki UW* (UW Annual), *Rozprawy UW* (UW Debates), and *Przegląd Humanistyczny* (Humanistic Review).

BIBLIOGRAPHY

Z dziejów polonistyki warszawskiej (From the History of Warsaw's Polish Studies), Warsaw, 1964.

J. Bieliński, *Królewski Uniwersytet Warszawski, 1816–1831* (The Royal University of Warsaw, 1816–1831), Volumes 1–3. Warsaw, 1907–12.

UNIVERSITY OF WROCŁAW (*UWr*) (in 1945–51 University and Polytechnic in Wrocław, since 1952 *UWr* of B. Bierut) was established in 1811 as a Prussian university under the name of its founder, Frederic Wilhelm III. Originally it had five faculties. In the early nineteenth century the school became a research center; it already had a large percentage of Polish students. In 1830 proposals were made to create a chair of Slavic Studies, finally only realized in 1841 because of the unfavorable political situation.

On August 24, 1945, the Polish *UWr* was established. Professors from other universities made up its faculty, mainly from Lvov (the biologist S. Kulczyński; the first rector, the medical scientist L. Hirszfeld; the mathematician H. Steinhaus; the historian W. Czapliński; and many others). At present the university has five faculties. Its library, which required re-Polonization after the losses suffered during the war, was augmented with books from Lvov (1947) and the collection from Ossolineum.

Polish Studies appeared in 1945 as part of the Institute of History of Polish Literature (with professors T. Mikulski, S. Kolbuszewski, and Julian Krzyżanowski* as a Visiting Professor). Other prominent scholars included Jan Kott* (1951–52), Rospond, Ossowski, Jakobiec, Kuraszkiewicz, and Floryan. In 1969 the present Institute of Polish Philology was created (the directors have included Zakrzewski, 1969–71, and Czesław Hernas after 1971). The institute has broadly based research interests; it is the coordinator of the Pan-Polish Project on "Polish National Culture. Its Tendencies and Development, and Its Perceptions." It has ties with several foreign schools, among others in Vilnius and Lille. Publications of the institute appear in *Prace Literackie* (Literary Research) of Acta Universitatis Wratislaviensis.

BIBLIOGRAPHY

M. Pater, *W murach uniwersytetu* (Within the Walls of the University), Wrocław, 1962.

URZAD (The Office) (see Breza).

V

VADE-MECUM (see Norwid).

W

WAŃKOWICZ, MELCHIOR (1892–1974), prose writer, reporter, and publicist, studied political science and law. He made his literary debut in an underground paper, *Wici* (Plait), of which he was editor from 1909 to 1911. In 1917–18 he enlisted as a soldier in the Polish Corps in Russia; later in the Polish Army he took part in the Polish-Soviet War of 1920; he used his experiences during the years of that war and the Russian Revolution in his first reportage novels, *Strzępy epopei* (Shreds of an Epos, 1923) and *Szpital w Cichiniczu* (The Hospital in Cichinicz, 1926). In 1924 he set up a lively printing house in Warsaw, whose successor exists to this day in New York—Roy Publishers. In 1923–26 he was head of the Press Department of the Home Office. He traveled to Mexico, dispatching reports later published as *W kościołach Meksyku* (In the Churches of Mexico, 1927). His trip to the Soviet Union resulted in the publication of *Opierzona rewolucja* (Full-Fledged Revolution, 1934). When World War II began he was able to escape to Romania: then to the Near East, Italy, France, Germany, and England. In 1943–45 he became a war correspondent. In 1949 he settled in the United States and visited Poland in 1956. He returned in 1958 and settled down in Poland permanently. Hounded by the authorities, who hindered the publication of some of his works (among others, *Bitwa o Monte Cassino* [The Battle for Monte Cassino]), in 1964 he was sentenced to three years in prison for voicing his opinions about the situation in Poland to the foreign press (the sentence was suspended after public outcry).

Wańkowicz created a unique type of nonfiction-tale, combining authentic facts with personal memories and unusual elements of plot and anecdote. He enchanted the reader with his vivid narration and his language—picturesque, fresh, juicy, and extraordinarily rich. He explored problems that he became personally involved in, employing semiepic, semilyrical forms, varying between irony and pathos, reaching back to the tradition of the tale. A participant in and keen observer of numerous historical events, he created a peculiar panorama of national history. He published his famous book *Na tropach Smętka* (On the Tracks of Sadness, 1936), attempting to preserve the national identity, revealing the vicissitudes of the Polish people in German East Prussia, and two works on the economic development of Poland between the wars: *C.O.P.—ognisko siły* (C.O.P.—A Bonfire of Force, 1938) and *Sztafeta* (Relay Race, 1939). His books devoted to the struggles of Polish soldiers during World War II include *Bitwa o Monte Cassino* (Battle of Monte Cassino, Volumes 1–3, 1945–47), a monumental epic-reportage of the famous battle in May 1944 on the Italian front by the Second Polish Corps, under the leadership of General Anders; *Wrzesień żagwiący* (Flaming September, London 1947), fragments of which were published in Poland in 1959 as *Hubalczycy* (Hubal's Men); and *Westerplatte.* His love of family tradition and the life in northeastern Poland is expressed in *Szczenięce lata* (The Raw Years, 1934), a humorous and sentimental description of the small gentry world which is slowly but invariably passing away. He also explored family memories in *Ziele na kraterze* (Herb on the Crater, 1951), dedicated largely to the dramatic fate of Warsaw youth who fought in the underground and in the Warsaw Uprising in 1944 (in which one of the writer's daughters lost her life). His observations regarding Polish emigrant centers in Canada and the history of the Poles dispersed by World War II throughout the world are presented in the cycle *Panorama losu polskiego: Tworzywo* (A Panorama of Polish Fate: Material, New York, 1954; in Poland in 1960), *Droga do Urzędowa* (New Road to Urzędów, New York, 1955), *Jak daleko?* (How Far?, New York, 1955). Completing the cycle is the story of the tragic fate of a Polish family sent deep inside the Soviet Union, *Dzieje rodziny Korzeniewskich* (The History of the Korzeniewski Family, 1945). After his return to Poland he published his memoirs and stories about former times and people: *Tędy i owędy* (Here and There, 1961) and *Zupa na gwoździu* (Nail Soup, 1976). He also published an American trilogy *W ślady Kolumba* (In the Tracks of Columbus, Part 1: *Atlantyk-Pacyfik* [Atlantic-Pacific], 1967; Part 2: *Królik i oceany* [Rabbit and Oceans], 1968; Part 3: *W pępku Ameryki* [In the Navel of America], 1969); a selection of reports from 1936 to 1958, *Od Stolpców po Kair* (From Stolpce to Cairo, 1969); and a review of his publicistic writings, *Przez cztery klimaty* (Through Four Seasons, 1972). His views of the work of a reporter and the theory of the genre are contained in *Karafka La Fontaine'a* (La Fontaine's Carafe, Volume 1, 1972; Volume 2, 1980). He also wrote two important polemic brochures (both published abroad), *Kundlizm* (Mongrelism, Rome-London, 1947) and *Klub Trzeciego Miejsca* (Club of the Third Place, Paris, 1949).

BIBLIOGRAPHY

English

Three Generations, translated by Krystyna Cękalska, Toronto: Canadian-Polish Research Institute in Canada, 1973.

The Hospital in Cichinicz (Szpital w Cichiniczach), Tokyo, 1938.

The History of the Korzeniewski Family (Dzieje rodziny Korzeniewskich), New York: National Committee of Americans of Public Descent, Inc., 1945; London: National Committee of Polish Descent, Inc., 1946.

WARIAT I ZAKONNICA (The Madman and the Nun) (see Witkiewicz, Stanisław Ignacy).

WAT, ALEKSANDER (Chwat) (1900–1967), a poet, prose writer, and translator, was cofounder of Polish futurism and coauthor of the Futurist one-day papers. He came from a partially assimilated Polish-Jewish family. He worked for the avant-garde magazines *Nowa Sztuka* (New Art) and *Almanach Nowej Sztuki* (Almanac of the New Art). From 1929 to 1931 he was coeditor of the leftist journal *Miesięcznik Literacki* (The Literary Monthly), the unofficial organ of the illegal Communist Party, and was employed by the Gebethner and Wolf Publishing House. After the outbreak of World War II, he found himself in Lvov; he was arrested by the Soviet secret police (NKVD) and transported to the Moscow prison Lubianka, and next to Kazakhstan, where under extremely difficult conditions he spent time in various prisons and camps, prepared to refuse Soviet citizenship. Released as a result of the amnesty in 1941, after treaty negotiations with the Polish government and the Soviet authorities, he remained in Kazakhstan until 1946. After his return to Poland, he at first took part in the literary life; however, in 1949, he withdrew from active participation, protesting against the forcing of the doctrine of socialist realism on writers. Extremely ill, from 1955 to 1957, he spent time in France recuperating; in 1959 he left for Italy, in 1961 for France; two years later he decided that he, together with his wife, Paulina (Ola), would emigrate. He published a volume of poetic prose influenced by dadaism, *Ja z jednej strony i Ja z drugiej strony mego mopsożelaznego piecyka* (I from One Side and I from the Other Side of My Pug-Iron Stove, 1920), and a collection of stories, *Bezrobotny Lucyfer* (Unemployed Lucifer, 1927, 1960), in which he presented a grotesque-fantastic vision of the crisis of contemporary civilization. In his later years he wrote numerous lyrics (*Wiersze* [Poems], 1957; *Wiersze śródziemnomorskie* [Mediterranean Poems], 1962; *Ciemne świecidło* [Dark Brightness], Paris, 1968), in which his poetic view of life sifted through constant illness and suffering appears along with reflections on art and history, with ample references to the Old Testament. In his "spoken memories," *Mój wiek* (My Century), published from a tape recording (starting

1964–65 during his stay at Berkeley, California), with an introduction by Czesław Miłosz (Volumes 1–2, London, 1978, Warsaw, 1990), he narrated his memories from his entire life to Miłosz, who prompted Wat with comments and questions. This intellectual confession—ideological sympathy with Communism, followed by his sacrifices and the prisons of the Soviet camps—constitutes one of the most important attempts in twentieth century literature to penetrate the secret of the Communist riddle—its alluring power, and at the same time its boundless criminality and the barbarism which it caused. Wat's analysis is rich in detail and striking honesty and at the same time does not avoid metaphysical interpretations: in his view Stalinist Communism is a twentieth century embodiment of Satan (there are certain analogies with Dostoevsky's theses, to which Wat constantly alludes). A continuation and supplement to these elements is contained in his essays, *Świat na haku i pod kluczem* (The World on a Hook and Under Lock and Key), published in London in 1985, and *Dziennik bez samogłosek* (Dictionary Without Vowels), published in London in 1986. His rich output of translations includes the works of Dostoyevsky (*The Brothers Karamazov,* 1928), Tolstoy (*Anna Karenina,* 1929), Turgenev, Ostrovsky, Korolenko, Chekhov, Ehrenburg, G. Bernanos, O. Henry, and Heinrich Mann.

(See Contemporary Polish Literature.)

BIBLIOGRAPHY

English

My Century: The Odyssey of a Polish Intellectual (Mój wiek), foreword by Czesław Miłosz, translated by Richard Lourie, Berkeley and Los Angeles, California: University of California Press, 1988.

Mediterranean Poems (Wiersze śródziemnomorskie), edited and translated by Czesław Miłosz, Ann Arbor, Michigan: Ardis, 1977.

WAŻYK, ADAM (1905–82), a poet, prose writer, essay writer, and translator, studied mathematics at the University of Warsaw. He was linked with the avant-garde poetic movement, was coeditor of *Almanach Nowej Sztuki* (Almanac of the New Art), and worked for *Zwrotnica* (Switch). During 1939–41 he lived in Lvov and was later transported to the Soviet Union, where he became a political officer in General Berling's army organized by Polish Communists. After the war, he settled in Łódź, where he worked for the Marxist weekly *Kuźnica* (Forge); as a journalist and a functionary of the Communist Party he performed the duties of one of the chief supervisors of the ideological law-abidingness of the literary milieu; from 1950 to 1954 he was chief editor of *Twórczość* (Creativity, or Creative Works). After 1956 he left the Communist Party, abandoned his Marxist convictions, and dedicated himself exclusively to literary works.

According to Ryszard Matuszewski, in his early poems, the collections *Semafory* (Semaphores, 1924) and *Oczy i usta* (Eyes and Lips, 1926), he developed a poetic theory based on loose associations, related to Apollinaire and early surrealism, described as an attempt to transfer cubism onto poetry. Later he began to concentrate on prose, ranging from avant-garde experiments to realistic convention in his psychological novel *Mity rodzinne* (Family Myths, 1938). His collection of war poetry, *Serce granatu* (Heart of a Grenade, published in Moscow in 1943; second edition, complete, 1944), consisted of patriotic and martial themes, as well as Classical conventions. These forms continue in his later poems, filled with rhetoric of political optimism, published in subsequent selections (1947, 1950, 1953). In his publicistic pieces in *Kuźnica* (The Forge) and in the collection *W stronę humanizmu* (Toward Humanism, 1949), he gave a Marxist interpretation of literary phenomena; he also appeared as a theoretician of socialist realism. In August 1955 he published his *Poemat dla dorosłych* (Narrative Poem for Adults), in which he expressed his bitter disappointment with the Communist base of his works and gave poetic testimony to the social conflicts of the Stalinist period. The publication of the poem brought on vehement debates, in which the official press accused Ważyk of betraying Marxist ideals and the image of the working class; in the emended edition of the work (1956) the poem *Qui tacent clamant,* in which Ważyk paid homage to the Hungarian insurgents who fought Soviet intervention in 1956, was added. In his later works he returned to his youthful intellectual experiences, publishing a poem, *Labirynt* (Labyrinth, 1961); a novel, *Epizod* (Episode, 1961), several volumes of poems, *Wagon* (The Wagon, 1963) and *Zdarzenia* (Happenings, 1977); and his literary autobiography, *Kwestia gustu* (A Matter of Taste, 1966). He also wrote essays on literature: *Dziwna historia awangardy* (The Strange History of the Avant-Garde, 1976), an anthology of poems; critical sketches on Polish and foreign authors, *Gra i doświadczenie* (Play and Experience, 1974); and essays on versification, *Esej o wierszu* (An Essay on Poetry, 1964) and *Amfion: Rozważania nad wierszem polskim* (Amphion: Considerations over Polish Poetry, 1983). He translated a great deal from French literature (Malraux, Rimbaud, Apollinaire, Eluard, Jacob, Cendrars), Pushkin, and the Roman poet Horace. He was the recipient of the PEN Club award for translation.

(See Contemporary Polish Literature.)

BIBLIOGRAPHY

Eseje literackie (Literary Essays), Warsaw, 1982.

WESELE (The Wedding) (see Wyspiański).

WIERZYŃSKI, KAZIMIERZ (born Wirstlein; name changed in 1912) (1894–1969), a poet, prose writer, essay writer, studied philosophy, literature, and history in Cracow and Vienna. During World War I he joined the legions struggling for Polish independence; in 1915 he was incarcerated as a war prisoner by the Russians. He returned to Warsaw in the fall of 1918 and soon began his association with the *Pod Picadorem* (Under the Picador) cabaret. He also became a member of the Skamander group in 1920. During the war with Russia in 1920 he became a propaganda officer, visited Switzerland and France, and eventually settled down in Warsaw, working as a publicist and literary and theatrical reviewer. He became a member of PAL in 1938. In September 1939 he was evacuated to Lvov, but was able to make his way to France; then through Portugal and Brazil to the United States, where he was a cofounder of the Polish émigré weekly *Tygodnik Polski* (Polish Weekly, 1943–46). He never returned to postwar Poland for political reasons (he was an ardent opponent of the Communist regime). For over twenty years he lived in Sag Harbor on Long Island, New York. He published his works in the London Polish publishing houses and the Parish Literary Institute. After 1964 he moved to Rome, then to London. He was the recipient of a medal in the literary competition of the Ninth Olympic Games in 1928, the Golden Wreath of PAL in 1935, and the State Award in 1936.

In 1913 he published several poems in magazines for young people, but his actual literary debut was with the collection *Wiosna i wino* (Spring and Wine, 1919), in which Wierzyński's joyful, vital, and enthusiastic tone gained him enormous popularity. The mood of euphoria, which was still dominant in *Wróble na dachu* (Sparrows on the Roof, 1912), was gradually toned down in subsequent volumes and replaced by a deeper meditation on the complex nature of life and the world: *Wielka Niedźwiedzica* (The Great Bear, 1923); a series of war poems, 1914–18; *Pamiętnik miłości* (A Diary of Love, 1925); *Rozmowa z puszczą* (A Conversation with the Wilderness, 1929); and a catastropic vision of modern civilization, *Pieśni fanatyczne* (Fanatic Songs, 1929) and *Gorzki urodzaj* (Bitter Harvest, 1933). According to Artur Hutnikiewicz, his volume *Laur olimpijski* (Olympic Laurel, 1927), a poetic projection of his sport experiences, was Wierzyński's most original achievement and considered by the author to be the work of his life. He also valued *Wolność tragiczna* (Tragic Freedom, 1936), a collection of poems in a Romantic style, whose hero was Piłsudski, and whose main theme explored the fate of the country—liberated so recently and already threatened again. The volume *Kurhany* (Grave Mounds, 1938), inspired by Romantic reminiscences, Cassandric in tone, foreshadowed the coming catastrophe. During the war Wierzyński became the embodiment of the poet who represented the struggling country, expressing tragedy and disappointment in his collections *Ziemia-Wilczyca* (Earth-Bitch Wolf, 1941), *Róża Wiatrów* (Wind Rose, 1942), and *Krzyże i miecze* (Crosses and Swords, 1946). The end of the war and its aftermath brought a virtual end to Wierzyński's artistic efforts: he had lost almost all of his family. He returned to writing, through music, publishing a book on Chopin (*Życie Chopina* [The Life of Chopin], English edition, 1949; Polish edition, 1953). His renewal in life and literature is reflected in the volumes *Korzec maku* (Bushel of Poppy Seed, 1951), *Siedem podków* (Seven Horseshoes, 1954), *Tkanka ziemi* (Tissue of Earth, 1960), *Kufer na plecach* (Chest on My Back, 1964), and *Sen mara* (The Sleep of Dreams, 1969). *Czarny polonez* (The Black Polonaise, Paris, 1968) differed from his former poems in its publicist tone and pamphletlike view of postwar Poland, subjected to the perverted influence of the Communist system. These works mark Wierzyński's second period, a second wind, as it were, stained with bitterness. He explored the meaning of art and poetry, adumbrating a stoical affirmation of life but expressing also his longing for, and his almost mystical ties to, his mother tongue and country. He spoke of the tragedy of exile, about the cruelty, violence, and self-destruction of the postwar world. He rejected Classical rigors and wrote poems in the form of intimate conversations, confessions, and meditations. He employed loose associations, contrast, poetic humor bathed in sarcasm and self-irony.

He also published several prose pieces: two volumes of stories on war themes, *Granice świata* (The Boundaries of the World, 1933) and *Pobojowisko* (Battlefield, 1944); several reviews (*W garderobie duchów* [In the Coat-Room of Ghosts, 1938]); a sketch, *Współczesna literatura polska na emigracji* (Contemporary Polish Literature in Emigration, 1943); a book, *Moja prywatna Ameryka* (My Private America, 1966); and a collection of essays, *Cygańskim wozem: Miasta, ludzie, książki* (Gypsy Wagon: Towns, People, Books, 1966).

(See Contemporary Polish Literature.)

BIBLIOGRAPHY

Poezje zebrane (Collected Poetry), London, 1959.

Utwory zebrane (Collected Works), fifth enlarged edition, Warsaw, 1939.

Poezja i proza (Poetry and Prose), Volumes 1–2, selected by and with comments by M. Sprusiński, Cracow, 1981.

English

Selected Poems, edited by Clark Mills and Ludwik Krzyżanowski, New York: Voyages Press, 1969.

WITKIEWICZ, STANISŁAW (1851–1915), the father of the notorious Stanisław Ignacy, was himself a painter, art critic, and prose writer. His father was sent to Siberia after the January Uprising of 1863. Witkiewicz spent three years in Tomsk, then studied art in Petersburg. In 1871 he made his way to Warsaw. From Warsaw he left for Munich to study. He worked as a painter and illustrator, publishing in various magazines. After 1890 he settled permanently in Zakopane. From 1908 he spent most of his time at the health resort Lovran on the Adriatic Sea, where he died of tuberculosis on the eve of World War I.

From 1884 he published his critical studies in the weekly *Wędrowiec* (The Wanderer), including a treatise on Mickiewicz's* imagery and color in *Pan Tadeusz.* He gained celebrity status with his collection of critical writings *Sztuka i krytyka u nas* (Art and Criticism in Poland, 1891), in which he fought a violent battle with the epigones of academic historical painting and defended the still underestimated paintings of Gierymski, Chełmoński, and others. He almost singlehandedly built the foundation of scientific theory of art in Poland. He claimed that the important aspect of art is not so much the theme as the artistic performance; he demanded objective and professional criticism. His aesthetic views were influenced by H. Taine and E. Veron, but he questioned Taine's underestimation of the role of the artist's individuality. For Witkiewicz and for naturalists, the basic criterion in art was agreement with nature, with truth. In his later works he emphasized the social and national functions of art. His monographs of great painters which attest to this fact are the most beautiful books on art in Polish literature: *Juliusz Kossak* (1900), *Aleksander Gierymski* (1903), and *Matejko* (1908). A great deal of his output is devoted to the region of the Tatra Mountains: in *Na przełęczy: Wrażenia i obrazy z Tatr* (In the Pass: Impressions and Pictures from the Tatras, 1891) he explores their landscapes and the life, language, and art of the highlanders; in *Po latach* (After Years, 1905) he expresses his fascination with their architecture and ornamentation. Witkiewicz himself was the creator of the so-called Zakopane style in architecture and he wrote about his ideas in *Styl zakopiański* (The Zakopane Style, 1901). In *Z Tatr* (From the Tatras, 1907) he included a translation of Tolstoy, transforming the latter's prose into the highlanders' dialect; he also included stories from the lives of the poor inhabitants of the Tatra region. Some of his works are devoted to moral and social issues; he also wrote a book about J. Siedlecki (*Dziwny człowiek* [A Strange Man], 1903), who was an avid art collector from Cracow. Witkiewicz was one of the most influential personages of his time.

(See Positivism.)

BIBLIOGRAPHY

Pisma zebrane (Collected Works), edited by J. Z. Jakubowski and M. Olszaniecka, introduction by J. Z. Jakubowski, Volumes 1–3, Cracow, 1970–74.

WITKIEWICZ, STANISŁAW IGNACY (1885–1939), (better known as Witkacy) the son of Stanisław Witkiewicz, was a playwright, prose writer, philosopher, theoretician of art, and painter. He spent his childhood and early years in Zakopane and was educated largely by his father. He studied art in Cracow and traveled to Italy, Germany, and France several times. He was brought up among the intellectual elite; among his friends were Karol Szymanowski, Tadeusz Miciński, Bronisław Malinowski, and Leon Chwistek. In 1909–12 he had a stormy love affair with the actress Irena Solska (a grotesque picture of his affair and the people involved in his and Solska's life was given in *622 upadki Bunga, czyli Demoniczna kobieta* [622 Falls of Bungo, or The Demonic Woman], written in 1910–11; published in 1972). In 1914 his fiancée committed suicide; in despair, he left for Australia with his friend Malinowski, sketching drawings and taking photographs. A Russian citizen, he fought in the Russian Army in World War I. He witnessed the collapse of the empire and the revolution, which had a strong influence on his catastrophic views. In 1918 he returned to Poland, to Zakopane. He gradually abandoned painting (except portrait painting, which he did for money) and turned toward literature, writing theoretical treatises and dramas. He was involved with the avant-garde group of Polish formists (*Formiści Polscy*). During 1918–26 and 1934 he wrote over thirty plays, some of which were lost. During 1925–32 he composed three novels. His later years were devoted almost exclusively to philosophy. He committed suicide, apparently upon learning of the Soviet invasion of Poland.

Witkacy's work is based on an elaborate system of philosophical and aesthetic views, presented in the sketches *Nowe formy w malarstwie i wynikające stąd nieporozumienia* (New Forms in Art and the Resulting Misunderstandings, 1919), *Szkice estetyczne* (Aesthetic Sketches, 1922), and *Teatr: Wstęp do teorii Czystej Formy w teatrze* (Theater: Introduction to the Theory of Pure Form in the Theater, 1923). According to Witkacy civilization is at a turning point: it had entered an epoch of equality, socialization, and mechanization, which would make the masses happy but would annihilate religion, philosophy, and art, through which an individual could experience "The Mystery of Existence." It is a mystery that a man experiences himself as a whole, even though he is composed of many qualities and impressions and even though his existence in the infinite existence of the world is finite. The "metaphysical fear related to the mystery of existence" is silenced in art, which preserves the unity of a personality through symbols connected in a preselected manner. The unity of a work of art is the work of art proper, for its figurative functions have only marginal meaning in comparison with the task of awakening metaphysical feelings (the slogan "Pure Form"). The growing complexity and social alienation of art are signs of its approaching demise: Witkacy's theory is avant-garde and catastrophic at the same time.

In his dramas Witkacy abandoned all realistic probability; the extraordinary events give an impression of a dream or hallucination. The characters, often fantastic and bigger than life, act cruelly and unpredictably, experiencing unusual amorous intrigues and emotional-erotic experiments; revolutionizing science, mathematics, or philosophy; creating fairy tale states or new religions. His heroes and heroines want to experience "the weirdness of existence," to create "artificial life." The plot often resembles a game, or a carnivallike improvisation; his dramas are precursors of the theater of the absurd. They seem to have been written by a contemporary writer. The themes are those that actually haunted their author: decadence, sexual deviation, the place of art in society, the essence of revolution, future shock, man's innate hatred of himself, the Genet-like theme of gender transfer, the impossibility of attaining catharsis or resolution in a work of art, and the search for metaphysical fulfillment. Only a handful of his "dramas" were either staged or published during his lifetime: *Pragmatyści* (The Pragmatists, 1920, staged in 1921), *Tumor Mózgowicz* (Tumor Brainstorm, published and staged in 1921), *Mister Price, czyli Bzik tropikalny* (Mister Price, or Tropical Madness, staged in 1926), *Nowe Wyzwolenie* (The New Deliverance, 1922–23; staged in 1925), *W małym dworku* (In a Small Manor-House, staged in 1923), *Metafizyka dwugłowego cielęcia* (The Metaphysics of a Two-Headed Calf, staged in 1928), *Kurka wodna* (The Water Hen, staged in 1922), *Mątwa, czyli Hyrkaniczny światopogląd* (The Cuttlefish, or Hyracanean Worldview, 1923; staged in 1933), *Jan Maciej Karol Wścieklica* (Jan Maciej Karol the Furious, staged in 1925), and *Wariat i zakonnica, czyli Nie ma złego co by na jeszcze gorsze nie wyszło* (The Madman and the Nun, or There's Nothing Bad That Couldn't Go Even Worse, 1925, staged in 1924). His plays which were produced after the war include *Oni* (They, staged in 1963); *Gyubal Wahazar, czyli Na przełęczach bezsensu* (Gyubal Wahazar, or In the Saddle of Nonsense, staged in 1966); *Bezimienne dzieło* (An Anonymous Work, staged in 1967); *Nadobnisie i koczkodany, czyli Zielona pigułka* (Belles and Dowdies, or The Green Pill, staged in 1967); *Szalona lokomotywa* (The Crazy Locomotive, staged in 1965); *Matka* (Mother, staged in 1964); *Sonata Belzebuba, czyli Prawdziwe zdarzenie w Mordowarze* (The Beelzebub Sonata, or A True Event in Mordowar, staged in 1966); and his most outstanding play, *Szewcy* (The Shoemakers, staged in 1957).

Considering theater to be the domain of pure form, Witkacy did not consider his novels to be works of art. In his novels he presents decadent characters longing for the "weirdness of existence," in a society heading for revolution which would put an end to any part of individuality. His heroes feverishly experience all possible erotic, narcotic, and artistic states, only to die or become insane at the moment of social change. Strange historiosophical ideas are combined in *Pożegnanie jesieni* (Farewell to Autumn, 1927, 1983; Lausanne, 1979) and *Nienasycenie* (Insatiability, 1930, 1957, 1982) with psychological considerations, while the uncompleted *Jedyne wyjście* (The Only Exit, written during 1931–33; published in 1968) presents Witkacy's philosophical views. He also wrote a book on narcotics and a series of sketches on irregularities and deviations in Polish culture and history (published jointly as *Narkotyki: Niemyte dusze* (Narcotics: Unwashed Souls, 1975). He developed his philosophical views throughout his life, attaining fullest expression in his final philosophical treatise, *Pojęcia i twierdzenia implikowane przez pojęcie istnienia* (Notions and Statements Implied Through an Understanding of Existence, 1935). Between the wars Witkacy was appreciated by few intellectuals and artists, often attacked by the critics (among others, Irzykowski*), and treated as a talented dilettante and perpetual avant-gardist, reveling in his own legend as an eccentric and scandalous whoremonger. The turning point of his postwar career came with the publication of his dramas by Konstanty Puzyna (1962, 1972). Witkacy has been lauded as a precursor of the theater of the absurd, an intellectual catastrophist, and the author of a prophetic vision of the fate of European civilization. Witkacy has gained a secure place in world literature and is one of the giants of modern theater and drama.

BIBLIOGRAPHY

Dramaty (Dramas), two volumes, Warsaw: Państwowy Instytut Wydawniczy, 1962; revised and emended, 1972.

Wybór dramatów (A Selection of Dramatic Works), edited and with an introduction by J. Błoński, Wrocław, 1983.

Dzieła wybrane (Selected Works), Volumes 1–5, Warsaw: 1985, Państwowy Instytut Wydawniczy, 1985.

Nienasycenie: powieść (Insatiability: A Novel), new edition, Warsaw: Państwowy Instytut Wydawniczy, 1957; two volumes, 1982.

Pożegnanie jesieni: powieść (Farewell to Autumn: A Novel), Warsaw: F. Hogsick, 1927; Państwowy Instytut Wydawniczy, 1983; Lausanne: L'Age d'Homme, 1979.

Dzieła wybrane (Selected Works), Volumes 1–5, Warsaw: Państwowy Instytut Wydawniczy, 1985.

English

Beelzebub Sonata (Sonata Belzebuba) (plays, essays, and documents), edited and translated by Daniel Gerould and Jadwiga Kosicka, New York: Performing Arts Journal Publications, 1980.

Insatiability (Nienasycenie) (a novel in two parts) translated, compiled and with an introduction by Louis Iribarne, Urbana: University of Illinois Press, 1976.

The Anonymous Work (Bezimienne dzieło), translated by Daniel C. Gerould and Eleanor Gerould, in *Twentieth Century Polish Avant-Garde Drama: Plays, Scenarios, Critical Documents,* Ithaca, New York and London: Cornell University Press, 1977.

The Madman and the Nun and Other Plays (Wariat i zakonnica i inne sztuki), translated by Daniel C. Gerould and C. S. Durer, Seattle: University of Washington Press, 1968.

Tropical Madness (Bzik tropikalny) (four plays), translated by Daniel and Eleanor Gerould, New York: Winter House, 1972.

The New Deliverance (Nowe Wyzwolenie), translated by Adam Tungu, *Polish Perspectives,* Number 6, 1963.

The Water Hen (Kurka Wodna), translated by C. S. Durer and Daniel C. Gerould, first staged, Summer 1967.

Daniel Gerould, *Witkacy: Stanisław Ignacy Witkiewicz as an Imaginative Writer,* Seattle: University of Washington Press, 1981.

The Witkiewicz Reader, edited by Daniel Gerould, Evanston, Illinois: Northwestern University Press, 1992.

WITTLIN, JÓZEF (1896–1976), a poet, novelist, translator, and critic, studied philosophy and linguistics in Vienna and in Lvov after World War I. During World War I, as an Austrian citizen, he was conscripted into the army and served on the front until 1918. After a brief encounter with the Poznań group of expressionists *Zdrój* (Spring), he became involved with the Skamander group in 1920. In 1935 he received a PEN Club award for his translation of *The Odyssey* and a year later was the recipient of an award from *Wiadomości Literackie* (Literary News) for his novel *Sól ziemi* (The Salt of the Earth). In 1937 he was awarded the Golden Wreath of PAL. In 1939 he emigrated to France, then Portugal, and finally, in 1941, to New York, where together with K. Wierzyński and J. Lechoń he founded *Tygodnik Polski* (Polish Weekly, 1941–43). He contributed to various émigré journals in London and Paris, worked with the Polish Section of Radio Free Europe, and was active in the international PEN Club. Wittlin's work is representative of the pacifist literature of antiwar protest of the 1920s and the 1930s. He was formally and ideologically influenced by German expressionism and the Polish variety of early expressionism (Jan Kasprowicz*). His *Hymny* (Hymns, 1920), written in free verse, are an example of the overlap of these two sources of inspiration. He later wrote under the influence of the Polish Renaissance and Baroque (*Poezje* [Poems], 1978). His pacifist tendencies can be seen in the collection of literary sketches *Wojna, pokój i dusza poety* (War, Peace, and the Soul of a Poet, 1925). His outstanding achievement was the novel *Sól ziemi* (Salt of the Earth, 1936), the first part of an intended cycle, O *cierpliwym piechurze* (About a Patient Foot Soldier), an expressionist novel about the beginning of World War I, presenting the fate of a simple soldier against the background of a grotesquely presented Austro-Hungarian monarchy and its army. The novel has been translated into more than ten languages and has received a number of awards, including those from the American Academy of Arts and Letters and the National Institute of Arts and Letters (1943). Wittlin also wrote his memoirs and essays, *Mój Lwów* (My Lvov, New York, 1946), and a collection of sketches, *Orfeusz w piekle XX wieku* (Orpheus in the Hell of the Twentieth Century, 1963). He translated the works of J. Roth, H. Hesse, and R. M. Rilke.

BIBLIOGRAPHY

English

Salt of the Earth (Sól ziemi), translated by Pauline De Chary, London: Methuen, 1940; Harrisburg, Pennsylvania: Stackpole Books, 1970.

WOJTYŁA, KAROL, POPE JOHN PAUL II (born 1920) (pseudonyms Andrzej Jawień, Stanisław A. Gruda, and Piotr Jasień), a theologian, philosopher, poet, and playwright, began his studies in Polish philology in 1938 at the Jagiellonian University. During the Nazi occupation he ran an underground theater in Cracow together with Mieczysław Kotlarczyk and worked as a laborer. In 1942 he entered an underground seminary in Cracow. Ordained in 1946, he studied for two years in Rome; in 1954 he joined the Philosophical Faculty of the Catholic University in Lublin, where he lectured and had other duties. In 1958 he was ordained a bishop; in 1963 archbishop of Cracow; and in 1967 a cardinal. On October 16, 1978, he was elected Pope of the Roman Catholic Church. He chose the name John Paul II. He published the theological and social encyclicals *Redemptor hominis* (1979), *Dives in misericordia* (1980), *Laborem exercens* (1981), *Slavorum Apostoli* (1985), *Redemptoris Mater* (1987), *Sollicitudo vei socialis* (1987), and *Centessimus annus* (1991).

Wojtyła's activity in literature and theater began during his school years in his native town Wadowice. As a student he wrote poems. In 1940 he wrote his first dramas, *Hiob* and *Jeremiasz* (Job and Jeremiah), published four decades later in *Poezje i dramaty* (Poetry and Dramas, 1980). The themes taken from the Old Testament and Polish history express the experiences of historical events. Both dramas are characterized by several layers of temporal structure with minimal plot and language heavily stylized and often discursive. During the early postwar years Wojtyła published his most ambitious literary work, the drama *Brat naszego Boga* (The Brother of Our God, in *Tygodnik Powszechny* [Universal Weekly], 1979; staged in 1980). The story concerns A. Chmielowski, later Brother Albert, founder of the Albertine Order, which cared for the poor and the homeless. Wojtyła juxtaposes an artist and a man of ethical action. According to Krzysztof Dybciak, the main issue, considered in social and moral as well as philosophical and theological terms, is the role of an individual in the process of history. In the poetics of Wojtyła's dramas the word is all-important: the central conflict is the conflict of ideas, while the action and plot complexities are very much reduced. After 1950 Wojtyła expressed himself primarily as a poet in contemplative poems quite akin to meditation. His treatises from this period are discursive, intellectual monologues, hardly what a contemporary reader would call poetry. The putative narrator undoubtedly presents the author's philosophical stand, which has often been referred to as active Christian personalism (first presented in his book

Osoba i czyn [Person and Action], 1969). Some poems are mystical in character, others dominated by ethical-existential considerations which explore social, moral, religious, and national issues, such as *Myśląc Ojczyzna* (Thinking, My country. . .). The dialogue-monologue "meditation on the sacrament of marriage," *Przed sklepem jubilera* (In Front of the Jewelry Shop), published in *Znak* (Mark, 1960), was staged in 1979. In all of his texts the author expresses the religious experience of human life: passing away and living on, life and eternity, death and resurrection.

Wojtyła's sermons also possess literary merit. The Polish Pope's literary output has been translated into all the major languages.

BIBLIOGRAPHY

Poezje i dramaty (Poetry and Dramas), selected by M. Skwarnicki and J. Turowicz, philological editor, J. Okoń, Cracow, 1980.

English

Collected Plays and Writings on Theatre, translated and edited by Bolesław Taborski, Cambridge: University of California Press, 1987.

The Jeweler's Shop, translated by Bolesław Taborski, New York: Random House, 1980.

WYKA, KAZIMIERZ (1910–75), a historian of literature, literary critic, and essay writer, studied Polish philology at the Jagiellonian University from 1928 to 1932. His mentors included I. Chrzanowski, S. Kołaczkowski, and K. Nitsch. He made his debut in 1932 in *Kultura* (Culture) with an article, *Czas i człowiek w "Nocach i dniach"* (Man and Time in "Nights and Days"). He continued his studies in Belgium and France. He became an assistant at the Jagiellonian University, where he also received his Ph.D. He spent the occupation near Cracow, teaching young candidates and writing in underground magazines. After the war he returned to the Jagiellonian and became full professor in 1948. During 1945–50 he was chief editor of the leading literary monthly *Twórczość* (Creativity). He was cofounder and from 1959 to 1970 director of the Institute of Literary Studies PAN. He continued his lectures at the Jagiellonian University (his students included J. Błoński, A. Kijowski, J. Kwiatkowski, H. Markiewicz, W. Maciąg, and K. Puzyna) and was a member of the *Sejm.*

Wyka's bibliography numbers over 950 entries. In his prewar writings he remained under the influence of Norwid* and Brzozowski*, championed the spirit of secular personalism, and emphasized the moral responsibility of literature. During 1945–48 he studied contemporary phenomena in prose (*Pogranicze powieści* [Borders of the Novel], 1948), arguing for realism in its broader sense. He became more active as a literary critic after the political breakthrough of 1956, openly praising the poetry of the postwar period, especially new currents in the poetry of the young generation, which during the years when the official doctrine of socialist realism reigned were condemned to silence (*Rzecz wyobraźni* [A Case for Imagination], 1959); he also devoted a great deal of attention to the writings of K. Baczyński* and T. Różewicz.*

His chief literary interests were history and theory. According to Henryk Markiewicz, he was fascinated by the role played by generations in the process of the historical changes in literature (*Pokolenia literackie* [Literary Generations], 1939, published in 1977). As a literary historian, he specialized in the literature of the nineteenth and twentieth centuries, concentrating, however, on Romanticism and Young Poland (*Modernizm polski* [Polish Modernism], 1939; published in 1959; *Cyprian Norwid poeta i sztukmistrz* [Cyprian Norwid, Poet and Master Dramatist], 1948; *Legenda i prawda Wesela* [Legend and Truth of The Wedding], 1950; studies of Żeromski,* Reymont,* Słowacki,* and Fredro;* and a comprehensive analysis of Mickiewicz's* *Pan Tadeusz,* Volumes 1–2, 1963).

Wyka's aesthetic sensitivity and his interpretative talent were combined with a keen sense of synthesis and stylistic ingenuity. He had a significant influence on the way Polish literature was viewed during his lifetime. Wyka also wrote studies on other forms of art—film, painting, various branches of history, culture, and Polish traditions (e.g., *Szkice literackie i artystyczne* [Literary and Artistic Sketches], Volumes 1–2, 1956), and even on the sociological and economic phenomena of the time of the German occupation. His literary talent was also revealed in his stories (*Opowiadania* [Short Stories], 1978) and pastiche and parodies (*Duchy poetów podsłuchane* [Spirits of Poets Overheard], 1959; 1962).

BIBLIOGRAPHY

Kazimierz Wyka: Charakterystyki, wzpomnienia, biografia (Kazimierz Wyka: Characteristics, Reminiscences, Biography), edited by H. Markiewicz and A. Fiut, Cracow, 1978.

WYSPIAŃSKI, STANISŁAW (1869–1907), a playwright, poet, painter, theater reformer, the son of a sculptor, was educated among the intellectual elite of Cracow. He studied painting in Cracow under the guidance of Jan Matejko, who allowed his young colleague to contribute to the redecoration of St. Mary's church. Later Wyspiański studied history, history of art, and literature at the Jagiellonian University. He traveled abroad and spent some time in Paris, studying and painting; he became acquainted with Gauguin and Puvis de Chavannes. An admirer of classical tragedy and of Shakespeare, he began to devote more and more time to the theater. His first dramatic works were begun in Paris but completed when he returned to Cracow (*Królowa Polskiej Korony* [The Queen of the Polish Crown] and early versions of *Legenda* [The Legend], *Warszawianka* [The Varsovienne], *Daniel,* and *Meleager,* 1892–94). His further artistic development was stimulated by his contacts with the City Theater in Cracow, first as a painter and scene designer, but soon as a director of his own dramas: *Warszawianka* in 1898; *Lelewel* a year later; then *Wesele* (The Wedding, 1901) and *Wyzwolenie* (Liberation, 1903). Meanwhile he started working on the graphic designs of *Życie** (Life) magazine; in 1902 he became a professor of the Academy of Fine Arts. He painted a great deal, chiefly portraits but also impressionistic landscapes. He was cofounder of the Art Association, innovator of book illustration, and one of the chief initiators of applied arts.

Wyspiański was truly a reformer of Polish theater and drama in the early twentieth century. His early works (*Legenda I,* 1898; *Daniel,* staged in 1932; *Protesilas i Laodamia,* 1899; and *Lelewel,* 1899) were still under the influence of foreign models, especially those of Wagner, Maeterlinck, and the French Classicists. In these works, however, are already discerned the motives of his later monumental dramas, which owe much to the tradition of the great national Romantic dramas. Exploring the traditional motives rooted in Romanticism, he introduced the great Romantics onto the stage proper: *Warszawianka, Lelewel,* and *Noc listopadowa* (November Night, 1904). He returned again and again to the November Uprising; *Legion* (1900) retells the story of Mickiewicz's Italian legion. What was more important, however, was the revival of the open structure of drama. Wyspiański gave voice to the issues essential to the survival of the nation, speaking of the past, prophetic in his assumptions, criticizing and advocating a program for the future, viewing Polish problems against the background of great philosophical issues. *Legion* presented a historical panorama of various epochs, while *Wesele* and *Wyzwolenie* were rooted in contemporary reality: their images, metaphors, and symbols, however, explored the great questions of national existence, the ideas and programs, the illusions and myths. Wyspiański's historiosophy was largely inspired by Nietzsche, especially the latter's postulate of monumental and critical history serving the future. The national myths appear in Wyspiański's dramas along with the great myths of the Mediterranean culture, especially that of ancient Greece (*Noc listopadowa* [November Night], *Akropolis* [Acropolis], 1904, *Protesilas i Laodamia* [Protesilaus and Laodamia], *Achilleis [Achilles],* 1903, and *Powrót Odysa* [The Return of Odysseus], 1907). The latter two works, especially, are concerned with Wyspiański's existential philosophy, which assumed the irreversibility of human fate, the unavoidability of evil, which always accompanied human deeds: he presented the heroic ethos as the only alternative in facing fate.

Wyspiański also reflected upon the earliest, legendary part of the history of Poland. After *Legenda* (Legend), he composed *Bolesław Śmiały* (Bolesław the Brave, 1903) and *Skałka* (The Little Rock, 1907), in which he explored the struggle of different concepts of life and different approaches to ethical action in history. The dramas created an original view of ancient Poland, but, at the same time, were also highly original achievements in the theater. Wyspiański was not only the author of the text but also costume and scene designer, as well as codirector; he was thus able to realize his vision of the theater. He led Polish theater out of nineteenth century *verismo,* by creating a uniform style of performance through a coherent blending of architecture, painting, music, words, actors, and movement on the stage: all these elements were subordinated to the main idea of the play and given a symbolic role. Wyspiański's concept of theater was one of the important elements in the great reform of the theater begun in Europe at the turn of the nineteenth and twentieth centuries. Wyspiański expressed his views on theater in *The Tragicall Historie of Hamlet . . . świeżo przeczytana i przemyślana przez St. Wyspiańskiego* (The Tragicall Historie of Hamlet . . . A Fresh and Original Reading, 1905).

Wyspiański also wrote two contemporary tragedies based on authentic events found in court-trial records: *Klątwa* (The Curse, 1899) and *Sędziowie* (The Judges, 1907), introducing everyday reality onto the stage, but endowing the plots with a tragic and metaphysical dimension.

A separate group of Wyspiański's works are *Rapsody* (Rhapsodies), inspired by Słowacki,* and in particular by his *Król-Duch* (King-Spirit)—lyrical-epic poems presenting visions of history centered around heroes and legends (*Kazimierz Wielki* [Casimir the Great], 1900, *Bolesław Śmiały* [Bolesław the Brave], 1900, *Wernyhora* [Wernyhora—Ukrainian Lyric Poet], 1900, *Święty Stanisław* [Saint Stanislaus], 1900–1902, *Henryk Pobożny pod Legnicą* [Henry the Pious at the Battlefield of Lignica], 1903, and *Piast* [Piast], 1903). Wyspiański also composed lyrics—intimate personal confessions, melancholy, reflective, ironical—in most cases not meant for publication.

In 1905 Wyspiański was selected as a candidate for the head of the City Theater in Cracow and presented a program for future reform. Unfortunately, the position was given to the actor Ludwik Solski. It should be added that Wyspiański was already seriously ill at the time; he was able only to dictate the final editings of his works that he had begun: an adaptation of Corneille's *Cyd* (Le Cid, 1907) and the drama *Zygmunt August* (1907). His funeral in Cracow was a national event. Wyspiański was certainly one of the most important creative personalities in Polish history.

Wesele (The Wedding), a drama in three acts, is considered by most critics one of the most important works in the history of Polish theater and literature; in terms of the Polish national consciousness its unique position remains unchallenged. The inspiration for the play was precipitated by the real wedding of the poet L. Rydel and Jadwiga Mikołajczykówna, a daughter of a peasant from the village of Bronowice, which took place on November 20, 1900, in Bronowice, in the house of a painter, W. Tetmajer, whose wife was an older sister of the bride. Three months after the actual wedding, rehearsals for the stage *Wesele* were begun. Opening night was an unprecedented event; authentic prototypes of characters in the play were fairly easy to recognize: *Gospodarz* (The Host) was Włodzimierz Tetmajer; *Poeta* (Poet), his brother Kazimierz; *Pan Młody* (The Young Bridegroom), Rydel; *Dziennikarz* (Journalist), R. Starzewski; and Czepiec, an old Jew, and his poetic, highly educated daughter, Rachel, kept their real names in the play. Other characteristic personages appear, such as the village priest. Act I, realistic in form, was composed of dialogues among the wedding guests appearing onstage in groups of two or three: among them were the representatives of the "city intelligentsia" and peasants from Bronowice. The lyrical charm of certain dialogues contrasts with the satirical and unmasking tone of other speeches, especially in the case of the "gentlemen" and the peasants. The composition of this section of the drama is stylized in the form of a *szopka* (a Christmas mummers' play), a popular form of Polish folk theater. Act II is transformed from the "real" wedding into a fantasy composed of unearthly visions. A little girl, Marysia, encounters the mysterious ghost; Dziennikarz (the Reporter) sees Stańczyk (King's Fool); Poeta (Poet) talks to Rycerz (The Knight); Pan Młody—to Hetman; Dziad (Old Beggar)—to Jakub Szela, a leader of the forgotten peasant rebellion against the gentry in Galicia; and in the final scene Gospodarz (Host) comes face to face with Wernyhora (a legendary national prophet). The dialogues reveal the hidden dreams, anxieties, and fears of the individuals; national myths and complexes are brought into the open. Two of the phantoms, Wernyhora and *Chochoł* (The Straw-Man), summoned from the garden, share a special role in the drama: they cannot be reduced to individual phantoms; they have a decisive influence on the course of events. Wernyhora gives Gospodarz a Golden Horn, the sound of which will summon people armed with scythes to battle. Gospodarz gives it to a young peasant, Jasiek. The conclusion is symbolic: Jasiek has lost the horn. The wedding guests, as if deep in their sleep, dance to the music of *Chochoł*, who is playing a melancholy soporific melody on a violin. The plot is nothing but a scaffolding for symbolically laden situations, dialogues, and images of metaphorical or symbolic character. The drama refers directly to the political and social situation in Galicia and is a warning to the intelligentsia, who continue to live with their myths and illusions, seemingly highly spiritual, but weak and decadent when contrasted with the primitive power of the simple folk. The old myth of victory at Racławice suggests that the peasants could be made to fight for freedom under the leadership of the intelligentsia. *Wesele,* however, shows the impotence of the intelligentsia at the moment of trial, and the immaturity of the peasants in spite of their readiness to act. The drama is constructed in symbolic poetic verse, full of allusions, understatements, and ambiguous images, impossible to interpret fully. The symbols in *Wesele* have become autonomous elements of national mythology (the Golden Horn, the dreamy dance sequence, *Cho-*

chol and his music). *Wesele* is a mine of excellent sayings, many of which, in fact, have become proverbs. Directed against myths, especially those of Romantic origin, it created myths of its own which are just as permanent and alive. The drama precipitated debates and arguments as soon as it was produced. A mountain of critical works has been devoted to the play. It is a truly national drama, one of the most important poetic analyses of society in Polish literature. It was made into an outstanding film by Andrzej Wajda, who himself has often borrowed "the dreamy dance sequence" in his other films (e.g., *Ashes and Diamonds*).

(See *Młoda Polska.*)

BIBLIOGRAPHY

Dzieła zebrane (Collected Works), Volumes 1–16, edited by L. Płoszewski and others, Cracow: Collected Edition, 1958–71.

English

Meleager, translated by G. R. Noyes and F. Noyes, Berkeley: University of California Press, 1933.

Protesilaus and Laodamia (Protesilas i Laodamia), translated by E. M. Clark and G. R. Noyes, London: *Slavonic Review*, London University, 1933.

The Return of Odysseus (Powrót Odysa), translated by Howard Clarke, Bloomington, Indiana: Indiana University Press, 1966.

The Wedding (Wesele), translated by Floryan Sobieniowski and Mesketh Parson, New York: Hart Stenographic Bureau, 1962.

The Wedding (Wesele), translated by Gerard T. Kapolka, Anne Arbor, Michigan: Ardis, 1990.

WYZWOLENIE (Liberation) (see Wyspiański).

Z

ZABŁOCKI, FRANCISZEK (1752–1821), a writer of comedies and a poet, was descended from an impoverished *szlachta* family and never completed his education. In 1774 he worked for the National Commission for Education. In spite of his contacts with the king and magnates, he lived on the outskirts of the "great world," among the intelligentsia. He undertook various types of literary work: he translated from Latin and French and wrote incidental poems, idylls, odes, poetic letters, fables, which appeared in *Zabawy Przyjemne i Pożyteczne* (Pleasant and Useful Playthings). His early writings (e.g., the satire *Duma ubogiego literata* [The Pride of a Poor Literary Person] and the mythological poem *Cztery żywioły* [Four Elements]) reveal the characteristic features of his style: the ability to create a mood, a free use of dialogue phraseology, a fluency of the verse, and a search for comic elements in the culture of the *szlachta* (nobility). He rarely wrote in a personal or intimate tone.

Zabłocki devoted the period from 1780 to 1788 almost exclusively to the theater. In accordance with theory and common practice, he employed the plots of French comedies and filled them with his own political, social, philosophical, and psychological observations. He wrote over fifty comedies, which, when viewed in their entirety, provide a unique panoply of character types, behavioral patterns, vices, masks, and conventions. Zabłocki made use of every model of comedy: Theatre Italien, Molière, sentimental comedy, new comedy (Diderot, Sedaine), and comic opera. He introduced Polish verse to the national stage.

The date of his theatrical debut is not known. In 1780 he published three works: the comedy *Dwojakie głupstwo* (Double Dupery), the comic opera *Balik gospodarski* (The Host's Little Ball), and *Ojciec dobry* (A Good Father) by Diderot (staged in 1782). In 1782 he published and staged the comedy *Zabobonnik* (The Superstitious One) and his greatest comedy, *Fir-*

cyk w zalotach (The Dandy Goes Awooing). In 1781–83 he wrote several farces: *Doktor lubelski* (Doctor from Lublin, published and staged in 1781), *Gdyracz* (Foul Mouth, published in 1781), and *Doktor z Musu* (The Doctor by Necessity, adapted from Molière, published and staged in 1782). He also wrote a number of sentimental comedies: *Filozof żonaty* (The Married Philosopher, staged and published in 1781), *Dziewczyna sędzia* (Female Judge, published in 1781; staged in 1783), and *Amfitrio* (adapted from Molière, staged in 1782; published in 1783), which also summed up his poetic credo. It is the most literary of his comedies, indicating a turning away from a veristic presentation of reality to allusion and metaphor. His later major comedies are *Sarmatyzm* (Sarmatism, staged in 1785; published in 1820) and *Król w Kraju Rozkoszy* (The King in the Kingdom of Bliss, staged in 1787; published in 1960).

According to Janina Pawłowiczowa, after 1788 Zabłocki's connection with the theater was almost severed: he became engaged more and more in public life; he worked for the Commission for Education and supported the Reform Party by writing pamphlets and satires. Zabłocki was also the author of a number of political poems. He took active part in the Kościuszko Uprising in 1784.

After 1795 Zabłocki abandoned literature altogether; he was ordained and worked as a priest in Góra and Końskowola. A few years before his death he prepared for publication several of his unpublished comedies, in which he expressed his doubt about the social value of literature.

Fircyk w zalotach (The Dandy Goes Awooing), a comedy in three acts, was an adaptation of a poor play by Romagnesi. It is considered the best Polish comedy prior to the works of Fredro.* The play preserves the Classical unities and precision of structure. The plot involves a love intrigue between a young widow, who hides her affection for the young dandy, Fircyk, under the guise of religious devotion and virtue. Fircyk, who follows her from Warsaw, is first attracted by her money; then more and more he becomes enamored of the person. The story is lively and clever, but everything is solved on the psychological level, without the intervention of outside events. Far from being didactic like his predecessors, Zabłocki fills the stage with multidimensional, ambiguous characters. His sympathy lies with the young dandy (Fircyk), who is bright and full of charm though not very serious until he is overcome for the first time in his life by love. The dialogues are brilliant, humorous, light, and literate. The play is performed on Polish stages to this date.

(See Enlightenment.)

BIBLIOGRAPHY

R. Kaleta, "Twórczość satyryczna Franciszka Zabłockiego" (Satirical Creativity of Franciszek Zabłocki), in *Oswieceni i sentymentalni* (The Enlightened and the Sentimental), Wrocław, 1971.

ZACZAROWANA DOROŻKA (The Enchanted Carriage) (see Gałczyński).

ZAGAJEWSKI, ADAM (born 1945), a poet, prose writer, and essayist, was born in Lvov, in an area appropriated by the Soviet Union. Soon after, his family moved to the western part of Poland. He studied psychology and philology at Jagiellonian University. He played an important role in the seventies in the poetic movement *Nowa Fala* (New Wave). Among other activities he was a member of the Cracow literary group *Teraz* (Now) and on the editorial board of the periodical *Student.* Persecuted by the Communist censor, at the end of 1982 he left Poland and settled in Paris, where since 1983 he has been coeditor of the quarterly *Zeszyty Literackie* (Literary Notebooks).

In his early works (the collections of poetry *Komunikat* [Bulletin], 1972, and *Sklepy mięsne* (Meat Markets], 1975), he employed the characteristic postulate of the New Wave—"telling it straight" about reality and about the unmasking of the falsity of the official language imposed by Communist ideology. Together with Julian Kornhauser, Zagajewski published a collection of critical sketches, *Świat nie przedstawiony* (A World Not Introduced, 1974), considered, alongside articles by Stanisław Barańczak, the most complete statement concerning the program of the New Wave, at the same time a polemic with the attitudes of the writers of the older generation accused of running away from problems in contemporary Poland into a sphere of contemplation cut off from real life (among those criticized was Zbigniew Herbert). He collected his sketches and published them in the volume *Drugi oddech* (Second Breath, 1978). In his later poetry Zagajewski evolved from generational confrontation and assumed a more reflective and moralistic pose, uniting the religious roots of the poet with the legacy threatened by the totalitarianism of European culture (*List: Oda do wielości* [Letter: Ode to Quantity], 1982, emended and published in Paris, 1983; the poem *Jechać do Lwowa* [To Ride to Lvov], London, 1985; and the collection *Płótno* [Canvas], Paris, 1990). His lyrical voice took on a very personal tone during this period, bordering on the metaphysical. His poetic style changed, taking on ascetic qualities and a precise mode of expression. His novels contain the responses of his generation, most significantly in *Ciepło, zimno* (Hot, Cold, 1975) and *Cienka kreska* (The Thin Line, 1983). In *Solidarność i samotność* (Solidarity and Solitude, Paris, 1990), he attempted to give a general view of the experiences of a normal citizen, a poet and émigré.

BIBLIOGRAPHY

English

"Adam Zagajewski's Poems," in *Spoiling Cannibals' Fun: Polish Poetry of the Last Two Decades of Communist Rule,* edited and translated by Stanisław Barańczak and Clare Cavanagh, with a foreword by Helen Vendler, Evanston, Illinois: Northwestern University Press, 1991, 152–61.

Shifting Borders: East European Poetries of the Eighties, edited by Walter Cummins, Rutherford, New Jersey: Fairleigh Dickinson University Press, 1993, 285–86.

ZALESKI, JÓZEF BOHDAN (1802–86), was chiefly a poet. He was the youngest of thirteen children of a modest *szlachcic* (noble) family. He spent part of his childhood in the Ukraine, the landscape and people of which he learned to admire. In school in Human he met S. Goszczyński,* with whom he shaped a group with literary ambitions. He made his literary debut in 1819 in *Dziennik Wileński* (The Vilnius Daily) with *Duma o Wacławie* (Lament About Wacław). In 1820, with his education uncompleted, he left for Warsaw. He published over thirty poems in various Warsaw magazines. They were highly regarded among the advocates of Romanticism (e.g., M. Mochnacki).

In his writings, especially during his early period, he wrote about his beloved Ukraine. Together with Malczewski and Goszczyński, they made up the Ukrainian School of poets. He was undoubtedly influenced by Mickiewicz,* but the master of his youth was K. Brodziński, whose poetic program Zaleski attempted to realize. His works represented a peculiar combination of sentimentalism and Romanticism, free of Promethean revolt and Byronic confusion. He mainly published historical *dumy* (laments) and reflective or love poems. His outstanding works of this period were *Rusałki* (Water Nymphs) and *Melitele* (1829).

He fought in the November Uprising; after the defeat he emigrated to France, where he spent the rest of his life. He later became a close friend of Mickiewicz.

Most of Zaleski's postuprising works were written during 1836–40 and in the early 1860s. In the poems he searched for a way to incorporate the Ukrainian spirit into Romantic national culture and for poetic expression of Romantically conceived folklore. He considered it his duty to maintain the link between the people and their traditions: in his poem *Duch od stepu* (The Spirit from the Steppes, 1836) he assumed the position of a *wieszcz* (national poet). In relation to the national tragedy he advocated a humble acceptance of God's will; he severed his ties to Mickiewicz and thought of entering a monastery. He also composed historical *dumy* (laments) (e.g., *Wyprawa chocimska* [The Chocim Expedition]) and religious poems and even tried his hand at writing an epic. His position in literature is secure, largely because of his stylizations and paraphrases of folk songs, in which he was able to preserve the specific mood of Ukrainian folk poetry. He made extremely successful transpositions of verse forms, in spite of the strong intonational differences between Polish and Ukrainian. Zaleski was very popular during his lifetime; however, his popularity declined with the end of Romanticism. Most of his works were published in a two-volume edition by E. Raczyński, (Poznań, 1841–91).

BIBLIOGRAPHY

Wybór poezji (Selected Poetry), second edition, edited and with an introduction by J. Tretiak, Cracow, 1925.

ZAMEK KANIOWSKI (Kaniowski Castle) (Goszczyński).

ZAPOLSKA, GABRIELA (Maria G. Janowska; pseudonyms Józef Maskoff and Walery Tomicki) (1857–1921), was a playwright, novelist, and short story writer. Born into a rich gentry family and forced into an unhappy marriage, she left her husband and severed family ties. In order to make a living, she worked for various magazines and as an actress (from 1882). Lack of success in the theater forced her to move to Paris (1889). After her return, she acted in Cracow and Lvov, but as a result of bad relations with theater directors, she had to give up acting altogether. She returned to journalism and, in time, set up a drama school. Together with her second husband, the painter S. Janowski, she organized a theater, which toured the provinces of Galicja.

She began her literary career writing novelettes but made her literary debut with a short story, *Jeden dzień z życia róży* (One Day from the Life of a Rose, 1881). After 1883 she began publishing stories in magazines. Those she published in *Przegląd Tygodniowy* (The Weekly Review)—*Malaszka* and *Kaska Kariatyda*—at the same time as her first full-length book, *Akwarele* (Watercolor, 1885), provoked the indignation of conservative critics and became objects of heated polemics. Considered to be a follower of Zola, she believed that naturalism included, above all, social goals. This idea permeates her publicistic and literary output, despite temporary lapses into modernism and her penchant for sentimental effects and pathos. Her major prose includes the following: a series of novelettes, *Menażeria ludzka* (The Human Menagerie, 1893), the novels *Janka* (Janka, 1895), *Fin-de-siècle'istka* (Fin-de-siècle'ette, 1897), and *Zaszumi las* (The Forest Will Rustle, 1899); and, above all, her social novel *Sezonowa miłość* (Seasonal Love, 1904), and its sequel, *Córka Tuski* (Tuska's Daughter, 1907). She also wrote two scandalous works on prostitution and venereal diseases: *O czym się nie mówi* (About Which One Does Not Speak, 1909) and *O czym się nawet mysleć nie chce* (About Which One Does Not Dare Even Think, 1914), and *Kobieta bez skazy* (A Woman Without Blame, 1913), which attempted to unmask the hypocrisy of the middle class.

In her dramatic works, according to Jadwiga Czachowska, Zapolska first came under the influence of the moralizing melodramas, then so popular. Possessing intuition and an excellent sense of current moods in society, she undertook contemporary patriotic themes in her melodramas *Tamten* (That One, staged in 1898) and *Sybir* (Siberia, staged in 1899). Such issues, however, seemed beyond her intellectual and artistic capacities. The same is true of her plays associated with her work as a publicist. Her sense of observation, sensitivity to human vice and funny aspects of human nature, and energy in unmasking those vices made her an outstanding writer of satirical social comedies, which unmasked the hypocrisy of the middle class: *Żabusia* (Tootsie, 1897), *Moralność pani Dulskiej* (The Morality of Mrs. Dulski, 1906), *Ich czworo* (The Four of Them, 1907), *Panna Maliczewska* (Miss Maliczewska, 1910), and a comedy about a marriage "quadrangle," *Skiz* (1909). These works attained great popularity and still appear on Polish stages.

Zapolska's works were controversial: they were subject to severe attacks by conservative critics. Tastes and customs have changed, however, and her work holds an important position in the development of Polish moral comedy and popular drama.

Moralność pani Dulskiej (The Morality of Mrs. Dulski), a comedy in three acts, is a satirical comedy with farcical elements. The story takes place in Lvov at the beginning of the twentieth century. The main problem is the crisis of middle-class morality, exemplified by a highly critical portrait of the Dulski family, in particular of Mrs. Dulski, a house owner, uneducated, ruthless, and hypocritical, who tolerates the seduction of her maid by her son and only worries that the affair not be revealed. The moral of the story is pessimistic: neither the rebellious son, Zbyszko, nor the more sensitive of the two daughters, Mela, has enough strength to oppose the milieu. The excellent structure of the play and clearly drawn characters made it very popular and caused *dulszczyzna* to become synonymous with priggishness, obscurantism, similar to Russian *poshlost'*—self-satisfied mediocrity, peppered with a dash of Tartuffeism.

(See *Młoda Polska.*)

BIBLIOGRAPHY

Dzieła wybrane (Selected Works), opracowanie T. Weiss, t. 1–16. Cracow, 1957–58.

English

"The Morality of Mrs. Dulski" (Moralność Pani Dulskiej), translated by Wiesława and Victor Contoski, *Slavic and East European Arts,* Volume I, Number 2, Spring 1983.

ZAWIEYSKI, JERZY (1902–69), a prose writer, playwright, and essay writer, was a graduate of a drama school. He worked for the theater almost all of his professional life; he was a friend of Schiller, Osterwa, and Jaracz. During the occupation he was a member of Underground Council for the

Theater and received numerous awards from underground dramatic competitions, in 1942 for *Masław* and in 1944 for *Dzień sądu* (Day of Judgment). After the war he became a lecturer at the Catholic University in Lublin. He was a member of the editorial board of the Catholic papers *Tygodnik Powszechny* (The Universal Weekly) and *Znak* (The Sign). He was also a member of the *Sejm* and the State Council, from which he was removed in 1968 by the Communist authorities because of his criticism of the persecution of the intellectuals and young students.

In his early works Zawieyski presented man lost in the contradictions of life. Many of his works arise from his fascination with Żeromski: the novels *Gdzie jesteś, przyjacielu* (Where Are You, Friend, 1932, 1956) and *Daleko do rana* (Long Till Morning, 1934) and his first drama, *Człowiek jest niepotrzebny* (Man Is Not Needed, staged in 1934). The drama *Powrót Przełęckiego* (Przełęcki's Return, staged in 1937; published in 1960) is a direct polemic with Żeromski. The dramatic element in Zawieyski's work is the conflict of conscience solved in terms of Christian ethics. His parabolic poetic dramas have their roots in European culture. Fascinated by the problem of faith, sin, suffering, guilt, and forgiveness, Zawieyski employed biblical themes to make his point: *Mąż doskonały* (A Splendid Husband, staged in 1945; published in 1946; definitive edition in 1948), *Ocalenie Jakuba* (The Salvation of Jacob, staged and published in 1947), *Pieśń o nadziei* (Song of Hope, 1948), and *Rzeka niedoli* (River of Misery, 1953). The themes to which he always returned—victory understood as faithfulness to one's truth; defeat with loyalty to one's beliefs; poetry which serves truth—are explored in his "ancient" dramas: *Sokrates* (Socrates, staged in 1950), *Niezwyciężony Herakles* (Hercules Undefeated, 1952), *Lament Orestesa* (Orestes' Lament, 1953), and *Tyrteusz* (1956). Lyrical and reflective motives are dominant in his dramas that explore contemporary themes: the most popular among these, *Rozdroże miłości* (Crossroads of Love, staged in 1946), emphasizes the superiority of forgiveness and creative love over abstractness and rigorism. His remaining dramas advocate the Christian view of reality.

According to Irena Sławińska, Zawieyski's historiosophical position, akin to existential personalism, is also developed in his novels, *Droga do domu* (The Way Home, 1946) and *Noc Huberta* (Hubert's Night, 1946). His prose is concerned with the historical genealogy of a contemporary Pole and with Norwid's concept of Romanticism as a permanent force that shapes national culture. He developed these ideas in the novel *Konrad nie chce zejść ze sceny* (Konrad Does Not Wish to Leave the Stage, 1966), which praised the heroic stand of symbolic Konrads who sacrificed their lives for the good of the nation. His conviction of the role of the ethical factor in history he embodied in his consideration of the vicissitudes of outstanding individuals of Polish cultural and social life: M. Mochnacki in *Romans z ojczyzną* (Romance with the Homeland, 1963); Mickiewicz* and the Polish Romantics, participants in the battle for freedom in the first half of the nineteenth century, in *Wawrzyny i Cyprysy* (Laurels and Cypresses, 1966); S. Brzozowski* and Z. Nałkowska* in *Korzenie* (Roots, 1969); T. Rejtan and T. Kościuszko in *Między plewą i manną* (Between Chaff and Manna, 1971); and J. Korczak* and others of his contemporaries in *Dobrze, że byli* (Good That They Were, 1974). His personal road from radical secularism to Christian attitudes he presented in *Droga Katechumena* (Road of the Catechumen, 1971), and his conception of the tasks of Catholic literature in *Próby ognia i czasu* (Trials of Fire and Time, 1958). He also left behind extensive diaries and reminiscences, gradually offered for publication.

BIBLIOGRAPHY

Dramaty (Dramas), Poznań, 1957.

ZEMSTA (Vengeance) (see Fredro).

ZIEMIA ULRO (The Land of Ulro) (see Miłosz).

ZNIEWOLONY UMYSŁ (The Captive Mind) (see Miłosz).

ZWIERCIADŁO (The Looking Glass) (see Rej).

ŻELEŃSKI, TADEUSZ (pseudonym Boy) (1874–1941), a critic, translator, and publicist, was the son of a composer and the cousin of Kazimierz Tetmajer.* He was brought up in an artistic milieu of Cracow and studied medicine from 1892 to 1900. He made his literary debut in 1895 as a poet. From 1901 to 1906 he worked as a doctor and published research papers in pediatrics but kept his ties with the Cracow *boheme*. After 1906 he became coauthor of the programs produced in the cabaret *Zielony Balonik* (The Little Green Balloon). He remained a physician until the end of World War I (in 1915 he was mobilized into the Austrian army as a doctor). He had earlier begun translating works from French, for which he received the award of the Academie Française in 1914 and a medal in 1922. In 1919 he began writing theater reviews, which he continued until the end of his life. After 1922 he lived in Warsaw, devoting all his time to literary work, publishing reviews, literary sketches, and critical studies. He was a member of PAL. After the outbreak of World War II he moved to Lvov (shortly thereafter he was taken hostage by the Red Army), where he held the Chair of French literature at the university. Arrested by the Nazis in 1941 after the German army made its way to Lvov, he was shot together with other prominent representatives of the Polish intelligentsia.

Boy's output is varied in form and genre. His popularity began with his cabaret pieces connected with *Zielony balonik* (The Little Green Balloon), published in the volume *Słówka* (Little Words, 1913), his most popular work, which displayed his unusual skill in the innovative use of language and in stylization. Boy translated over a hundred of the greatest works of French literature, including those of Balzac, Molière, and Proust. He also edited *Antologia literatury francuskiej* (An Anthology of French Literature, 1922). He wrote critical studies on the works of authors he had translated, including introductions to his translations published in the volume *Studia i szkice z literatury francuskiej* (Studies and Sketches from French Literature, 1920) and *Nowe studia z literatury francuskiej* (New Studies from French Literature, 1922). He also wrote monographs on Molière and Balzac. His theatrical reviews are contained in ten volumes entitled *Flirt z Melpomeną* (Carrying on with Melpomene, 1920–32) and an additional seven volumes published from 1933 to 1939, making up a unique document of theatrical life in Cracow and Warsaw during 1919–39. He also wrote feuilletons on contemporary social themes (published in ten volumes) which, according to Andrzej Z. Makowiecki, were often an attack on anachronistic views and forms of social life. Among the best known sketches are his articles advocating a reform of the marriage laws and a defense of birth control (*Dziewice konsystorskie* [Consistorial Virgins], 1929, and *Piekło kobiet* [The Hell of Women], 1930). His unique output also includes works on Polish literature, especially biographical works, which revised long-held views and contradicted opinions held by academics. In the volumes *Ludzie żywi* (Living People, 1929) and *Brązownicy* (The Braziers, 1930), he took on such respected personages as Żmichowska,* Przybyszewski,* and Mickiewicz,* revealing features of their character that were never touched upon before. His most outstanding work in the history of literature is *Obrachunki fredrowskie* (Fredro's Reckonings, 1924), which painted a portrait of Fredro* that went against all stereotypes. Boy-Żeleński's works are unconventional and seem refreshingly open compared with more traditional and official studies that seem somewhat hypocritical in their approach, presenting only one point of view. Boy-Żeleński was also interested in his contemporaries: he wrote numerous sketches and studies and published memoirs (*Znasz li ten kraj?* . . . (Do You Know This Country?. . . , 1931) in which he painted a colorful picture of the artistic community of Young Poland, and an anthology, *Młoda Polska* (Young Poland, 1939).

(See *Młoda Polska.*)

BIBLIOGRAPHY

Pisma (Works), Volumes 1–28, edited by H. Markiewicz, Warsaw, 1956–75.

ŻEROMSKI, STEFAN (pseudonyms Maurycy Zych and Józef Katerla) (1864–1925), novelist, short-story writer, playwright, and publicist, came from an impoverished family with patriotic traditions; he spent his childhood at the foot of the Holy Cross Mountains in central Poland. He early became an orphan and acquired his education under severe financial difficulties. He studied only for a short time, and the period made his social views more radical. He worked mainly as a private teacher in gentry homes, among others in Nałęczów. In 1892 he traveled abroad; after his marriage he returned to Rappersvil in Switzerland to work as a librarian in the Polish National Museum. He became acquainted with the new Socialist generation of émigrés (G. Narutowicz, J. Marchlewski, and E. Abramowski). After his return to Poland he was still unable to devote all his time to literature. Only after the publication of *Popioły* (Ashes) in 1904 was he able to write full time. It was then that he moved to Zakopane, largely because of his poor health (tuberculosis). In 1905 he returned to Nałęczów and worked as a social and patriotic activist, together with the local democratic intelligentsia. In 1908 he left the Kingdom of Poland under police pressure and lived in Paris from 1909 to 1912; he then returned to Zakopane. In 1913 he married again. At the outbreak of World War I, he found himself in Zakopane. He tried to get to the front, but after the evacuation of Cracow, he returned to Zakopane and became active on the local level. In 1919 he settled in Warsaw, participating in the literary life of the revived country (he was the initiator of the Polish Academy of Literature [PAL], president of the Writers' Union, and founder of the Polish PEN Club). Nominated for the Nobel Prize in 1924, he did not receive it, mainly as a result of the opposition of the Germans, who critically attacked him after the publication of *Wiatr od morza* (The Wind from the Sea, 1922). In 1925 his health deteriorated and the greatest of contemporary Polish writers was laid to rest. His funeral became a great national event.

Żeromski's first published works were poems written during his school years. During this period he also published letters and stories in various magazines. In 1882 he began keeping his diaries, which he continued until 1891. Published in 1953–56, the diaries became an important literary event. In 1895 he published his first collection of stories, *Opowiadania* (Short Stories), which included *Zapomnienie* (Forgetfulness); *Doktor Piotr* (Doctor Peter); *Ananke; Zmierzch* (Twilight); *Złe przeczucie* (Misgivings); *Po Sedanie* (After the Sedan); *Pokusa* (Temptation); and *Siłaczka* (Mighty Woman). During the same year he published the volume *Rozdziobią nas kruki, wrony* (They'll Peck Us to Bits, Ravens, Crows), which included *Mogiła* (The Tomb), *Źródło* (The Spring), *W sidłach niedoli* (In the Snares of Adversity), *Poganin* (The Pagan), and *Do swego Boga* (To One's God). Both collections were highly appreciated by readers and critics, regarded as the voice of the generation, an expression of moral and social anxiety. The themes are varied: social injustice, especially in the country; heroes' fight against evil, sacrificing their own happiness. These problems are intertwined with the struggle for independence. Glorifying the heroes of the national uprisings, Żeromski saw the reason for defeat in the anachronous social structure and the selfishness of the upper classes. A synthesis of his early output can be found in the novel *Syzyfowe prace* (Sysyphian Labors, 1897), in which he painted a realistic image of school in the Russian partition, with its unsuccessful aim of denationalizing students and imposing on them the idea of Russian statehood. It is a novel about growing up, about the anxiety of youth, the birth of national rebellion and social consciousness, and friendship and first love.

A new period in Żeromski's output began with the novel *Ludzie bezdomi* (Homeless People, 1899, published in 1900). The novel was a protest against social conditions and the demoralization of the world, which gives the impression that the best people feel uprooted. It was a new type of social novel, deeply rooted in the reality of the late nineteenth century but centered around ideas, not a complex plot. Żeromski's fame rests on his subsequent novel, *Popioły* (Ashes, 1904), a historical epic which takes place in the late eighteenth and early nineteenth centuries, mainly during the Napoleonic Wars. It opened a new stage in the development of the Polish historical novel: the narration is interspersed with lyrical episodes, with discursive elements of a philosophical and moral character. Epic images and fragments of the plot appear interchangeably with digressions, reflections on the sense of human existence, on the conflict between aims and means. *Ludzie bezdomni* and *Popioły* established the main tendencies of Żeromski's later writings. He returned to the tragic conflict of good and evil, of the ethical ideal and biological vitality in his legend *Aryman mści się* (Aryman Avenges Himself, 1904). As a historical novelist he undertook themes which allowed him to penetrate and explore the problems of the nation. The legend *Powieść o Udałym Walgierzu* (The Story About Udał Walgierz), which appeared in *Chimera** in 1905, described in poetic summary the rise of the Polish state and the moral transformation of the hero against this background. His descriptions of the struggle for independence were accompanied by daring insights into various aspects of contemporary life, especially social and cultural backwardness. These themes appear in his novellas and novels, and in his publicistic writings as well, combining the elements of the pamphlet and lyricism. In 1905 he wrote the novella *Echa leśne* (Forest Echoes), devoted to the January Uprising of 1963. This was followed by *Sen o szpadzie* (Dream of a Sword, 1905), *Nagi bruk* (Bare Pavement, 1906), *Nokturn* (Nocturne, 1907), and *Słowo o bandosie* (Word About the Hired Harvester, 1908), where he attempted to bridge the gap between the former struggle for independence and contemporary social revolution. His memories of the January Uprising found expression in *Wierna rzeka* (Faithful River, 1912), a beautiful story about heroism and love of one's country.

Żeromski's attitude toward revolution was complex. It grew out of his solidarity with human suffering and his understanding of the historical role of the lower classes, but it was also marked by an underlying fear. The defeat of the 1905–7 revolution brought on moral depression and forced Żeromski to reconsider the basic problems of life in Poland. These painful experiences are reflected in *Dzieje grzechu* (History of Sin, 1908), a social novel with naturalist underpinnings, a shocking testimony of the triumph of evil, not only in human relations, but also in the very nature of man. The novel does not make overt allusions to the revolution, but its deep pessimism stemmed from the collapse of the hopes the writer attached to the year 1905. The same disappointment can be found in *Duma o hetmanie* (Ballad of a Hetman, 1908), which described the defeat at Cecora. The drama *Róża* (Rose, 1909) is one of the most complete accounts of the 1905 Revolution in Polish literature. The problem of the fate of the nation and of individuals who sacrifice their lives for independence and for a dignified life for the oppressed is the principal theme in Żeromski's writings. The theme is further explored in the tragedy *Sułkowski* (1910), the novel *Uroda życia* (The Beauty of Life, 1912), and the trilogy *Walka z szatanem* (Battle with Satan, 1916–19). The final period of Żeromski's work brought several journalistic works, *Początek świata pracy* (The Beginning of the World of the Working Class, 1919), *Organizacja inteligencji zawodowej* (The Organization of the Vocational Intelligentsia, 1919), and *Snobizm i postęp* (Snobbism and Progress, 1923); the prose poems *Wisła* (Vistula, 1918) and *Międzymorze* (The Isthmus, 1924); the prose novel from the borderline of journalism *Wiatr od morza* (Wind from the Sea); the collection of stories *Pomyłki* (Mistakes, 1923); and the dramas *Ponad śnieg bielszym się stanę* (I'll Become Whiter Beyond Snow, 1921), *A Christmas Mummer's Play* (1923), and *Uciekła mi przepióreczka* (The Quail Got Away from Me, 1924). The main achievement of his late period is the novel *Przedwiośnie* (Early Spring, 1924), which caused a great deal of controversy with its daring claims about the great social expectations raised by Poland's regained independence and the subsequent disappointment. In 1925 he published the prose poem *Puszcza jodłowa* (Fir-Tree Forest), his farewell to the country of his childhood and youth. Żeromski's involvement with the problems of the nation is inseparable from his artistic accomplishments. He could have been a great writer in any country: fate and love destined him for Poland.

Przedwiośnie (Early Spring) grew out of the writer's anxiety about the political and social turmoil present in the newly revived Polish state. Internal political conflicts, an inefficient government, an irresponsible parliament, a deteriorating economy, inflation, unemployment, and strikes—these seemed to presage a catastrophe or revolution. *Przedwiośnie* painted a picture of contemporary Poland but also expressed the writer's opinion on burning questions.

The problems are dramatized in the rather typical ordinary life of Cezary

Baryka, a young man born and brought up in Russia, for whom Poland was an idealized legend, which inspired curiosity and distrust. The distrust is deepened with the advent of the Russian October Revolution. His hero constantly confronts dream and reality, his father's utopian vision of "glass houses," and the truth of life. Having spent some time in Warsaw, Baryka takes part in the war with Russia in 1920. After the campaign he is invited by his friend to an old gentry house in Nawłoć, where he becomes acquainted with the Poland of the gentry, which is slowly passing away. The beauty of the place and a love affair with Laura, the owner of a neighboring estate, attract Cezary cursorily, but not sufficiently to allow him to be blind to the poverty of the peasants and the wastefulness of life in Nawłoć. During his next stay in Warsaw he is presented as a man torn between contradictory ideas, approving of one view, and then the other, eventually to reject all views. Two colleagues represent his dilemma: on the one hand, Szymon Gajowiec, who assures him that the only way is slow peaceful work; on the other hand, Baryka's university colleague, Antoni Lulek, an admirer of the revolution, who aggravates Cezary's bitterness with insistent arguments. In a fit of rebellion and despair Baryka joins a demonstration of workers.

The novel does not give an unequivocal answer to the questions it raises: it is a call to acknowledge personal sins, and, although flawed, several fragments of the novel contain incomparable beauty. Its publication was both a political and a literary event. It was received by a segment of society as a call for revolution and raised violent criticism in conservative circles. Żeromski admitted in his *List otwarty do Arcybaszewa* (An Open Letter to Arcybaszew) that the controversial last scene of the novel was meant as a dramatic warning, a signal of alarm. He called for immediate and daring reforms. The novel was admired by many readers, and Cezary Baryka became the symbolic embodiment of the youthful drive to rebuild the world in the name of social justice. Żeromski clearly explained his relation to the Russian Revolution and Communism in his journalistic coverage *Na probostwie w Wyszkowie* (At the Presbytery at Wyszków, 1920), in which he paid homage to the Polish people engaged in mortal battle with the Bolshevik invasion in 1920 and condemned Polish Bolsheviks as betraying the people (like the notorious chief of CZEKA, Feliks Dzierżyński, whose statue in Moscow was toppled in 1991); in postwar Poland the work was forbidden by the Communist censor and could only appear with the establishment of *Drugi obieg* (Alternative Press). Żeromski's personal notes, from the age of eighteen to twenty-seven, published posthumously from 1963 to 1970 (*Dzienniki* [Diaries]), proved to be a highly interesting "confession" of his youthful period, touching upon his personal and deeply felt psychological analysis.

(See *Młoda Polska.*)

BIBLIOGRAPHY

Dzieła (Works) edited by Stanisław Pigoń and with an introduction by H. Markiewicz, S. I–V, Volumes 1–32, Warsaw, 1956–57; 1963–70.

English

Ashes (Popioły), two volumes translated by Helen Stankiewicz Zand, New York: A. A. Knopf, 1928.

ŻMICHOWSKA, NARCYZA (pseudonym Gabryella) (1819–76), a novelist, poet, and pedagogue, was educated to be a teacher. She was employed by the Zamoyski family and traveled to Paris with them. Her democratic views, however, led to a conflict with her employers, and she returned to Poland in 1839. Her poem *Szczęście poety* (The Luck of a Poet), published in *Pierwiosnek* (Primrose) in 1841, brought her instant popularity and effected her entry into literary and cultural magazines. She worked in Warsaw as a publicist, initiating a women's movement later referred to as "enthusiasts." From 1844 to 1845 she lived in Wielkopolska; in 1845 she moved to Poznań. It was then that she published a volume of poetry and prose, *Wolne chwile Gabryelli* (Free Moments of Gabryella).

In 1846 she returned to Warsaw; here she published her best novel, *Poganka* (The Pagan Lady), in *Przegląd Naukowy* (Scholarly Review). The novel explored themes of interest among the second generation of Romantics, which centered around the dilemma of Romantic individualism versus ties to the fate of the nation, the borders of sovereignty of art and the artist. Żmichowska gave a straightforward answer to the question, and the novel received different interpretations. Daring in its formulation of current problems, psychologically revealing, and containing interesting fantastic elements, it is one of the outstanding works of Polish Romanticism. She published *Książka pamiątek* (A Book of Mementos), a work written for the so-called conspiracy of craftsmen—an underground organization headed by H. Krajewski, with whom Żmichowska collaborated after her return. In October 1849, the conspiracy was uncovered and Żmichowska was imprisoned until February 1852. According to Marian Stępień, during the investigation she displayed unusual moral fortitude and courage.

Having returned to Warsaw, she resumed her work as a pedagogue. Her chief work during this period was the novel *Biała róża* (White Rose, published together with a short story, *Stary dwór w Świerszczowej* [The Old Mansion in Świerszczowa], under the rubric *Nieznane pisma bezimiennej autorki* ([The Unknown Writings of an Anonymous Author], Volume 4 of *Pisma Gabryelli* [The Writings of Gabryella], 1861).

During 1863–74 she lived with her family in the country. She became more interested in positivist ideology but expressed her dissatisfaction with the positivist roman a thèse in *Czy to powieść* (Is This a Novel, written during 1875–76). She was working on an anthology of Polish nineteenth century poetry (published in 1882 as *Kwiaty rodzinne* [Family Flowers] after her death). She also edited several textbooks, wrote a number of didactic works, and translated Thomas Macaulay's *History of England.*

BIBLIOGRAPHY

Pisma (Works), Volumes 1–5, edited and with an introduction by P. Chmielowski, Warsaw, 1885–86.

Wybór powieści (Selected Novels), Volumes 1–2, edited by M. Olszaniecka, Warsaw, 1953.

ŻYCIE (Life), a literary-artistic journal, was published in Cracow from 1897 to 1900, first as a weekly, then from 1899 as a biweekly, and later as a monthly. The founder and first editor was L. Szczepański (1897–98), followed by I. Maciejowski, A. Górski (1898), and A. Grzymała-Siedlecki and A. Wysocki. Stanisław Przybyszewski* became editor in 1898, with the artistic collaboration of Stanisław Wyspiański.* In its early stages the magazine had an electric character; apart from the literary and artistic sections it also contained social and scientific commentaries; along with writers of the older generation, most notably from the circle of naturalists (A. Dygasiński,* G. Zapolska,* W. Orkan*), he gathered together young authors who represented various modernist tendencies (Z. "Miriam" Przesmycki, K. Tetmajer,* L. Rydel, F. Merandola). Several important critics provided literary and theater criticism (P. Chmielowski,* A. Potocki, A. Górski, J. Lorentowicz, A. Łada, W. Feldman*). The cycle of articles by Górski (pseudonym Quasimodo) became the theoretical justifications of aims of the young generation of writers, entitled *Młoda Polska** (Young Poland) and published in 1989. Górski validated the new, universal interests of the young poetry, but at the same time demanded ties with the independent (national) trends of Polish Romanticism. The profile of the journal changed radically after Przybyszewski assumed its editorship. He wanted *Życie* to be a programmatic journal, devoted exclusively to modernism. Przybyszewski himself published his two famous manifestos in *Życie: Confiteor* and *O "nową" sztukę* (About the "New" Art), in which he accepted for publication Wyspiański's* dramas *Warszawianka* (Varsovienne) and *Klątwa* (The Curse); the poetry of S. and W. Korab-Brzozowski, A. Lange,* T. Miciński,* K. Zawistowski, J. Żuławski, M. Komornicka, and B. Leśmian;* the prose of A. Kisielewski, T. Rittner,* W. Sieroszewski*). He included the basic thesis of his program, the phrase "Art for Art's Sake"; the need for metaphysical content, drawn from the penetration of the unconscious; the freedom of individual quest; and the cult of the artist. During Przybyszewski's editorship works of preexpressionist and symbolist poetry appeared predominantly. The journal published numerous poems, prose works, and essays of the editor, and hymns on religious themes by J. Kasprowicz,* as well as translations of the most famous symbolists and Parnassists, French and Belgian. The artistic style was decided by Wyspiański,* J. Stanisławski, J. Mehoffer, E. Muench, and G. Vigeland. Wyspiański provided an artistic design that made each issue a harmonious artistic whole. *Życie* stopped publication because of permanent financial difficulties and because of constant interventions by the Austrian censors. In spite of its small circulation (one thousand copies) the journal exerted a significant influence on the development of Polish modernism.

BIBLIOGRAPHY

S. Przybyszewski, *Moi współczesni* (My Contemporaries), Warsaw, 1959.

ŻYWE KAMIENIE (Living Stones) (see Berent).

General Reference Bibliography

Bruckner, Aleksander. *Dzieje kultury polskiej* (History of Polish Culture). Warsaw, Cracow: Książka i Wiedza, F. Pieczatkowski, 1946–58.

Bruckner, Aleksander. *Geschichte der polnischen Literatur*. Second edition. Leipzig: C. F. Amelung, 1909.

Budzyk, Kazimierz, and other editors. *Bibliographia literatury polskiej, "Nowy Korbut"* (A Bibliography of Polish Literature, "The New Korbut"). Warsaw: Państwowy Instytut Wydawniczy, 1963, five volumes, plus Volume 12.

Czerwinski, Edward J. *Contemporary Polish Theater and Drama (1956–1984)*. Westport, Connecticut: Greenwood Press, 1988.

Davies, Norman. *God's Playground: A History of Poland*. New York: Columbia University Press, 1982, two volumes.

Dyboski, Roman. *Periods of Polish Literary History*. The Ilchester lectures for the year 1923. London: Humphrey Milford, Oxford University Press, 1923.

Gerould, Daniel, ed. *Twentieth Century Polish Avant-Garde Drama: Plays, Scenarios, Critical Documents*. Daniel and Eleanor Gerould, trans. Introduction by Daniel Gerould. Ithaca, New York: Cornell University Press, 1977.

Gillon, Adam and Krzyżanowski, Ludwik, eds. *Introduction to Modern Polish Literature: An Anthology of Fiction and Poetry*. New York: Twayne, 1964.

Holton, Milne and Vangelisti, Paul, eds. *The New Polish Poetry*. Pittsburgh: University of Pittsburgh Press, 1978.

Korbut, Gabriel. *Literatura polska od początkow do wojny światowej* (Polish Literature from Its Beginnings to the World War). Warsaw: General editorship of Mianowski Publishers, 1929–31, four volumes.

Korzeniewska, Ewa, and other editors. *Słownik współczesnych pisarzy polskich* (A Dictionary of Polish Writers). Warsaw: Państwowe Wydawnictwo Naukowe, 1963, four volumes.

Kridl, Manfred. *A Survey of Polish Literature and Culture*. Olga Scherer-Virski, trans. The Hague: Mouton and Co., 1956.

Krzyżanowski, Julian. *Historia literatury polskiej: Alegoryzm–Preromantyzm* (A

History of Polish Literature: Allegorism–Preromanticism). Third edition. Warsaw: Państwowy Instytut Wydawniczy, 1966.

Krzyżanowski, Julian. *A History of Polish Literature.* Doris Ronowicz, trans. Warsaw: Polish Scientific Publishers, 1978.

Kuncewicz, Maria, ed. *The Modern Polish Mind: An Anthology of Stories and Essays.* Boston: Little, Brown and Co., 1962.

Kutrzeba, Stanisław. *Historia ustroju Polski w zarysie* (A History of Political Institutions in Poland in Survey Form). Lwów: Gebethner and Wolff, B. Poloniecki, 1905–17, four volumes.

Lednicki, Wacław. *Life and Culture of Poland as Reflected in Polish Literature.* New York: Roy Publishers, 1944.

Levine, Madeline G. *Contemporary Polish Poetry, 1925–1975.* Boston: Twayne Publishers, 1981.

Literatura polska: Przewodnik encyklopedyczny (Polish Literature: Encyclopedic Guide). Warsaw: Państwowe Wydawnictwo Naukowe, 1984–85, two volumes and a supplement.

Matuszewski, Ryszard and Pollak, Seweryn, eds. *Poezja polska 1914–1939* (Polish Poetry 1914–1939). Warsaw: Czytelnik, 1962.

Mayewski, Pawel, ed. *The Broken Mirror: A Collection of Writing from Contemporary Poland.* New York: Random House, 1958.

Peterkiewicz, Jerzy and Singer, Burns, eds. and trans. *Five Centuries of Polish Poetry, 1450–1950: An Anthology with Introduction and Notes.* London: Secker and Warburg, 1950; London and New York: Oxford University Press, 1970; Westport, Connecticut: Greenwood Press, 1979.

Scherer-Virski, Olga. *The Modern Polish Short Story.* The Hague: Mouton, 1955.

Segel, Harold B. *Polish Romantic Drama.* Ithaca, New York: Cornell University Press, 1977. Translation of three plays: Mickiewicz's *Forefathers' Eve, Part III,* Krasiński's *The Un-Divine Comedy,* and Słowacki's *Fantazy.*

Suchodolski, Bogdan. *A History of Polish Culture.* E. J. Czerwinski, trans. Warsaw: Interpress Publishers, 1987.

Terlecki, Tymon, ed. *Literatura polska na obczyźnie 1940–1960* (Polish Literature Abroad, 1940–1960). London: B. Swiderski, 1964–1965, two volumes.

Tyrmand, Leopold, ed. *Explorations in Freedom: Prose, Narrative and Poetry from Kultura.* New York: Free Press, 1970.

Kultura Essays. New York: Free Press, 1970.

Wieniewska, Celina, ed. *Polish Writing Today.* Baltimore: Penguin Books, 1967.

Index

Page numbers in *italic* indicate main entries.

About the Editor

E. J. CZERWINSKI is Professor Emeritus of Slavic and Comparative Literature at the State University of New York at Stony Brook. His many articles have appeared in journals such as *The Polish Review, Comparative Drama, Modern Drama,* and *World Literature Today*. His books include *Contemporary Polish Theatre and Drama, 1956–1984* (Greenwood Press, 1988).

ISBN 0-313-26222-5
90000>
EAN
9 780313 262227
HARDCOVER BAR CODE